# The 10X Compounding Blueprint

***How to Aggressively 10X Your Trading Capital ($100K to $1M) in Six Months With High-Velocity Setups, Tactical Leverage, and the Iron Vice of Risk Management***

By

**Frank Ikechukwu Igwealor**

**Attorney, Economist, CPA, CMA, CFM**

***This is high-risk territory — most aggressive traders blow up***

Educational Purposes Only — No Investment, Legal, Tax, or Professional Advice. This book is provided solely for educational and informational purposes. It is intended to explain the principles, mathematics, psychology, historical examples, and risk-management concepts associated with aggressive stock market speculation. Nothing in this book constitutes financial, investment, legal, accounting, tax, or other professional advice, nor should any discussion be interpreted as a recommendation, solicitation, or offer to buy, sell, or hold any security or financial instrument.

The strategies discussed—including, but not limited to, common stocks, ETFs, leveraged ETFs (2× and 3×), options, warrants, margin, and other leveraged instruments—involve substantial risk. Trading these instruments may result in partial or total loss of capital in a very short period. In some circumstances, losses may exceed the initial investment.

The objective referenced throughout this book—growing $100,000 into $1,000,000 in approximately six months—is presented solely as an illustration of the mathematics of exponential compounding and the market conditions under which extraordinary returns have occasionally occurred. It is not a prediction, guarantee, promise, expectation, or representation of likely or typical results. Such outcomes are exceptionally rare and depend upon numerous unpredictable factors, including market conditions, liquidity, volatility, execution quality, risk management, timing, and luck. Most traders attempting highly aggressive strategies lose money, and many lose all of their trading capital.

Past performance, historical examples, case studies, charts, market events, and discussions of individual securities should not be interpreted as evidence of future performance. Financial markets are uncertain, constantly changing, and influenced by factors beyond anyone's control.

Readers are solely responsible for their own investment and trading decisions. Before acting on any information contained in this book, readers should conduct their own independent research and consult qualified financial, legal, accounting, and tax professionals who understand their individual circumstances. The author and publisher expressly disclaim any liability for any direct, indirect, incidental, consequential, or other loss or damage arising from the use of, or reliance upon, the information contained in this publication.

By reading this book, you acknowledge that you understand the substantial risks associated with speculative trading, accept full responsibility for your own decisions, and agree that the author and publisher shall not be liable for any losses, damages, or claims arising from the application of the ideas or strategies discussed herein. Trade only with capital you can afford to lose. Capital preservation always comes before capital appreciation.

First Edition: 2026
Published in the United States of America
ISBN: 979-8-951213-03-7

## Table of Contents

# INTRODUCTION

## Why/How 10X (1,000%) Compounding Is Rare — But Possible

The idea of turning $100,000 into $1,000,000 in six months sounds absurd to most people — and statistically it should. Most market participants never achieve it. Most professionals never achieve it. Most traders who attempt it lose money, often catastrophically. This book does not sell fantasy. It examines the narrow conditions, disciplines, instruments, market environments, and psychological behaviors under which extreme compounding occasionally becomes possible. A 1,000% return in six months is not ordinary investing. It is calculated aggression against the laws of average market returns, permanently balanced on the knife's edge of total account liquidation.

## The Mathematics: What 10X Actually Requires

Strip away the emotion and the goal reduces to a single multiplication problem. Turning $100,000 into $1,000,000 means growing capital tenfold — a 900% net gain. Assuming a standard 20 trading days per month, six months gives you roughly 120 trading sessions to execute the campaign. There are two useful ways to model what that demands.

Track A: The Monthly Milestone Model. To reach $1,000,000 in six months, the account must compound at a net rate of approximately 46.8% per month. Each month's milestone becomes the next month's starting line:

| Month | Starting Capital | Target Ending Capital |
|---|---|---|
| Month 1 | $100,000 | $146,800 |
| Month 2 | $146,800 | $215,502 |
| Month 3 | $215,502 | $316,357 |
| Month 4 | $316,357 | $464,412 |
| Month 5 | $464,412 | $681,757 |
| Month 6 | $681,757 | $1,000,000 |

To put the target in perspective, the S&P 500 has averaged about 10% annually, and even the best hedge funds rarely sustain 30–40% annualized over long periods. Here, the objective is 46.8% per month, repeated six times. Traditional portfolio management targeting 8–15% annually cannot produce this outcome.

Track B: The Per-Trade R-Multiple Model. Viewed trade by trade, the objective is less intimidating. A 1,000% return does not require one spectacular winner or 120 consecutive winning days. It requires roughly 36R, where 1R is the maximum risk per trade. Just twelve 3R trades—each earning three times the initial risk—can mathematically reach the goal. This reframes the challenge: success comes not from perfection, but from accumulating a number of high-quality, asymmetric winners while strictly limiting losses.

## Why 10X (1,000%) Compounding Is Rare

The math above explains the ambition. The obstacles are mathematical, structural, and psychological.

The Mathematical Barrier. The required return forces traders beyond conventional investing into instruments capable of nonlinear gains: options, warrants, leveraged ETFs, high-beta momentum stocks, gamma squeezes, short squeezes, low-float breakouts, and volatility expansions. A stock gaining 15% can send a near-dated call option up 100–300%, while a sustained sector trend can dramatically compound a 3× ETF. The same convexity that creates opportunity also creates danger.

The Leverage Trap and Volatility Drag. Many traders assume aggressive growth requires maximum leverage. Chasing 3× ETFs such as SOXL or out-of-the-money options, they overlook volatility drag, path dependency, and theta. In choppy markets, daily ETF resets and option time decay steadily erode capital, even if the underlying eventually moves correctly. A 10–15% adverse move can erase 30–100% of a leveraged position.

The Mathematics of Ruin. Compounding cannot survive repeated large losses. A 50% drawdown requires a 100% gain just to break even. As losses mount, traders often increase position size, abandon stops, and revenge trade, turning a manageable setback into a path toward insolvency.

The Diversification Dilemma. Diversification reduces volatility but also reduces velocity. It is mathematically impossible to turn $100,000 into $1,000,000 in 180 days by spreading capital across large-cap blue chips. Hyper-growth requires disciplined concentration—which is precisely what makes it hazardous.

The Psychological Barrier. The greatest obstacle is emotional. Many traders cannot tolerate the volatility required. Conservative thinking causes premature exits; undisciplined aggression leads to ruin. Large unrealized swings tempt traders into large positions, emotional exits, and revenge trades.

The Statistical Reality. The statistics are unforgiving. Studies consistently find that 70–97% of active day traders and retail speculators lose money, while only about 1–3% remain consistently profitable after fees. Most aggressive accounts fail within months. Survival is rare—and survival is the prerequisite for every extraordinary return. Traders who survive can compound again; those who blow up are permanently removed from the game.

## How 10X (1,000%) Compounding Is Possible

Rare is not impossible. It is narrow, volatile, psychologically demanding, and unforgiving of error. Achieving a **1,000%** return requires thinking less like a retail trader and more like a disciplined micro-hedge fund—combining market timing, instrument selection, position sizing, and rigorous risk control.

Trade the Regime, Not Just the Stock. Extreme compounding depends on market environment. It is most achievable during periods of abundant liquidity, strong speculation, sector manias, and broad momentum—not in stagnant markets. History repeatedly provides such windows: technology and biotech booms, AI rallies, semiconductor supercycles, commodity shocks, meme-stock manias, crypto-linked surges, and post-crash liquidity rebounds.

The goal is not to predict tops and bottoms, but to recognize when liquidity, volatility, and crowd psychology favor aggression.

Convexity and Pure-Play Vehicles. Generating 46.8% per month requires instruments with nonlinear upside: LEAPS, in-the-money options, warrants, and tactical 2×/3× sector ETFs used only in confirmed, high-volume uptrends and exited as soon as distribution begins.

Asymmetric Sizing: A Modified Kelly Approach. Position size should be dynamic, not fixed. Increase exposure only when probability is unusually high—for example, after a confirmed 52-week-high breakout, strong institutional volume, and a 1:4 reward-to-risk setup. Reduce exposure—or move to cash—when conditions deteriorate.

Riding Institutional Momentum. The 10x campaign follows institutional money, not stagnant value stocks. It targets high-velocity themes such as AI hardware, silicon photonics, and high-probability biotech catalysts, riding multi-billion-dollar momentum rather than fighting it.

Ironclad Drawdown Governance. Hyper-aggressive growth depends on defensive discipline. Every trade requires a hard stop-loss, while account-level circuit breakers halt trading whenever equity falls more than 10% from its peak, preventing one losing streak from becoming ruin.

How It Has Actually Happened. These outcomes are rare but real. The 2021 GameStop squeeze and other short squeezes turned some small accounts into millions within weeks. Biotech, meme stocks, and skilled options traders have captured multi-bagger gains around earnings, mergers, and macro events. Early crypto and technology booms also created fortunes, though many were later lost.

The common threads in the genuine successes are consistent: near-perfect (or lucky) timing of a powerful trend; extreme concentration in one to five names; aggressive but deliberate use of leverage; strict exit discipline before the reversal; and enough starting capital and risk tolerance to survive the volatility. It is essential to remember the survivorship bias at work here — these outcomes are highly visible, while the thousands of accounts destroyed in the same environments are invisible.

The Profile of the Survivor. The rare trader who compounds aggressively and survives tends to combine eight traits: (1) uncompromising risk management; (2) rapid adaptability as conditions change; (3) concentration in high-conviction setups; (4) willingness to hold winners aggressively; (5) emotional discipline under violent volatility; (6) a deep, intuitive understanding of momentum; (7) awareness of which market regime is in force; and (8) the humility to reduce exposure when conditions deteriorate.

## The Realistic Blueprint Mindset

The governing principle is controlled aggression. A trader must think simultaneously like a speculator and a risk manager. A 1,000% return is possible only during extraordinary market conditions, with elite execution, iron discipline, and some luck. It is neither reliable nor consistently repeatable.

Treat this book as a high-risk playbook for asymmetric opportunities. Its purpose is to maximize probability in favorable regimes while using strict risk rules, drawdown limits, and disciplined review to prevent ruin.

A core warning, worth repeating throughout: you can lose 100% of your capital, and many have. Never trade money you cannot afford to lose. Past outliers do not predict your results. Paper trade and size small until you have proven consistency.

## The Difference Between Gambling and Aggressive Professional Speculation

To outsiders, aggressive trading and gambling look alike. Both involve risk, uncertainty, large gains or losses, and emotional swings. Those similarities lead many to conclude that aggressive trading is simply financial gambling.

That conclusion is wrong. Turning $100,000 into $1,000,000 in six months is not investing—it is aggressive speculation. But speculation differs from gambling in the same way a casino patron differs from a professional poker player who has spent 10,000 hours mastering probability, psychology, and bankroll management. The difference is not the size of the risk, but the structure of the risk, the quality of the edge, disciplined execution, probability management, and a repeatable process.

## One Seeks Excitement, the Other Expectancy

A gambler risks money for excitement, entertainment, or hope. A professional speculator risks capital to exploit **asymmetric probabilities** under controlled conditions. One seeks excitement; the other seeks **expectancy**.

The gambler plays a game with a built-in negative edge. The professional trades only when probability, momentum, liquidity, volatility, positioning, and reward-to-risk temporarily favor him. The gambler plays every hand; the professional waits for specific setups. In casino terms, the gambler bets against the house; the professional tries to become the house.

The contrast runs all the way down: (1) The gambler acts impulsively; (2) **The professional acts selectively; (3)** The gambler increases risk after losses; (4) **The professional reduces exposure when conditions deteriorate; (5)** The gambler seeks certainty where none exists; (6) **The professional manages uncertainty deliberately; (7)** The gambler needs to be right; but (8) **The professional needs to survive.**

## Edge vs. Hope

The first divide is mathematical. The gambler plays a **negative-expectancy** game, hoping for one big win. Buying short-dated out-of-the-money options or chasing a hyped small-cap without a tested edge is gambling from the outset.

The professional trades only with a verified **positive expectancy**. He seeks setups where reward greatly exceeds defined risk and enters only when historical testing, the current market regime, and a clear catalyst align. He understands that repeating a positive-expectancy setup hundreds of times builds the equity curve, even if individual trades fail.

The difference is reflected in their language. The gambler says, "This 3x ETF looks like it's going up today — I'm going all in." The professional says, "This sector is breaking out on heavy volume with institutional sponsorship; my backtested system shows a 62% win rate at 3.8-to-1 reward-to-risk, so I'll risk 1% of capital with a hard stop." Same instrument, opposite activity.

This is why the simplest honest test of any trade is one question: if I made this exact trade one hundred times, would I expect to come out ahead? If the answer is "no" or "I don't know," it is gambling. If the answer is "yes, based on a tested edge," it is professional speculation.

## Process vs. Emotion

Professionals trade from a written blueprint that removes emotion from execution. Entries, exits, position size, stop-losses, scaling rules, and risk limits are defined before the trade, allowing the system—not emotion—to govern decisions. Gamblers trade on instinct, **FOMO**, or the urge to recover losses.

A handful of rules separate the two, and the professional treats them as non-negotiable:

- Never risk more than 1–2% of total capital on a single trade.
- Predefine entry, stop-loss, and profit target before entering.
- Cut losses mechanically — never "this time is different."
- Scale in only on proven strength, pyramiding winners rather than losers.
- Keep a daily journal recording every trade's rationale, outcome, and lesson.

## Sizing and Leverage: Weapon vs. Suicide

Position sizing best reveals the difference. Gamblers size by conviction, greed, or revenge, often risking **20%, 50%,** or even **100%** of capital on a single biotech approval or earnings report, inviting ruin.

Professionals size mathematically. In a **$100,000** account with a **5%** stop and a **2%** maximum account risk (**$2,000**), the position is **$40,000**—no more. Position size is calculated, never guessed.

Leverage follows the same principle. **2× and 3× ETFs, options,** and **margin** can accelerate **1,000%** compounding—or wipe out an account. Professionals use leverage selectively, only when reward is highly asymmetric and risk tightly defined, while accounting for **volatility decay** in leveraged ETFs and **time decay** in options. Even a worst-case overnight gap should never be capable of destroying the account.

## The Three Pillars of Professional Speculation

To compound $100,000 into $1,000,000 in 180 days, speculation has to be conducted under corporate-grade governance. Three foundational rules separate the sovereign speculator from the gambler — rules the gambler violates by default.

| THE SOVEREIGN SPECULATOR |
|---|
| 1. Calculated Asymmetric Edge (risk 1 to win 3+) |
| 2. Automated Hard Technical Stop-Loss |
| 3. Account-Level Circuit Breakers |

**Pillar 1 — Asymmetric Edge.** Gamblers accept symmetric—or even negative—payoffs, risking $1 to make $1, or worse, risking $5 to make $1 by averaging down. Professionals demand asymmetry: every trade must offer at least 3R–5R of upside relative to risk. With a 3R structure, a trader can be wrong 70% of the time and still grow the account because occasional large winners outweigh frequent small losses. The goal is not to win often, but to lose small and win big.

**Pillar 2 — The Sacred Stop-Loss.** Gamblers remove stops and hope for reversals, turning small mistakes into catastrophic losses. Professionals treat the stop-loss as a binding exit, entered automatically with the trade through the execution platform or API. If price reaches the stop, the position is closed without hesitation. The loss is simply a predetermined business expense.

**Pillar 3 — Account-Level Circuit Breakers.** Gamblers increase size after losses. Professionals install institutional circuit breakers: if account equity falls by a predetermined amount—say **10%** from its peak—all trading stops until a mandatory review of market conditions and execution prevents a losing streak from becoming ruin.

## The Freight Train Rule

Never stand in front of a freight train—but ride one when conditions are right. Gambling fights the trend or jumps aboard randomly. Professional speculation identifies powerful trends early, enters with defined risk, rides momentum aggressively, and protects profits. Environment matters. Aggressive trading works best during periods of abundant liquidity, expanding volatility, institutional momentum, sector rotation, and broad speculation. When conditions deteriorate, professionals reduce exposure, preserve capital, and wait. Gamblers keep trading because the action itself has become the objective.

## Survival Is the Foundation

Every rule rests on one principle: **survival**. An **80%** loss requires a **400%** gain just to break even, making catastrophic drawdowns devastating to future compounding. Professionals think first about survival, liquidity, position sizing, and risk containment—then about profits. This is why elite **hedge funds**, **proprietary trading firms**, and **family offices** focus more on risk management than prediction. Amateurs believe success comes from forecasting markets. Professionals know it comes from surviving long enough for a genuine edge to compound.

Professional speculation also compounds **skill**. Thousands of hours build pattern recognition, execution discipline, risk awareness, regime recognition, and emotional stability. None guarantees certainty, but together they create a **probabilistic edge**. Professionals do not control outcomes—they control process. They do not win every trade—they control losses. They do not predict every move—they act when probabilities favor them.

## When Speculation Mutates into Gambling

The line is thin and crossed quietly. Speculation becomes gambling when position sizes become reckless, leverage excessive, trades emotional, rules abandoned, losses trigger revenge trading, or the trader seeks stimulation instead of process. At that point, speculation ceases to be a profession and becomes emotional self-destruction financed by the market.

Emotional control is therefore structural, not optional. Successful aggressive traders balance two opposing traits: enough aggression to seize rare asymmetric opportunities and enough discipline to survive when conditions turn hostile.

## At a Glance: The Operational Divide

| Operational Variable | The Retail Gambler | The Professional Speculator |
|---|---|---|
| **Primary Motivation** | Excitement, thrill, hope, rapid riches, emotional validation | Cold execution of a systematic, probability-based edge |
| **Mathematical Edge** | Negative expectancy; relies on "the big hit" | Quantified positive expectancy over a large sample |
| **Decision Process** | Emotion, hunches, hot tips, FOMO | Written rules, tested process, predefined criteria |
| **Position Sizing** | Arbitrary; driven by greed or conviction | Calculated from account risk limits and volatility (ATR) |
| **Leverage Behavior** | Maximum leverage on every idea, blindly | Selective convexity, aware of decay and theta |
| **Response to Losses** | Denial, averaging down, revenge trading | Mechanical stop-loss, reduced size, post-mortem audit |
| **Time Horizon** | One exciting bet at a time | A series of high-conviction asymmetric bets |
| **Record Keeping** | None or casual | Detailed journal plus performance statistics |
| **Concentration** | Unhedged, random chaos | Concentrated, but strictly fenced by risk parameters |
| **Long-Term Outcome** | Near-certain ruin | Survivable drawdowns with potential for outlier gains |

## A Final Warning

Even with flawless process, aggressive professional speculation remains extraordinarily dangerous; a hostile regime can take most or all of your capital in a matter of weeks. The traders who have actually produced 1,000%-plus gains in short windows are the extreme minority who survived several near-death experiences through iron discipline and a measure of luck. This book does not promise that you will turn $100,000 into $1,000,000. It hands you the same blueprint the rare winners used — combined with the risk rules they too often ignored until the day they blew up. Master the difference between gambling and professional speculation first; only then do the aggressive tools in the chapters ahead become weapons instead of liabilities.

- Why Most Traders Never Achieve Exponential Returns

If turning $100,000 into $1,000,000 in six months were easy, everyone would do it. Instead, studies across countries and decades reach the same conclusion:

- **70–97%** of active day traders lose money.
- About **80%** quit within two years.
- Only **1–3%** remain consistently profitable.
- In a major study of Brazilian day traders active beyond **300 days**, **97%** still lost money.
- After commissions, slippage, and taxes, the average retail trader's returns are deeply negative.

A **900%+** return in six months is not merely rare—it is a statistical outlier. Most traders think success depends on finding the right stock, indicator, guru, or strategy. In reality, the barriers are structural, mathematical, and psychological. Most are undercapitalized intellectually long before they are undercapitalized financially.

## Exponential Growth Is a Different Regime

The first failure is conceptual. Exponential growth is not linear growth accelerated—it is a different mathematical regime. Human intuition expects steady, linear progress; compounding does not behave that way. Early in a **10×** campaign, gains appear disappointingly small even when execution is excellent. Many traders respond by increasing position size too early or abandoning a profitable edge just before compounding accelerates. Extreme returns come from a handful of concentrated, asymmetric opportunities captured during unusually favorable market environments. That requires surviving long enough to reach those environments—and having the skill and emotional discipline to exploit them. Most traders fail at one or both.

## The Structural Killers

Before psychology takes over, several structural forces quietly destroy aggressive accounts. They are mathematical, not emotional.

Volatility Drag and Path Dependency. High-velocity instruments such as 2× and 3× ETFs and short-dated options carry hidden costs. Leveraged ETFs reset daily, making returns path-dependent. If a 3× semiconductor ETF rises 5% one day and falls 5% the next, the underlying index may finish near breakeven, but the leveraged ETF suffers a structural loss from volatility. In trendless markets, this silent decay steadily erodes the capital base required for exponential compounding:

| **Account Volatility / Churn** | → | **Daily Leveraged Reset** | → | **Structural Capital Decay** |
|---|---|---|---|---|

The Mathematics of Ruin. Drawdowns compound geometrically. A 50% loss requires a 100% gain to recover; 75% requires 300%; 90% requires 900%. In leveraged instruments, a single adverse move or overnight gap can produce such losses within hours. Without drawdown limits, disciplined position sizing, and account-level circuit breakers, most traders are mathematically eliminated long before they realize it. One freight train in the wrong direction ends the campaign.

The 1:1 Fallacy. Many retail traders accept 1:1—or worse, negative—reward-to-risk ratios, risking $2,000 to make $1,000. At 1:1, maintaining profitability requires an exceptionally high win rate—typically above 60–70% after commissions and slippage. Exponential compounding requires deliberate asymmetry: risking 1R to pursue 3R–5R. Without it, an ordinary losing streak permanently damages the equity curve.

Margin Ruin and Forced Liquidation. Many traders pursue 10× returns in 180 days by maximizing broker margin, giving the brokerage the power to end the campaign. A routine stop-run or overnight macro gap can trigger forced liquidation at the worst possible moment, converting a temporary drawdown into permanent capital destruction.

## Hope Instead of Edge

Most traders enter with hope rather than edge. They chase tips, **FOMO**, revenge-trade, and size positions emotionally instead of probabilistically. Professional speculation requires **positive expectancy**—a tested process whose long-term gains outweigh losses, costs, and drawdowns.

A feeling is not an edge, nor is following a guru. A genuine edge comes from **backtested, statistically validated setups**, understanding how instruments behave (including **leveraged ETF decay** and **option Greeks**), and recognizing the current market regime. Professionals judge success over hundreds of trades, not one. Losses are business expenses; amateurs take them personally.

## The Psychological Killers

Large returns require enduring large volatility, which produces fear, greed, panic, euphoria, hesitation, and fatigue. Many traders can discuss aggressive strategies calmly; far fewer can execute them while their accounts swing violently. Those who cannot tolerate volatility eventually sabotage their own system.

The Cognitive Decay of the Equity Curve. As an account grows, dollar swings become emotionally harder to manage. A trader comfortable risking $1,000 in a $100,000 account may panic when the same percentage becomes $5,000–10,000 in a $500,000 account. The result is predictable: taking profits too early or refusing to honor stops, turning routine losses into catastrophic ones.

Emotional Instability Under Volatility. Fear and greed produce familiar mistakes: (1) Selling winners too early; (2) Holding losers too long; (3) Revenge trading; (4) Increasing size after wins; and (5) Becoming addicted to constant action. Eventually, the market punishes every one of them.

Confusing Activity with Productivity. Many traders mistake activity for progress. They overtrade, chase momentum, react to every headline, switch strategies constantly, and quietly lose money through spreads, commissions, and slippage. Professionals know the largest gains come from a few exceptional opportunities, not constant participation. They wait, then press hard when conditions strongly favor aggression.

Survivorship Bias. Social media showcases winning screenshots while hiding thousands of blown-up accounts. Traders compare themselves to survivors rather than the full population, badly misjudging the true odds.

Abandoning Discipline in Success. Success often destroys more traders than failure. Large gains breed overconfidence, oversized positions, ignored stops, and excessive concentration. Many careers end not because of early losses, but because traders mistake a favorable market for permanent skill. Markets have a long history of humbling those who confuse momentum with mastery.

A Performance Discipline, Not Just a Skill. Sustained execution requires a stable operator. Elite trading demands concentration, emotional regulation, energy management, sleep, and resilience. Chronic stress, financial pressure, relationship turmoil, addiction, or exhaustion erode decision quality under pressure. That is why many top traders organize their lives around protecting psychological clarity. Trading is not merely a technical skill—it is a performance discipline.

## The Environment Decides — and the Discipline of Restraint

Aggressive compounding is highly **regime-dependent**. It thrives during expanding liquidity, strong momentum, elevated volatility, sector manias, institutional rotation, and speculative participation. In choppy or illiquid markets, the same tactics can fail catastrophically. Professionals adapt to the regime; amateurs apply the same strategy regardless of conditions.

Leverage magnifies not only gains, but mistakes and emotional instability. A survivable unleveraged trade can become fatal when leveraged. The irony is that aggressive compounding requires equal measures of aggression and restraint. Professionals know when to press and when to move to cash. Most traders know only one speed, and markets eventually punish that rigidity.

## The Rare Winners: What They Do Differently

Exponential returns remain possible because markets periodically create extraordinary asymmetric opportunities. Successful traders are distinguished not by secret indicators but by disciplined execution:

- Risking only **1–2%** of capital per trade, often less.
- Mastering **1–3** high-probability setups.

- Maintaining detailed journals and honest reviews.
- Waiting patiently during unfavorable markets.
- Recognizing psychological biases.
- Adapting to changing market regimes.
- Treating every trade as one data point in a large sample.
- Protecting survival above all else.

They still experience major drawdowns. The difference is that they survive them. Extraordinary returns come from disciplined execution under extreme uncertainty—not excitement.

## The Hard Truth

Exponential returns are rare not because opportunities are scarce, but because most traders run an undisciplined operation. They misuse leverage, ignore path-dependent decay, accept poor reward-to-risk ratios, rely on margin, and size positions emotionally instead of systematically. A **1,000%** compounding campaign requires replacing prediction with disciplined enforcement of mathematical risk limits. This book will not sugarcoat the challenge. The strategies ahead are powerful only when paired with professional discipline. The road to **1,000%** in six months is littered with failed accounts. To join the **1–3%** who succeed rather than the **97%** who fail, you must build unbreakable rules, respect the mathematics of ruin, master your psychology, and treat trading as a high-stakes profession.

## Survival Before Compounding

Every trader enters the market dreaming of compounding; few understand survival. That misunderstanding destroys more accounts than poor stock selection, weak indicators, bad timing, or lack of intelligence. Most traders focus on making money instead of avoiding elimination, yet survival is the foundation of compounding. Without it, compounding never has time to work.

This is the first law of aggressive trading: **You cannot compound from zero.** Once the account is destroyed, the game is over, regardless of how brilliant the strategy was. Institutional traders understand that permanently impairing capital in the first **30–60 days** prevents exponential growth from ever taking hold. Traders who survive retain the ability to compound; traders who blow up are permanently removed from the game. The governing principle of this book is simple: First, do not die. Then compound aggressively.

## The Mathematics of Ruin

The math alone should permanently change how a serious trader thinks about risk, because compounding is exponential – but so is destruction. Losses do not punish symmetrically; the deeper the hole, the more violently the recovery math turns against you.

| Drawdown | Remaining Capital (on $100,000) | Gain Needed to Recover |
|---|---|---|
| **–10%** | $90,000 | +11.1% |

| Drawdown | Remaining Capital (on $100,000) | Gain Needed to Recover |
|---|---|---|
| **−25%** | $75,000 | +33.3% |
| **−50%** | $50,000 | +100% |
| **−75%** | $25,000 | +300% |
| **−90%** | $10,000 | +900% |

In a six-month campaign, these numbers are decisive. A 10× objective requires roughly **46.8% monthly** compounding. A single **50% drawdown** demands a **100% gain** just to break even. Leverage magnifies the damage: **3× ETFs** and options can lose **70–100%** in one violent move, wiping out months of gains—or the entire account—in days. A **50% drawdown** destroys more than capital; it destroys time. It delays or derails the compounding curve's acceleration while inflicting mathematical, psychological, and emotional damage. Every legendary aggressive trader who endured made capital preservation the first priority, even while employing high-conviction, leveraged strategies.

## Aggression, Not Recklessness

Many traders mistake aggression for recklessness. They assume extraordinary returns require maximum exposure, excessive leverage, oversized positions, and constant trading. Professionals think the opposite: **offensive growth is governed by defensive boundaries.** Before an account can compound, it must survive. Retail traders often postpone discipline until the account grows larger. There is no later if the account is gone. Aggressive compounding is therefore built on **selective aggression**—protecting capital during unfavorable markets so you remain funded when rare, high-probability opportunities appear.

## The Survival Architecture

Survival is not willpower but structure. Professional trading desks operate within non-negotiable, predefined risk limits established before trading begins, preventing emotions from dictating decisions during drawdowns.

**The 1% Risk Unit.** Aggressive speculation does not justify risking large portions of capital on one trade. Even with high-convexity instruments—short-dated options, warrants, and 3× leveraged ETFs—maximum loss at the stop should be limited to 1% of total equity, never more than 2%. Position size is the mathematical result of that rule.

**Total Account Equity** → **Extract 1% Risk Unit ($1,000)** → **Measure Distance to Technical Stop** → **Output Position Size**

On a $100,000 account, maximum loss per trade is $1,000. A 5% stop permits a $20,000 position; a 10% stop, required by higher volatility or a wider Average True Range, reduces it to $10,000. At 1% risk, five consecutive losses reduce equity by only about 5%, leaving 95% of the compounding engine intact. As equity grows to $200,000, $400,000, and beyond, the 1% risk unit is recalculated. Many traders fail not on the way down but on the way up, increasing size emotionally instead of mathematically.

Graduated Circuit Breakers. Traders should not wait for a margin call to halt a losing streak. Drawdown is met with a pre-set, automated ladder of de-risking:

| Trigger (peak-to-trough) | Mandatory Action |
|---|---|
| **Down 10%** | Halve all position sizes |
| **Down 20%** | Cut risk to 0.5% per trade, or stop trading for the week |
| **Hard ceiling (≈25–30%)** | Total account lockdown: liquidate to cash, revoke API order-routing keys, freeze operations for a 48-hour audit |

These safeguards prevent recoverable setbacks from becoming terminal losses. If you feel compelled to override them, they are doing their job.

**Leverage as a Scalpel, Not a Sledgehammer.** Leverage is dangerous only when misused. Applied within confirmed, high-momentum trends, it accelerates compounding; applied emotionally, it destroys accounts. Use leverage only after trend confirmation, with predefined stops, and increase size gradually as discipline and consistency are proven. Most traders encounter leverage before developing the maturity to manage it.

**The Path-Dependent Liquidation Filter.** Path-dependent instruments require both price and time limits. Exit leveraged momentum trades that stall for more than 48–72 hours, even if the stop remains intact. In a six-month campaign, dead time is risk. Sideways markets erode leveraged ETFs through volatility decay and options through theta decay. Survival requires keeping capital liquid and deployed only in assets that are moving.

**Cash Is a Position.** In low-edge markets, cash is professional risk management, not fear. Many elite traders hold 30–70% cash during choppy conditions, preserving both capital and psychological readiness to exploit higher-probability opportunities.

## Some Environments Reward Aggression; Others Punish It

Markets move through cycles of momentum, liquidity, volatility, speculation, sector leadership, macroeconomics, and psychology. Some reward aggression; others punish it. Professionals recognize regime changes, reduce exposure, and wait. **Hedge funds** and **family offices** do the same. The greatest compounding periods often arrive suddenly during liquidity surges, momentum manias, technological revolutions, sector explosions, and volatility expansions. Only traders who remain solvent can exploit them.

## The Psychological War of Survival

A **1,000%** campaign tests every aspect of your psychology. Expect 30–50% drawdowns, rapid swings of thousands of dollars, and alternating confidence and doubt. Volatility breeds fear, greed, euphoria, frustration, revenge trading, and exhaustion. Many traders understand risk intellectually but fail emotionally.

Emotional stability is part of the survival architecture. Panic during losses and euphoria after wins both destroy discipline. Survival requires emotional neutrality.

Position sizing is equally critical. Most disasters result not from being wrong but from being oversized. Even excellent analysis can be overwhelmed by macro shocks, liquidity collapses, earnings surprises, or abrupt shifts in sentiment. Small positions keep you in the game.

Patience is another survival skill. Many traders fail from boredom rather than poor analysis, forcing trades instead of waiting for asymmetric opportunities. Often, the most profitable trade is no trade.

Three principles reinforce discipline:

- Losses are tuition, not personal failure.
- Your job is not to be right, but to preserve your edge.
- When you become angry, euphoric, or emotionally tilted, stop trading.

Above all, remain humble. Traders who become attached to an opinion, position, sector, or forecast stop adapting. Professionals survive by admitting mistakes quickly, reducing exposure as conditions deteriorate, and changing with the market. Adaptability is the hidden foundation of extraordinary compounding.

## Survival Is the Real Edge

The traders who achieve **10×** returns are not always the smartest or luckiest. They survive long enough for their edge to compound. While amateurs focus on the **1,000%** upside, professionals focus first on **not going to zero**. Great fortunes are built through long periods of disciplined survival interrupted by the aggressive exploitation of rarc opportunities.

Master survival first — iron risk rules, drawdown governance, emotional control, and process discipline — and the aggressive tactics in the chapters ahead become genuine weapons. Ignore it, and even the best setups in this book will eventually destroy you. Everything that follows is built on this foundation: break the survival rules and the blueprint collapses; respect them, and you give yourself the only real chance at the returns this book was written for. Survival comes first. Compounding comes second. Always.

## The Philosophy of Controlled Aggression

At first glance, controlled aggression seems contradictory. Aggression implies bold action; control implies restraint. Yet extraordinary returns require both. To turn $100,000 into $1,000,000 in six months, you must be neither a conservative investor nor a reckless gambler, but a controlled aggressor—someone who pursues explosive returns within ironclad risk limits.

This is the central principle of the blueprint: Aggression without control is gambling. Control without aggression produces mediocrity. Retail traders equate aggression with oversized positions, excessive margin, and blind faith. Professionals define it as the calculated escalation of risk only when rare, high-probability conditions justify it.

## What Controlled Aggression Is

Controlled aggression combines two opposing forces:

- **Aggression:** Concentrated positions in high-conviction setups using **2× and 3× ETFs, options, warrants,** and momentum breakouts.
- **Control:** Strict position limits, risk rules, stop-losses, drawdown breakers, and disciplined execution that prevent one mistake from destroying the account.

It is neither emotional trading nor YOLO speculation. It is professional-grade aggression—focused, disciplined, and rule-bound.** **The distinction shows up on every operational dimension:

| Dimension | Reckless Trading (Gambling) | Controlled Aggression (Professional) |
|---|---|---|
| **Position Size** | Emotional, "all in" | 1% risk maximum per trade, mathematically calculated |
| **Leverage** | Maximum at all times | Selective, regime-dependent, tightly bounded |
| **Conviction** | "This feels like it" | Backtested edge + clear catalyst + favorable regime |
| **Response to Loss** | Revenge trade, double down | Cut the loss immediately, reduce size, or stop |
| **Drawdown** | No plan — "it'll come back" | Graduated circuit breakers (10%, 20%, hard lockdown) |
| **Mindset** | Hope and thrill | Probability, process, survival first |

## Why It Is the Only Path to 1,000% in Six Months

Controlled aggression is not optional—it is essential.

First, the mathematics demand it. A **900%+** gain in six months—about **46.8%** monthly—cannot come from small, diversified positions. It requires a handful of exceptional winners and the willingness to press hard when the odds are unusually favorable.

Second, control ensures survival. The same leverage capable of producing a **300%** month can also produce an **80–100%** loss. Without strict risk controls, the instruments capable of delivering **10×** returns are the same ones that destroy most traders.

Third, history supports it. The traders who achieved extraordinary short-term gains—certain **2021 GameStop** traders, skilled options traders, and momentum specialists during powerful bull markets—all practiced some form of controlled aggression, whether they named it or not.

## The Sniper, Not the Machine Gunner

Retail traders often behave like machine gunners—constantly trading, accumulating fees, and slowly bleeding capital. Controlled aggression is the discipline of the sniper.

Focus on a small group of high-velocity instruments—**3× sector ETFs**, short-dated options, and leading momentum stocks. Wait patiently. When key signals align—**relative-volume surges, 52-week-high breakouts,** and **institutional sector inflows**—deploy capital aggressively within predefined risk limits.

Elite military strategy follows the same principle: conserve resources, study conditions, and commit overwhelming force only when the odds favor success. Professional traders preserve capital during low-probability periods, then attack decisively when momentum and asymmetry align.

This creates a paradox many traders cannot tolerate. Professionals may appear inactive for long periods, then become highly aggressive during brief windows that generate most of their returns. Human nature craves constant activity; controlled aggression demands the opposite—**patience most of the time, aggression only at the right time.**

That requires emotional neutrality. Traders must shift seamlessly between offense and defense without becoming fearful after losses or reckless after wins, and without becoming attached to any trend, sector, narrative, or position.

## The Twin Engines: Offense and Defense

Controlled aggression resembles a high-performance race car: the engine provides the speed for extraordinary compounding; the brakes and steering make that speed survivable. Offense and defense are complementary. Without offense, exceptional returns are impossible. Without defense, survival is impossible.

| CONTROLLED AGGRESSION |
| --- |
| **OFFENSIVE ENGINE** |
| Deep in-the-money options (convex, fixed downside) |
| Concentrated 3x tactical sector ETFs |
| Dynamic capital scale (modified Kelly) |
| **DEFENSIVE BRAKES** |

| CONTROLLED AGGRESSION |
| --- |
| Automated hard API stop-losses |
| Graduated account-level circuit breaker |
| Mandatory 48-hour lockdown protocol |

The Offensive Engine. When the market enters a confirmed, high-volume uptrend, controlled aggression abandons broad diversification. Diversification preserves wealth; concentration builds it. Using a modified Kelly framework, capital is concentrated in the 2–3 highest-velocity catalyst stocks riding institutional accumulation. The aggression remains survivable through convexity. Long in-the-money options, warrants, and selective leverage cap downside at a predefined 1R while preserving upside of 3R, 5R, or even 10R. Leverage is tactical—it expands only when probability, liquidity, volatility, and reward-to-risk favor continuation, and contracts immediately when they do not.

The Defensive Brakes. While the offensive engine accelerates, the defensive system becomes fully mechanical. Stop-losses are hard bracket orders routed automatically through the execution platform or API. Above them sit graduated account-level circuit breakers that progressively reduce risk, ultimately moving the portfolio to cash and triggering a mandatory trading review. Aggression remains controlled because no single market sequence can destroy the capital base.

## The Five Tenets

Distilled, the five operating tenets that thread through every later chapter:

1. **Survival is the foundation.** You are permitted to be aggressive only because you have first built an unbreakable defense — the subject of the chapter on survival before compounding.

2. **Edge before size.** Never deploy aggression without a proven, high-conviction edge; aggression without edge is just expensive gambling.

3. **Asymmetry is king.** Seek setups where defined risk is small but potential reward is enormous — 3:1, 5:1, or better. This is where leverage becomes an ally instead of an executioner.

4. **Process over outcome.** Judge each day by whether you followed your rules, not by the P&L. A losing day that obeyed the rules is a good day; a winning day that broke them is a dangerous one.

5. **Adapt or die.** Be ferocious in favorable regimes and extremely patient — or fully in cash — when conditions deteriorate. Knowing when not to be aggressive is part of the aggression.

## Operating Inside Uncertainty

Controlled aggression begins with humility. Uncertainty never disappears, losses are inevitable, no setup is guaranteed, no strategy lasts forever, and every market regime eventually changes. Humility prevents aggression from becoming arrogance. Extraordinary returns exist because uncertainty exists. Without volatility, fear, greed, and asymmetry, there would be no exceptional opportunities. Controlled aggression does not eliminate uncertainty—it manages it by surviving hostile markets, preserving capital, and attacking decisively when rare, favorable conditions emerge.

> ***"I will attack the market with maximum force when conditions align with my proven edge. I will defend my capital with ruthless discipline at all other times. I accept that massive wins and painful drawdowns are both part of this path. My job is not to be right every day — my job is to survive long enough for the math of controlled aggression to work in my favor."***

This philosophy runs through every chapter that follows — stock selection, options strategies, 3x ETF tactics, position sizing, psychology, drawdown management, and exit rules. Each is an application of the same idea. The trader who masters only aggression eventually blows up; the trader who masters only caution never compounds enough to reach the goal. The rare trader who sustains exponential growth holds both at once, and understands the deepest truth in aggressive speculation: the goal is not to be aggressive all the time — it is to be aggressively right when the moment finally comes. Master that, and the tactics in the rest of this book become genuine weapons. Ignore it, and even the best setups here will eventually destroy you.

# PART I — THE MATHEMATICS OF 1,000% COMPOUNDING

**Chapter 1**

# Understanding Exponential Wealth

## The Power of Compounding

Compounding is the engine of this blueprint: it can turn profitable months into a 10× return, and it punishes mistakes just as relentlessly—one catastrophic drawdown can erase months in days. Most investors know only its slow form, retirement accounts growing over decades; aggressive speculation runs the same mathematics on a compressed timeline, where each profit enlarges the base that produces the next. That acceleration is what makes turning **$100,000** into **$1,000,000** in six months mathematically possible.

### You Are Not Earning 1,000% at Once

You are not earning **1,000%** on the original **$100,000** in one trade; you are compounding controlled gains on an expanding base: **$100,000** → **$130,000** → **$175,000** → **$260,000** → **$400,000** → **$650,000** → **$1,000,000**. No single trade approaches 1,000%—sequential compounding does the work. The account must compound about **46.8% per month**, roughly **9.3% per week** or **1.3% per day** – a path traced month by month in the milestone table later in this chapter.

The curve is heavily back-loaded. The first three months reach only about **$316,000**; the final two generate more than **$535,000**—over half the ending account, and more than the first four months combined. This is where many traders fail: impatient with modest early gains, they over-leverage, force trades, or abandon risk rules just before compounding accelerates.

### Compounding Applies to the Risk Unit

You don't hit 46.8% a month by finding a stock that conveniently rises 46% every twenty days; you apply compounding to your **risk unit**. A professional defines **1R** as the most capital he'll lose on a trade at its stop—typically **1%** of equity. As the curve climbs, 1R expands automatically: 1% of **$100,000** is **$1,000**; at **$500,000** the same rule makes 1R **$5,000**. You never raise the percentage you risk—the base scales it for you.

| **Current Account Balance** | → | **Extract 1% Risk Unit (1R)** | → | **Capture ~3R Profit Setup** | → | **Account Compounds** |
|---|---|---|---|---|---|---|

*Each cycle then* ***resets*** *a larger 1R on the new, expanded base – and repeats.*

With a structural edge in which the average winner captures roughly **3R**, reaching the target needs no flawless win rate: a net **~36R** across the campaign's **~120 sessions** is mathematically enough. Because each win enlarges the base, the same rule deploys progressively larger blocks into the same high-velocity setups—without raising the account's percentage risk. That is professional velocity: you scale your parameters, not the wildness of your trades.

## How the Instruments Amplify It

Here stocks, 2× and 3× ETFs, options, and warrants become powerful. Strong momentum stocks and 3× sector ETFs can move **30–100%+**; options can turn a **20–30%** move in the underlying into **200–1,000%+** through leverage, volatility, and gamma; warrants amplify further. As the account grows, ordinary percentages produce extraordinary dollars: a **20%** gain on **$100,000** earns **$20,000**; the same gain on **$500,000** earns **$100,000**. Eventually the expanding base is the primary growth engine.

## Losses Compound Too

Compounding runs in reverse just as well. A **50%** drawdown halves both capital and future earning power, demanding a **100%** gain just to recover. Sequence matters: because the curve is back-loaded, a major early drawdown can make the six-month objective nearly impossible even with flawless execution afterward. Leveraged products worsen this through **path dependency, daily resets, volatility drag,** and **theta decay**. You are protecting more than capital—you are protecting future compounding.

## The Psychology of the Curve

The uneven curve imposes two opposite tests. Early, when gains feel trivial against the goal, the danger is impatience—forcing trades and over-leveraging to "speed things up," the most common way the engine gets interrupted. Once acceleration arrives and the dollar swings turn enormous, the danger flips to over-protection—cutting winners short out of fear of giving back gains. You have to stay stable across all three phases: the slow grind, the accelerating middle, and the high-volatility large-capital stage. This is why consistency beats occasional brilliance—exponential growth rarely comes from one massive trade, but from repeated asymmetrical setups, disciplined risk control, and, above all, surviving long enough for the curve to steepen.

## Protecting the Engine

Harnessing compounding while surviving it comes down to a few non-negotiables:

- **Protect the base.** Never risk more than 1% per trade; a damaged base compounds slower.
- **Compound winners aggressively.** Pyramid into confirmed strength and let winners run behind trailing stops—the large R-multiples bend the curve upward.
- **Cut losers instantly.** A small mechanical loss protects the whole trajectory.
- **Use leverage selectively.** Only when a setup offers extreme asymmetry, never as a constant state.
- **Reinvest religiously.** Never withdraw early; every dollar left is fuel for next month's expansion.

Compounding is not magic; it is mathematics meeting discipline. Most traders never see exponential returns because they break the survival rules before the math can work—over-leveraging, revenge-trading, or absorbing one **70%** drawdown that ends the game. Those who reach this level treat every trade as if it affects the next five months of compounding: ferocious offense when the edge is present, extreme defense the rest of the time. Master survival, respect the math, then unleash controlled aggression with the instruments in this book.

*The amateur compounds by chasing bigger and bigger percentage moves. The sovereign speculator compounds by scaling his operational parameters. When equity grows from $100,000 to $500,000, you don't hunt crazier stocks; you deploy the same 1% risk on the same institutional setups and let the geometric expansion of position size do the heavy lifting.*

## Why Repeated 25% Gains Matter More Than Single Jackpots

Inexperienced traders believe wealth comes from a single trade—one perfect option, one short squeeze, one biotech approval, one overnight gap. The fantasy dominates speculative culture because it promises an enormous reward without long-term discipline. Professional compounding almost never works that way: survivors rely not on one miracle but on repeated asymmetric gains compounded over time.

The distinction matters more than almost anything in this book. Turning $100,000 into $1,000,000 on one trade is gambling on prediction; reaching it through repeated controlled gains is building through mathematics—far more reliable than miracles. Jackpot strategies depend on rare, low-probability anomalies that expose the account to terminal ruin; the repeated-25% strategy depends on high-probability velocity, positive expectancy, and geometric compounding.

### The Math: Eleven Tranches of 25%

To turn $100,000 into $1,000,000 you don't need a stock that rises 1,000%. In a concentrated, sequential model, just eleven consecutive 25% tranches cross the million-dollar mark:

| Tranche | Start of Tranche | After +25% |
|---|---|---|
| 1 | $100,000 | $125,000 |
| 2 | $125,000 | $156,250 |
| 3 | $156,250 | $195,312 |
| 4 | $195,312 | $244,140 |
| 5 | $244,140 | $305,175 |
| 6 | $305,175 | $381,469 |
| 7 | $381,469 | $476,837 |
| 8 | $476,837 | $596,046 |
| 9 | $596,046 | $745,058 |

| Tranche | Start of Tranche | After +25% |
|---|---|---|
| 10 | $745,058 | $931,322 |
| 11 | $931,322 | **$1,164,153** |

Nothing spectacular happens in any step—a 25% gain is ordinary—yet eleven of them carry $100,000 past $1,000,000. Acceleration is the point: the same 25% that adds $25,000 to the first tranche adds nearly $187,000 to the tenth, because each gain sits on a larger base.

In time terms, across roughly 120 sessions eleven tranches means harvesting 25% about once every ten or eleven trading days—and a 25% move in the right vehicle is common: a liquid 3× sector ETF (SOXL in a semiconductor breakout) or a high-delta in-the-money option can deliver it inside a normal momentum window. That is the model's quiet genius: it re-engineers an impossible-looking target into a repeatable, almost assembly-line process—the same 10x goal, viewed as a series of harvests rather than a monthly rate.

## Why Jackpots Kill, While 25% Gains Build

This is the technical heart of the gambling-versus-speculation divide. Chasing jackpots destroys capital velocity three ways.

**Probability, not outlier dependence.** To make 1,000% on one trade you must use deeply speculative, illiquid, or far-out-of-the-money instruments—0DTE options, penny stocks—whose payoff probability is typically under 5%. The chaser loses most of the time, and those micro-losses bleed the base dry. The 25% speculator works where institutional volume is densest: a 25% move in a high-beta stock or 3× ETF happens routinely on earnings breakouts and sector rotations, keeping expectancy positive.

**The asymmetry moat.** Because a 25% target lives close to the action, the stop stays tight—often just 3–5% below entry—producing a 5R-to-8R reward-to-risk. Fail, and you exit with a scratch loss; succeed, and the payoff dwarfs the risk. Jackpot instruments offer no such moat: binary by nature, they routinely gap down 50% or expire worthless overnight, exposing your account to ruin.

| Path | The Setup | The Outcome |
|---|---|---|
| **Speculator** | Tight 3–5% stop beneath a 25% target | Scratch loss if wrong; +5R to +8R if right |
| **Gambler** | No real stop; binary, decaying instrument | Gap-down or worthless expiry – risk of ruin |

**Scalability.** A jackpot strategy doesn't scale. Growing from **$100,000** to **$500,000**, you can't push half a million into illiquid penny stocks or thin options chains without severe slippage. You can deploy it into liquid **3× ETFs** or mega-caps and capture repeated **25%** moves. The tranche model scales; the jackpot model collapses under its own size.

### The Hidden Cost of the Jackpot

Jackpots breed excitement, not discipline—overconfidence, oversized positions, reckless leverage. Many who win big early lose everything because the money arrived before the discipline. Repeated **25%** gains build the opposite: consistency, emotional control, scalability, survival. A trader who gains **300%** then loses **80%** has interrupted the engine and often finishes behind the steady compounder. The objective is **optimal compounding**—maximizing long-term growth without sacrificing survival.

### Trader A and Trader B

Two traders over the same market. Trader A compounds 25% repeatedly with disciplined risk, avoids catastrophic drawdowns, and survives into the acceleration phase. Trader B occasionally doubles the account spectacularly but repeatedly collapses, rebuilding from a smaller base each time. Trader B gets the screenshots; Trader A very often finishes wealthier, because uninterrupted compounding is powerful and a single deep collapse can erase years of it. Continuity beats intensity.

### Continuity Is the Real Edge

This is why elite traders look less aggressive than amateurs expect: protecting the engine matters more than chasing excitement. The amateur seeks thrills; the professional seeks continuity. Repeated controlled gains also create psychological stability—jackpot trading produces euphoria, despair, **FOMO**, revenge trading, and dependence on action, while consistent gains build confidence in process over luck. The calmer trader survives longer, and survival gives compounding the time it needs.

### One Jackpot, or a Lifetime

The goal is not one perfect trade but repeatedly exploiting high-probability, asymmetric opportunities while preventing catastrophic interruption. **One jackpot can change a month; repeated compounding can change a lifetime.** Master repeated **25%** gains—high-probability, tightly risk-controlled, scalable—and you replace lottery thinking with a disciplined engineering process that survives real markets.

## The Mathematical Path from $100,000 to $1,000,000 in Six Months

This is the blueprint in numbers. To compound 10x, the account must grow tenfold—not a 100% gain but a **900%** net gain, a final value equal to **1,000%** of the start. The arithmetic is simple: **$100,000 × 10 = $1,000,000**. The execution is brutal.

As a rate, that's roughly **+46.8% per month**, about **+9.3% per week**, or near **+1.94% per session** across 120 sessions. No single 900% trade hides in that figure; it demands repeated controlled gains with almost no interruption from large losses. View the target through three lenses: the geometric milestone path, the daily velocity it implies, and the R-multiple engine that delivers it.

### The Geometric Milestone Path

Compounded at 46.8% a month, **$100,000 × 1.468⁶** lands almost exactly on **$1,000,000**:

| Month | Monthly Return | Ending Balance | Capital Added |
|---|---|---|---|
| **Start** | — | $100,000 | — |
| 1 | +46.8% | $146,800 | +$46,800 |
| 2 | +46.8% | $215,502 | +$68,702 |
| 3 | +46.8% | $316,357 | +$100,855 |
| 4 | +46.8% | $464,412 | +$148,055 |
| 5 | +46.8% | $681,757 | +$217,345 |
| 6 | +46.8% | $1,000,000 | +$318,243 |

Shape matters as much as destination. **Month 6** alone generates more than **$318,000**—exceeding the original **$100,000**—and over half of the **$1,000,000** is created in the final two months. The first **90 days** look deceptively slow, leading many to abandon risk rules in **Months 2–3**, destroying the engine just before the curve turns vertical.

### A Realistic, Lumpy Path

Real markets never deliver a smooth 46.8%. A more believable route averages roughly **+48%** through uneven results—the kind a strong trending market produces with leveraged instruments:

| Month | Return | Ending Balance | Character of the Month |
|---|---|---|---|
| 1 | +55% | $155,000 | Strong breakout month |
| 2 | +40% | $217,000 | Solid follow-through |
| 3 | +65% | $358,050 | Major trend acceleration |
| 4 | +35% | $483,368 | Consolidation month |
| 5 | +50% | $725,052 | Big catalyst move |
| 6 | +45% | $1,051,324 | Final push past the goal |

This reaches—and slightly exceeds—the target with realistic volatility, no miracle month; the largest gain is **+65%**, well within a **3× ETF** or well-timed options trade in a strong trend. What it requires is avoiding catastrophic losses, because the curve has little room for major drawdowns.

## Daily Velocity and the Expectancy Formula

Across roughly **120 sessions**, the pace averages about **+1.94%** per session (**$100,000 × 1.0194$^{120}$ ≈ $1,000,000**). Markets don't rise in equal increments, so professionals focus on **expectancy**, not daily targets: **Expectancy = (Win Rate × Average Win) – (Loss Rate × Average Loss).**

A trader with just a **40%** win rate can still run positive expectancy with a reward-to-risk near **3.5:1**—winners several times larger than losers. The win rate matters far less than the size of winners relative to losers; that asymmetry is the entire game.

## The R-Multiple Engine

The most practical way to execute across stocks, 3× ETFs, options, and warrants is to drop percentage targets and manage in R-multiples. **1R** is your risk unit—the most you'll lose on a trade at its hard stop, about **1%** of equity. As equity compounds, 1R scales automatically: at **$100,000**, 1R is **$1,000**; at **$500,000**, **$5,000**. You never raise the percentage; the expanding base does the work.

Because each loss is capped at one robotic 1R while winners run into large multiples—the 20R, 40R moves convex instruments produce—the account compounds on a small number of outsized wins, not a high win rate. The point is positive expectancy, not perfect prediction:

| Metric | Illustrative Allocation over 120 Sessions |
|---|---|
| **Total executed trades** | 60 (about one entry every two sessions) |
| **Win rate** | 45% — 27 winning trades, 33 losing trades |
| **Average loss** | −1R (robotic stop-loss enforcement) |
| **Average win** | +3R (profits taken at structural extensions) |
| **Gross wins** | 27 × 3R = +81R |
| **Gross losses** | 33 × (−1R) = −33R |
| **Net result** | +48R — strongly positive expectancy |

A **45%** win rate still produces exceptional returns because winners average **three times** the losers. That expectancy, compounded on a growing base, powers the whole curve—and the larger the winners (especially with **options** and **3× ETFs**), the fewer are needed.

## How the Instruments Make It Possible

The velocity the math demands is reachable only because the toolkit manufactures large asymmetric winners:

- **3x ETFs and leveraged products.** TQQQ or SOXL can move 40–100%+ inside a strong trend—one large-R win from a sector run.

- **Options (long calls and call spreads).** A well-timed 20–30% move in the underlying can mean 200–800%+ on the position.
- **Warrants and high-beta stocks.** Extreme convex asymmetry in bull runs—small defined risk, large upside.
- **Pyramiding.** Adding to winners as they prove themselves stacks size into what's already working.

Used with disciplined risk management, these tools make the path mathematically possible.

### Critical Warnings About This Path

- **Extraordinarily difficult:** sustaining **46.8%** monthly ranks among the highest levels of trading performance. Treat **10×** as a stretch goal, not an expectation.
- **Drawdowns are inevitable:** even successful campaigns may see **20–40%** drawdowns; without strict controls, reaching **Month 6** is unlikely.
- **Sequence risk is critical:** because the curve is back-loaded, an early **-60%** loss can make the objective nearly impossible. Protect early capital.
- **Taxes matter:** in the **U.S.**, short-term gains are taxed as ordinary income; frequent trading can create substantial liabilities.

### The Controlled-Aggression Approach to the Math

The numbers become reachable only atop the disciplines from earlier chapters—four standing commitments:

- **Survive every month first.** Enforce the 1% rule and graduated drawdown circuit breakers before chasing any target.
- **Compound winners ruthlessly when the freight train is running.** Press hard only when the regime genuinely favors aggression.
- **Stay patient, and in cash, when there is no edge.**
- **Reinvest every dollar.** Never withdraw early; each dollar left is fuel for next month.

The mathematics, instruments, and strategy all exist; what separates the few who succeed is execution—holding discipline through the first **90** deceptively slow days, enduring drawdowns, and resisting the urge to force results. This chapter is the map; the rest is disciplined execution.

## Why and How Drawdowns Destroy Compounding

You can have the best setups, timing, and instruments—3× ETFs, options, warrants—and still lose a 1,000% campaign through one catastrophic drawdown. Amateurs focus on upside; professionals focus on drawdowns, because compounding is brutally asymmetric: gains build slowly, large losses destroy fast. The real danger isn't the loss—it's damaging the engine. Exponential growth depends on reinvesting an expanding base; a deep drawdown doesn't just cut capital, it breaks the mathematical path, making a 180-day campaign increasingly unattainable.

## The Asymmetric Tyranny of Recovery Math

Losses and gains are profoundly unequal: the return needed to climb back to a prior peak scales exponentially, and in a six-month sprint every point of recovery also burns calendar you can't replace:

| Drawdown | Capital Left | Gain Needed to Recover | Months at +46.8%/mo |
|---|---|---|---|
| **–10%** | $90,000 | +11.1% | ~0.2 |
| **–20%** | $80,000 | +25% | ~0.5 |
| **–30%** | $70,000 | +42.9% | ~0.9 |
| **–40%** | $60,000 | +66.7% | ~1.3 |
| **–50%** | **$50,000** | **+100%** | ~1.8 |
| **–60%** | $40,000 | +150% | ~2.4 |
| **–70%** | $30,000 | +233% | ~3.2 |
| **–80%** | $20,000 | +400% | ~4.3 |
| **–90%** | $10,000 | +900% | 6+ |

Read the final column: a **10%** loss costs about one-fifth of a month; a **50%** drawdown consumes nearly two months of maximum-rate compounding just to break even; a **90%** collapse eats the entire campaign. A trader who grows **$100,000** to **$300,000** then loses **70%** falls back to **$90,000**—months of progress gone, but the clock doesn't reset.

## Drawdowns Starve the Engine

There's a second, mechanical way drawdowns break compounding. Position size is a fraction of equity, so when equity shrinks, the weapon shrinks with it. A drawdown doesn't just lower your balance—it starves the engine of fuel:

| Account | Position Size (10%) | On a +50% Move | Harvested |
|---|---|---|---|
| **$100,000 (healthy base)** | $10,000 | +50% | +$5,000 |
| **$50,000 (after –50% DD)** | $5,000 | +50% | +$2,500 |

The same winning trade now yields half the dollars. After a **50%** drawdown, you need twice as many equivalent winners to restore the same growth rate. A drawdown doesn't merely reduce capital—it weakens every future opportunity.

## The Leverage Amplifier

The instruments that enable a **10×** campaign also magnify drawdowns. **3× ETFs** can lose **60–90%** in sharp reversals while the index falls only **20–30%**; options can expire worthless overnight; warrants can collapse in ordinary corrections.

Leveraged ETFs also suffer **volatility drag** from daily resets. If an index falls **10%** then rises **11.11%**, it breaks even; a **3× ETF** falls **30%** then rises **33.33%**:

- **$100,000 → $70,000 → $93,331**

The index breaks even; the leveraged account permanently loses **$6,669** through path dependency alone. In choppy markets this silent decay steadily erodes capital.

## Why a Six-Month Sprint Has No Margin

Time normally heals drawdowns; a **six-month** campaign has no such luxury. Every month recovering is one less month compounding, and because the curve is back-loaded, early losses are especially destructive.

Suppose **$100,000** grows to **$180,000** by **Month 3** (**+80%**), then suffers a **55%** drawdown to **$81,000**. Reaching **$1,000,000** now needs roughly **+1,135%** in the final three months—no longer a trading plan but a lottery ticket. The drawdown didn't just cost **$99,000**; it ended the campaign.

## The Deficit Paradox

Deep drawdowns damage psychology as much as capital. Traders abandon sizing rules, pull stops, and chase recovery through oversized options and warrants—speculation quietly becomes gambling. The paradox: one loss often creates the conditions for a larger one, as fear, hesitation, and revenge trading follow. Many never recover because the account survives but the decision-maker doesn't.

## Drawdown Control Is the Compounding Strategy

This leads to the reframe that separates professionals from amateurs. The amateur asks, "How much can I make?" The professional asks, "How much can I lose without interrupting future compounding?" Survival is mathematically welded to growth: protecting capital isn't defensive thinking, it's offensive mathematics. Missing an opportunity is survivable; destroying the account is not. This is why elite funds often look conservative—avoiding catastrophic drawdowns matters more than capturing every gain, and a trader banking **15–30%** without collapses will bury the one chasing **300%** jackpots between crashes.

You can't eliminate drawdowns, but you can keep them survivable, and a few hard rules do most of the work:

- **The 1% risk rule.** Never risk more than 1% on a trade, so no position can open a crater.
- **Graduated circuit breakers.** Down 10% from peak, halve sizes; down 20%, cut risk to 0.5% per trade; by 25–30%, move fully to cash and reassess.

- **Position limits.** No more than four to eight positions at once, and no more than 25–30% in any single name or theme.
- **Daily and weekly loss limits.** Hit a preset daily or weekly loss and you stop until the next session.

These rules convert an account-killer into a manageable setback. The goal isn't to never lose; it's to never let a loss reach the depth from which the math can't recover inside six months.

Drawdowns don't simply reduce capital—they steal time and dismantle the path to $1,000,000. Amateurs fixate on upside; professionals obsess first over the downside, knowing one bad sequence can erase a string of brilliant trades and no late genius outruns an early collapse. Master drawdown control and you give compounding room to work. Survival isn't the conservative choice—it's the ultimate edge.

## CAGR vs. Aggressive Compounding

Most investors think in **CAGR**—the Compound Annual Growth Rate. Wall Street quotes it, advisors live by it, long-term investors treat it as gospel, and across decades that reverence is earned. But in a six-month sprint to turn **$100,000** into **$1,000,000**, CAGR thinking is not merely inadequate—it can be actively dangerous.

The error runs both ways: many apply slow long-term logic to aggressive speculation, and just as many apply speculation psychology to long-term investing. Before engineering a 10x return over 180 days, you must see exactly where traditional compounding ends and aggressive compounding begins—they run on different machinery, governed by velocity, concentration, and parameter scaling.

**Deconstructing CAGR: the linear anchor.** CAGR is the geometric mean progression rate over a period longer than a year, assuming steady, smoothed compounding:

*CAGR = (Ending Value / Beginning Value)^(1/n) – 1*, where *n* is years.

It's the native language of pension funds, endowments, mutual funds, and conservative wealth managers—built for passive long-term allocations where volatility smooths across cycles and capital stays largely static and diversified.

Across long horizons its power is real. **$100,000** at **10%** annually:

- roughly **$259,000** in 10 years,
- roughly **$673,000** in 20 years,
- roughly **$1.74 million** in 30 years.

An annual CAGR of **8%–12%** is considered highly successful in family-office practice. But notice the timescale: at **10%**, that **$100,000** takes roughly **24 years** to reach **$1,000,000**. Traditional CAGR prioritizes survivability, diversification, preservation, tax efficiency, and low volatility—steady accumulation with time doing the work.

### The Numbers Behind a Six-Month 10x

Now compress that 24-year journey into 120 sessions:

- Starting capital: **$100,000**
- Ending capital: **$1,000,000**
- Time: **6 months (0.5 years)**

- Total return: **+900%**

Annualized, the result is staggering:

*Annualized Return = ($1,000,000 / $100,000)^(1/0.5) − 1 = 10² − 1 = 9,900%*

That's not a typo: a 10x return in six months equals a **9,900% annualized CAGR**. For context, Warren Buffett's lifetime CAGR sits near **20%**, and the best hedge funds rarely sustain **30–40%** annualized for long. A **9,900%** CAGR is extreme-outlier territory—financial miracles, not financial planning.

In the cadence you'll actually trade, the target is a net monthly rate of about **46.78%**:

*Monthly Return = 10^(1/6) − 1 ≈ 46.78%*

Because a 9,900% annualized figure is meaningless to a daily trader, aggressive compounding discards annualized thinking for something more granular: the **Compounding Tranche Model**.

## The Velocity Engine: The Compounding Tranche Model

Traditional compounding waits a year for one growth cycle; aggressive compounding refuses to wait. Instead of one annual cycle, the operator treats every trade liquidation as a milestone: realized cash is immediately recycled into the next high-velocity setup, and the base grows tranche by tranche. You're not earning a return on static capital—you're rotating a liquid base through asymmetric opportunities as fast as disciplined execution allows. The unit shifts from years to sessions, and the engine runs only as long as the base stays alive to feed it.

## CAGR vs. Aggressive Compounding: Side by Side

The two models differ on nearly every operational axis:

| Dimension | Traditional CAGR | Aggressive Compounding |
|---|---|---|
| **Primary time unit** | Years (n) | Trading sessions / tranches |
| **Target horizon** | 10 to 30 years | 6 months (120 sessions) |
| **Required return** | ~8–12% per year (≈1–2% / month) | ~46.8% per month (+900% total) |
| **Asset distribution** | Broadly diversified (smooths volatility) | Highly concentrated (exploits volatility) |
| **Core instruments** | Blue-chip equities, fixed income, index ETFs | 3x ETFs, options, warrants, high-beta catalysts |
| **Leverage use** | Minimal | Heavy and selective (2x / 3x ETFs, options) |
| **Reinvestment trigger** | Quarterly dividends / annual rebalancing | Immediate realization / intraday liquidation |

| Dimension | Traditional CAGR | Aggressive Compounding |
|---|---|---|
| **Volatility tolerance** | Low (smooth equity curve) | Extremely high (large swings expected) |
| **Drawdown impact** | Painful but recoverable | Potentially fatal if not tightly controlled |
| **Mindset** | Steady, patient growth | Controlled aggression, survival first |
| **Realism** | Sustainable for institutions | Extreme-outlier territory for individuals |

## Volatility: Smoothing vs. Exploitation

The deepest difference is each model's relationship with volatility. Traditional CAGR thrives on low variance: deep drawdowns drag the geometric mean, so managers diversify specifically to suppress standard deviation and engineer a steady climb—volatility is a cost to smooth away. Aggressive compounding inverts that: volatility is the raw fuel of velocity. You can't manufacture **40–100%** months from stagnant, low-beta assets; a **~46.8%** monthly target demands high-beta vehicles—**3× ETFs**, high-gamma options, warrants, momentum equities—during confirmed breakouts. But the same leverage that amplifies upside amplifies downside; these instruments suffer severe path dependency and drag in sideways markets, so the moment a position stalls or rolls into distribution, it's liquidated to cash. You embrace volatility—but only on your terms.

## Why Aggressive Compounding Is Harder

Compressing time does more than raise the target—it changes the physics of the account.

1. **The curve steepens late.** Gains compound on a fast-growing base, so the final months dwarf the early ones—a single strong month near the end can exceed your starting capital. Slow early progress is normal.
2. **Sequence of returns is everything.** Traditional CAGR assumes a smooth path; aggressive compounding depends on order. A large early loss shrinks the base; a large early gain accelerates everything after. The same returns, reordered, can mean **$1,000,000** or failure.
3. **Leverage amplifies both sides. 3× ETFs, options, and warrants** make **40–100%** months possible—and **30–50%** drawdowns. Leverage magnifies edge and mistakes alike.
4. **The psychological load is brutal.** A long-term investor may tolerate a **−20%** year; an aggressive trader may endure multiple **−30% to −50%** drawdowns while executing flawlessly. One week can move an account more than a traditional portfolio moves in years.

**Dynamic position sizing.** Traditional investing uses static sizing—a 5% allocation rebalanced annually. Aggressive compounding is dynamic: position size grows with equity. A **1R** unit is **$1,000** in a **$100,000** account; by

**Month 4**, near **$464,000**, the same 1R is **$4,640**. You aren't taking greater risk—you're applying the same edge to a larger base, and the mathematics magnify absolute dollar gains.

## A Realistic (Volatile) Compounding Path

A perfectly smooth 46.8% exists only on a spreadsheet. A more realistic path fluctuates around the required rate and includes one significant drawdown:

| Month | Return | Balance | Notes |
|---|---|---|---|
| 1 | +55% | $155,000 | Strong trend entry |
| 2 | +35% | $209,250 | Consolidation |
| 3 | +70% | $355,725 | Major breakout |
| 4 | **−25%** | $266,794 | Drawdown test |
| 5 | +65% | $440,210 | Recovery + momentum |
| 6 | +55% | $682,326 | Final push (size up to close the gap) |

Even with a **−25%** month, disciplined execution still carries the account most of the way to **$1,000,000**; the final stretch becomes a matter of position sizing. The deeper lesson is what did **not** happen: without strict controls, that **−25%** month could easily have become **−60%**, ending the run. The drawdown was survivable because it was controlled.

## Survival Is the Real Engine

Both systems rest on the same foundation—capital generating more capital through compounding. What differs is speed, volatility, leverage, time compression, and concentration, not the mathematics. Traditional CAGR is built for stability, retirement, and multi-decade accumulation; aggressive compounding is built for accelerated expansion over compressed timeframes. Think of two vessels: traditional investing is a cargo ship—slow, steady, hard to sink; aggressive compounding is a racing boat—extraordinary speed, but equally capable of self-destruction without skilled navigation. That's why survival comes first. A traditional investor recovers gradually because time is on their side; an aggressive trader may not survive repeated catastrophic drawdowns long enough for compounding to work. The mathematics are identical regardless of speed—and they punish recklessness without mercy:

- *Aggressive compounding without discipline is gambling.*
- *Disciplined aggressive compounding is professional speculation.*

That difference decides who stays in the game long enough to benefit. It's why the chapters on **Survival, Drawdown Management,** and **Controlled Aggression** are essential: without them, the same mathematics that builds wealth destroys it even faster.

## Chapter 2
# The Compounding Mindset
## Thinking in Account Growth Cycles

Inexperienced traders imagine account growth as a straight line; professionals know it almost never is. Turning $100,000 into $1,000,000 in six months is not a smooth ascent—the account moves through recurring cycles of expansion, stagnation, consolidation, volatility, drawdown, and occasional explosive acceleration. Reading those cycles in advance is what separates the traders who ride to $1M from those wiped out midway.

There is a subtler mistake too: assuming an account at $800,000 trades just like one at $100,000, only with bigger numbers. It doesn't. As equity scales through geometric compounding, the relationship between liquidity, leverage, instrument selection, and psychological friction shifts beneath your feet.

So two cycles run at once. The **Scale Cycle** tracks *where your money is*—which instruments you can use and how large your risk unit becomes. The **Journey Cycle** tracks *where you are in the run*—how aggressive to be and which psychological trap is waiting. Master the campaign by navigating both, never conflating them.

### Framework One — The Scale Cycle

As equity compounds it passes through three scale cycles, each altering what you can trade, how much you can move without distorting the market, and which failure mode is most likely to break the engine:

| | Cycle 1: Incubation | Cycle 2: Acceleration | Cycle 3: Sovereign Capacity |
|---|---|---|---|
| **Equity band** | $100k – $250k | $250k – $600k | $600k – $1M |
| **Strategic mandate** | Maximize convexity & capital efficiency | Tactical sector rotation & capital preservation | Institutional slippage protection & scale governance |
| **Primary vehicles** | ITM options, warrants, 3x ETFs (SOXL, TQQQ) | 2x/3x sector ETFs, mega-cap deep-ITM options, liquid momentum equities | High-volume liquid equities, broad-index leveraged ETFs, institutional derivatives |
| **Risk unit (1R)** | $1,000 – $2,500 | $2,500 – $6,000 | $6,000 – $10,000 |

### Cycle 1 — Incubation ($100,000 to $250,000)

In **Incubation**, the constraint is time, not liquidity. To hit early milestones within 180 days, deploy capital into high-convexity instruments while avoiding broker margin and forced liquidation—use embedded leverage (options, warrants, leveraged ETFs) where downside is capped at the 1% risk unit ($1,000–$2,500) but upside stays asymmetric.

*Danger — the Small-Numbers Delusion:* because a 1% loss feels small in dollars, traders get careless, overtrade mediocre setups, and rack up a 15% drawdown before compounding gains momentum.

### Cycle 2 — Acceleration ($250,000 to $600,000)

Above $250,000, the 1% risk unit expands to $2,500–$6,000—the most efficient compounding phase. Concentrated positions in high-momentum sectors (semiconductors, AI infrastructure, biopharma catalysts) generate meaningful dollars; a single 3R winner may add $15,000–18,000. The strategy is rotating capital aggressively between leading sectors—harvest, return to cash, redeploy into the next breakout.

*Danger — Psychological Friction:* traders who tolerated $1,000 swings panic over routine $10,000 moves on a $500,000 account, leading to premature profit-taking or abandoned stops.

### Cycle 3 — Sovereign Capacity ($600,000 to $1,000,000)

Beyond $600,000, operate like an institutional micro-hedge fund. The 1% unit rises to $6,000–10,000, allowing $300,000–500,000 positions with a 2% stop. Liquidity now governs everything: illiquid warrants and thin options chains create slippage, so confine capital to mega-cap technology and the most liquid sector ETFs and eliminate low-volume instruments above roughly $600,000.

*Danger — the Finish-Line Delusion:* as $1,000,000 nears in Months 5–6, many abandon discipline, take oversized shortcut trades for the final $100,000, and suffer the late-stage drawdown that destroys the campaign.

## Framework Two — The Journey Cycle

Where the Scale Cycle governs your *tools*, the Journey Cycle governs your *aggression and psychology*. Almost every explosive compounding story unfolds through the same five-phase rhythm; knowing it in advance removes the shock when volatility hits:

| Phase | Month | Account (approx.) | Character | Mindset & rule |
|---|---|---|---|---|
| **1. Ignition** | 1 | $100k → $160k | First big winners; confidence builds | Strict 1% risk. Prove the edge. |
| **2. Momentum Expansion** | 2–3 | $160k → $400k+ | Compounding kicks in hard | Pyramid winners. Increase aggression selectively. |
| **3. Testing** | 3–4 | Volatile (20–40% drawdown ) | Pullbacks, consolidation, doubt | Activate circuit breakers. Protect gains. |
| **4. Re-Expansion** | 4–5 | $350k → $700k+ | Recovery + new momentum | Re-engage on confirmed setups only. |
| **5. Final Surge** | 6 | $700k → $1M+ | Parabolic moves | Scale out partially. Lock in profits. |

**Ignition (Month 1).** The account is smallest and most vulnerable, and the temptation is to oversize or reach for leverage. Resist it—this phase builds the engine: discipline, repeatable execution, survival. Trade only high-conviction setups, keep size modest until consistency is proven, target **+40–60%** if conditions allow. The danger is early overconfidence.

**Momentum Expansion (Months 2–3).** Compounding becomes visible as gains apply to a larger base: a **20%** gain on **$100,000** earns **$20,000**; the same on **$400,000** earns **$80,000**. Pyramid winners and selectively use **2×/3× ETFs** and longer-dated options, but never exceed **1%** risk. Success breeds more recklessness than failure.

**Testing (Months 3–4).** Most **10×** campaigns fail here: momentum fades, volatility contracts, **20–40%** drawdowns are common. The amateur revenge-trades; the professional activates circuit breakers, cuts exposure or moves to cash, and treats the slowdown as preservation. This phase separates professionals from gamblers.

**Re-Expansion (Months 4–5).** Survivors often see their strongest gains here as fresh momentum emerges and a larger base magnifies ordinary moves into substantial dollars. Re-engage aggressively only on confirmed trends, using **warrants** or high-delta **options** when appropriate.

**Final Surge / Harvest (Month 6).** Parabolic moves appear late in strong trends; the danger is greed—forcing the final push to **$1,000,000**. Harvest systematically: scale out **30–50%** into strength, trail stops on the rest, secure the milestone rather than gambling it.

## Managing the Cycles: Four Operating Principles

Both frameworks converge on the same disciplines—the controls that keep the engine alive long enough to compound.

**1. Dynamic position sizing—hold the 1% rule religiously.** Keep maximum risk at **1%** of total capital. As the account grows from **$100,000** to **$300,000** to **$600,000**, dollar exposure rises automatically while percentage risk stays fixed.

**2. Name the phase you are in.** Recognize euphoria versus adversity: in winning streaks follow rules relentlessly; in drawdowns obey circuit breakers. Greed and fear interrupt compounding equally.

**3. Instrument rotation—match the vehicle to the phase.**

- **Ignition:** stocks and 2x ETFs.
- **Momentum Expansion:** 3x ETFs and options.
- **Testing:** cash or inverse hedges.
- **Re-Expansion / Final Surge:** warrants and aggressive options.

This dovetails with the Scale Cycle: the larger your equity, the more you migrate toward deep-liquidity instruments regardless of phase.

**4. Track your cycle position weekly.** Each week locate yourself on both maps—which Scale Cycle your equity sits in, which Journey phase the run is in—and set aggression accordingly: attack during Momentum Expansion and Re-Expansion, defend during Testing.

> **THE CONTROLLED AGGRESSION RULE**
> ***"Ride the cycles with maximum force when momentum confirms your edge—and defend ruthlessly the moment the cycle turns against you."***

### The Hidden Truth About Growth Cycles

Most traders expect growth to feel smooth; aggressive compounding usually feels chaotic—explosive growth, then consolidation, then stagnation, then acceleration. That is normal, because markets themselves move in cycles of momentum, volatility, liquidity, speculation, and macro. This is why emotional stability is the deepest edge: not every week is an expansion week, and the professional adapts rather than forcing consistency onto an inconsistent market. Extraordinary growth comes not from one perfect trade but from surviving enough cycles, long enough, for compounding to turn explosive.

## Small Edges Compounded Aggressively

The retail public assumes a **1,000%** return in six months requires miraculous predictions or a **500%** penny-stock jackpot. Professionals don't chase magical trades—they exploit **small, repeatable edges**. Hyper-velocity compounding is built on **expectancy**, not prediction: a modest statistical advantage, repeated with disciplined execution and rapid capital turnover, turns ordinary price inefficiencies into an exponential curve.

### The Anatomy of an Edge

An edge is not a guaranteed winner or a secret pattern. It is **verified positive expectancy** over many trades—total gains consistently exceed total losses across a large sample—governed by your win rate (W) and your reward-to-risk ratio (the R-multiple):

*Expectancy (E) = (Win % × Average Win) – (Loss % × Average Loss)*

### The Realist's Edge Profile

Turning **$100,000** into **$1,000,000** in roughly **120 trading sessions** does **not** require a **90%** win rate; chasing one leads traders to take small profits while letting losses grow. A genuine edge looks surprisingly modest:

- **Win rate (W):** 45% — you are wrong more often than you are right.
- **Loss size:** strictly capped at −1R (your 1% risk unit, e.g. $1,000).
- **Win size:** averaging +3R, taken at clean technical extensions (e.g. $3,000).

*E = (0.45 × $3,000) – (0.55 × $1,000) = $1,350 – $550 = +$800 per trade***

A net **+0.80R per execution** is, by design, a "small" edge—a minor tilt in your favor, much like the house edge over a blackjack player. Unremarkable on any single trade; executed with disciplined velocity, an unstoppable compounding juggernaut.

### The Velocity Multiplier: Frequency and Turnover

A small edge stays a small return if you execute it once a month. Compounding accelerates not by maximizing win size but by **maximizing how often the capital base is rotated through the edge**. Consider two traders running the *same* positive expectancy:

| | Trader A — Linear Accumulator | Trader B — Hyper-Velocity Speculator |
|---|---|---|
| **Approach** | One large breakout setup per month | Quick 2-to-3-day structural swings |
| **Instruments** | Standard positions held through slow moves | 3x leveraged sector ETFs, short-dated ITM options |
| **Typical hold** | ~30 days | 2–3 days |
| **Turnover (6 months)** | 6 rotations | 60 rotations |
| **Same edge → result** | Modest, near-linear growth | Geometric compounding ignites |

Every time Trader B liquidates to cash, the expanded equity base is instantly recalculated into position sizing and the dollar value of 1R grows with it. By raising rotation frequency, the geometric curve is triggered on a compressed timeline—letting a series of minor 2% to 5% moves multiply the base tenfold.

## Why Small Beats Spectacular

Casinos understand this: the house edge on a blackjack hand may be a few percentage points, but across enormous volume it becomes a fortune with near-statistical inevitability. Professional trading works the same way—whether the edge comes from timing, momentum, volatility, liquidity, asymmetric positioning, disciplined exits, sector rotation, or behavioral psychology. Each looks small; aggressively compounded, they become extraordinary.

Compounding is what makes a modest percentage nonlinear. The same 20% gain produces radically different dollars as the base expands:

- 20% on $100,000 → $20,000
- 20% on $200,000 → $40,000
- 20% on $500,000 → $100,000
- 20% on $1,000,000 → $200,000

The account itself becomes the growth engine, which is why repeated moderate gains routinely outperform occasional jackpots. The jackpot trader lives with unstable curves, emotional chaos, and catastrophic reversals; the edge-based compounder gets controlled, repeatable, scalable growth—far more sustainable when the timeline is this compressed.

## Protecting the Engine: Drawdown and Parameter Control

A small edge is mathematically fragile; it compounds only if you refuse operational friction, because one careless loss can erase many disciplined wins. A 50% loss requires a 100% gain just to break even—large losses don't just hurt, they cripple future compounding by leaving the engine less mass to work with. This is why elite traders obsess over asymmetry, expectancy, reward-to-risk, sizing, and capital preservation rather than excitement.

If your edge assumes an average loss of −1R, letting a single trade run to −3R or −5R out of "hope" invalidates the math—one emotional drawdown can destroy the expectancy of your next five winners. The defense is mechanical, not emotional, resting on two pillars:

**Robotic API Stops** Stop-loss routed via API the millisecond the entry fills. No "mental" targets; no manual execution delay. No hoping a −1R loss back toward breakeven.

**Cash-Drag Elimination** Idle capital is an operational loss, not a rest. Sideways for more than 48 hours → liquidate to cash. Immediate re-allocation into the next active catalyst.

In a hyper-velocity campaign, idle capital is an operational loss; compounding mass cannot stagnate in an asset that has stopped yielding velocity—claw it back to cash and rotate into the next catalyst.

## Controlled, Adaptive Aggression

Small edges become powerful combined with leverage, volatility, concentration, and disciplined scaling: an 8% stock move can produce a far larger options gain, a sector rotation is amplified through 2x and 3x ETFs, warrants magnify upside in expansions. But aggression is applied selectively, only when probabilities visibly favor it.

This is controlled, not permanent, aggression. Permanent aggression destroys accounts, because no edge is static: a strategy brilliant in speculative bull markets can fail in volatility contractions or defensive regimes. So increase aggression when the edge strengthens and cut it when the edge weakens—that adaptability keeps the edge alive long enough for compounding to turn extraordinary.

THE ADAPTIVE-AGGRESSION RULE

***"Press hardest when the edge is strongest, and retreat to cash the moment it weakens. Aggression is a dial, never a switch."***

## The Psychology of Boring

Here is the trap: small edges feel unimpressive, so most traders abandon them. The mind craves dramatic stories—giant wins, overnight fortunes—but professional wealth creation is mathematically boring. A trader who simply repeats disciplined entries, controlled exits, proper sizing, and moderate consistent gains quietly outperforms far more dramatic traders. The market rewards mathematical consistency, not emotional excitement.

The compounding curve rewards patience before anything else: growth appears slow, then gradual, then noticeable, then suddenly nonlinear. The first phase tests your patience; the later phase rewards your survival. One edge, repeated hundreds of times with discipline and protected from catastrophic drawdowns, is enough to produce extraordinary expansion. The path to extraordinary returns is built on ordinary, repeated advantages.

**Small edges. Repeated consistently. Scaled intelligently. Protected ruthlessly. Compounded aggressively.** *That is how large fortunes are actually built in speculation.*

## Professional vs. Emotional Trading

Across a **1,000%** campaign in **120 trading sessions**, success depends less on intelligence than on emotional discipline. Markets rarely destroy traders for lacking analytical ability; they destroy them because they can't manage themselves under uncertainty. Two traders can use the same charts, instruments, and leverage and reach opposite outcomes—one seeks validation or rescue, the other sees only probabilities governed by predefined rules.

### The Psychological Divide: Validation vs. Probability

**The emotional trader — the ego-driven operator.** Every trade becomes a judgment of self-worth: winners breed euphoria, overconfidence, and oversized positions; losers trigger denial, revenge trading, and the urge to remove stops. The market becomes stimulation rather than **positive expectancy**, and in a high-velocity campaign that path ends in liquidation.

**The professional speculator — the parametric trustee.** Thinks like an auditor, not a gambler: any single trade is unpredictable, so the focus is strict compliance with the system. Losses are operating expenses, not personal failures, and across a large sample one stopped-out position barely registers. The goal isn't to eliminate emotion—it's to keep emotion from controlling execution.

### The Operational Comparison

The divide shows up on every axis of how the two operators behave:

| Operational axis | The Emotional Trader | The Professional Speculator |
|---|---|---|
| **Decision driver** | Fear, greed, FOMO, revenge | Written rules and a tested edge |
| **Relationship with the market** | Adversarial — trying to beat or outsmart the tape | Fiduciary — extracting premium from verified footprints |
| **View of a loss** | A personal failure to hide or chase | A pre-calculated operational cost of doing business |
| **Position sizing** | Conviction, or "I need to make it back" | Fixed 1% risk, from equity and ATR volatility |
| **Stop-loss enforcement** | Mental, flexible, ignored out of hope | Automated via API, executed instantly |
| **Response to a win** | Sell too early, or turn euphoric and | Scale out systematically; let equity scale size |

| Operational axis | The Emotional Trader | The Professional Speculator |
|---|---|---|
| | overtrade | |
| **Response to a drawdown** | Panic, denial, revenge trading | Activate pre-defined circuit breakers |
| **Leverage use** | Maximum, especially when emotional | Selective — only in high-asymmetry setups |
| **Journaling and review** | None or sporadic | Honest written review after every trade |
| **Daily metric** | Dollar P&L — "Did I make money today?" | Compliance:"Did I execute the plan flawlessly?" |
| **Long-term result** | Account blow-up or slow bleed | Survival and compounding toward $1M |

## Execution Under Stress

A 10x run guarantees periods of high dollar volatility, and behavior at peak stress reveals the profile:

> **TWO PATHWAYS THROUGH THE SAME VOLATILITY**
> **Emotional:** Volatility → Panic / euphoria → Parameter violation → **RUIN** **Professional:** Volatility → Robotic execution → Parameter adherence → **COMPOUNDING**

After several **3R** winners, the emotional trader thinks they've "cracked the code," sizes up, abandons risk rules, and overcommits to marginal setups—often just before a reversal. The professional treats winning streaks no differently than losing ones: risk stays fixed at **1R**, and account growth, not emotion, increases position size.

Facing losses, the emotional trader revenge-trades with oversized exposure to short-dated options or volatile **3× ETFs**, accelerating the decline. The professional does the opposite: a predetermined drawdown automatically cuts the risk unit from **1R** to **0.5R** after a **5%** decline, and at a **15%** drawdown trading stops through an API-enforced **48-hour** review—preserving capital until conditions realign with the edge.

## Why Emotion Wins by Default — and Destroys

Most traders attempting aggressive 10x runs are driven by emotion, and the patterns are consistent:

- A stock is running and they feel they're "missing out" → oversized FOMO entry.
- They're down big and feel desperate → revenge trade with even larger size.

- They're up big and feel invincible → remove stops or pile on reckless leverage.
- They fall in love with a position → quietly convert a trade into an "investment."

Leveraged instruments—3× ETFs, options, warrants—magnify both volatility and emotional mistakes; one impulsive decision can erase 30–70% of an account within hours.

## Engineering Process to Defeat Emotion

The professional doesn't rely on willpower in the moment—they build systems that reduce emotional interference, anchored in a few non-negotiables:

**1. Pre-defined rules beat real-time judgment.** Every setup has a written entry, stop, target, and max size *before* the trade—no exceptions, because stress corrupts real-time judgment.

**2. Process over P&L.** A "bad" day that followed the rules is a good day; a "good" day that broke them is dangerous.

**3. Emotional awareness as a risk tool.** When you feel tilted, euphoric, or desperate, you stop trading.

**4. Ego management.** You don't need to be right; you need the account to grow. Wrong small is routine; wrong big is the one unforgivable error.

**5. Routine and discipline.** A pre-market checklist, a post-market review and journal, and a weekly cycle assessment turn good behavior into reflex rather than daily willpower.

The emotional trader resists structure because it feels restrictive—but structure is exactly what protects the trader from themselves and creates long-term freedom. Build systems that survive emotion, and emotion stops running the account.

## Two Traders, One Move

The same opportunity, handled two ways—the entry was never the difference:

| The Emotional Trader | The Professional |
|---|---|
| Catches a strong 3x ETF move and turns $100k into $280k in three weeks. Euphoria takes over: he triples his size on the next "sure thing" and ignores his stop. One reversal later he is back to $65k—emotionally devastated, and now chasing even harder. | Catches the same move and turns $100k into $250k. He holds his 1% risk rule, scales out partially, and journals every trade. When the market shifts he cuts size immediately, preserves capital, and waits for the next high-probability setup—surviving the drawdown and compounding onward toward $1M. |

Both caught the identical 3x ETF move. One let the win become a feeling and gave it all back; the other let it become a larger, well-protected base and kept compounding. Short-term they looked the same; structurally they were never playing the same game.

## Short-Term Profit Is Not Professionalism

A trader can be repeatedly stopped out and temporarily underperforming while operating professionally, and another can post explosive gains while operating emotionally and unsustainably. Short-term profitability often just reflects a favorable regime rewarding reckless behavior—then conditions change. Emotional traders shine during manias and liquidity surges and disappear in volatility contractions; the professional survives both, and survival is the precondition for compounding to ever become extraordinary.

### The Deepest Difference

Strip everything away and one line remains: the professional builds systems that survive emotion, while the emotional trader lets emotion become the system. One compounds; the other self-destructs. Every strategy and instrument in this book works only when executed professionally.

> THE CONTROLLED-AGGRESSION STANDARD
> ***"I trade the plan, not my feelings. Emotion is allowed in preparation and in review—never in execution."***

**Master your psychology first.** *The mathematics and the instruments will then do the rest.*

## The Compounding Mindset

This may be the most important chapter in the book. Aggressive trading attracts brilliant, high-IQ traders chasing legendary home runs, yet 10× compounding over six months rewards relentless consistency, not occasional brilliance. Faced with a 1,000% target, most search for one perfect trade—a 1,000% option, a penny-stock explosion, a flawless prediction. That mindset is a mathematical dead end. Extraordinary wealth is built through disciplined execution, careful risk management, and the compounding of consistent gains.

### The Myth of the Home-Run Trade

Many traders spend careers chasing the perfect stock, option, catalyst, or prediction. Occasionally they succeed; more often they fail, and the graveyard is full of jackpot-chasers. A single **500%** winner means little if followed by two **70%** losses—the disciplined trader banking **25–35%** repeatedly usually finishes far ahead.

### The Mathematics of Survival

The amateur doesn't grasp the brutal asymmetry of losses—that a 50% loss requires a 100% gain just to break even. As drawdowns deepen, the recovery grows exponentially:

| Drawdown taken | Gain required just to break even |
|---|---|
| −10% | +11% |
| −20% | +25% |
| −50% | +100% |
| −75% | +300% |

This is why *sequence of returns* is everything. A few large early losses—common with brilliant but undisciplined bets—make recovery mathematically brutal and can knock you out before compounding begins. Survival is the first requirement of compounding: without capital, compounding cannot occur.

## The Real Roadmap: 15% × 17

Here is the liberating truth. To grow $100,000 into $1,000,000 in 180 days you don't need a 1,000% winner. You need a net **15%**, compounded just **seventeen** times:

*$100,000 × (1.15)**17** ≈ $1,076,000*

A 15% gain from a quality mid-cap breakout or 3× ETF swing is realistic. Repeat it 17 times while tightly controlling downside, and compounding does its job—you're harvesting **repeatable gains**, not swinging for home runs.

## Two Equity Curves

Two traders start from the same $100,000. The brilliant one earns +80%, −40%, +50%, −30%—spectacular gains followed by devastating losses, a roller-coaster curve. The consistent one compounds steady gains while cutting losses fast: a 65% win rate, +35% average winner, −8% average loser, smooth compounding. The brilliant trader's 200–400% winners are erased by a few 40–60% drawdowns. Compounding rewards consistency, not brilliance.

*Same $100,000 start. The grinder's smooth +15% cycles clear $1M; the gambler's spikes and crashes end near $62k.*

## The Tragedy of the Genius

Brilliance breeds ego. A hunch-based winner delivers a dopamine hit, and the trader starts believing they can outsmart the market's plumbing; a single 300% win can convince them risk management is optional—and overconfidence reliably precedes the major loss. The brilliant trader tries to call exact tops and bottoms or bets the ledger on an unconfirmed earnings print, then clings to the failing position when the market shifts. The consistent allocator has no desire to be right—only to execute the rules to the penny: enter if the setup prints, exit instantly if the structural floor cracks, feel no highs or lows, because any trade is one data point of a thousand.

## Building the Compounding Mindset

Consistency is not a personality trait; it is an operating system you install. Five habits hold it together.

**Process over outcome.** Judge each day by whether you followed your checklist—relative strength, volume, ATR-based sizing, 1% risk, catalyst alignment—not by P&L. A good process can still lose a trade and a bad one can still win; over enough repetitions, process determines outcome.

**Ruthless risk discipline.** Never risk more than 1% per idea—the rule that turns 3x ETFs, OTM calls, and small-cap runners into survivable weapons.

**Emotional detachment.** No FOMO entries without confirmation, no revenge trading, no falling in love with a position. Discipline is hardest during success—respect risk most when you feel invincible.

**Journaling and review.** A mandatory end-of-day review plus a weekly equity-curve and win-rate analysis. What gets measured gets repeated.

**Rotation and capital recycling.** Profits are redeployed immediately into the next high-probability setup. Cash is a position; a stagnant winner is capital that has stopped working.

### The Ten Non-Negotiables

Distilled to commandments, the entire book reduces to these:

- Never risk more than 1% of the account on a single idea.
- Cut every loser at its predefined stop—no exceptions, no "hope."
- Never move a stop away from danger; move it toward profit.
- Judge the day by the process followed, not the dollars made.
- Rotate on schedule; never marry a position.
- Recycle profits into the next high-probability setup.
- No FOMO entries; no revenge trades after a loss.
- Respect risk most during winning streaks.
- Treat each trade as one data point in a large sample.
- Survive first. Compounding can only work on an account that is still alive.

### An Honest Reality Check

A 1,000% return in six months is an extreme outlier. Most who attempt it lose money—many lose most of their capital—and 3× ETFs, options, and warrants magnify both gains and losses. Most fail not from low intelligence but from chasing jackpots instead of compounding disciplined gains. The rare survivors aren't the smartest—they're the most disciplined, running trading as a high-performance system. Nothing here is investment advice; its value is the mindset that separates survivors from statistics.

### Consistency Is the Secret Sauce

Extraordinary wealth rarely comes from doing one thing brilliantly once. It comes from doing many things reasonably well, repeatedly, long enough for compounding to work its quiet magic. Brilliance creates a spectacular gain; consistency creates a sustainable fortune—and it's what ties regimes, growth cycles, small edges, allocation, and psychology into one repeatable system.

> THE CONSISTENCY RULE
>
> ***"I do not need to be brilliant. I need to be repeatable. Survive, execute the plan to the penny, and let the compounding math do the rest."***

**Brilliance gets you noticed. Consistency gets you to $1,000,000.**

## Trading as Capital Allocation

The biggest mental shift required to turn $100,000 into $1,000,000 in six months is to stop thinking like a trader and start thinking like a capital allocator. Amateurs ask, *"What stock will go up?"* Professionals ask, *"Where can I deploy capital for the best risk-adjusted return?"* A position is not a bet—it is a capital allocation with an expected return, defined risk, and opportunity cost. Your job is to manage capital, not predict markets.

## The Identity Shift: You Are the CEO of a Hedge Fund

To compress a 10x return into 120 sessions, you must genuinely change identity. You are no longer a retail trader hunting tips—you are the Chief Executive and Chief Risk Officer of an agile, hyper-velocity treasury desk, and every variable is redefined:

| Old variable | Reframed under the new mandate |
|---|---|
| **Your $100,000 base** | Corporate inventory and working liquidity—raw material to deploy where it yields the highest velocity of return, never money for consumption or entertainment. |
| **The financial markets** | A wholesale marketplace where sectors, instruments, and trend regimes compete to rent your capital. |
| **A trade entry** | A capital-allocation contract—a temporary lease on an asset's momentum that meets your underwriting criteria. |
| **A stop-loss** | A risk-mitigation contract—the instant termination of an underperforming deployment before it can impair the balance sheet. |

## Capital Is Inventory

Every dollar carries four costs: **opportunity cost, risk exposure, volatility exposure,** and **expected return**. The question is never *"Do I like this stock?"* but *"Is this my highest-quality capital allocation?"* Professionals abandon weak positions fast because trapped capital can't be deployed elsewhere. Emotional traders hope; capital allocators reallocate.

## Trader vs. Allocator: The Full Contrast

The two mindsets diverge on every axis that matters:

## The Three Directives of Professional Allocation

An elite allocator runs every opportunity through a matrix balancing asset safety against velocity. Three mandates are non-negotiable.

> THE CAPITAL ALLOCATION MATRIX
> **1. Capital Velocity** – how fast, not just how much, an allocation yields. **2. Convexity Optimization** – bounded downside, uncapped upside on every deployment. **3. Opportunistic Liquidity** – cash held as an active, strategic weapon.

**1. Capital Velocity – the asset-turnover mandate.** Judge positions by **speed** as well as return: if a **stock, warrant, or 3× ETF** stays sideways **48–72 hours**, liquidate and redeploy. Dead capital is expensive.

**2. Convexity Optimization – the asymmetry shield.** Risk only **1R** (1% of equity) to pursue **3R–5R+** using **deep in-the-money options** or **specialized warrants** with automated stops.

**3. Opportunistic Liquidity — cash as a weapon.** During **CPI releases, Fed decisions**, or broad distribution, move aggressively to cash; preserved capital provides maximum flexibility when momentum returns.

## The Core Allocation Rules

Those directives become operational through a short set of rules.

**The 1% risk rule.** Never allocate more than 1% of total capital to any single idea—so a $150,000 account risks at most $1,500 per position—always recalculated against *current* size, never your starting size, so dollar risk scales automatically.

**Tiered capital structure.** - **Core capital (60–80%):** deployed in high-conviction setups. - **Dry powder (20–40%):** cash reserved for superior opportunities or recovery. - **Aggressive capital (variable):** only in Acceleration or Expansion phases with extreme asymmetry.

**Opportunity-cost discipline.** Before any entry, force the comparison: is this the best use of capital right now versus other setups, or versus cash? Then reallocate continuously—pyramid winners under strict rules, cut losers immediately and recycle the capital, sit in cash when there's no edge. The envelope scales with the account:

| Account size | Max risk / trade | Max positions | Allocation style |
|---|---|---|---|
| $100k – $200k | $1,000 – $2,000 | 6 – 10 | High-conviction, selective |
| $200k – $500k | $2,000 – $5,000 | 8 – 12 | Pyramid winners aggressively |
| $500k – $1M | $5,000 – $10,000 | 10 – 15 | Scale out profits, protect base |

## Ranking Opportunities Like a Venture Investor

Because every position competes against every other use of capital, the professional is always ranking. Each candidate is screened like a venture deal: upside asymmetry, downside exposure, probability distribution, liquidity profile, what would invalidate the thesis, what alternative uses exist. Capital then flows aggressively toward strength and asymmetry and rotates away the instant conditions deteriorate—concentrate in the strongest momentum and highest expectancy, reduce or eliminate weaker ones immediately.

## The Allocator's Edge in Leveraged Instruments

Within this framework, leveraged instruments are tools for capital deployment, never gambling tickets—each plays a role:

- **3x ETFs and options:** powerful amplifiers, but only allocated surgically with bounded risk.
- **Warrants:** extreme leverage with defined risk when structured correctly.

- **Stocks and 2x ETFs:** a lower-volatility base for steadier compounding.

The allocator never reaches for raw margin loans, which carry existential liquidation risk; they use embedded derivatives precisely because the downside is bounded by structure. The instrument is just a terminal through which capital flows to multiply.

## Allocation Is Survival Plus Compounding

Every chapter resolves back into better capital allocation. Survival rules protect the base; small edges and consistency are repeatable positive allocation decisions; controlled aggression is knowing when, and how much, to deploy. Hold the line on one honest question, day after day for six months:

> THE ULTIMATE ALLOCATION QUESTION
> ***"If I allocate capital to this idea, am I making the highest-probability, highest-asymmetry use of my limited resources right now—versus every other setup, or simply holding cash?"***

Answer it honestly while following the risk rules in this book, and you will have executed the true blueprint for 1,000% compounding.

**Trade less like a speculator. Allocate more like a professional.**

## Chapter 3

# The Truth About Aggressive Trading

Let us be brutally honest from the first page. Turning $100,000 into $1,000,000 in six months through aggressive trading is possible—but extraordinarily rare. The overwhelming majority who attempt anything close fail; most lose a large portion, many lose all, of their capital. That is statistical reality, and any honest blueprint must begin there. Retail literature blames the wrong things—the wrong pattern, the wrong indicator, a failure of willpower. The truth is structural: traders don't fail because their upside targets are too aggressive. **They fail because their defensive parameters are non-existent.** Compress a 1,000% return into roughly 120 sessions and the margin for operational error is zero.

### The Harsh Statistics

The base rates are sobering: **70–97%** of active retail traders lose money over time, about **80%** quit within their first two years, and only **1–3%** reach lasting, consistent profitability. In leveraged products specifically—the 2x and 3x ETFs, options, and warrants this book relies on—failure rates run higher still, because losses are magnified and arrive faster. The tiny minority who succeed do so not because they are smarter, but because they bring a professional discipline most traders refuse to adopt.

### The Core Paradox: Offense Is Dictated by Defense

Your offensive velocity is dictated by your defensive boundaries. Amateurs attack like drag racers, maximizing leverage and chasing speed; professionals think like Formula 1 engineers—speed exists only because the brakes and chassis are built to survive it. Most 10× campaigns fail not because traders can't find winning stocks, but because weak risk controls turn normal drawdowns into liquidation. Master the brakes, and the speed follows.

### Why Most Traders Fail: The Real Mechanics

Most failures trace to the same structural mistakes:

1. **They gamble instead of speculate.** They chase tips, **FOMO** into momentum, and size emotionally, treating **3× ETFs** and **options** as lottery tickets instead of capital-allocation tools.
2. **The tyranny of asymmetric drawdown math.** Losses are exponentially harder to recover than wins, consuming both **capital** and **time** and making exponential compounding increasingly unattainable.
3. **They ignore path dependency—the volatility-drag tax.** **3× ETFs** reset daily; in sideways markets, **volatility drag** erodes capital even if the index finishes unchanged.
4. **They size by conviction, not risk.** Amateurs commit **50–100%** to single ideas; professionals risk only **1–2%** and let stop distance and volatility set position size.

**5. Emotional trading destroys them—the revenge loop.** Winning streaks breed overconfidence; losing streaks trigger revenge trading, oversized positions, and abandoned stops.

**6. No edge, no process, no framework.** They switch strategies constantly, keep no journal, follow no written rules, and chase home runs instead of compounding a repeatable edge.

> **ONE BAD GAP, TWO OUTCOMES Sizes by conviction:** Deploys 50% of cash → One bad gap → CATASTROPHIC RUIN Sizes by parameter: Deploys a fixed 1% risk → One bad gap → MINOR COST (−1R)

## Leverage Is a Mirror

Leverage exposes and magnifies every weakness—fear, greed, ego, impatience, overconfidence. As exposure grows from $20,000 to $300,000 through leverage, large option positions, or volatile 3× ETFs, weaknesses hidden at smaller size emerge. Many traders are emotionally—not financially—undercapitalized, burdened by desperation and unrealistic expectations that erode judgment. Markets reward execution, adaptability, emotional control, risk management, and timing. Leverage simply magnifies what the trader is.

## Prediction vs. Risk Management

Amateurs ask, "What will happen next?" Professionals ask, "What happens if I'm wrong?" No one—not hedge funds, family offices, or legendary speculators—forecasts consistently. Professionals structure losses as manageable business costs; amateurs structure them as catastrophes. Compounding requires surviving enough cycles, volatility, mistakes, and emotional pressure for the mathematics to work.

## The Rare Winners: What They Do Differently

The few who achieve large short-term gains share a recognizable profile:

- They treat trading as professional capital allocation, not entertainment.
- They operate with controlled aggression—ferocious when the edge is present, disciplined or fully in cash when it is not.
- They run ironclad risk rules: roughly 1% risk per trade, with predefined drawdown circuit breakers.
- They obsess over process and consistency more than being right on any single trade.
- They journal everything and review performance ruthlessly.
- They respect the mathematics of ruin and protect the compounding base.

The survivors end up calmer, more selective, and less ego-driven than beginners expect. They learned the order of operations the hard way: discipline before leverage, process before aggression, survival before compounding, emotional control before position size.

### The Reality Checklist

The contrast that decides who survives, line by line:

| The Amateur Trap — why they fail | The Sovereign Blueprint — how to win |
|---|---|
| Fixates on win metrics and profit targets | Fixates on maximum-drawdown boundaries and risk limits |
| Uses raw broker margin—instant liquidation risk | Uses embedded derivatives for bounded convexity |
| Relies on "mental stops" and hopes for a reversal | Enforces automated bracket orders, routed via API at entry |
| Lets capital stagnate in sideways, dead positions | Demands capital velocity; flushes dead positions to cash |
| Treats trading as a casino for personal validation | Runs the account as an audited corporate treasury desk |

### The Hard Truth for This Book

This blueprint is not for everyone. It is for the small minority willing to accept frequent losses as a cost of doing business, follow rules when emotions demand otherwise, stay in cash when no edge exists, survive painful drawdowns without abandoning discipline, and treat every dollar as professionally allocated capital. If you cannot commit to that, this book will not help you—and aggressive trading will likely hurt you. Everything that follows—market regimes, instruments, position sizing, psychology—is written for those who can.

## The Dangers of Leverage

Leverage is the rocket fuel of this blueprint—and its fastest path to zero. Without **2x/3x ETFs, options, warrants, or margin**, turning **$100,000 into $1,000,000 in six months** is highly unlikely; used improperly, it can destroy most or all of your capital within weeks. Leverage does not create edge—it amplifies volatility, compresses time to ruin, and magnifies gains, losses, emotions, and mistakes alike.

### The Dual-Edged Sword: Amplification, Not Edge

Leverage is a mathematically neutral multiplier: Leveraged Return = Underlying Return × Leverage Factor (λ). The catastrophic retail mistake is calculating only the upside: a **3× ETF** turns a **10%** gain into **+30%**, but a routine **5%** pullback becomes **−15%**, immediately raising recovery difficulty. It amplifies whatever is already there, in both directions.

## How Each Instrument Behaves

Each leveraged vehicle multiplies returns differently—and carries some hidden cost:

| Instrument | Leverage effect | Hidden danger | Typical bad-move outcome |
|---|---|---|---|
| **2x ETFs** | 2× the daily move | Volatility decay (beta slippage) | −30% when the index drops 15% |
| **3x ETFs** | 3× the daily move | Severe decay in choppy markets | −60%+ when the index drops 20% |
| **Long calls** | 5–20x+ effective leverage | Theta decay + volatility crush | Can go to zero overnight |
| **Warrants** | Extreme leverage | Expiration and dilution risk | Total loss is common |
| **Margin** | 2–4x+ buying power | Margin calls and forced liquidation | Account can even go negative |

## The Three Structural Killers

Beyond simple amplification, leverage destroys accounts through three hidden mechanical forces.

**1. The margin trap and forced liquidation.** Raw margin creates existential risk: a sharp decline can breach maintenance requirements, triggering automatic broker liquidation at the worst possible price.

> **THE MARGIN-CALL DEATH SPIRAL** Macro gap down → Maintenance threshold breached → Automated broker flash-liquidation → **PERMANENT CAPITAL RUIN**

**2. Volatility drag and path dependency (the silent tax).** Leveraged ETFs multiply an index's *daily* move, resetting their base each close. In a choppy phase, that daily reset turns leverage into an active drain—watch a two-day sequence in a 3x ETF:

| Day | Base index | Your 3x ETF account |
|---|---|---|
| **Day 0** | 100.0 | **$100,000** |
| **Day 1 (−10%)** | 90.0 | **$70,000 (−30%)** |
| **Day 2 (+11.1%)** | 100.0 (flat) | **$93,333 (+33.3%)** |

The index finished perfectly flat—net 0%—yet the leveraged account suffered a permanent structural erosion of roughly $6,667 in just 48 hours. This "beta slippage" bleeds leveraged holders to death through trendless regimes. It is not theoretical: during the 2022 bear market, many 3x ETFs (e.g. SOXL) lost 80–95% while their underlying indexes fell roughly 50–60%.

**3. Theta decay and the options mirage.** Options and warrants avoid margin calls but introduce theta decay: short-dated, out-of-the-money contracts lose value fast as expiration nears, and without an quick explosive move many expire worthless. Warrants add expiration and dilution risk.

## Leverage Compresses Time, Liquidity, and Judgment

Leverage compresses months into hours and magnifies liquidity risk as spreads widen and exits vanish under stress. Its greatest danger is psychological: a trader comfortable with $20,000 of exposure may panic at $300,000, and large wins breed overconfidence and progressively larger bets until discipline collapses. Leverage reveals character—it does not create it.

## The Blueprint Directive: Bounded Convexity

Use leverage only within controlled aggression. The professional bans raw broker margin and short-dated out-of-the-money flyers, and enforces bounded convexity:

- **Deep in-the-money options:** high deltas (0.80+) with long expirations—stock-like exposure, downside limited to the premium.
- **Regime-locked 3x ETFs:** deploy only during confirmed, high-volume institutional momentum; exit immediately when distribution or sideways action appears.
- **Use it selectively** — heavy leverage only in clear, high-momentum "freight-train" regimes.
- **Size it conservatively** — never risk more than 1% of total capital on a single leveraged position.
- **Define risk first** — know your maximum loss before entry, use hard stops, never move them emotionally.
- **Monitor daily** — set alerts and be ready to exit or hedge fast.

And enforce hard drawdown circuit breakers across the whole account, without negotiation:

| Account drawdown | Required action |
|---|---|
| **−10%** | Cut total leverage in half. |
| **−20%** | Reduce to minimal leverage, or move to cash. |
| **−30%** | Stop. Flatten the book and reassess from scratch. |

## The Bottom Line

Leverage amplifies whatever is already there. With positive expectancy and strict rules, it accelerates you toward $1,000,000; traded emotionally, it accelerates you toward zero faster than almost any other force in markets. This is why the chapters on Survival, Capital Allocation, Controlled Aggression, and Consistency are non-negotiable—they are the guardrails. The purpose of leverage is never maximum exposure; it is efficient exposure.

> **THE LEVERAGE LAW** ***"Leverage does not create edge or character—it amplifies whatever is already there. Bring discipline and it compounds you toward $1M; bring emotion and it accelerates you to zero."***

## The Psychology of Fast Money

Fast money is seductive. Few experiences rewire the brain like watching **$100,000 become $250,000** in weeks through **3x ETFs, options, or warrants**—dopamine surges, and you feel invincible. That is exactly where most aggressive traders are destroyed. Advice to "control greed" barely scratches the surface, because fast money creates measurable **neurochemical and cognitive distortions**: over a **120-session** campaign, rapid turnover systematically degrades judgment. Most traders fear losses most, but sudden success is often more dangerous—many survive failure but not winning.

### The Neurochemical Trap: The Dopamine Deficit Loop

Rapid gains activate the brain's reward system much like powerful stimulants. A string of wins in high-convexity instruments resets the brain's expectation for excitement—and that reset becomes the trap.

> **THE DOPAMINE DEFICIT LOOP** Rapid wins → **dopamine spike** → the natural market pause → **boredom misread as deficit** → forced over-trading → **RUIN** *↺** Each unmet craving demands bigger size. The loop tightens until it breaks the account.*

When markets consolidate—or you move to cash to protect capital—dopamine falls, and the brain misreads a healthy pause as deprivation, driving traders to force marginal setups to recreate the high. Wealth creation quietly becomes excitement-seeking, and trading begins resembling addiction more than professional speculation.

### How Fast Money Warps the Mind

Beneath the chemistry sit five predictable distortions.

**Euphoria and overconfidence.** After several large wins, traders believe they've "figured it out." Sizes expand, stops disappear, rules are abandoned—which is why many blow up right after their best month.

**The identity trap.** Fast money becomes identity: "I'm the trader who turned $100k into $400k." Drawdowns feel like attacks on self-worth, so traders defend losing positions and trade to protect ego instead of capital.

**FOMO on steroids.** You watch a 3x ETF ripping, feel physical discomfort at missing it, and jump in late and oversized—usually right before the reversal.

**Revenge trading.** After a sharp loss, the urge to "get it back quickly" takes over: bigger size, lower standards, deeper hole.

**The normalization of risk.** What once felt reckless starts to feel normal after a winning streak; risk tolerance calibrates upward at exactly the wrong moment, and you believe the current regime will last forever. It never does.

## The Typical Fast-Money Cycle

Strung together, these distortions produce a remarkably consistent arc:

| Phase | What happens |
|---|---|
| **Months 1–2 — Euphoria** | Strong wins; the account doubles; you feel invincible. |
| **Month 3 — Overconfidence** | Oversized leveraged bets into a marginal setup; then a sharp reversal. |
| **Month 4 — Panic** | Revenge trading; a major 30–70% drawdown. |
| **Months 5–6 — Fallout** | A blown-up account, or an emotionally exhausted trader who quits. |

This cycle has destroyed far more accounts than bad setups ever have. The Month-3 reversal is rarely a bad trade—it is the predictable consequence of the euphoria in Months 1–2.

## The Cognitive Distortions of High-Velocity Capital

Three specific failure points appear where psychology meets a fast-moving equity curve.

**1. The house-money fallacy.** When $100,000 compounds to $250,000, the trader mentally splits the account into "hard-earned principal" and "house money." Every dollar has identical risk; treating profits with less respect loosens parameters and lets one drawdown erase months of gains.

**2. Dollar-volatility desensitization (scale shock).** A trader calm with $1,000 risk (1% of $100k) freezes at a $6,000 swing on $600k or $8,000 on $800k, producing premature profit-taking on strong 5R trades and refusal to honor stops—turning routine losses into terminal impairments.

**3. The closeness-to-the-goal delusion.** Nearing $800k–$1M in Months 5–6, focus shifts from process to outcome; the trader drops filters, takes oversized bets, and over-leverages at peak account size—walking into a late-stage shock.

## The Blueprint Antidote: Sterilize the Desk

You don't overcome these distortions by feeling them less—you engineer them out by decoupling emotion from the ledger.

**The fiduciary bracket.** Every entry carries a hard stop and a structural target, routed via API simultaneously; your hands leave the keyboard the moment the order fills. The decision is made while you are calm; the machine executes while you are not.

**The P&L blackout.** Lock the terminal to show only R-multiples and technical percentages—never the live dollar balance. If you can't see the $10,000 fluctuation, your brain can't experience the shock that triggers or greed.

**Process-driven auditing.** Grade each day by compliance, not profit: a session where you lost a pre-calculated 1R but executed every rule is a

**success**, while one where you broke the rules, averaged down, and pulled a stop—yet made $20,000 on luck—is a **failure**. Process adherence is your only scoreboard.

- Pre-commit to rules when calm; never adjust them when emotional.
- Treat big wins as data, not validation of genius; never raise your risk percentage after one.
- When euphoric, reduce size or take the day off; when desperate or angry, stop trading immediately.
- Take mandatory cool-offs after any oversized win or loss.
- Keep 20–30% in cash as a psychological safety valve.
- Anchor your identity to your process, never your profits.

### Win the Wins

The goal is not to feel rich in Month 2—it is to be rich, and still in the game, in Month 6. The ability to stay disciplined after success is rarer than the ability to survive failure, and it is the single biggest obstacle between you and $1,000,000. Master the psychology of fast money and you remove it; ignore it, and no strategy, instrument, or edge will save you. **Kill the thrill, or the thrill will kill the account.**

## Survival Rates Among Active Traders

The public sees the winners; the market quietly buries the rest. Before attempting to turn **$100,000 into $1,000,000 in six months**, confront one of finance's hardest truths: **most aggressive traders fail**—decades of evidence across multiple countries say so. New traders see screenshots and overnight fortunes; they rarely see the survival statistics. Yet survival, not profits, is what matters: the first rule of compounding is that you must remain in the game long enough for compounding to work.

### The Brutal Statistics

A forensic look at broker ledgers, academic studies, and regulatory data tells a story the marketing never does (figures vary; the direction never does):

| Source / Population | Finding |
|---|---|
| U.S. active day traders | ~72–80% end the year with net losses |
| Taiwan (long-run studies, Barber & Odean) | Under 1% achieve consistent positive returns net of fees |
| Brazil (traders persisting >300 days) | 97% lost money; only ~1.1% earned more than minimum wage |
| Broad retail (broker disclosures, SEC, ESMA) | ~70–95% lose money over multi-year horizons |
| Options & leveraged products | Worse still — theta decay, volatility crush, and magnified losses |

## The Survival Curve: 100 Traders, Five Years

Attrition is the headline. Track a cohort of 100 fresh aggressive traders and the curve is merciless:

| Milestone | Still Standing (of 100) | What Happened |
|---|---|---|
| Day 1 | **100** | Funded the account, full of conviction |
| 1 month | **~60** | ~40% quit almost immediately |
| 2 years | **~20** | ~80% gone — blown up or walked away |
| 3 years | **~13** | Only ~13% remain active |
| 5 years | **~1–5** | ~1–5% consistently profitable after fees |

## The 90/90/90 Rule and the 180-Day Sieve

Institutional desks summarize retail speculation with the **90/90/90 Rule**: roughly **90%** of active traders lose about **90%** of their capital within **90 days**. Over this book's six-month horizon, failure is front-loaded—nearly **80%** quit or blow up within **180 days**, while fewer than **1%** achieve sustained exponential returns. Most fail not from weak algorithms or slow data, but from poor execution, psychological instability, and a failure to understand expectancy.

## Why the Crowd Fails — by Design, Not Accident

Traders fail not because markets are an unbeatable casino, but because they step onto an institutional battlefield carrying predictable, structural flaws:

- **Over-leverage (the gambler's fallacy).** A **20%** decline in the underlying can erase **60%+** of a **3x ETF** position.
- **Trader's Ruin (statistical certainty).** Finite capital with neutral or negative expectancy trends toward bankruptcy; risking **10–20%** per trade makes an ordinary streak of **5–6 consecutive losses** catastrophic.
- **The friction tax.** Across 120 sessions, spreads and slippage in illiquid options, warrants, and leveraged ETFs can consume **10–20%** of a **$100,000** account before any profit.
- **Negative expectancy (the disposition effect).** Fear cuts winners quickly while hope keeps losers alive—small gains and large losses guarantee failure.
- **Structural decay.** Theta decay and volatility drag make time itself work against poorly managed positions.
- **No process, wrong opponent.** They chase tips, revenge trade, and succumb to FOMO while competing against hedge funds, market makers, and quant firms.

> **Expectancy = (Win rate × Avg win) – (Loss rate × Avg loss)** *Keep wins small and let losses run, and this number is negative by construction. No entry signal can save it.*

## Two Paths Through 180 Days

The same starting capital, the same market, two operators, two endings:

| Phase | The Gambler (95% pathway) | The Allocator (<1–5% pathway) |
|---|---|---|
| Days 1–30 | Over-trades out of excitement; hits a normal 3-trade losing streak, panics, removes stops, takes a 30% drawdown | Sets a fixed 1% risk unit ($1,000); accepts small scratch losses with robotic indifference |
| Days 31–90 | Falls into revenge trading; uses raw margin to force wins in illiquid assets; takes a margin call and forced liquidation | Equity curve trends out of incubation; reinvests realized tranches into deep, liquid names |
| Days 91–180 | Account abandoned or liquidated — destroyed by recovery math and volatility drag | Milestone progress compounds cleanly; manages liquidity rather than chasing hype |

## The Mathematics of Destruction

Survival is a mathematical advantage, because losses compound differently than gains: a 20% loss needs +25% to recover, a 50% loss +100%, a 75% loss +300%, a 90% loss +900%. Months of careful gains can vanish in one undisciplined period, and each deep loss slashes future compounding power. *The full recovery mathematics are developed in the Risk of Ruin chapter*—here the point is simply that avoiding the deep hole is worth more than any single brilliant trade.

## Survival Is the Edge

The amateur asks, "How much can I make?" The professional asks, "How much can I survive?" That single difference explains who is still standing in year five. Two illusions destroy most traders: the **illusion of skill**, which mistakes a favorable market for competence, and **survivorship bias**, which highlights the few spectacular winners while hiding the thousands who failed. Most blowups occur *after* success, when confidence expands leverage and leverage invites ruin. Opportunities are unlimited; capital is not.

## The 1–5% Who Survive

The tiny minority who last share exactly the profile sketched earlier—capital allocation over entertainment, controlled aggression, ironclad 1%-or-less risk with predefined circuit breakers, a written process executed through ruthless rotation, obsessive journaling, and the humility to prioritize survival over ego. **They rely not on brilliance or luck but on structure that lets a small**

**edge compound—and on the discipline to follow it when it is boring and when it is terrifying.**

### The Survival Cycle

Most enduring careers move through the same progression—learning, costly mistakes, improving risk control, consistency, confidence without arrogance, rapid compounding on a preserved base, and finally longevity, where survival itself becomes the compounding advantage. Those who reach the late stages almost always survived the early ones.

### The Honest Message of This Book

This blueprint is written for the **1–5%**—the rare trader willing to embrace extreme discipline in pursuit of extreme returns. It is **not for everyone**, and pretending otherwise would set you up for slaughter.

Be clear-eyed about the goal: growing **$100,000 into $1,000,000 in six months** is exceptionally ambitious, requiring rare conditions, flawless execution, disciplined risk management, and exceptional opportunities. The pursuit of extraordinary returns must never come at the expense of survival. Stocks, **2x/3x ETFs**, options, and warrants offer tremendous upside—but only when managed professionally. Survival is the rarest skill: you don't need to win every trade, only to stay solvent long enough for compounding to work. **Survive first. Compound second. Everything else is noise.**

## Importance of Capital Preservation

Retail traders hear *aggressive trading* and imagine relentless offense—explosive assets, maximum leverage, constant action. Professionals understand the opposite: **capital preservation is your primary offensive weapon.** The amateur asks, *"How much can I make?"* the professional, *"How much can I lose without crippling the compounding engine?"* Lose the capital and the campaign ends. Across a **120-session** sprint, your ability to exploit market velocity depends entirely on protecting the underlying capital.

### The Preservation Paradox: Defense Dictates Offense

Amateurs associate preservation with holding bonds; in high-velocity trading, preservation powers aggression, because compounding requires continuity and continuity requires survival. Fail to protect the **$100,000** base and every drawdown forces smaller future positions, starving the engine just as major opportunities emerge. Traders most obsessed with protecting capital often compound fastest, because uninterrupted compounding beats temporary explosiveness.

### The Mathematical Iron Law

The primary threat is not a low win rate—it is the asymmetric tyranny of drawdown math. Allow a concentrated **3x ETF**, option, or warrant to produce a **30%** drawdown and you now need **42.9%** simply to recover; compounding time becomes recovery time, undermining the **180-day** objective. Small losses are operating expenses; large losses are existential. Deep drawdowns also destroy confidence and sizing—an account may survive financially while collapsing psychologically.

## The Infrastructure of Sovereign Preservation

To make preservation operational rather than aspirational, the blueprint enforces three institutional-grade parameters.

**1. The fixed risk unit (1R).** Size by permissible loss, not expected gain: no trade risks more than **1%** of equity, so on a **$100,000** account **1R = $1,000**. Even after five consecutive losses—statistically normal—you retain roughly **95%** of capital.

**2. The time stop.** Time is capital: if a position goes sideways or trendless, exit to cash. Cash is a high-optionality position that preserves capital for the next breakout.

**3. The account-level circuit breaker.** If a correlated macro event or overnight gap drags total equity **15%** below its peak, an API protocol flushes the book to cash and locks the terminal for a mandatory **48-hour** audit—isolating the parent capital from the revenge-trading loop.

> **THE ACCOUNT-LEVEL CIRCUIT BREAKER** Total equity −15% from peak → automated API protocol → flush the book to 100% cash → **48-HOUR LOCKDOWN**

## Preservation Is a Philosophy, Not a Technique

Once preservation becomes instinctive it changes every decision: the trader asks what if I'm wrong, what's the maximum loss, can the account survive, will this drawdown interrupt compounding. The danger peaks during winning streaks, when success quietly increases size, leverage, and complacency until an adverse move inflicts severe losses—many traders fail not from lack of opportunity but from abandoning preservation after success. Preserved capital also preserves calm, and calm preserves disciplined execution.

## Cash Is Stored Opportunity

Optionality is the hidden power of preservation. A trader with capital intact can wait, survive difficult cycles, capitalize on panic, and deploy aggressively the moment opportunity appears; the trader who has destroyed capital loses this entirely. Real professional aggression is selective, not constant—maximum exposure only when liquidity is strong, volatility supports the strategy, momentum confirms, and asymmetry is clearly favorable. Outside those windows, exposure contracts fast, and that flexibility is what preserves capital through unfavorable regimes.

## Protect the Capital First

A final truth reaches beyond the ledger: preservation protects not only the account but the trader. Losses that spiral out of control produce stress, instability, damaged relationships, and burnout. The greatest traders in history shared one trait above all—they survived: not every trade or month, but long enough for their edge and compounding to become extraordinary. **Protect the capital first; everything else depends on it.**

# Chapter 4
# Risk of Ruin Mathematics

## Risk of Ruin & Position Sizing

Most traders believe success is about stock selection, timing, and finding the next explosive setup. Professionals understand something deeper: position sizing often matters more than the trade itself. An excellent strategy can be destroyed by catastrophic sizing; an imperfect one can survive and compound if sizing is disciplined. In a 10x campaign the greatest threat is not a bad trade—it is **Risk of Ruin**, the probability that a perfectly normal losing streak reduces your account to a point where recovery becomes impossible. The market rewards surviving long enough for your edge to compound. Position sizing is not a technical detail; it is survival mathematics.

### What Risk of Ruin Actually Is

Every trader has a risk of ruin; the only question is whether they understand it. In probability terms it depends on your net edge and how many "risk units" of capital you have before bankruptcy:

$$RoR = \left( (1 - A) / (1 + A) \right) U$$

where $A$ is your net statistical edge and $U$ is the number of risk units before bankruptcy (total capital ÷ position-risk size).

The counterintuitive takeaway: **if your sizing exposes too much capital per trade, risk of ruin approaches 100%—even with a highly profitable edge.** A trader with a phenomenal 55% win rate and 2R wins can easily hit a random seven-trade losing streak—ordinary variance. Risk 10% per trade and that normal streak compounds into a 50%+ drawdown, after which asymmetric recovery math finishes the job. The relationship between risk-per-trade and ruin is wildly nonlinear; the illustrative ranges below (for a solid ≈55% win rate, 2.5-to-1 payoff) show the shape:

| Risk per trade | Approximate risk of ruin |
|---|---|
| **5%** | **60–80%+ (very high)** |
| **3%** | **25–40%** |
| **2%** | **8–15%** |
| **1%** | **under 1% (excellent)** |
| **0.5%** | **near zero** |

The lesson is unambiguous: risking more than 1–2% per trade in an aggressive, leveraged strategy converts a survivable edge into near-certain ruin. It is especially fatal here—reaching $1,000,000 from $100,000 requires roughly +46.8% per month, and a single 60% drawdown early forces +150% on the remaining capital just to break even.

## The Fixed-Risk Position-Sizing Engine

The blueprint rejects amateur "dollar-amount sizing" and enforces fixed-risk sizing, where position size is the output of two variables: the risk unit (1R, fixed at 1–2% of equity) and the technical stop-loss distance (entry to invalidation, set by ATR or recent structural lows):

*Position Size = (Account Equity × Risk %) ÷ (Entry Price − Stop-Loss Price)*

On a $150,000 account, a 1% risk unit is $1,500. If your stop sits 8% below entry, position size is $1,500 ÷ 0.08 = $18,750. The stop distance, not your excitement, determines how much you deploy.

## The Engine in Action Across Growth Cycles

Watch the same rule protect the base while scaling the offense. Take a liquid 3x ETF breaking out at $50.00 with a stop at $47.50—a 5%, $2.50-per-share risk distance—at two account sizes:

| | Incubation phase | Acceleration phase |
|---|---|---|
| **Account equity** | $100,000 | $500,000 |
| **1R risk unit (1%)** | $1,000 | $5,000 |
| **Risk per share ($50 – $47.50)** | $2.50 | $2.50 |
| **Shares deployed** | 400 | 2,000 |
| **Capital exposed (× $50)** | $20,000 | $100,000 |
| **Loss if stopped out** | $1,000 (1%) | $5,000 (1%) |

In both phases a stop-out loses **exactly 1%** of the active ledger—$1,000 or $5,000. Position mass scaled up fivefold automatically because the base grew, but vulnerability to a ruin event stayed pinned near zero. You command a far larger block of market equity without ever raising the parent account's percentage risk.

## The 1% Rule: Your Mathematical Shield

Distilled to one sentence: never risk more than 1% of your current equity on any one trade. As the account compounds, the dollar figure scales with it—$1,000 at $100k, $2,500 at $250k, $6,000 at $600k—while the percentage stays fixed. That keeps risk of ruin extremely low, lets you survive 50 to 100+ losing trades without structural damage, and gives you the psychological freedom to trade aggressively when the edge is strong.

## The Sizing Toolkit

**Volatility-based (ATR) sizing.** Size against the instrument's Average True Range so every trade carries similar risk—a wild 3x ETF and a calm large-cap should expose the same 1R, which means different share counts.

**The pyramiding rule.** Only ever add to winners, never to losers; keep total risk across all open positions capped near 6–8% of equity so a correlated reversal can't threaten the account.

**Correlation and portfolio-level risk.** Several positions aren't diversification if they share a theme, momentum regime, or liquidity cycle—your true exposure is far larger than it looks. Evaluate exposure at the portfolio level, not position by position.

**Sizing by instrument.** 3x ETFs: very volatile—tight stops, smaller size. Options: max loss is the premium, never above 1% of equity. Warrants: treat like high-leverage options, size very conservatively. Stocks and 2x ETFs: slightly larger, still under the 1% rule.

### The Kelly Criterion — and Why You Use a Fraction of It

To optimize growth velocity the blueprint borrows from the Kelly Criterion, which gives the mathematically optimal fraction of capital to allocate to an edge:

*K% = W – ( (1 – W) ÷ **R )*

With a 45% win rate and 3R payoff, full Kelly is K% = 0.45 – (0.55 ÷ 3) = **26.7%**—a warning, not an instruction. Raw Kelly assumes perfect execution and zero friction; deploying 26.7% on a single edge invites violent volatility and scale shock. So the blueprint uses **fractional Kelly**—roughly a tenth of the raw figure—capping the active risk unit near 2–3% in peak regimes and defaulting to 1% otherwise. A fraction of Kelly captures most of the growth for a small fraction of the ruin risk.

### Sizing Is Emotional Management Disguised as Math

There is a psychological layer beneath the formulas: large exposure changes the person holding it. A trader calm risking 2% can become impulsive, fearful, or frozen risking 30%, and that instability degrades execution itself. Many traders fail psychologically before they fail mathematically. So size to your emotional tolerance as well as your strategy—a position you can't hold calmly is too large, whatever the spreadsheet says. The objective is never to maximize a single trade; it is to maximize long-term compounding survival through volatility, drawdowns, and uncertainty.

> **THE POSITION-SIZING CREED**
> ***"I size every trade so that even a complete loss cannot meaningfully threaten my ability to keep compounding. My aggression lives in the quality of my setups and the leverage I selectively apply—never in reckless risk per trade."***

## Maximum Acceptable Drawdowns

Every aggressive trader learns a brutal truth: the size of the drawdown determines the difficulty of the recovery. That is not psychology—it is mathematics, and mathematics does not negotiate. Your most dangerous enemy is not a single bad trade but an unmanaged drawdown, because drawdowns don't subtract capital linearly—they alter the compounding engine itself. So the blueprint defines and enforces a hard **Maximum Acceptable Drawdown**.

## Why Drawdowns Are Lethal to a 10x Plan

In a six-month campaign you have little time to recover, and every point lost early sharply raises the return required on what remains:

| Drawdown | Capital left | Return then needed for $1M | Feasible in time? |
|---|---|---|---|
| **−10%** | $90,000 | **+1,011%** | Extremely hard |
| **−20%** | $80,000 | **+1,150%** | Nearly impossible |
| **−30%** | $70,000 | **+1,329%** | Practically impossible |
| **−40%** | $60,000 | **+1,567%** | No |
| **−50%** | $50,000 | **+1,900%** | No |
| **−60%** | $40,000 | **+2,400%** | No |

Any drawdown deeper than roughly 25–30% in the first three or four months essentially ends your 10x attempt, even if you trade flawlessly afterward. A 15% drawdown needs only about 17.6% to recover—inside a normal edge—while 30% already demands roughly 42.9%, and past that the math turns openly hostile.

## The Line of No Return: A 15% Hard Floor

For a $100,000 campaign, the Maximum Acceptable Drawdown is capped at **15% ($15,000)** from any historic peak. There, the 17.6% recovery stays within your asymmetric edge—you climb back without anything heroic. Drop past 20% or 30% and you're forced to hunt low-probability outliers or expand size drastically, converting controlled aggression into terminal gambling. The 15% line is a hard, concrete wall.

## The Multi-Layered Drawdown Defense

To make sure you never breach the floor, the blueprint engineers a tiered, automated defense that runs independently of emotion.

> **THE DRAWDOWN-CELL PARAMETERS**
> **1. Maximum risk per trade** – 1% of equity (1R). **2. Maximum daily loss** – 3%, then the desk locks for the day. **3. Maximum peak-to-trough** – 15% – the hard floor.

**1. The micro-layer: the 1% trade guard.** Every trade limits loss to 1% of current equity; reaching the 15% floor on stops alone would take fifteen consecutive losers—a statistical anomaly if you filter strictly for high-volume momentum.

**2. The mezzo-layer: the 3% daily churn limit.** When correlated assets gap down together and stops cluster, realized losses hitting 3% of the day's opening balance trigger an automated protocol that cancels all orders and locks the terminal for the session.

**3. The macro-layer: the 15% systemic circuit breaker.** If total equity contracts 15% from peak, a systemic lockdown flushes the book to cash and locks you out for a mandatory 48-hour audit to determine whether the drawdown came from non-compliance or regime misalignment.

## The Dynamic Risk Downscaler

The circuit breaker is the last line of defense; the downscaler makes reaching it almost impossible. Instead of holding your risk unit static while underperforming, cut it as the ledger slips from its peak:

| Distance from peak | Risk per trade | Posture |
|---|---|---|
| **At peak** | **1.0%** | Full deployment |
| **−5% drawdown** | **0.5%** | Buffer widens |
| **−10% drawdown** | **0.25%** | Maximum moat |

By shrinking exposure precisely as the account enters a deficit, you extend your survival runway: a normal losing streak that would have marched a static account into the 15% floor now stalls out well short of it, because each step costs less ground than the last.

## Drawdowns Are Psychological, Too

A drawdown is never only a number—it compresses psychology. Reduced capital, flexibility, and confidence and elevated pressure arrive at once, and the trader starts forcing trades or freezing. A trader can survive a 60% drawdown mathematically while never recovering psychologically. This is why the worst blowups come after success: big gains lower fear, lower fear raises exposure, and one sharp reversal does disproportionate damage. The defense is to define your Maximum Acceptable Drawdown *before* trading begins, pre-committed in writing and obeyed mechanically.

## Enforcement in Practice

- Track your high-water mark every day.
- When you hit a threshold, exposure reduces automatically—no debate, no "just one more."
- Use 3x ETFs and options progressively more conservatively as the drawdown deepens.
- Keep meaningful dry powder—25–40% cash—during choppy phases.

## Keep Drawdowns Survivable

The traders who succeed at extreme compounding don't try to avoid every drawdown—that's impossible—they keep drawdowns survivable. Deep drawdowns don't merely dent the balance sheet; they steal time, corrode psychology, and push required recovery returns past anything achievable in the months left. The goal was never to avoid losses, but to avoid losses large enough to stop compounding—and that battle is decided by drawdown management. **Protect the floor; the ceiling takes care of itself.**

> **THE DRAWDOWN CREED**
> ***"I accept that drawdowns are normal, even healthy, in aggressive trading. I will never let one breach my 15% floor—because beyond it, the mathematical path to $1,000,000 quietly dies."***

## Recovery Mathematics

Surviving a drawdown is not the question; in a six-month **10×** campaign the question is whether you can recover fast enough to still reach **$1,000,000.** Most traders think linearly—a **20%** loss needs a **20%** gain. Recovery is **non-linear**: as capital falls, required returns rise exponentially. Over **120 sessions**, ignoring this asymmetry is a leading cause of account failure.

### The Non-Linear Math of Capital Destruction

Gains and losses do not share a 1:1 reciprocal relationship, because losing capital erodes your **compounding base mass**—fewer dollars remain active, forcing the survivors to work far harder. The exact recovery required is governed by one formula:

> **Required Recovery (%) = [ Drawdown % ÷ (1 − Drawdown %) ] × 100**

Plotted across deepening drawdowns from a $100,000 base, the formula exposes why aggressive traders run a fanatical capital defense—the hill steepens until it becomes a vertical cliff:

| Drawdown | Capital Left | Recovery to Even | Req. Monthly Return* | Verdict |
|---|---|---|---|---|
| **-5%** | $95,000 | +5.3% | ~1.0% / mo | **Trivial** |
| **-10%** | $90,000 | +11.1% | ~2.1% / mo | **Easy** |
| **-15%** | $85,000 | +17.6% | ~3.3% / mo | **Manageable** |
| **-20%** | $80,000 | +25.0% | ~4.6% / mo | **Doable** |
| **-25%** | $75,000 | +33.3% | ~5.9% / mo | **Demanding** |
| **-30%** | $70,000 | +42.9% | ~7.4% / mo | **Hard** |
| **-40%** | $60,000 | +66.7% | ~10.8% / mo | **Very Hard** |
| **-50%** | $50,000 | **+100.0%** | ~14.9% / mo | **Extremely Difficult** |
| **-60%** | $40,000 | **+150.0%** | ~20.1% / mo | **Nearly Impossible** |
| **-70%** | $30,000 | **+233.0%** | ~27.2% / mo | **Impossible in window** |

| Drawdown | Capital Left | Recovery to Even | Req. Monthly Return* | Verdict |
|---|---|---|---|---|
| **-80%** | $20,000 | **+400.0%** | ~38.0% / mo | **Impossible** |
| **-90%** | $10,000 | **+900.0%** | ~58.5% / mo | **Terminal** |

## The Milestone That Decides the Campaign

Up to about a **15%** drawdown, recovery (**17.6%**) stays achievable with a strong edge. Beyond **20–30%**, recovery becomes statistically improbable within six months—a trader down **50%** must **double** the remaining account just to break even. Practical rule: any drawdown deeper than 25–30% early usually ends the 10x attempt mathematically, even with flawless subsequent execution.

## The Mechanical Squeeze on Position Mass

Behind the percentages sits a physical mechanism: position size is a direct percentage of equity, so a drawdown shrinks your position mass and starves the engine of fuel. Under a strict 10%-per-trade rule:

> **PRISTINE BASE** Account: $100,000 10% block: $10,000 25% move → **+$2,500**
>
> **IMPAIRED BASE (–50%)** Account: $50,000 10% block: $5,000 25% move → **+$1,250**

Same brilliant 25% move, half the reward. Because the drawdown halved your position mass, you must execute twice as many identical winners to claw back the same dollars—permanently altering your timeline and quietly converting a six-month 10x target into an impossibility.

## Why Recovery Is So Much Harder in Aggressive Trading

- **Time compression.** No multi-year runway; every month clawing back to even is a month not compounding forward.
- **Leverage amplifies losses.** 3x ETFs, options, and warrants can turn an ordinary correction into a 50–90% loss in days.
- **Psychological damage.** After a deep drawdown most traders quit or revenge-trade—both make recovery less likely.
- **Opportunity cost.** While digging out of a –50% hole, the strong trends that could have compounded you pass by.

## The Behavioral Hazard: The Deficit Mutation Loop

The most lethal element of recovery mathematics is how it compromises executive function. Staring at a deep deficit, a trader's cognitive parameters fracture and they enter a destructive loop of emotional compensation:

> **Deep Capital Deficit → Panic & Urgency → Rule Violation / Over-Leverage → Liquidation**

To escape the pain fast, the trader abandons the playbook—the 1% unit is dropped, stops are pulled, and capital is over-allocated into binary short-dated options or thin warrants chasing one redeeming "jackpot." Emotional overexposure inside a live mathematical deficit is the exact tipping point where capital allocation ends and terminal gambling begins.

### Consistency Beats Brilliance: The Two-Trader Proof

Recovery mathematics explain why steadiness compounds better than fireworks:

> **Trader A** gains 100%, then loses 50%. The account sits exactly at breakeven. The spectacular run accomplished nothing. **Trader B** compounds +15%, +20%, +12%, +18% while guarding the downside carefully — and finishes well ahead of Trader A.

It is also why hedge funds and prop desks automatically **reduce exposure after a drawdown**—not because opportunity vanished, but because mathematical and emotional instability rise together after losses. Stabilize first; resume aggression later.

### The Controlled-Aggression Recovery Rules

- **The 1% risk rule—your primary defense.** Small individual losses are what keep drawdowns shallow.
- **Hard circuit breakers, tiered to the peak:** −10% → cut sizes 50%; −20% → risk 0.5% per trade; −25% → 70%+ cash and reassess; −30% → full stop, go to cash and rebuild.
- **Pyramid only on winners.** Never add to a loser hoping for rescue.
- **Accept small losses quickly.** A string of −8% to −12% losses is survivable; one −55% loss is not.

### The Bottom Line

Recovery mathematics is unforgiving inside six months. The traders who reach $1,000,000 are not the ones who avoid every loss—they are the ones who **never allow a drawdown so deep that recovery becomes unrealistic.** A 10% loss leaves you in control; an 80% loss leaves you fighting mathematics itself, the one opponent no trader defeats emotionally. **Protect your capital aggressively. Keep drawdowns survivable. Let compounding do the rest.**

## Volatility Drag

One of aggressive trading's most misunderstood forces is **volatility drag**—also called **variance drain** or **beta slippage**. Few understand its mathematics, yet it quietly destroys compounding, reducing returns even when markets finish flat. Institutional managers treat volatility as a **geometric tax**: because compounding depends on the geometric, not arithmetic, mean, higher variance structurally lowers long-term growth. In a **180-day** campaign using daily-reset **leveraged ETFs**, ignoring drag guarantees weaker—or negative—results despite a positive win rate.

## The Geometric Tax: Why Gains and Losses Don't Offset

Arithmetic averages mislead. A **$100,000** account that gains **50%** then loses **50%** doesn't break even—it falls to **$75,000**, a permanent **25%** loss. Likewise **+10%/−10%** leaves **$99,000** (−1%), and **+20%/−20%** leaves **$96,000** (−4%). Drag rises with the square of volatility:

*Volatility Drag* $\approx \sigma^2 / 2$

where $\sigma^2$ is the variance of your return stream. The objective is twofold: maximize asset momentum while minimizing the volatility of your **equity curve**.

## The Leveraged-ETF Trap: Path Dependency

**2×** and **3× ETFs** reset daily, making returns **path dependent**—they deliver multiples of *daily*, not long-term, returns. In strong trends they compound well; in volatile, sideways markets the daily reset becomes a persistent drain. The single-cycle block makes it concrete: an index rises 10% then falls 9.09%, ending flat, while the 3x ETF goes +30% then −27.27% and lands at −5.45%. Now watch four days of churn that nets the index to zero:

| Day | Index move | Index level | 3x ETF move | 3x ETF value |
|---|---|---|---|---|
| **Day 0** | baseline | 100.00 | baseline | **$100,000** |
| **Day 1** | +10.00% | 110.00 | +30.00% | **$130,000** |
| **Day 2** | −9.09% | 100.00 | −27.27% | **$94,545** |
| **Day 3** | +10.00% | 110.00 | +30.00% | **$122,909** |
| **Day 4** | −9.09% | 100.00 | −27.27% | **$89,388** |

The index finishes unchanged, yet the **3× ETF** loses **$10,612 (10.6%)** solely from variance.

## Why It Is Deadly for a 10x Goal

- **It compounds against you** through daily rebalancing.
- **It turns flat markets into losses**—in sideways conditions, 3x ETFs can shed 10–30%+ while the underlying barely moves.
- **It magnifies risk of ruin**—you can be right on the trend and still lose capital to drag, forcing larger recovery on a smaller base.
- **It strikes when traders get greedy**—holding 3x ETFs too long through consolidation lets drag destroy the gains.

By **Month 3**, **$100,000** has grown to **$180,000 (+80%)**; three weeks of consolidation and drag cut it **25%** to **$135,000**, leaving roughly **+640%** still needed to reach **$1,000,000**.

## Immunizing the Ledger From Drag

You must still harness the velocity of 2x/3x ETFs and options—but only behind strict parameters that immunize the portfolio against drag:

> **THE VOLATILITY-DRAG INSULATION 1. Regime locking** – no leveraged allocations in sideways markets. **2. Maximum capital velocity** – leveraged holds of just 2–5 sessions. **3. The cash safe-haven** – flush to 100% cash through the chop.

**Regime locking.** Ban 2x/3x ETFs and options when an asset trades inside a sideways consolidation or below rising short-term averages (e.g. the 10-day EMA); allocate only during confirmed, high-volume blue-sky breakouts where directional velocity overpowers the daily-reset friction.

**Maximum capital velocity.** Treat leveraged positions as short-term captures of two to five sessions: scale into the breakout, harvest a rapid tranche, liquidate to cash before path-dependent decay engages. Never marry a 3x ETF for weeks.

**Cash as a pristine buffer.** In a high-variance distribution phase, flush the book to 100% cash—its volatility coefficient is exactly zero, freezing your variance and preserving base mass for when clean momentum resumes.

**Two more habits.** Monitor realized beta—if drag is eating the 2–3× you expect, cut exposure—and mix instrument types: stocks and 2x ETFs carry lower drag, 3x ETFs offer high power at high drag, options give defined risk where the cost is time decay rather than beta slippage.

## Smooth Compounds Faster Than Explosive

This reframes the goal. Many chase high volatility believing it creates wealth; in reality uncontrolled volatility destroys compounding efficiency, and smooth growth often compounds faster than explosive, unstable performance. A trader earning 80% with controlled volatility can outperform one posting 200% punctuated by collapses, because the path of returns matters as much as the destination and the smoother curve survives long enough for the math to work. Volatility also drags on you psychologically—violent swings breed fatigue and impulsiveness that degrade execution. Aggressive compounding does not require maximum chaos; it requires controlled offensive pressure with survivable volatility.

# Why Avoiding Catastrophic Loss Matters More Than Maximizing Gains

In aggressive trading, one mathematical truth outranks every other: **avoiding a single catastrophic loss is worth more than capturing ten large wins.** This is the precise, unsentimental reason a tiny minority ever reach a 10x return while the majority blow up trying.

> *The retail public reads the phrase "1,000% Compounding" and assumes the strategy belongs to a hyper-aggressive profit maximizer. The institutional allocator knows the opposite is true: the speculator who turns $100,000 into $1,000,000 in six months is not a genius at finding winners — they are a fanatic about avoiding ruin.*

Across a 120-session campaign, large gains are largely a byproduct of market velocity meeting a positive-expectancy edge; avoiding catastrophic loss is a non-negotiable structural mandate. Permit one defensive breach and the arithmetic of the ledger strips your engine of power, rendering the target mathematically impossible.

## The Amateur Mind vs. the Professional Mind

Most inexperienced traders enter obsessed with upside; professionals become obsessed with survivability. A trader who books +50%, +80%, but later takes a catastrophic drawdown often ends up worse off than one producing smaller, steadier gains—because losses damage the compounding engine itself.

## The Asymmetric Mathematics of Gains and Losses

Gains and losses do not carry equal mathematical gravity, and the gap widens viciously inside a six-month sprint:

> Make 100% on $100,000 and your base scales to $200,000. Suffer a 50% loss on that new balance and you are not back to $150,000 — you are wiped all the way down to **$100,000.** A 50% down-move completely erased a 100% up-move.

Because defense always holds the mathematical upper hand, a trader who maximizes gains over capping losses is engineering their own ruin. The full break-even ledger appears earlier in this chapter; the point bears repeating: a single **−50%** drawdown forces you to double the surviving capital just to break even, and **−90%** demands **+900%**—essentially the whole campaign spent climbing back to zero. Recovery is rarely impossible in theory; it simply grows exponentially harder as capital shrinks, because the trader faces reduced capital, flexibility, emotional stability, and opportunity all at once.

## Why One Catastrophic Loss Destroys the Entire Blueprint

1. **It steals your compounding base.** A catastrophic loss shrinks the capital every future gain must compound on. It causes capital collapse.

2. **It creates impossible recovery math.** Beyond roughly **−50%**, recovery becomes unrealistic within the remaining time.

3. **Leverage magnifies the wound.** A single move in a **3× ETF, option, or warrant** can inflict a **−60% to −90%** loss in one session.

4. **It triggers the psychological spiral.** Large losses damage capital and judgment—fear, revenge trading, and abandoned systems often produce a second, fatal loss. Capital preservation is psychological preservation.

## The Geometric Engine: Fuel vs. Friction

Picture two opposing forces. Capital mass is fuel: run a strict 1R unit with an asymmetric edge (average win near +3R) and the account scales through frequent modular tranches; because the defensive boundaries are ironclad, the base stays un-impaired and can safely deploy large equity blocks in explosive regimes. Catastrophic loss is friction: a 40% loss reduces a $100,000 account to $60,000, requiring +66.7% merely to break even—time spent recovering instead of compounding toward $1,000,000.

## The Hidden Cycle: Why Traders Blow Up After Winning

Many traders lose fortunes not during difficult markets but immediately after extraordinary success: success reduces fear, reduced fear expands exposure, expanded exposure magnifies fragility, and one violent reversal erases all progress. Bull markets make leverage feel safe and momentum permanent until one reversal erases years of gains. Elite traders look conservative because they prioritize survival over short-term excitement.

## The Survivor's Edge: Optionality and Continuity

Markets reward continuity more than brilliance: traders who survive multiple cycles compound steadily, while those destroyed by one catastrophic loss never reach future opportunities. Preserved capital also means preserved optionality—the ability to exploit dislocations, adapt to regimes, and act rationally. This is the central paradox: traders most focused on avoiding catastrophic loss often compound fastest, because uninterrupted compounding is exponentially powerful.

## Controlled Aggression: The Priority Order

Aggressive trading does not require accepting unlimited volatility—that is a myth. Professional aggression follows a strict sequence:

- **Avoid catastrophic loss.** Non-negotiable, before anything else.
- **Survive normal drawdowns of 15–25%.** Plan for them.
- **Maximize gains—only after the first two are secured.**

Most traders reverse this order, chasing gains and hoping survival follows—which usually ends in ruin. Restraint is not weakness; it is risk management.

## The Defensive Framework: Three Pillars

You don't maximize gains by taking wider risks. You maximize gains by enforcing three unyielding pillars that elevate capital preservation to a mandate:

**PILLAR 1 The Asymmetric Payoff Mandate (3R Minimum)**

Trade only when potential reward is at least **3R**. One routine winner can offset three consecutive losses.

**PILLAR 2 Automated Invalidation Stops**

Every stock, **leveraged ETF**, or option is entered with an automated hard stop. No mental stops. No hope.

**PILLAR 3 Regime-Locked Allocation Discipline**

Avoid leverage in choppy, sideways, high-variance markets. Move toward cash

**PILLAR 1 The Asymmetric Payoff Mandate (3R Minimum)**

until clean momentum returns. Cash preserves maximum optionality.

- **The 1% risk rule.** Never risk more than 1% of total capital per trade.
- **Hard circuit breakers.** Automatic de-risking at −10%, −20%, and −25% drawdowns.
- **No martingale, no averaging down.** Never add to a loser.
- Define maximum loss before every trade, especially with options and warrants.
- **Maximum portfolio heat.** Total risk across all open positions stays at or below 6–8% of equity.

> **"In aggressive trading, the difference between success and failure is not how big your winners are: it is how small your losers stay."**

One catastrophic loss can erase ten outstanding trades; ten disciplined winners can absorb many small losses. That is why elite traders obsess over capital preservation and **risk of ruin** more than the next **10-bagger**. Master this and **2×/3× ETFs, options, and warrants** become wealth-building tools instead of wealth-destroying weapons. Traders survive missed opportunities; they rarely survive catastrophic losses. **Protect first. Compound second—the sustainable path to $1,000,000 in six months.**

# PART II – THE MARKET ENVIRONMENT

# Chapter 5
# Understanding Market Regimes

## A. Bull Markets

Not all market environments are equal, and the single biggest determinant of whether **$100,000** can become **$1,000,000 in six months** is the market regime. A **bull market** is the only environment where aggressive, leveraged compounding has a genuine mathematical chance; choppy, bearish, or high-uncertainty markets sharply raise the **risk of ruin**. Structurally, a bull is a **high-liquidity, parameter-stable regime** where persistent institutional buying exceeds supply, letting high-beta instruments deliver full compounding power—yet the same forgiving conditions breed overconfidence, leverage addiction, and risk blindness. The objective is to exploit the bull without becoming its victim.

> **And yet: every aggressive trader loves bull markets — and most aggressive traders are ultimately destroyed by them.** The same forgiving conditions that fortunes also breed overconfidence, leverage, and risk blindness. This chapter teaches you to hold both truths at once: attack the bull while it lasts, and never forget what it is doing to your judgment.

### What Defines a Bull Regime

A true bull is more than rising prices—it is a psychological and liquidity environment: a sustained uptrend of **higher highs and higher lows**; broad participation with **most sectors rising together**; expanding money flow and **rising volume on up-days**; a risk-on appetite paying higher multiples for growth; and momentum persistence—**breakouts follow through** and dips are bought quickly. The freight train runs powerfully for extended periods, and aggression is rewarded.

### Identifying a Bull Regime: Objective Filters

Confirm the regime with verifiable metrics, never sentiment, and never on a single signal—require at least four before deploying maximum aggression:

- Major indexes above rising 21-day EMA and 200-day SMA with higher highs.
- The 200-day average sloping upward with price well above it.
- Volume expanding on up-days and contracting on orderly pullbacks.
- A rising advance-decline line and new 52-week highs swamping new lows.
- Leadership from growth sectors — technology, semiconductors, biotech, consumer discretionary.
- The VIX staying relatively low and subdued.

### Why Bull Markets Are Built for 1,000%

- **Asymmetric upside.** Strong trends produce frequent 20–100%+ moves in individual names and sectors.

- **Leverage works for you.** In a confirmed, linear bull, the daily reset of 2x/3x ETFs and options compounds in your favor.
- **Momentum compounds naturally.** Winners keep winning, so you can pyramid into strength.
- **Trend-following wins more often.** Breakouts, pullback buys, and rotation all perform better when the tide is rising.

### Best Instruments and Tactics

Each high-beta vehicle has a role—higher aggression means higher risk:

| Instrument | Best Use in a Bull Regime | Aggression |
|---|---|---|
| Momentum stocks | Leading growth names with strong catalysts | **High** |
| 2x ETFs | Smoother compounding vehicle | **High** |
| 3x ETFs (TQQQ, SOXL) | Core trend amplifier | **Very High** |
| Warrants | Asymmetric lottery tickets on leaders | **Very High** |
| Long calls / call spreads | High-conviction directional bets | **Extreme** |

*Tickers and leverage factors change and vary by jurisdiction; verify each fund before trading.*

Core tactics stay simple: buy relative-strength leaders, buy pullbacks within strong trends, pyramid into confirmed strength, and trail stops or scale profits.

### The Velocity Playbook: Maximum Deployment

A confirmed bull suppresses catastrophic overnight gaps, so the risk environment lets you shift from defense to maximum-velocity deployment:

> **Bull regime confirmed → Unlock embedded leverage → Maximize capital turnover → Tranche compounding**

The 3x ETFs and options that are toxic in chop become primary wealth accelerators in a confirmed linear bull. Hunt 52-week blue-sky breakouts and high-relative-volume flags clearing resistance on heavy volume—with no overhead supply they expand vertically over 2-to-5-day windows. Scale your fixed 1% risk unit (1R) into the breakout, capture a clean +3R to +5R, then liquidate to cash and recalculate your expanded base.

### The Stages of a Bull Market

Bull markets evolve, and the stage governs how much leverage is prudent:

| Stage | What Drives It | Your Posture |
|---|---|---|

| Stage | What Drives It | Your Posture |
|---|---|---|
| Early | Fear fading, recovery expectations, institutional accumulation | Build aggressively into emerging leadership |
| Middle | Broad participation expansion across sectors | Full deployment; pyramid confirmed trends |
| Late | Speculative mania – valuations disconnect, retail euphoria, greed | Tighten risk; the greatest hidden danger lives here |

## The Blindspots: Why Bull Markets Destroy Traders

Bull markets hide risk exceptionally well, which is why inexperienced traders often post their largest gains just before their largest losses. Three blindspots do the damage:

- **The ego-attribution error.** Because the regime is forgiving, even poor entries resolve profitably and the trader concludes they've "cracked the code," loosening risk and over-leveraging. The antidote is one constant question: "Is my strategy working because I'm skilled, or because of the market?"
- **Bad habits made profitable.** Oversizing, ignoring stops, averaging down, and over-concentrating all still make money in a powerful bull—so the trader mistakes survival for skill until the regime changes and the identical behavior turns catastrophic.
- **Volatility desensitization.** Used to every dip being bought, the trader treats the first toxic counter-trend move as a "healthy pullback," freezes, fails to execute stops, and lets a routine cost mutate into a huge drawdown.

## Dangers Even in a Bull

A bull is not risk-free: sharp 10–20% corrections happen regularly, sector rotations punish laggards without warning, and late-stage euphoria breeds blow-off tops. **This is precisely why the 1% risk rule and predefined circuit breakers stay active even at the height of the run**—discipline is never suspended just because the tape is green.

## The Controlled-Aggression Pledge

> *"When the regime is clearly bullish and momentum confirmed, I will deploy maximum controlled aggression using leverage and pyramiding. When conditions deteriorate, I will immediately reduce exposure and protect capital."*

## The Regime Governance Matrix

| Parameter | The Retail Gambler | The Blueprint Allocator |
|---|---|---|
| Allocation | Chases extended, over- | Concentrates in the top 3 high- |

| Parameter | The Retail Gambler | The Blueprint Allocator |
|---|---|---|
| focus | hyped laggards on FOMO | volume momentum sectors |
| Instruments | Over-leverages via raw margin or cheap OTM options | Uses deep-ITM options and regime-locked 2x/3x ETFs for bounded convexity |
| Position sizing | Scales absolute size up on emotional confidence | Keeps the risk unit fixed at 1% (1R); lets the math scale the block |
| Exit strategy | Holds indefinitely out of greed, expecting eternal growth | Takes robotic profits at pre-calculated asymmetric extensions |

### Final Principle

Bull markets are where fortunes are built and where overconfidence, leverage addiction, and recklessness silently prepare traders for destruction. The difference between those who reach 10x and those who don't: **the winners aggressively ride the bull while it lasts; the losers fight the regime, stay aggressive through the chop, or get euphoric at the worst moment.** The goal is not merely surviving the bull—it is surviving what comes after it. **Attack while the tide is rising—with both hands on the risk controls.**

## B. Bear Markets

**Bull markets build confidence; bear markets reveal truth.** If bulls fuel **10×** returns, bears are where most aggressive traders fail—nothing exposes weak discipline, excessive leverage, and false confidence faster than a sustained decline. Bear markets are more than falling prices: liquidity contracts, fear rises, volatility expands, correlations tighten, and breakouts fail. Strategies that thrived in the bull suddenly break, because **every strategy is regime-dependent.** Rather than fight the decline, professionals shift from high-velocity deployment to capital preservation and short-duration tactical trades.

### Identifying a Bear Regime: Objective Filters

Bears begin quietly—leadership weakens, breakouts fail, defensives outperform—all easily dismissed as "just a pullback." Watch internals, not headlines; require at least four of these before de-risking:

- Major indexes holding below declining 21-day EMA and 200-day SMA
- Lower highs and lower lows on the weekly charts
- VIX sustained above 25 (severe stress above 30)
- Distribution dominance: heavy volume on down-days, drying up on relief rallies

- Defensive leadership — utilities, staples, and healthcare outperforming
- Negative advance-decline line, new 52-week lows swamping new highs (5:1)

## Why Bear Markets Are Hostile to 10x Goals

- **Leverage works against you.** A 20% index drop can produce 50–70%+ losses in a 3x product.
- **Recovery math becomes nearly impossible.** A 40–60% early drawdown makes the required returns unrealistic.
- **Correlation expands.** Diversification evaporates—high-beta and leveraged positions collapse together.
- **Emotional pressure peaks.** Fast losses trigger revenge trading and rule-breaking at the worst moment.
- **Bull strategies fail.** Breakouts fail, momentum reverses violently, and "buy the dip" becomes a trap.

## The False Rally Trap

Bears don't slide down smoothly. Institutional short-covering and sudden retail FOMO make **bear markets produce the most explosive upward relief rallies in financial history**—and those rallies are the trap:

> **Anatomy of a trapped allocation** An amateur sees a high-beta index surge 6% in a single session and, driven by fear of missing out, deploys heavy capital into 3x ETFs or short-dated calls at the top of the intraday spike. Because the macro regime is under institutional distribution, the rally has no structural liquidity. Within 48 hours the market reverses to fresh lower lows — the trader is caught in a liquidity trap, absorbs an unmanaged 20% drawdown, and triggers the asymmetric recovery math that stalls the entire compounding engine.

These violent rallies are repeatedly mistaken for permanent bottoms; then the downtrend resumes. Don't fight the tide, and don't guess the bottom.

## The Bear Market Playbook

Under a confirmed bear, the bull's offensive levers are locked and replaced by a defensive cage on three pillars:

> **1. Cash asset superiority** — a volatility coefficient of exactly zero **2. Short-duration horizons** — hit-and-run strikes of 1–2 sessions **3. Inverse vehicle architecture** — defined-risk downside exposure

**1. Cash is an aggressive position.** Cash is a zero-volatility holding; flushing to 50–100% cash during macro distribution insulates your base. While the herd loses 30% of net worth, your pristine $100,000 base stays intact—raising your relative purchasing power at the eventual bottom.

**2. Compress time horizons (hit-and-run).** If you trade a tactical long—an isolated high-volume catalyst breaking to blue-sky highs against the market—downscale to half size (risking 0.5R, or 0.5% of equity), hold one to two sessions, harvest the expansion, return to 100% cash.

**3. Activate inverse and convex downside vehicles.** Because panic moves roughly three times faster than greed, a bear unlocks high-velocity downside tools: inverse leveraged ETFs (SQQQ, SOXS, SPXS) for short exposure without raw margin, and deep in-the-money puts or defined-risk bear spreads on weak laggards breaking support. Defined-risk downside is the best asymmetric tool in a bear.

## The Instrument Map

| Instrument | In a Confirmed Bear | Why |
|---|---|---|
| Long equity positions | Dramatically reduce or go to cash | High risk of ruin |
| 3x bull ETFs | Avoid — or tiny size, tight stops | Severe downside decay |
| Long calls (OTM) | Very limited or none | Theta decay kills |
| Inverse / bear ETFs | Selective short exposure | High reward, still dangerous |
| Put options / bear spreads | High-conviction, defined-risk | Best asymmetric tool |
| Cash | **50–80%+ allocation** | Best position in most bears |

## The Controlled-Aggression Pledge

> ***"I will not fight a clear bear market with leveraged long positions. I will preserve capital aggressively and wait for the regime to shift back to bullish before resuming full aggression."***

## Survival Is Offensive Preparation

Bear markets are environments of **transfer**: weak hands liquidate and over-leveraged participants fail, while the disciplined survive and inherit the next opportunity—many great fortunes are built in the transitions out of bears, which reset valuations and excess. So preservation is not retreat but offensive preparation: the trader who protects capital, stability, and optionality through the collapse is positioned to attack the recovery; cash buys strategic freedom exactly when the fully-invested trader loses it.

## The Psychology of the Decline

Long declines exhaust participants—optimism fades, discipline erodes into revenge trading and panic—and near the bottom, when pessimism is overwhelming, many capitulate believing "this time is permanent," often near the start of the next opportunity. The professional cultivates disciplined adaptability: bull and bear are both temporary, and the ability to stay rational while others panic becomes extraordinarily valuable when the cycle turns.

### The Regime Alignment Matrix

| Parameter | The Retail Gambler | The Blueprint Allocator |
|---|---|---|
| Primary posture | Buys the dip on hope; averages down into bleeding assets | Prioritizes capital insulation; elevates cash to a strategic stronghold |
| Risk unit | Maintains or expands size to force losses back to break-even | Downscales the risk unit by 50% (1R → 0.5R) to preserve mass |
| Holding horizon | Turns short-term trades into long-term "investments" out of denial | Restricts operations to ultra-short 1–2 day tactical strikes |
| Instruments | Long-only margin or decaying OTM calls | Inverse ETFs and high-delta puts to capture downside velocity |

### Final Principle

Bull markets reward participation; **bear markets reward professionalism.** A bear will punish overconfidence and regime denial more violently than any other environment. Read the regime, de-risk ruthlessly, and preserve capital so you're still in the game when the next bull arrives—knowing when *not* to be aggressive often separates the traders who reach 10x from those who blow up trying. **Don't fight the tide. Insulate the capital. Strike short, or stand in cash.**

## C. High-Volatility Markets

**High-volatility regimes are the silent killers of aggressive compounding plans.** They feel exciting—big swings, frequent "opportunities," massive daily moves in 3x ETFs and options—but beneath the surface they are often the worst possible environment for turning $100,000 into $1,000,000. Retail treats them like an adrenaline casino; the clinical truth is colder: a high-volatility regime is structural liquidity fragmentation, severe price variance, and an unstable distribution of expectancy. Volatility must be respected, not worshipped.

### What High Volatility Actually Is

A high-volatility market is not simply a fast market, and not the same as a down market—volatility can occur upward, downward, or sideways. Daily ranges widen, gaps increase, stops trigger constantly, and sentiment flips in hours. These regimes emerge during crises, manias, liquidity shocks, policy transitions, earnings seasons, squeezes, and geopolitical events. Volatility is neither good nor bad—it is amplified movement, magnifying both opportunity and error—so the professional associates it with required precision, because mistakes become far more expensive on an unstable tape.

## Identifying a High-Volatility Regime

Quantify volatility as a structural barrier, not an emotional state. Confirm at least four of these objective signatures:

- VIX sustained above 25–30 (and expanding, often spiking above 35)
- ATR on leading ETFs and momentum names expanded 100–300% above its 20-day baseline
- Indexes stuck in wide ranges with frequent fakeouts, no sustained trend
- Alternating strong up and down days with no follow-through
- Order-book fragmentation — widening spreads, thinning liquidity, violent gaps
- Mean-reversion shocks that violate the 9- and 21-day EMAs in both directions within one week
- Poor momentum / 3x ETF performance, elevated put-call ratio, fear-driven headlines

## Why High Volatility Is Hostile to 10x Goals

- **Variance drag crushes leveraged products.** A 3x fund can shed 20–40% while the index moves only a few percent.
- **Whipsaws trigger stops repeatedly**—you get stopped on both longs and shorts, bleeding capital through costs and slippage.
- **Options decay accelerates.** High implied volatility makes options expensive, and the subsequent IV crush destroys long-premium positions.
- **Recovery becomes nearly impossible.** Several 15–30% drawdowns in quick succession make the required returns unrealistic.
- **Correlation instability and liquidity traps.** Diversification fails, spreads widen, and stops fail—worst in small-caps, options, low-float names, warrants, and leveraged products.

## The Variance Tax on Compounding

There is an exact mathematical reason high volatility poisons a compounding engine—compounding depends on the geometric mean, not the arithmetic average, and volatility drives a wedge between them:

> **Geometric growth rate ≈ Arithmetic average return – $\sigma^2$ / 2**
> *where* $\sigma^2$ *is the variance of your return stream*

If you let your own equity-curve volatility expand with the market's, variance drag flattens or decays your base even when your win rate stays positive. Thin order books add slippage on top: poor fills widen losses and clip targets, systematically dismantling a small statistical edge.

## Productive vs. Destructive Volatility

High volatility does not always mean high opportunity. The professional distinguishes the two faces of a violent tape and pursues asymmetric opportunity, not random chaos:

| Productive Volatility (attack selectively) | Destructive Volatility (stand aside) |
|---|---|
| Trend persistence and clean directional expansion | Whipsaws and unstable, violent reversals |
| Deep liquidity and tradable dislocations | False breakouts and failed follow-through |
| Forced-liquidation and panic-pricing asymmetry | Illiquid, random chaos that invites overtrading |

## The High-Volatility Playbook: Risk Containment

Under a confirmed high-volatility regime, standard long-duration momentum is forbidden; the portfolio deploys a containment framework built to neutralize variance drag:

> **1. Risk-unit downscaling** – cut to 0.25–0.50% per trade **2. Parameter expansion** – wider ATR brackets, smaller blocks **3. Tactical profit compressing** – hit-and-run, 1–2 sessions

**1. Radical risk-unit downscaling.** Because intraday variance is wildly expanded, cut the active risk unit by 50–75%—risking a strict 0.25% to 0.50% of equity per trade—so a normal sequence of choppy stop-outs can't inflict a catastrophic drawdown.

**2. Parameter expansion (wider stops, smaller size).** Calculate stops from expanded volatility (e.g. 2.5x ATR rather than a tight percentage); the wider stop automatically downscales the share or contract count, holding a smaller, safer block with dollar risk capped.

**3. Tactical profit compressing (hit-and-run).** Hold a maximum of one to two sessions or take profits at pre-calculated +2R to +3R targets, converting paper exposure back to 100% cash before a mean-reversion shock claws it back.

## The Instrument Map

| Instrument | In Confirmed High Volatility | Why |
|---|---|---|
| Long 3x ETFs | Avoid – or very small size only | Severe drag and whipsaw risk |
| Long options | Limited, short-dated, defined-risk spreads | High premium plus IV crush |

| Instrument | In Confirmed High Volatility | Why |
|---|---|---|
| Low-beta stocks | Selective, with tight stops | Safer but slow |
| Volatility products (VXX, UVXY, put spreads) | Advanced only | Can profit from volatility itself |
| Short / inverse | Very selective, tight risk | Dangerous in violent reversals |
| Cash | **50–80%+ allocation** | Best default position |

## The Controlled-Aggression Pledge

> ***"I will not fight volatility with heavy leverage. I will reduce position size dramatically, increase cash, and wait for the regime to clarify into a trending bull market before resuming full aggression."***

## Liquidity, Correlation, and the Mind

Three traps compound the math. **Correlation instability:** calm-market relationships break and "uncorrelated" positions collapse together—so reduce exposure, leverage, and concentration. **Liquidity traps:** a name that looked liquid becomes impossible to exit cleanly, so evaluate liquidity quality, not just price movement. **Psychological magnification:** fear, greed, and impatience all intensify. Calm markets hide psychological weakness; volatile markets expose it instantly, which is why disciplined traders reduce exposure after any emotional destabilization—the objective becomes preserving clarity, not merely capital.

## Transition Signals: When to Re-Engage

Treat a high-volatility stretch as a recovery and preparation phase, not a compounding phase. Begin increasing aggression only when the regime clarifies:

- VIX declining and stabilizing below 20–22
- Indexes breaking out of their ranges with conviction
- Rising momentum and relative strength in the leading sectors
- Daily whipsaw action visibly decreasing

| Parameter | The Retail Gambler | The Blueprint Allocator |
|---|---|---|
| Position sizing | Keeps identical or larger size to chase "bigger intraday moves" | Shrinks size automatically via wider ATR-based stop brackets |
| Risk unit | Exposes 5–10% of equity out of | Downscales the risk unit to |

| Parameter | The Retail Gambler | The Blueprint Allocator |
|---|---|---|
| | greed, risking rapid ruin | 0.25–0.50% to insulate the base |
| Target | Chases over-extended multi-day breakouts at vertical highs | Executes mean-reversion pullbacks or clear channel boundaries |
| Holding horizon | Holds through massive intraday swings out of hope | Compresses to ultra-short 1–2 day cash tranches |

### Final Principle

High-volatility markets are where most aggressive traders give back their bull-market gains—usually expensive noise that erodes capital through drag, whipsaws, and emotional error, though for the prepared trader they also create dislocations and oversized asymmetric opportunity. The edge is the discipline to **stand aside through destructive volatility, strike only at productive volatility, and preserve the capital needed to compound when the next clear bull arrives.** Here, emotional stability is a competitive advantage as valuable as any strategy.

## D. Liquidity-Driven Rallies

**Liquidity-driven rallies are the highest-octane regime for aggressive compounding—and one of the most treacherous.** The media attributes massive advances to earnings or technology; the clinical truth is that the most violent vertical expansions are driven by pure institutional liquidity. When central banks and capital flows flood the system, they put an artificial floor under prices, and 10x in six months moves from "extremely difficult" to "genuinely possible." Think of the 2020–2021 stimulus melt-up—meme stocks, ARKK, Tesla—as the archetype. But the upside is available only to those who trade the regime with strict discipline.

### What Drives a Liquidity Rally

Liquidity rallies occur when easy conditions—falling rates, fiscal stimulus, QE, short covering, monetary expansion—push capital into risk assets faster than sellers can absorb it. Prices rise because liquidity expands, not necessarily because earnings improve, and liquidity can overpower valuation far longer than most traders expect.

### Identifying the Regime: Objective Filters

Confirm a liquidity surge with macro and technical signatures, not sentiment:

- Central-bank accommodation (QE, repo operations, rate cuts).
- Falling DXY and 2-year Treasury yields. Capital fleeing safe havens for risk.
- Indexes and high-beta sectors above rising 9- and 21-day EMAs.
- A volume-price disconnect — the market rallies through bad news.

The behavioral fingerprints are just as clear: explosive upward momentum with gap-ups and parabolic moves, retail and speculative frenzy, prices decoupling from fundamentals, extreme concentration in a few names, high volatility with an upside bias, and frequent short and gamma squeezes accelerating the advance.

## The Engine: Multiple Expansion and the Reflexive Loop

Two mechanisms power the move. The first is multiple expansion—a stock's price is its earnings times the multiple investors will pay:

> **Stock Price = Earnings Per Share (EPS) × Price-to-Earnings Multiple (P/E)**

When the system is flooded with cheap credit, managers must deploy immediately to avoid cash drag; share supply is fixed but liquidity demand is near-infinite, so the P/E expands rapidly, independent of corporate performance. The second mechanism is reflexivity—a self-reinforcing loop:

> **Rising prices → Attention → Capital inflow → Higher prices → More attention**

The professional doesn't waste time fighting this or moralizing about a "bubble." The market is a matching engine for capital flows; your job is to exploit the structural trend, not argue with it.

## Why This Regime Is Built for 10x

- **Massive asymmetric moves.** Individual stocks and 3x ETFs can deliver 50–300%+ in weeks.
- **Leverage works extremely well. 3× ETFs, long calls, and warrants** can convert **20–40%** underlying moves into **100–1,000%**+ returns.
- **Momentum persists.** Breakouts follow through, allowing safe pyramiding.
- **Fast capital rotation.** Money flows quickly into new themes, creating sequenced opportunities.

## Best Instruments and Tactics

Higher aggression means higher risk:

| Instrument | Best Use | Aggression |
|---|---|---|
| Momentum stocks | Leading names with strong narratives | **Very High** |
| Short-term options | Gamma scalping and momentum bursts | **High** |
| Warrants | Asymmetric bets on leaders | **Very High** |
| 3x sector ETFs (TQQQ, SOXL) | Core trend amplifiers | **Extreme** |
| Long calls / LEAPS | High-conviction leaders | **Extreme** |

Favor **0.70–0.80 delta**, **30–60-day** in-the-money calls for stock-like exposure with defined downside. Concentrate in the strongest **2–3** sectors, pyramid into strength, scale out into parabolic moves, and rotate back to cash.

### The Velocity Playbook

With the capital flood confirmed and systemic liquidity dampening the odds of an extended pullback, shift to maximum capital acceleration:

> **Capital flood confirmed → Lock top high-beta sectors → Deploy embedded leverage → Rapid 2–5 day turnovers**

Capital pours into the highest-beta, most speculative vehicles. Ignore defensive value, concentrate active tranches into the top three relative-strength sectors, **deploy 3x ETFs and high-delta call brackets, and recycle capital through rapid turnovers, pyramiding winners and harvesting into strength**.

### The Breadth-Expansion Warning Sign

Watch how breadth evolves, because it dates the rally. Early, leadership stays concentrated in genuinely strong companies; as liquidity expands, speculation broadens—weaker, unprofitable, heavily shorted, and meme names rise simply because liquidity overwhelms restraint. **That degradation in quality is a late-stage tell.**

### The Liquidity-Attribution Trap

Liquidity rallies reward bad habits temporarily—excessive leverage looks brilliant, sloppy risk management looks harmless—so the trader mistakes regime tailwinds for genius; then liquidity contracts and the identical behavior turns catastrophic overnight. The protective question is the same one that governs the bull: **"Is my strategy genuinely strong, or is liquidity temporarily hiding its weakness?"**

### It Always Ends — Often Violently

Liquidity rallies end abruptly with **rate hikes, tapering, risk-off shocks,** or a **VIX** spike, and the same loop that drove prices up accelerates the collapse down—many fortunes made during **2020–2021** disappeared when the regime changed. The specific hazards: liquidity can dry up overnight, stretched valuations snap back in violent mean-reversion crashes, volatility drag bites during choppy intervals, and retail herding creates crowded trades and brutal two-way squeezes.

### The Exit Discipline

The traders who succeed don't ride these regimes to the very top—they ride hard while it lasts, take profits systematically, and protect capital the moment the tide turns: increase aggression only while clear liquidity and momentum hold; scale out 30–50% into parabolic strength; tighten stops as the rally matures; and de-risk or go heavily to cash the instant liquidity weakens.

### The Controlled-Aggression Pledge

> ***"When liquidity is flooding the market and momentum is confirmed, I will attack with maximum controlled force using leverage and pyramiding. I will remain paranoid about regime shifts and protect profits aggressively."***

### The Liquidity Regime Governance Matrix

| Parameter | The Retail Gambler | The Blueprint Allocator |
|---|---|---|
| Market philosophy | Shorts the market because "prices are too high and disconnected" | Accepts the liquidity trend as reality and rides the institutional wave |
| Asset concentration | Scatters capital across 20 laggards hoping they catch up | Concentrates in the top 2–3 highest-velocity momentum sectors |
| Risk management | Grows complacent and raises absolute risk units out of greed | Keeps the risk unit fixed at 1% (1R); lets equity scale the block |
| Exit execution | Holds forever, expecting the central bank to support prices eternally | Takes robotic profits at pre-calculated +3R to +5R targets |

### Final Principle

Liquidity-driven rallies are environments of accelerated opportunity and explosive compounding—the best friend of the six-month 10x trader, when they last—but they almost always end abruptly. The enduring mindset every regime returns to: participate aggressively, compound intelligently, respect liquidity deeply, and never forget that regimes change. Recognize the flood, attack it hard, and exit before the tide turns—because liquidity leaves far faster than it arrived. **Ride the flood hard—and be gone before the tide turns.**

## E. AI, Biotech, Crypto, and Momentum Cycles

One of the greatest mistakes aggressive traders make is assuming markets behave the same way at all times. They don't—markets move in cycles, and every major wealth-creation period was driven by a dominant regime. To compound $100,000 into $1,000,000 in six months, understanding regimes is foundational: aggressive compounding depends less on predicting the future than on identifying **where speculative capital is flowing right now**. Timing the regime is often more important than timing the exact stock.

### What a Market Regime Is

A market regime is a broad phase defined by economic conditions, sentiment, capital flows, liquidity, volatility, and sector leadership—trending, sideways, high- or low-volatility, risk-on or risk-off, sector-specific. Reading the current regime tells you when to be aggressive, when to reduce exposure, which sectors deserve capital, and when the market is sliding into exhaustion.

## The Mechanics of Hyper-Velocity Sectors

To compound at a 1,000% rate, capital cannot sit in slow, mature assets—it must route into environments defined by **reflexivity and high narrative delta**, where valuation metrics are abandoned and prices move vertically. The mechanism is consistent:

> **Narrative shock → Institutional FOMO → Illiquid float squeeze → Vertical price extension**

These thematic sectors—AI, biotech, crypto, and the broader momentum complex—are the primary velocity domains where a fixed 1% risk unit (1R) can yield explosive +5R to +10R payoffs over days. They are also where most accounts die.

## The Four Regimes at a Glance

| Regime | What Drives It | Favored Instruments | Defining Risk |
|---|---|---|---|
| AI / Technology | Capex supercycles; infrastructure & compute demand | 3x tech/semi ETFs, high-delta calls, leaders | Valuation air-pocket on growth slowdown |
| Biotech | Binary catalysts: FDA, trial data, M&A | Defined-risk options, warrants, event swings | A failed trial gaps the stock down 50–90% |
| Crypto | Liquidity, halving cycles, reflexivity | Crypto/miner equities, leveraged crypto ETFs, spreads | Violent leverage unwind; liquidity vanishes |
| Momentum / liquidity | Loose money, FOMO, self-fulfilling breakouts | Low-float breakouts, squeezes, leveraged ETFs | Sudden momentum crash on reversal |

## The AI Regime — The Infrastructure Expansion Cycle

Artificial intelligence is one of modern markets' strongest capital-attraction forces. Massive capex cycles concentrate liquidity in semiconductors, data centers, cloud, networking, cybersecurity, robotics, AI software, and quantum—sustained inflows create unusually persistent momentum, well suited for 3× tech ETFs and high-delta calls. Leaders can rise several hundred percent while disconnecting from valuation; hallmarks include Nasdaq leadership, semiconductor strength, elevated call activity, and persistent dip-buying. Risk emerges when expectations outrun reality, growth slows, or the Fed tightens, turning "AI bubble" into distribution.

## The Biotech Regime — The Binary Catalyst Cycle

Biotech is the market's most explosive catalyst-driven sector, depending on **FDA decisions, Phase 1/2/3 results, partnerships, breakthrough designations,** and **acquisitions**. Positive news can lift stocks or warrants **100–300%** overnight; failed trials erase **50–90%**. The best environments feature abundant liquidity and strong risk appetite; traders monitor catalyst calendars, FDA dates, float, short interest, cash runway, and institutional ownership. Because downside is binary, professionals use tight sizing and defined-risk options or warrants.

## The Crypto Regime — The Pure Reflexivity Cycle

Crypto combines technology speculation, monetary ideology, leverage, social media, and **24-hour** trading; miners, exchanges, infrastructure, and leveraged crypto ETFs run largely on **reflexivity**, not earnings. Bull cycles fueled by **halvings**, adoption, or expanding liquidity generate extraordinary turnover and implied volatility, ideal for option spreads. The danger is sudden reversal—when momentum breaks, leverage unwinds and liquidity disappears within days. Monitor **Bitcoin dominance, ETF flows, on-chain data, Fed policy, the U.S. dollar, derivatives leverage, regulation**, and **Fear & Greed** extremes.

## Momentum Cycles — Loyalty to Momentum Itself

Some of history's greatest rallies were driven by liquidity and momentum rather than fundamentals—**meme stocks, gamma squeezes, short squeezes,** and low-float runs become self-reinforcing as price attracts capital. Momentum rotates continuously among **AI, biotech, crypto, semiconductors, small-cap growth, clean energy**, **quantum,** and **defense**; the edge is loyalty to momentum itself, not any single sector, and success requires disciplined trend following, rapid profit-taking, and strict risk control.

## The Velocity Playbook

Once your macro screen confirms a sub-sector has entered an active institutional momentum cycle, execution is mechanical:

1. **Filter for relative volume and blue-sky highs.** Focus on stocks with relative volume ≥3.0× the 20-day average making 52-week or all-time highs; favor genuine leaders over sympathy plays.
2. **The 9-day EMA anchor and tight stops.** Enter on pullbacks to a rising 9-day EMA with stops just below the prior session's low—tight stops allow larger positions while keeping the 1% (1R) limit.

## Reading the Regime: Identification Tools

Identify the environment before sizing into it: **bull regimes** show low volatility and positive returns, **sideways** show chop, **bear** show high volatility and negative returns. Use relative-strength ranking versus the S&P, moving averages, VIX levels, and volume/breakout filters to classify the tape, scanning weekly across the broad market, sector rotation, and macro, then combining the regime filter with momentum signals to avoid whipsaws.

### Position Sizing and the Regime-Shift Principle

Increase exposure, leverage, and holding periods only in strong momentum regimes; in weak or uncertain environments, reduce size, shorten holds, raise cash, and protect capital. Every regime ends—successful traders recognize transitions early, preserve capital, and rotate into emerging leadership. Markets continually transfer wealth from rigid participants to adaptable ones.

### The Momentum Sector Governance Matrix

| Parameter | The Retail Gambler | The Blueprint Allocator |
|---|---|---|
| Asset selection | Buys dying low-volume laggards that "feel cheap" vs. the leaders | Concentrates in the top 1–2 relative-strength leaders with massive RVOL |
| Risk parameter | Pushes the risk unit to 5–10% out of greed and hype | Keeps it fixed at 1% (1R); lets the math scale the block safely |
| Holding protocol | Converts a broken momentum trade into a "long-term investment" | Enforces time stops; flushes stagnant or breaking names to cash within ~48 hours |
| Derivatives | Buys hyper-extended, short-dated, far-OTM options | Uses high-delta ITM options or structural warrants for pure price delta |

### This Is High-Risk Territory

**Say it plainly: these high-velocity sectors are where most aggressive traders blow up.** The same reflexivity that produces vertical rallies produces 80% distribution crashes — and leverage, binary catalysts, and crypto liquidations magnify every error. Size small, prefer defined-risk options for binary events, enforce time stops, keep stops tight, and never marry a narrative. (See the Survival Rates and Decay Risks chapters.)

### Final Principle

Aggressive compounding is not merely selecting stocks—it is understanding where speculative capital is flowing, where momentum is accelerating, and where institutional and retail psychology converge. AI, biotech, crypto, and momentum cycles are the recurring engines of explosive movement; the trader who reads liquidity expansion, narrative dominance, and crowd psychology captures extraordinary asymmetric opportunities. **Trade the regime, not the story. Rotate with the capital, not against it.**

## Sector Rotation

Money rarely flows into every sector equally. **Institutions, hedge funds, pensions, algorithms,** and **retail** constantly rotate capital toward stronger returns, momentum, or safety. In a six-month **10×** campaign, sitting in lagging sectors while leadership advances is costly. Sector rotation is institutional liquidity migration—professionals don't marry sectors, they follow capital.

## The Law of Liquidity Conservation

Institutional liquidity is usually **redistributed**, not destroyed. Except during systemic panics, capital rotates continuously:

| |
|---|
| **RISK-ON → capital flees defensive anchors → floods high-beta growth (AI, tech, crypto)** |
| **RISK-OFF → capital flees growth premium → floods defensive value (utilities, staples)** |

## The Sector Rotation Clock

Institutional managers rotate between cyclical, growth, and defensive sectors based on interest-rate trajectory and economic output—a four-stage clock that maps where capital floods next:

| Stage | Macro Environment | Where Capital Floods | Blueprint Posture |
|---|---|---|---|
| 1. Early-bull accumulation | Rates bottoming; central banks accommodative | Cyclicals — Financials, Consumer Discretionary, Industrials, early Tech | Build; options + 3x for trend initiation |
| 2. Mid-bull acceleration | Expansion confirmed; demand surges | Growth — AI, advanced semiconductors, emerging tech | **Peak window — maximum velocity** |
| 3. Late-bull distribution | Overheating, inflation rising, tightening begins | Inflation hedges — Energy, Materials, Commodities | Scale back growth; rotate to hedges |
| 4. Bear contraction | Growth flatlines / recession; max risk aversion | Defensives — Utilities, Staples, Healthcare | **Primarily 100% cash; tactical shorts only** |

## The Relative-Strength Engine

You confirm rotation with one pure metric: the **relative-strength (RS) line.** Never read a sector chart in isolation—divide the sector ETF by the benchmark (XLF ÷ SPY or XLK ÷ SPY) and read the slope:

| RS Line | What It Means | Action |
|---|---|---|
| **Rising** | Sector outperforming; institutions gathering here | **Mandatory long-allocation zone** |

| RS Line | What It Means | Action |
|---|---|---|
| **Declining** | Sector underperforming; institutions fleeing | **Strict capital-exclusion zone** |

This is why **strength beats valuation**: a "cheap" stock can keep falling for months if capital is leaving its sector, while a strong sector extends far beyond textbook valuation. Rank sectors by 1-to-12-month momentum and RS ratio, plot them on a Relative Rotation Graph, route capital to the top one or two, and rebalance weekly.

## Confirming a Rotation

False rotations kill accounts, so demand a stack of confirmations before committing leverage—require several together:

- A rising RS line versus the S&P 500
- Unusual volume spikes and repeated breakouts across the sector
- Sector-ETF outperformance and visible ETF inflows / institutional accumulation
- Strong earnings reactions and a supportive macro or catalyst backdrop
- A risk-on regime filter (e.g. VIX below ~20)

## Instruments and Execution

Express the rotation through liquid, high-beta vehicles—leveraged sector ETFs (SOXL for semis, LABU for biotech, leveraged energy and financial funds), single-name 2x products where they exist, and directional calls or spreads on leaders for defined-risk asymmetry:

> **Example:** A $100,000 account identifies an Energy/Utilities rotation from AI-capex and power-demand themes. Allocate 30-50% to leveraged ETFs or defined-risk calls, harvest 20-50% gains, then rotate into the next confirmed leader (e.g., biotech during an M&A cycle). Sequential 20-100%+ sector advances compound rapidly when driven by confirmed institutional rotation.

## Risk and the Old-Leadership Trap

- **Leverage decay.** 2x/3x ETFs erode in choppy rotations—deploy only in confirmed strong trends.
- **Whipsaws.** False rotations are account-killers; require momentum plus volume plus macro before committing.
- **Correlation spikes.** Risk-off events drag everything down together, so rotation alone is no hedge in a panic.
- **Sizing and stops.** Risk ≤1% per rotation idea, cap any one sector at 20–30% at peak conviction, use hard stops or options.

The most destructive mistake is emotional attachment to old leadership—**yesterday's winning sector becomes tomorrow's underperformer** (internet after dot-com, solar after its peak, crypto after liquidity collapses, meme stocks after the retail tide receded). Enforce time stops: flush a dead or stagnant sectoral allocation to cash within 48–72 hours. In rotation, position sizing beats prediction and adaptation beats stubbornness.

### The Sector Rotation Governance Matrix

| Parameter | The Retail Gambler | The Blueprint Allocator |
|---|---|---|
| Response to rotation | Stays trapped in a bleeding sector, "hoping" it recovers | Instantly liquidates breaking assets; follows the liquidity footprint |
| Asset selection | Guesses the next sector from social-media hype | Uses RS filters to isolate confirmed, high-volume institutional inflows |
| Capital distribution | Over-diversifies across all 11 sectors, diluting growth | Concentrates active liquidity in the top 1–2 leading sectors |
| Holding horizon | Turns a failed momentum trade into a long-term "investment" | Enforces time stops; flushes stagnant allocations within 48–72 hours |

### Final Principle

Sector rotation is one of the hidden engines of aggressive wealth creation: it lets you identify emerging opportunities, avoid weakening environments, align with institutional flows, and exploit momentum while the regime is favorable. The trader who understands rotation is no longer randomly selecting stocks—**he is tracking the movement of money itself. Follow the flood. Cut the line when the tide rotates out.**

# Chapter 6
# Momentum: The Engine of Fast Compounding

## Why Momentum Dominates Short-Term Markets

If long-term investing is driven by fundamentals, short-term aggressive trading is driven by momentum, and that distinction has to be settled first—because the literature most readers were raised on points the wrong way, conditioning the public to hunt undervalued stocks and wait for the market to recognize "true worth." For a six-month campaign that is a structural mismatch: to cross a 1,000% threshold in roughly 120 sessions you cannot buy *cheap* assets, you must buy *fast* ones. Momentum—the well-documented tendency of strong performers to keep performing, driven by institutional order flow, retail FOMO, and scarce liquid float—is the single variable that correlates directly with capital velocity, and it is the engine every later chapter bolts onto.

### The Law of Financial Inertia

An object in motion tends to stay in motion until an external force acts on it, and price obeys an almost identical law: in a bull market, stocks with strong volume, accelerating price, institutional accumulation, and a live catalyst continue far longer than most traders expect. **New highs are not "expensive."** A stock printing a fresh 52-week high has *cleared its overhead supply*—no trapped historic buyers wait to sell at break-even—so institutional sweeps translate directly into vertical acceleration, while the amateur's falling laggard carries trapped supply and dead capital. And **under-reaction is the exploitable glitch**: institutions can't deploy billions instantly, so they accumulate over days or weeks, creating the sustained trends momentum traders exploit.

### Why Momentum Exists: Behavior, Institutions, and Algorithms

Markets are emotional, liquidity-driven, and shaped by crowd behavior, and in the short term price movement itself becomes the catalyst: a stock moving higher attracts institutions, retail, algorithms, options desks, and media at once, in a self-reinforcing cycle. **Humans** react to greed, fear, and FOMO; **institutions** chase relative strength and add to winners because they can't look under-allocated against benchmarks; **algorithms** amplify both, triggering automated buys as levels break. Strength attracts strength, volume attracts volume.

### The Three Structural Engines of Velocity

Beneath the psychology sit three mechanical forces that drive a momentum asset vertical over a compressed timeline.

1. **Institutional order-book sweeping.** Funds under strict performance benchmarks can't sit in cash when a sector shows alpha—they deploy algorithms that *sweep the offer*, buying every available block, which forces competing algos to trigger their own buys.

**2. Reflexivity and the float squeeze.** Many high-velocity vehicles—specialized warrants, emerging-tech names, high-beta option chains—carry a tightly constrained float. When a narrative catches fire, incoming capital overwhelms supply: price surges, short sellers are liquidated, and their forced buy-backs cascade, while options market makers buy the underlying to hedge deltas (the **gamma squeeze**), detaching the asset from fundamentals.

**3. The velocity premium (time deflation).** In a 180-day campaign your enemy is *dead time*: a fairly-valued utility may take eighteen months to unlock value, while momentum assets execute large percentage moves over two to five sessions. Rotating capital through these high-velocity funnels maximizes turnover—and turnover is what reaches compounding's vertical inflection.

## Liquidity: The Fuel of Momentum

Liquidity is the fuel the engine burns. Momentum thrives when central banks are accommodative, rates are low, leverage is abundant, and speculative appetite rises—which is why the strongest momentum eras coincided with loose policy and technology revolutions. The corollary is a warning: when liquidity contracts, momentum frequently collapses. In trending regimes, 2x and 3x ETFs and options turn a 10–20% underlying move into a 30–100%-plus swing—the point of using them, and exactly why they must be confined to genuine trends.

## Why Fundamentals Matter Less in the Short Run

The hardest idea for a new trader to accept is that short-term price action is not governed by valuation. Stocks can become dramatically overvalued, stay elevated, and keep rising on weak fundamentals, because near-term markets run on narrative dominance, momentum psychology, liquidity, and positioning. Markets can remain irrational far longer than traders can remain solvent betting against them—so during a momentum phase, the trader who fights price with a valuation spreadsheet gets run over.

## Sector Momentum and Thematic Expansion

Momentum rarely occurs in isolation—it spreads across sectors and sympathy plays: an AI rally radiates through semiconductors, cloud, optics, cybersecurity, and data-center infrastructure; crypto moves spread to miners and exchanges; biotech strength lifts small-cap healthcare. A trader who misses the leader can still profit from related names, leveraged ETFs, warrants, or low-float sympathy plays. The 2026 backdrop sharpens this—widening dispersion between winners (AI infrastructure, select energy) and losers rewards rotation over a single static bet.

## The Signals That Confirm Momentum

To make entries timely rather than hopeful, momentum is confirmed through a compact signal set:

- **Price and volume breakouts.** New highs on surging volume; look for 20–50%-plus moves in the leaders.

- **Relative strength.** Sector or stock outperforming its benchmark over a 1–6-month window—rank and rotate into the top performers.
- **Technical confirmation.** MACD crossovers with histogram expansion, RSI holding 50–70 within an uptrend, and ADX above 20–25 to confirm trend strength.
- **Earnings and catalysts.** Positive surprises, guidance raises, contract wins, and re-rating news flow.
- **Timeframes.** A 6–12-month lookback for ranking; daily and weekly charts for execution.
- **Regime awareness.** Momentum rules in strong trends; mean reversion dominates choppy tape—deploying leverage into chop is how the engine stalls.

## Deploying Capital: Instruments

The instrument menu maps momentum onto asymmetric exposure: **3x ETFs** (SOXL, LABU, TQQQ) in strong trends only, pyramided on breakouts and ridden until momentum fades; **2x ETFs** for slightly longer holds in themes like AI or energy; **options** (long calls or call spreads) on leaders for defined risk, bought on the post-breakout volume spike; and **stocks and warrants** for individual high-momentum names, with warrants adding leverage on smaller caps.

## The Momentum Velocity Matrix

| Operational Vector | The Retail Gambler | The Blueprint Allocator |
|---|---|---|
| **Entry logic** | Buys "cheap" falling knives, averaging down into an active downtrend. | Enters high-volume assets printing fresh 52-week or all-time highs. |
| **Primary metric** | Imaginary "intrinsic value" from outdated balance sheets. | Relative Strength and Relative Volume. |
| **View of price** | Believes a stock that has doubled is "too high" to buy. | Knows strength breeds strength; buys the line of least resistance. |
| **Capital allocation** | Stagnates capital in sideways assets out of emotional loyalty. | Enforces a time stop; flushes any asset that loses vertical acceleration within 48 hours. |

## The Momentum Life Cycle

Most momentum moves travel a recognizable arc—**accumulation** (institutions quietly build), **breakout** (price clears resistance and accelerates), **public participation** (retail and media amplify), **euphoria** (valuation disconnects), **exhaustion** (buying weakens, volatility rises), and **collapse or consolidation** (momentum fades, capital rotates). The greatest risk appears precisely at maximum excitement—the moment the move feels safest to chase.

### The Dark Side: Momentum Crashes and Survival

The same force that produces rapid gains produces devastating collapses. Momentum carries severe tail risk—infrequent but brutal crashes, often when a beaten-down market rebounds and prior losers snap back hardest. When momentum breaks, buyers vanish, liquidity evaporates, and reversals turn violent and illiquid. So survival is the strategy, not a footnote: **hard stops** (5–10% or ATR-based, set before entry), **position sizing** (risk ~1% per idea), **regime filters** (reduce or invert in high-VIX or post-crash conditions), and **disciplined diversification** (three to five ideas, pyramid only winners). A **1,000%** return requires either consistently high win rates with controlled losses or a few exceptional winners held with discipline.

### How the Momentum Trader Thinks

The momentum trader asks a different question than the investor. Not "what is this company worth?" but: where is money flowing, where is volume expanding, which sectors are accelerating, which names are breaking out? It is a discipline of probability—the trader accepts missing some moves, entering late, and facing reversals, because the objective is not perfection but repeated, controlled-risk participation in explosive trends.

### Final Principle

Momentum is the engine of aggressive compounding because short-term markets are governed by psychology, liquidity, speculation, and capital flow rather than valuation—it is the financial expression of collective human behavior under greed, fear, urgency, and opportunity. This chapter is the thesis; the rest of the section is the machinery. **Relative Strength** answers *where* to attack, and **Volume Expansion** answers *when, and how big.*

## Relative Strength — Isolating the Alpha Footprint

Of all the tools an aggressive trader can carry, none is more decisive than **Relative Strength**—the precision-targeting system of momentum trading, the filter that tells you *where* the strongest money is concentrating. In a compressed timeline you cannot afford to be early, contrarian, or sentimental; RS turns broad momentum into an actionable rotation map. But first the term has to be rescued from retail confusion.

### What Relative Strength Actually Is — and What It Is Not

Retail platforms confuse **Relative Strength (RS)** with the **Relative Strength Index (RSI)**—they are not the same. RSI is a bound mean-reversion oscillator pinned between 0 and 100, telling you whether one stock looks "overbought" in isolation; serious allocators largely ignore it. True Relative Strength is an **unbounded comparative measure of one asset's performance against a benchmark.** It doesn't ask whether a stock is cheap—it asks whether it is *outperforming*, and whether that outperformance is accelerating. Strong stocks tend to get stronger.

Separate RS from raw momentum, too. *Absolute momentum* is an asset's own price performance; *relative strength* is comparative—the asset's return against a benchmark over defined lookbacks (1-, 3-, 6-, 12-month). A stock up 20% while the index is up 30% has *weak* RS and should be avoided, however impressive its chart. Reduced to one expression, RS is a ratio:

***Relative Strength Line = Price of Target Asset ÷ Price of Benchmark Index***

When that line rises, the asset is gaining on the market; plotted over time, it is the cleanest footprint of where institutional capital is hunting.

## The Law of Outperformance: Why Strength Breeds Strength

The core thesis: **the assets that show the greatest resilience during market duress lead with the greatest magnitude during expansion.** A stock lagging its benchmark is under systematic institutional distribution—toxic dead weight, "cheap" for a reason. Look for the inverse: the name trading sideways or printing higher lows while the S&P 500 or Nasdaq-100 cascades. When the index stabilizes and stages even an ordinary relief rally, the stored energy in that high-RS asset uncoils into a vertical, high-volume breakout—precisely the velocity a tranche needs for a +3R to +5R payout. This is behavioral persistence: capital chases strength, and the chase is self-reinforcing.

## Relative Strength as the Footprint of Institutional Capital

Institutions move enormous size and can't hide it forever. When a fund accumulates, volume expands, price stabilizes, pullbacks turn shallow, and breakouts become forceful—institutional buying *creates* relative strength, and a stock outperforming during difficult conditions often signals hidden accumulation long before the news. Retail reacts to headlines; professionals read money flow, and RS is one of the clearest footprints flow leaves behind.

## The Dual-Layer Filter: Sector First, Then the Apex Stock

To make this a repeatable workflow, apply RS in two layers—macro before micro.

**Layer 1 — sector-to-market RS.** Before analyzing individual stocks, compare each of the eleven major sectors to the S&P 500 (SPY); avoid declining-RS sectors and concentrate in the two or three with rising, accelerating RS—often semiconductors, AI infrastructure, biotech, and, in the 2026 rotation, parts of energy (XLE), industrials (XLI), materials, and utilities riding AI-power demand.

**Layer 2 — stock-to-sector RS.** Within leading sectors, compare each stock to its sector ETF (NVDA ÷ SMH) and seek the apex stock—the strongest name in the strongest group, where institutional inflows concentrate.

The highest-probability trades occur only when all three align: a **strong market**, a **strong sector** (rising RS line), and the **strongest stock** (the apex leader).

## The Quantitative Signatures of Alpha

Three behaviors confirm genuine relative strength—treat them as a checklist before risk goes on.

**1. High-base retention during corrections.** When the index takes a routine 5–10% correction, watch for assets that refuse to print lower lows—a tight, horizontal consolidation while the benchmark cascades means institutional algorithms are absorbing every share offered. The floor is structurally locked.

**2. The first-responder breakout.** The instant the index prints its first stabilizing green day, the high-RS asset prints a definitive high-volume breakout to fresh 52-week or all-time highs—clearing resistance days ahead of the broader market.

**3. The moving-average slope lock.** Price holds cleanly above a rising 50-day SMA carrying a steep positive slope even while the benchmark's 200-day is flat or declining—the mathematical signature of sustained, multi-month accumulation.

Relative strength becomes far more powerful paired with **relative volume**: explosive momentum names routinely trade at 2x, 3x, 5x, even 10x average volume, because major moves require participation and aggressive buying. Volume validates an RS signal—without it, a breakout is a guess.

## The Professional's Toolkit

A handful of tools turn relative strength into a scannable discipline:

- **RS Ratio / RS Line.** Plot the asset against its benchmark (SOXL ÷ SPY); a cross of the ratio above its own 50-day average is a clean entry trigger.
- **Relative Rotation Graphs (RRG).** Track securities through Leading, Weakening, Lagging, and Improving quadrants—buy Improving→Leading, exit Leading→Weakening.
- **Ranking systems.** Scan for the top RS percentile across timeframes (a combined 3-month and 6-month score works well), or use an IBD-style RS Rating from 1–99.
- **Scanner setup.** In TradingView or Finviz, filter for RS above benchmark, a volume surge, and ADX above 20; rebalance weekly.

Elite traders confirm RS across multiple timeframes—when daily, weekly, and sector leadership align, trends are far more durable than isolated short-term strength.

## Deploying Leverage on High-RS Names

Relative strength matters most when you add leverage, because leverage magnifies gains, losses, and emotional pressure alike—so the rule is absolute: **leverage is reserved for the strongest sectors, trends, and breakouts only.** The menu: **3x/2x leveraged ETFs** (SOXL for semis/AI, LABU for biotech) pyramided as RS strengthens; **options** (long calls or debit spreads) on high-RS leaders post-breakout; **stocks and warrants** on top-RS names with warrants adding torque on smaller plays; and **sector ETFs** rotating core capital into the top two or three RS sectors. Some of the strongest RS emerges from **short squeezes**—high short interest, low float, a real catalyst—among the strongest names in the market, and the most dangerous to overstay.

## Strength vs. "Cheap": The Most Expensive Mistake

One of the biggest mistakes is confusing weakness with value. "Cheap" stocks often keep falling while stocks near new highs keep making higher highs—markets reward demand, not discounts. The strongest stocks *appear* expensive precisely because institutions keep accumulating them; successful traders follow price action, not opinions. The RS life cycle mirrors the momentum arc (quiet accumulation → early outperformance → breakout → momentum expansion → euphoria → exhaustion); the aggressive edge lives in the breakout and expansion phases—the first two are for the patient, the last two are where capital is destroyed.

| Tactical Axis | The Retail Gambler | The Blueprint Allocator |
|---|---|---|
| **Screening metric** | Bound oscillators (RSI, stochastics) to find "oversold" laggards. | Unbounded comparative metrics (the RS line) to locate institutional leaders. |
| **Reaction to dips** | Buys the stocks that dropped the most — absorbing the market's trash. | Buys the stocks that refused to drop — riding the institutional shield. |
| **Trend definition** | Trapped in names breaking below their 200-day averages. | Locked into names printing blue-sky breakouts ahead of the index. |
| **Capital efficiency** | Stagnates in lagging sectors out of loyalty and hope. | Enforces a strict RS filter; flushes weak lines to cash instantly. |

## Risk, Survival, and Position Discipline

Relative strength plus leverage is rocket fuel, explosive in both directions. Respect the failure modes: RS is a *lagging* signal that confirms strength but doesn't predict the top; high-RS winners can suddenly lag hard in post-bear or high-volatility regimes; leveraged products bleed in sideways chop and demand a confirmed trend; and sizing discipline means risking 1–2% per idea, diversifying across four to six positions, and cutting weak RS the moment it appears.

## Final Principle

Relative Strength reveals where institutional money, momentum, and demand are concentrating. In a six-month campaign targeting 1,000%, it provides the framework to identify leadership early, avoid laggards, deploy leverage selectively, and align with institutional capital while controlling risk. It is the tactical heart of momentum investing.

## Volume Expansion — The Catalyst of Structural Breakouts

Price movement attracts attention; volume reveals conviction. If Relative Strength tells you *where* the strongest money is concentrating, Volume Expansion is the ignition switch that tells you *when* it is firing—and how large you can be. Price and RS may hint at strength, but only a clear volume surge proves real institutional and crowd participation, turning a potential breakout into one worthy of 2x/3x leverage, options, and rapid pyramiding. Without it, breakouts fizzle and aggressive traders bleed capital one "quiet" failure at a time.

### What Volume Expansion Actually Represents

Volume expansion occurs when activity rises significantly above normal—a stock averaging two million shares may suddenly trade ten, twenty, or a hundred million during a major event—reflecting rising urgency, institutional involvement, and expanding liquidity. **Volume is the only true validator of price velocity:** price can be pushed on thin liquidity, but volume represents actual capital expenditure. A technical breakout is essentially meaningless unless massive volume accompanies it—amateurs buy quiet breakouts on light volume, then watch the asset mean-revert into their stop. The metric that captures this is **Relative Volume**, a ratio of current activity to the historical norm:

***Relative Volume (RVOL) = Current Session Volume ÷ Average Volume of the Past N Sessions***

True institutional accumulation leaves an un-fakeable footprint: a vertical volume expansion that dwarfs the baseline, proof that asset managers are using market orders to sweep the ask and overwhelm the float—the linear trajectory that 3x ETFs and deep ITM options are built to exploit.

### Why Volume Dominates Short-Term Momentum

Price shows **what** is happening; volume shows **how much conviction** is behind it. Rising prices on weak volume reflect speculation or thin liquidity; rising prices on explosive volume signal institutional accumulation and urgency. Volume is the dominant short-term filter because it provides:

- **Institutional validation.** Breakouts on **2x–5x+** average volume reveal genuine institutional buying.
- **Leverage amplification.** SOXL, LABU, and options perform best on strong volume and decay during low-volume chop—volume determines when leverage is justified.
- **The behavioral edge.** Rising volume on advances and declining volume on pullbacks signals healthy momentum; falling volume during rallies warns of exhaustion.
- **Dispersion in 2026.** Amid broadening leadership—AI infrastructure and power, energy, biotech M&A—volume surges separate true rotations from low-float hype.

High-volume breakouts consistently produce higher success rates, stronger follow-through, and better Sharpe ratios than low-volume breakouts.

## The Operational Signals: Reading the Tape

Reduce volume analysis to four repeatable signals:

**1. Relative Volume (RVOL) as the alpha filter.** Use a screener and require RVOL ≥ 3.0—within the first 30–60 minutes the stock should already trade near 300% of its normal volume for that time of day. Treat 2x–3x RVOL as the floor, not the target.

**2. The breakout volume surge.** When price clears resistance, a pivot, or a major moving average, require a 3x–10x-plus volume spike with closing strength—the bar finishing near its highs with minimal upper wick. Volume confirms the breakout; price alone does not.

**3. The volume pocket (supply starvation).** During the consolidation, volume should dry up entirely—tiny, below-average bars meaning previous buyers refuse to sell and the float shrinks to almost nothing. When the breakout hits on massive expansion, incoming capital slams into a vacuum and price launches vertically over a tight two-to-five-day window.

**4. The distribution scan (the guardrail).** If your stock or 3x ETF prints an exceptionally heavy volume day while price stalls or closes near the bottom of its range—an institutional churn candle—execute your trailing stop immediately. Smart money is liquidating to the retail public.

## The Engines of Explosive Volume

Volume expansion rarely appears at random—a handful of recurring mechanisms generate the largest surges, each a distinct opportunity and hazard. **Short squeezes:** heavy shorts rush to cover as a stock rises, momentum and retail pile in, options activity expands. **Gamma squeezes:** aggressive call buying forces market makers to hedge by buying shares, a self-feeding loop of exploding options and share volume. **Sector rotation:** rising volume across an entire sector signals institutional rotation rather than a single-name story. **News catalysts:** earnings surprises, FDA approvals, acquisitions, and contracts create urgency, and volume separates a real catalyst from a weak news pop.

## Climax, Distribution, and the Healthy Dry-Up

Volume expansion is bullish only in context. Late in a cycle, climactic volume and parabolic price often reflect emotional retail buying while professionals distribute. Healthy leaders consolidate quietly, pull back on declining volume, hold support, and launch again. Intraday, strong momentum shows heavy opening volume, sustained midday participation, and strong closing accumulation—the close matters most, since institutions execute late-day, so a strong close on heavy volume signals continued demand while a weak close after heavy volume signals distribution.

## Volume in Leveraged Instruments

Volume matters even more once you add leverage, because leverage amplifies movement, emotion, and **liquidity risk** alike: weak volume in a leveraged instrument produces wide spreads, poor fills, and outright liquidity traps, while strong volume delivers smoother fills and more durable momentum. In leveraged trading, liquidity is survival—deploy only into liquid instruments showing expanding participation: **3x/2x ETFs** (SOXL, LABU) on volume-backed breakouts, pyramided only as volume confirms; **options** on high-RVOL leaders post-surge; and **stocks and warrants** on names showing volume spikes for asymmetry.

### The Volume Governance Matrix

| Tactical Axis | The Retail Gambler | The Blueprint Allocator |
|---|---|---|
| **Breakout entry logic** | Buys any price breakout, ignoring the volume histogram entirely. | Enforces a strict RVOL ≥ 3.0 mandate before allocating a single dollar. |
| **Consolidation view** | Panics when volume drops in a consolidation, assuming the asset is dead. | Reads supply starvation as the calm before an explosive vertical launch. |
| **Heavy down-days** | "Buys the dip" on massive red volume, absorbing institutional liquidation. | Obeys stops and locks profits the instant distribution volume triggers. |
| **Capital efficiency** | Ties up capital in low-volume, illiquid tickers that chop for weeks. | Rotates exclusively through high-volume, high-velocity institutional funnels. |

### The Psychology Behind Volume

Volume is a direct expression of urgency, FOMO, institutional conviction, greed, and panic—a real-time readout of collective psychology, not merely a technical indicator. FOMO without volume is a trap; conviction *confirmed* by volume is an edge.

### Risk and Ironclad Rules

The same fuel that compounds an account can detonate it. Respect the failure modes: **false breakouts** (low-volume teases fail often—require multi-bar confirmation), **climax exhaustion** (parabolic spikes frequently mark tops—scale out into them), **leverage decay** (low-volume chop destroys 2x/3x products), **sizing** (risk ≤1% per idea, cap any single surge at 20–30% of the portfolio), and **2026 crowding** (leveraged-ETF volumes are booming—use the liquidity but stay alert to overcrowding).

### Final Principle

Volume expansion is one of the clearest confirmations of genuine momentum: price movement attracts attention, volume reveals conviction. The greatest momentum moves in history occurred with extraordinary participation, and volume is the footprint participation leaves. In this blueprint, volume is the bridge between the two halves of the engine: Relative Strength tells you *where* to attack, Volume Expansion *when, and how big*.

## Institutional Accumulation

One of the most expensive beliefs a trader can hold is that retail buyers drive the market's largest moves. They don't—retail creates volatility, noise, and the occasional viral frenzy, but **institutions create sustained momentum.** The vertical, hyper-velocity trends that turn a $100,000 account into something far larger are the product of systematic, multi-day deployment of institutional capital—hedge funds, mutual funds, pensions, sovereign wealth, banks, and algo firms aggressively building positions over time. That money leaves footprints, and the trader who reads them gains a durable edge: positioning ahead of the volume expansion, the breakout, and the crowd.

### What Institutional Accumulation Really Is

Institutional accumulation is the process by which large investors steadily purchase shares over an extended period. Because they control enormous capital, they cannot buy a full position instantly without driving price against themselves, so they accumulate gradually—buying consolidations, absorbing selling pressure, defending support, increasing exposure session after session. That patient pressure leaves a residue: rising volume, improving relative strength, tight ranges, and persistent strong closes—and accumulation frequently precedes major breakouts, which is the lead time the aggressive trader hunts.

### The Elephant in the Bathtub

The defining constraint is scale. A retail trader puts $20,000 into a 3x ETF in a millisecond; a multi-billion-dollar fund building a 5% stake may need to deploy $200,000,000, and firing that as one market order drives price 40% against itself, destroying its own cost basis. So institutions hide, breaking block orders into thousands of tranches via stealth algorithms—VWAP, TWAP, and iceberg orders. But no algorithm repeals supply and demand: an institution accumulating a massive stake is an elephant hiding in a bathtub, and the overflow onto the tape is the footprint.

### Why Accumulation Is the Engine of Fast Compounding

Momentum develops when institutional demand overwhelms available supply: sellers vanish, prices rise, volume expands. Three properties make accumulation valuable: **scale and conviction** (their buying absorbs selling pressure during consolidation, then ignites momentum once complete), a **lead-time edge** (you front-run the obvious move by detecting the footprint while the stock is quiet), and **leverage synergy** (true accumulation produces tight price action on rising up-day volume—exactly where leveraged instruments deploy without immediate decay). The greatest momentum stocks often see weeks or months of persistent buying, and that sustained demand produces the trend continuation behind extraordinary compounding.

## The Forensic Footprints of Smart Money

No matter how sophisticated their execution, institutions cannot fully erase their tracks. Four un-fakeable signatures confirm active accumulation: **pocket pivots** (volume surges on tight, quiet days), the **rising floor** (higher lows anchored to moving averages), **clean closes** (price pinned at the highs into the bell), and **float scarcity** (supply removed until a vortex forms).

1. **Pocket pivots.** An asset in a tight range suddenly prints a volume bar larger than any down-volume bar of the prior 10–15 sessions while price barely moves—an institution stepping into the bid and absorbing every offered share without letting price escape. The **Accumulation/Distribution (A/D) line** and **On-Balance Volume (OBV)** measure exactly this: when price drifts flat while A/D or OBV climbs, you have textbook quiet accumulation, reinforced by relative volume expanding even as price stays calm.

2. **The rising floor.** Institutional algorithms buy the instant an asset pulls back to an anchor—most often the **10-day EMA or 50-day SMA**—producing a clean sequence of higher lows. Inside that base, weak holders exit, institutions build, and floating supply is exhausted; the range tightens and pullbacks grow shallow until accumulation overwhelms supply. *The bigger the base, the bigger the breakout.*

3. **Clean closes.** Retail dominates the open on overnight headlines; institutions dominate the **close**—the final thirty minutes, when liquidity is deepest and block adjustments are finalized. A stock repeatedly closing at or near its daily high on heavy volume shows institutional conviction; weak closes after large intraday rallies hint at distribution. The close reveals who controlled the session.

4. **Float scarcity and the vortex effect.** As an institution locks up 10%, 15%, or 20% of a company's liquid float, it removes those shares from circulation, and even a minor influx of buying triggers a structural vortex—price leaps vertically because there is almost no supply to block it. The effect turns most violent when accumulation overlaps high short interest and a limited float: as supply is removed, shorts are forced to cover into a market with no sellers.

## Confirming the Footprint: Tools and Lagged Data

The four signatures work in real time; secondary tools confirm them. **Order-flow analysis** (delta, footprint charts, volume clusters) reveals absorption directly, with platforms like Bookmap and TrendSpider surfacing block trades and dark-pool prints. **Dark-pool activity** conceals individual prints but the aggregate still bleeds onto the tape. **Lagged confirmation** from quarterly 13F filings and ETF inflows shows rotation after the fact—treat it as confirmation, never a trigger, since by the time a 13F prints the footprint is months old.

## Relative Strength, Leadership, and Sponsorship

Strong relative strength is itself a footprint: a stock outperforming the market, its sector, and its peers is usually absorbing concentrated professional demand. Institutions prefer liquid leaders with dominant growth narratives and accumulate the strongest names in the strongest sectors—and sponsorship compounds on itself, as analysts turn bullish, targets rise, and retail expands. So hunt for stocks that refuse to weaken: names that decline less, recover faster, and keep outperforming under pressure.

## The 2026 Accumulation Map

In the current regime, institutions are overweight U.S. equities and concentrated in real-economy themes. The heaviest flows move into AI infrastructure and the power demand behind it—utilities, nuclear, and renewables tied to the data-center buildout—alongside biotech (M&A and the GLP-1/obesity wave) and broader energy rotations. The watchlist nearly writes itself: hunt accumulation signatures in the names anchoring these narratives.

## The Accumulation Governance Matrix

| Tactical Axis | The Retail Gambler | The Blueprint Capital Allocator |
|---|---|---|
| **Market thesis** | Believes he can outsmart institutions by buying what the smart money is dumping. | Identifies the institutional footprint and aligns capital with the smart money. |
| **Volume analysis** | Watches price ticks and ignores the volume behind the move. | Scans for institutional relative-volume expansions (RVOL ≥ 3.0). |
| **Reaction to consolidation** | Gets bored and exits just before the accumulation phase resolves. | Identifies pocket pivots and front-runs the breakout alongside the algorithms. |
| **Capital positioning** | Exposes capital to illiquid tickers with no institutional sponsorship. | Rotates liquidity exclusively through names showing genuine block accumulation. |

## Trading the Footprint: Aggressive Setups

Detection is half the blueprint; the other half is converting a confirmed footprint into a position sized for fast compounding—**3x and 2x ETFs** (SOXL, LABU, leveraged energy) pyramided as volume expands once the stock breaks out; **options** on names showing A/D divergence plus improving RS for defined-risk exposure during the quiet phase; and **stocks and warrants** on high-conviction leaders or smaller caps for added leverage during the buildup.

> **Execution Sequence — from a $100,000 base** Your scan flags rising OBV and A/D in an AI-infrastructure or energy-utility name consolidating on power-demand news. Price is holding VWAP and printing higher lows — the rising floor. You wait. On the breakout above resistance, volume surges and the stock closes clean at its high. Allocate 20–35% to a 3x sector ETF or to long calls, then scale in as further accumulation signals confirm. You trail your stop below the accumulation zone, rotate the gain into the next setup, and repeat. Sequential 40–150% swings, compounded back to back, are what bend the curve from $100k toward $1M.

## When the Giants Leave: Recognizing Distribution

Institutions accumulate, then eventually distribute—the same process in reverse: heavy selling volume, weak closes, failed breakouts, rising volatility, and repeated rejection at resistance, with the key tell being divergence on high volume (price pushing to new highs while A/D and OBV roll over). Recognizing the shift is non-negotiable; ignoring it is how traders give back in a few sessions what took months to build. The same footprints that got you in must get you out.

## Risk, Discipline, and Survival

Leverage amplifies error as readily as edge, so: **demand confirmation** (multiple independent signals plus a catalyst—a single indicator is a hypothesis, not a trade), **trade real time, not lagged data**, **respect the over-leverage trap** (don't size up fully until the breakout confirms), and **size for survival** (risk ~1% per idea, cap exposure during the accumulation-to-breakout transition near 25–30%, use hard stops or defined-risk options on every position).

## The Psychology of the Herd of Giants

Institutions are run by professionals under intense performance pressure, benchmark tracking, career risk, and a human fear of missing the trend—so when they collectively identify a dominant narrative, they compete for exposure, and that competition *is* the momentum, feeding itself far longer than valuation would justify. Understanding that lets you hold a winner while the crowd second-guesses it: you are not predicting the whale's mood, you are reading where it is already feeding.

## Final Principle: Swim with the Whale

Institutional accumulation is one of the hidden engines behind sustained momentum: the largest moves occur because professional money is aggressively building, revealing itself through volume expansion, relative strength, breakout persistence, and clean closes. **Retail traders create noise. Institutions create trends**—and in aggressive trading, trends are where extraordinary wealth is made.

## Breakout Behavior

**Breakout behavior is the ignition point where momentum converts into explosive, tradable gains.** A breakout marks the transition from quiet accumulation to public momentum expansion—the moment relative strength accelerates, volume expands, and institutional conviction becomes visible. Retail calls a fresh 52-week or all-time high "too expensive" and waits for a pullback; the allocator knows a breakout is the definitive transition from accumulation to rapid capital expansion. In a compressed campaign you trade assets at the exact moment their directional velocity explodes.

### What a Breakout Actually Is

A breakout occurs when price moves above resistance, a consolidation range, prior highs, a trendline, or a key moving average. That resistance is a concentration of institutional supply—short-sellers defending positions and historic buyers waiting to exit at break-even. During consolidation, buyers and sellers balance and volatility contracts; when price punches through on massive volume, balance disappears and a structural shift unfolds:

> **Resistance breached → Overhead supply evaporates → Short sellers squeezed → Buy algos trigger**

With no overhead supply left, the asset enters a **blue-sky regime**—a frictionless environment allowing massive vertical extension over a compressed 2-to-5-day window, the velocity required to turn over a tranche for a +3R to +5R payout.

### Why Breakouts Drive Fast Compounding

Consolidation builds tension as sellers exhaust and buyers coil; a decisive breakout releases that pent-up demand, triggering FOMO, stop hunts, and short covering that fuel multi-leg moves. **Clean breakouts often deliver 20–100%+ underlying moves in weeks, amplified 2–3x by leveraged ETFs or further by options**—and crucially, they compress time, turning slow appreciation into explosive expansion, exactly what a six-month campaign needs.

### The Anatomy of a High-Velocity Breakout

A valid breakout unfolds in three chronological phases:

**1. The setup – volatility contraction (the coiled spring).** Look for the Volatility Contraction Pattern (VCP), where intraday swings narrow from left to right—a 20% correction, then a 10% pullback, then a tight 3% squeeze—as the float is locked up; volume should dry up almost entirely during the final squeeze.

**2. The flashpoint – the high-volume sweep.** Execution occurs when price crosses the absolute pivot high with an immediate explosion in relative volume (RVOL ≥ 3.0) within the first hour, proving institutional blocks are sweeping the offer and insulating the breakout from mean-reversion failure.

**3. Continuation – the 3-day velocity window.** A genuine breakout follows through immediately, trading cleanly outside old resistance and refusing to fill the gap; the first three days hold the steepest gains, making this the premier window for short-dated high-delta calls or 3x ETFs, whose speed overpowers theta and variance drag.

### The Confirmation Stack

Never trade a breakout on price alone—before committing leverage, require the full stack: a rising **RS** line (or RRG rotating into Leading), **volume expansion** (2–5x+ average on the breakout candle, RVOL ≥ 3.0 intraday), an **institutional footprint** (rising OBV / advance-decline through the base, higher lows), **momentum filters** (ADX > 25, a bullish MACD crossover, price above the 20- and 50-day averages), and **a genuine catalyst** (earnings, news, or sector rotation).

### Breakout Patterns

The recurring high-probability structures and what each signals:

| Pattern | What It Is / What It Signals |
|---|---|
| Horizontal resistance break | Price clears multi-month, high-volume resistance on a volume surge |
| Flag / pennant / trendline | Continuation after an orderly pullback within an established uptrend |
| Cup-with-handle / base break | Price exits a large consolidation built over weeks or months (a tight handle plus volume) |
| Volatility contraction (VCP) | A coiled squeeze — narrowing swings and drying volume — then expansion |
| Moving-average reclaim | Price reclaims a key moving average and triggers momentum buying |
| All-time-high / blue-sky | Price enters discovery with little or no overhead resistance — strongest with RS leadership |

Some of the market's strongest momentum begins at an **all-time high**: with overhead resistance eliminated and few trapped sellers, price enters true discovery, institutions chase performance, and continuation becomes more likely. Breakouts go vertical when extra pressure develops—**short squeezes** force shorts to cover and **gamma squeezes** force market makers to buy shares for hedging—so a low-float stock with a strong catalyst, heavy short interest, and a clean breakout can become extraordinarily volatile; monitor options volume, open interest, and implied volatility alongside price.

### The Forensic Defense: Diagnosing the False Breakout

Not every breakout succeeds. Bull traps usually show one or more warning signs: a breakout on weak or average volume, price breaking resistance but closing near the session low back inside the base, or a failed retest instead of renewed buying. Successful retests hold support on renewed demand; failed retests signal distribution. The response is always the same—**exit immediately, never average down.** Most failed breakouts stem from weak volume, poor market conditions, absent institutional participation, or exhaustion after an extended advance.

## The Breakout Cycle

Most breakout behavior follows a recognizable cycle—knowing the stage keeps you from chasing the late, emotional part of the move:

| | |
|---|---|
| 1 | **Accumulation** — Institutions quietly build positions. |
| 2 | **Consolidation** — Volatility contracts and supply weakens. |
| 3 | **Breakout** — Price clears resistance with volume expansion. |
| 4 | **Momentum expansion** — Retail, media, and institutional buying accelerate. |
| 5 | **Euphoria** — Speculation intensifies and the move turns emotional. |
| 6 | **Exhaustion** — Buying pressure fades and reversal becomes likely. |

## Instruments and Execution

Express confirmed breakouts through **leveraged ETFs** (SOXL, LABU, leveraged energy and small-cap funds), **options** (long calls or call debit spreads; high-delta calls during the first **3-day** breakout window), and **warrants** (asymmetric leverage on smaller momentum names). Route capital only into confirmed leaders.

> **Worked example — $100,000 account** A small-cap or energy name shows improving relative strength and accumulation (rising OBV through the base). Price breaks multi-week resistance on 4x volume amid a sector catalyst. Allocate 20–40% to a 3x sector ETF or out-of-the-money calls on the leader, scaling in on follow-through (higher highs plus volume). Trail stops below the breakout level or by ATR / prior low, targeting a 30–100%+ swing, then rotate proceeds into the next confirmed setup. Sequential clean breakouts compound aggressively — but only when each one clears the full confirmation stack.

## Risk and Survival Rules

- **Whipsaws and traps.** Many breakouts retrace to shake out weak hands—use tight initial stops below the breakout level, or options for defined risk.
- **Leverage decay.** Never hold 3x products through post-breakout chop—they belong only in strong, trending follow-through.
- **Overcrowding.** Popular themes fail faster the moment volume fades.

- **Discipline.** Risk ≤1% per breakout, cap any one theme at 25–35% of the portfolio, require the full confirmation stack, never chase, and pair every setup with a VIX / regime filter.

## Final Principle

Breakout behavior is one of the clearest expressions of momentum acceleration—a signal of increasing demand, institutional participation, expanding liquidity, and changing psychology at once. It ties the engine together: **relative strength identifies the candidates, volume and accumulation confirm readiness, and the breakout launches the leveraged rocket. Enter at the pivot. Demand the volume. Cut the trap. Ride the velocity.**

# Chapter 7
# Volatility as Opportunity

## A. Trading Volatility Intelligently

Most investors fear volatility; aggressive traders study, respect, and profit from it. Volatility—the speed and magnitude of price movement—reflects uncertainty, emotion, and liquidity imbalance, and without it extraordinary short-term compounding is nearly impossible. Retail mistakes volatility for danger; professionals recognize it as pricing inefficiency and capital velocity. Low-volatility markets stagnate capital; high-volatility markets accelerate compounding—provided you trade the structure, not the chaos. Turning **$100,000 into $1,000,000 in six months** depends entirely on harnessing it.

### Volatility Is Not Risk

Build this distinction into bedrock. **Volatility** is the statistical dispersion of an asset's returns; **risk** is the permanent impairment of capital. They are not synonyms, and conflating them keeps the retail crowd out of exactly the conditions that compound fastest. A **3x ETF**, high-beta stock, or option chain wrapped inside a disciplined **1% (1R)** framework does not become riskier simply because volatility rises: fixed stops keep downside constant while larger swings let positions reach **+3R to +5R** targets in hours instead of weeks.

***Volatility = dispersion of returns (the opportunity) · Risk = permanent loss of capital (the enemy)***

### Why Volatility Creates Opportunity

Large returns require large price movement—stocks moving **10%, 20%, 50%, or 100%** within days compress years of traditional investing into weeks. This is why aggressive capital concentrates in momentum stocks, low-float breakouts, sector catalysts, AI speculation, data-center equities, options, leveraged ETFs, and high-beta sectors. Volatility is the raw material of rapid compounding.

### Volatility Is Mean-Reverting: Expansion and Contraction

Volatility is among the most reliably **mean-reverting** metrics in markets, moving in a rhythm of contraction (quiet consolidation) and expansion (high-velocity bursts) that is itself tradable. The directional application developed here forbids chasing assets already at peak expansion; instead you screen for deep **volatility contraction**—the VCP pattern—and load the position while the asset is quiet, *before* the catalyst is priced in. When volatility reverts toward its mean, that expansion launches price vertically. You are buying the calm to sell the storm.

### The VIX and the Volatility Regime

Above any single stock sits the market's overall volatility, most visibly the **VIX**. A **low-to-moderate VIX (below ~20)** is a trending, lower-variance backdrop that favors aggressively long leveraged ETFs on momentum breakouts; a **high VIX (above ~25–30)** signals stress—shift toward protective puts, short-volatility structures, or defensive rotation, and cut leverage materially. One filter sharpens the read: deploying long leverage is most favorable when **realized** volatility sits below **implied** within an uptrend—you are being paid to take directional risk the market is overpricing.

### Pure Volatility Instruments

Beyond trading volatility *through* stocks, you can trade it directly. VIX futures, options, and ETFs/ETNs let you take a position on variance itself: **VXX** and **UVXY** rise as volatility spikes (long vol), while **SVXY** profits as it subsides (short vol). These are tactical instruments for swings around known events, not buy-and-hold—long-volatility products suffer brutal decay and contango in calm markets, bleeding value simply by being held, and leveraged versions magnify both the move and the decay. Use them only directionally, in short bursts, with tight stops.

### Options and Implied Volatility

Options are the purest expression of volatility trading, because volatility is priced directly into them. **Implied volatility (IV)** reflects expected future movement and skyrockets ahead of flashpoints—earnings, FDA decisions, Fed announcements—inflating premiums. This creates the most common trap: amateurs buy hyper-inflated options at peak hype and suffer an **IV crush** the next morning, destroying capital *even when they guessed direction correctly.* The intelligent approach trades volatility deliberately: **long volatility** (buy straddles or strangles before a catalyst when IV is cheap, or debit spreads for defined risk), **short volatility** (sell premium through credit spreads or iron condors in low-VIX regimes, or into an overextended spike), and **bounded structures** (vertical spreads, iron condors, structural warrants that insulate the ledger from variance drain). On leveraged ETFs, options on SOXL, LABU, and TQQQ offer extreme convexity for pyramiding a winner.

### Leveraged ETF Rebalancing Velocity

Daily rebalancing cuts both ways: during sustained trends, **2x** and **3x ETFs** can outperform their nominal leverage through positive geometric compounding, but in sideways markets the same mechanism causes volatility decay regardless of where the index finishes. Rule: hold leveraged ETFs only during strong, confirmed trends.

### Volatility, Liquidity, and Instrument Selection

Volatility without liquidity is a trap—illiquid assets produce wide spreads, poor fills, and violent reversals, random chaos rather than productive variance. The professional insists on volatility accompanied by strong volume and reliable liquidity, because liquidity is what makes clean entries, clean exits, and real risk management possible. Each instrument expresses volatility differently: **stocks** give direct exposure; **2x/3x ETFs** amplify daily exposure for confirmed trends only; **options** give asymmetric leverage with defined risk; **warrants** add longer-duration speculative leverage; and **crypto**

**equities and small-cap momentum** deliver the most extreme expansion—highest reward, highest danger.

## The Volatility Cycle

Most volatility moves travel a recognizable arc—compression, catalyst emergence, expansion, momentum acceleration, emotional euphoria, then collapse as momentum weakens and reversals emerge—and knowing the phase keeps you from entering late or holding into the collapse.

## The Volatility Governance Matrix

| Tactical Axis | The Retail Gambler | The Blueprint Allocator |
|---|---|---|
| **View of chaos** | Reacts emotionally — chases vertical spikes, panic-sells the bottom. | Reads chaos as structural liquidity and rapid target-attainment velocity. |
| **Position sizing** | Holds massive size through wide swings. | Shrinks absolute share size as ATR expands. |
| **Option execution** | Buys short-dated OTM options at peak IV. | High-delta Low-IV ITM or defined-risk spreads. |
| **Horizon** | Long-term hope | 1–2 day tactical execution |

## Risk, Psychology, and Intelligent Discipline

The difference between intelligent volatility trading and gambling is discipline: asymmetric setups, controlled risk, managed size, and alignment with momentum, versus oversized positions and emotional chasing. The survival rules are non-negotiable: **size to the variance** (shrink exposure as ATR expands, stand aside when volatility turns irrational), **cap the risk** (≤1% per idea, ≤20–30% of the portfolio in high-volatility setups at once), **define risk with structure** (defined-risk options and ATR-based stops over naked exposure), **respect decay** (limit leveraged ETFs and vol products to strong trends), and **journal the regime** behind every trade.

## Final Principle

Volatility is neither good nor bad—it magnifies opportunity, providing momentum, leverage, asymmetry, and accelerated compounding, but rewarding only disciplined traders who control risk and align with market structure. **ATR** measures variance; **gamma squeezes**, **short squeezes**, and **momentum ignition** express it; disciplined risk management harnesses it. **Trade the structure of volatility, cage the risk, harvest the velocity, and let the market's waves do the compounding.**

## B. ATR and Price Expansion — The Volatility Governor

Volatility creates movement; price expansion creates opportunity. The retail public judges a move as "big" or "small" by visual bias or the raw dollar size of the day's gain—guesswork. The allocator relies instead on an objective, volatility-normalized metric: the **Average True Range (ATR)**. In a compressed six-month campaign, ATR is your **position-sizing and volatility governor**, defining the exact baseline of normal noise for any asset and pinpointing the precise moment a price-expansion event is occurring.

### What ATR Actually Measures

ATR measures the average amount an asset moves over a chosen period, and unlike a simple high-minus-low range it accounts for intraday range, gaps, and overnight volatility. A low-ATR stock moves slowly; a high-ATR stock swings hard, and aggressive traders gravitate toward expanding ATR because larger movement creates larger profit potential. The foundation is the **True Range (TR)**, engineered by J. Welles Wilder to respect overnight gap risk—the very risk that defines leveraged ETFs, options, and high-beta names—as the greatest of three spreads:

$$\textbf{True Range (TR)} = \max\left[\,(H - L),\ |H - C_{prev}|,\ |L - C_{prev}|\,\right]$$

where H is the current high, L the current low, and $C_{prev}$ the previous close. The Average True Range is a moving average of these values over a lookback window—the blueprint enforces a strict **14-period (14-ATR)** default—telling you precisely how many points the asset travels in a normal session.

### Why ATR Is the Aggressive Trader's Edge

Fast compounding requires movement, and ATR measures whether enough exists to justify aggressive positioning. A $50 stock carrying a 2.5 ATR has roughly a $5 daily range, so you size accordingly. Read as a trend, ATR becomes a regime signal: **rising ATR** (expansion) signals increasing momentum and the ideal backdrop for breakouts and leveraged entries; **contracting ATR** warns of consolidation, where leverage decays and exposure should be reduced. It answers the question relative strength, volume, and accumulation leave open: how far, and how fast.

### Price Expansion: Identifying the Launchpad

Price expansion occurs when an asset moves more aggressively than its own baseline—during breakouts, earnings reactions, short squeezes, sector rotations, or AI-driven momentum waves—and ATR rises sharply, signaling accelerating participation. Many explosive moves are preceded by gradually rising ATR, the market quietly "waking up" as institutions accumulate before the catalyst detonates the range. In a 120-session sprint you deploy at the flashpoint: a **volatility-contraction** phase (daily range under 1× ATR) resolves through a **flashpoint breakout** into a **price-expansion** phase (daily range above 2× ATR).

### The 2-ATR Expansion Rule

A valid, high-conviction breakout occurs when the asset punches through a key pivot high and the daily bar expands to **2× ATR or greater in a single session**, backed by a surge in relative volume (RVOL ≥ 3.0). That expansion is proof the old baseline of variance has fractured—institutional blocks have overwhelmed the float and generated the directional velocity that fuels compounding. Expansion without volume confirmation is a false signal.

### The Position-Sizing Engine: Volatility Equalization

This is the most important idea in the chapter: **ATR lets you trade hyper-volatile 3x ETFs, options, and warrants with the same controlled risk profile as a conservative index fund.** Instead of an arbitrary 5% or 10% stop, the blueprint sets a *volatility-based invalidation bracket* at a multiple of current ATR, typically 2.0× to 2.5× ATR below the entry pivot. Two formulas drive it:

***Stop-Loss Distance ($) = Multiplier × 14-ATR***

***Position Size (shares) = (Account Equity × Risk Unit) ÷ Stop-Loss Distance ($)***

Because the ATR-derived stop distance is embedded in a fixed-risk model, your position mass scales down automatically as volatility expands. On a $100,000 account risking 1% ($1,000), a stock with a $3 ATR and a 2× stop ($6 risk per share) supports roughly 167 shares—the more volatile the asset, the smaller the block, without any change to the dollar risk accepted.

### The Comparative Proof

Consider a $100,000 account running a strict 1% risk unit ($1,000), choosing between two momentum assets that break out simultaneously at an identical $100.00 entry—one calm, one wild:

| Characteristic | Asset A: Stable Tech ETF (XLK) | Asset B: 3x Semis ETF (SOXL) |
|---|---|---|
| **Entry price** | $100.00 | $100.00 |
| **Current 14-ATR** | $2.00 (low variance) | $6.00 (extreme variance) |
| **Stop bracket (2× ATR)** | $4.00 → $96.00 stop | $12.00 → $88.00 stop |
| **Risk unit (1R)** | $1,000 | $1,000 |
| **Max allocation** | **$1,000 ÷ $4 = 250 shares** | **$1,000 ÷ $12 = 83 shares** |
| **Total capital exposed** | **$25,000** | **$8,300** |

If a macro shock triggers both stops, the trader loses exactly $1,000—1% of capital—on each. The algorithm automatically shrank the SOXL block to neutralize its extreme variance, letting you command the upside of a 3x ETF without exposing the core ledger to a catastrophic risk-of-ruin event.

## ATR in Practice: Stops, Targets, and Pyramiding

Set the initial stop 1–2× ATR below the entry or breakout low, widening to 2–3× ATR for 3x ETFs whose amplified moves demand more room. To ride extended trends, use the **Chandelier Exit**—a trailing stop pinned to the highest high minus 2–3× ATR. Tight fixed stops in a high-ATR name guarantee premature exits; ATR-based stops breathe with the asset's normal noise and keep you in the move.

Scale profit targets to risk—2–4× the risk taken (2–4 ATR of favorable movement). Confirm entries by buying expansion breakouts only—a close more than 1 ATR above the recent range, with a volume surge and improving relative strength—then pyramid into winners exclusively while ATR is still rising; the moment ATR contracts, stop adding and begin scaling out.

## Instruments

The menu: **2x/3x ETFs** (SOXL, LABU, leveraged energy) entered on ATR-confirmed breakouts and trailed with 2–3× ATR; **options** bought during ATR expansion for convexity, using ATR to choose strikes targeting a 2–3 ATR move; and **stocks and warrants** on high-ATR leaders in AI power or biotech.

## ATR Across Market Regimes

ATR behaves differently by environment, and reading that context separates constructive volatility from dangerous volatility. In **bullish momentum markets** expansion tends to be directional and constructive; in **bear markets** it turns chaotic; during **speculative liquidity expansions** it can explode across entire sectors; under **tight monetary conditions** it becomes erratic. The essential judgment is whether rising volatility reflects healthy momentum or underlying panic. Most expansions travel a recognizable sequence—compression, accumulation, catalyst, ATR expansion, momentum acceleration, exhaustion, then collapse back toward baseline.

## The ATR Governance Matrix

| Operational Vector | The Retail Gambler | The Blueprint Allocator |
|---|---|---|
| **Stop-loss definition** | A rigid, unadjusted percentage rule (e.g., 5%) applied to every asset. | Stops linked to active volatility via 2× ATR brackets. |
| **Position-sizing logic** | Identical dollar amounts into every asset, regardless of volatility. | Share size scales down automatically as ATR expands. |

| Operational Vector | The Retail Gambler | The Blueprint Allocator |
|---|---|---|
| **Breakout assessment** | Chases any green day, blind to structural variance. | Verifies the move through a strict 2× ATR expansion filter. |
| **Trailing strategy** | Clings to a stop too tight, getting chopped out by normal noise. | Uses a 3× ATR volatility guard from peak equity to ride trends. |

### Psychology, Pitfalls, and Intelligent Rules

ATR expansion is a readout of changing psychology: as volatility rises, fear, greed, and urgency climb, drawing in retail, institutions, and algorithms, which feeds still more expansion. It is also where undisciplined traders are destroyed through oversized positions and poor stops. The rules follow directly: **confirm expansion** (spikes without volume or RS are false signals), **avoid leverage in chop** (require ADX > 25), **always ATR-adjust size**, and **cap and journal** (risk 1–2% per trade, avoid trading when ATR is extremely elevated without direction).

### Final Principle

ATR converts the abstract fear of a "risky" chart into a precise, governed risk decision: rising ATR signals expanding participation, and ATR-based sizing and stops keep that power survivable. Within this blueprint, ATR is the *how far and how much* calibrator: momentum says strength persists, relative strength says *where*, volume says *when*, and ATR says *how far the move can travel and exactly how large to size for it.*

## C. Gamma Squeezes — Weaponizing Structural Options Plumbing

Few forces create explosive short-term movement as violently as a gamma squeeze—and few are as misunderstood. The retail public attributes a vertical 50% spike to short covering or hype; that is a fraction of the story. **A gamma squeeze is a structural liquidity loop forced by the mechanical, automated hedging requirements of options market makers.** Short covering and hype ride along, but the engine is options plumbing. In a six-month sprint it is the ultimate time-compressor—the derivatives market actively forcing the underlying to launch vertically—and among the most dangerous environments in the market, where reversals are brutal and liquidity can vanish in minutes.

### The Mechanics: Delta, Gamma, and the Market Maker

When you buy a call, you buy from an institutional market maker whose mandate is to stay *market-neutral.* **Delta (Δ)** measures the expected change in an option's price per $1.00 move in the underlying; having sold you a call, the maker is short delta and immediately buys a fraction of the underlying to hedge (a 0.20-delta option means 20 shares per contract). **Gamma (Γ)** is the acceleration metric—the rate of change of delta per $1.00 move:

***Gamma (Γ) = ∂Δ / ∂S — the rate of change of Delta per $1 move in the underlying***

Gamma is the maker's compounding risk: as the stock climbs toward the strike, delta expands rapidly—0.20 to 0.40 to 0.60—forcing the maker to buy more and more shares to keep the hedge neutral. That forced, accelerating buying is the raw material of the squeeze.

## The Reflexive Feedback Loop: Anatomy of the Squeeze

A gamma squeeze ignites when a massive cluster of short-dated, out-of-the-money calls is aggressively bought across a concentrated, low-float equity: aggressive call buying forces makers to buy stock to hedge, the buying drives price up, the rising price accelerates delta (the high-gamma zone), and the higher delta forces makers to buy still more. Because the float is restricted, those automated market orders act like a vacuum cleaner sweeping the order book, forcing a near-vertical extension. The move turns truly explosive when retail call buying, institutional momentum, algorithms, and forced hedging all fire at once—and gamma squeezes frequently overlap with **short squeezes**, compounding the buying pressure.

## Spotting the Squeeze Before It Cascades

The edge lies in locating the **incubation flashpoint** before the cascade, where certain conditions cluster: **float scarcity** (a liquid float under roughly 50 million shares), **option-volume inversion** (daily call volume exceeding the 20-day average equity volume by 2x or more), **high open interest** clustered just above price, **IV skew** (short-dated OTM calls priced at markedly higher IV than ATM), **high short interest**, and **a coiled technical base** beneath a breakout level with a live catalyst. Read the options plumbing directly with gamma-exposure (GEX) tools such as SpotGamma or Unusual Whales.

## The Convexity Entry: Positioning Ahead of the Cascade

Once the signature is verified, the blueprint allows a few entries. **Stock/warrant:** buy at the volatility-contraction pivot high, using the makers' hedging blocks as a structural shield beneath your 1% risk unit. **High-delta option:** buy in-the-money calls (0.70–0.80 delta) 30–60 days out for stock-like velocity at a fraction of the capital—as the squeeze fires and IV skyrockets, the inflating premium can hand an explosive **+5R to +10R** over a 48-to-72-hour window. **Targeted convexity:** long OTM calls or debit spreads for limited risk and outsized upside, pyramided on follow-through; when gamma spills into a theme, 2x/3x sector ETFs (SOXL, LABU) or single-stock leveraged products (NVDL) capture the overflow.

## Price Expansion, Intraday Behavior, and Exhaustion

A gamma squeeze is price expansion in its purest modern form—repeated gap-ups, expanding ATR, widening ranges, and vertical movement, here driven by hedging demand rather than ordinary momentum. Intraday it is treacherous: explosive opening momentum, violent reversals, and repeated bursts as makers continuously rebalance. Volatility expansion cuts both ways—as momentum accelerates, IV rises and premiums swell; when the squeeze weakens, that same IV collapses and premiums can evaporate in hours. Every squeeze exhausts itself, typically when calls expire or profit-taking hits, traveling the familiar arc from quiet options accumulation through euphoria to collapse, with the greatest danger appearing precisely at maximum excitement.

## The Gamma Squeeze Governance Matrix

| Operational Vector | The Retail Gambler | The Blueprint Allocator |
|---|---|---|
| **Entry profile** | Chases the asset after it has already run 100% vertical, on pure FOMO. | Enters at the incubation flashpoint, before the loop cascades. |
| **Instrument choice** | Buys hyper-lottery far-OTM calls expiring in 48 hours. | Uses raw stock, warrants, or deep high-delta ITM calls. |
| **Risk managemen t** | Removes stops, assuming the vertical spike runs forever. | Holds the risk unit fixed at 1% via automated invalidation stops. |
| **Exit execution** | Holds through the inevitable crash out of greed. | Executes a hard time-stop or robotic profit-take within 2–5 sessions. |

### Risk, Survival, and Psychology

Gamma squeezes reflect mass psychology under greed and FOMO, which is exactly what makes them lethal to the undisciplined. Treat every squeeze as a high-conviction, short-duration trade: **expect rapid collapse** (squeezes unwind violently after expiration; theta destroys long options the moment momentum stalls), **demand the full confirmation stack**, **respect liquidity** (plan the exit before the entry in thin names), **never over-leverage** (risk ≤1% per idea, 0.5–1% on pure option plays), and **kill the FOMO** (take profits into strength, don't marry the trade).

### Final Principle

Gamma squeezes are among the most powerful volatility-expansion events in modern markets, combining aggressive options buying, forced hedging, momentum, and speculative psychology into self-reinforcing upward pressure. Within this section the gamma squeeze is the **ultimate accelerator**: detected through *volume* and *ATR* expansion, aimed by *relative strength*, and governed by the same volatility-based sizing that lets you stand in front of a vertical move. Master the plumbing, position at the flashpoint, harvest the cascade—then vanish back into cash before the wave crests.

## D. Short Squeezes — Harvesting Enforced Buying Panics

Among the most explosive wealth-creation events is the short squeeze: traders who bet against a stock are forced to buy shares back as price rises, their buying pushes price higher, which forces still more shorts to cover. Where retail sees a broken company or a meme, the allocator sees **a compressed spring of guaranteed, price-insensitive buying demand.** It is also one of the most dangerous environments in the market, where reversals are devastating—so the goal is to *understand* short squeezes, not merely chase them.

### The Mechanics of the Trapped Speculator

A short borrows shares and sells them expecting to buy back cheaper—sell at $20, repurchase at $10, keep the $10. The reversal is brutal: where a long can lose at most 100%, a short faces **theoretically unlimited loss** because a stock can rise without ceiling. Shorting is a high-friction operation: the speculator must **borrow** the shares and pay an annualized Cost to Borrow that in heavily shorted names can spike past 50% or even 100%, and if price surges the broker issues a margin call or executes a forced liquidation, *buying the stock back at the market ask.* The trapped short does not choose to buy; the system buys for them.

### The Anatomy of the Chain Reaction

A high-velocity squeeze is a reflexive liquidity cascade: a catalyst pushes a heavily shorted stock up, trapped shorts come under margin stress, forced liquidations follow, brokers place urgent market orders to cover, the buying spikes price further, and that spike triggers the next wave of higher-cost shorts. **Forced buying is far more powerful than discretionary buying**—in a squeeze, buyers buy because they are *compelled* to, ignoring valuation and paying almost any price, which pushes price into the stop clusters of shorts who entered higher, sweeping the offer book clean.

### Short Interest as Stored Energy

Think of short interest as stored energy: **every short seller is a future buyer**—the only questions are when and at what price. A stock carrying significant short interest contains latent, built-in buying pressure like a compressed spring; when a catalyst triggers panic, it releases all at once. The larger the short position, the more violent the release.

### The Ingredients of a Powerful Squeeze

Not every heavily shorted stock squeezes. The strongest setups combine several conditions: **high short interest** (ideally 20%+ of float), **limited float** (so demand exhausts supply quickly), **elevated Days to Cover** (the short ratio—a reading of 4–5 or higher means shorts can't all escape quickly),

**surging Cost to Borrow** (proving share supply is drying up), **a positive catalyst**, and **strong momentum and a coiled base** (a tight VCP directly beneath a breakout line). Days to Cover is computed as:

## The Amplifiers: Options, Institutions, and Volume

Three forces turn a squeeze from sharp to historic. **Options** stack a gamma squeeze on top—aggressive call buying forces makers to hedge—and when both fire together the move becomes parabolic. **Institutions** identify vulnerable short positioning early and absorb supply, making borrow harder to locate. And **volume** is the unmistakable footprint—powerful squeezes trade at multiples of normal volume with sustained buying and rising ATR.

## The Squeeze Playbook: Screening and Execution

The blueprint forbids chasing a squeeze already gone vertical into the top 1% of its historical ATR. Instead, screen for names coiling at the incubation flashpoint: short interest of 20%+ of float, Days to Cover of 4–5 or higher, a rising cost to borrow, and a catalyst-and-pivot confluence. Read short data with Ortex, ShortSqueeze.com, and Finviz alongside unusual options flow. Enter at the technical pivot breakout, and because a squeeze is driven by panic rather than durable accumulation it tends to be violent but short-lived—capture it with short-dated high-delta calls (or OTM calls and debit spreads), or a direct equity or warrant block, protected by a tight trailing 2× ATR guard, for a **+4R to +8R** expansion over a three-to-five-day window.

Squeeze conditions cluster when aggregate short positioning runs high—in the 2026 environment, hedge-fund shorts have sat near multi-year highs in pockets of the market, concentrated in AI and technology, biotech, energy and power, and small- and mid-caps. The classic case studies—GameStop in 2021, Volkswagen in 2008—remain the clearest illustrations of how far a fully loaded spring can travel.

## Genuine Squeezes vs. False Setups

No single factor guarantees a squeeze, and many high-short stocks simply grind lower for months. **Genuine** setups show multiple factors aligning—elevated short interest, low float, unusual volume, strong relative strength, a real catalyst, supportive options flow, and a clean breakout. The fatal error is entering **late**, when emotional buying and parabolic charts coincide with early participants taking profits. Every squeeze ends—declining volume, repeated failure at higher prices, and weakening momentum signal exhaustion as shorts finish covering, and the move travels the familiar arc from heavy short positioning through euphoria to reversal.

## The Short Squeeze Governance Matrix

| Tactical Axis | The Retail Gambler | The Blueprint Allocator |
|---|---|---|
| **Asset selection** | Buys bankrupt, delisted shells on social-media hype. | Screens liquid names for short interest ≥ 20% and Days to Cover ≥ 4. |

| Tactical Axis | The Retail Gambler | The Blueprint Allocator |
|---|---|---|
| **Entry execution** | Buys at the parabolic peak out of FOMO. | Enters at the technical pivot flashpoint, before the cascade. |
| **Risk management** | Runs with no stop, certain the stock "will go to the moon." | Cages the trade in a rigid 1% account-risk bracket. |
| **Monetization** | Holds through the entire downside crash, turning a win into a loss. | Harvests profits into the vertical acceleration window (2–5 days). |

### Psychology, Risk, and Iron Discipline

A short squeeze is fundamentally a psychological event—fear among trapped shorts, greed and FOMO among longs—and those emotional extremes amplify the volatility that destroys the undisciplined. Treat every squeeze as a high-conviction, short-duration trade: **expect the sudden reversal** (time exits on volume fade or ATR contraction), **respect liquidity** (plan the exit before the entry), **assume most fail** (require the full stack, never chase), **never overexpose** (≤1% per idea, avoid holding through expiration), and **size for the lottery** (high-variance setups paired with strict sizing, not hope).

### Final Principle

Short squeezes occur when heavily shorted stocks rise, shorts become trapped, and forced buying accelerates momentum—the strongest combining high short interest, low float, a real catalyst, volume expansion, and institutional accumulation. The short squeeze and the gamma squeeze are the two **forced-buying engines** of this section—one driven by trapped shorts, the other by hedging dealers, most violent when they fire together. Identify the loaded spring, enter at the flashpoint with caged risk, harvest the enforced panic—and be in cash before the spring fully unwinds.

## E. Momentum Ignition — Catching the Liquidity Cascade

Momentum is rarely created by accident—major moves almost always begin with a catalyst or imbalance that makes buyers suddenly more aggressive than sellers, and that initial burst is **momentum ignition:** the spark that starts the fire, the phase in which an asset transitions from quiet and range-bound to active and momentum-driven. The retail crowd assumes a stock moves because of good earnings or an upgrade; the allocator knows news is merely data, and ignition is the high-volume injection of capital that fractures price structure and pulls participation in behind it. Your job is to **detect and ride** naturally occurring ignition events—never to manufacture one, which is manipulation and a regulatory red line.

## What Momentum Ignition Is

Momentum ignition is the event that causes an asset to begin attracting sustained buying, when demand suddenly overwhelms supply—producing increased volume, rising volatility, expanding ranges, improving relative strength, and accelerating momentum. Crucially, ignition is not the entire trend; it is the *beginning* of one, and the greatest percentage gains tend to occur in its earliest stage. By the time the broader market recognizes the opportunity, much of the low-risk entry is already gone.

## The Mechanics of the Spark: The Three-Layer Cascade

For days or weeks an asset rests in volatility contraction; ignition fires when that equilibrium is shocked, and the move propagates through three layers in rapid succession. **Layer 1 – the ignition spark:** a large participant or genuine catalyst drives aggressive market orders that sweep the sell-side in a compressed window, breaking the asset out of its resting state. **Layer 2 – algorithmic propulsion:** momentum scanners flash the anomaly, high-frequency systems flood the bid, and breakout algorithms trigger, converting a single shove into a self-reinforcing wave. **Layer 3 – behavioral foam:** retail FOMO ignites and social media chases the move, so by the time the public arrives, early entrants sit on floating profits cushioned by a thick layer of algorithmic buying.

## Why Ignition Matters: The Catalysts and the Early-Entry Edge

The largest gains cluster near the beginning of a move, which is why early entry is so valuable—a trader entering shortly after ignition enjoys lower risk, a better entry, and a far stronger reward-to-risk ratio than one arriving after the media and crowd. Ignition almost always begins with a catalyst: **earnings surprises**, **AI announcements**, **FDA approvals**, **acquisitions and M&A**, **government contracts**, or **product launches and regulatory shifts**. It is most violent where supply is thinnest—in **low-float** names, where fewer shares mean demand impacts price disproportionately, which is why so many of the market's largest percentage gainers originate in small-caps and speculative sectors.

## The Ignition Signature: Verifying the Flashpoint

The blueprint forbids buying low-volume "drift." Verify true ignition by tracking a strict multi-variable signature in the first 5 to 30 minutes: **the RVOL shock** (relative volume of 5.0 or greater), **range displacement** (long-bodied candles slicing through resistance, pushing beyond the 2× ATR envelope within the opening hour), **options-volume inversion** (near-term OTM call volume spiking, pulling in gamma hedging), **relative strength and structure** (RS shifting into the Leading quadrant, higher lows, a clean VCP base), and **accumulation and short pressure** (rising OBV plus high short interest). The signal is the convergence—no single line, but the whole stack firing together.

## Genuine Ignition vs. False Sparks

**Genuine ignition** shows multiple confirming factors at once—a real catalyst, volume expansion, improving relative strength, institutional participation, a clean breakout, and sector support—while **false ignition** shows brief excitement and volume that fades within minutes, traceable to a weak catalyst or absent institutional support. Separating the two is much of what separates winners from losers.

## The Tactical Playbook: Trading the Shockwave

When a valid signature is confirmed, execution is clinical and dual-pronged. **The immediate delta entry:** bypass limit orders and use a stop-market order one tick above the consolidation pivot high so you are filled as the flashpoint confirms, anchoring the stop at the low of the ignition candle to hold risk to your 1% unit (1R). **The high-convexity derivative play:** on assets with liquid options, buy at-the-money calls in the nearest 7-to-14-day window, or OTM calls and debit spreads at ignition for maximum convexity—because ignition spikes implied volatility, the contracts gain from both the price delta and the inflating Vega premium. The menu is familiar: 2x/3x ETFs (SOXL, LABU, leveraged energy), options, and stocks or warrants on low-float leaders.

## The Momentum Ignition Cycle

Most ignitions follow a recognizable progression—accumulation, catalyst emergence, volume expansion, breakout, public awareness, momentum expansion, euphoria, then exhaustion—and locating an asset within it is what lets you act before euphoria and exit before exhaustion.

## The Momentum Ignition Governance Matrix

| Tactical Axis | The Retail Gambler | The Blueprint Allocator |
|---|---|---|
| **Trigger recognition** | Waits for a lagging headline or social post to explain why a stock is moving. | Relies on real-time scanners tracking RVOL ≥ 5.0 and ATR displacement. |
| **Order routing** | Uses passive limit orders that go unfilled, or panics and buys the peak. | Uses programmatic stop-market orders to clip the exact flashpoint. |
| **Risk insulation** | Chases without a plan, widening the stop as the position moves against them. | Pins risk to the ignition-candle low, never exceeding 1R. |

| Tactical Axis | The Retail Gambler | The Blueprint Allocator |
|---|---|---|
| **Monetization window** | Falls in love with the asset and holds into the mean-reversion. | Treats it as a velocity play, exiting into peak acceleration (1–3 days). |

## Risk, Discipline, and the Regulatory Line

Ignition is the highest-reward entry in the book and one of the most dangerous. **Require the full stack** (catalyst, volume, RS, and structure together—never chase a single green candle), **expect rapid reversals** (treat it as a 1–3-day velocity play), **control leverage** (3x products and short-dated options punish a stalled move; favor defined-risk options in the most volatile ignitions), **cap and journal** (≤1% per idea), and **stay inside the line** (detect and ride natural ignitions only—never act to create artificial price movement).

## Final Principle

Momentum ignition is the spark that begins major trends, transforming quiet stocks into active ones and ordinary price action into extraordinary volatility. Within this blueprint it is the **action trigger** atop everything already built: momentum establishes that strength persists, relative strength tells you *where*, volume and ATR tell you *when* and *how far*, the gamma squeeze provides the accelerator, and ignition is the precise flashpoint where all of it converges into an entry. Detect the spark within the rules, clamp onto the cascade with controlled risk, harvest the velocity—then rotate to the next one.

# Chapter 8
# Liquidity and Market Structure

## A. Market Makers — The Invisible Architects of Liquidity

When you flip capital tranches aggressively across high-beta stocks, leveraged ETFs, and options, you cannot treat the market like a vending machine. Behind every trade sits a structure, and at its center is the **market maker (MM)**—simultaneously your most vital partner and most dangerous adversary. Understanding how makers manage inventory, handle order flow, and extract their "tax" through the bid-ask spread is what separates a disciplined allocator from a retail gambler who gets quietly cannibalized by toxic liquidity. One clarification frames the chapter: market makers are not the enemy—they are mechanics who manage risk by rigid rules, and many of the most explosive opportunities in this book exist precisely because of how they hedge. Align with their flows; never fight them.

### What a Market Maker Is, and the Inventory Mandate

A market maker continuously quotes both a bid and an ask, standing ready to buy when others sell and sell when others buy—without that two-sided presence, many securities would suffer wider spreads and thinner liquidity. The modern makers—Citadel Securities, Virtu, Jane Street—are high-frequency operations dominating liquidity provision. Shatter the retail myth: makers are **not directional speculators**. Their model is non-directional—a buyer pays the ask, a seller hits the bid, and the maker pockets the spread.

***Retail buys at the ask and sells at the bid; the market maker captures the spread on both sides, thousands of times a day.***

That spread is not free money: to provide it, the maker takes the other side of order flow, exposing it to **inventory risk**. When an aggressive wave hits, the maker accumulates a large opposite position and must neutralize it before the market moves against it—continuously adjusting bids, asks, and hedges, which is how it participates in price discovery. The lesson is profound: many short-term price movements reflect maker inventory management rather than any fundamental development. The wiggle you are agonizing over is often just a desk rebalancing its book.

### Adverse Selection and Liquidity Holes

Two structural phenomena govern volatile, low-float instruments. **Adverse selection** is the maker's fear of informed order flow—filling an uninformed retail order is welcome, but discovering they are selling into a massive institutional block is adverse selection, so they widen the spread and pull quotes away from the toxic buying, which accelerates the very upward move you are riding. **Liquidity holes** form when, during macro shocks or violent ignition events, makers step away or widen spreads to extremes—a structural void where an asset skips multiple price points. Fire a lazy market order into that void and you absorb 2–5% of instant slippage. The hole is self-preservation, but it empties your account just the same.

## Market Makers in Volatility and Low-Float Names

Makers prefer orderly markets, so during earnings, FDA decisions, Fed meetings, and panics they widen spreads, reduce displayed liquidity, and turn defensive—exactly why traders see wider spreads and worse fills in those windows. In strong momentum stocks they become *reactive rather than predictive*, adjusting quotes as price runs, which itself fuels volatility expansion. Low-float names magnify everything: with few shares available, liquidity vanishes quickly and makers must adjust aggressively—which is why low floats produce explosive breakouts and squeezes *and* the worst slippage. Bigger squeeze potential and bigger execution danger travel together.

## The Options Engine: Delta Hedging and the Squeeze Connection

In the options market, makers are frequently the counterparty: when traders buy calls, makers sell them and hedge their short-delta exposure by **buying the underlying (delta hedging)**—mechanical flow that adds real buying and volatility independent of any opinion. This is the engine behind the squeezes covered earlier: in a **gamma squeeze**, call buying forces makers to buy stock, the rising price expands delta, and they must buy still more; in a **short squeeze**, maker hedging stacks on top of short covering. Tracking options flow and gamma exposure (GEX) is really tracking where maker hedging is about to fire.

## The Bid-Ask Spread: The Market Maker's Tax

The spread is the price of immediate liquidity, and it varies enormously: liquid 3x ETFs like TQQQ or SOXL trade penny-wide, allowing nearly friction-free compounding, while warrants and OTM options can carry spreads of 10% or more—meaning you begin already deep in the red. Never assume the posted bid and ask represent true depth; they are quotes, not guarantees. The discipline follows: **the blueprint forbids trading any instrument whose bid-ask spread exceeds 2% of the underlying price.** If the toll to enter is that high, the road is not worth taking.

## The Execution Playbook: Trading Around the Plumbing

Protecting the parent capital comes down to strict execution protocols. **The crossing-order rule:** use limit or marketable-limit orders (a limit slightly above the ask or below the bid for a fast fill without unlimited slippage); raw market orders are outlawed except when an automated trailing stop fires. **Exploit maker-taker fees:** a passive resting limit order earns a small rebate as a liquidity "maker," lowering frictional drag. **Respect order-book depth:** scale order blocks to the depth actually available—tight spreads and high volume allow confident pyramiding, thin conditions demand smaller size and patient limits. **Time the spread:** avoid the first couple of minutes after the open, when spreads are widest.

## Common Misconceptions

Many traders believe makers manipulate every stock and target retail. In reality they provide liquidity, manage risk, and earn spreads; they influence *short-term* behavior through hedging but do not determine long-term trends, which remain driven by earnings, growth, and institutional capital. Psychologically they are the opposite of the retail crowd—not bullish, bearish, or narrative-driven, but focused entirely on risk, inventory, and hedging—which is why understanding their mechanics lets you interpret unusual moves and liquidity shifts with far more accuracy.

### The Market Structure Governance Matrix

| Operational Axis | The Retail Gambler | The Blueprint Allocator |
|---|---|---|
| **Order routing** | Throws market orders into the book, treating slippage as a minor annoyance. | Deploys limit and marketable-limit orders to command the fill price. |
| **Spread assessment** | Chases illiquid warrants and options with 15% spreads, starting at a deep loss. | Filters for tight, institutional-grade liquidity; rejects spreads over 2%. |
| **Inventory awareness** | Assumes infinite depth that can absorb any size anytime. | Scales order blocks to the active order-book depth. |
| **Execution timing** | Trades the first two minutes when maker spreads are widest. | Waits for spreads to tighten or trades in peak-volume windows. |

### Risk, Survival, and the Execution Edge

Makers are not adversaries to defeat, but their mechanics punish carelessness: **slippage and adverse selection** (enter with limits, not market orders), **liquidity withdrawal** (in stress they widen spreads or pull quotes—avoid oversized positions you cannot exit cleanly), **fakeouts** (maker algorithms can manufacture brief momentum that reverses—demand the full confirmation stack), and **discipline** (risk ≤1% per idea, favor defined-risk options, monitor days-to-expiry). Treat execution like a surgical extraction.

### Final Principle

Market makers are the hidden infrastructure of modern markets, providing liquidity, price discovery, and continuity while shaping volatility, spreads, options pricing, and both gamma and short squeezes. The aggressive trader who understands them gains insight into how liquidity actually moves and why certain momentum events turn explosive—because behind every breakout and squeeze stands a market structure, and the maker is one of its principal architects. They are mechanics to align with, never enemies to fight.

## B. Dark Pools — Navigating the Institutional Shadows

To push a $100,000 portfolio to $1,000,000 in 180 days, you must track where institutional capital actually moves—and that is rarely where retail is looking. The retail trader stares at the lit order book believing it shows the entire market; the allocator knows the visible market is often a sideshow. **Dark pools are the hidden plumbing where institutional block orders are quietly matched outside the public eye to avoid moving the price.** The term provokes suspicion, but understanding them is not conspiracy thinking—it is tracking the footprints of giant participants accumulating or distributing *before* that activity registers on a retail chart.

## What a Dark Pool Is

Formally, dark pools are **Alternative Trading Systems (ATS)**—private, regulated venues that do not publish a visible real-time order book; matching happens privately and the completed trade is reported publicly only afterward. A dark-pool trade is not invisible forever, just not visible *before* it executes. They come in several forms: broker-dealer internalization pools (Citadel, Virtu), independent crossing networks (Liquidnet), exchange-owned, and hybrid venues. The scale is underestimated: off-exchange and dark trading now frequently runs around **40–45%** or more of total U.S. equity volume on heavy days, meaning the "public" lit price reflects only a little over half of true activity. This fragmentation is precisely why some breakouts seem to come from nowhere.

## Why Dark Pools Exist: Block Execution and Market Impact

Picture a fund wanting to buy two million shares of a mid-cap. Placing that openly on a lit exchange would trigger a liquidity panic—HFT algorithms front-run the giant bid and send price soaring, inflicting severe **adverse price slippage**. Dark pools solve this: the order is matched privately, frequently at the midpoint of the national best bid and offer, leaving only a post-trade print and essentially zero pre-trade impact. Users are overwhelmingly institutional, and the larger the order, the greater the value of dark execution.

## Reading the Shadow Tape: Form T Prints and the TRF

Hidden though they are before execution, dark pools cannot stay hidden afterward. By FINRA mandate, every dark-pool transaction is reported to a **Trade Reporting Facility (TRF)** and printed to the public tape within seconds, showing up as **Form T** or late prints—trades appearing outside regular hours, or massive blocks at identical price points mid-session. They are the ink the giants leave behind.

***You cannot see the order resting in the dark pool — but you can always read the ink it leaves on the tape after it executes.***

**The footprint of accumulation:** when a stock trades flat inside a tight 1% range while TRF data shows millions of shares quietly printing in blocks that dwarf normal retail flow, an institution is absorbing the float. **The footprint of distribution** is the inverse: a stock hovering near its highs while massive blocks keep hitting the tape *without* pushing price higher means a giant is liquidating into retail. Same large prints, opposite meaning—so direction, not just size, is what you read.

## How Dark Flow Creates Tradable Edges

Because dark prints often reveal institutional intent before it appears in price or lit volume, they slot into the momentum engine: large buy-side dark prints during a tight consolidation signal smart money building ahead of a breakout (**accumulation**); a surge in dark volume followed by a catalyst frequently precedes a lit breakout (**ignition precursor**); hidden buying in a high-short name quietly builds **squeeze fuel**; and a thin lit book plus heavy dark activity warns of an explosive move when that hidden liquidity surfaces (**liquidity insight**).

## The Tactical Playbook: Trading the Block Shadow

You do not trade *inside* dark pools—you read the prints through aggregators as a directional leading indicator. **The block-shadow breakout:** find a low-float equity or leveraged ETF showing a massive, uncharacteristic spike in dark block volume (often 200–500% above its normal trailing dark volume) while price stays compressed—an institutional floor being built in the shadows—then enter aggressively when it breaks on the lit exchange. **The dark-pool level defense:** if a large slice of a stock's weekly float (say 30%) was accumulated at a specific price (e.g., $45.00), that coordinate becomes ironclad structural support; on a pullback to it, enter with leverage and a tight stop just below the print, letting the institution's own risk management defend your entry.

## Tools and Signals for the Retail Trader

FINRA publishes ATS data on a two-to-four-week delay; near-real-time platforms (TradeAlgo, Unusual Whales, Cheddar Flow, Bookmap, TrendSpider, FlowAlgo) close the gap. Watch dark volume as a percentage of total, block size and direction (buy versus sell prints mean opposite things), divergence (heavy dark buying while lit price stays flat is the highest-quality tell), and liquidity heatmaps. None stands alone—read dark data alongside relative strength, volume, ATR, and options flow, letting it confirm a thesis rather than create one.

## Common Misconceptions

Four myths cause more bad trades than any data limitation. Dark pools are **not illegal**—they are regulated venues under FINRA and SEC oversight. **Not every dark print is bullish**—institutions sell through them as readily as buy. They **do not control prices**—long-run prices are still driven by earnings and capital flows. And dark activity **guarantees nothing**—it is one data point, never a standalone signal. The transparency debate is real: supporters say dark pools protect institutions from market impact and improve execution; critics say they erode pre-trade transparency and weaken public price discovery. Both are partly right, and the regulatory balance keeps evolving.

### The Dark Pool Governance Matrix

| Tactical Vector | The Retail Gambler | The Blueprint Allocator |
|---|---|---|
| **Market perception** | Believes dark pools are an illegal, rigged system built to steal from them. | Sees a regulated, predictable mechanism for institutional liquidity. |
| **Data interpretation** | Watches only retail chart patterns and lagging social sentiment. | Tracks TRF tape prints to see where the largest blocks are printing. |
| **Execution timing** | Chases breakouts blind to whether institutions are buying or selling. | Enters after confirming dark accumulation beneath a consolidation. |
| **Risk placement** | Sets stops at arbitrary percentages or generic moving averages. | Anchors stops tightly beneath heavy institutional dark-print clusters. |

### Risk, Discipline, and the Limits of Dark Data

Dark data is a powerful confirmation layer but incomplete in retail hands. The picture is **partial** (delayed, incomplete—use as confirmation, never a standalone signal), **asymmetry persists** (you read footprints, not access), **prints can deceive** (a block may be a sell, hedge, or distribution—read direction), and you must **demand multi-confirmation** (dark activity plus lit volume plus relative strength plus a catalyst, risk ≤1% per idea).

### Final Principle

Dark pools let institutions execute large trades and accumulate positions, and for the aggressive trader they offer a window into how professional money moves beneath the surface. Dark activity alone predicts nothing, but combined with institutional accumulation, relative strength, volume expansion, and breakout behavior, it becomes powerful context—because some of the most important activity in any market happens long before it becomes visible to the crowd, and the dark pools are often where it begins.

## C. Institutional Flows — Riding the Tides of Mega-Capital

If retail traders are the waves of the market, institutions are the tides—retail creates noise, institutions create trends. To transform $100,000 into $1,000,000 in 180 days, abandon the fantasy of "predicting" prices and master the physics of **institutional flows**. The secular moves that expand a stock 50%, 100%, or 500% are driven by the giant, slow-moving tides of institutional capital, which cannot move at the press of a button—it deploys over days, weeks, or months. Tracking that high-volume footprint is how you hook a lean portfolio block to an unstoppable locomotive.

## The Nature of the Whale: Why Institutional Accumulation Persists

Institutions operate under rules retail does not, and those rules make their buying persistent and predictable. **The allocation mandate:** a fund mandated to raise exposure to a theme is effectively *required* to buy regardless of "overbought" conditions. **The multiday execution footprint:** acquiring five million shares, it uses TWAP and VWAP algorithms to slice the order into small continuous blocks across many sessions. **The structural support floor:** because these programs run continuously, each dip toward the institution's average entry reactivates the algorithm, absorbing retail selling and defending the level—which is why strong stocks keep bouncing off support that looks arbitrary on a chart.

## What Institutional Flows Are — and Why They Move Markets

Institutional flows are the movement of large pools of capital into and out of stocks, sectors, and themes. Because the sums are vast, even small allocation changes have enormous impact—a pension fund shifting just 2% of a $100 billion portfolio represents $2 billion of pressure. The institutions in question—pension, mutual, hedge, and sovereign funds, insurers, endowments, banks, and ETFs—collectively manage tens of trillions and dominate ownership. Most traders fixate on news and indicators; professionals focus first on where the institutional money is moving, because capital flow consistently matters more than opinion.

***Price follows money — and institutional flows decide where the money goes.***

## Accumulation and Distribution: The Two Footprints

**Accumulation** is large investors building positions gradually across sessions, through dark pools, via algorithmic execution—its footprint shows as rising volume, strong closes, improving relative strength, shallow pullbacks, and repeated defense of support. Momentum follows accumulation. **Distribution** is the inverse—heavy selling volume, weak closes, repeated failures near resistance, declining RS, and rising volatility—and the edge is that it usually begins before the broader market notices, because price behavior reveals institutional intent before the news does.

## Sector Rotation and Theme-Based Flows

Capital rotates systematically: technology leads during innovation cycles, energy during commodity and power-demand booms, financials in rising-rate environments, defensives during uncertainty. Modern markets increasingly organize around **themes**—AI, semiconductors, cloud, cybersecurity, robotics, quantum, biotech, defense, renewables, digital assets—and when institutions embrace one, capital concentrates and momentum develops. In the 2026 landscape, leadership has broadened out of mega-cap tech into "real economy" beneficiaries—energy and utilities on AI data-center power demand, infrastructure, industrials, select biotech, and small- and mid-caps—alongside record ETF inflows.

## ETF Flows and the Visible Footprints

ETF flows have become one of the most powerful forces in modern markets: when money enters an ETF, the manager must buy the underlying holdings, creating buying pressure across an entire sector at once, amplifying trends (and outflows do the opposite, warning of distribution). Two visible footprints betray the hidden flow before filings confirm it: **relative strength** (stocks absorbing inflows outperform, resist weakness, and lead—the visible shadow of hidden capital) and **volume expansion** (repeated accumulation days and elevated relative volume). Price reveals direction; volume reveals commitment.

## The Footprint Metrics: Confirming the Flow

To verify heavy capital is flowing before a vertical expansion, look for three signatures together: **the block-trade count** (a spike in single trades exceeding roughly 10,000 shares or $100,000 in value—an institutional calling card retail can't match), **accumulation days at a 3:1 ratio** (over a 20-day window, up-days on massive volume and down-days on thin volume), and **rising institutional sponsorship** (an accelerating net-positive increase in funds reporting new long positions via 13F—focusing on the changes, not static holdings). The toolkit is now retail-accessible: ETF flow reports, 13F trackers like WhaleWisdom and Fintel (delayed ~45 days, for confirmation not timing), and dark-pool platforms. Flows accelerate hardest when they overlap a catalyst—earnings, M&A, policy, or AI-capex news.

## The Tactical Playbook: Riding the Tide

You do not step in front of the institutional freight train—you jump on the caboose. Enter at the **initial institutional breakout flashpoint:** price clearing a long-term consolidation on volume at least 100% above its 50-day average. Because institutional flows are large and persistent, these moves can trend smoothly for two to six weeks—an ideal environment for leverage. Rather than raw equity, capitalize with 60-delta options 30–45 days out, or compound through 3x leveraged ETFs (TQQQ, SOXL, leveraged energy) when the flow is theme-wide; warrants add asymmetry on smaller names. Keep capital risk anchored to a trailing 1% (1R) technical buffer.

## The Institutional Flow Governance Matrix

| Operational Dimension | The Retail Speculator | The Blueprint Allocator |
|---|---|---|
| **Trend stance** | Fades strong trends, shorts a stock simply because it "looks too high." | Aligns with the trend, knowing heavy inflows create an unstoppable engine. |

| Operational Dimension | The Retail Speculator | The Blueprint Allocator |
|---|---|---|
| **Volume analysis** | Watches price alone, ignoring whether volume is expanding or contracting. | Treats volume as the truth, verifying flow via block counts and accumulation ratios. |
| **Position sizing** | Gambles random percentages on gut feel and emotional conviction. | Scales size to the liquidity and average daily volume the inflow generates. |
| **Exit execution** | Sells at the first minor pullback out of fear, missing the macro move. | Trails a stop tied to institutional moving averages to ride the full trend. |

### Risk, Regimes, and Discipline

Institutional behavior shifts with the regime—adding risk in bulls, preserving capital in bears, chasing speculative sectors in liquidity expansions, rotating defensive in uncertainty. Following smart money is powerful but not infallible: **respect the lag and the crowd** (13F data is delayed; overcrowded flows reverse sharply), **demand confirmation** (pair inflows with RS, ATR expansion, and a clean breakout), **plan for risk-off** (flows can vanish in a high-VIX session), and **size and diversify** (≤1% per idea, cap any theme at 25–35% of the portfolio).

### Final Principle

Institutional flows determine where capital concentrates, which sectors lead, and which trends persist. Retail contributes volatility; institutions provide the sustained pressure that drives the major moves. The trader who reads flows can align with powerful capital movements, recognize accumulation early, and detect distribution before it is obvious—because in modern markets, price follows money.

## D. Options Dealer Hedging — The Invisible Hand of Forced Flows

Many traders believe stocks move primarily on earnings, reports, and sentiment. Those forces matter—but in modern markets, short-term price action is increasingly dictated by options activity and the hedging decisions of the dealers who sell those options. When traders flood an options chain, the dealers on the other side do not take a directional bet—they are forced, by their own risk systems, to buy or sell the underlying to stay neutral, and that forced, programmatic flow is one of the most powerful hidden engines in the market.

### The Forced Counterparty: Delta Hedging in Brief

When a trader buys a call, a dealer is almost always the writer, and by selling it the dealer becomes short the stock's direction. Because the business is collecting premium rather than gambling on direction, the dealer immediately neutralizes the exposure through **delta hedging**. Delta measures how much an option moves per $1.00 move in the underlying: a far-OTM call might carry a 0.10 delta (like 10 shares), an at-the-money call a 0.50 delta (50 shares). The instant a dealer sells a 0.50-delta call, it buys roughly 50 shares to flatten—so a desk selling 1,000 such contracts buys on the order of 50,000 shares. That is real, mechanical buying pressure, driven purely by risk management.

## Gamma: Why Hedging Becomes Self-Reinforcing

Delta is not static. **Gamma** measures how fast delta changes as the stock moves, and it is where the explosive energy is born: as price rises toward a cluster of heavily-owned call strikes, those deltas climb rapidly—0.10 to 0.30 to 0.50 to 0.90—and to stay neutral the dealer's algorithms buy more and more shares, pushing price higher, which expands deltas further, which forces still more buying. Pushed to its extreme this loop is the gamma squeeze; but the same mechanism operates, more quietly, every single day.

## Gamma Exposure and the Two Regimes

The aggregate of all this hedging can be estimated as **Gamma Exposure (GEX)**—roughly, how many shares the dealer community must buy or sell for each 1% move. It resolves into two opposite regimes, and knowing which one you are in is as important as any chart pattern:

***Positive GEX: dealers sell strength and buy weakness — volatility is dampened, price pins. Negative GEX: dealers buy strength and sell weakness — volatility is amplified, price explodes.***

In a **positive-gamma** regime, dealers lean against every move—selling strength, buying dips—which dampens volatility and produces "pinning" near high-open-interest strikes. In a **negative-gamma** regime, dealers are forced to chase—buying strength, selling weakness—which amplifies every move and manufactures the large swings and violent reversals that define explosive momentum. Aggressive traders thrive in negative-gamma conditions, because that is where variance expands; the regime is to dealer hedging what the VIX regime is to volatility.

## Strike Magnets, Pinning, and Expiration Flows

Open interest concentrates at round strikes—$50, $100, $150, $200—and heavy positioning there generates hedging that turns them into support, resistance, or trigger points; in a positive-gamma regime this actively **pins** price toward the high-open-interest strike into expiration. Expiration itself—**OPEX**—is now a major structural event: as contracts expire, hedges roll off and dealer exposure shifts abruptly, producing unusual volatility and sharp reversals. The explosion of **0DTE and short-dated options** intensifies all of this, their gamma changing so rapidly that hedging flows can dominate short-term price action far more than fundamentals. Dealer hedging is not confined to single names—the largest options markets sit on broad-market, tech, and sector ETFs, transmitting pressure across entire sectors, which is why an index move can seem strangely disconnected from any headline.

### Reading Dealer Positioning: The Toolkit

Dealer positioning is partly observable. Monitor **the core metrics** (options volume, open interest, implied volatility, aggregate GEX, dealer positioning, the expiration calendar), **the gamma-inversion trigger** (scan for assets entering short-gamma territory, typically when price breaks above a major strike carrying heavy open interest), and **the options-to-share volume ratio** (names where the options market's dollar volume exceeds the underlying equity's—when the options tail wags the equity dog, a burst of call buying overwhelms the float). Tools: SpotGamma, Unusual Whales, GEX monitors, and options-flow scanners.

### The Tactical Playbook: Trading the Hedging Flow

Align dealer flows with the full stack—relative strength, volume, dark-pool accumulation, institutional flows, and ATR—and let the hedging supply the propulsion. **Gamma-squeeze setup:** heavy call buying drives GEX negative and dealer hedging accelerates the upside—express it with OTM calls, debit spreads, warrants, or 3x ETFs. **Hedging-defined levels:** positive GEX builds floors and ceilings around big strikes, and a decisive break leads to accelerated movement as the regime flips. **Positioning for velocity:** buy short-dated, high-gamma options (7–14 days) just ahead of a major resistance or gamma-flip level, where dealer hedging can supply jet fuel carrying the trade 100–300% within 48 hours.

### The Dealer Hedging Governance Matrix

| Tactical Parameter | The Retail Speculator | The Blueprint Allocator |
|---|---|---|
| **Market viewpoint** | Believes stocks move only on earnings, news, or chart patterns. | Knows derivative flows and forced hedging often dictate short-term action. |
| **Strike selection** | Buys cheap, far-OTM 0.02-delta calls that expire worthless. | Buys at the gamma-flip zone to trigger the dealer buying engine. |
| **Volatility awareness** | Pays inflated premiums to dealers at peak retail hype. | Tracks IV skew, entering when dealer pricing is misaligned. |
| **Monetization** | Holds the squeeze too long and is crushed as dealers unwind hedges. | Sells into peak vertical acceleration, exiting as hedging exhausts. |

### Risk, Discipline, and the Mechanical Mindset

Dealer hedging is mechanical and cuts both ways: **expect the unwind** (hedging flows reverse violently after expiration or a gamma flip), **mind**

**theta** (long options bleed if momentum stalls), **respect amplification** (a short-gamma regime magnifies losses just as eagerly as gains), **don't fight the pin** (avoid fighting positive-GEX pinning without a strong catalyst), and **survive** (≤1% per idea, favor defined-risk spreads in high-gamma setups, monitor days-to-expiry).

### Final Principle

Options dealer hedging has become one of the most influential forces in modern markets, shaping liquidity, volatility, momentum, and both gamma and short squeezes. Dealers are not predicting direction—they are managing risk—yet that risk management generates pressure powerful enough to move entire stocks, sectors, and indexes. Price is increasingly the product of options positioning, dealer hedging, and market structure interacting, and reading that interaction is a genuine edge.

## E. Short Interest Dynamics — Reading the Pressure Gauge

Among the most misunderstood forces in modern markets is short interest. Most traders see it as a bearish bet against a company; in reality it is **stored market pressure**—a reservoir of future demand that can release with extraordinary violence. Where the Short Squeezes chapter dissected the squeeze *event*, this is the standing **pressure gauge:** how to read short positioning as a structural metric, quantify how loaded a spring is, and know *which* springs are most compressed before any fire. Preparation, not prediction.

### What Short Interest Is — and Why It Is Future Demand

Short interest is the total shares borrowed, sold short, and not yet repurchased—a direct measure of capital betting against a stock, and of potential future buying, because closing a short *requires buying stock*. When a heavily shorted stock begins rising, new buyers enter, institutions accumulate, shorts cover, and momentum traders pile in—demand spikes from multiple sources at once while available supply shrinks. That imbalance produces the explosive moves heavily shorted stocks are famous for.

***Every short position is a future buy order — short interest is stored demand waiting for a catalyst.***

### The Lending Market: Three Vectors That Load the Spring

To short, a trader borrows shares, sells them, and hopes to buy back cheaper—introducing three risk vectors, each a **measurable pain threshold**. **Cost to Borrow (CTB):** as short interest explodes, lendable supply collapses and the annualized borrow fee climbs from a routine 1% to over 100% on hard-to-borrow names, burning the short's capital daily. **Maintenance margin:** a short is marked to market daily, and once rising price breaches the threshold the broker issues a margin call. **The forced buy-in:** if the lender recalls shares, the broker buys the stock back at any price. Together these convert rising price mechanically into short buying.

## The Metrics: Quantifying the Pressure

Four metrics turn short positioning into a structural diagnostic, screened together. **Short interest as a percentage of float:** below 5% is low, 5–10% moderate, 10–20% elevated, above 20% significant squeeze potential, above 30% highly vulnerable (aggressive targets show 20%+ in mid- and large-caps, 15%+ in thin micro-caps). **Days to Cover** (the short ratio) estimates how many days of normal volume it would take for every short to exit:

***Days to Cover = Total Shares Sold Short ÷ Average Daily Trading Volume***

A reading above 5.0 signals a severe bottleneck; above 10.0, explosive potential. **Utilization rate** is the percentage of the lendable pool actually borrowed—**100% utilization** means the cupboard is bare, so no new shorts can enter and the asset is wholly exposed to an upward demand shock. The crucial caveat across all four: high readings are *potential energy*, not a buy signal. Without a catalyst, that energy may never release.

## Why High Short Interest Exists, and the Sentiment Gauge

Never assume a heavily shorted stock is automatically attractive—stocks become heavily shorted for reasons (deteriorating earnings, dilution risk, slowing growth), and sometimes the bears are simply right. It matters *who* is short: many positions belong to hedge funds and institutions with deep capital and conviction, which cuts both ways—when those institutions are wrong, their eventual covering in size becomes extraordinarily powerful buying. Extremely high readings also signal skepticism and disbelief, and paradoxically some of the strongest rallies begin precisely when sentiment is most negative, because a positive surprise lands with disproportionate force on crowded pessimism. Unlike a long who can hold forever, the short faces unlimited loss, mounting margin pressure, and daily borrow cost—so as losses accumulate, covering becomes involuntary, and the stock stops trading on valuation and starts trading on the survival of the people trapped against it.

## Short Interest Within the Structure: How the Layers Combine

Short interest rarely acts alone—it is the loaded-spring layer the rest of the section's machinery compresses and releases. The most explosive setups occur when it stacks with **institutional accumulation** (absorbing shares, leaving shorts vulnerable), **low float** (amplifying everything), **options dealer hedging** (call buying forces dealers to buy shares while shorts cover, stacking gamma and short pressure), and **dark-pool accumulation** (building hidden demand before lit price moves). Short interest is not a standalone bet but a coordinate on the structural map—it tells you which springs are most compressed.

## The Tactical Playbook: Reading the Gauge, Trading the Release

You never buy a stock simply because it is shorted—that is the trap. You wait for the **catalyst flashpoint** that triggers the reflexive loop: a real catalyst sparks long buying, rising price pushes shorts into their margin thresholds, brokers issue calls, and forced buy-ins hit—covering that then triggers dealer hedging and sends price vertical. The entry signature: a name with high short interest and elevated days-to-cover breaking above its 20-day relative high on volume at least 200% of its 50-day average. To maximize yield on forced capitulation, bypass the underlying and deploy into OTM, near-dated calls (roughly 0.30–0.40 delta)—as the squeeze triggers, exploding spot combines with an IV spike to expand those contracts 200–500% in days. Scale out ruthlessly into the vertical volume climax.

### The Short Interest Governance Matrix

| Tactical Parameter | The Retail Speculator | The Blueprint Allocator |
|---|---|---|
| **Asset selection** | Chases broken, bankrupt names with high short interest, ignoring borrow fees. | Targets turning or high-momentum names with tight utilization and a real bottleneck. |
| **Catalyst verification** | Buys blindly on social-media hype, hoping a squeeze appears. | Waits for a quantifiable volume explosion and breakout confirming shorts are squeezed. |
| **Risk management** | Holds through deep drawdowns, sure "shorts must cover eventually." | Anchors a stop below the breakout candle, risking 1–2R at most. |
| **Take-profit** | Holds for infinite gains and is caught in the violent post-squeeze collapse. | Scales out into peak volume acceleration and the liquidity climax. |

### Risk, Data, and Ironclad Rules

Short interest is potential energy, not a timing signal. **It can grind lower** (high short interest persists if the bears are right—require a catalyst plus technical confirmation), **unwinds are rapid** (exit ruthlessly on momentum divergence), **mind the liquidity trap** (thin floats inflict savage slippage—plan the exit before the entry), **beware overcrowding** (copycats produce fakeouts), and **respect the data lag** (reported roughly twice a month; near-real-time estimates from Ortex, ShortSqueeze.com, or Finviz help; risk ≤1% per idea, cap high-short themes at 20–25%).

### Final Principle

Short interest is powerful precisely because it is two things at once: current bearish positioning and future buying pressure. The strongest opportunities arrive when catalysts emerge, institutions accumulate, volume expands, and momentum accelerates together—the moment short sellers become unwilling participants in the very rally they bet against, and their simultaneous rush for the exit becomes one of the most explosive engines of price appreciation in all of finance. The bears' pain is the bulls' liquidity.

## F. Float Rotation — The Mechanics of Supply Exhaustion

Price movement is a pure function of supply and demand. In a typical large-cap, supply is vast—it takes billions to move price—but in high-velocity trading the gold standard is the opposite condition, and few concepts are as important, or as overlooked, as **float rotation**: the mechanical process in which a stock's entire tradable supply changes hands one or more times within a single session. When structural volume turns over the float, supply-and-demand dynamics permanently fracture—old overhead resistance vanishes because the entire shareholder base resets at a higher floor. This is why some stocks move 20%, 50%, 100%, or several hundred percent in days: price is driven not by value but by the speed at which ownership changes hands.

### Float vs. Authorized Shares: The Real Battleground

Separate corporate share structure from real tradable supply. **Authorized and outstanding shares** are the total a company may issue, including insider and lock-up stock—largely illiquid. The **public float** is the actual battleground: the unrestricted shares available for trading. A company with 100 million shares outstanding but 85 million locked up has a public float of just 15 million. The **micro-float sandbox**—public floats under 20 million shares, ideally under 10 million, common in small-cap growth, recent SPACs, and detached warrants—is a high-priority hunting ground, because institutional-grade volume hitting a micro-float guarantees a structural supply shock.

### What Float Rotation Is

Float rotation measures how many times the public float changes hands in a period:

***Float Rotation = Trading Volume ÷ Public Float***

If a stock with a 10-million-share float trades 50 million shares in a day, its float has rotated five times. This is *not* simply volume—it is how frequently the available supply turns over. Read the multiple as a live demand meter: **~1×** is normal elevated activity; **2–4×** is strong momentum; **5–10×** is extreme conviction tied to a squeeze or major catalyst, the fuel for parabolic moves; **10×+ over a few days** is extraordinary speculation. A stock trading 5% of its float attracts little interest; one trading 300% has become a market focus; one trading 1,000% is in a full speculative frenzy.

### The Mechanics of Supply Exhaustion: The Shareholder Reset

When a float rotates multiple times in a session, a complete shareholder reset occurs: a flood of volume overwhelms the small float, short sellers are run over with no shares to borrow or buy back, early retail buyers sell into the move for a quick 10–20% gain, and those blocks are instantly absorbed by high-conviction institutional and algorithmic buyers near the top of the range who have no incentive to sell. The cost basis of the entire market has shifted upward—the old sellers are gone, the old shorts are dead, and a new marketplace is established at a higher tier. This is **supply exhaustion:** with no overhead resistance left and the float held by fresh, committed hands, it takes only a microscopic amount of additional buying to send the asset vertical on thin liquidity.

### Why Float Rotation Drives Aggressive Compounding

Float rotation influences supply, demand, liquidity, and psychology at once. **Supply scarcity:** high rotation on a low float forces buyers to bid aggressively for a shrinking pool, powering breakouts. **Momentum confirmation:** rotation above 1–2× alongside improving RS, a volume surge, and ATR expansion validates real institutional or dark-pool flow. **Liquidity insight:** rotation signals genuine buying before price fully reflects it. Float size also dictates magnitude—large-float names travel slowly, while small-float names move dramatically on modest buying, which is why so many of the market's largest percentage gainers originate from low floats.

### Float Rotation and the Squeeze Engines

Float rotation is the connective tissue between the forced-buying events covered earlier. Paired with high **short interest**, a low float becomes combustible—as the float rotates, shares grow scarce and covering pressure detonates a squeeze. In a **gamma squeeze**, call buying forces dealers to hedge, further draining float availability. And persistent **institutional accumulation** (often visible first in dark-pool prints) shrinks the tradable float, raising sensitivity so future rotation becomes even more explosive.

### The Tactical Playbook: Trading the Rotation Flashpoint

The objective is to identify the precise moment of supply exhaustion. **The float-rotation screen** flags three intraday criteria at once: a public float under 20 million shares (ideally under 10 million), relative volume above 5.0, and intraday float turnover of 50% or more within the first 30 minutes pacing toward 150%+ by the close. **The high-leverage protocol:** once an asset has rotated its float past 100% while holding above VWAP, old resistance lines are irrelevant—weaponize the setup with at-the-money weekly options, or scale into a correlated 2x/3x sector ETF (LABU, SOXL, leveraged energy) if the rotation is theme-wide. Because the float has already turned over, a minor inflow can drive the asset 50–100% in hours, inflating ATM premiums by 300% or more.

### Liquidity Traps and the Float Rotation Cycle

The same conditions that create extraordinary upside create extraordinary downside. Rapid rotation produces **liquidity traps:** as volatility expands, liquidity appears abundant and participation accelerates—but the instant momentum weakens, buyers vanish, liquidity evaporates, and price collapses as fast as it rose. The thin float that powers the ascent makes the descent brutal, which is why your position in the cycle must be read continuously.

### The Float Rotation Governance Matrix

| Tactical Parameter | The Retail Speculator | The Blueprint Allocator |
|---|---|---|
| **Volume analysis** | Sees high volume and assumes the stock is overbought, about to crash. | Calculates volume-to-float ratios to detect a permanent supply dislocation. |
| **Resistance mapping** | Fears old resistance lines drawn from old charts months ago. | Knows 100%+ rotation wipes out historical overhead resistance. |
| **Risk management** | Sets wide, arbitrary stops, blind to the asset's intraday structure. | Anchors the stop at the VWAP or the high volume node of the rotation. |
| **Order execution** | Uses market orders at peak volume and absorbs heavy slippage. | Uses limit or stop-limit orders to enter at the structural breakout keys. |

### Risk, Psychology, and Discipline

Float rotation is psychology in motion, and that emotional acceleration is what makes low-float trading so dangerous. **Respect the two-way speed** (tight stops essential), **manage illiquidity** (thin floats gap—use limit orders and smaller size), **treat 5×+ as a climax warning** (extreme rotation often marks the top—scale out aggressively into it), **filter false rotations** (require the full stack—RS, ATR, options flow, a real catalyst), and **size for survival** (≤1% per idea, defined-risk options in low-float plays, avoid overnight holds unless the close is strong).

### Final Principle

Float rotation is one of the purest expressions of supply-and-demand dynamics—a direct measure of how aggressively participants compete for a finite pool of shares. The most explosive stocks share the same fingerprints: a low float, rising volume, a strong catalyst, elevated short interest, increasing options activity, and a rapidly rotating float.

This completes *Liquidity and Market Structure*, and the layers now interlock: **dark pools** reveal *who* is quietly accumulating, **institutional flows** are the macro tide beneath everything, **market makers** are the plumbing that processes every order, **dealer hedging** turns that plumbing from passive into actively propulsive, **short interest** is the loaded-spring gauge, and **float rotation** is the demand meter showing how violently a finite supply is consumed. Together they convert raw liquidity mechanics into a real-time map of conviction—align your entries with the footprints of the smartest money, route every order with surgical discipline, and let supply exhaustion do the heavy lifting toward the target.

# PART III – INSTRUMENTS OF AGGRESSIVE COMPOUNDING

# Chapter 9
# Trading Common Stocks Aggressively

## Momentum Stocks — The Individual-Equity Execution Layer

If long-term investing rewards patience, momentum trading rewards speed. In a **180-day** campaign, common stocks become high-velocity vehicles, and a momentum stock is more than a rising stock—it is an equity in rapid expansion driven by a powerful catalyst, institutional accumulation, and a structural supply imbalance. These are the market's thoroughbreds, attracting capital, volume, media attention, and new highs at once. This chapter unifies the Momentum, Catalyst, Gap-and-Go, Mid-Cap, and Market Structure sections into one objective: identifying, ranking, and trading the market's strongest momentum leader.

### What a Momentum Stock Is — and the Anomaly Behind It

A momentum stock shows sustained price appreciation with strong volume, rising demand, institutional buying, and superior relative strength—it rises faster than almost everything else. This rests on the momentum anomaly: assets moving fastest tend to continue short-term, fueled by institutional chasing and behavioral bias, and trends persist longer than expected, which is why amateurs sell leaders too early claiming they've "already moved too much."

### The Anatomy of Hyper-Momentum: The Velocity Signature

A tradable momentum stock has a recognizable structure built on three pillars. **The primary catalyst:** an undeniable structural change—an earnings blowout, a regulatory approval, a paradigm shift—that justifies institutions chasing at any price. **Elite relative strength:** complete independence from the index, so when the market is down 2% and the stock is flat or up 5%, institutional engines are absorbing market-wide selling. **The EMA ride:** the stock is in high-angle acceleration with the 8-day and 21-day EMAs fanned out above the longer anchors as a dynamic floor. The full sequence runs from a catalyst and volume surge triggering a high-angle breakout (RVOL above 2.5), into expansion where price rides the 8-day EMA and dislocates from the S&P 500 and Nasdaq, and finally into disposal once price extends more than three ATRs above the 21-day EMA—the visual fingerprint that separates a live momentum stock from one that has merely gone up.

### The Hyper-Momentum Screen: Finding the Top 1%

You do not guess which stocks become monsters—you use rigid filters to capture the top fraction of the tape. The screen flags names with **relative strength in the top percentile** over 1-, 3-, 6-, and 12-month windows (RS line breaking out or in the Leading quadrant of an RRG), **ATR greater than ~4% of price** for the range needed inside a 2-to-5-day hold, **volume intensity at or above 250%** of the 3-month average (RVOL above 2.5), **new highs or clean base breakouts** with rising ATR and ADX above 25, and **a fundamentals tilt** toward accelerating revenue in a hot theme. Scanners like Finviz, TradingView, and IBD relative-strength lists surface candidates daily.

## Stock Selection: Picking the Leader

The screen produces a list; selection is the art of ranking it. Focus on names printing new highs, new relative-strength highs, and clear sector leadership—leaders decline less during pullbacks, recover faster, and outperform consistently. Trade *with* sector leadership, never against it: the strongest stocks emerge from the strongest sectors—semiconductors during an AI build-out, biotech during breakthroughs, energy during a demand surge. Layer on **narrative**, because investors buy stories before they buy earnings. In the current cycle, leadership has broadened beyond mega-caps into AI power and infrastructure, biotech catalysts, and select high-growth small-caps.

## The Convergence Point: Where the Whole Toolkit Stacks

What makes the momentum stock the centerpiece is that it is the single ticker on which every force in this book stacks at once—institutional accumulation (the durable buyer), volume expansion (the confirmation), a tight float (the amplifier), elevated short interest (the squeeze fuel), dealer hedging (the gamma engine), and the catalyst (the ignition). The skill is recognizing their *convergence:*

***A true momentum stock is the one ticker where catalyst, relative strength, volume, float, short interest, and dealer hedging all stack at the same time.***

Highest conviction comes precisely when multiple forces align on the same name—the momentum stock is where the abstract structural forces of the earlier sections collapse into one concrete, tradable decision.

## The Execution and Compounding Protocol

Enter at the **momentum flashpoint**—the high-volume breakout of a pristine base, or the first structural pullback to the 8-day EMA—never by chasing a stock already extended 200% without a pause. Because deep-liquidity leaders permit it, deploy concentrated size: 10–25% of account equity per name (up to ~20–25% on the cleanest setups), held to 4–8 positions. Size every position by ATR so each trade risks the same fixed dollar unit, and anchor a razor-thin stop at the breakout-candle low or just below VWAP—limiting total risk to 0.5–1% of account equity per trade while leaving upside uncapped. Realize profits mechanically: sell roughly two-thirds into peak vertical acceleration (two to three ATRs above the 21-day EMA), trail the remainder on the 8-day EMA, then **rotate** the proceeds into the next qualifying leader. Sequential wins across three to five strong names—amplified where appropriate with long calls, debit spreads, warrants, or a thematic 2x/3x sector ETF—produce the outsized compounding math. Never fall in love with a winner.

## The Momentum Cycle

Most momentum stocks travel a recognizable progression—accumulation, ignition, breakout, momentum expansion, public participation, euphoria, exhaustion, then correction—and knowing the stage keeps you buying early-to-middle rather than into the top.

## The Momentum Stock Governance Matrix

| Operational Parameter | The Retail Speculator | The Blueprint Allocator |
|---|---|---|
| **Entry timing** | Chases a stock after it has run 200% without a pause, buying the top. | Enters at the flashpoint – the base breakout or first pullback to the 8-EMA. |
| **Risk management** | Uses no stop or a loose mental one, letting a failed trade become a bagholder. | Enforces an automated stop at a structural level, cutting at 1R without emotion. |
| **Position scaling** | Risks the same dollars on a quiet stock as on a volatile one. | Uses ATR-based sizing so every trade risks an identical dollar unit. |
| **Profit realization** | Holds for infinite gains and is wiped out when momentum reverses. | Sells two-thirds into peak acceleration, trailing the rest on the 8-EMA. |

## Risk, Psychology, and Survival

Momentum is as dangerous as it is powerful—the same volatility that creates extraordinary gains creates extraordinary losses. **Cut reversals ruthlessly** (momentum names can drop 30–70% fast on a missed catalyst—honor the stop), **respect overcrowding** (the most popular names suffer the most violent unwinds), **demand liquidity** (favor names with ~1M+ shares average daily volume), **cage and diversify** (≤1% per stock, cap the momentum basket at 30–40%, require the full stack, never chase an extended name), and **master the psychology** (sell strength into weakness and rotate; selectivity creates consistency).

## Final Principle

Momentum stocks are the engines of aggressive stock-market compounding—not every one becomes a major winner, but nearly every major winner was once a momentum stock. This is the **individual-equity execution layer** of the section, where the conceptual forces, the specific setups, and the structural toolkit converge on selecting and sequencing single-name leaders. Screen for the top fraction of the tape, rank for the genuine leader, concentrate at the flashpoint with risk caged to the penny, ride the 8-day EMA, sell into the vertical, and rotate into the next.

## Small-Cap Runners — Trading the Liquidity Vacuum

If momentum stocks are the engines of aggressive trading, small-cap runners are the rocket ships. Some of the largest short-term percentage gains in market history—100%, 300%, 500%, occasionally 1,000% in remarkably short periods—have come not from giants but from small companies hit by a sudden surge of interest. The blueprint reframes them: not speculative gambles but **highly localized liquidity vacuums** capable of booking 50–300% gains in a multi-day cycle—the most explosive and most dangerous vehicle in the book, traded with mechanical execution and zero emotional attachment, or not at all.

### What a Small-Cap Runner Is — and Why It Moves So Fast

A small-cap runner is a relatively small company—typically under $2 billion in market cap, often $300 million to $1 billion—whose stock enters a momentum phase where buying overwhelms supply. They move faster than anything else for a structural reason: a trillion-dollar company needs billions of fresh buying to move, but a small-cap with few shares and low institutional ownership can be dislocated by modest demand. A $50 million inflow barely registers on a $1 trillion giant but transforms a $100 million company—small size creates sensitivity, and sensitivity creates opportunity.

### The Liquidity Vacuum: Anatomy of a Runner

A true runner is born from a precise structural recipe. **The micro-float threshold:** a public float under 10 million shares, ideally under 5 million, so a sudden influx of buyers creates an immediate inventory crisis for market makers. **The low-dollar-volume illusion:** before the run these stocks trade under 100,000 shares a day, off the institutional radar, so when a headline drops there is no institutional block-selling to damp the velocity. **The structural catalyst:** explosive and easily digestible by retail and algorithmic scanners—a biotech FDA approval, a surprise government contract, an AI licensing deal—need not guarantee profitability, only attention. When millions of dollars of volume collide with a three-to-five-million-share float, ordinary matching breaks down and a runner is born.

***Small-cap runners aren't traded because they're cheap — they're traded because they're empty: price becomes a measure of physical scarcity, not corporate value.***

A runner ignites when the structural forces stack on one tiny name. **Low float** is the volatility amplifier (a 5-million-share float needs a fraction of the buying a 500-million-share float would), **float rotation** confirms the frenzy when the stock trades several times its float in a session, **volume expansion** of 5x, 10x, or 20x normal validates the move, **elevated short interest** of 20–30%+ adds squeeze fuel, and heavy call buying drags in **dealer hedging**. Layer on exceptional relative strength and a hot theme—AI power, biotech, quantum, energy—and the move can turn parabolic. The explosive runners are where several stack at once.

## The Three-Phase Execution Protocol

You operate like an assassin on a rigid three-phase lifecycle. **Phase 1 — the alert and absorption scan (9:30–10:00 AM):** scanners flag any $1–$15 name showing intraday relative volume above 10.0; rather than chasing the first print, wait for early volatility to settle and watch the first wave of retail buying get absorbed into a clean high-volume hold above VWAP. **Phase 2 — the float-turnover entry:** the entry triggers when the stock breaks its opening 15-minute high on volume proving at least 30% of the public float has changed hands, ideally above VWAP; allocate 10–15% of account equity on the riskiest micro-floats, stretching toward 20–25% only on the most liquid confirmed runners, held to 4–8 names, with the stop at intraday VWAP or the breakout-candle low. **Phase 3 — the parabolic scaling disposal:** runners spike vertically and end in halts or reversals, so scale out 50% into the first 50% move, raise the stop to break-even, and liquidate the rest into the afternoon volume climax (three to four times daily ATR), layering OTM calls, warrants, or a 3x sector ETF where it fits.

## The Dilution Trap: The Risk Unique to Small-Caps

The most important risk specific to small-caps is the **dilutive share offering.** Cash-burning companies use the very run you are trading to raise capital, issuing new shares through S-1 or S-3 shelf registrations or at-the-market (ATM) offerings—a surprise offering instantly floods the float, crushes the price, and pulls the floor out from beneath the crowd. The allocator evaluates cash burn and SEC filings *before* entering, confirming no active dilution can fire during the window. This is why you rent the scarcity, and vanish into the volume climax before the offering hits.

## The Small-Cap Runner Cycle

Most runners follow a recognizable sequence—dormancy, catalyst, momentum ignition, breakout, acceleration, public participation, euphoria, exhaustion, then correction or collapse—and the best opportunities come before public euphoria develops.

## The Small-Cap Runner Governance Matrix

| Operational Parameter | The Retail Speculator | The Blueprint Allocator |
|---|---|---|
| **Asset philosophy** | Falls in love with the drug or tech, sure it is the next giant. | Rents an illiquid chip in a temporary vacuum for hours — never owns it. |
| **Risk management** | Buys the parabolic peak on FOMO, then averages down into the crash. | Enters at defined pivots with an automated stop that cuts at 1R. |
| **Dilution** | Is blind to S-1/S-3 shelves | Checks cash burn and |

| Operational Parameter | The Retail Speculator | The Blueprint Allocator |
|---|---|---|
| **awareness** | and is wiped out by a surprise offering. | filings to rule out dilution during the window. |
| **Exit strategy** | Holds through the backside, watching a 100% gain become a loss. | Scales out into peak liquidity, exploiting the covering frenzy. |

### Risk, Psychology, and Survival

Small-cap runners are psychological events, and the same feedback loop that accelerates the rise makes the fall just as violent. **Respect the gaps** (runners can drop 50%+ intraday or overnight—use defined-risk options, never oversize), **demand liquidity** (favor runners with ~500k–1M shares or more), **treat rotation as a top signal** (extreme float rotation often marks the climax—scale out into strength), **filter false runners** (catalyst-less gaps fade fast), and **cage and journal** (≤1% per idea, cap the small-cap basket at 30–40%, cut losses fast, never average down).

### Final Principle

Small-cap runners combine small capitalization, limited float, powerful catalysts, volume expansion, momentum, and raw investor psychology—when those forces align, extraordinary appreciation can occur, but the same characteristics create extraordinary risk. This is the **high-velocity, high-risk extreme** of the section—the liquidity vacuum you step into as the float rotates and vanish from before the offering hits. Rent the scarcity, extract the multiplier, and disappear—the rocket fuel, used sparingly and never with reverence.

## Mid-Cap Breakouts — The Institutional Sweet Spot

Small-cap runners produce the rawest percentage gains but lack the liquidity to absorb large positions as your capital scales; large-caps offer effectively infinite liquidity but lack the daily volatility for rapid compounding. Between them sits the structural sweet spot: the **mid-cap breakout.** Mid-caps—broadly $2 billion to $10 billion, with looser definitions stretching toward $20 billion—have the institutional liquidity to let you deploy heavy concentrated slices without moving the market, yet retain enough elasticity to rip 20–50%, sometimes 30–150%, in a multi-day-to-multi-week burst. In this blueprint the mid-cap breakout is the primary compounding engine once an account grows too large for micro-cap constraints.

### What a Mid-Cap Is — and Why It's the Sweet Spot

A mid-cap sits in a distinct phase of the corporate lifecycle—larger than a speculative startup, smaller than a mature leader, frequently entering rapid expansion—which is precisely what makes it the market's sweet spot: the intersection of growth, liquidity, and institutional interest. Small-caps often lack liquidity and coverage; large-caps often lack explosive growth. Mid-caps frequently have both—proven models, accelerating revenues, expanding margins, rising institutional ownership—combined with the capacity for extraordinary moves. They have survived the most dangerous stages of development yet remain small enough to double.

### Why Mid-Cap Breakouts Work: Institutional Sponsorship Mechanics

Unlike small-caps, driven largely by retail and algorithms, mid-cap expansions are fueled by **institutional sponsorship shifts**, and three mechanics make them violent. **The mandate-restriction catalyst:** many large funds and ETFs are prohibited by charter from buying stocks below roughly $2 billion in market cap or under $5 a share, so the moment a high-growth company crosses into the mid-cap universe it unlocks a wave of mandated demand. **The liquidity pocket:** floats of roughly 20 to 100 million shares are tight enough that when three or four institutions build simultaneously, their combined buying forces an extended multi-week trend. **The catalyst trigger:** mid-cap breakouts anchor to high-quality institutional catalysts—accelerating earnings, margin expansion, a new product cycle, M&A, or AI-capex wins—rather than social-media hype. This accumulation, often visible first in dark-pool prints and ETF inflows, gives mid-cap trends their durability.

### The Confirmation Stack: Volume, Relative Strength, Narrative

No breakout should be trusted without **volume:** a move through resistance on two-to-five-times normal volume signals genuine participation, while a breakout on average volume frequently fails. **Relative strength** is the second confirmation—future leaders display exceptional RS before their largest advances, ideally rotating into the Leading quadrant of an RRG. Layered on top are **earnings acceleration** (beats that pull upgrades) and **narrative** (the strongest breakouts sit at the center of a major theme—AI infrastructure, semiconductors, cybersecurity, biotech, defense, energy). Trade in the direction of sector leadership.

### The Breakout Structures: VCP and the Base Patterns

Mid-cap breakouts emerge from recognizable bases—flat bases, cup-and-handle, ascending triangles, 52-week-high breakouts—but the premier setup is the **Volatility Contraction Pattern (VCP)**, because it compresses risk to its minimum before expansion. The sequence is precise: a primary uptrend advances 30–100% on heavy volume; volatility contracts through progressively shallower pullbacks—a first of perhaps 15–20% that shakes out weak hands, a second of 7–10%, a final of just 2–4% on which *volume dries to near zero*; then the pivot breakout crosses clean horizontal resistance on greater than 200% of normal volume. That volume pocket proves overhead supply is exhausted—there is no one left to sell, so it takes little fresh buying to send the stock vertical.

## The Execution Protocol: Concentration and the Razor-Thin Stop

The mid-cap setup permits the most aggressive concentration in the book, because deep liquidity lets you size up without destroying your entry. **Identification:** market cap $2–$10 billion, a multi-week base with two to four contractions each shallower than the last, a near-zero volume pocket on the final contraction, a float of 20–100 million shares, relative-strength leadership, and a breakout on expanding ATR with ADX above 25. **Allocation:** 15–30% of account equity per high-conviction name, up to ~25% on a pristine VCP, held to 4–8 positions. **The razor-thin stop:** just 1–2% below the breakout pivot or the low of the final cheat candle. That combination—heavy size, tiny stop—is what makes the mid-cap breakout the most capital-efficient setup available:

***A 25% position with a 2% technical stop risks just 0.5% of total account equity — maximum concentration, minimum risk.***

If the breakout is real, institutional algorithms hit the ask and the trade moves green within minutes, all but eliminating slippage. Hold the core as long as the stock closes above its 21-day EMA—capturing the full structural move—and pyramid into follow-through on rising volume and continued relative strength.

## Momentum Persistence: Why Mid-Caps Compound

The single greatest advantage of the mid-cap breakout is **momentum persistence.** Small-cap rallies explode and collapse within days; mid-cap breakouts, carried by institutional accumulation rather than retail froth, trend for weeks or months in an orderly fashion. That persistence is what makes them ideal compounding vehicles—it gives you time to pyramid into winners and let a single decision compound, because compounding thrives on persistence and mid-caps supply it more reliably than any other aggressive vehicle.

## The Mid-Cap Breakout Cycle

Most mid-cap leaders travel a recognizable progression—business improvement, institutional accumulation, emerging relative strength, base formation, breakout, momentum expansion, growing sponsorship, public recognition, then trend maturity—and the edge lies in identifying it before the breakout is obvious.

## The Mid-Cap Breakout Governance Matrix

| Operational Parameter | The Retail Speculator | The Blueprint Allocator |
|---|---|---|
| **Base analysis** | Buys wide, loose, erratic patterns and gets chopped up by intraday noise. | Waits for extreme volatility contraction proving supply is exhausted. |
| **Position sizing** | Stays small out of fear, never meaningfully scaling | Concentrates heavily (up to ~25%), leveraging deep |

| Operational Parameter | The Retail Speculator | The Blueprint Allocator |
|---|---|---|
| | the account. | liquidity for dollar gains. |
| **Risk management** | Uses wide, arbitrary 7–10% stops to compensate for poor entries. | Enforces a tight 1–2% stop right below the structural pivot. |
| **Selling protocol** | Sells for a quick 5% gain, missing the institutional trend. | Holds while price closes above the 21-day EMA, capturing the macro-move. |

### Risk, Discipline, and Survival

Not every breakout succeeds. **Filter false breakouts** (whipsaws are common during rotations—require volume and a real catalyst), **watch rotation risk** (leadership can shift abruptly—monitor sector RS and flows), **respect gap risk** (use limit orders and defined-risk options), **cage the capital** (≤1% per position, cap the mid-cap basket at ~40%, never average down, cut on a decisive close back below the breakout, never let a loss run past ~8%), and **stay mechanical** (sell into strength when momentum diverges).

### Final Principle

Mid-cap breakouts occupy a unique position: more stability than small-caps, more upside than large-caps, stronger institutional sponsorship, and greater trend persistence. This is the **scalable compounding engine** of the section—where the catalyst is the trigger and the gap-and-go is the intraday burst, the mid-cap breakout supplies the multi-week structural trend that lets a growing account deploy real size without choking on liquidity. Find the contraction, verify the exhausted supply, concentrate into the pivot with microscopic risk, and let the multi-billion-dollar funds escort your ledger toward the target.

## Gap-and-Go Setups — Exploiting the Overnight Liquidity Shock

Among short-term patterns, few have produced more explosive gains than the gap-and-go—stocks that gap up before the open, attract extraordinary volume, and keep advancing after the bell, routinely the biggest percentage gainers of the day. The retail public sees a stock open 10–15% higher and reacts with terror, assuming they "missed the move"; the aggressive speculator sees a **definitive catalyst shock** that bypassed the normal auction, trapped overnight short sellers, and forced institutional chasing from the first second. But one distinction governs everything: many stocks gap; only a few *gap and go*. The entire skill is separating genuine continuation from a gap destined to fade.

## What a Gap-and-Go Is — and Why It Works

A gap-and-go occurs when a stock opens significantly above its previous close *and then continues higher*. The gap forms because material new information arrives while the market is closed—an earnings beat, FDA approval, AI development, acquisition, government contract, or upgrade—and the market instantly reprices. The setup compresses opportunity: instead of waiting weeks, the trader encounters extraordinary volume, volatility, momentum, and institutional participation inside a single session, and where attention concentrates, capital follows.

## The Mechanics of the Overnight Shock

The gap forces an immediate structural crisis along two fault lines. **The short trap:** every overnight short is instantly pushed into a deep loss, and their protective stops—which are buy orders—cluster just above the open, waiting to cascade. **The institutional inflow bottleneck:** allocators waiting for confirmation are suddenly under-allocated and cannot wait for a dip, so they program algorithms to sweep the available ask from the opening bell. Together these create a violent liquidity vacuum with forced buyers stacked on both sides.

## Gap-and-Go vs. Gap-and-Fade

Not every gap continues. Many become **gap-and-fade** setups—early buyers take profits, enthusiasm cools, and the stock bleeds lower, often filling the gap entirely—usually from a weak catalyst, excessive pre-market speculation that exhausts demand, poor market conditions, absent institutional interest, or a gap running into major resistance. Distinguishing a genuine gap-and-go from temporary excitement is the most valuable skill in this chapter.

## The Pre-Market Qualification Matrix

Before the bell, the candidate must clear a baseline filter. **Gap magnitude:** roughly 4%+ for mid- and large-caps, or 12%+ for small-cap runners (broadly the 4–15% zone)—too small and it fills, too large and it risks opening exhausted. **Pre-market volume:** at least ~200,000 shares (ideally 3–10x average), proving deep overnight participation. **Structure and catalyst alignment:** the gap should break cleanly above a multi-week base or psychological resistance, powered by a real catalyst. **Supporting signals:** relative-strength leadership, bullish options flow, dark-pool accumulation, and elevated short interest. The disqualifiers matter as much: avoid low-volume gaps, gaps into major resistance, and any gap without a clear news catalyst.

## The Execution Trigger: The Opening Range Breakout

When the bell rings, an intense battle erupts between early profit-takers and institutional buyers, and the blueprint demands patience through it. Rather than buying the chaotic first print, let the **opening range** establish—the high and low of roughly the first 5 minutes (stretching to 10–15 on the most volatile names). The 5-minute high becomes the trigger pivot; the 5-minute low becomes the ironclad stop. Place a buy stop-market or marketable-limit order one tick above the range high, and the moment it fills, anchor the stop at the range low. A break of the range high on heavy volume proves institutional buying has absorbed the early profit-taking. For setups that never give a clean range break, a secondary entry is the **VWAP hold**—entering on a controlled bounce off VWAP with the same stop discipline.

## Position Sizing and the Monetization Protocol

Because gap-and-go setups run at extreme velocity, size every trade around the opening range's width using the fixed 1% risk unit (on a $100,000 account, 1R = $1,000):

***Stop Distance = 5-Min High − 5-Min Low · Position Size = 1R ÷ Stop Distance***

A wide opening range automatically downsizes the share count to keep dollar risk caged at 1R; a tight one allows a larger position. These are pure velocity plays, so the blueprint enforces a **momentum time-stop:** if the asset has not reached its +3R to +5R target within the first 60–90 minutes, trail the stop to the 15-minute VWAP or liquidate to cash. Scale out in tranches—perhaps a third into the first 20–30% surge—and liquidate into peak vertical acceleration rather than holding the gain until it evaporates by the close.

## What Makes the Gap "Go": The Confirming Forces

Continuation is never random. **Volume is everything**—extraordinary pre-market and opening volume and sustained participation confirm conviction; without it the breakout dies. **Relative strength**—gap-and-go winners become the strongest stocks that day, pulling in momentum traders, institutions, and fresh liquidity. **Low float and short interest** turn demand into scarcity, with covering adding a feedback loop. **Institutional participation and gamma**—sustained volume signals institutions sustaining the trend retail ignited, while heavy call buying forces dealer hedging. Low-float small-caps generate the largest moves, but mid- and large-cap gaps offer greater liquidity and more sustainable continuation.

## The Gap-and-Go Cycle

Most gap-and-go stocks travel a recognizable progression—catalyst, pre-market gap, volume expansion, opening-range formation, breakout, momentum expansion, public attention, exhaustion, then consolidation or reversal.

## The Gap-and-Go Governance Matrix

| Operational Parameter | The Retail Gambler | The Blueprint Allocator |
|---|---|---|
| **Opening behavior** | Panics and buys the 9:30 open without verifying the gap will hold. | Waits for the opening-range candle to close, defining a clear bracket. |

| Operational Parameter | The Retail Gambler | The Blueprint Allocator |
|---|---|---|
| **Risk insulation** | Trades with no stop and is wiped out when the gap fades and fills. | Anchors the stop at the opening-range low, capping downside at 1R. |
| **Volume analysis** | Ignores liquidity, chasing low-volume gaps with no backing. | Enforces a pre-market volume filter before allocating a dollar. |
| **Monetization** | Holds out of greed, watching the morning gain vanish by the close. | Liquidates into peak acceleration or the VWAP time-stop within hours. |

### Risk, Psychology, and Survival

Gap-and-go trading is as dangerous as it is profitable. **Expect fills and reversals** (require volume and momentum confirmation—never assume green at the open means up for the day), **respect the volatility** (lean on defined-risk options on the most volatile names), **mind liquidity** (stick to adequate average volume, plan the exit before the entry), **cap the activity** (≤1% per setup, two to four trades per day, never revenge-trade a faded gap), and **stay mechanical**.

### Final Principle

Gap-and-go setups are one of the purest expressions of momentum: a significant catalyst emerges, demand overwhelms supply, volume expands, and momentum continues after the bell. Within the section, the gap-and-go is the highest-velocity intraday expression of the catalyst—the overnight shock that compresses an entire revaluation into a single session. Caged by the opening-range breakout and fixed 1R sizing, governed by the momentum time-stop, it turns overnight news into intraday compounding rockets. Qualify the gap before the bell, let the range define your bracket, strike only the highest-quality continuations—and be back in cash before the move matures.

## Catalyst Trading — Weaponizing the Revaluation Event

If momentum is the engine of aggressive stock trading, catalysts are the ignition source. Nearly every major winner begins with one: before the rally, the breakout, the volume surge, there is almost always a catalyst that changes perception, expectations, and capital flows—and price follows expectations. Catalyst trading is the act of front-running the institutional revaluation of an asset: when a quantifiable catalyst hits the tape, it opens a gap between current price and new perceived fair value, and the market's scramble to bridge that gap creates a predictable, high-velocity trend.

## What a Catalyst Is — and Why Catalyst Trading Works

A catalyst is any event that causes investors to reassess a company's future—raising earnings expectations, reducing uncertainty, creating a competitive advantage, or shifting sentiment. The key concept is *change*. Stocks do not move on current reality—they move on future expectations: a stock at $10 reflects what investors currently believe, and when new information arrives, models are rebuilt, positioning changes, and price adjusts. Catalyst trading identifies those shifts before they are fully priced, and the larger the shift, the larger the potential move.

## The Catalyst Taxonomy: Noise vs. Alpha

Not all news moves stocks. Classify every catalyst by institutional impact into three tiers. **Tier 1 — structural/binary (high impact):** undeniable events that force immediate reallocation—FDA approvals or denials, pivotal Phase 3 readouts, confirmed acquisitions, major regulatory breakthroughs, and surprise earnings beats with raised guidance. **Tier 2 — tactical (moderate impact):** events that spark momentum but usually need a technical breakout to sustain—large contract or AI-capex wins, government and defense deals, confirmed M&A rumors, tier-one analyst initiations. **Tier 3 — retail noise (zero or negative impact):** generic press releases, vague "strategic partnership" announcements, and pure social-media hype, frequently trap catalysts engineered to provide exit liquidity for insiders. The magnitude of the catalyst tends to determine the magnitude of the move.

## The Anatomy of a Revaluation

When a Tier 1 catalyst hits, the asset undergoes a **phase transition:** its price is no longer governed by the old technical trend but by the urgent need for funds to adjust sector weightings. The catalyst disseminates instantly, high-frequency algorithms trigger off sentiment while institutional block desks scale positions, and the dislocation breaks resistance, squeezes shorts, and drives vertical expansion. Crucially, the move does not end when the headline goes stale—because institutional buying executes over days, weeks, or months, a major catalyst's impact persists far longer than retail expects, and underestimating that persistence is one of the most common ways traders exit too early.

## Confirmation: Volume, Relative Strength, and Reaction

The market's reaction—not the headline—reveals a catalyst's true significance, because the market sometimes sells good news and sometimes ignores it. **Volume** validates the catalyst (a move on 3x, 5x, or 10x normal volume signals genuine participation), **relative strength** confirms it (a stock responding to meaningful news outperforms its peers and sector), and the **reaction** itself is the final arbiter—trade what the tape does, not what the press release says it should.

***Trade the market's reaction to the catalyst — the volume, the relative strength, the price — never the headline alone.***

## The Execution Framework: Trading the Discovery Window

You follow a mechanical protocol that captures the institutional wave while minimizing exposure to the "sell-the-news" reversal. **Step 1 — the pre-trade qualifier:** evaluate the sentiment-to-price delta—if the stock has already run into the event, the catalyst is priced in and the trade is a fade; favor catalysts on names consolidating for 10–20 sessions, and for scheduled events build a partial pre-event position through defined-risk options. **Step 2 — the discovery window (9:30–10:00 AM):** never market-buy the first second; let the 15-minute opening range establish, and if price holds above morning VWAP and breaks the 15-minute high on relative volume above 3.0, the catalyst has institutional validation. **Step 3 — scaling and sell-the-news protection:** enter on the break with a tight stop at the 15-minute low (1R), sell roughly half into the first major exhaustion spike one to two hours after the open, and exit the rest if price closes back below the 30-minute VWAP. Scale the hold to the tier—a Tier 3 catalyst is a same-day event never held overnight, while a Tier 1 structural revaluation can be pyramided for days or weeks as long as RS and volume confirm. Pure binary events can gap 30–70% overnight, so size small and express them through straddles, strangles, or capped-risk debit spreads.

## Catalyst Interactions: Stacking the Probabilities

A catalyst is most explosive when it lands on the structural forces built earlier. On a heavily shorted name, a positive surprise forces covering; options markets frequently move *before* the stock, with unusual call volume and rising IV acting as an early-warning system and the dealer hedging that follows amplifying the move; and dark-pool prints reveal pre-positioning before the lit price reacts. The edge comes from stacking probabilities—relative strength plus flows plus short interest plus a real catalyst, all pointing the same way.

## The Catalyst Trading Cycle

Most catalyst trades travel a recognizable arc—catalyst emerges, market notices, volume expands, momentum ignites, institutional participation, public awareness, momentum expansion, exhaustion, then consolidation or reversal.

## The Catalyst Governance Matrix

| Operational Axis | The Retail Gambler | The Blueprint Allocator |
|---|---|---|
| **Information processing** | Reads the headline and buys on a gut feeling about the news. | Quantifies impact via RVOL and price displacement in the first 15 minutes. |
| **Position timing** | Chases the stock while it spikes 20%+, buying the local top. | Enters only after a 15-minute base confirms institutional absorption. |
| **Risk** | Removes stops, hoping a | Cuts at 1R the instant price fails |

| Operational Axis | The Retail Gambler | The Blueprint Allocator |
|---|---|---|
| **management** | bad reaction recovers. | to hold VWAP, regardless of the news. |
| **Duration** | Hopes the stock grows long-term because of the news. | Scales the hold to the catalyst tier, exiting before the hype peaks. |

## Risk, Psychology, and Survival

Not every catalyst produces a profitable trade. **Respect the negative surprise** (a wrong-way binary move can erase 30–70% overnight—size small, lean on defined-risk options), **anticipate the volatility crush** (post-event IV collapses and can destroy long premium even on a correct call—exit or roll quickly), **assume fading momentum** (many catalysts produce a one-day pop—require confirmation before holding multiple days), **keep a catalyst calendar** (≤1% per idea, limit concurrent events, never revenge-trade a miss), and **stay probabilistic** (a headline is not a business model).

## Final Principle

Catalyst trading identifies events capable of changing market expectations and capitalizes on the momentum that follows—the strongest become extraordinary opportunities when they combine with institutional accumulation, volume expansion, relative strength, and favorable conditions. This chapter opens *Trading Common Stocks Aggressively*, where structural understanding becomes a repeatable machine: the catalyst is the trigger, and momentum, relative strength, volume, ATR, dark pools, institutional flows, dealer hedging, and short interest are the confirmation stack that tells you which catalysts are real. Classify the event honestly, demand confirmation from the reaction, execute through the discovery window with caged risk, and scale the hold to the tier.

# Chapter 10
# ETFs and Leveraged ETFs

## A. Sector ETFs

To scale $100,000 toward $1,000,000 in 180 days, a trader cannot diversify across the whole market—**diversification breeds average returns.** In this blueprint, sector ETFs and their leveraged counterparts are systemic macro-shuttles, the tactical backbone of rotation. When a powerful catalyst hits an entire industry, picking a single stock injects idiosyncratic risk—an accounting scandal or operational failure while the rest of the sector rockets upward. A sector ETF removes that risk and captures the pure beta of the macro-theme: treat the unleveraged fund as the base layer and the 2x/3x version as the accelerator.

### What a Sector ETF Is

A sector ETF tracks a specific industry, so instead of one stock you own a basket—instant diversification within a targeted slice. The standard sectors span technology, semiconductors, financials, healthcare, biotech, energy, utilities, industrials, materials, consumer discretionary and staples, real estate, and communications, with thematic overlays like cybersecurity and AI.

### Why Sectors Lead Stocks

Professionals watch sectors first, for one reason: **money usually flows into a sector before it flows into its stocks.** When institutions add exposure to AI, semiconductors, biotech, or energy, they frequently begin by buying the sector ETF, and those flows lift the underlying names. Strong stocks come from strong sectors—identify the leading sector and the stock-selection problem mostly solves itself.

### Sector Rotation: The Core Mechanic

Markets rotate continuously as conditions evolve, and recognizing rotation early lets you stand in front of the next wave rather than chase the last. **Economic expansion** favors technology, consumer discretionary, and industrials; **rising commodity prices** favor energy, materials, and natural resources; **economic uncertainty** favors healthcare, utilities, and staples. The trigger you trade is **relative strength**: track each sector index against the S&P 500 (SPY), and when a sector's RS line breaks out to multi-month highs versus SPY, institutions are rotating into that group—the cleanest signal a fresh leadership wave has begun.

### The Leverage Overlay

Overlay 2x or 3x leverage and a sector wave becomes a velocity engine—a sector gaining 5% can produce roughly +10% in a 2x fund and +15% in a 3x fund over short periods. The full daily-rebalancing mathematics live in the 2x and 3x chapters; the short version is that **leverage rewards persistent direction and punishes sideways noise.**

> **The overlay rule:** leverage the sector, not the stock. When an institutional wave hits an industry, the whole tide rises — so you capture the entire fund flow through a liquid leveraged ETF and bypass single-company landmines entirely. Use leveraged sector funds only for short-to-medium trending moves (days to a few weeks) in confirmed regimes; never camp in them through chop.

## A Field Guide to the Major Sectors

| Sector | What It Tracks and What Moves It |
|---|---|
| Technology | Software, cloud, hardware, networking, digital infrastructure; leads risk appetite and produces many of the market's largest winners |
| Semiconductors | The center of AI, data centers, autonomous vehicles, robotics; a frequent leadership vehicle that often leads both up and down |
| Biotech / Healthcare | Pharma, devices, diagnostics, innovators; driven by FDA approvals, trial results, M&A, and demographics — high volatility, sharp momentum |
| Energy | Producers, refiners, pipelines, infrastructure; driven by commodity prices, geopolitics, and supply shocks — a leader during commodity booms |
| Utilities | Regulated power and electricity; an increasingly structural play on AI-driven data-center power demand |
| Financials | Banks, insurers, brokers, asset managers; benefit from rising rates, expansion, and active capital markets |
| Industrials / Materials | Infrastructure, defense, reshoring, capex cycles; geared to the "real economy" build-out |
| Cybersecurity | Network, cloud, and endpoint defense; a durable structural-growth theme tracked as a basket rather than one name |
| Artificial Intelligence | Chips, cloud, software, data centers, AI infrastructure; thematic flows often begin at the ETF level |

## Key Sector Vehicles

*Core (unleveraged) — the base layer: high liquidity, tight spreads, low decay, deep options chains.*

| Ticker | Sector / Use |
|---|---|
| XLE — Energy Select Sector SPDR | Oil, power demand, and energy services |

| Ticker | Sector / Use |
|---|---|
| XLU – Utilities Select Sector SPDR | Direct AI-power play; multi-year structural shift |
| XLI – Industrials Select Sector SPDR | Infrastructure, defense, reshoring |
| XBI / IBB – Biotech | Catalyst-driven: M&A and clinical trials |
| XLK – Technology (with SMH for semis) | AI / semiconductor core; use selectively in rotations |

*Leveraged (2x/3x) – the accelerator, for short-to-medium trending moves only:*

| Ticker | Sector / Use |
|---|---|
| SOXL – Direxion Daily Semiconductor Bull 3X | AI / semiconductor rocket; frequent top performer in rallies |
| UTSL – Direxion Daily Utilities Bull 3X | Pure power / AI-demand leverage |
| LABU – Direxion Daily S&P Biotech Bull 3X | Biotech catalyst amplifier |
| Energy leveraged (e.g., NRGU 3X; ERX 2X) | Oil and power-services spikes – confirm true multiple |
| DFEN, TECL, and sector 2x/3x | Defense, technology, industrials, and materials strikes in rotations |

## The Tactical Playbook: The Sector Rotation Engine

You do not buy leveraged sector ETFs because you "feel bullish"—you wait for a measurable institutional wave. **The relative-strength trigger:** the sector must print a multi-month breakout on its RS line versus SPY, with the leveraged ETF's volume surging well above normal (a 200%+ surge is a strong tell) and regime filters confirming (ADX above 25, rising volume). **Entry:** stack confirmations—breakout, volume surge, genuine catalyst—building the unleveraged base first, then adding leverage on confirmed strength. **Sizing:** because a sector ETF carries no single-stock bankruptcy risk, concentrate—commonly 30–40% of the account into a single liquid 3x sector ETF during a prime rotation—while capping any one sector at 30–50%, risking ≤1% per idea, and trading only top-tier vehicles (~$50M+ daily dollar-volume). **The risk and exit matrix:** anchor protection to the unleveraged sector chart (a ~2x ATR stop or a line below structural support), and once the move goes vertical, trail with a 10-day moving average—the moment the ETF closes below it, the macro-wave is fragmenting, so liquidate to cash.

**Worked example — $100,000 account** An energy/utilities rotation strengthens on ETF inflows and AI power-demand news. Allocate ~25% to an XLE/XLU base plus 15–25% to a leveraged vehicle (UTSL or an energy 2x/3x) or calls on the leaders. Trail with ATR-based stops anchored to the unleveraged chart, and scale out on momentum divergence or a rotation signal. Then rotate realized gains into the next sector — say biotech on an M&A wave. Sequential 30–100%+ sector swings compound rapidly when each entry is a confirmed institutional wave rather than a guess.

## The Leveraged Sector Governance Matrix

| Parameter | The Retail Speculator | The Blueprint Allocator |
|---|---|---|
| Holding horizon | Holds a 3x sector ETF for months through choppy tape, letting decay destroy principal | Rents the vehicle strictly during directional trends; intraday to multi-day |
| Asset selection | Trades illiquid leveraged ETFs with wide spreads, bleeding to slippage | Uses only top-tier, ultra-liquid vehicles ($50M+ daily dollar-volume) |
| Risk insulation | Averages down on a declining fund inside a structural downtrend | Never averages down; stops dictated by the unleveraged index chart |
| Objective focus | Guesses which micro-cap wins the sector race — often the one that fails | Captures the entire institutional flow, bypassing company-specific landmines |

## Risk, Liquidity, and Survival

**Leverage decay:** 2x/3x products erode in chop—deploy only in confirmed trends (ADX above 25, strong volume). **Whipsaw rotations:** false leadership changes are common—require relative strength plus flows plus a catalyst. **Liquidity and correlation:** sector ETFs are liquid but can gap hard on macro shocks. **Discipline:** cap any one sector at 30–50% at peak conviction, risk ≤1% per idea, keep stops mechanical.

## The Psychology of Sector Leadership

Sector leadership is collective belief made visible: investors constantly ask which industries will grow fastest, and capital flows toward the answers, so price becomes a real-time readout of expectations. Reading that readout, rather than arguing with it, is the edge.

## The Sector ETF Cycle

Most sector trends follow a recognizable progression—narrative emerges, institutional interest develops, ETF inflows increase, relative strength appears, stock leadership develops, public participation increases, momentum accelerates, saturation stretches valuations, then rotation begins as leadership shifts elsewhere.

### Final Principle

Sector ETFs align you with one of the most powerful forces in markets—institutional capital flows. The strongest winners emerge from sectors attracting money, attention, and momentum, so learn to read sector leadership and relative strength and you participate in an entire wave instead of betting on a single name. Used as the base layer with leverage as the accelerator, sector ETFs are the executable core of the rotation framework. **Buy the haystack. Ride the wave. Rotate on the crack.**

## B. 2x Leveraged ETFs

*If momentum stocks are race cars, 2x leveraged ETFs are race cars with turbochargers*. The retail crowd dismisses 2x funds as a boring middle ground between 1x tracking and the hyper-volatile 3x rockets; the allocator knows better. In a compressed sprint, 2x ETFs are your high-capacity structural anchors during intermediate regimes—the "cruising gear." When a segment is in a strong, persistent trend but ATR is historically high, a 3x vehicle exposes the ledger to catastrophic intraday stop-out risk, while the 2x grants double the directional velocity with enough breathing room to avoid being shaken out by noise. Used recklessly, they accelerate losses just as fast.

### What a 2x ETF Actually Is

A 2x ETF delivers approximately twice the *daily* performance of a benchmark—the index rises 1%, the fund seeks +2%; it falls 1%, the fund seeks −2%. The key word is **daily**, and that single word governs everything. The leverage is manufactured through derivatives—swaps, futures, options—not by borrowing cash, so the trader obtains leveraged participation through an ordinary brokerage account.

### Why Aggressive Traders Use 2x ETFs

Aggressive traders use 2x ETFs for **enhanced returns** (a sustained trend produces materially larger gains on the same view), **capital efficiency** (less capital controls greater exposure), **diversification** (a whole sector rather than one name), **liquidity** (the major funds trade millions of shares with active options chains), and **simplicity** (no margin account required).

### The Mathematics of Leverage — and of Decay

Leverage magnifies both directions: an index up 10% may lift a 2x fund ~20% before fees, and a 10% drop cuts it ~20%. Because leverage resets every day, returns are **path-dependent**—a 2x ETF promises only approximately twice the move *each day*, so over time the sequence of up and down days, not just net direction, determines the result. Critically, volatility decay does not scale linearly—it scales roughly with the *square* of the leverage factor. Watch a choppy two-day round trip that returns the index to break-even (Day 1: +10%, Day 2: −9.09%):

| Instrument | Day 1 | Day 2 | Capital Retained | Volatility Penalty |
|---|---|---|---|---|

| Instrument | Day 1 | Day 2 | Capital Retained | Volatility Penalty |
|---|---|---|---|---|
| 1x (unleveraged) | +10% | −9.09% | **100.00%** | none |
| 2x leveraged | +20% | −18.18% | **98.18%** | −1.82% |
| 3x leveraged | +30% | −27.27% | **94.55%** | **−5.45%** |

This is why the 2x fund is the allocator's scale engine: it **mutes structural erosion**, letting you camp on a major macro-trend without watching principal evaporate during routine pullbacks.

### Why 2x Often Beats 3x

2x often beats 3x: **lower volatility drag** (it erodes far more gently in choppy tape, capturing most of the intended multiple with a smoother curve), **better for rotation** (easier to hold through minor pullbacks and sector shifts), **liquidity and options** (active chains allow call overlays without the hair-trigger sensitivity of 3x), and a **holdable horizon** (suited to multi-day and multi-week holds where 3x decay becomes punishing).

### Where 2x ETFs Shine: Trends, Sectors, and Rotation

Strong, sustained trends are the lifeblood of leveraged-ETF trading—trend persistence is the friend of leverage, choppy stagnation its enemy. The greatest structural edge is **sector rotation**: when institutional capital rotates toward technology, semis, energy, or AI infrastructure, a leveraged sector fund amplifies the whole wave. And leverage runs both ways—bullish 2x funds profit from rising prices, inverse 2x funds from falling ones.

> **Counterintuitive but true:** a 2x sector ETF can be safer than a single stock. A lone name can be wrecked by an earnings miss, a lawsuit, an accounting scandal, or a product failure; a sector basket diffuses that idiosyncratic risk across many holdings. You accept higher volatility from leverage in exchange for shedding single-company blow-up risk – often a favorable trade for an aggressive trader.

### Key 2x Vehicles for the Blueprint

| Theme | Representative 2x Vehicles |
|---|---|
| AI / Tech / Semiconductors | Direxion Daily AI & Big Data Bull 2X (AIBU); select single-stock 2x (NVDA, GOOGL, ARM) |
| Biotech / Healthcare | ProShares Ultra Nasdaq Biotechnology (BIB); 2x healthcare plays |
| Energy / Utilities (power demand) | ProShares Ultra Bloomberg WTI Crude (UCO); Ultra Energy (DIG); 2x utilities |

| Theme | Representative 2x Vehicles |
|---|---|
| Broad / Thematic | Ultra S&P 500 (SSO); Ultra QQQ (QLD); sector Ultra funds (industrials, materials) |
| Single-stock 2x (selective) | Leveraged single names (e.g., Tesla, Nvidia) – extra torque, higher idiosyncratic risk |

### The Tactical Playbook

You deploy 2x leverage as a specific position-sizing alternative when conditions call for size over raw speed. **The volatility-swapping rule:** when a core index breaks out but its 14-period ATR is highly expanded, a technical stop on a 3x fund must sit extraordinarily wide, forcing the sizing algorithm to shrink the share count under a fixed 1% risk unit (1R = $1,000); swap to the 2x alternative (QLD, SSO) and intraday variance is effectively halved, letting you deploy **double the position mass inside the same 1R cash boundary. The trend-splicing protocol:** during a healthy pullback to a rising 50-day MA, avoid options (IV over-inflates premium) and 3x (a further dip could trigger an account-shredding stop-out)—instead accumulate a concentrated 30% block of the 2x ETF at the touchpoint. **Execution:** use 2x as the core leveraged layer (~15–40%) on top of unleveraged ETFs or stock, entering on breakout + catalyst + flows in trending regimes (low-to-moderate VIX, ADX above 25), risking 1% max with ATR-based stops.

> **Worked example — $100,000 account** An AI-power rotation strengthens as utilities and energy see data-center-driven inflows. Allocate ~20% to an unleveraged XLU/XLE base plus 20–30% to a 2x utilities or energy vehicle (e.g., DIG or UCO), adding modest call overlays for gamma. Risk 1% max with ATR-based stops. Pyramid on follow-through, trail on divergence, then rotate realized gains into the next 2x theme (say biotech on M&A). Sequential 25–80% swings in 2x vehicles compound efficiently – with materially less decay risk than 3x.

### The 2x Leverage Governance Matrix

| Parameter | The Retail Speculator | The Blueprint Allocator |
|---|---|---|
| Asset selection | Calls 2x "inefficient"; chases the flashiest daily gainer | Deploys 2x intentionally to optimize position sizing in high-ATR trends |
| Decay mitigation | Holds leveraged funds through deep sideways chop, ignoring slippage | Uses 2x to minimize beta drag when an index enters wider consolidation |
| Risk insulation | Averages down as the trend breaks, expanding exposure into weakness | Locks initial risk at 1R, with stops based on the unleveraged index floor |

| Parameter | The Retail Speculator | The Blueprint Allocator |
|---|---|---|
| Capital mobilization | Commits a slice too small to move the ledger | Concentrates liquid blocks up to ~30% to scale the account safely |

### Risk, Discipline, and Survival

Because leverage magnifies mistakes, risk management is the strategy, and survival is the first priority. **Cap risk at 1% per idea**, **cap total leveraged exposure** at roughly 40–50% of the portfolio, **favor 2x over 3x** whenever trend strength is moderate or the hold exceeds one to two weeks, and **demand a trend** (avoid long holds in choppy tape). The recurring errors—ignoring decay, oversizing, trading without a confirmed trend, holding through consolidations—are all magnified by leverage, which is exactly why discipline matters more, not less. **Emotion is the enemy of compounding.**

### The 2x ETF Cycle

Most leveraged-ETF trades follow a recognizable progression—sector leadership emerges, institutional flows increase, momentum accelerates, trader participation expands, leveraged-ETF demand grows, the trend matures, then rotation begins as leadership shifts.

### Final Principle

2x ETFs are the versatile middle ground between common-stock runners (high alpha) and 3x funds (pure rocket fuel), bundling leverage, diversification, liquidity, and sector exposure into one instrument—but **leverage is a tool, not a strategy. Smoother torque. Less decay. Survivable risk.**

## C. 3x Leveraged ETFs

*If the 2x fund is the cruising gear, the 3x leveraged ETF is the booster rocket.* These funds deliver roughly triple the daily return of an index or sector, turning a moderate 5–15% move in a strong trend into a 15–45%+ swing that can accelerate a $100k → $1M path in days or weeks. They are not buy-and-hold assets—they are high-velocity instruments engineered for explosive expansion during strong, highly directional regimes, the high-octane finisher for confirmed momentum, breakouts, and catalyst-driven moves.

### What a 3x ETF Actually Is

A 3x ETF produces approximately three times the *daily* return—the index gains 2%, the fund seeks +6%; it loses 2%, the fund seeks −6%. The emphasis on **daily** is critical: many wrongly assume it delivers exactly triple the long-term return, and it does not. The leverage is manufactured internally through OTC equity swaps, futures, and options with prime-brokerage counterparties—exposure substantially larger than the capital invested—so both gains and losses are magnified threefold.

### Why Aggressive Traders Reach for 3x

Aggressive traders reach for 3x for **maximum torque** (in strong directional moves it amplifies compounding faster than 2x), a **short-duration edge** (best for 1–10 day holds during momentum ignition, gap-and-go, or catalyst events, minimizing daily-reset decay), and **capital efficiency** (a small amount expresses a large macro view).

### The Two Faces of Path Dependency

Because a 3x fund rebalances at the close of every day, its multi-day result depends on the *path*, not just the destination—and compounding works **in both directions. The parabolic tailwind (clean trends):** in a persistent multi-day trend a 3x ETF actually outperforms its theoretical multiple, because it is contractually forced to buy more exposure at the end of every green day. If the underlying gains +5% per day for three days, the index rises 15.76% and a naive non-rebalanced 3x would be 47.28%—but the fund, compounding +15% daily, does better:

| Trading Day | Starting Equity | Daily 3x Move | Ending Equity |
|---|---|---|---|
| Day 1 | $100,000.00 | +15% | $115,000.00 |
| Day 2 | $115,000.00 | +15% | $132,250.00 |
| Day 3 | $132,250.00 | +15% | **$152,087.50** |

**The decay penalty (choppy tape):** the same mechanism turns vicious sideways. If an index swings +10% on Day 1 and −9.09% on Day 2, it ends flat, yet the 3x fund moves +30% then −27.27%, finishing at 94.55%—a 5.45% destruction of capital in 48 hours with zero net movement:

| Scenario | Underlying Index | Naive 3x (linear) | Actual 3x Fund | Net Effect |
|---|---|---|---|---|
| Clean trend: +5%/day × 3 | +15.76% | +47.28% | **+52.09%** | **+4.81% bonus alpha** |
| Chop: +10%, then −9.09% | 0.00% | 0.00% | **94.55% retained** | **−5.45% capital bleed** |

The discipline writes itself: **deploy 3x only when the path is likely to be clean and directional, and exit the instant it is not.**

### Where 3x ETFs Thrive: Trends, Sectors, Rotation

Momentum is the natural habitat of leveraged ETFs—the longer the trend persists, the more powerful the compounding, while trendless markets are where these vehicles quietly die. Technology and semiconductors are the recurring leadership categories, combining high growth, heavy institutional participation, and elevated volatility, but the deepest edge is **sector rotation**.

And leverage runs both ways—bullish 3x funds profit from rising prices, inverse 3x funds from falling ones.

### Key 3x Vehicles for the Blueprint

| Vehicle | Use Case |
|---|---|
| SOXL – Direxion Daily Semiconductor Bull 3X | Core AI / semiconductor play; explosive during tech-infrastructure rallies |
| TQQQ – ProShares UltraPro QQQ | Broad Nasdaq leverage for market-wide momentum and AI rotations |
| LABU – Direxion Daily S&P Biotech Bull 3X | Biotech M&A and clinical-catalyst waves |
| UTSL – Direxion Daily Utilities Bull 3X | High-conviction AI power / electricity-demand play |
| Energy / power (e.g., NRGU, 3x infrastructure) | Energy and power-capex rotations; verify true 3x vs 2x equivalents |
| FNGU (3x FANG+), WEBL, DFEN, and similar | Thematic and sector strikes during confirmed rotations |

### The Tactical Playbook: The Confirmed-Regime Blitz

The blueprint outlaws camping in 3x through sideways consolidations—they deploy only behind an ironclad regime filter. **The regime filter:** initiate only when the unleveraged index breaks cleanly above a multi-week base while trading above its rising 21-day EMA, ADX reads above 20–25 with +DI above −DI, and the 14-period ATR is stable or contracting rather than expanding into chaos. **The entry signature:** stack a confirmed breakout, volume surge, relative-strength leadership, and a genuine catalyst. **Position sizing:** use 3x as the **attack layer**—roughly 10–30% on top of unleveraged ETFs or stock, up to ~30% in a single vehicle only in prime regimes, capping total 3x exposure at 25–40% of the portfolio and risking 0.5–1% per position. **The dynamic volatility guard:** never set stops on the erratic 3x fund itself—map the stop to the unleveraged index, and if it closes below structural support or its rising 8-day EMA, liquidate the 3x robotically and return to cash.

> **Worked example — $100,000 account** An AI-power rotation accelerates on utilities/energy inflows and capex news. SOXL or UTSL breaks out on volume with relative-strength leadership. Allocate 15–25% to the 3x ETF plus modest call overlays for convexity. Risk 0.5–1% max, with an ATR-based stop just below the breakout low (anchored to the unleveraged index). Pyramid on continued expansion, then trail aggressively or scale out at 30–80%+ per leg. Rotate proceeds into the next 3x theme – say LABU on a biotech-M&A wave. A few clean 40–150%+ 3x swings in genuinely trending regimes produce the large compounding jumps the blueprint depends on.

## The 3x ETF Governance Matrix

| Dimension | The Retail Speculator | The Blueprint Allocator |
|---|---|---|
| Holding strategy | Buys and holds through a bear market, suffering a ~90% unrecoverable drawdown | Rents the vehicle only during high-conviction trends; returns to cash on trend cracks |
| Market-condition logic | Buys 3x in wide, choppy consolidations, letting beta slippage bleed the ledger | Executes only when ADX and EMA filters confirm a directional, non-choppy regime |
| Risk engine | Averages down on a crashing 3x fund, accelerating toward Risk of Ruin | Anchors stops to the unleveraged index; caps portfolio risk at 1R |
| Monetization | Gets greedy at the parabolic peak and watches it reverse into a loss | Scales out systematically into vertical daily expansions stretched ~3 ATR past the 21-EMA |

## Critical Risks and Survival Rules

With 3x leverage the math is unforgiving and mistakes are amplified threefold. **Volatility decay** can lose 5–20%+ even when the underlying ends flat—never hold without a confirmed trend. **Amplified drawdowns:** a 10% sector drop is roughly a 30% loss before fees. **Path dependency:** in non-trending markets the compounding math works viciously against you. The iron-discipline checklist: risk ≤1% per position (0.5–1% on the highest-leverage strikes), cap total 3x exposure at 25–40%, trade only in high-conviction trending regimes, and treat strict stops and daily regime checks as mandatory. **Treat 3x as surgical strikes, never as buy-and-hold.**

## The 3x ETF Trading Cycle

Most leveraged-ETF trades follow a recognizable arc—sector leadership emerges, institutional flows increase, momentum accelerates, volume expands, leveraged-ETF demand increases, the trend matures, exhaustion develops, then rotation begins—and the late stages matter most with 3x.

## Final Principle

3x ETFs bundle leverage, liquidity, diversification, sector exposure, and trend participation into one security, and deployed during strong environments and sustained momentum they can dramatically accelerate wealth creation—but **leverage is not a substitute for skill.** Used as disciplined short-burst weapons inside the full system, 3x ETFs turn confirmed momentum into life-changing velocity; used carelessly, they are the fastest way to ruin in this book. **Clip to the trend. Extract the move. Vanish into cash.**

## D. Decay Risks — Neutralizing the Silent Assassin of Leverage

Leverage is a double-edged sword. The 2x and 3x ETFs in this book deliver exponential trend velocity, but they carry a silent assassin that can destroy a compounding sprint **without the underlying index ever moving against you**: leverage decay, known mathematically as beta slippage or volatility drag. This is the chapter every other leveraged-ETF chapter points back to. The central, counterintuitive truth: you can be perfectly correct about direction—the right sector, the right theme, the right trend—and still lose money. Master decay and you separate the traders who achieve explosive 1,000% runs from those who blow up.

> **The warning that frames the chapter:** most retail traders who buy leveraged ETFs lose money — not because they pick the wrong direction, but because decay quietly bleeds them in the chop between trends. Treat 3x funds as surgical weapons engaged for short, clean bursts, never as core holdings.

### What Decay Actually Is

Decay is the gradual erosion of returns caused by daily rebalancing, volatility, compounding mathematics, tracking inefficiencies, and fund expenses. It is not a defect—the funds work exactly as designed, delivering a multiple of **daily** returns, not long-term returns. That single design choice is why "if the index gains 20%, a 3x ETF gains 60%" is true sometimes and false often: the path the market takes is what decides which.

### The Daily Reset, Path Dependency, and the Mechanism

Every leveraged ETF resets its exposure at each day's close, so returns are path-dependent—the sequence of gains and losses matters as much as the destination. Picture two markets that both start at 100 and end at 100: one rises smoothly, the other lurches violently. The index outcome is identical, but the more volatile journey produces far greater decay. The mechanism is the engineering: to hold its ratio fixed, the fund must add exposure at the end of every green day (after price has risen) and cut it at the end of every red day (after price has fallen)—harmless in a clean trend, but in choppy tape a machine that systematically buys high and sells low every session at 4:00 PM.

### The Variance-Drag Math

The degradation can be quantified by the variance-drag approximation:

> **Drag ≈ ½ · L (L – 1) · $\sigma^2$** *where L is the leverage factor and* $\sigma^2$ *is the daily variance of the underlying*

The drag scales with the *square* of the leverage factor (for L = 2 the drag is $\sigma^2$; for L = 3 it is $3\sigma^2$—three times as much). Watch a choppy two-day round trip that returns the index to break-even (Day 1: +10%, Day 2: −9.09%):

| Instrument | Day 1 | Day 2 | Capital Retained | Penalty |
|---|---|---|---|---|

| Instrument | Day 1 | Day 2 | Capital Retained | Penalty |
|---|---|---|---|---|
| 1x (unleveraged) | +10% | −9.09% | **100.00% ($100,000)** | none |
| 2x leveraged | +20% | −18.18% | **98.18% ($98,180)** | −1.82% |
| 3x leveraged | +30% | −27.27% | **94.55% ($94,550)** | **−5.45%** |

## The Same Effect Across Realistic Regimes

Illustrative simulated outcomes for a 3x fund over a five-day window show how completely the regime, not the direction, drives the result:

| Regime | Underlying | 3x ETF Outcome | Verdict |
|---|---|---|---|
| Strong trend (clean breakout) | +10.4% | **≈ +31–35%** | decay minimal |
| Sideways chop (rotation) | ≈ 0% | **−5% to −15%+** | decay bleeds capital |
| Volatile recovery | +2.7% | **flat to negative** | right direction, lost money |

## Why Volatility Hurts Compounding

Underneath decay sits the asymmetry of losses: a 50% loss requires a 100% gain to recover, and leverage forces a fund to climb out of amplified drawdowns again and again, so repeated large swings erode the compounding base far more than their average would suggest. Two smaller drains compound it—**fees** (leveraged ETFs carry higher expense ratios, often ~0.9–1.1%) and **tracking error** (swaps and futures push realized performance slightly off the theoretical multiple)—but volatility compounding is the true killer. Decay is not a fee; it is mathematical.

## 2x vs 3x Decay

Decay rises with leverage quadratically: a 3x fund demands larger daily adjustments and bleeds roughly three times as fast as a 2x in the same chop, so the more leverage you use, the more trend quality you must demand before deploying it.

| Leverage | Relative Decay | Implication |
|---|---|---|
| 2x | Lower ($\approx \sigma^2$) | More forgiving; holdable across longer, moderate trends |
| 3x | ~3× higher ($\approx 3\sigma^2$) | Unforgiving; reserve for short, clean, high-conviction bursts |

## Time Is Not Always Your Friend

Traditional investing rewards patience; leveraged ETFs invert that rule—the longer one is held, the greater the cumulative impact of volatility, fees, and decay. This does not forbid multi-day holds; it means continuously re-testing whether the trend is intact, momentum is strong, and the environment still favors leverage.

## Four Myths About Decay

| The Myth | The Reality |
|---|---|
| "Leveraged ETFs are broken." | They function exactly as designed — to track a daily multiple. |
| "Decay happens every day." | A strong, persistent trend overcomes decay and can produce extraordinary returns. |
| "Decay makes them unusable." | Many traders use them effectively — inside trends, with discipline. |
| "Direction is all that matters." | Path matters as much as destination; and decay is mathematical, not a fee. |

## The Mitigation Toolkit

Treat leveraged ETFs as short-term rentals behind a rigid filter. **Trend-only rule:** deploy 3x only with ADX above 25, strong relative strength, volume expansion, and confirmed momentum ignition—never in low-VIX chop. **Volatility filter and downshift:** when realized volatility spikes, evacuate 3x to cash or 1x, or if the trend is intact but variance has expanded, swap down to 2x (which suffers under half the drag). **Time-stop discipline:** 3x for 1–10 day strikes, 2x for 1–4 week rotations, unleveraged when in doubt—if a position has not broken cleanly into a low-variance trend within 3–5 sessions, close it. **Sizing and stops:** risk 0.5–1% per leveraged idea with tight ATR-based stops (1–1.5x ATR). **Options overlays:** calls or debit spreads give defined risk plus gamma without daily-reset decay, though option theta still applies. **Monitor and rotate** daily.

> **Worked example — $100,000 account** An AI-power theme breaks out (UTSL or an energy 3x) on strong volume, relative strength, and a catalyst. Allocate 15–25% to the 3x ETF for 3–7 days maximum, risking 0.75% with an ATR-based stop. Pyramid on follow-through; scale out 50% at +30–50% and trail the rest. The instant chop develops and ADX drops, exit immediately — even at breakeven — and rotate to unleveraged or 2x. You forfeit a little upside to keep decay from converting a winning theme into a loss, preserving capital for the next high-conviction trend.

### The Leverage Decay Governance Matrix

| Parameter | The Retail Speculator | The Blueprint Allocator |
|---|---|---|
| Holding strategy | Buys a 3x ETF and "hopes" over a multi-year horizon, blind to drag | Rents leveraged vehicles only during high-conviction, low-variance trends |
| Market-condition logic | Camps in 3x through wide sideways chop, bleeding to slippage | Returns to cash or 2x the moment volatility indices spike |
| Risk engine | Averages down on a declining leveraged fund toward Risk of Ruin | Anchors stops to the unleveraged index; caps risk at 1R |
| Mathematical awareness | Assumes 3x always returns 300% of the multi-month move | Computes path-dependency to time precise exits |

### The Decay Cycle

Leveraged-ETF performance moves through a recognizable sequence—a trend begins, leverage amplifies gains, volatility appears as the move ages, rebalancing recalibrates exposure at each close, compounding effects accumulate and diverge from the naive multiple, the trend persists or fails, and decay accelerates or stays minimal depending on volatility—so exit before it compounds.

### Final Principle

Decay is the tax aggressive traders pay for leverage. The greatest mistake is to obsess over leverage while ignoring decay; the professionals respect both, deploying leverage into strong trends and favorable regimes and refusing it in volatile, trendless tape. Respect decay ruthlessly and it stops being a threat and becomes a **filter**—one that keeps you in only the highest-probability setups. **Engage on a clear runway. Extract the burst. Decouple before the friction.**

## E. Swing Trading Leveraged Instruments

This chapter pivots from intraday velocity to multi-day positioning. The retail crowd refuses to hold a leveraged ETF past a single session, conditioned by the blanket warning that *"leveraged instruments are intraday vehicles only"*—a massive source of inefficiency. You never buy and *hold* a 3x ETF passively, but **renting** a 2x or 3x vehicle for a hyper-focused 3-to-15-day swing is one of the most repeatable ways to scale a $100,000 ledger, turning a 10–25% underlying swing into a 20–75%+ gain. Held across a confirmed, low-variance trend, the daily-rebalancing engine works *for* you while you sidestep the theta and IV crush that plague options swing traders. Above all: **leverage is the accelerator, not the strategy.**

## The Strategic Mandate: Why Leveraged Swings Beat Options

For a multi-day swing, an aggressive allocator chooses a leveraged ETF over call options for three structural reasons:

| Factor | Call-Option Swing | Leveraged-ETF Swing |
|---|---|---|
| Time decay (theta) | Loses value every day held; a 4-day stall erodes the premium | Zero time decay — hold the trend without a clock |
| Implied volatility | Premium inflates pre-event, then IV collapses — can lose even when right on direction | Tracks pure price delta — immune to IV crush |
| Expiration | Hard expiry forces your timing | No expiration — exit on your signal, not the calendar |
| Clean multi-day trend | Convexity helps, but decay and IV fight you | **Daily rebalancing compounds in your favor** |

## What Swing Trading Actually Is

Swing trading captures intermediate price movements lasting several days to several weeks—the meaningful middle of a larger trend, rather than intraday noise. The objective: identify a trend early, participate while momentum is strong, and exit before it deteriorates. **Trends beat leverage**—a trader with a strong trend, disciplined risk, and moderate leverage routinely outperforms one with excessive leverage, poor timing, and weak trends.

## 2x vs 3x for Swings

Match the leverage to the swing—the two tiers serve different hold lengths and temperaments:

| Leverage | Best Swing Length | Profile |
|---|---|---|
| 2x | 5–25 days | Smoother, lower decay, more holding flexibility — the longer-swing workhorse |
| 3x | 3–15 days | More torque and faster compounding, but larger drawdowns, more decay, and heavier emotional load — needs active management |

## Best Vehicles

Keep a themed watchlist and treat each fund as a rental, not a holding:

| Tier | Representative Vehicles |
|---|---|
| 3x — higher torque, shorter swings | SOXL (semis/AI), LABU (biotech), UTSL (utilities), NRGU or energy 3x; broad: TQQQ, FAS |

| Tier | Representative Vehicles |
|---|---|
| 2x — smoother, longer swings | QLD (Nasdaq), DIG (energy), BIB (biotech), thematic 2x AI/power and sector funds |

## The Tactical Playbook: The 3-to-15 Day Swing Protocol

Never guess when a swing begins—run a mechanical sequence that enters as an index transitions from quiet consolidation into a structural multi-day wave. **The entry stack (full stack required):** the sector sits in a confirmed uptrend and leading RS versus SPY (RRG leading quadrant); the unleveraged underlying closes above its rising 8-day and 21-day EMAs; daily ADX reads at least 20–25 and slopes up with volume and ATR expansion; a genuine catalyst or inflow underwrites it; and you enter on the first minor pullback to the rising 8-day EMA. **Sizing:** deploy an initial 15–30% block into a single qualified vehicle (toward ~25% only for a prime 3x setup), pyramid 10–15% on confirmed follow-through, map the stop to the unleveraged daily chart (~1–2x ATR below entry or one tick below the prior day's low / 21-day EMA), keep total account risk at 0.75–1% per swing, and cap combined leveraged exposure at 30–40%. **The exit engine:** scale out in tranches—a first tranche into strength (e.g., one-third at +25–40%), harvest the bulk (~75%) at a 3R–4R return or when the underlying stretches ~3x ATR above its 21-day EMA, and trail the runner, liquidating it fully when the underlying closes below its 8-day EMA. Respect the ceilings: ~3–15 days for 3x, 5–25 days for 2x.

> **Worked example — $100,000 account** An AI power/utilities rotation strengthens on capex news. UTSL (3x) or a 2x utilities fund breaks out on volume with relative-strength confirmation. Allocate ~20% to the leveraged ETF plus ~10% in calls for extra convexity. Risk 0.75% with an ATR-based stop on the unleveraged chart. Pyramid on continued expansion and institutional inflows, hold 5–12 days through the swing, and scale out at 30–70%+ as momentum fades or a rotation signal appears. Rotate proceeds into the next swing — say LABU on a biotech-M&A catalyst. Several sequenced 35–100%+ swings across four to six themes can drive large compounding jumps while sidestepping decay.

## The Leveraged Swing Governance Matrix

| Dimension | The Retail Speculator | The Blueprint Allocator |
|---|---|---|
| Holding horizon | Buys at random and leaves it on for weeks through deep corrections | Enforces a strict 3-to-15 day window; exits the moment momentum cools |
| Overnight risk | Swings high-premium options, bleeding to hidden theta and IV decay | Swings leveraged ETFs, capturing pure directional delta with no decay drag |
| Risk management | Panics in normal volatility and dumps, or uses no stops at all | Anchors stops to the unleveraged index chart; risk locked at 1R |

| Dimension | The Retail Speculator | The Blueprint Allocator |
|---|---|---|
| Monetization | Hopes a trend lasts forever and round-trips an explosive gain into a loss | Extracts profits into vertical ATR extensions or a daily close below the 8-EMA |

### Risk and Iron Discipline

**Decay in non-trending swings:** even 5–10 days of chop can erode 8–20%+ in a 3x product—exit fast if ADX drops below 20. **Gap and overnight risk:** news can reverse a swing between sessions—use smaller size or options, and never hold through major OPEX. **Leverage amplification:** never exceed 1% risk per swing. **Overexposure:** keep combined leveraged exposure to 30–40%, favoring 2x for longer swings and 3x for explosive short bursts. Swing trading rewards **patience between setups**—most damage is done by forcing entries out of greed and panicking out of exits from fear.

### The Leveraged Swing Trading Cycle

Most leveraged swing trades follow a familiar arc—catalyst emerges, institutional flows develop, relative strength appears, momentum accelerates, leverage amplifies gains, the trend matures, risk management takes priority, then capital rotates into the next swing.

### Final Principle

Swing trading leveraged instruments is not about maximizing leverage—it is about applying leverage to the right trend at the right time, where institutional flows are strong, sector leadership is clear, and risk can be tightly managed. **Leverage magnifies outcomes; trend selection determines direction; risk management determines survival. Rent the trend. Compound the run. Return to cash.**

## F. Tactical Leverage

The retail crowd treats leverage like a volume knob—turning it up to 3x when they feel aggressive and down to 1x when timid. **The allocator treats leverage as a sensitive variable that must be synchronized with market-regime volatility.** This is the chapter that governs all the others: across a 180-day sprint the market changes character repeatedly, and tactical leverage dictates exactly when to deploy 1x, 2x, or 3x based on one question—how efficient is the directional trend relative to the underlying variance? The objective is never maximum leverage; it is optimal leverage.

### Leverage Is a Tool, Not a Lifestyle

The best traders use leverage tactically rather than continuously—raising exposure when probabilities, momentum, and flows align, and cutting it when uncertainty rises. The defining mental shift: **the leverage attaches to the opportunity, not to the account.** A setup with a strong trend, clear sector leadership, a real catalyst, and high relative strength earns far more leverage than a choppy tape with mixed signals.

## The Volatility-Leverage Inversion Law

The core axiom of tactical leverage is an inversion—leverage and volatility move in opposite directions:

> **As underlying variance (ATR) expands, the leverage you deploy must contract. As variance compresses into a tight, efficient directional channel, leverage scales to its maximum.**

The reasoning is pure probability: high volatility brings noise and deep mean-reversion spikes, so coupling a violent tape with a 3x supercharger forces your stops to widen dramatically, slashing the share count to hold the fixed 1% risk unit—you end up risking the same cash on a far more erratic, decay-prone asset. This is why not all volatility is equal: **constructive volatility** (orderly trends, healthy pullbacks) rewards leverage, while **destructive volatility** (violent reversals, weak follow-through) punishes it.

## The Tactical Leverage Matrix: Three Regime Channels

Translate the Inversion Law into three operational channels—read the regime, then deploy the matching vehicle:

> **GREEN CHANNEL Hyper-Velocity Blitz — 3x Leverage Regime:** Index trades cleanly above its rising 8- and 21-day EMAs; daily ADX ≥ 25 and rising; 14-day ATR stable or contracting. **Vehicle:** 3x leveraged ETFs (e.g., TQQQ, SOXL, LABU). **Execution:** The runway is straight and efficient — decay risk near zero, path dependency working for you. Deploy heavy concentration (up to ~35% account mass) with tight stops anchored to the daily index lows.

> **YELLOW CHANNEL High-Variance Scaling — 2x Leverage Regime:** Primary uptrend intact (price above the 50-day SMA) but volatility has expanded; ATR rises and the index prints wide, alternating candles. **Vehicle:** 2x leveraged ETFs (e.g., QLD, SSO). **Execution:** Downgrade immediately from 3x to 2x, halving beta exposure. This keeps large absolute share mass while giving the trade the breathing room to survive high-ATR pullbacks without premature stop-outs or 3x decay.

> **RED CHANNEL Capital-Preservation Lock — 1x or Cash Regime:** Index closes below its 50- and 200-day SMAs, ADX shows a bearish expansion, or the tape enters a choppy sideways distribution box. **Vehicle:** Unleveraged 1x sector ETFs (e.g., XLK, SMH) — or 100% pristine cash. **Execution:** Leverage is outlawed here. Gap-downs and decay will systematically liquidate an account. Lock the ledger in cash or 1x exposure and wait for the market's structure to reset.

## 2x vs 3x: Matching Torque to the Trend

Within the Green and Yellow channels, match leverage tier to the expected hold and trend quality:

| Tier | Best Window | Profile |
|---|---|---|
| 2x | 5–20 days | Smoother in moderate trends; lower decay; the scalable workhorse |

| Tier | Best Window | Profile |
|---|---|---|
| 3x | 2–10 days | Maximum torque for explosive moves; higher decay — use surgically |

## Key Instruments by Channel

Key instruments by channel:

| Channel | Representative Vehicles |
|---|---|
| Green — 3x tactical | SOXL (semis/AI), LABU (biotech), UTSL (utilities/power), NRGU (energy); broad TQQQ |
| Yellow — 2x tactical | QLD (Nasdaq), SSO (S&P 500), DIG (energy), thematic AI/utilities 2x |
| Red — 1x / defensive | Unleveraged sector ETFs (XLK, SMH) or 100% cash |

## The Decision Protocol

Tactical leverage is a repeatable loop run daily, not a one-time choice. **Read the regime** (index structure, breadth, and the ATR/ADX volatility signature place you in Green, Yellow, or Red). **Confirm leadership and flow** (sector RS leading, institutional participation, a genuine catalyst). **Assess momentum quality** (volume expansion and clean follow-through, not a single extended candle). **Select the channel** (deploy the matching vehicle and allocation, risking 0.5–1% per setup with ATR stops). **Monitor continuously, then downshift**—the instant variance expands or the regime cracks, step down a channel (3x → 2x → cash) without hesitation.

> **Worked example — $100,000 account (the same hit-and-rotate engine, with the leverage dial set by regime)** An AI power/utilities rotation accelerates on fresh capex news while the index sits in a clean, low-ATR Green-channel trend. UTSL (3x) breaks out on 3–4x volume with relative-strength confirmation and institutional inflows. Allocate 15–25% to the leveraged ETF plus ~10% in out-of-the-money calls for convexity, risking 0.75% with a tight ATR stop below the breakout low. Pyramid 10–15% on follow-through, hold 4–12 days, and scale out in tranches (one-third at +25%, one-third at +45%, trail the rest) for a 35–90%+ position return. Then rotate immediately into the next setup — say LABU on a biotech-M&A catalyst. If ATR suddenly expands mid-trade, the Inversion Law downshifts you to a 2x vehicle or to cash before the decay does its damage.

## The Tactical Leverage Governance Matrix

| Parameter | The Retail Speculator | The Blueprint Allocator |
|---|---|---|
| Leverage selection | Static 3x in all conditions because they want "big gains" | Modulates 3x → 2x → 1x by active regime-volatility readings |
| Risk | Couples max leverage with a | Uses 2x in high-ATR regimes to |

| Parameter | The Retail Speculator | The Blueprint Allocator |
|---|---|---|
| insulation | high-ATR tape and gets stopped out | compress variance behind fixed cash stops |
| Capital efficiency | Shrinks size out of fear when volatility spikes, nullifying the leverage | Switches vehicle to maximize share mass inside a fixed 1R cage |
| Regime adaptability | Holds melting 3x through a bear market and wipes out the base | Returns to 100% cash the moment macro support cracks |

## Risk, Capital Preservation, and the Hit-and-Rotate Mindset

Tactical leverage rests on one foundation: **preserve capital during unfavorable conditions.** Cutting leverage in hostile regimes preserves the capital—and the optionality—needed to strike when the next clean trend arrives. **Decay amplification:** even short holds in chop bleed 3x products—never hold through low-ADX periods. **Whipsaws:** false breakouts demand multi-signal confirmation. **Gap and overnight risk:** use smaller size or defined-risk options around events. **Exposure cap:** keep combined tactical leveraged positions to 25–35% of the portfolio, risk ≤1% per trade. The best practitioners adopt a **"hit-and-rotate"** mindset—striking hard when the channel is Green, downshifting without ego when it turns Yellow, and sitting patiently in cash when it goes Red.

## The Tactical Leverage Cycle

Most applications follow a recognizable progression—opportunity emerges, institutional flows develop, momentum strengthens, leverage is increased to align with the channel, compounding accelerates, the trend matures, exposure is reduced, and capital is preserved for the next opportunity—and the discipline lives in the back half.

## Final Principle

Tactical leverage is the disciplined application of amplified exposure during the windows when opportunity is unusually favorable—governed by regime, sector leadership, flows, momentum, and risk. The best traders seek not maximum leverage but **optimal leverage**, raising exposure as probabilities improve and cutting it as they decay. It is the repeatable engine that turns short-term dispersion into exponential growth while preserving the capital needed to seize the next opportunity. **Green: strike. Yellow: scale down. Red: cash.**

# Chapter 11
# Options for Accelerated Returns

## A. Long Calls

Among every instrument available to an aggressive trader, few offer more explosive upside than the long call. A stock might rise 10, 20, or 30 percent over weeks; a well-selected call on it can rise 50, 100, 300 percent or more over the same window—and for a campaign built to transform $100,000 into $1,000,000 in six months, that convexity is the engine. But there is a hard line between using calls and being used by them. The retail crowd treats OTM calls as lottery tickets and watches them incinerated by options math; in this blueprint, long calls are asymmetric capital-replacement tools—a way to control large blocks of high-beta equity with a fraction of the capital while anchoring maximum risk to a tight, predefined cash border.

### What a Call Option Actually Is

A call gives the buyer the right, but not the obligation, to purchase shares at a predetermined strike before expiration. Unlike a shareholder, a call buyer is never forced to take delivery—it is that optionality which creates leverage. Every call is defined by five components: the **underlying** security, the **strike** price, the **expiration** date, the **premium** (its cost), and the **contract size** (standardized at 100 shares). A call has **intrinsic value** when the stock trades above the strike (a $120 stock with a $100 strike carries $20 of intrinsic value), and on top sits **time value**—premium for the time remaining and volatility expected, which erodes as expiration nears.

### Why Calls Create Leverage and Asymmetric Risk

Leverage is the primary attraction. A $100 stock costs $10,000 for 100 shares; a call on those shares may cost a few hundred dollars, and a $5 premium on a $50 stock delivers roughly 20x notional leverage without a margin loan. Just as important is the shape of the risk: maximum loss is capped at the premium paid, while maximum gain is theoretically unbounded. And as the underlying rises, the option's delta increases, so gains accelerate—that convexity, driven by gamma, is why a 15 percent move in a stock can become a 150 percent move in the right call.

### The Greeks That Govern a Call

A call is a decaying asset governed by precise forces. **Delta** measures how much the option moves per $1.00 move in the underlying: a far-OTM call carries a weak delta of 0.10 to 0.30 (the stock must make a large fast move just to break even), so the blueprint commands the opposite—buy in-the-money or deep-ITM calls with strong delta that track the stock nearly dollar-for-dollar. **Theta** is the silent daily bleed of premium, and its decay curve accelerates sharply inside the final 30 days, so a trader can be right about direction and still lose if the move arrives too slowly. **Vega** measures sensitivity to implied volatility (IV): buying into a hype cycle means overpaying for inflated IV, and when the news drops the resulting **IV crush** can destroy premium even when the stock moves your way—so enter when IV is compressed relative to its own history, not spiking at peak attention.

### The Tactical Playbook: The Delta-60 Protocol

Readers do not guess at strikes—they apply the **Delta-60 Protocol**. **Maturity (DTE):** 30 to 45 days for core swings, keeping the entry outside the toxic final-30-day theta cliff (longer multi-week swings extend toward 60–90 DTE; 0DTE contracts are reserved for defined-catalyst gamma plays). **Strike:** the strike registering a delta of 0.60 or greater, typically one to two strikes in-the-money. A 0.60-delta contract with 45 days of life behaves almost like the underlying on the upside yet costs a fraction of the share price—if the stock rips 10 percent, the premium can easily expand 100 to 150 percent.

### Capital Allocation and Risk Control

Because options carry built-in leverage, the binding constraint is never how much you can deploy—it is how much you can lose. The rule is fixed: no single call may risk more than 1 percent of total account equity—$1,000 on a $100,000 base, your one R. Allocation flows out of that rule: with a tight stop a position might use 5 percent of the account; with a wider high-conviction setup, 10 to 20 percent—but the dollar at risk never changes. The stop is mapped not to the option but to the underlying's technical floor (the breakout-candle low or intraday VWAP).

> **THE RISK-UNIT EQUATION: $5,000 allocation × 20% contract stop-loss = $1,000 at risk (1R)**

Exits are mechanical: scale out of 50 percent on the first 100 percent premium double, then trail the remainder; or harvest in thirds. Pyramid into confirmed strength as rising delta works in your favor, then rotate realized profit into the next setup—it is the sequencing of many controlled 100-to-400-percent wins, not a single heroic trade, that produces compounding velocity.

### Where Calls Work Best

Calls reward environments where price moves fast and conviction is rising: **momentum leaders** (rapid movement and expanding volatility make premiums explode), **breakouts** (amplify participation without a large share position), **catalysts** (earnings, FDA decisions, M&A, contracts, AI announcements create sudden volatility), **sector leadership** (calls magnify the move when institutions accumulate a hot group's leaders), and **leveraged-ETF overlays** (calls on SOXL, LABU, UTSL, or TQQQ stack convexity on convexity—powerful, to be sized with extra respect). In the 2026 landscape, elevated options volume across AI infrastructure and power, biotech M&A, and small- and mid-cap rotation creates an unusually rich field—which makes selection discipline more important, not less.

### A Worked Execution Example

Consider a mid- or small-cap AI-power or biotech name printing a relative-strength breakout on a volume surge alongside a genuine catalyst. The stock trades at $45. You buy slightly OTM $48 calls, 30 to 45 days out, at a $3.50

premium ($350 per contract), sizing so total risk stays near 1 percent. Over five to eight sessions the stock advances 15 percent, and the call expands to between $8 and $12—a 130 to 240 percent return on premium. You pyramid into follow-through, then scale out in thirds as momentum cools, and rotate the profit into the next high-conviction call.

### Retail Speculator vs. Blueprint Allocator

| Dimension | The Retail Speculator | The Blueprint Allocator |
|---|---|---|
| Strike selection | Buys cheap, far-OTM calls (~0.10 delta) hoping for a miracle headline. | Buys ITM/DITM calls (≥ 0.60 delta) to replicate equity movement. |
| Maturity | Buys 0–7 DTE lottery weeklies and lets theta destroy the principal. | Selects 30–45 DTE to neutralize the near-term decay slope. |
| Volatility | Chases calls into vertical spikes, buying at peak implied volatility. | Enters when IV is compressed, sidestepping the IV crush. |
| Monetization | Holds to expiration, watching intraday gains melt back to zero. | Scales out of 50% on a 100% double, trails the rest. |

## Common Mistakes and the Iron Discipline Rules

Most traders lose with calls not because the instrument is flawed but because they misuse it—buying expirations too short, ignoring volatility and overpaying, chasing extended stocks, oversizing, and ignoring theta. Against those stand the survival rules: never risk more than 1 percent of the account on a single call; favor 30–90 DTE for swings; use bull call (debit) spreads to cut cost and cap loss further; trade only liquid underlyings and strikes; respect IV-crush risk around catalysts; and exit ruthlessly on momentum divergence or broken support, keeping a live catalyst calendar at all times.

## The Life Cycle of a Call Trade

Most winning call trades move through a recognizable sequence—an opportunity emerges as a catalyst develops, calls are purchased on confirmation, momentum and volatility expand, option value accelerates as gamma compounds the gains, public participation grows, the trend matures, profits are scaled down, and capital is redeployed into the next high-conviction setup.

## The Psychology of Buying Calls

A call buyer is purchasing possibility. The successful stay anchored to probabilities, catalysts, momentum, and timing; the unsuccessful fixate only on the size of the payoff. The right frame is a “lottery ticket with an edge”: patience to wait for genuinely high-conviction setups, paired with the ruthlessness to act and exit on plan.

### The Final Principle

Call options offer leverage, capital efficiency, defined downside, and substantial upside, and they pair naturally with common stocks, sector ETFs, and leveraged instruments to turn a momentum-and-catalyst framework into high-convexity engines. The best opportunities arrive when strong catalysts emerge, momentum accelerates, institutions accumulate, volatility expands, and sector leadership is clear—get those conditions right, manage risk to the dollar, and string enough controlled wins together with discipline, and the result is one of the most powerful engines of accelerated wealth creation available to a private trader.

*Production notes (for design): option payoff diagrams and annotated before/after charts of representative call wins; a strike-selection guide (ITM/ATM/OTM by timeframe) with breakeven and theta-by-DTE; unusual-options-flow scanners (Unusual Whales, TradeAlert) for sourcing; and prominent, unambiguous risk disclaimers on options and leverage.*

## B. Long Puts

If calls let a trader profit from rising markets, puts let a trader profit from falling ones—and they do something calls cannot: defend the account when the tide turns. The retail crowd files puts under "doom-and-gloom insurance," which is half the picture. In a six-month sprint, puts play two roles: as **offense**, high-velocity instruments engineered to exploit panic (fear is a more powerful catalyst than greed, and stocks cascade downward several times faster than they climb); as **defense**, the insurance that keeps a 30-to-50-percent drawdown from ending the campaign.

### What a Put Option Is

A put gives the buyer the right, but not the obligation, to sell shares at a predetermined strike before expiration, profiting as the underlying declines. It is defined by the same five components as a call, and like a call it delivers leverage—control over 100, 500, or 1,000 shares for a fraction of the cost of shorting—with one decisive advantage over short selling: the maximum loss is capped at the premium paid, where a short sale carries theoretically unlimited loss.

### Why Markets Fall Faster Than They Rise

Human psychology explains the edge. Bull markets run on optimism and gradual accumulation; bear markets run on fear, forced selling, and margin calls—reflexive and self-amplifying—so declines arrive faster than advances. Three structural forces make a flush efficient: **the velocity of fear** (dealers unwind hedges as delta collapses, brokers force-liquidate margin accounts—mechanical selling begets more selling), **the implied-volatility tailwind** (collapsing stocks spike the VIX and single-name IV, so vega inflates put premium from both the falling price and the surging volatility), and **the gamma-squeeze inversion** (an avalanche of panicked put buying forces dealers to short the underlying to stay delta-neutral, manufacturing a violent downward spiral).

> **1.** A major support level or moving-average floor cracks on heavy volume. ▼ **2.** Dealers short the underlying to hedge collapsing delta; brokers liquidate margin accounts. ▼ **3.** Forced selling drives the price down faster — looping back to step 2. ▼ **4.** IV spikes as fear rises, inflating put premiums on top of the price drop — a double compounding for the put holder.

## Two Jobs: Defense and Offense

The blueprint deploys puts for two distinct purposes. **Defense — protecting the compounding base:** the biggest threat to 1,000 percent compounding is drawdown math (a 30-to-50-percent loss requires a 50-to-100-percent gain just to return to even), so protective puts bought against long stock, a 3x ETF (SOXL, LABU, UTSL), or a sector basket collar the downside while leaving the upside open. **Offense — profiting from the drop:** in risk-off shifts, on overextended names, or during sector rotations, puts let a trader profit from the downside directly while rotating capital.

## The Tactical Playbook: The Inverted Delta-60 Protocol

For the offensive trade, readers wait for a definitive structural fracture. **The short-side qualification scan:** a clean daily close below the declining 8-day and 21-day EMAs with the 50-day SMA flattening (the regime anchor), and a breakdown through major support on volume of at least 150 percent of the 50-day average (the volume catalyst). **Contract selection:** 21 to 35 days to expiration with an ITM put at a delta of about −0.60 or steeper for near dollar-for-dollar replication; for insurance or slower swings, extend to 30 to 60 days with slightly OTM puts. **The wider menu:** protective (married) puts against a long position; directional bearish puts on weakening-RS names; bear put (debit) spreads (the default for defined-risk downside capture); and volatility plays when IV is low but expected to spike. **Sizing:** a maximum ~5 percent of account mass to a directional put chain with loss held to the fixed 1 percent (1R), and protective puts sized smaller at 0.5 to 1 percent.

## Where Puts Work Best

The richest put opportunities cluster where selling becomes mechanical and volatility expands—market corrections, earnings disappointments, sector weakness opening ETF and leveraged-ETF plays, and genuine crashes, where fear dominates and downside momentum accelerates into the most substantial gains of all. Because IV expands with fear, a put can gain value even before a large price decline fully develops. For a worked case: long SOXL during a power rotation with the VIX creeping higher and RS weakening, you buy slightly OTM puts 30 to 45 days out for 0.5 to 1 percent of account risk as insurance—if the sector pulls back 8 to 12 percent, those puts can return 80 to 250 percent or more, offsetting the long-side losses and freeing capital to rotate into the next leader.

### Calls Versus Puts

| Dimension | Calls | Puts |
|---|---|---|
| Profit from | Rising prices and bullish momentum. | Falling prices and bearish momentum. |
| Driven by | Optimism, gradual accumulation, positive catalysts. | Fear, forced selling, negative catalysts. |
| Speed | Slower ascent; greed moves gradually. | Faster descent; fear moves quickly. |
| Role here | Offense — upside torque. | Defense and the tactical counter-punch. |

### Retail Speculator vs. Blueprint Allocator

| Dimension | The Retail Speculator | The Blueprint Allocator |
|---|---|---|
| Trigger logic | Buys puts on a stock making new highs, guessing the top out of ego. | Enters only when an asset fractures its floor (21-EMA / support) on heavy volume. |
| Strike selection | Buys cheap OTM puts (~0.10 delta) that need a bankruptcy to pay. | Uses ITM puts (≥ −0.60 delta) to capture the immediate drop. |
| IV awareness | Buys after the VIX has doubled, overpaying right before an IV crush. | Enters as the pivot cracks, before IV fully expands. |
| Monetization | Holds too long; watches the gain evaporate in a relief rally. | Scales out 75% into the first parabolic flush, back to cash. |

### Risks and the Iron Discipline Rules

Puts reduce some risks and introduce others. **Time decay:** puts bleed aggressively, especially OTM—favor 30 to 60 DTE and avoid long holds without volatility expansion. **Volatility crush:** buying after the VIX has already spiked is the classic way to overpay. **Wrong-way risk:** markets can stay irrational longer than expected—size small. **Liquidity:** stick to liquid underlyings. The survival rules: risk no more than 1 percent on any directional put (0.5 to 1 percent on protective puts); never use a protective put as an excuse to oversize the underlying long; exit or roll on a momentum reversal; pair every put with an ATR-based stop; and track net portfolio delta and gamma daily.

### The Put Cycle

Most successful put trades move through a recognizable progression—weakness emerges as technical deterioration appears, selling accelerates as institutional distribution begins, volatility expands as fear increases, put values rise as leverage works, public panic intensifies the selling, momentum peaks at extremes, profits are realized as the risk-reward flips, and capital is redeployed.

### The Psychology of Trading Puts

The amateur is conditioned to make money only when markets rise and treats a red screen as a crisis; the disciplined trader understands that gravity is faster, cleaner, and more predictable than ascent—and that staying solvent through the drop is what funds the next advance. In compounding, defense wins championships.

### The Final Principle

Put options provide leverage, capital efficiency, defined risk, and substantial upside during bearish conditions, with the best opportunities emerging when momentum breaks down, institutions distribute, volatility expands, and fear takes hold. The trader who commands both calls and puts can pursue opportunity regardless of whether optimism or fear rules the tape—and that two-sided flexibility is a decisive competitive advantage.

*Production notes (for design): payoff diagrams for protective vs. naked puts vs. bear put spreads; a strike/DTE selection guide by scenario; integration showing how puts protect the long-biased engine; and prominent risk disclaimers—puts decay fast, IV crush can wipe a correct directional call, and a hedge must never justify oversizing the underlying.*

## C. LEAPS

LEAPS—Long-Term Equity Anticipation Securities—are simply long-dated options (calls and occasionally puts) with expirations one to three years out. The retail crowd files them under "conservative, slow, for long-term investors" and misreads the instrument entirely. For a 180-day campaign, LEAPS are the patient accelerator: a deep-liquidity capital-replacement tool combining much of stock ownership's upside with the leverage and defined risk of options. They resolve a paradox—a 45-day call exposes the ledger to brutal decay if the asset consolidates, and buying shares drains cash, while LEAPS thread the needle with deep intrinsic delta and near-zero near-term decay.

### What LEAPS Are, and Why They Exist

LEAPS were created to solve options trading's oldest problem: time. Short-dated contracts bleed value rapidly, and a trader can correctly identify the company, trend, catalyst, and direction yet still lose because the move took longer than expected—so by extending expiration far into the future, LEAPS turn time from an enemy into a non-issue. The cleanest way to think about a deep LEAPS call is as synthetic stock ownership: instead of 100 shares, you buy one LEAPS call controlling the same 100 shares, capturing the upside and leverage while committing far less cash.

### The LEAPS Paradox: Long-Dated Options for a Short Sprint

Readers are not holding these for two years—they exploit a long-dated contract's mathematical properties over a window that lasts as long as the regime thesis holds. **The flattened theta slope:** for contracts under 45 days, theta is a steep accelerating cliff, but for LEAPS with 300 to 700 days remaining, daily theta is negligible—so if a stock chops sideways for three weeks before breaking out, the premium stays insulated. **The high-intrinsic-delta engine:** the blueprint outlaws OTM LEAPS and targets deep-ITM strikes at a delta of roughly 0.80 to 0.90, a near-direct proxy for the stock. **The leverage-efficiency ratio:** a deep-ITM LEAPS on a $100 stock might cost $25, controlling the same 100 shares for $2,500 rather than $10,000 and freeing ~$7,500 of cash—on the order of 3x to 4x structural leverage (as much as 3x to 8x depending on strike and time) with no margin interest and no liquidation risk.

### Strike Geometry: Deep, Balanced, or Speculative

Where you place the strike defines the instrument. **Deep-in-the-money (the blueprint default):** substantial intrinsic value, high delta (0.80–0.90), slow theta, reduced volatility sensitivity—the closest thing to leveraged stock ownership. **At-the-money:** a middle ground balancing leverage, cost, and responsiveness, used selectively for a higher-conviction tilt. **Out-of-the-money:** cheapest and highest percentage upside but lowest probability—treated as speculation, not capital replacement, and effectively off the table for the core allocation.

### The Tactical Playbook: The Blue-Chip Proxy Protocol

LEAPS are used on high-liquidity mega-cap leaders, strong-RS names, and broad sector trackers undergoing a structural trend shift—never on thin small-cap runners where wide spreads distort pricing. When a regime filter confirms a low-variance bull expansion: **expiration** of the furthest liquid January cycle (a minimum of ~270 to 360 days, often 12 to 36 months out), **strike** at a delta between 0.80 and 0.90 (typically 15 to 20 percent below spot), and a **spread threshold** of no more than ~2 percent of the premium. Within the system they serve four roles: core long-biased positions, rotation and regime anchors, synthetic stock replacement, and the hybrid stack (roughly 60 to 70 percent of the options allocation in core LEAPS, 30 to 40 percent in short-term tactical calls and puts).

### A Worked Execution Example

A worked case: the AI-power and utilities regime strengthens with sustained institutional flows. Rather than buying 1,000 shares of an $80 leader, or holding a 3x utilities ETF through the whole move, you buy a January 2027 or 2028 LEAPS at the $65–$70 strike for an $18–$25 premium—a delta near 0.75 to 0.85—allocating 15 to 25 percent of the account (40 to 60 contracts) with total risk near 1 to 1.5 percent of equity. Over four to six months, if the underlying rises 35 to 60 percent, the LEAPS can expand 80 to 200 percent or more through delta expansion and retained time value, with short-term calls added on breakouts for torque and protective puts bought if the VIX spikes—a lower-maintenance compounding engine running underneath the faster tactical book.

## Capital Deployment and the Risk Cage

Because LEAPS mimic the stock closely while costing a fraction, they permit safe concentration—a 15 to 25 percent capital block across two or three highly liquid positions, with risk per position kept to roughly 1 to 1.5 percent (slightly wider than the strict 1 percent, because a deep-ITM LEAPS carries real intrinsic value and will not evaporate to zero on a normal technical stop).

> **1.** Macro breakout: the leader closes above its rising 200-day moving average. ▼ **2.** Deploy capital proxies: buy deep-ITM LEAPS (~0.85 delta, 300+ DTE) on the leader. ▼ **3.** Preserve cash: roughly 75% of the equivalent share cost stays in liquid reserve for tactical setups. ▼ **4.** Mechanical stop: exit if the underlying closes below its rising 50-day moving average — loss contained within the 1R–1.5R boundary.

The stop is never on the option—it is tied to the underlying's daily chart: if the asset closes below its rising 50-day moving average, the macro-wave is invalid and the LEAPS is liquidated. With no accelerating decay distorting the premium, the exit is clean and the loss stays caged.

## Where LEAPS Work Best

Most great winners take months or quarters to realize their potential—precisely the terrain LEAPS are built for. The richest opportunities cluster in long-duration secular trends (AI, advanced semiconductors, cloud, robotics, cybersecurity, biotech, defense, energy) and durable sector leadership. The 2026 edge is structural: multi-month regimes like the AI infrastructure and power buildout, biotech M&A cycles, and energy rotation play out over quarters, and LEAPS let readers stay positioned without rolling every few weeks, less vulnerable to short-term volatility noise.

## LEAPS Versus Short-Term Calls

| Dimension | Short-Term Calls | LEAPS |
|---|---|---|
| Edge | Explosive leverage, rapid gains, sharp catalyst plays. | Slow decay, flexibility, time for the thesis to develop. |
| Cost | Low upfront premium. | Higher upfront premium, lower % leverage. |
| Time risk | Severe theta; small margin for error on timing. | Minimal near-term theta; long runway. |
| Role | Tactical torque around momentum bursts and catalysts. | Core conviction base and regime anchor. |

**Retail Speculator vs. Blueprint Allocator**

| Parameter | The Retail Speculator | The Blueprint Allocator |
|---|---|---|
| Strike geometry | Buys OTM LEAPS out of greed and watches them expire worthless. | Buys deep-ITM strikes (0.80–0.90 delta) for an immediate equity proxy. |
| Holding strategy | Buys and forgets for two years, blind to changing structure. | Holds while the regime is valid — weeks to months — as a leverage tool. |
| Capital | Ties up the whole account in one chain, no cash for fast setups. | Uses LEAPS efficiency to free ~75% of cash for nimble trades. |
| Risk | Tolerates a 50% drawdown because there's still time left | Enforces a technical stop on the underlying's chart. |

## Risks and the Discipline Rules

LEAPS reduce some risks but eliminate none—they **still decay** (theta and vega matter if IV collapses or the thesis takes longer), a **wrong thesis** is not saved by time alone, **opportunity cost** locks capital, and **liquidity** still matters. The rules: risk no more than 1 to 1.5 percent per position; pair every LEAPS with an ATR-based stop or shorter-dated protective puts; review monthly and roll or exit if the thesis weakens (they are not "set and forget"); avoid speculative strikes and over-concentration; and never let the long runway justify oversized conviction.

## The LEAPS Cycle

Most successful LEAPS trades move through a recognizable progression—a long-term opportunity is identified as a major trend emerges, the position acquires long-duration exposure, institutional participation expands, fundamentals improve and validate the thesis, momentum develops, leverage amplifies the gains, public recognition arrives, and profits are realized and redeployed into the next regime.

## The Psychology of Trading LEAPS

LEAPS reward a different temperament than weeklies—they encourage institutional thinking about competitive advantage, earnings growth, and long-term catalysts rather than daily ticks, which tends to surface higher-quality opportunities. Patience with a high-conviction LEAPS is strength, not weakness.

## The Final Principle

LEAPS combine leverage, time, capital efficiency, and defined risk in a single contract, letting a trader participate in major long-term opportunities without the relentless pressure of short-dated options. The best setups appear when transformational trends are developing, institutions are accumulating, and sector leadership is strengthening—weekly options may deliver the fastest gains, but LEAPS provide time, the most underestimated asset of all.

## D. Spreads

Many traders are drawn to options for leverage, but leverage is never free: options can be expensive, time decay is relentless, and volatility distorts pricing. While naked long calls and puts deliver raw uncapped convexity, they expose the trader to the two great wealth-destroying forces—**Theta** (the daily bleed of time decay) and **Vega** (the brutal collapse of value when IV is crushed after a catalyst). This is where spreads become the precision scalpel: **a vertical spread is a structural volatility-mitigation engine.** By simultaneously buying and selling contracts in the same cycle, readers offset time decay, cap the cost of entry, and engineer asymmetric risk-and-reward profiles with a maximum loss known to the penny.

### What Is an Option Spread? Why They Exist

An option spread involves simultaneously buying and selling options on the same underlying, differing by strike, expiration, or both, to deliberately reshape the trade's cost, risk, profit potential, and volatility sensitivity. Spreads were developed to manage the tradeoffs every option carries, letting traders do five things at once: reduce cost, define risk precisely before a dollar is committed, improve capital efficiency, manage time decay rather than fall victim to it, and create more favorable, repeatable risk-reward structures.

### The Philosophy and Architecture of Spreads

The speculator asks "How much can I make?"; the professional asks "How much risk am I taking to make it?" Spreads enforce the professional question structurally, because the answer is fixed at entry. Every vertical spread is built from two opposing components: **the directional engine** (the long wing—an ITM option securing a high directional delta), **the decay sponge** (the short wing—an OTM option whose theta partially offsets the long option's decay), and **the IV insulator** (because both legs sit on the same underlying, a sudden IV crush hits both, so the long leg's loss is cushioned by the short leg's drop—which makes spreads the preferred tool for high-velocity catalysts).

### The Spread Family

The most important distinction is vertical versus the rest, and debit versus credit. The **vertical spread** is the workhorse—same expiration, different strikes, in bull (profiting as the underlying rises) and bear (profiting as it falls) forms. The **bull call spread** buys a call and sells a higher-strike call, profiting on a rise with reduced cost, lower decay, and defined risk (profit capped at the higher strike)—the primary offensive weapon for breakouts, gap-and-go, and catalysts. The **bear put spread** buys a put and sells a lower-strike put for efficient bearish exposure during RS weakening, on overextended names, or to hedge a long book.

## Debit Spreads versus Credit Spreads

When the option you buy costs more than the one you sell, you pay to enter—a **debit spread**, with defined risk, defined reward, limited capital, and clear directional exposure (the primary vehicle here). When the option you sell generates more premium than the one you buy, you are paid to enter—a **credit spread**, benefiting from premium collection and time decay, used sparingly to monetize high-IV environments or as hedges.

## The Full Toolkit at a Glance

| Strategy | Role |
|---|---|
| Bull Call Spread | Bullish directional trade. The primary offensive weapon for breakouts and catalysts. |
| Bear Put Spread | Bearish directional trade. Tactical shorts and portfolio hedges. |
| Bull Put Spread | Income-oriented bullish trade. Collect premium when expecting price to hold above a level. |
| Bear Call Spread | Income-oriented bearish trade. Collect premium on overextended names. |
| Calendar Spread | Same strike, different expirations. Exploits the term structure of time decay. |
| Diagonal Spread | Different strikes and different expirations. A blend of directional and time-based exposure. |

## Why Spreads Improve Capital Efficiency, Decay, and Volatility

The single greatest advantage of a spread is cost reduction: by partially financing the long option with the short, the trader discounts the entry cost meaningfully, freeing capital for the next opportunity—and it is the redeployment of capital, again and again, that produces compounding velocity. Spreads also soften time decay (the short option's theta income offsets the long option's theta expense) and control volatility exposure (holding both a long and short option makes pricing more predictable). Heading into earnings, premiums and IV expand and outright options become expensive—a spread offsets much of that cost while insulating against the post-earnings crush, which is exactly why momentum traders construct a bull call spread rather than buying expensive calls outright.

## The Tactical Playbook: The Bull Vertical Blitz

Readers stay with highly liquid debit vertical spreads. **The spread configuration:** 14 to 60 DTE (spreads mitigate decay, so shorter-dated contracts than a naked buyer would dare are viable); the **long strike** one step in-the-money at a delta of roughly 0.55 to 0.60; the **short strike** out-of-the-money at the next major resistance tier or target ATR extension. The beauty is that maximum loss is strictly capped at the net debit, both numbers known before entry:

**Maximum Risk = Net Debit Paid = Premium Paid (long) – Premium Received (short)**

**Maximum Reward = ( Width Between Strikes – Net Debit ) × 100**

The blueprint mandates a risk-to-reward ratio of at least 1:2. Because the net debit is the entire maximum loss, position sizing and risk sizing are the same decision. Worked example: a stock at $50, buy the $48 call and sell the $55 call, 30 to 45 DTE, for a $2.80 net debit—maximum risk $280 per contract, maximum reward $420 if the stock closes above $55, a return on risk of roughly 150%. In an aggressive rotation, a mid-cap leader at $62 prints a breakout; buy the $60 call and sell the $70 call, 45 DTE, for a $3.20 net debit—if the underlying moves 18% over twelve days, the spread can expand toward $7.00 to $8.50, a 120% to 165% return on risk. A disciplined allocator might commit 5% of a $100,000 base into a single high-conviction spread, knowing the entire block is the capped maximum loss—if it reaches target, that block can triple while total portfolio risk stays locked to the penny.

## The Vertical Spread Governance Matrix

| Operational Parameter | The Retail Speculator | The Blueprint Capital Allocator |
|---|---|---|
| Premium cost control | Buys expensive naked calls, overpaying for time insurance they do not need. | Uses a short wing to discount the entry cost of the directional position substantially. |
| Theta management | Watches premium melt away every night the stock consolidates. | Turns time decay into an ally, letting the short contract insulate the ledger against minor stalls. |
| Volatility exposure | Gets wiped out by an IV crush after an earnings or catalyst announcement. | Enters a spread to neutralize much of the Vega exposure, keeping the leg values structurally aligned. |
| Monetization discipline | Holds out for infinite gains, watching a winner reverse into a total loss near expiration. | Robotically liquidates as the spread approaches its maximum mathematical value, returning to cash. |

## Risk Management and Iron Discipline

Every spread has a maximum gain, a maximum loss, and a fully defined risk profile, but a defined-risk structure is only as safe as the discipline around it: risk no more than ~1 percent (measured at the defined maximum loss) per position; favor 30 to 60 DTE for swings; exit early on momentum divergence rather than holding into expiration; pair every spread with an ATR-based stop on the underlying; and track net Greeks (delta, theta, vega) across the entire portfolio. The recurring mistakes—poor strike selection, entering too close to expiration, ignoring the volatility regime, oversizing, and misunderstanding the payoff—are all preventable, and a post-catalyst crush still hurts a debit spread, just far less than a naked long.

### The Spread Trading Cycle

Successful spread trades follow a repeatable process—an opportunity is identified, a spread is constructed to fit the thesis, the maximum loss is known and accepted before entry, capital is deployed at the sized level, the thesis plays out, option values adjust, risk is managed on plan rather than emotion, and proceeds rotate into the next opportunity.

### Spreads Versus Naked Options

Both naked options and spreads have a role—the question is which fits the setup, the volatility regime, and the risk you are willing to define:

| Structure | Advantages | Disadvantages |
|---|---|---|
| Naked long options | Uncapped upside; maximum leverage and convexity. | Expensive premiums; severe time decay; lower probability of profit; full exposure to IV crush. |
| Spreads | Lower cost; defined risk; improved capital efficiency; reduced Theta and Vega exposure. | Capped profit; somewhat greater structural complexity. |

### The Psychology of Discipline

Spreads demand a different mindset—focusing on probabilities, efficiency, and repeatability rather than dreaming of unlimited profits, which tends to produce better decisions. Capping upside is professional discipline, not weakness: brilliant traders chase unlimited gains and blow up; consistent compounders engineer repeatable edges. Spreads turn aggressive options trading from a lottery into a high-edge business.

### Final Principle: Law of Premium Arbitrage

Option spreads represent the evolution from raw speculation toward structured risk management, letting traders reduce cost, define risk, improve capital efficiency, manage volatility, and still participate fully in directional opportunity. The most successful traders eventually discover that extraordinary compounding is not merely about finding extraordinary opportunities—it is about managing risk intelligently enough to remain in the game long enough for compounding to work, and few strategies serve that objective as well as a well-constructed spread.

## E. Volatility Trading

Most traders believe they are trading direction, asking only whether the stock will rise, fall, or go nowhere. Professional options traders often focus on something else entirely: volatility—the magnitude of movement rather than its vector. Often the largest profits come not from predicting direction but from correctly predicting how far an asset will travel. **Volatility trading is the act of betting on the magnitude of an asset's move, independent of its direction**—when an asset sits under a coiled spring (an FDA decision, a contested earnings report, a macro release), the market knows a violent dislocation is coming but cannot map the vector, and the right structures let readers trade that pure kinetic expansion in either direction.

## What Is Volatility? Historical versus Implied

Volatility measures the rate and magnitude of price movement—a stock drifting 1% a day is far less volatile than one swinging 5%—and it is, in essence, the market's measure of uncertainty: the greater the uncertainty, the larger the expected move and the more expensive the options. Two measures anchor the discipline: **historical volatility** looks backward (how much a stock has actually moved), providing context but not pricing; **implied volatility (IV)**, derived from current option prices, looks forward, representing the market's expectation of future movement. The craft begins with reading IV correctly.

## The Mechanics of Vega and Gamma

To trade volatility with authority, stop seeing IV as a static statistic and start seeing it as a mean-reverting wave—it compresses into tight ranges of quiet equilibrium, then explodes into expansion before contracting again. Two derivative mechanics harvest the cycle. **The Vega engine:** vega measures how much premium changes per one-point shift in IV, so buying options while IV is historically crushed means buying artificially underpriced premium that inflates the moment uncertainty enters the tape, even before the underlying moves. **The Gamma explosion:** when an asset breaks out hard after a catalyst, gamma drives deltas toward 1.00 or 0.00 at extreme speed, transforming cheap contracts into highly reactive equity proxies within minutes. Vega captures the inflation of fear before the move; gamma captures the violence of the move itself.

## The Volatility Cycle

Because volatility mean-reverts, it travels a recognizable cycle readers can anticipate—calm conditions with cheap premiums, uncertainty emerging, volatility expanding and premiums rising, the catalyst arriving, resolution developing, then volatility contracting as premiums collapse in the crush.

## Why Volatility Creates Opportunity, and the Earnings Crush

Opportunity exists because markets routinely misprice uncertainty—options become excessively expensive, fear becomes exaggerated, or expectations detach from reality—and the volatility trader exploits the gap between expected volatility and the volatility that actually arrives. **Earnings and the volatility crush:** heading into a print, uncertainty rises, demand climbs, and IV expands; once the numbers are out, uncertainty evaporates and IV frequently collapses, so a trader can correctly predict direction and still lose because the IV that inflated the premium drains out the instant the news is known. Understanding the crush is the price of admission to event trading.

## Long Volatility and Short Volatility

Every volatility strategy falls on one side of a divide: you are either buying volatility or selling it. **Long volatility** wants to own options before a major move, benefiting from expanding IV and larger-than-expected movement—straddles and strangles (the purest magnitude bets), long calls and puts (directional but still long volatility), and calendar spreads (selling a near-term option and buying a longer-dated one to stay net long vega). **Short volatility** wants to sell expensive options and let them decay, benefiting from time decay and contracting IV—iron condors and credit spreads (defined-risk premium collection in a range), and covered calls. A non-negotiable rule: **never sell volatility naked**—always express a short view through defined-risk structures.

## The Tactical Playbook: Straddle versus Strangle

Readers deploy two market-neutral weapons, choosing on capital efficiency and the size of the expected move. **The long straddle** buys an ATM call and ATM put at the same strike (both near 0.50 delta), so the instant the underlying breaks out, one side ignites hyper-drive gamma that can eclipse the losing side's premium—reached for on high-liquidity mega-caps and index ETFs ahead of binary macro events. **The long strangle** buys an OTM call and OTM put, drastically lowering entry cost and maximizing leverage—reserved for high-beta mid-caps and biotech approaching binary catalysts where the expected move is enormous. **The selection protocol:** enter only when IV Rank is roughly 20% or lower over a 52-week window (volatility at wholesale), select 14 to 30 DTE (close enough for gamma velocity, far enough to avoid terminal theta), and cap risk at ~1% of the account per structure. Before entering, estimate how far the market is already pricing the move:

**Implied Move ≈ Stock Price × IV × √( Days to Event / 365 )**

A straddle or strangle only pays if the realized move exceeds this implied move. Two distinct plays: **the pre-event Vega play** (enter when IV Rank is low, then liquidate the afternoon before the event, capturing the run-up in premium from Vega expansion alone and sidestepping the crush—never holding through the news); and **the through-the-event move play** (hold through the catalyst and rely on a move large enough to overwhelm the crush—for example, an ATM straddle 20 to 30 DTE for a $6.50 net debit ahead of a Phase 3 readout, which can expand 80% to 250% if the stock gaps 15% to 25%, because the realized move dwarfs the lost Vega). Decide which one you are in before you enter, and never let a pre-event Vega play drift into an unplanned hold through the announcement.

## The Volatility Trading Governance Matrix

| Tactical Axis | The Retail Speculator | The Blueprint Capital Allocator |
|---|---|---|
| Directional bias | Picks a side on a binary earnings report, treating the catalyst like a coin flip. | Stays direction-agnostic, betting strictly on the magnitude of the information shock. |

| Tactical Axis | The Retail Speculator | The Blueprint Capital Allocator |
|---|---|---|
| IV timing | Buys at the peak of an IV spike (IV Rank near 95%) and is decimated by the crush. | Enters only when IV Rank is compressed (around 20% or lower), exploiting cheap premium. |
| Execution architecture | Holds through the announcement, praying for an impossibly large move. | On a Vega play, often liquidates the afternoon before the event to bank pre-event expansion. |
| Risk insulation | Allocates large, unhedged sizes to naked options, exposing the book to ruin. | Caps maximum risk at the structure's defined net debit, holding portfolio risk to a tight 1R. |

## Volatility and Market Regimes

Different environments produce different volatility profiles: low-volatility regimes (stable trends, predictable movement) favor selling premium through defined-risk condors, while high-volatility regimes (large swings, rapid shifts) favor owning premium ahead of moves. The blueprint trader keeps both modes loaded—long volatility into building catalysts, defined-risk short volatility to harvest premium after spikes—recycling the income from one into the funding of the other. Both fear and greed expand volatility, and both create the dislocations the volatility trader is built to exploit.

## Risk Management and Iron Discipline

Volatility trading can be extraordinarily profitable and dangerous in the same week. Risk no more than ~1% (at the structure's maximum defined loss) per volatility trade; use straddles and strangles only around high-conviction catalysts confirmed by volume and relative strength; respect theta (long-volatility positions bleed daily); never short volatility naked or into uncertain macro events or high-short-interest squeezes; and track portfolio vega and net Greeks daily. The five amateur errors—buying expensive options when the move is already priced, ignoring the crush, assuming a correct direction is enough, oversizing event trades, and trading options without understanding IV—separate professionals from the crowd.

## The Psychology of Volatility

Volatility trading trains a rare posture: neutrality. The beginner asks "Will the stock go up or down?"; the experienced volatility trader asks "Will the stock move more or less than the market expects?" That reframing is the whole game—the market has already priced the expected move, and profit lives in the gap between expectation and reality. Institutions treat volatility as a tradable asset class in its own right, and aggressive individuals can adopt the same perspective.

### Final Principle: The Law of Volatility Arbitrage

Volatility trading is the practice of trading expectations rather than direction, drawing value from uncertainty, implied volatility, event risk, and the architecture of option pricing—sources of profit invisible to the trader who watches only price. It is the tool that keeps readers alive and earning between the big directional swings, completing a toolkit in which calls and spreads play offense while volatility structures play both defense and opportunistic offense.

## F. Gamma Exposure

Among all the forces that move option prices, few are as powerful—or as poorly understood—as gamma. Most traders buy options for leverage, then treat gamma as an afterthought; the aggressive allocator knows it is the true kinetic engine of a 1,000 percent sprint, granting not simply leverage but *accelerating* leverage. When an asset breaks out with force, gamma bends the delta curve upward, turning a cheap contract into a hyper-reactive equity proxy in minutes. Where delta gives directional exposure, gamma decides how fast that exposure grows—the explosive convexity behind breakouts, momentum ignitions, gap-and-go setups, and squeezes.

### The Mathematics of Acceleration: What Gamma Is

Gamma cannot be understood without anchoring delta. Delta measures how much an option's value changes per $1.00 move in the underlying (a 0.50 delta means ~$0.50 of premium gain per $1.00 of stock), but delta is not fixed—as the stock moves, delta moves too, and gamma measures the speed of that change. In plain terms, delta is your velocity and gamma is your acceleration:

**New Delta = Original Delta + ( Gamma × Change in Stock Price )**

Two structural facts govern everything: gamma is highest for at-the-money contracts and tapers sharply as an option moves deep in- or out-of-the-money, and it is acutely sensitive to time—as expiration approaches, the gamma of ATM contracts explodes into a razor-thin needle. Near-term, at-the-money options therefore carry the highest kinetic energy on the chain, which is why they are both the sharpest tool and the most dangerous.

### The Market-Maker Sandbox: Forced Hedging

To trade gamma, readers must understand they are trading against options market makers, not other speculators. Market makers are risk-neutral: when a trader buys a call, the maker sells it and is left exposed if the stock rockets, so it buys shares of the underlying to stay delta-neutral. This continuous rebalancing is delta hedging, and gamma determines how fast the required hedging changes.

### The Gamma-Squeeze Feedback Loop

When a wave of aggressive speculators floods an asset with short-dated, near-the-money calls, dealers become deeply short gamma, and a self-reinforcing loop can ignite:

> **1.** Speculators flood near-term ATM and OTM call chains. ▼ **2.** Dealers, now short those calls, are short gamma. ▼ **3.** The stock ticks higher and option deltas accelerate vertically via gamma. ▼ **4.** To stay delta-neutral, dealer algorithms are forced to buy more underlying shares. ▼ **5.** That forced buying drives the stock higher — looping back to step 3 and compounding into a parabolic melt-up.

This is a gamma squeeze, among the fastest ways to book a 300 to 500 percent premium return—the buying is mechanical and non-discretionary, because dealers hedge when their risk models require it. **Positive (long) gamma:** you own the options, and as the stock moves in your favor delta increases rapidly—convexity working for you. **Negative (short) gamma:** dealers sit here when retail buys calls heavily, and their hedging manufactures the self-reinforcing move a long-gamma trader aims to front-run. Heavy put buying flips the machine into a downside cascade—gamma is a force, not a direction. Gamma effects are magnified when the float is scarce, which is why a gamma squeeze and a short squeeze so often travel together.

## The Tactical Playbook

Readers target setups where dealer vulnerability is highest, in two modes. **Mode 1 — the near-term gamma strike** (the pure squeeze play at the peak of the terminal gamma curve, for high-volume intraday breakouts and post-catalyst gap-and-go): 3 to 7 DTE weeklies sitting on the terminal gamma spike, strikes exactly ATM or one step OTM where gamma is maximized, open interest on the strike exceeding the stock's average daily share volume, and a 60-minute time-stop—if the breakout fails to produce vertical velocity, liquidate before overnight decay. **Mode 2 — long-gamma swing and volatility plays:** slightly OTM calls or a bull call spread 30 to 45 days out on RS breakouts; straddles or strangles ahead of binary events; gamma scalping (delta-hedging the underlying intraday while keeping the long-gamma exposure); and riding dealer gamma by front-running building negative GEX with long calls.

## Position Sizing and Risk Control

As always, the binding constraint is the loss, not the allocation: no single gamma position may risk more than 1 percent of total account equity ($1,000 on a $100,000 base). A near-term strike with a 60-minute time-stop might commit a 3 percent block while risking only 1 percent; a swing runs roughly 0.75 to 1 percent at risk. Exits are mechanical—scale out in tranches (a third near +80 percent, a third near +150 percent, a trailing stop on the rest), pyramid into confirmed acceleration never into hope, then rotate. One or two clean gamma-driven moves of 150 to 400 percent supply enormous compounding steps while defined risk keeps the account intact.

## Recognizing a Gamma Setup

No single indicator guarantees a squeeze, but the more that stack, the higher the probability hedging flows amplify price: elevated call volume and rising open interest concentrated at specific strikes; expanding IV and ATR confirming a real move; a genuine catalyst plus clear RS leadership; a constrained float; and open interest on the key strike exceeding average daily share volume. Large open-interest concentrations create magnetic price levels, and dealer-positioning tools (SpotGamma, Unusual Whales) add context on where gamma is concentrated—but they are context, never a standalone signal. A worked case: a low-float AI-power or biotech name prints an RS breakout on a volume surge with heavy call flow building negative dealer GEX; you buy 30-to-45-day slightly OTM calls (or a bull call spread) sizing for 0.75 to 1 percent risk, and as the stock runs 8 to 12 percent over one to three days, gamma ramps delta from ~0.45 toward 0.75+, converting that 10 percent stock move into a 120 to 300 percent gain on the option.

### Where Gamma Matters Most

Gamma effects concentrate in identifiable regimes—earnings season, AI momentum cycles and the power theme, biotech catalysts, meme-stock episodes, and broad corrections where put activity intensifies the downside machine. In 2026 specifically, heavy options flow across AI infrastructure, biotech catalysts, small- and mid-cap runners, and power names is producing frequent gamma clusters. Near-term expirations (0DTE through 30 DTE) amplify the effect, while LEAPS provide smoother, longer-dated gamma without the terminal decay.

### Retail Speculator vs. Blueprint Allocator

| Parameter | The Retail Speculator | The Blueprint Allocator |
|---|---|---|
| Mechanism | Buys weeklies because they are “cheap,” blind to the Greek dynamics. | Targets weeklies to exploit maximum gamma acceleration on confirmed breakouts. |
| Counterparty | Sees the options market as a casino, blind to dealer order books. | Tracks short-gamma thresholds to anticipate forced dealer buying. |
| Risk insulation | Holds bleeding weeklies overnight through chop; theta does the rest. | Enforces a strict ~60-minute intraday time-stop to insulate the ledger. |
| Monetization | Waits for infinite gains; lets a 400% expansion round-trip to zero by Friday. | Liquidates 50% into the peak hedging cascade, trails the rest. |

### Risks and the Iron Discipline Rules

Gamma creates opportunity and danger in equal measure, and gamma-driven moves reverse as fast as they develop. **Gamma decay:** long gamma is expensive and bleeds fast when the move stalls—limit hold time. **Volatility crush** can offset gamma gains even when direction is right. **Whipsaw** punishes long gamma hard—demand the full confirmation stack. The survival rules: risk no more than 1 percent per gamma position; use GEX tools for context but never trade on them alone; exit ruthlessly on momentum divergence (gamma works both ways); pair with protective spreads in uncertain regimes; track total portfolio gamma daily; and never chase a late-stage move—entering after most of the squeeze is the most common way to give the gains back.

### The Gamma Cycle

Most gamma-driven moves follow a recognizable progression—a catalyst emerges, call buying accelerates, dealers hedge and share purchases begin, the stock rises, gamma exposure increases and expands hedging demand further, public participation arrives, momentum peaks at volatility extremes, hedging pressure subsides, and consolidation or reversal sets in as the move unwinds.

### The Psychology of Trading Gamma

Gamma trading trains a single discipline: ride the acceleration, do not fight it. The best traders do not predict direction perfectly—they position for convexity when probability tilts in their favor, then let the math do the work, with the humility to accept that not every options-heavy chart will squeeze and the ruthlessness to exit the instant momentum diverges.

### The Final Principle

Gamma exposure shapes dealer hedging, stock-price movement, volatility, momentum, and liquidity all at once, and when it aligns with strong catalysts, heavy call activity, institutional participation, and a constrained float, it can produce some of the market's most explosive advances. Price is driven not only by what investors believe but by how dealers are forced to respond to those beliefs—and that forced response is where extraordinary, compoundable opportunities are born.

## G. Risk-Defined Strategies

One of the greatest misconceptions in aggressive trading is that extraordinary returns require unlimited risk—the reality is the opposite. To push a $100,000 ledger into seven figures in 180 days, readers cannot afford a single catastrophic drawdown, and the biggest flaw in most aggressive manuals is the glorification of naked, unhedged options that expose the trader to total premium wipeouts on every position. Risk-defined strategies are the structural shield—the mathematical act of placing an absolute, ironclad ceiling on the loss at the exact moment of entry. Using multi-leg structures eliminates catastrophic tail risk while keeping the explosive, asymmetric leverage the campaign requires.

### The Fallacy of the Naked Option

A speculator holding a naked option is exposed to vulnerabilities no stop-loss can fully contain. **The overnight gap:** a macro shock or surprise earnings leak can gap a stock down 30 percent before the open, bypassing standard stops entirely and erasing half the capital base. **The theta and vega tax:** a naked long option fights a ticking clock and shifting volatility at the same time. Risk-defined strategies solve this with a second contract that absorbs the risk—you give up a fraction of an "infinite" upside that seldom arrives for a clearinghouse-guaranteed ceiling on maximum loss.

## What a Risk-Defined Strategy Is, and the Mathematics of Survival

A risk-defined strategy is any option position where the maximum possible loss is known before entry: the trader knows the maximum risk, maximum reward, breakeven levels, and precise exposure. That predictability is not a constraint on aggression—it is what makes disciplined aggression possible, converting every trade into a known, repeatable bet rather than an open-ended gamble. The case is arithmetic, because losses and the gains required to recover them are not symmetric:

| Drawdown suffered | Gain required to recover |
|---|---|
| 20% | 25% |
| 50% | 100% |
| 75% | 300% |
| 90% | 900% |

A single uncontrolled position can wipe out months of progress and leave a mathematically punishing recovery burden—which is why survival comes first. Defined risk also creates psychological stability: with the worst case locked to a single 1R unit at entry, readers can sleep through overnight headlines, and that calm is itself an edge.

## The Core Risk-Defined Toolkit

Readers use directional, highly asymmetric structures built to maximize return on capital while caging the cash risk. **The debit vertical (the directional scalpel):** instead of buying a naked call, sell a further-OTM call against it, forming a bull call debit spread (or bear put debit spread on the short side)—maximum risk is strictly the net debit, the short leg drops capital required by as much as 40 percent, and the structure lifts into a clean 2:1 or 3:1 reward-to-risk. **Credit spreads (premium collection with a floor):** a bull put credit spread sold when you expect the stock to hold above support, a bear call credit spread when you expect it to stay below resistance—maximum loss capped at the strike width minus the credit, benefiting from time decay (an IV crush hurts debit spreads but helps credit spreads). **The iron condor (the volatility cage):** when a major index sits in a wide, sideways box, combine a bear call spread and a bull put spread, collecting a net credit on both sides while the long wings define the risk:

> **Maximum Risk = Width of the Spread – Net Credit Received**

If price stays inside the technical cage to expiration, the options decay to zero and the reader keeps the full credit. The butterfly is the condor's tightly targeted cousin—low cost, limited risk, and a sharp payoff peak when a stock gravitates toward a specific price. The standalone instruments already covered (a long call, long put, and LEAPS) are themselves risk-defined, capping loss at the premium paid; the spreads extend that principle, trading a piece of the upside for lower cost, lower decay, and a tighter box. The structures combine: layer a bull call debit spread on top of a core LEAPS or 3x ETF holding to add controlled, defined-risk torque without uncapping the downside.

### Execution and Position Sizing

Favor 30 to 60 DTE for swing structures; size every structure so the net debit (or capped credit-spread loss) is no more than ~0.5 to 1 percent of the account; pair each spread with an ATR-based stop on the underlying; and exit early on momentum divergence. Defined-risk trades aligned with momentum, relative strength, and a real catalyst frequently carry 55 to 70 percent win rates—but only when the structure sits on a genuine thesis. Worked example: an AI-power or biotech mid-cap prints a breakout with a real catalyst; the stock trades at $62, and you buy the $60 call and sell the $70 call, 45 days out, for a $3.80 net debit ($380 of risk per spread), sizing 15 to 25 percent of the account into ~40 to 65 spreads to keep total risk near 0.8 to 1 percent. Maximum reward is about $620 per spread if the stock finishes above $70 (~163 percent return on risk), and in practice an 18 percent run in ten to twelve days often carries the spread to 100 to 180 percent before expiry—every single trade with a hard floor on the loss.

### Retail Speculator vs. Blueprint Allocator

| Dimension | The Retail Speculator | The Blueprint Allocator |
|---|---|---|
| Downside | Naked equity or options, exposed to catastrophic overnight gaps. | Structural cap on every trade; max loss guaranteed at entry. |
| Capital efficiency | Ties up large margin in single positions, slowing compounding. | Uses defined wings to cut margin and lift return on capital. |
| Catalysts | Gambles binary events naked; falls victim to IV crush. | Uses hedged multi-leg structures to blunt IV swings. |
| Psychology | Stressed by overnight news into erratic decisions. | Sleeps with the worst case locked to 1R. |

### Where Risk-Defined Structures Shine

Volatile markets create extraordinary opportunity and danger at once, which is exactly where defined risk earns its keep—earnings season, biotech catalysts, AI momentum cycles, corrections, and any high-volatility environment. The 2026 backdrop fits: rotational markets with frequent breakouts and catalysts reward bull call debit spreads on the upside, while bear put spreads and iron condors handle hedges and range plays.

## Risks and the Iron Discipline Rules

Defined risk is not the same as no risk. **Capped upside:** you surrender some unlimited gain for safety—accept it as professional risk management. **Assignment risk:** monitor short legs near expiration. **Volatility direction:** IV crush hurts debit spreads and helps credit spreads—match the structure to the volatility you expect. The survival rules: never risk more than 1 percent on any single structure; prefer 30 to 60 DTE for swings; exit early on momentum divergence; track portfolio Greeks (especially net delta and theta); pair every spread with an ATR-based stop; and keep structures simple—a clean two-leg spread beats an over-complex one most of the time.

## The Risk-Defined Trading Cycle

Most successful risk-defined trades move through a repeatable process—an opportunity is identified, the appropriate structure is selected, maximum loss is calculated before entry, the position is established, the thesis unfolds, exposure remains controlled throughout, profits or losses are realized within the predefined box, and capital is redeployed.

## The Psychology of Capping Upside

The hardest lesson for an aggressive trader is that capping the upside is not weakness—it is the discipline that separates the survivors who reach $1,000,000 from the brilliant traders who blow up on the way there. Extraordinary wealth is not made by finding one exceptional opportunity; it is made by surviving long enough to exploit many. Risk-defined strategies turn the blueprint from a high-stakes gamble into a repeatable, high-edge business.

## The Final Principle

Risk-defined strategies let a trader combine leverage, flexibility, capital efficiency, and opportunity with a clearly defined downside. The best traders understand that extraordinary returns are not created merely by finding exceptional setups, but by surviving long enough to exploit many of them. For a campaign chasing accelerated returns, this is the framework that balances aggression with discipline—because the goal is not simply to win big, but to win big while ensuring that no single mistake ever has the power to end the journey.

## Chapter 12
# Warrants and Structured Speculation

## A. SPAC Warrants

Among the most misunderstood instruments in speculative finance are SPAC warrants. During the 2020–21 boom, some traders generated extraordinary returns while others suffered devastating losses, and the dividing line was almost always whether they understood how the instrument worked. The retail public ignores warrants for their complexity, and many institutions are legally restricted from holding them—and that neglect is precisely what creates the opportunity. For the aggressive speculator, a SPAC warrant is best understood as **the ultimate penny-option hybrid**: a long-dated, asset-backed call option granting hyper-leveraged exposure to small- and mid-cap mergers, where a handful of winners returning several hundred to over a thousand percent can reshape the compounding curve while each loss is capped at the small amount committed. They are never core capital.

### What Is a SPAC, and Its Structure

A SPAC (Special Purpose Acquisition Company) is a publicly traded shell formed for a single purpose: to acquire or merge with a private company and take it public. At IPO it has no operating business, no revenues—its primary asset is cash held in trust—and the objective is to find a target, complete a business combination, and bring that company public (the de-SPAC). The IPO is sold in **units** bundling a share of common with a warrant or fraction of a warrant; after a defined period the units separate and trade independently, creating multiple ways to participate in the same transaction.

### The Anatomy of a SPAC Warrant

See a SPAC warrant not as a stock but as a long-dated call option issued by the company itself—a contractual right to buy common shares at a predetermined price, exercisable once the combination closes. Three features define it. **The strike-price baseline:** by near-universal convention, standard SPAC warrants carry an exercise price of $11.50 per share. **The maturity runway:** they typically run roughly five years from merger completion, giving the business years to execute. **The leveraged catch-up:** because the warrant is a fixed-strike right, it moves with enormous convexity—if a hot target announces a merger and the common climbs from a $10.00 baseline to $20.00 (a 100% move), a warrant struck at $11.50 might travel from $0.50 toward its intrinsic value of $8.50, a roughly 1,600% return on the identical corporate event.

### Warrants Versus Common Shares and Call Options

Picture two traders in the same name: one buys common, the other warrants. If the stock rises moderately, both profit; if it rises dramatically, the warrant holder captures a far larger percentage gain through embedded leverage. SPAC warrants share much DNA with call options—leveraged upside, defined capital commitment—but the differences are structural: warrants are far longer-dated and are issued *about* the company rather than written by other participants, which means exercise can create new shares. One correction worth making explicitly: a warrant is *not* free of time decay—as a long-dated option it carries time value that erodes slowly when expiration is years away, then faster as the runway shortens. The advantage over a short-dated option is not the absence of decay but its pace; treat the long runway as patience, not immunity.

## The Leverage Effect and the Merger Target

The primary attraction is leverage: a warrant near a dollar can generate extraordinary percentage gains if the merged company becomes a genuine success, which is why warrant traders gravitate toward disruptive themes—AI, EVs and autonomous systems, fintech, biotech, cybersecurity, robotics, space. This is the asymmetry aggressive traders prize: downside limited to the small premium committed, paired with upside that can run to several multiples. A single multi-bagger can pay for many losing positions. But none of this matters if the underlying business is weak—the warrant's value rests on the quality of the merger target. Low price is not low risk; you buy a warrant because you believe the company can become substantially more valuable, not because the ticket is cheap.

## The Tactical Playbook: The Definitive-Agreement Shock

Readers never buy blindly during the quiet blank-check phase, which ties up capital for months on a rumor—they trade a datable event: the **Definitive Agreement**. **Stage 1 — the shock:** a SPAC announces a definitive merger with a high-conviction target, and the common gaps up on heavy volume, clearing $12.00 and pulling the $11.50-strike warrant into the money. **Stage 2 — the disconnect:** with the common at, say, $15.00, the warrant's intrinsic value is roughly $3.50, yet it may still trade well below that, at perhaps $1.50, because retail cannot price warrants and restricted institutions cannot accumulate them. **Stage 3 — the concentration blitz:** into that gap, deploy a single defined capital block using staggered limit orders, capturing the convergence toward intrinsic value and the momentum that follows, then exit into strength.

## The Disconnect Qualification Matrix

A setup qualifies only when two structural conditions are present together: **common-stock confirmation** (the common clears roughly $12.00 on heavy volume, pulling the warrant inherently into the money) and **a genuine warrant discount** (the warrant trades at a meaningful discount to its theoretical intrinsic value, common-stock price minus $11.50). Without that disconnect, there is no edge, only a leveraged directional bet.

## Sizing and Risk Caging

Because warrants trade with thin liquidity and wide spreads, position sizing is the difference between a satellite bet and a portfolio wound. **Treat the entire allocation as the maximum loss**—a warrant can go to zero, so cap that risk at roughly 1% of the account per position (some traders use as little as

0.5%) and size the number of warrants to that risk. **Use a thesis-based stop, not a percentage stop**—standard percentage stops are useless inside wide spreads, so map the technical stop to the common: if it breaks back below its $10.00 trust floor, the merger thesis is likely failing and the warrants are liquidated immediately.

### The Redemption Trap and Other Structural Risks

SPAC warrants carry structural risks that can erase value overnight. **The redemption guard:** most charters contain a company call provision—if the common trades above roughly $18.00 for 20 of 30 consecutive trading days, the company can force holders to exercise or redeem, often for as little as $0.01 to $0.10. The rule is absolute: never hold a warrant past a corporate redemption notice; monetize into the peak of the hype and exit before forced conversion. **Redemption of shares and failed mergers:** shareholders can redeem for cash rather than participate, and heavy redemptions drain capital and can sink both the deal and the warrants. **Dilution:** exercising warrants creates new shares. **Liquidity:** thin trading produces wide spreads that bite hardest precisely when you most need to get out.

### The 2026 Market Context

SPAC activity has rebounded from its post-boom collapse into a more disciplined regime—tighter regulation, higher-quality sponsors, more real businesses—with well over a hundred SPAC IPOs in the most recent year raising tens of billions. Warrants remain deeply speculative and many still carry live redemption risk; the edge is selectivity, with warrants tied to credible sponsors and genuine execution stories in AI and data-center enablement, power, biotech, and industrials able to explode on results while the rest expire worthless. Quality of deal, not cheapness of ticket, is the filter.

### The SPAC Warrant Governance Matrix

| Operational Parameter | The Retail Gambler | The Blueprint Capital Allocator |
|---|---|---|
| Timing alignment | Buys at the IPO stage and leaves capital dead for years hoping for a rumor. | Strikes only on Definitive Agreement confirmation, when a real catalyst is on the tape. |
| Pricing execution | Fires market orders into wide spreads, surrendering size instantly to slippage. | Accumulates with staggered limit orders inside the liquidity pocket. |
| Risk insulation | Ignores filings and is caught flat-footed by a forced redemption call. | Tracks the $18.00 redemption threshold and exits before forced conversion. |
| Portfolio role | Treats the warrant as a permanent holding and falls in love with the target. | Treats it as a short-term, high-leverage chip to fund a specific milestone. |

### Risk Management and Iron Discipline

Warrants are the highest-octane layer of the toolkit. Risk no more than about 0.5% to 1% of the account (measured as the full allocation) on any single warrant; focus only on high-conviction sponsors and themes confirmed by relative strength and volume on the common; exit ruthlessly on a broken thesis or an approaching redemption trigger; use warrants strictly as satellite bets, never core capital; and journal every warrant with its exact terms, catalyst timeline, and exit plan before entering. Most losses trace to buying purely because a warrant looks cheap, ignoring business quality, overlooking redemption and expiration terms, underestimating illiquidity, and overconcentrating.

### The Psychology of SPAC Warrants

Warrants combine low prices, high leverage, and large upside narratives—a potent emotional cocktail that tempts excessive optimism, overconcentration, and dependence on a single outcome. The successful warrant trader feels the excitement and acts against it: small size, predefined exits, and a willingness to be wrong cheaply many times in exchange for being right enormously a few times.

### The SPAC Warrant Cycle

Most successful warrant trades move through a recognizable arc—SPAC formation raises capital into trust, management searches for a target, the merger announcement lands and attention spikes, investors run due diligence, the business combination closes, growth execution proves the thesis, institutional participation expands and liquidity improves, valuation re-rates, and warrant appreciation accelerates as embedded leverage amplifies the move.

### Final Principle: The Law of Structured Inefficiency

SPAC warrants blend long-duration leverage, merger catalysts, growth-company exposure, and asymmetric return potential into one instrument. For the aggressive trader they open opportunities common stock cannot, but leverage magnifies both insight and error—success depends on business quality, management execution, market conditions, valuation discipline, and risk management, in that order. The most successful warrant traders never buy simply because a warrant is cheap; they buy because they believe the company can become far more valuable, and they size so that being wrong is survivable.

## B. Penny Warrants

Among the most speculative instruments available, few rival the explosive potential of penny warrants. They trade for pennies—sometimes only a few cents—yet can occasionally produce returns measured in hundreds or thousands of percent. They are a lottery ticket with structure, sitting at the very top of this book's risk ladder, the higher-octane sibling of SPAC warrants. Where the retail public gambles blindly on low-float penny stocks, the disciplined speculator reaches for the penny warrant as a **micro-cap asymmetry engine**—long-dated call options tied to micro-cap, small-cap, and pre-revenue companies, priced in literal pennies, where a modest recovery in the underlying can send the warrant up many hundreds of percent with downside capped at the small amount committed. Most eventually expire worthless, and sizing for both realities is the entire discipline of the asset class.

## What Is a Penny Warrant, and Why They Exist

A penny warrant is simply a warrant trading at a low market price—typically below a dollar, often below $0.50, sometimes below $0.10. Like every warrant it grants the right to buy common shares at a predetermined exercise price before expiration; the warrant is not ownership but a contractual right whose value depends almost entirely on the underlying's future performance. Many are detachable and trade separately, often for two to five years or more.

Penny warrants arise through two routes. The first is **collapse**—a warrant becomes a penny warrant when the underlying declines substantially, but not every distressed warrant stays distressed, and opportunity is born from those depressed levels when circumstances change. The second is **structural**, where the deeper edge lives: micro-cap companies raise capital by issuing units to accredited investors and funds, a unit bundling one common share with a full or fractional warrant (the sweetener). The funds often dump the common immediately to recover principal, keeping the warrants at essentially no cost—and because those warrants then trade on thin, lightly followed boards ignored by institutional algorithms, they are prone to extreme structural mispricing.

## The Mathematics of Asymmetry and Leverage

The attraction reduces to a single comparison. Suppose a common stock rises from $2 to $4: the holder earns 100%, an excellent result. Now suppose a warrant on that same stock rises from $0.10 to $1.00 over the move: the holder earns 900%. The underlying merely doubled, yet the warrant multiplied many times over through embedded leverage—but that leverage is symmetric in its indifference, amplifying failure exactly as readily as success: the same structure that can return 900% usually returns negative one hundred percent.

## Why Time and Exercise Prices Matter

Warrants often run several years, buying time for execution, financing, and adoption to unfold—but long-dated is not decay-free, and a warrant's time value erodes slowly while expiration is distant and faster as the runway shortens. Every warrant carries an **exercise price**, and a low warrant price means nothing in isolation; what matters is the relationship between stock price, exercise price, and time remaining. A cheap warrant struck far above an achievable stock price is not a bargain—it is a slow expiration.

## The Importance of Catalysts

Penny warrants need **catalysts** to reprice; without one, even a genuinely cheap warrant can stay cheap until it expires. The events that ignite them include successful financings, revenue acceleration, regulatory approvals, major contracts, M&A, uplistings, partnerships, and breakthroughs. The largest gains come from turnaround stories—companies that fell, then reversed—because expectations there begin from the floor: when expectations are depressed, positive surprises carry disproportionate weight, and the warrant's embedded leverage magnifies the repricing dramatically. Emerging-technology names in AI, quantum computing, advanced semiconductors, biotech, robotics, energy innovation, cybersecurity, and aerospace supply a steady stream of such depressed-then-revalued situations.

## The Tactical Playbook: The Micro-Cap Coiled Spring

Readers never buy a penny warrant on a dying business hoping for a miracle—they treat it as a pure structural option and wait for an unmistakable inflection on the underlying common. The setup is a coiled spring: a long base, then a violent release on real information. **Stage 1 – the catalyst:** the company announces a genuine, material event (a major resource find, a surprise clinical clearance, a government contract) that rewrites the story. **Stage 2 – the equity inflection:** the common breaks out of a multi-month base on overwhelming volume while the warrant still trades at an extreme discount to model value. **Stage 3 – the asymmetric deployment:** commit a single, deliberately tiny capital block through patient tiered limit orders, treating the entire allocation as a max-loss premium, then scale out into the strength.

## The Dynamic Entry Filter

A penny warrant qualifies only after the underlying common clears a strict momentum gate: **the volume shock** (the common prints a breakout day exceeding its 50-day average volume by roughly 500% or more, evidence of a real information shock rather than forum chatter) and **the warrant-price and runway floor** (the warrant trades between about $0.05 and $0.50, with at least 12 to 24 months of life remaining, capturing maximal structural leverage before terminal time decay surfaces).

## Sizing, Risk Caging, and the Max-Loss Proxy

Because penny warrants carry wide spreads and fragmented order books, conventional percentage stops are actively harmful—a 10% stop on a $0.10 warrant can be triggered by a single stray quote—so the blueprint replaces the price stop with a max-loss option-proxy framework. **The allocation cap:** keep each position small and never let the entire penny-warrant sleeve exceed roughly 5% of the account (draft sizing for individual bets ranges from about 0.5% up to 2%—settle on a single figure and treat it as a hard ceiling). **The risk rule:** treat the chosen allocation as already spent at entry—the small size is the stop, and what remains is a thesis-and-volume exit, cut immediately if the catalyst proves false or breakout volume collapses.

The payoff, in a successful case: if a low-float micro-cap runs from $0.40 to $2.00 on a momentum squeeze, a warrant carrying heavy delta and gamma acceleration might travel from $0.05 toward $1.05, so a $2,000 block would expand toward $42,000—a milestone-class compounding step—while maximum downside stayed locked at a small fraction of the portfolio. Such outcomes are the exception, not the expectation; most positions are written off, which is exactly why each one must be small enough to lose without flinching.

### The Penny Warrant Governance Matrix

| Operational Parameter | The Retail Gambler | The Blueprint Capital Allocator |
|---|---|---|
| Asset evaluation | Buys on anonymous forum hype, praying to ride a pump-and-dump. | Enters only after a roughly 500% volume shock validates a real catalyst. |
| Order execution | Surrenders the edge with reckless market orders inside wide spreads. | Accumulates only through patient, passive tiered limit orders. |
| Risk management | Bets an outsized share of the account on one micro-cap and courts ruin. | Caps each position to a tiny max-loss proxy, insulating the core capital base. |
| Monetization | Holds the illiquid warrant out of greed, watching a multi-bagger round-trip to zero. | Scales out into the vertical volume on the way up, returning to cash. |

### The 2026 Market Context

Penny-warrant activity remains alive in the speculative corners—biotech micro-caps on clinical catalysts, AI micro-infrastructure, energy-transition plays, and classic turnarounds. Tighter regulatory scrutiny has cleaned up some of the worst promotion schemes, but genuine high-asymmetry opportunities persist for the disciplined: a handful of names tied to real catalysts can explode while the broad universe drifts to zero. Quality of catalyst, not cheapness of the ticket, is the filter.

### The Structural Risks

Penny warrants carry risks severe enough that most positions fail. **Wipeout rate:** most go to zero—failed catalysts, poor execution, dilution, and forced redemption routinely destroy the entire position, and this is the base case, not the tail. **Liquidity and manipulation:** extremely thin markets produce wide spreads and fertile ground for pump-and-dump activity. **Dilution:** most structures imply future share issuance on exercise. **Time and expiration:** even long-dated penny warrants remain subject to theta.

### Risk Management and Iron Discipline

This is the highest-risk layer of the toolkit, and the discipline must be the strictest in the book. Keep total exposure across all penny warrants at or below roughly 5% of the account, each position far smaller; require a full confirmation stack before entry (volume expansion, a credible catalyst, improving relative strength, signs of institutional or dark-pool interest); hold a strict predefined exit plan; never use margin and never oversize; and journal every position with its exact terms, exercise price, expiration, dilution profile, catalyst timeline, and exit plan before committing a dollar.

### The Psychology and Portfolio Role

Few instruments tempt the emotions like a five- or ten-cent warrant—the low absolute price invites a trader to imagine immediate riches and forget that low price is not low risk. That fantasy is precisely what funds the losses of the crowd. Because penny warrants are so speculative, position sizing is not a detail—it is the strategy: treat them as satellite positions orbiting a solid core, so the inevitable losers never threaten that core while the winners deliver outsized compounding steps.

### The Penny Warrant Cycle

Most successful penny-warrant trades move through a recognizable arc—expectations collapse and speculation drains away, a catalyst emerges as business conditions improve, investors rediscover the story, the stock advances, warrant leverage activates and percentage gains accelerate, momentum expands as new participants pile in, and warrant appreciation multiplies.

### Final Principle: The Law of Micro-Cap Asymmetry

Penny warrants are the most speculative yet potentially rewarding instrument available, combining low entry cost, embedded leverage, long-duration optionality, and asymmetric return potential. The best opportunities appear when expectations are depressed, a catalyst is developing, management is executing, fundamentals are improving, and the market has not yet noticed—but success depends on identifying a company whose future will prove dramatically more valuable than the market believes, and sizing so that being wrong, repeatedly, costs almost nothing.

## C. Deep Optionality

Among the most powerful concepts in speculative investing is **deep optionality**—the pursuit of positions where downside is relatively limited, upside is potentially enormous, and the future contains multiple pathways to success. Some of the greatest fortunes were built not by forecasting every detail correctly, but by owning assets with extraordinary optionality and letting an uncertain future resolve favorably. Warrants are among the purest optionality instruments available, and deep optionality reframes the central question: instead of asking *"what is this company worth today?"* the trader asks *"what could this company become if several favorable outcomes occur?"* For an aggressive campaign, it is the patient, high-conviction structure that compounds in the background while the tactical engine runs at full throttle around it.

### What Is Optionality?

Optionality is the value created by uncertainty—when future outcomes vary widely, opportunity emerges. A mature, predictable company has little; a company facing a future ranging from outright failure to industry domination is riskier, yet that very uncertainty creates its optionality, and a warrant lets a trader participate in the full spread of outcomes rather than betting on a single forecast. A warrant is fundamentally an option on a future outcome: the holder pays not mainly for present value but for future possibility, and because warrants are leveraged, they magnify successful outcomes.

### The Power of Multiple Pathways and Why Markets Misprice It

The most attractive feature of deep optionality is several independent routes to success—a company might win because its technology works, demand accelerates, a strategic partner emerges, a major customer signs, regulation turns favorable, the industry consolidates, or a catalyst no one anticipated arrives. The more independent ways an outcome can break right, the greater the embedded optionality. Markets are excellent at pricing current conditions and far weaker at pricing distant possibilities, so warrants occasionally trade at a structural pricing disconnect: because they trade on thin secondary boards, are poorly understood by retail, and are off-limits to many institutions, their premium can decouple from model value, occasionally leaving a meaningful discount—which can be a genuine margin of safety or the market correctly pricing real risk, and telling the two apart is the whole skill.

### The Venture-Capital Mindset and Optionality Versus Probability

Most investors think linearly; markets often move exponentially—a company generating a million dollars of revenue may eventually generate ten million, a hundred million, or a billion—and when a warrant is attached to a business capable of exponential growth, the combination of that nonlinearity with the warrant's leverage is where the largest returns originate. Deep optionality resembles venture-capital investing: many bets fail, some survive, and a rare few generate extraordinary returns that pay for all the losers. And probability is not payoff—a 10% chance of rising twenty-fold may carry higher expected value than an 80% chance of doubling. Deep optionality deliberately hunts that second kind of situation; the objective is to maximize expected opportunity, not certainty.

### The Core Mechanics of Deep Optionality

Two structural properties give deep optionality its teeth, both flowing from years of remaining life. **The quiet clock (near-zero near-term decay):** a 45-day option bleeds time value daily, but a corporate warrant carrying three to seven years of life sees negligible decay over a 30-to-90-day window—not literally zero theta, but small enough to ignore in practice, so the holder buys directional leverage without a meaningful ticking clock. **The delta slingshot (convexity from a coiled spring):** deep optionality targets warrants whose underlying sits just below or at the exercise strike (around $11.50 for many SPACs, anywhere from a couple of dollars to ten or more for micro-cap raises), where delta might sit near 0.30 to 0.40—but because years of life remain, a sharp breakout triggers rapid gamma acceleration toward 0.80, so a 50% move in the stock can translate into a several-hundred-percent expansion in the warrant.

## Key Forms of Deep Optionality

Deep optionality shows up in several recognizable structures: **long-dated company warrants** (issued by micro- and mid-cap growth companies after a financing or turnaround, exercise prices commonly in the low-single to low-double digits, expirations of roughly four to seven years), **structured or pre-funded warrants** (bundled with debt or equity raises, sometimes carrying cashless-exercise or variable-share provisions that deepen convexity), and **special-situation warrants** (from distressed restructurings, mergers, or PIPE financings, occasionally with terms unusually favorable to the holder).

## Optionality, Narratives, and Identifying It

Markets are driven by narratives as well as fundamentals, and because leverage amplifies shifts in expectation, warrants are exquisitely sensitive to changing stories—a strengthening narrative can re-rate a warrant violently upward, just as a fading one can collapse it. Real optionality clusters around a recognizable set of business characteristics; the strongest setups combine most of the following:

| Characteristic | What it signals |
|---|---|
| Large addressable market | Room for the business to grow many times over. |
| Scalable business model | Revenue can expand rapidly without proportional cost. |
| Transformational product | The offering can change industry behavior, not just compete within it. |
| Strong management team | Execution capability to convert possibility into results. |
| Financial survivability | Enough resources or funding to reach the key milestones. |
| Long-duration warrants | Time remaining for the thesis to actually develop. |

## The Danger of False Optionality

Not every cheap warrant is deep optionality—many are simply permanent impairment wearing a low price tag. A company with declining revenue, no financing, weak management, and no credible catalyst has little genuine optionality, no matter how inviting the warrant looks. The distinction between real and false optionality is the difference between a venture bet and a donation, and learning to tell them apart, by insisting on a business capable of meaningful transformation, is the core analytical task of the chapter.

## The Tactical Playbook: The Deep-Optionality Capture

Readers never buy illiquid warrants on stagnant companies—they wait for the underlying to prove a regime shift before deploying a dollar. **Regime inflection detected:** the common breaks out to multi-month highs on volume expansion of roughly 300% or more of its 50-day average. **Evaluate the deep optionality:** verify the warrant trades at a meaningful discount (the blueprint looks for 30% or more) to its theoretical option value, and has at least 18 months of runway remaining. **Position asymmetrically:** deploy a single, deliberately small capital block through patient limit orders, treating the entire allocation as a capped max-loss premium.

## Sizing and Risk Insulation

Because these warrants have fragmented order books, conventional percentage stops are forbidden—a random spread expansion would strip the position out—so the blueprint substitutes a max-loss option-proxy framework. **Per-position risk:** keep each deep-optionality position small, on the order of 0.75% to 1% of the account, treated as fully at risk from entry (one draft sizes individual blocks far larger, at 4% or more—settle on a single figure and treat it as a hard ceiling). **Total bucket:** keep the entire deep-optionality and structured-speculation sleeve at or below roughly 10% to 12% of the account. **Exit, not stop:** the small size is the stop; govern the position with milestone-based scaling and a thesis-and-time exit, cut on a broken thesis, a dilution announcement, or dwindling runway.

Illustrative example: identify a mid- or small-cap AI-power, biotech, or energy-transition company with real fundamentals, a near-term catalyst, improving relative strength, and long-dated warrants trading at roughly $1.20 to $2.80, struck above the current stock but reachable within twelve to twenty-four months. You enter at conservative size, and as the company executes and the common rises 50% to 150% over three to six months, the warrant's convexity and delta expansion can produce several hundred percent—you scale out in tranches and rotate proceeds into core momentum positions, 3x ETF swings, or options spreads.

## The Deep-Optionality Governance Matrix

| Operational Parameter | The Retail Speculator | The Blueprint Capital Allocator |
|---|---|---|
| Asset selection | Buys cheap, far-out-of-the-money warrants on failing businesses, as lottery tickets. | Targets warrants where the underlying has validated an active institutional trend shift. |
| Risk management | Uses market stops on illiquid boards and is wiped out by random spread noise. | Treats the small allocation as a fixed max-loss proxy, removing stop-hunt vulnerability. |
| Pricing awareness | Assumes the warrant tracks the stock's daily percentage | Exploits structural pricing discounts to secure a margin |

| Operational Parameter | The Retail Speculator | The Blueprint Capital Allocator |
|---|---|---|
| | moves one-for-one. | of safety at entry. |
| Portfolio role | Either bets too small to matter or concentrates recklessly into one name. | Sizes a calculated, capped block within a diversified optionality sleeve. |

## Risk, Dilution, Discipline, and the Portfolio Approach

Deep optionality is the highest-convexity layer of the toolkit, and its risks compound accordingly. Dilution is foremost—companies can issue new shares and heavily erode warrant value, and many underlying businesses simply fail. Forced or cashless redemption can end a position abruptly when the stock trades well above the strike, and the same illiquidity that creates the pricing discount also makes entry and exit slippage brutal. Cap total deep-optionality exposure at roughly 10% to 12% of the account with each position far smaller; require strong confirmation (relative-strength leadership, institutional flows, a real catalyst pipeline, favorable warrant terms); hold a strict exit and scale plan tied to milestones and remaining time; never chase hype; and journal every term sheet and redemption trigger before committing.

Warrants let a trader express high-conviction views with far less capital than the equivalent stock, which makes deep optionality naturally a portfolio strategy rather than a single bet. Because individual outcomes are so uncertain, the right structure is several positions across multiple industries, catalysts, and timelines, so failures are expected and survivable while any one breakout can move the whole ledger.

## The Deep-Optionality Cycle

Most successful optionality trades move through a recognizable progression—opportunity is ignored and expectations stay low, catalysts begin emerging, the market notices and narratives strengthen, capital flows accelerate as institutional participation rises, valuations re-rate, warrant leverage activates, and optionality becomes reality as the market prices success rather than mere possibility.

## Final Principle: The Law of Deep Optionality

Deep optionality is the art of investing in possibilities rather than certainties—asymmetric outcomes, transformational opportunities, long-duration catalysts, and extraordinary upside. Warrants express this philosophy better than almost any other instrument because they bundle leverage, time, capital efficiency, and exposure to future success into a single low-cost claim. The richest opportunities appear exactly where expectations are low, uncertainty is high, and attention is scarce—which is why they are so often overlooked, and why a disciplined framework for finding and sizing them is such an edge.

## D. Dilution Risks

One of the most overlooked dangers in warrant investing is dilution. Traders pour attention into leverage, upside, catalysts, and growth, and far too few think about what happens when warrants are actually exercised—yet dilution is the most common reason a warrant position ends up worthless. The retail public assumes a warrant is simply a permanent proxy for a long-dated call option. It is not: **a listed option is a contract written between speculators; a warrant is a contract written directly with the issuing corporation.** When a listed option is exercised, no new shares are created; when a warrant is exercised, the company mints brand-new shares. Leverage creates opportunity; dilution reduces ownership; their interaction usually determines whether a warrant becomes an engine of wealth or a slow trap.

### What Is Dilution, and Why Warrants Create It

Dilution occurs when additional shares are issued: as the share count rises, ownership percentages fall, earnings per share can decline, and value is spread across a larger base. Own 10% of a company with one million shares; if it later issues another million, your stake falls to 5%—you hold the same number of shares but own a smaller slice. Every warrant represents the potential creation of new shares: when holders exercise, they pay the exercise price, fresh shares are issued, and total shares outstanding climb. A warrant is not a discounted share; it is a future claim on equity, and the apparent leverage must always be weighed against the dilution it implies.

### What Dilution Does to a Warrant

Dilution attacks a warrant through three reinforcing channels: **immediate price pressure** (more shares mean a lower ownership percentage per share, pushing the stock down), **reduced intrinsic value** (a falling stock pushes the warrant toward or below its strike, where intrinsic value vanishes), and **psychological and liquidity damage** (wider spreads, thinner volume, and lost confidence compound the decline).

A simplified illustration: a stock trades at $4.00 with a warrant exercise price of $2.50, so the warrant carries $1.50 of intrinsic value and might trade around $1.65 with a little time value. The company then dilutes by 30%—common in cash-burning micro-cap biotech or capital-hungry AI names—and the stock falls to roughly $3.10. The warrant's intrinsic value collapses from $1.50 to about $0.60, and the warrant itself may trade down toward $0.70: a 30% dilution has produced a roughly 55% to 60% drop in the warrant, and in harsher cases a 50% to 80% loss, turning a would-be multi-bagger into a deep loser almost overnight.

### The Anatomy of the Dilution Landmine

Beyond ordinary issuance, structured warrants carry two specific dilution vectors. **The share-count explosion (the float flood):** when an underlying rockets past its warrant strike, a wave of holders exercises at once—picture a tight, low-float company with 10 million common shares and 5 million trading warrants; if the stock surges and those warrants convert, the share count expands by 50% in short order, inflating the float and unleashing a wall of selling that caps the parabolic move. **The cashless-exercise trap:** buried in many warrant agreements is a provision that delivers only a fractional share based on a fair-market-value formula written to protect the corporation—in practice it can strip the warrant of its remaining time premium and shut down its non-linear leverage in a single event, so readers must know whether it exists before they buy.

### Fully Diluted Share Count, and Why It Matters

The most important number most speculators never check is the **fully diluted share count**—the total shares that could exist once warrants and options are exercised and convertibles converted. Beginners look only at current shares outstanding; professionals look at the fully diluted figure, and the gap can be enormous. Two companies each with 50 million shares outstanding look comparable, but if Company B has 100 million warrants outstanding, exercise could eventually carry it to 150 million shares, and every per-share metric shifts dramatically. A low share price tells you nothing about whether a company is cheap, because market cap is price times shares.

### Convertible Debt, Shelf Registrations, and the Modern Dilution Toolkit

Warrants are only one source of new shares. Many speculative companies finance through convertible notes that let lenders convert debt into stock at favorable, sometimes low, prices, and the modern micro-cap dilution toolkit is broader still—in the current environment, biotech with heavy trial burn, AI infrastructure with heavy capex, and speculative energy names lean on equity raises, especially below roughly $500 million in market value. The specific structures to watch: frequent S-3 shelf registrations, at-the-market (ATM) offerings that drip new stock continuously, convertible notes with low conversion prices, and PIPE deals that often arrive with their own discounted warrants attached.

### Good Dilution Versus Bad, the Overhang, and Reading the Capital Structure

Not all dilution is harmful—many growth companies issue equity to fund expansion, acquisitions, R&D, or capacity, and if that capital is invested well, shareholder value can rise even as ownership is diluted. The decisive question is always whether the value created exceeds the ownership surrendered: good dilution accelerates growth and long-term value; bad dilution merely funds losses, props up weak operations, or enriches insiders. A large **warrant overhang** can suppress valuation and create persistent selling pressure well before any exercise occurs, and management compensation—options, restricted units, performance awards—adds another layer of new-share issuance to weigh. Skilled investors read a capital structure the way an auditor reads a ledger: how many warrants and options exist, what convertibles are outstanding, the fully diluted count, and when and at what prices these become exercisable.

## The Tactical Playbook: The Dilution-Avoidance Protocol

Readers never fall in love with a corporate narrative and never hold a warrant into a known dilution window—they treat warrants as high-velocity rentals governed by due diligence, strict sizing, catalyst timing, and ruthless exits. **Step one — pre-trade due diligence:** before buying any warrant, read the latest 10-Q, 10-K, and the warrant agreement itself (searching SEC EDGAR for the company name with "warrant"), and run the result against this red-flag/green-flag checklist:

| Red Flags (caution or skip) | Green Flags (proceed carefully) |
|---|---|
| Cash runway under ~12–18 months with no clear path to profitability | Strong institutional ownership and recent insider buying |
| A history of multiple offerings in the past 12–24 months | A near-term catalyst strong enough to outweigh likely dilution |
| Authorized share count far above shares outstanding | Favorable warrant terms (anti-dilution protection) |
| Management selling shares while promoting the story | Cashless-exercise and ratchet terms that protect the holder |
| Weak or absent anti-dilution protection in the warrant agreement | Underlying business genuinely funded for its catalyst path |

**Step two — strict sizing:** size so a dilution shock cannot breach the risk budget—roughly 0.5% to 0.75% of account risk per individual warrant, with the total warrant and structured-speculation bucket no more than about 8% to 12% of the account. **Step three — catalyst-driven timing:** enter only when a major catalyst is roughly two to eight weeks away and capable of driving the stock well above the exercise price quickly, to be in for the repricing and out before the dilution machinery engages. **Step four — watch the filings and price thresholds:** the **S-1 effectiveness trigger** (a warrant generally cannot be exercised until its registration is declared effective—the day the SEC issues the Notice of Effectiveness, the gate opens for mass conversion, so cut size the moment it drops) and **the redemption red-line** (the company may call the warrants, often for about $0.01, once the common trades at or above roughly $18.00 for 20 of 30 consecutive days—treat the met condition as a non-negotiable command to liquidate into the peak volume).

**Step five — dynamic exit discipline:** scale out of 30% to 50% of the position on the first major move; exit or sharply reduce immediately on any new dilution announcement (an ATM, shelf takedown, convertible, or PIPE); and trail a stop on the underlying, for example below key support or on a 20% to 25% drawdown from the peak. Illustrative example: a biotech micro-cap with promising Phase 2 data has warrants at $0.45; you enter with about 0.6% account risk. The data is positive, the stock gaps 90%, and the warrant surges roughly 450%—you scale out half into the spike. Two weeks later the company announces a $25 million ATM offering, and you exit the remainder at a net 180% gain rather than holding for a 1,000% that the dilution will now never deliver.

## The Dilution-Risk Governance Matrix

| Operational Dimension | The Retail Speculator | The Blueprint Capital Allocator |
|---|---|---|
| SEC-filing literacy | Ignores filings, unaware an effectiveness notice has unlocked dilution. | Tracks EDGAR and anticipates the institutional supply shock. |
| Price-target logic | Holds past the redemption threshold out of greed, hoping for more. | Treats the redemption trigger as an absolute command to take profits. |
| Asset conception | Assumes warrants behave like options, with no impact on the float. | Recognizes warrants as dilutive claims with a finite operational shelf life. |
| Holding strategy | Holds through forced or cashless exercise and watches the premium get crushed. | Extracts the momentum, then returns to cash before the cap table changes. |

## Common Mistakes

Dilution losses cluster around a familiar set of errors—focusing only on current shares outstanding while ignoring the fully diluted count, assuming warrant exercise will not matter, overlooking convertible debt as a source of future shares, mistaking a low share price for a cheap valuation, and failing to account for management's future issuance—each avoidable with the capital-structure analysis above.

## The Dilution Cycle

Speculative companies tend to move through a recognizable dilution cycle—capital is needed for growth plans, securities (warrants, options, convertibles) are issued, capital is raised and the business develops, the share price appreciates, the securities become valuable enough to incentivize exercise, additional shares are issued, and the ownership structure changes as economic interests are redistributed.

## Final Principle: The Law of Capital Fluidity

Dilution is the hidden counterweight to leverage: warrants offer extraordinary upside, embedded leverage, and deep optionality, while dilution erodes ownership and future earnings participation. The most successful warrant investors evaluate both forces at once, asking not only what a warrant could become but how many additional shares could eventually exist. The objective is never to find leverage alone, but leverage attached to a business whose value can grow faster than dilution can erode it.

## E. Liquidity Risks

Most traders pour their energy into charts, catalysts, and valuation, and far too few give liquidity the attention it deserves. A warrant can offer tremendous upside, an attractive catalyst, and compelling optionality, and still become a trap if it cannot be sold efficiently—a position that is profitable on paper is worthless if it cannot be turned back into cash. For a 180-day compounding sprint, **liquidity is the governor of capital mobility**: the entire engine depends on entering efficiently, exiting efficiently, preserving the gain, and rotating into the next setup fast, so liquidity must be treated not as a passive metric but as an active risk boundary that dictates sizing and execution before a single share is bought.

### What Is Liquidity, and Why Warrants Often Lack It

Liquidity is the ease with which a security can be bought or sold without materially moving its price—a liquid security shows frequent trading, narrow spreads, and clean execution, while an illiquid one shows sparse activity, wide spreads, and erratic pricing. Many warrants fall squarely into the second category, and the cheapest, highest-asymmetry warrants are usually the thinnest of all. Warrants are structurally less liquid than common stock: the investor base is smaller, many institutions are restricted, fewer market makers quote them, and their non-standard terms prevent standardization—on top of which many trade on OTC markets with tiny floats. The most dangerous trait is the **illusion of cheapness**: a warrant quoted at $0.10, $0.25, or $0.50 may not reflect executable value, because the true cost of getting out can be wildly different once the thin book is tested.

### The Anatomy of the Liquidity Vacuum

Warrants expose the trader to two structural hazards. **The bid-ask spread tax:** in a liquid name the spread is often a single penny, but in corporate and SPAC warrants it routinely widens to 10%, 20%, even 30% or more—a warrant quoted $1.00 bid / $1.20 ask, bought at the ask, is instantly worth only the $1.00 bid, a 16.7% loss the millisecond the order fills. **The mirage of paper wealth:** a position is only ever worth what the market will pay *right now* for the entire share mass. Accumulate 50,000 warrants at $0.50 and watch the last trade tick to $1.50, and the dashboard shows $75,000 of equity—but if the live bid shows buyers for only 5,000 shares at $1.50 with the rest tiered down toward $0.60, market-selling the whole position crashes the price into something near break-even. Buy 50,000 warrants at $0.35 ($17,500 committed), watch the quote climb to $2.80, then try to sell 20,000 and see the price collapse to $1.80–$2.10: you realize far less than the theoretical 700%, and the shortfall damages every link in the compounding sequence that follows.

### Liquidity, Position Size, and Market Stress

Liquidity risk scales directly with position size, and it has a cruel habit of vanishing exactly when it is needed most—in a correction, buyers grow scarce, spreads blow out, and a warrant that looked tradable in calm conditions becomes a tar pit. Before establishing any warrant position, four questions must have answers: Who will buy this from me? How much volume actually exists? How quickly can I get out? And what happens to all of that in a correction? Low float is a double-edged sword—it can produce explosive rallies and just as easily violent declines and manipulation, where small transactions move price enough to create false breakouts. The uncomfortable tension at the heart of the asset class is that the deepest optionality usually exists precisely where liquidity is weakest; this chapter resolves it not by avoiding thin names but by sizing and executing so that thinness cannot trap the account.

## The Tactical Playbook: The Liquidity Optimization Protocol

Readers never cross the spread carelessly. **Cap one — the 5% daily-volume ceiling:** the maximum share mass in any single warrant is capped against its trailing liquidity, so the entire position can be exited inside one normal session without driving the price against the seller.

**Maximum Share Mass = Trailing 10-Day Average Daily Volume × 0.05**

Owning no more than roughly 5% of a warrant's average daily volume means you can step out of the order book quietly rather than becoming the order book on the way down. **Cap two — size for slippage within the risk budget:** size every warrant position so that even with 30% to 50% slippage on exit, the realized loss still stays within roughly 0.5% to 1% of the account. **Execution:** market orders are outlawed—every transaction uses disciplined tiered limit orders. **Inbound accumulation:** place limits at the bid or mid-point in smaller tranches across multiple days, never chasing across the spread. **Outbound distribution:** when a catalyst drives a vertical move, offer liquidity to the frantic buyers by placing limit sells inside the rising ask, scaling out in three or four stages. And make **liquidity a top-three filter** (after catalyst strength and dilution risk), keep a backup plan (exercising and selling the common if warrant liquidity dries up), and pair an illiquid warrant with liquid instruments so overall portfolio liquidity stays healthy.

## A Worked Example

Illustrative example: a biotech micro-cap with strong upcoming data has warrants at $0.28 on roughly 80,000 shares of daily volume. You enter with about 0.6% account risk ($600). On positive news the common gaps 70% and the warrant prints $1.60 in quotes—rather than dumping, you scale out in four tranches over two days to avoid crushing the thin book, realizing roughly 420% net after slippage instead of a theoretical 600%-plus, then immediately rotate the proceeds into a more liquid options spread or 3x ETF swing.

## The Liquidity-Risk Checklist

Before buying any warrant, run it against this scorecard—red flags are reasons to shrink size or walk away, green flags signal a book you can actually trade in size:

| Red Flags (caution or skip) | Green Flags (tradable) |
|---|---|
| Average daily volume below | Consistent daily volume above ~200,000 |

| Red Flags (caution or skip) | Green Flags (tradable) |
|---|---|
| ~50,000–100,000 warrants | warrants |
| Bid-ask spread wider than ~15–20% | Tight spreads, under ~10% |
| Price lurches wildly on small prints | Orderly price action on normal prints |
| No market makers actively quoting | Visible institutional or active-trader interest |
| OTC Pink Sheets or a very low exchange tier | Underlying common is itself highly liquid (easy to hedge or exit via stock) |

## The Liquidity-Risk Governance Matrix

| Operational Dimension | The Retail Gambler | The Blueprint Capital Allocator |
|---|---|---|
| Order architecture | Fires panicked market orders, surrendering capital to the spread. | Uses staggered limit orders to capture pricing at the bid or mid-point. |
| Position-sizing logic | Over-allocates off a chart, blind to the asset's daily volume. | Caps share mass at the 5% daily-volume ceiling to guarantee exit liquidity. |
| Dashboard illusion | Celebrates paper profits it cannot actually exit at. | Computes realizable value from true order-book depth, not the last print. |
| Liquidity-crisis action | Dumps the whole position into a thin market, self-inflicting a drawdown. | Scales out incrementally into catalyst-driven volume expansions. |

## Common Mistakes

Liquidity losses cluster around predictable errors—ignoring the bid-ask spread, buying positions too large to exit, assuming liquidity will always be there, ignoring volume trends that warn of deteriorating depth, and using market orders that wreck execution—each avoidable with the protocol above.

## The Liquidity Cycle

Speculative warrants tend to move through a recognizable liquidity cycle—limited interest and low activity, a catalyst emerges and attention builds, volume expands and liquidity improves, momentum develops, institutional interest appears and depth improves, peak enthusiasm brings maximum liquidity, sentiment changes, and liquidity contracts as exits become difficult again. The lesson is timing the exit: the deepest liquidity coincides with peak enthusiasm, which is precisely when the disciplined allocator is distributing into the crowd.

### Final Principle: The Law of Order Book Depth

A warrant can offer tremendous upside and still trap the trader who cannot exit, so liquidity is not a technical footnote but a fundamental risk factor—the governor of whether a paper gain ever becomes a real one. The disciplined allocator evaluates liquidity before upside, caps share mass against daily volume, executes only through limit orders, and treats the ability to get out as inseparable from the decision to get in.

## F. Timing Asymmetry

One of the most powerful yet least understood advantages of warrants is **timing asymmetry**. Most investors fixate on price, valuation, catalysts, and leverage; sophisticated speculators give equal weight to time. A trader can identify the right company, technology, management, and trend, and still lose money if the timing is wrong. But the word "timing" pulls in two directions: **timing asymmetry has two faces.** On one side, a warrant's long life lets you be early, survive the wait, and be right eventually—time as an ally. On the other, a warrant spends most of its life dormant and reprices violently in brief bursts, so the disciplined trader can rent only the acceleration and refuse to pay the opportunity cost of the dead stretches—time as the enemy. The unifying principle: **patience on structure, aggression on execution.**

### What Is Timing Asymmetry?

Timing asymmetry exists when downside is limited, upside is substantial, and the holder has meaningful time for the thesis to develop—the cost of being early is reduced while the reward for eventually being right stays large. Warrants supply this because they typically run far longer than listed options, often three to seven years: where a short-dated option forces you to be right about direction, magnitude, and timing all at once, a long-dated warrant can require only that you be right about direction and outcome. The difficulty being-right-too-early solves is real—markets often need months or years to price a transformational development, and in practice being early feels almost identical to being wrong. A warrant is a way to buy that time cheaply, and its slow theta lets it survive the normal pullbacks, rotations, and macro noise that routinely destroy short-dated premium.

### The Two Faces of Timing Asymmetry

Because this chapter draws on two genuinely different ways of exploiting time, separate them cleanly. **Face one — the duration edge (patient capital):** time is the ally—buy a long-dated warrant ahead of a multi-quarter catalyst horizon and let the runway absorb the flat stretches and drawdowns, positioned for when recognition finally arrives. This is the warrant as a core conviction anchor, held for months, exited on milestones rather than daily noise; its enemy is not time but a broken thesis. **Face two — the velocity edge (renting the acceleration):** time is the enemy, specifically the dead time of dormancy—the same instrument that rewards patience spends most of its life flat on microscopic volume, then reprices in a violent burst when an information shock hits, so you wait in cash, strike at the velocity flashpoint, ride the repricing for days, and liquidate. The discipline that keeps these coherent: **decide which face you are trading before you enter, and never let one drift into the other.** The classic account-draining error is to open a three-to-fifteen-day velocity rental, watch it move against you, and reassure yourself that "it's long-dated, I'll just hold it," silently converting a tactical rental into an unvetted anchor.

## The Anatomy of a Warrant's Lifecycle

Both faces rest on the same fact: a warrant's price efficiency is highly non-linear and bound to corporate events, not a smooth clock, and its life typically moves through three phases. **Phase 1 — dormancy:** while a SPAC searches or a micro-cap quietly executes a pivot, the warrant trades on microscopic volume and flat price action—the outlawed zone for the velocity trader, the cost of admission for the patient anchor. **Phase 2 — the information shock:** the moment a definitive agreement is announced or a breakthrough hits the tape, the thin-float asset awakens and races toward theoretical value in days. **Phase 3 — the convexity squeeze:** as the common pushes through the fixed strike, the warrant enters its prime window and exhibits positive convexity, a modest move in the equity translating into a far larger expansion in the warrant as it transitions from out-of-the-money toward deep in-the-money.

## The Patience Premium and Market Cycles

A hidden advantage of the duration edge is the **patience premium**: most participants capitulate when prices stagnate or catalysts slip, so a holder with enough time can simply outlast them, and patience itself becomes a competitive edge. Paired with deep optionality, time raises the probability that a favorable outcome eventually emerges, giving exposure to multiple potential paths over an extended development period. Every major theme travels from skepticism through curiosity, adoption, and enthusiasm to euphoria, and a long-dated warrant is a bridge across that gap—it keeps the holder positioned from skepticism to recognition without forcing a perfectly timed re-entry.

## The Tactical Playbook A: The Core Conviction Anchor

Because there are two faces, there are two playbooks sharing entry discipline but differing in horizon. **Playbook A — the duration play (the core conviction anchor):** use long-dated warrants as the patient base of the sleeve through **core conviction anchors** (long-dated warrants on high-quality companies inside a strong regime, with short-term calls and spreads for the momentum bursts around them), **catalyst-horizon plays** (warrants bought three to twelve months ahead of a major expected event—clinical data, a large contract, an uplisting), and **post-dilution recovery** (after a company dilutes but the thesis remains intact, long-dated warrants can offer better risk-reward than buying fresh equity).

Illustrative example: a mid-cap AI-power or biotech name with strong intellectual property has four-year warrants trading at $1.80 (exercise price $6.50, stock at $4.20). You believe regime tailwinds and upcoming catalysts can drive the stock to the mid-teens over twelve to eighteen months, so you commit a measured allocation—and over the following four to six months, as catalysts land and the stock rises 80% to 150%, the warrant can deliver several hundred percent through delta expansion and slow theta. You scale out in tranches against milestones, freeing capital for tactical trades while a runner keeps compounding with minimal daily decay; re-evaluate quarterly and never treat it as a permanent holding.

## The Tactical Playbook B: The Velocity Play

**Playbook B — the velocity play (the catalyst-timing protocol):** when the goal is to rent the acceleration rather than anchor a thesis, the protocol is strict and short. **Trigger — the 500% volume shock:** enter only when the warrant or its underlying common prints an intraday volume expansion of roughly 500% or more above its 20-day average, accompanied by a clean technical breakout and, for the convexity case, the common clearing the strike. **Horizon — the compressed holding window:** trade strictly as a short-term vehicle on a three-to-fifteen-day horizon, capturing the initial vertical repricing fueled by the shock and market-maker hedging, and when the move stretches to an extreme (the daily range extends roughly three ATRs above the eight-day EMA) or volume begins to taper, liquidate into the strength. Compressing the window is what lets the velocity trader extract a sharp milestone while sidestepping the dilution, cashless-exercise, and redemption risks that accumulate the longer a warrant is held.

## Capital Efficiency, Time, and When the Edge Fails

Timing asymmetry also improves capital efficiency: because a warrant costs far less than the equivalent common exposure, the holder can diversify across multiple themes and pursue several optionality bets at once while most of the account stays free for tactical 3x ETF swings, options spreads, and pyramiding. But the edge is not infallible—time can work against you, capital tied up in a flat warrant carries real opportunity cost, redemption clauses can force conversion, and time alone never creates value: a flawed business, weak management, insufficient financing, or structural industry decline will defeat any amount of runway. The underlying business remains decisive.

## The Timing Asymmetry Governance Matrix

| Operational Axis | The Retail Gambler | The Blueprint Capital Allocator |
|---|---|---|
| Allocation timing | Buys deep in the dormancy phase, leaving capital dead for months on hope. | Anchors deliberately ahead of a vetted catalyst horizon, or strikes velocity plays only at the validated flashpoint. |
| Holding horizon | Holds blindly through deep corrections, letting opportunity cost drain the ledger. | Matches horizon to intent: a 3-to-15-day rental for velocity, milestone-based scaling for anchors. |
| Catalyst | Chases after the asset has | Positions ahead of, or at the |

| Operational Axis | The Retail Gambler | The Blueprint Capital Allocator |
|---|---|---|
| response | gone parabolic for days, buying the top. | inception of, the volume shock, not after the crowd. |
| Monetization logic | Falls in love with the story and holds into dilution and redemption traps. | Scales out against milestones or into vertical volume, returning capital to work. |

## Risk Management and Discipline

The same rules apply to both faces, scaled to the longer exposure of the anchor play: cap total long-dated warrant exposure at a defined ceiling and keep each position small (draft sizing ranges from roughly 0.75% to several percent per position—settle on one figure); require clear multi-quarter catalysts and improving fundamentals before establishing an anchor, and a validated volume shock before opening a velocity rental; set milestone-based exits in advance (for example, begin scaling out as the stock approaches twice the exercise price); re-evaluate every anchor quarterly; and never use margin or oversize. Timing-asymmetry losses cluster around confusing time with quality, ignoring dilution, ignoring liquidity, overestimating catalysts, and overconcentrating.

## The Timing Asymmetry Cycle

Most successful long-dated warrant trades move through a recognizable progression—opportunity identified while the market is still skeptical, position established, time passes as development quietly continues, catalysts emerge and progress becomes visible, market recognition develops, momentum accelerates as capital flows increase, valuation re-rates, and optionality converts to value as warrant appreciation accelerates. The holder benefits not from perfect timing, but from having enough time.

## Final Principle: The Law of Temporal Velocity

Timing asymmetry is among the most powerful advantages available to the warrant trader, but its lesson is double-sided. The duration edge says the objective is not always to be right immediately, but to be right eventually while retaining the ability to stay positioned until the opportunity unfolds. The velocity edge says that in a compressed sprint you cannot afford to pay for dead time, so you rent only the acceleration. Held together by a single rule—patience on structure, aggression on execution—they let a high-conviction thesis mature on the warrant's long runway while the rest of the toolkit generates the rapid, sequential wins the timeline demands.

# Chapter 13
# Synthetic Leverage

## A. Margin

Leverage has built fortunes and destroyed accounts, often in the same cycle, and margin sits at the center of that reality because it is usually the first form of synthetic leverage a trader ever encounters. This chapter opens the Synthetic Leverage section, so a precise definition matters: **synthetic leverage means controlling more market exposure than your cash alone could buy.** Margin is its oldest form—a broker loan against your securities—and like all leverage it is neither good nor bad, simply powerful: for a campaign attempting to turn $100,000 into $1,000,000 in six months it can accelerate returns dramatically, or accelerate losses just as fast.

### What Is Margin, and How It Works

Margin is borrowed capital. A brokerage lets a trader buy securities using a mix of personal cash and borrowed funds, so instead of buying only what cash allows, the trader controls a larger position—increased buying power is leverage. A $100,000 cash account has $100,000 of purchasing power; a $100,000 margin account may have $200,000 or more, meaning the trader controls assets worth more than the capital invested. That gap between capital and controlled exposure is the leverage, and every advantage and danger in this chapter flows from it. Three numbers govern a margin account:

| Mechanism | What it means |
|---|---|
| Reg T (initial) margin | Standard US rule: 50% initial requirement, roughly 2:1 leverage. Post $50,000 to control $100,000 of stock or ETFs. |
| Portfolio margin | Risk-based requirement for qualified, experienced accounts, often 15–30%, permitting materially higher effective leverage on diversified books. |
| Maintenance margin | Usually 25–30%. If account equity falls below this floor, the broker issues a margin call demanding cash or liquidation. |

### Why Margin Accelerates Gains, and Losses

The appeal is straightforward arithmetic: buy $100,000 of stock that rises 20% and you gain $20,000; use margin to buy $200,000 and the same move yields $40,000. But the mathematics are pitilessly symmetric—a leveraged position cannot distinguish a correct decision from a mistake. If that $200,000 position falls 20%, the loss is $40,000, and on 2:1 margin a 10% drop in the underlying is roughly a 20% hit to the account before interest. Margin magnifies error with exactly the same efficiency it magnifies success, which is why everything that follows is about risk control, not return.

## The Margin Call and Forced Liquidation

The most feared phrase in leveraged trading is the margin call: when account equity falls below the maintenance requirement, the broker may demand cash, force reductions, or liquidate. The distinction to internalize is brutal—the market decides your profits, but the broker decides your margin requirements, and if you fail to meet a call, the broker's automated algorithm market-dumps shares at the worst possible price, frequently the exact bottom of an intraday flush. This is why a leveraged trader can be fundamentally, technically, and ultimately right and still lose everything, because leverage shortens the time horizon and removes staying power. A call can also strike overnight on a gap, wiping out months of gains before the trader can react.

## The Interest Tax, the Psychology, and the Escalation Trap

Borrowed cash is not free: brokers charge variable interest, often high single digits to low double digits annually, and in a short sprint that drag eats into compounding velocity every day a position is held—the quiet tax that turns a marginal edge into a losing one over time. Margin also changes behavior more than it changes mathematics, producing greater emotional intensity, twitchier decisions, and stronger reactions to volatility. And it introduces timing risk: without leverage a trader can usually ride out temporary volatility, but with leverage a drawdown that would merely sting in a cash account can breach a maintenance threshold. Worst of all is the escalation trap: **success breeds confidence, confidence breeds overconfidence, overconfidence breeds excessive leverage, and excessive leverage breeds the major loss that ends the run.**

## An Alternative to Borrowed Cash: The Synthetic Long

There is a way to obtain stock-like leverage without borrowing cash from the broker at all, by building the exposure out of options. To replicate owning 100 shares, a trader can construct a **synthetic long** within a single expiration cycle: buy one at-the-money call (delta roughly +0.50) and sell one at-the-money put at the same strike (delta roughly +0.50 to the position, since a short put is positive delta). Combined, the two legs produce a position delta of about 1.00, so the structure moves nearly dollar-for-dollar with the stock:

**Position Delta = (+0.50, long call) + (+0.50, short put) ≈ 1.00**

Two genuine advantages follow: because the premium received for the short put largely offsets the premium paid for the long call, the net debit to enter is close to zero, so the trader controls 100 shares' worth of exposure while posting only the broker's margin on the short put (often 10–20%); and the position carries no margin interest and approximately neutral net time decay, since the long call's and short put's theta largely cancel. What it does *not* do is remove risk: the synthetic long reproduces the full downside of owning the stock, the short put can be assigned, it still requires margin that can be called, and because it lets a trader control far more notional per dollar posted, it can be *more* dangerous than ordinary margin if oversized. It eliminates the interest cost and the cash loan, not the loss—treat it as leverage to be sized and stopped like any other.

## The Professional Approach: Surgical Use Only

Professionals rarely treat margin as a license to maximize exposure—they treat it as a tactical, capital-efficiency, and above all risk-management problem, asking before every use whether leverage is justified, what the downside is, and whether the account can survive an adverse path. Crucially, margin availability does not determine position size, risk tolerance does. In this blueprint margin is a precision instrument deployed in narrow circumstances—amplifying a high-conviction core position in a strong, confirmed regime; pairing margined stock with risk-defined options (a protective spread or married put); and short-term tactical boosts during confirmed breakouts, not long-term holds that accrue interest. Illustrative example: a confirmed AI-power rotation might justify holding $150,000 to $180,000 of notional in a liquid mid-cap leader or sector ETF—only about 1.5x to 1.8x leverage—with risk strictly capped at 1% of the account ($1,000) via a tight ATR-based stop, downside further limited by a protective bull call spread or married put, the margin paid down quickly with profits. One or two clean margined swings of 30% to 70% can meaningfully lift the compounding curve, but the leverage is the booster, never the engine.

## Critical Risks and Iron Survival Rules

Margin turns small mistakes into catastrophic ones—the amplified-loss math, overnight gap risk, interest drag, and correlation risk all compound each other. The rules are non-negotiable: never exceed roughly 1.5x to 2x overall portfolio leverage (counting margin, leveraged ETFs, and options delta together—though individual structures like the synthetic long can carry far higher embedded leverage, the cap is on total portfolio exposure and the total cap always wins); risk no more than about 1% of the account per margined idea; use margin only in strong trending regimes with clear relative-strength leadership; keep a minimum 40–50% cash buffer; pay down margin aggressively on every winner; and never stack leverage on leverage—no margin on 3x ETFs, penny warrants, or illiquid names, where double leverage is blow-up math. Margin losses cluster around borrowing the maximum, assuming normal conditions persist, concentrating leverage, letting fear and greed drive decisions, and entering without a predetermined exit.

## The Leverage Governance Matrix

| Operational Dimension | The Retail Speculator | The Blueprint Capital Allocator |
|---|---|---|
| Funding mechanism | Borrows raw cash from the broker, paying margin interest every day a position is held. | Uses margin sparingly and surgically, or builds exposure synthetically to avoid the interest cost. |
| Liquidation exposure | Maxes out leverage and is exposed to broker-controlled forced liquidation at the worst price. | Caps total leverage near 1.5–2x and holds a large cash buffer, so a normal drawdown never triggers a call. |

| Operational Dimension | The Retail Speculator | The Blueprint Capital Allocator |
|---|---|---|
| Sizing logic | Lets broker-permitted leverage dictate size, treating availability as permission. | Lets risk tolerance dictate size, capping risk near 1% per idea regardless of what the broker allows. |
| Debt discipline | Carries margin balances indefinitely, letting interest erode the edge. | Pays margin down aggressively on every winner; leverage is a temporary booster, not standing debt. |

### Margin During Market Corrections

Corrections are where weak risk management is exposed: as volatility rises and liquidity thins, brokers may tighten margin requirements precisely as prices fall, and forced selling cascades through over-leveraged accounts, pushing the leveraged trader to become a seller at the exact moment flexibility would be most valuable. The cash buffer and the leverage cap exist for precisely this scenario.

### The Margin Cycle

Most leverage-related outcomes follow a recognizable arc—capital is established, margin is introduced and buying power expands, opportunities are pursued and exposure increases, results improve and confidence grows, leverage expands and risk increases, volatility arrives and pressure intensifies, discipline determines the outcome, and capital survives or disappears. The difference between success and ruin is almost always made at the discipline step, before the volatility has fully passed.

### Final Principle: The Law of Synthetic Efficiency

Margin lets a trader control larger positions, improve capital efficiency, and accelerate gains, and it magnifies losses, volatility, emotional pressure, and risk in equal measure. It can be a powerful ally in the campaign from $100,000 to $1,000,000, but it is never a substitute for discipline—leverage does not create skill; it amplifies whatever skill, or lack of it, already exists, which is why the best aggressive traders tend to use margin least.

## B. Portfolio Margin

If ordinary margin is a powerful tool, portfolio margin is leverage on a different level—one of the most important tools used by professional traders, hedge funds, and sophisticated options traders, yet far less understood. The core idea is a shift in how risk is measured: **standard Regulation T margin evaluates positions in isolation with rigid, fixed formulas; portfolio margin evaluates the entire account as a single, risk-modeled entity.** That shift can unlock opportunities a conventional account cannot, and it can also produce losses that escalate far faster—in equal measure the most sophisticated and the most dangerous form of synthetic leverage in this section.

## What Is Portfolio Margin? Reg T Versus Portfolio Margin

Portfolio margin is a risk-based system: instead of applying a simple borrowing formula to each position, it evaluates total portfolio risk, correlations, hedging relationships, and stress-test scenarios, then sets the requirement based on the estimated worst-case loss. The clearinghouse engine—typically a model such as TIMS or a value-at-risk calculation—simulates a matrix of market-shock scenarios across roughly a 10 to 20 step range, asking one cold question: what is the maximum theoretical loss this account would suffer if the underlying market dropped or rose sharply, on the order of 12% to 15%, at tomorrow's open? For a well-hedged book, that number can be far smaller than Reg T would demand. The contrast is structural—Reg T is binary, while portfolio margin abandons that fixed tax for a dynamic estimate of real risk:

**Reg T Margin = Σ ( Position Value × Fixed % )**

**Portfolio Margin = Maximum Theoretical Loss across the simulated ±15% shocks**

| Dimension | Regulation T | Portfolio Margin |
|---|---|---|
| Risk view | Each position in isolation. | The whole portfolio as one risk-modeled entity. |
| Requirement | Fixed (~50% on equities), static. | Risk-based (~15–30% on diversified books), dynamic. |
| Hedges | Largely ignored; a protective put just costs extra cash. | Recognized; a hedge can lower the requirement. |
| Typical leverage | About 2:1. | Roughly 3x to 6x or more on low-risk, hedged portfolios. |
| Behavior in volatility | Stable requirement. | Requirement can rise sharply and fast. |

## Synthetic Leverage Through Efficiency, and Why Professionals Prefer It

Portfolio margin creates synthetic leverage not by increasing borrowing directly, but by reducing the capital a position ties up—the leverage emerges from the risk calculation rather than a borrowing formula. Buying power expands precisely where risk is genuinely lower: hedged positions, diversified books, and defined-risk options structures all reduce the modeled worst-case loss, and the engine releases capital in proportion. Reg T routinely misreads the true risk of a book of long and short options, spreads, and hedges, and while most traders are first drawn to portfolio margin for raw buying power, the experienced come to value something subtler—flexibility, the ability to deploy capital wherever the best opportunity appears, which often proves more valuable than leverage itself.

### The Qualification Barrier

Because portfolio margin grants institutional-grade power, regulators enforce a hard gate: the FINRA minimum equity is generally $125,000, with many brokers requiring $150,000 or more, alongside advanced options approval and demonstrated experience, with stricter maintenance rules than Reg T. For a book that begins at $100,000, this creates a sequencing reality: **it is a tool for a later, scaled-up phase, not the starting line**—early gains must first carry the account above the qualification threshold. A caution worth making explicit: the high-velocity instruments that might get an account there fastest—short-dated options and micro-cap warrants—are also the highest-risk in this book, and clearing a regulatory threshold is never a guarantee of having the skill to wield what lies beyond it.

### The Tactical Playbook: Hedged Leverage, Not Naked Leverage

The most important rule of portfolio margin is what *not* to do with it: readers do not use the expanded buying power to blindly buy six times more common stock, which is a recipe for an immediate, unrecoverable wipeout the first time the market gaps. The power is meant to be spent on hedged and defined-risk structures, where the risk model rewards the protection with released capital. The paired structure that exploits the model is simple: hold a long position (a high-beta leader or liquid ETF) and simultaneously buy out-of-the-money protective puts—because the model recognizes the floor, a position that would lock up $50,000 under Reg T might require only a small fraction, freeing the difference as liquid capital. The freed capital is not free money; it is unused borrowing capacity, and every dollar of additional exposure it funds is additional risk.

### Where It Works, and Where It Does Not

The legitimate uses are narrow: **core regime plays** (larger positions in strong-RS leaders or sector ETFs during confirmed rotations), a **pyramiding booster** (adding size on a winner faster than Reg T allows, within the risk cap), and **hybrid setups** (margin on liquid stocks or ETFs paired with protective spreads or married puts). Equally important is what to keep out: high-volatility names, 3x leveraged ETFs (stacking leverage on leverage), illiquid warrants, and naked short options, each of which can make the dynamic risk model turn violently against the account. Illustrative example: under portfolio margin a trader might control a far larger notional position in a liquid mid-cap leader or utilities ETF than Reg T would permit, with risk still capped near 0.75% to 1% via tight ATR stops and downside defined by bull call spreads or protective puts, paying the margin down aggressively after each swing to reset buying power.

### The Dangers

Portfolio margin's advantages come bundled with risks easy to underestimate precisely because the margin number looks small. **The illusion of safety:** a low requirement is an estimate produced by a model, while the risk is reality, and extreme markets routinely exceed model assumptions—"my requirement is low, therefore my risk is low" is backwards reasoning. **Correlation risk:**

the system leans on correlation assumptions that break in a crisis, when correlations converge toward one and a book that looked balanced becomes dangerously concentrated. **Volatility expansion:** when volatility expands, modeled risk rises, requirements increase, and buying power contracts all at once—leverage is most available when least needed and least available when most desired—and unlike many Reg T requirements, portfolio-margin requirements change rapidly at the broker's discretion. **Market crashes** reveal the true nature of leverage: a trader who looked conservative in calm markets is suddenly, involuntarily, highly leveraged.

## The Portfolio-Margin Governance Matrix

| Operational Parameter | The Reg T Retail Speculator | The Disciplined PM Allocator |
|---|---|---|
| Capital utilization | Ties up ~50% of position value in static collateral. | Releases capital via risk-based pricing on hedged positions, redeploying it carefully. |
| Leverage architecture | Relies on static cash borrowing with ongoing interest. | Uses dynamic, risk-modeled leverage, but caps total exposure to the book's global limit. |
| Hedging incentive | Sees hedging as a cost, since a put drains extra cash under Reg T. | Sees hedging as a requirement-reducer, and as genuine downside protection first. |
| Liquidation reality | Faces per-position margin calls on single-stock moves. | Holds large cash buffer and monitors, to address portfolio-wide calls when volatility spikes,. |

## Critical Risks and Iron Survival Rules

Portfolio margin is a double-edged sword—a 10% adverse move can trigger massive calls, a correlation shock can liquidate positions automatically, intraday requirements can change at the broker's discretion, and margin interest still applies. Maintain a minimum 40% to 50% cash or equity buffer at all times; cap overall portfolio leverage (counting embedded leverage from 3x ETFs and options delta) at the book's single global ceiling; risk no more than about 0.75% per idea, tighter than under Reg T because portfolio-margin calls arrive faster; use it only after mastering Reg T and proving consistent profitability; and review portfolio risk daily, stress-testing against a 15% decline. Failures cluster around treating buying power as available risk capacity, ignoring correlation and volatility risk, over-concentrating despite the diversified appearance, and letting leverage create the illusion of skill.

### The Portfolio-Margin Cycle

Most portfolio-margin experiences follow a recognizable arc—capital is established and the account qualifies, buying power expands and leverage increases, opportunities multiply and flexibility improves, exposure grows and positions become larger, conditions change and volatility emerges, risk is tested as stress scenarios become real, and capital compounds or contracts—with the outcome decided not when leverage is acquired but when it is tested. Professionals rarely ask "how much leverage can I obtain?" but "how much risk can I survive?"

### Final Principle: The Law of Capital Density

Portfolio margin offers greater capital efficiency, flexibility, buying power, and a more realistic portfolio-level view of risk, while introducing correlation risk, volatility risk, model risk, and the constant temptation of excess. For a trader who has already mastered risk and process, it can be a powerful accelerator, but it must never be mistaken for free leverage, because the market—not the margin formula—ultimately decides risk.

## C. Leveraged Instruments

One of the fastest ways to accelerate returns is through leveraged instruments—tools that let a trader control exposure far greater than the capital committed. They can be powerful accelerators of profit, capital efficiency, and compounding, and equally powerful accelerators of loss and account destruction. This is the capstone of the Synthetic Leverage section, and it does two things: **first, it treats the leveraged ETF, the 2x and 3x funds, in depth, because they carry a specific, lethal mathematical hazard; second, it draws the section together**, mapping every form of leverage already covered into a single toolkit and drawing the line between leverage you buy off the shelf and leverage you engineer yourself.

### What Is a Leveraged Instrument? Embedded Versus Synthetic

A leveraged instrument provides economic exposure that exceeds the capital invested. The mechanism varies—a margin loan, a fund's internal structure, an option's premium, a warrant's contract—but the result is identical: with no leverage, $100,000 that rises 10% earns $10,000; with 2x leverage, $200,000 of exposure earns $20,000 on the same move. The return doubles, and so does the loss. **Embedded leverage** is pre-packaged—a 2x or 3x ETF delivers a fixed daily multiple in a single, liquid ticker, simple to buy but blunt and subject to a corrosive daily-reset decay. **Synthetic leverage** is engineered—the trader builds the exposure deliberately from combinations of stock, margin, options, and warrants, accepting more complexity in exchange for precise control over the leverage ratio, duration, decay profile, and defined-risk shape. The blunt instrument is faster to deploy; the engineered one is a scalpel, and both are governed by the same risk ceiling.

## The Leverage Toolkit: A Map of the Section

Every instrument below creates leverage by a different route; this map shows how they fit together rather than re-explaining each (futures are a further high-leverage instrument used heavily by professionals, sitting outside this book's core toolkit but obeying the same amplifier logic). The point is that all of these can combine, and combining them is where the real danger lives:

| Instrument | How it creates leverage | Covered in |
|---|---|---|
| Margin | Borrowed broker cash against securities (about 2:1). | Margin chapter |
| Portfolio margin | Risk-based requirements on a hedged book (3–6x+). | Portfolio Margin chapter |
| Leveraged ETFs | Built-in daily multiple (2x/3x), no borrowing by the trader. | This chapter |
| Options | A small premium controls large exposure; defined risk on long options. | Spreads and Volatility chapters |
| Warrants | Long-dated, leveraged claims on a company's stock. | Warrants section |
| Synthetic stock | Long call plus short put, or stock-plus-option combinations. | Margin chapter; below |

## Leveraged ETFs and the Volatility-Decay Tax

Leveraged ETFs are the section's signature instrument and its most misunderstood. A 3x Nasdaq-100 or 3x semiconductor ETF is engineered to deliver three times the return of its index for one single day, and because the leverage resets daily, holding one through a choppy market exposes the account to a severe geometric tax known as volatility decay, or beta slippage. The mechanism is best seen in numbers—take an index at 100 that drops 10% on Day 1, then rises 11.11% on Day 2, returning exactly to 100 (a flat 0% round trip), and watch the unhedged 3x ETF:

| | Index | 3x ETF |
|---|---|---|
| **Start** | 100.00 | 100.00 |
| Day 1 (index −10%, ETF −30%) | 90.00 | 70.00 |
| Day 2 (index +11.11%, ETF +33.33%) | 100.00 | 93.33 |
| Net result | Flat (0%) | −6.67% |

The index broke even; the 3x ETF lost 6.67% of its capital in 48 hours, with no trend at all, purely from the mathematics of daily resets. Compounded across weeks of chop, this tax systematically incinerates capital, which is why leveraged ETFs are not investments but short-horizon trading vehicles—treating them otherwise is a near-guarantee of erosion.

## The Tactical Playbook: The High-Angle Regime Sprint

Because of the daily-reset physics, the rule is strict: rent leveraged ETFs only during confirmed, low-variance, high-angle trends, and outlaw them the moment the market turns choppy—the same daily compounding that destroys capital in chop compounds powerfully in your favor during a smooth, linear melt-up, so the entire edge is in the regime filter. **The trend anchor:** the underlying index must trade cleanly above its rising 21-day EMA and 50-day SMA. **The volatility screen:** market or sector implied volatility must be compressed (for example the VIX below roughly 18 and sloping down). **The sprint deployment:** only when both conditions hold does capital go in, tracking the daily moving average, with a hard exit at the first decisive trend break.

## Sizing, Stops, and the Cash Rule

Leveraged ETFs carry no option-style expiration, permitting larger concentration during a pristine regime, but that flexibility must not override the book's risk limits. **Allocation versus risk:** the blueprint may commit a sizable block, on the order of a fifth of the account, to a single high-conviction 3x setup, but the risk on that position must still be capped near 1% of the account through the stop, and the allocation contributes meaningfully to total portfolio leverage. **The hard stop:** exit instantly if the asset closes below its rising 8-day EMA or a defined support shelf—and note that a gap through the stop can realize a larger loss than planned, especially on a 3x instrument, so size for that possibility. **Buy with cash, never stack margin:** a leveraged ETF bought with cash cannot be margin-called and cannot lose more than the amount invested, which is the entire point of using it instead of broker margin; buying a 3x ETF on margin re-introduces interest and liquidation risk and stacks leverage on leverage, and is forbidden. "No margin call" is not "low risk"—the instrument itself can still fall 30%-plus in a single day.

## Engineering Synthetic Leverage

Where the leveraged ETF is blunt, synthetic leverage is surgical. By constructing exposure from combinations of stock, margin, options, and warrants, a trader can dial in an exact effective leverage, manage theta and gamma intelligently, build defined-risk profiles even at high leverage, and largely sidestep the volatility drag that plagues leveraged ETFs. Several engineered setups recur:

| Synthetic setup | Construction and purpose |
|---|---|
| Protective synthetic | Margined stock or ETF + a married protective put: leveraged upside with a hard downside floor. |
| LEAPS + margin | Deep-ITM long-dated calls held on margin: stock-like behavior at roughly 3–6x with slower decay than short options. |
| Spread on margin | A bull call debit spread on a margined liquid name or ETF: controlled, high-convexity exposure. |

| Synthetic setup | Construction and purpose |
|---|---|
| Warrant + overlay | A long-dated warrant as base leverage + short-term calls or spreads layered on for gamma bursts. |

Illustrative example: rather than buying a 3x utilities ETF outright during a confirmed AI-power rotation, a trader uses margin to hold a larger notional position in a liquid mid-cap power name or sector ETF, simultaneously buys protective OTM puts or a collar to define maximum loss near 1% of the account, and on the breakout pyramids by adding a bull call debit spread—roughly 2.5x to 4x effective synthetic leverage with defined risk, scaled out in tranches, margin paid down afterward. One or two clean synthetic swings of 40% to 120% can add large equity jumps while preserving capital far better than a naked 3x hold through the same period.

## The Hidden Cost, Psychology, and Best Conditions for Leverage

Leverage is never free; the cost simply takes different forms—margin interest, option premium, volatility decay, financing charges, opportunity cost, or simply increased risk. Amateurs fixate on the benefits; professionals weigh both sides, asking what the amplification actually costs before deciding whether the trade is worth it. Leverage also changes behavior as much as mathematics: as it rises, fear, greed, and stress rise with it while decision quality falls, and the trader who cannot stay calm at a given size has, in practice, exceeded their real leverage limit regardless of what the math allows. It works best when trends are strong, momentum is accelerating, volatility is manageable, and risk is clearly defined—timing the regime, not maximizing the multiple, is where the advantage lives.

## Risk Stacking: The Hidden Danger

The greatest danger in an aggressive book is hidden, accumulated leverage: a trader may simultaneously hold margined stock, a leveraged ETF, options, and warrants, each carrying its own leverage, and the combined exposure can be far greater than any of them appears in isolation. This is risk stacking, treated at length in the Position Stacking chapter, and it is how accounts that felt prudent position by position blow up all at once. The discipline is constant: evaluate total portfolio exposure, correlation-adjusted, not instrument by instrument.

## The Leveraged-Instrument Governance Matrix

| Operational Parameter | The Retail Spectator | The Blueprint Capital Allocator |
|---|---|---|
| Holding horizon | Treats a 3xETF as a long-term investment, holding through bear markets. | Treats it as a short-term velocity rental over a compressed window. |

| Operational Parameter | The Retail Spectator | The Blueprint Capital Allocator |
|---|---|---|
| Regime awareness | Buys leveraged ETFs in choppy, sideways ranges and is ground down by decay. | Deploys in low-variance, high-angle expansions when volatility is crushed. |
| Risk architecture | Over-allocates with no plan; a 10% index pullback can erase 30% of the position. | Caps risk near 1% per idea with hard stops, within the global leverage cap. |
| Cost profile | Pays margin interest chasing single stocks on borrowed cash. | Uses built-in or defined-risk leverage and prices the premium cost in advance. |

## Critical Risks and Iron Survival Rules

Synthetic and embedded leverage share the same failure modes: a margin-call cascade that can liquidate engineered positions faster than a simple ETF; correlation and gap risk; and complexity risk, where more moving parts mean more that can go wrong. Cap overall portfolio leverage (including embedded leverage from leveraged ETFs and options delta) at the book's single global ceiling; risk no more than about 0.75% to 1% per leveraged idea; maintain a 35% to 50% cash or equity buffer; review net Greeks and margin usage daily and prefer defined-risk overlays on every margined position; and pay down borrowed capital aggressively after every winner, never holding a leveraged ETF through a choppy or falling regime.

**A reconciliation note for the manuscript, and the natural place to settle it:** this is the final chapter of the Synthetic Leverage section, and the book's total-leverage ceiling is now stated four different ways across it—1.5x to 2x in the Margin chapter, 3x to 3.5x in Position Stacking, and 2.5x to 3.5x in both Portfolio Margin and here. Three of the four cluster near 3x to 3.5x, with the Margin chapter the conservative outlier. Portfolio margin can technically *permit* far higher leverage still, on the order of 6x to 8x on hedged equity, which is exactly why a single, firm, book-wide cap matters. Choose one global maximum, apply it identically across all four leverage chapters, and let the lower, safer figure govern until it is set.

## Survival and Leverage

Leverage losses cluster around excessive concentration, ignoring volatility, chasing returns so that leverage substitutes for analysis, risk stacking multiple forms of leverage on one thesis, and entering without an exit plan. The core principle reduces to one line: **leverage should enhance skill, not replace it.** A trader without an edge cannot borrow one—if the strategy is sound, leverage accelerates success; if flawed, it accelerates ruin—so the most successful traders use the least leverage necessary, because survival is the precondition for compounding.

### The Leverage Escalation Cycle

Most leverage failures follow the same arc—initial success and developing confidence, increased exposure as position size expands, larger gains, overconfidence as risk awareness declines, excessive leverage as exposure becomes dangerous, a market reversal, and significant losses as capital contracts rapidly.

### Final Principle: The Law of Leveraged Decay

Leveraged instruments let a trader control larger positions and accelerate compounding while introducing greater volatility, risk, and emotional pressure. For the campaign from $100,000 to $1,000,000 they can be genuine engines of growth, but leverage is not a source of returns—it is an amplifier of returns, and amplifiers raise both the music and the noise. Whether the result is wealth or wreckage depends entirely on the discipline behind the tool.

## D. Position Stacking

One of the most powerful, and most dangerous, techniques in aggressive trading is position stacking. Many traders imagine leverage comes from a single source, when in reality the largest gains and the largest blowups occur when multiple forms of leverage are layered on top of one another around the same idea. **Stacking has one dangerous face and two disciplined ones.** The dangerous face is accidental: a trader unknowingly accumulates correlated exposure across several instruments and mistakes it for diversification. The two disciplined faces are deliberate: pyramiding additional layers into a trade that is already winning, and engineering a custom multi-instrument structure at entry. All three are the same act—layering exposure on a single thesis—and all three are governed by one rule: what matters is your true, correlation-adjusted exposure, never the number of tickets you hold.

### The Danger: Hidden Concentration

Position stacking, in its most lethal form, occurs whenever multiple positions create exposure to the same underlying theme, stock, sector, or direction. The trader believes several independent trades exist; the market sees a single concentrated bet. Owning the stock, buying its calls, holding its warrants, and adding a leveraged ETF on its sector are not four positions—they are one position expressed four times. Accidental stacking usually grows out of conviction: a strong thesis breeds confidence, confidence invites additional exposure, the trader seeks confirming information, and a reversal multiplies the losses across the whole stack. It accumulates through familiar combinations that look diversified and are not—stock plus calls, a leveraged ETF plus sector options, stock plus warrants plus calls on one name, several companies within one sector, or broad theme stacking across AI software, hardware, infrastructure, and ETF exposure all at once. Stacking turns toxic when correlations rise: in a correction they converge toward one and everything falls together.

## Stress-Testing True Exposure

The defense is to interrogate the portfolio honestly before the market does it for you: What if the primary thesis is wrong? What if volatility doubles? What if liquidity disappears? What if correlations converge and every related position moves together? These questions reveal real exposure, which almost always exceeds what position count alone suggests. The professional asks "what is my actual risk?" rather than "how many positions do I own?", monitoring gross, net, sector, correlation, and leverage exposure together.

## The Discipline, Form A: Pyramiding Into Winners

Used consciously and bounded by risk, the same layering becomes a precision tool. **Form A — pyramiding into winners:** the retail amateur stacks when losing, averaging down out of ego; the disciplined trader does the opposite, keeping the initial risk tiny and using the unrealized profit of a winning position to fund each subsequent layer. The absolute rule is mechanical: you may only add size if the total net risk of the entire unified trade remains at or below your baseline risk unit (1R, roughly 1% of capital). Layers are added in sequence as the trend proves itself:

| Layer | Instrument | Entry trigger | Risk rule |
|---|---|---|---|
| 1 — Core anchor | Common stock or 3x ETF | Breakout above the 21-day EMA on strong volume. | Hard stop under the breakout candle; max risk locked at 1R. |
| 2 — Delta boost | ITM option (~0.80 delta) or vertical spread | Asset clears the first minor consolidation flag. | Trail Layer 1 to lock in +1R; Layer 2 risk subsidized by Layer 1 profit. |
| 3 — Gamm a strike | Near-term ATM weekly option | Asset enters a vertical, parabolic expansion. | Move the unified trailing stop to the 8-EMA; treat Layer 3 as an execution. |

The intended effect is a near free-roll—if the trend reverses, the trailing stop on Layer 1 has already locked in profit that absorbs the loss on later layers; if it continues, the combined delta engine compounds rapidly. But this must be stated honestly: stops rarely fill exactly at plan, a violent reversal gaps through trailing stops, slippage widens on the leveraged later layers, and a near-term gamma option can lose far more, far faster, than a model assumes. Pyramiding genuinely reduces reversal risk and is vastly safer than averaging down, but it never eliminates the possibility of a real loss—size every layer as if the stop could slip. Maturity is the moment of maximum danger, because the layered totals create a top-heavy, inverted pyramid: the instant the stack prints a vertical climax, the entire structure is liquidated at once and risk resets to baseline.

## The Discipline, Form B: Engineering a Stack at Entry

**Form B — engineering a stack at entry:** the second discipline composes leverage deliberately, combining instruments to fine-tune effective leverage and manage the Greeks—mixing low-theta long-dated exposure with high-gamma short-dated exposure and defined-risk hedges, all inside the 1% risk rule. Several recipes recur by regime:

| Stack | Composition | Best for |
|---|---|---|
| Core + protection | Margined stock or sector ETF + a married protective put or collar. | Trending markets where you want defined downside. |
| Anchor + overlay | ITM LEAPS or a structured warrant (base leverage) + short-term bull call spreads or OTM calls (gamma). | Multi-month theses with tactical bursts. |
| Triple synthetic | Portfolio-margin position in a liquid leader + deep-ITM LEAPS + a protective put spread. | High-conviction core in a strong regime. |
| Volatility-adjusted | 2x/3x ETF core + a long straddle or strangle around a catalyst. | Event-driven, volatility-expansion setups. |

Illustrative example: rather than simply buying a 3x utilities ETF during a confirmed AI-power rotation, a trader builds a stack—a margined position in a liquid power or utilities name, a deep-ITM 2027 LEAPS on the same theme for low-decay base leverage, a 30-to-45-day bull call spread for tactical gamma on the breakout, and a small protective put spread defining maximum portfolio risk near 0.8%. Effective leverage on the thesis lands around 3.5x to 4.5x, and on a 15% to 25% move over a week or two the stacked position can return well over 100% on the capital deployed, with the winner pyramided, scaled out in tranches, and the margin paid down.

## The Unifying Rule: Measure True Exposure, Cap Total Leverage

Both disciplined forms, and the avoidance of the dangerous one, reduce to a single governing discipline: size to true, correlation-adjusted exposure, and cap total leverage hard. Two limits do the work—per-position risk no more than about 0.75% to 1% (1R) on any single stacked idea, measured at the unified position's true stop rather than leg by leg; and a firm portfolio-wide ceiling on combined effective leverage from margin, leveraged ETFs, options delta, and stacks together. (The book's single global leverage ceiling is the one settled in the reconciliation note in the Leveraged Instruments chapter; no combination of stacked layers may push total portfolio leverage past it.) Daily, the disciplined stacker reviews net Greeks across the whole book and stress-tests against a sharp drop, and any stack too complex to monitor is simplified or unwound.

## The Position-Stacking Governance Matrix

| Operational Parameter | The Retail Spectator | The Blueprint Capital Allocator |
|---|---|---|

| Operational Parameter | The Retail Spectator | The Blueprint Capital Allocator |
|---|---|---|
| Sizing direction | Averages down into losing positions out of denial, multiplying the risk of ruin. | Pyramids up only into winning, structurally sound trends that have validated the edge. |
| Risk allocation | Adds size on gut feeling, leaving the account exposed to a sudden reversal. | Restricts new layers to the locked-in profit of preceding layers, never breaching 1R net. |
| Leverage coordination | Maxes out margin at entry, exposed to immediate broker liquidation. | Coordinates distinct layers and caps total portfolio leverage to the book's global limit. |
| Monetization | Holds a top-heavy position through a full reversal, turning a win into a loss. | Liquidates the whole unified stack into peak volume, locking the milestone in cash. |

## Risks and Iron Survival Rules

Stacking multiplies not only exposure but the number of things that can fail—complexity risk grows with every leg, margin amplification means a sudden gap can trigger cascading liquidations, and a Greeks mismatch can convert a position you believed was hedged into a directional bet. Keep total effective leverage within the book's single global ceiling; risk no more than roughly 0.75% to 1% per stacked position, measured on the unified structure; review net Greeks daily and stress-test against a sharp drop (for example a 12% market decline); hold a 35% to 45% cash buffer; and simplify or unwind any stack too complex to monitor. Most blowups trace to false diversification, excessive leverage, ignoring correlation, risk stacking, and emotional attachment—clustering near market extremes, exactly when their cost is highest.

## The Position-Stacking Cycle

Aggressive traders tend to move through a recognizable stacking arc—an opportunity is identified, an initial position is established, additional instruments are added and leverage expands, confidence increases, exposure becomes concentrated as risk accumulates often unseen, the market decides, and outcomes are magnified across every layer—with the result decided by whether discipline holds as exposure concentrates.

## Final Principle: The Law of Capital Layering

Position stacking occurs whenever multiple positions express the same underlying view, whether the trader intends it or not. Used intelligently—pyramiding into proven winners and engineering risk-bounded structures—it accelerates returns; used recklessly, it manufactures hidden concentration and destroys capital with astonishing speed. The decisive insight is that the number of positions held matters far less than the number of genuinely independent outcomes they represent.

## E. Controlled Concentration

To turn one hundred thousand dollars into one million in a hundred and eighty days, readers must first confront the most comfortable lie in retail finance: that broad diversification is a virtue. For a pension fund with a thirty-year horizon, scattering capital across thirty unrelated assets is sound counsel; for a six-month, ten-fold sprint, it is a mathematical death sentence. Here is the paradox: extraordinary wealth is almost always created through concentration—and extraordinary losses are almost always caused by it. The entire difference reduces to a single word: **control.** Readers do not diversify—they practice **controlled concentration through synthetic leverage**: pinning a large share of the portfolio's firepower onto one to three high-velocity, asymmetric setups at any given time, while keeping the dollars they can actually lose locked inside an ironclad, quantified cage. The amateur concentrates blindly; the disciplined speculator uses synthetic structures to command enormous positions while bounding real risk to a rounding error. Both concentrate; only one survives.

### What Controlled Concentration Actually Is, and the Limits of Diversification

Controlled concentration is the deliberate allocation of significant capital toward a limited number of high-conviction opportunities while strict risk controls remain in force—engineered to maximize opportunity, conviction, focus, and compounding while minimizing catastrophic loss, emotional decision-making, and uncontrolled exposure. The gambler and the blueprint allocator may hold positions of identical size, but one is exposed and the other is fenced; one hopes, the other has calculated. Traditional diversification works beautifully for retirement portfolios whose objective is steady growth, but average is precisely the problem: owning twenty mediocre ideas reliably produces mediocre, index-tracking results, and almost no one has ever transformed a hundred thousand dollars into a million in six months by being well diversified. Hold ten positions at once and attention fragments, fees multiply, and capital is too diluted for any single winner to move the account curve.

### Conviction, Hope, and the Right to Concentrate

Concentration itself is not dangerous—uncontrolled concentration is. The dividing line is conviction versus hope. Conviction is built from research, preparation, evidence, observed market behavior, and a sober risk assessment; hope is built from emotion, wishful thinking, and attachment. What converts conviction into a license to concentrate is **edge**—from superior research, timing, understanding of a theme, execution, or risk management. Without an edge, concentration is merely speculation wearing a confident face; with a real edge, the larger and more durable it is, the more concentration it justifies.

### The Mathematics of Capital Density: The Three-Basket Rule

A manuscript built on aggression still needs a rigid operational boundary, and the blueprint enforces one: the **Three-Basket Rule.** At no point during the campaign may the ledger hold more than three active, core structural setups at once—smaller satellite positions are permitted, but the heavy capital lives in no more than three baskets. Two forces justify the limit: the **saturated delta engine** (capping at three core positions gives each enough capital density that a single milestone meaningfully bends the account curve, whereas spread across ten names every winner becomes a rounding error) and the **cognitive advantage** (three positions can be executed flawlessly; ten guarantee operational errors at exactly the moments that matter). The principle reduces to four words: quality, not quantity.

## Fencing the Risk: Nominal Exposure Versus Risk Exposure

The engine that makes safe concentration possible is the strict separation of two numbers amateurs treat as one: **nominal exposure** (the total dollar value of the shares a structure controls) and **risk exposure** (the maximum cash the ledger can actually lose if the trade fails).

*Nominal Exposure = Shares Controlled × Current Stock Price*
*Risk Exposure (1R) = Total Portfolio Mass × 0.01*

On a hundred-thousand-dollar account, one risk unit (1R) equals one thousand dollars. A reader might deploy a synthetic long structure to control $150,000 of a high-beta semiconductor leader—a position that, bought outright, would consume the entire account—paired with a hard technical stop or a defined long-put wing, so that if the trade fails the loss is capped at exactly 1R regardless of how large the nominal position was. Nominal exposure can be enormous; real risk stays microscopic, and that decoupling is the whole game.

## Expressing One Thesis Through Many Instruments

Controlled concentration does not require owning a single security—a single thesis can be expressed through common shares, options, warrants, and leveraged ETFs simultaneously—but the danger is that this flexibility hides the true size of the bet. A trader holding the stock, calls, warrants, and a leveraged ETF on the same name does not own four diversified positions; he owns one concentrated position wearing four costumes. **Always measure aggregate exposure, not position count**: if four instruments depend on the same move in the same stock, they are one basket. Readers achieve high exposure without draining cash by building synthetic stacks: **margin plus protective spread** (margin for reach on a liquid leader, downside capped with a collar or bear-put spread), **LEAPS or warrant anchor plus tactical calls** (a long-dated base with short-dated bull-call spreads layered on for gamma), and **3x ETF core plus options overlay** (a leveraged sector vehicle like SOXL, LABU, or UTSL during a strong trend, hedged at all times with defined-risk spreads).

## The Allocation Matrix

Allocation is governed by conviction and measured two ways that must never be confused: **equity allocation** (the share of actual account equity a position represents) and **capital power** (the buying power deployed, including synthetic leverage, which can exceed one hundred percent of equity precisely because the structures are fenced). By conviction tier on a $100k–$250k account: **Tier 1** (highest conviction—strong regime alignment, RS breakout, volume expansion, catalyst clarity) at 20–35% of equity each; **Tier 2** (good setups) at 10–18% each; **satellite** (warrants and high-gamma plays) at 3–8% each, no more than 12% combined. Portfolio heat at peak runs 45–55% of equity in concentrated and synthetic positions; in normal conditions hold 30–40% in cash or low-risk instruments, and never let the pristine cash reserve fall below roughly a quarter of the account.

| Configuration | Basket 1 | Basket 2 | Basket 3 | Cash Reserve |
|---|---|---|---|---|
| **Triple Threat (standard)** | 25% capital power — hedged 3x ETF | 25% — vertical debit spread | 25% — deep-ITM LEAPS proxy | 25% pristine cash |
| **Apex Focus (maximum)** | 60% capital power — asymmetric synthetic-long network | 15% — gamma squeeze strike | Empty (dormant) | 25% pristine cash |

Even in Apex mode, where capital power concentrates behind a single dominant thesis, real ledger risk stays tightly bounded—the large allocation funds margin requirements and option premium, not raw downside—and a hard rule overrides everything in the table: **no single position's equity may exceed 35% of the account, and no single idea may ever risk more than 1R.**

## A Live Campaign: An Aggressive Execution Example

A live campaign: suppose an AI-power rotation confirms with strong institutional flows, clear relative-strength leadership, and catalyst momentum on a $100k account. The reader allocates 28% synthetically—roughly $18k of margined long exposure on a liquid power-sector leader, anchored by deep-ITM LEAPS and topped with a bull-call debit-spread overlay—so effective exposure lands near $220k–$280k notional while the protective layers cap maximum risk at about 0.9% of the account. The theme runs 22% over ten days, and the stacked position returns somewhere between 65% and 140%. The reader scales out across three or four tranches, pays down the margin, and rotates the freed capital into the next Tier 1 concentration—perhaps a biotech M&A wave expressed through a LABU stack. String six to ten of these together with disciplined risk, and the ten-fold target stops being a fantasy and becomes arithmetic.

## Position Sizing, the Exit, and Hidden Concentration

Position sizing is the single skill that most reliably separates professionals from amateurs—even the highest-conviction idea requires a hard limit, set by answering four questions before entry: how much capital is genuinely at risk, what is the maximum acceptable loss, how volatile is the position, and what happens if the thesis is simply wrong. The exit matters even more than the entry: before committing a dollar, the disciplined reader has already defined profit objectives, stop-loss levels, a scaling plan, and contingency actions—

many traders enter intelligently and then exit emotionally, surrendering in panic the gains their analysis earned.

Concentration hides at levels most traders never check: a reader who owns five semiconductor names, four AI companies, or a basket of biotech firms feels diversified but is deeply concentrated within a single theme, and when the market turns risk-off those correlated positions fall together. Concentration crosses into recklessness when leverage becomes excessive, risk is ignored, emotion takes the wheel, or liquidity is poor—leverage deserves particular caution because it magnifies everything concentration already amplifies. The warning signs are behavioral and consistent across every blown-up account: refusing to reduce a losing position, rationalizing losses, averaging down again and again, and ignoring market conditions that have plainly changed.

## The Iron Discipline Rules and the Professional Framework

The protections collapse without a short list of non-negotiable rules enforced mechanically: never risk more than 1% of the account on any single concentrated idea (and no more than 0.75% on higher-volatility stacks); hold no more than three Tier 1 positions at once; review portfolio correlation and aggregate Greeks every day; force a reduction the moment any position exceeds 35% of account equity; and always have an exit plan defined before entry. Professionals do not ask "how many positions do I own?" but "how much of my future depends on a single outcome?" The complete discipline reduces to a six-part framework: high conviction backed by strong evidence, defined risk, adequate liquidity, clear catalysts, continuous monitoring, and emotional discipline. When all six are present, concentration is no longer a gamble—it is a strategy.

## The Governance Matrix

| Operational Dimension | The Retail Gambler | The Blueprint Capital Allocator |
|---|---|---|
| **Asset Distribution** | Over-diversifies into twenty positions to feel safe, guaranteeing mediocre, index-tracking returns. | Concentrates into a maximum of three high-velocity baskets to maximize compounding power. |
| **Risk Definition** | Confuses size with risk, assuming that concentrating capital means accepting certain ruin. | Decouples nominal exposure from risk exposure, capping absolute downside to a single 1R unit. |
| **Execution Focus** | Scans hundreds of charts daily and misses key turns through cognitive fatigue. | Hyper-focuses on the order book and technical levels of three concentrated targets. |
| **Drawdown Mitigation** | Suffers total liquidation when a single unhedged position gaps against him. | Protects concentration with synthetic option wings or hard, asset-linked time-stops. |

## Final Principle

Compounding accelerates when capital is deployed efficiently, and controlled concentration is the multiplier that makes a ten-fold, six-month result mathematically plausible—not by taking on more risk, but by routing more capital to the highest-quality opportunities while the risk rules protect the engine. It rests on a single truth: extraordinary returns rarely come from excessive diversification, and extraordinary losses almost always come from uncontrolled concentration. In the pursuit of turning one hundred thousand dollars into one million, concentration supplies the acceleration—but control alone decides whether the journey ends in wealth creation or capital destruction. The secret was never concentration. **The secret is concentration under control.**

# PART IV – THE PROFESSIONAL TRADER'S PLAYBOOK

# Chapter 14
# Building a High-Velocity Watchlist

## A. Relative Volume Screens

### Why Relative Volume Is the Engine

A high-velocity watchlist is the engine of aggressive momentum trading, and the objective is narrower than most traders assume: not to predict which stocks might move, but to identify the stocks already moving with institutional participation. The most effective tool for that is the relative volume (RVOL) screen—your primary behavioral scanner. A breakout without a volume surge is a retail illusion; price is the argument, volume is the verdict. When an institutional order-flow engine begins aggressively accumulating, it cannot hide, leaving an immediate vertical distortion in the relative-volume reading. One honest note: turning $100,000 into $1,000,000 in six months demands roughly 1,000% returns, near-perfect execution, real leverage, and luck—most traders attempting this style lose money, and 50%-plus drawdowns are common. RVOL improves where you point capital; it does not repeal that risk.

### What Is Relative Volume?

Relative volume compares an asset's current trading volume to its own average over a recent lookback window—typically the 20-, 30-, or 50-day average.

*RVOL = Current Volume ÷ Average Historical Volume*

| Today's Volume | Average Daily Volume | RVOL |
|---|---|---|
| 2 million | 1 million | 2.0 |
| 12 million | 3 million | 4.0 |
| 50 million | 5 million | 10.0 |

A reading of 2.0 means twice the normal pace: near 1.0 is normal, 2.0 is twice normal, 5.0 signals exceptional institutional participation, and 10.0 or more points to unusual, event-driven demand. Large moves rarely occur without unusually high volume.

### The Mathematics of the Volume Distortion

The central lesson is that absolute volume is nearly meaningless without context—a stock trading five million shares may be dead if its baseline is ten million, while a thin name printing one million against a 50,000-share baseline is undergoing an immense structural shift:

| Stock | Today's Volume | Average Volume | RVOL |
|---|---|---|---|
| Stock A | 80 million | 75 million | 1.07 |
| Stock B | 9 million | 800,000 | 11.25 |

Most beginners screen for "most active" and choose Stock A; the professional chooses Stock B, an eleven-fold surge in demand—the kind of distortion where explosive moves begin. Institutions, hedge funds, and algorithmic desks cannot quietly buy millions of shares, and their footprints appear as unusually high relative volume.

### The RVOL Threshold Scale

| RVOL | Interpretation |
|---|---|
| Below 1.5 | Ignore |
| 2.0 | Interesting |
| 3.0 | Strong |
| 5.0 | Excellent |
| 8.0+ | Exceptional |
| 10.0+ | Potential momentum explosion |

Different traders use different cutoffs; for aggressive momentum work, read 2.0 and above as conservative, and 3.0 to 5.0-plus as true velocity. Many of the biggest winners begin with RVOL above 5—but a high reading is a signal to investigate, never an automatic buy.

### The U-Shaped Curve: RVOL by Time of Day

Early-session volume is naturally elevated, so a raw comparison to the full-day average is misleading. Trading volume follows a U-shaped curve—spiking in the opening and closing thirty minutes and drying up through midday—so the Blueprint scanner never compares 9:45 AM volume to yesterday's total, but to the historical average for 9:45 AM:

| Time of Day | Strong RVOL Signal |
|---|---|
| First 15 minutes | Above 3 |
| First hour | Above 2.5 |
| Midday | Sustained above 2 |
| Final hour | Rising volume confirms continuation |

Names that hold elevated RVOL through the whole day usually carry stronger institutional sponsorship than those that fade after the open. For intraday decisions, lean on "pace" RVOL—a projected end-of-day figure—rather than the raw running total.

### Combining RVOL with Price, Breakouts, and Other Signals

High volume without price movement usually means nothing. The combination you want pairs a high RVOL reading with strong price appreciation, a breakout above resistance, and an expanding intraday range: a break of $30 resistance on average volume often fails, while a break on five times average volume has a far higher chance of holding. RVOL grows far more powerful when several independent signals align:

| Confirming Signal | Why It Matters |
|---|---|
| New 52-week high | Indicates trend leadership |
| Breakout from consolidation | Suggests fresh institutional buying |
| Gap-up on news | Introduces a new catalyst |
| Tight float | Amplifies price movement when demand surges |
| Strong sector | Institutional money flows into leading groups |
| Expanding options activity | Reinforces directional momentum |

The most explosive setups stack these—a low float with high RVOL and a real catalyst, an options-flow overlay flagging unusual sweeps for a potential gamma squeeze, or high short interest meeting a volume spike. Momentum is strongest when the evidence converges.

## The Tactical Playbook: The RVOL Baseline Setup

Readers run a restrictive, multi-stage filter at specific windows rather than scanning at random. **The opening print scan (9:45 AM EST):** fifteen minutes after the bell, automated scanners sweep the entire equity and derivative universe against three constraints—RVOL ≥ 3.0 (three times its norm in the first fifteen minutes), a price move of at least 3% above the prior close or a clean breakout from a multi-week base, and a liquidity floor of roughly 500,000 shares average daily volume. **The mid-day consolidation scan (11:30 AM EST):** scan the morning's breakout list for a specific institutional signature—price consolidation on deflating volume:

> **THE MID-DAY RE-ENGAGEMENT FLOW 9:30 AM BREAKOUT PRINT** → Stock surges +6% on RVOL 4.5 (institutional sweep) ↓ **MID-DAY BULL FLAG** • Price action – orderly drift/pullback holds the 8-period EMA • Volume action – RVOL falls below 1.0 (retail churn, no institutional selling) ↓ **THE SECONDARY TRIGGER** Afternoon volume re-engages → RVOL crosses > 2.0 → execute the stacking protocol

When price holds its morning gains while RVOL drops sharply through the lunch hour, institutional buyers have paused their algorithms and are holding rather than dumping—a textbook bull flag, and the afternoon re-engagement of volume is the trigger to add.

## The Core Screen and Enhanced Filters

One effective momentum screen narrows thousands of names to a manageable group, used daily and intraday: price above $5 (a practical $2–$100 band avoids illiquid pennies and inert mega-caps), average daily volume above 500,000–1,000,000 shares, relative volume above 3, price up more than 5% on the day, a new 20-day high, float under 50–100 million shares, a bid-ask spread below 0.5%, and no imminent earnings (unless deliberately trading the earnings catalyst). Sort survivors by RVOL descending—a tight list of a few names that clear every filter beats a chaotic list of a hundred.

Layer these on for maximum velocity: **low float + high RVOL** (a float under 10–20 million with RVOL above 5 and a catalyst can run 2–10x), **pre-market focus** (scan pre-market volume spikes to find the day's setups early), **sector and theme rotation** (group by hot themes—AI, biotech, EV—and screen the leveraged ETFs like TQQQ and SOXL), **options-flow overlay** (high RVOL plus unusual options volume flags gamma-squeeze potential), and **technical confirmation** (require price above VWAP, a break of resistance, or a flag/cup on high RVOL before acting). For leveraged plays, screen the underlying's RVOL and trade the derivative—a high-RVOL move in QQQ points toward TQQQ or QQQ calls. Run real-time scans on Finviz, Trade Ideas, thinkorswim, TradingView, Scanz, or TrendSpider, with alerts on RVOL thresholds and price-plus-volume combinations.

## The Daily Watchlist Routine

Every session opens with the same sequence. **Pre-market:** scan for stocks gapping up on news, rank by pre-market RVOL, and note earnings, upgrades, FDA decisions, or contracts. **After the open:** drop names whose RVOL fades, promote those holding above 3 while breaking key levels, and track sector leaders and laggards. **End of day:** save the strongest closers (finishing near highs on elevated RVOL) and build a secondary continuation list. Structurally, run a layered watchlist—a core list of 50–100 liquid, volatile names and leveraged ETFs, a daily velocity layer fed by the RVOL scanners, and an alert layer watching thresholds and volume pace—cross-checking every promotion against catalysts, short interest, and chart patterns before it earns aggressive size.

## RVOL Across Market Regimes

The same reading means different things by tape: in bull markets high RVOL fuels multi-day trends and breakouts follow through more reliably; in choppy markets it still produces sharp moves but gains are shorter-lived and tight risk management is essential; in bear markets it often accompanies panic selling and violent short-covering rallies, so distinguish genuine accumulation from a temporary rebound before committing.

## The Watchlist Filtration Governance Matrix

| Watchlist Parameter | The Retail Spectator | The Blueprint Capital Allocator |
|---|---|---|

| Watchlist Parameter | The Retail Spectator | The Blueprint Capital Allocator |
|---|---|---|
| Scanner Architecture | Watches "most active" lists, chasing bloated billion-share names with no institutional backing. | Runs time-adjusted RVOL screens to capture precise behavioral anomalies. |
| Volume Interpretation | Assumes high absolute volume means a stock is ready to run, ignoring historical context. | Requires an RVOL multiplier of 3.0 or more to confirm a genuine information shock. |
| Time-of-Day Discipline | Scans at random, buying late-day fading breakouts at the top of the range. | Scans at 9:45 and 11:30 AM EST to match institutional algorithmic cycles. |
| List Management | Keeps 100 tickers on a chaotic list, fragmenting attention and conviction. | Maintains a tight list of a handful of names that clear every structural filter. |

### Risk, Discipline, and Common Mistakes

RVOL points your capital at the right names; it does not guarantee the trade. **False signals:** a high reading can mark exhaustion as easily as a launch—confirm with price action, never buy on RVOL alone. **Don't chase extension:** avoid stocks already stretched far from key moving averages. **Mind the float and the source:** in thinly traded names a huge RVOL can come from a tiny share count, not real demand. **Leverage amplification:** 2x and 3x ETFs decay in chop and options carry time and volatility risk—size small. **Psychology and sizing:** high velocity demands pre-defined rules—a clear entry (RVOL above 3 plus a breakout), tight stops (5–10%), scaled targets, and risk of roughly 1–5% per trade. Most traders lose money in this style and 50%-plus drawdowns are common; let survival, not any single trade, govern your sizing.

**Blueprint Principle:** Price tells you what is happening. Relative volume tells you how much conviction is behind the move. Build your watchlist around measurable demand today—not predictions.

## B. Catalyst Detection

### Why Catalysts Sit at the Center of the Blueprint

Your relative-volume screens are the radar—they tell you something is happening. But a volume spike alone is a question, not an answer; catalyst detection supplies the *why*, and whether the move has structural backing. In a six-month sprint you cannot deploy capital into random, unexplained spikes, which lack institutional staying power and mean-revert. What you hunt instead are high-impact, asymmetric fundamental triggers—**Information Shocks**—events powerful enough to make Wall Street re-price an asset overnight. This is why, for aggressive compounding, **catalyst detection is arguably more important than chart analysis**: technical patterns describe how a stock is moving; catalysts explain why institutions are willing to pay progressively higher prices. A strong catalyst plus high RVOL plus technical confirmation can produce moves of 20–100% or more in days, sometimes hours—which is exactly why it demands tight risk control.

## What Is a Catalyst? The Anatomy of an Information Shock

A catalyst is any new development that forces participants to rapidly reassess a company's or sector's value—an unexpected piece of fundamental data that renders prior valuation models obsolete, compelling analysts and algorithmic market makers to re-price in real time. The market is a forward-looking discounting mechanism: prices rise because investors believe tomorrow will be materially better, and a catalyst is what changes that expectation, creating a surge in institutional buying, unusually high volume, momentum and volatility, and sustained trends. The Blueprint forbids chasing generic noise, sensational headlines, or unverified rumor and mandates an explicit, identifiable trigger you can name and source before risking a dollar. The strongest catalysts share a signature—they are unexpected, measurable, scalable, earnings-altering, and expectation-altering.

## The Hierarchy of Market Catalysts

Not all catalysts carry equal force. At the top sit the **Big Four Institutional Catalysts** most likely to force programmatic, multi-day accumulation. **Tier 1 — earnings surprises (the Triple-Beat):** nothing moves stocks more consistently than unexpected earnings growth—target a beat on top-line revenue, a beat on bottom-line EPS, and an upward revision of forward guidance, which compels funds to recalculate position sizes. **Tier 2 — FDA and clinical milestones (the binary multiplier):** especially potent in biotech and small-caps, a Phase II or III success, a fast-track or breakthrough designation, or an approval can create instantaneous re-pricing—and are also the most dangerous, since a disappointing readout erases the position just as violently. **Tier 3 — major product launches. Tier 4 — structural contracts and OEM partnerships** (often the contract value exceeds the company's entire market cap). Below them: **Tier 5 — analyst upgrades**, **Tier 6 — M&A**, **Tier 7 — industry and sector rotation** (often traded through 2x/3x ETFs), **Tier 8 — regulatory and legislative winds**, **Tier 9 — short squeezes** (driven by mechanics, not fundamentals—treat with caution), and **Tier 10 — the artificial-intelligence narrative** (GPUs, optical networking, cloud, data centers, cybersecurity, robotics, power infrastructure).

## A Second Lens: Categorizing Catalysts for Scanning

For day-to-day scanning, sort catalysts by predictability: **scheduled (calendar-based)**—earnings dates, FDA/PDUFA decisions, clinical readouts, FOMC and economic data, conferences, lock-up expirations (preparable in advance); **unscheduled/breaking**—M&A, contract wins, launches, regulatory rulings, insider buying, surprise upgrades (react in real time); and **sector/thematic**—hot themes that drive sympathy plays across related names. Front-running a scheduled catalyst and riding the initial reaction to a breaking one are two different skills, and a complete watchlist accounts for both.

## Detecting Catalysts Before Everyone Else

Professionals build systems; they do not rely on luck. The edge is extracted before the opening bell, when a verified catalyst can be matched to a position map while the rest of the market is still asleep:

> **THE PRE-MARKET DETECTION FLOW 06:00–08:30 AM EST** → Run SEC EDGAR scanners & global news feeds ↓ **FILTER CATALYST SIGNATURE** • Step 1 — Verify explicit catalyst type (Triple-Beat, FDA, Major Contract, Regulatory) • Step 2 — Confirm float < 50M shares (low supply = maximum volatility) ↓ **INTRADAY VELOCITY CROSS** Market opens → match catalyst to RVOL ≥ 3.0 → deploy fenced capital

**The pre-market filtration protocol (6:00–8:30 AM EST):** deploy automated RSS feeds and SEC filing scrapers targeting Form 8-K (material events), Form 4 (insider buying), and the major news wires, stripping out editorial commentary. Each morning, review companies reporting before the open, pre-market news, new 8-Ks, analyst upgrades/downgrades, unusual options activity and insider purchases, government-contract and regulatory decisions, and major economic data. The 2026 stack blends news terminals (Benzinga Pro, Scanz, Trade Ideas), calendars and filings (Yahoo/EarningsWhispers, MarketChameleon, BioPharma Catalyst, SEC EDGAR), and social/sentiment tools (X advanced search, StockTwits, Reddit—for awareness, never confirmation). A sample workflow: pre-market (7–9 AM) scan earnings and FDA calendars plus news for gappers, filtering for high projected RVOL, price roughly $2–$100, and float under 50 million; intraday set alerts for 8-Ks and cross-check every signal against the RVOL spike; evening rebuild the watchlist.

## The Float-to-Catalyst Alignment

A catalyst is only as explosive as the supply structure it acts upon—the same news that barely moves a billion-share mega-cap can send a low-float name vertical, because there is not enough stock to absorb demand. Apply the **Float Constraint Filter**: the ideal target carries a free float under roughly 50 million shares, where a major Information Shock collides with a restricted float to enter its most convex state.

## Combining Catalysts with Technical Confirmation

The highest-probability trades occur when the fundamental and technical pictures agree. Pair a compelling catalyst with relative volume above 3 (often above 5 for the most aggressive setups), a breakout above resistance or VWAP or a clean gap-and-go, a new 52-week high, strong sector leadership and visible institutional accumulation, and expanding options volume. Liquidity is non-negotiable whenever you intend to use options or leveraged ETFs—average volume above 500k–1M shares and tight spreads.

## The Catalyst Checklist

Before entering, run the catalyst through seven questions: Is it genuinely unexpected? Is it likely to increase future earnings or cash flow? Will institutions care? Is the stock on unusually high relative volume? Is price confirming with a breakout? Is the broader market supportive? Is there enough liquidity to enter and exit efficiently? If several answers are "no," the catalyst probably lacks the power to sustain a trend—pass.

## Avoid Weak Catalysts and False Positives

Many headlines look exciting but carry little lasting impact, because the market quickly discounts news that does not materially improve future earnings. Be skeptical of routine conference presentations and investor-day fluff, ordinary press releases, minor management changes, speculative rumors without evidence, and small customer wins or vague partnerships with no disclosed financials. A genuine 8-K is not the same as an anonymous post, and front-running a pump-and-dump is the fastest way to hand your capital to someone else.

## Building the Daily Catalyst Watchlist

Maintain a dynamic, tiered watchlist rebuilt every session. **Tier 1 — immediate opportunities:** five to ten names with a major catalyst announced today, RVOL above 5, price gains above 7%, breakout patterns, and visible institutional buying. **Tier 2 — developing stories:** emerging catalysts, improving technicals, rising institutional ownership. **Tier 3 — future candidates:** upcoming earnings, launches, pending regulatory decisions, or scheduled conferences. A parallel **sector basket** of leveraged ETFs tied to thematic catalysts lets you express a sector view when no single name stands out. Even powerful stories exhaust themselves—watch for catalyst fatigue (declining RVOL, repeated failures to make new highs, weakening institutional participation, negative revisions, gap-ups sold into through the day) and step aside before reversion. Retail asks "has the stock gone up too much?"; institutions ask "has the long-term earnings outlook fundamentally changed?"—train yourself to ask the institutional question.

## The Catalyst Detection Governance Matrix

| Operational Dimension | The Retail Spectator | The Blueprint Capital Allocator |
|---|---|---|
| Catalyst Sourcing | Relies on speculative internet forums, sensational media articles, and late-day hype videos. | Scrapes raw SEC filings (Form 8-K), regulatory notices, and official corporate press wires. |
| Validation Filter | Chases any stock up 10% on the day, blind to the underlying reason for the move. | Demands an explicit, un-arbitraged corporate milestone before acting on the price action. |

| Operational Dimension | The Retail Spectator | The Blueprint Capital Allocator |
|---|---|---|
| Supply Awareness | Buys heavily diluted, bloated structures, then wonders why the price won't move. | Aligns high-impact catalysts with a restricted float ceiling (< 50M shares) to maximize velocity. |
| Execution Timing | Gets trapped buying the top of a dead rumor right before a secondary offering drops. | Positions at the inception of verified news, preserving a mathematical margin of safety. |

### Risk and Execution Discipline

Everything here cuts both ways—the same forces that drive a 20–100% move can reverse just as violently. **Overhype and "sell the news":** many catalysts are already priced in by the headline—use tight stops, risking no more than 5–10% per trade. **Leverage danger:** options, warrants, and 3x ETFs can decay or gap to near-zero—size small, on the order of 1–2% of capital at risk. **False positives:** verify the source; avoid unverified rumors and pump-and-dump dynamics. **Psychology:** catalyst chasing breeds FOMO—define rules in advance and follow them. The objective is never to trade every headline; it is to act only on catalysts that materially improve a company's prospects and are confirmed by institutional buying, strong relative volume, and disciplined risk management.

**Blueprint Principle:** Catalysts ignite momentum. Relative volume confirms participation. Price confirms conviction. When all three align—and only then—a stock may become an exceptional compounder.

## C. Earnings Momentum

### Why Earnings Momentum Anchors the Blueprint

If one factor consistently separates ordinary stocks from exceptional performers, it is earnings momentum. Sustained advances of 200%, 500%, or even 1,000% are almost always supported by rapidly improving corporate earnings—institutions ultimately buy earnings growth, and price follows. It is also the most predictable, institution-backed catalyst, and that predictability is the edge. The retail amateur treats a report like a coin flip, gambling the night before; the Blueprint allocator waits for the numbers to clear, lets the Information Shock hit the tape, and systematically exploits the Post-Earnings Announcement Drift (PEAD), because a multi-billion-dollar fund cannot buy in a single session without spiking the price—its algorithms accumulate over days or weeks. The move can be expressed across every instrument: a positive surprise plus a low float for explosive runners, or 2x/3x ETFs like SOXL on a semiconductor beat, with post-earnings IV collapse favoring directional calls on *continuation* rather than gambles through the report.

## What Is Earnings Momentum, and the Science of PEAD

Earnings momentum is the continuous improvement in financial performance that exceeds market expectations—accelerating EPS, rapidly growing revenue, expanding margins and free cash flow, improving return on equity, and rising estimates and guidance revisions. Over the long run, stock prices follow earnings, which is why retail fixates on today's price while professionals focus on next quarter, next year, and the long-term trajectory. **Post-Earnings Announcement Drift** is a well-documented inefficiency: stocks reporting significant positive surprises tend to drift upward for a prolonged period rather than re-pricing instantly, because large funds must adjust valuation models, secure committee approval, and split multi-million-share orders into small blocks—programmatic buying that builds a floor under the asset:

One honest caveat: PEAD is real, but markets have grown more efficient, and a portion of the drift now compresses into the first session—an argument for tighter execution and confirmation, not for abandoning the edge.

## Reading Earnings Quality

Not every beat deserves capital. The market rewards **acceleration** more than absolute growth, because a rising growth rate signals improving competitive strength—consider a company whose year-over-year EPS growth climbs each quarter:

| Quarter | Year-over-Year EPS Growth |
|---|---|
| Q1 | 18% |
| Q2 | 32% |
| Q3 | 61% |
| Q4 | 105% |

The absolute numbers matter, but the slope matters more; institutions notice when the second derivative turns positive. **Revenue confirms the story:** earnings can be flattered temporarily through cost cuts, buybacks, or accounting, but revenue is far harder to manipulate, so the strongest companies pair EPS beats with accelerating sales and growing recurring revenue. **Guidance drives price:** a company that beats but lowers guidance can fall sharply, while one that modestly beats and substantially raises guidance can rally hard—track estimate revisions and upgrades, since institutional models automatically adjust to higher expected profits. And beware low-quality earnings driven by one-time asset sales, tax benefits, aggressive buybacks, or weak year-ago comparisons.

## The Three Levels of Earnings Momentum

Earnings momentum matures through recognizable stages, and position size and conviction should scale with the level. **Level one — emerging momentum:** a first significant beat, initial upgrades, moderate institutional buying—often the start of entirely new uptrends. **Level two — confirmed**

**momentum:** multiple consecutive beats, strong revenue acceleration, raised guidance, expanding margins, and RVOL above 3—frequently where sustained accumulation begins. **Level three — elite momentum:** the market's biggest winners, with exceptional EPS and revenue growth, industry leadership, repeated guidance increases, continuous upgrades, heavy institutional sponsorship, and persistent new highs.

## The Tactical Screen and Execution

Readers do not guess which companies will report well—they scan roughly 15 minutes before the open and 30 minutes after the close to isolate confirmed earnings-power shifts. **The quantitative surprise filter:** EPS and revenue both beat consensus by roughly 5–10% or more (a true Triple-Beat, not a one-cent headline); management explicitly raises forward guidance; and the stock gaps up by roughly 5% or more, clearing the 50- and 200-day moving averages or breaking a multi-month base. **The liquidity and velocity overlay:** RVOL above 3–5x with price holding above VWAP, price roughly $5–$150, average volume above 500k–1M shares, float under 50M for explosive small-caps (or liquid large-caps and ETFs for size), and confirming context. Sort by surprise magnitude, then RVOL, then percentage move from the open. **Execution** runs on a two-stage matrix: the **Day-1 Opening Range Breakout** (if the stock gaps up on RVOL ≥ 3.0, wait for the first 5-minute candle to close and enter on a breach of its high on accelerating volume, risk capped at the low of that print) and the **Day-2 to Day-5 continuation** (if Day 1 finishes at the top of its range on heavy volume, accumulate on the first minor pullback to the 8-period EMA, riding the institutional wave across a three-to-five-day arc).

## Expressing the Trade Across Instruments

Express the trade across instruments: **stocks** as the core breakout vehicle, scaling in on pullbacks to VWAP; **leveraged ETFs** (TQQQ or SOXL on clustered tech or semiconductor beats, respecting decay); **options** (calls on continuation or credit spreads to fade—avoid long straddles through the event, where IV crush works against you); and **warrants** for longer-dated leverage on durable post-earnings trends. Example: a low-float biotech pairs a Phase III milestone with its report and gaps 30% on 10x volume—enter long stock or calls on the first flag breakout, target a 50–100% move, and keep a tight stop below the gap low. The highest-probability trades occur when an earnings beat and raised guidance are confirmed by a breakout, a new 52-week high, strong relative volume, visible accumulation, and clear sector leadership—a great report inside a leading sector (semiconductors, AI, cloud, cybersecurity, defense, automation, medtech, energy infrastructure, fintech) is worth more than the same report in a laggard.

## The Earnings Momentum Checklist

Before adding a stock, confirm most of the following: quarterly EPS growth above 30%, revenue growth above 20%, a clear positive surprise, raised forward guidance, expanding gross and operating margins, strong free cash flow, analyst estimate upgrades, increasing institutional ownership, and relative volume above 3. When several align, the probability of sustained momentum rises sharply; when most are absent, the beat likely lacks the fuel to drift.

## Detection and the Daily Routine

Professionals review earnings daily, layered on the RVOL and catalyst screens. Before the open, compare actuals against consensus and flag strong historical-surprise records; during the session, watch whether strong earnings are confirmed by rising RVOL, gaps, breakouts, and sustained intraday strength; after the close, review after-hours reporters and rebuild tomorrow's list—the goal is not to know who reported, but which reports fundamentally changed expectations. Tools: TradingView, Benzinga Pro, Yahoo Finance, and EarningsWhispers for calendars and surprise history; thinkorswim, Trade Ideas, Scanz, or TC2000 for post-earnings filtering. Run a tiered watchlist—**Tier 1 (Velocity)** fresh beats with gap-and-go on 5x-plus RVOL, **Tier 2 (Developing)** pre-earnings momentum entered cautiously with defined-risk options, and a **sector basket** for broad earnings waves through TQQQ, SOXL, or other 3x ETFs.

## The Institutional Accumulation Cycle

Most major advances follow a recognizable sequence—revenue begins accelerating, earnings exceed expectations, management raises guidance, analysts increase estimates, institutions accumulate as RVOL expands, the stock breaks out to new highs and momentum traders join, and financial media amplifies the story as additional institutional capital follows.

## The Earnings Momentum Governance Matrix

| Operational Dimension | The Retail Spectator | The Blueprint Capital Allocator |
|---|---|---|
| Chronological Timing | Gambles before the announcement, exposing capital to binary, un-hedged option crushes. | Strikes after the announcement, exploiting the verified Post-Earnings Announcement Drift. |
| Data Interpretation | Buys simply because a company beat historical EPS, ignoring forward-guidance downgrades. | Demands a Triple-Beat signature — top-line, bottom-line, and an upward guidance revision. |
| Risk Insulation | Chases a massive gap-up blindly, far above the daily ATR, with no structural stop. | Uses precise 5-minute ORB thresholds or EMA pullbacks to tightly fence capital risk. |
| Capital Rotation | Holds indefinitely out of hope, letting capital stall as the drift phase fades. | Harvests the move over a defined 3-to-5-day window, returning capital to cash. |

### Risk, Discipline, and Common Mistakes

Earnings momentum is a genuine edge, but only inside a hard risk framework—many "beats" sell off, gaps can open against you, and leverage compresses every mistake. Cap risk at 5–10% per trade and scale out into strength; favor momentum continuation over pre-earnings longs and avoid straddles through the event, since post-earnings IV collapses fast; keep effective leverage modest and size derivatives tiny (1–2% of capital at risk); and avoid the classic errors—don't buy on a one-penny beat, don't ignore deteriorating revenue behind a higher EPS, don't chase extended gaps with no defined risk, and don't assume every beat leads to a rally.

**Blueprint Principle:** Earnings create conviction. Revenue validates the story. Guidance shapes expectations. Institutions supply the buying power. Price reflects the result.

## D. Sector Leadership

### Why Sector Leadership Anchors the Watchlist

One of the costliest mistakes a trader can make is studying individual stocks while ignoring the sector they live in—the strongest stocks almost always emerge from the strongest sectors. Institutional money rarely buys a single company in isolation; capital floods entire industries when investors believe an economic, technological, or regulatory trend will drive sustained growth. A stock can carry a flawless chart and stellar catalyst, but if it sits in a hated, stagnant sector, institutional capital passes it by. The logic of the chapter reduces to one line: top-down to a strong sector, then down to the strong stocks and ETFs inside it, confirmed by RVOL and a catalyst—which concentrates aggressive capital where momentum and compounding velocity are highest and can deliver moves of 20–100% or more faster than chasing isolated names.

### Sector Leadership Is Institutional Leadership

Markets move in waves, and money rotates from one sector to another as conditions, rates, innovation, and sentiment evolve. Institutions almost never buy a single semiconductor company—they buy the whole ecosystem (chip manufacturers, equipment suppliers, optical networking, memory makers, AI-infrastructure names), because a portfolio manager running billions cannot take meaningful positions in hundreds of unrelated industries and builds thematic exposure instead. A view as simple as "AI spending will double" translates into chip designers, memory makers, networking suppliers, cloud providers, cooling and electrical-equipment firms, and data-center REITs all at once. Picture two companies with identical earnings growth—one in the strongest industry, one in the weakest: the stronger sector attracts greater institutional buying, higher volume, deeper coverage, richer multiples, and more durable momentum, so a merely good company in a powerful sector can become an exceptional performer.

## The Market Moves in Groups: A Short History of Leadership

Every major bull market develops identifiable leadership groups—the faces change, the pattern does not:

| Era | Leadership Groups |
|---|---|
| 1990s | Internet, networking, software, telecommunications |
| 2003–2007 | Energy, commodities, mining, homebuilders |
| 2009–2015 | Cloud computing, social media, mobile technology |
| 2020–2021 | Electric vehicles, clean energy, e-commerce, biotechnology |
| 2023–present | AI, semiconductor design and equipment, optical networking, data centers, cybersecurity, power infrastructure |

Each cycle crowns its leaders, and the largest, most durable advances cluster inside them. The objective is not merely to find good companies but to identify the industries likely to attract sustained institutional investment—and to find them early.

## The Mathematics of Sector Alpha: The 80/20 Rule and the RS Line

Empirical study points to an **80/20 dominance rule**: during a high-velocity expansion, roughly 80% of the explosive moves concentrate in about 20% of active sectors. To exploit that, the Blueprint bypasses bloated, market-cap-weighted sector funds and measures sub-sector industry groups against the broad market with a relative-strength (RS) line:

*Relative Strength = Price of the Sub-Sector (ETF or Stock) ÷ Price of the SPY Index*

The scanner does not hunt the highest absolute price—it tracks the steepest angle of outperformance versus the S&P 500, typically over rolling 5-, 10-, 20-, and 60-day windows. This is most valuable during a pullback: when the broad market corrects, a leading sector that refuses to break—holding flat-to-rising relative strength—is a coiled spring that tends to release first and fastest when the index stabilizes. Watching for this hidden strength during corrections is one of the highest-value habits in the chapter.

## The Leadership Pyramid

Institutional buying inside a sector tends to descend the capitalization ladder in a predictable order: money first enters the broad **sector ETF**, then the industry's **large-cap leaders** that establish the trend, then **mid-caps** for higher growth potential, and finally **small-caps**—frequently where the most explosive percentage gains occur, because a small capitalization can re-rate violently when institutional demand arrives.

## The Tactical Playbook: Top-Down Selection

Readers run a strict top-down extraction every weekend and pre-market session, filtering the universe down to a handful of high-velocity targets:

> **THE TOP-DOWN SELECTION MATRIX STEP 1 — INDEX OVERVIEW** → Confirm SPY/QQQ are in a healthy, bullish regime ↓ **STEP 2 — SECTOR EXTRACTION** • Rank sub-sectors by RS line (20-day vs. 50-day lookback) • Keep the top sectors showing heavy institutional accumulation ↓ **STEP 3 — THE APEX SELECTION** Isolate stocks/warrants printing RVOL ≥ 3.0 inside those top sectors

**The sector rotation filter:** the sub-sector must rank in the top tier of all industry groups over trailing 20- and 60-day windows, and the sector ETF or proxy must trade cleanly above its rising 21-day EMA and 50-day SMA (if the sector line sits below its 50-day SMA, the entire industry is blacklisted regardless of individual-stock hype). **The apex selection:** within the top two or three sectors, drill into the components for the highest RVOL (≥ 3.0), lowest float (under ~50M shares), and most disruptive catalysts—requiring the sector to outperform SPY over 5–20 days, the name to show RS above 1.0 against its own sector, price above $5, average volume above 1M, momentum confirmation, and RVOL above 2–3x. Build the top-down read on TradingView, thinkorswim, Benzinga Pro, Finviz, StockCharts, or TrendSpider, anchored by the standard ETF proxies (XLK technology, XLF financials, XLE energy) and their 2x and 3x versions.

## Reading a Leading Sector: Breadth and Confirmation

Leadership is rarely confined to one company, so never judge a sector by its largest name—ask how many stocks in the group are advancing. A genuinely strong sector shows broad participation: multiple stocks making new highs, high relative volume across the group, positive earnings momentum and upward analyst revisions, visible institutional buying, positive news flow and strong sector-ETF performance, and expanding market breadth. When company-specific and sector-specific momentum align, institutional buying becomes self-reinforcing and your probability of success rises sharply.

## Building a Sector-Based Watchlist

Organize the watchlist by industry rather than alphabetically, so you can see an entire group catch fire at once—grouping sub-themes under each leading sector (Artificial Intelligence: chip designers, optical networking, AI software, data-center infrastructure; Cybersecurity: endpoint, identity, cloud security; Aerospace & Defense: contractors, drones, satellite comms; Healthcare Innovation: medical devices, biotech, diagnostics; Financial Technology: payment processors, digital banking, financial software). Run it as a tiered process: pre-market, review heatmaps and RS rankings to identify two to four leading sectors, drill to the top five to ten stocks and leveraged ETFs in each, and promote only names that also carry an RVOL spike, a catalyst, or earnings momentum. Reserve Tier 1 for leaders inside leading sectors, keep emerging rotation candidates on Tier 2, and avoid laggard sectors entirely unless shorting them.

## Integrating Across Instruments

Sector leadership expresses itself across the toolkit, and the leveraged vehicles are often the point: **leveraged ETFs** (SOXL for semis, TNA for small caps, or a sector-specific 2x) as the primary velocity vehicle; **stocks** (the highest-RS leaders, traded on breakouts); **options** (calls on sector leaders or ETFs); **warrants** (longer-dated plays on select leadership); and **sympathy plays** (weaker names that catch up as rotation broadens). The prime setup is a sector leader plus high RVOL plus a catalyst or earnings beat—sector supplies the "where," RVOL flags the activity, the catalyst provides the "why."

## Sector Rotation and the Institutional Rotation Cycle

Markets rotate constantly—financials to technology, technology to energy, and onward—and successful momentum traders rotate with institutional capital, never growing emotionally attached to a sector. Most leadership follows a recognizable arc: a major catalyst emerges, institutions accumulate sector ETFs, large-cap leaders break out and analysts raise forecasts, mid-caps then small-caps see explosive momentum, media amplifies the story and retail enters, and valuations stretch as institutions rotate into the next theme. The greatest opportunities cluster in the early-to-middle stages—rank top sectors by momentum and rotate on a defined cadence, always toward where the money is going rather than where it has been. Be cautious of sectors showing declining revenues, regulatory pressure, deteriorating earnings, or persistent institutional outflows.

## The Sector Leadership Governance Matrix

| Watchlist Parameter | The Retail Spectator | The Blueprint Capital Allocator |
|---|---|---|
| Selection Orientation | Bottom-up guessing — picks charts in beaten-down sectors hoping for a reversal. | Top-down extraction — isolates institutional money flows at the sector level first. |
| Relative-Strength IQ | Blind to correlation, buying stocks that are actively lagging the S&P 500. | Requires a rising RS line, parking capital only in the top tier of industries. |
| Correction Response | Panics and liquidates at random when the index pulls back. | Hunts hidden strength — watches which groups refuse to drop during corrections. |
| Capital Focus | Spreads capital thin across unrelated, lagging sectors, diluting velocity. | Practices controlled concentration in the one or two dominant sectors. |

### Risk, Discipline, and Common Mistakes

Sector leadership tilts probability in your favor but does not suspend risk—and leadership can change faster than any other layer. **Rotation risk:** leadership shifts quickly—use stops and watch for exhaustion rather than staying loyal to yesterday's group. **Leverage decay:** 3x ETFs erode in sideways tape—reserve them for confirmed leadership. **Overconcentration:** cap total exposure to top themes at roughly 30–50% of capital and risk about 1–3% per trade, since sector reversals can be swift. **Confirm, don't assume:** not every stock in a hot sector deserves capital—still require earnings growth, relative volume, and price confirmation. Strong relative strength sometimes trumps a fundamental opinion—follow the money flow over your bias.

**Blueprint Principle:** Strong stocks lead strong sectors, and strong sectors lead strong markets. Institutional capital does not search at random—it concentrates where earnings, innovation, and economic trends intersect.

## E. Social Sentiment

### Why Social Sentiment Completes the Watchlist

Information now travels at the speed of a smartphone notification—millions of traders and algorithms react to the same headline at once, creating feedback loops that can drive a stock dramatically higher or sharply lower in hours. Social sentiment is the real-time crowd-psychology layer of your watchlist, capturing hype, FOMO, and fear as they build, and by 2026 retail traders drive an estimated 30–40% of volume in the most volatile names. The amateur treats social platforms like a casino floor, chasing late-stage hype; the Blueprint reader quantifies the crowd, confirms it against the harder layers, and acts with cold exit discipline. Sentiment plays two roles: its rate of change is an early radar for the RVOL spikes and catalyst moves that can precede surges of 20–100% or more, and its presence is a final confirmation that an existing setup has caught broad participation. What it is not is a standalone buy signal.

### What Is Social Sentiment? Leads, but Usually Confirms

Social sentiment measures the collective attitude toward a stock, sector, or theme, read across FinTwit, trading communities (Reddit's r/WallStreetBets, StockTwits), news commentary, search trends, influencer activity, and options chatter—reflecting where attention is flowing, which in the modern market frequently precedes liquidity. Institutional sentiment develops through earnings revisions, research, and reallocations; retail sentiment is driven by social discussion, breaking news, and viral ideas—and the most powerful momentum appears when the two align. That alignment usually unfolds in order: institutions recognize improving fundamentals, price rises, RVOL increases, analysts upgrade, media notices, social discussion expands, and only then does retail accelerate. So social sentiment normally *confirms* a trend rather than starting it—amplification layered on conviction, not the thesis itself.

## The Mathematics of Sentiment: Acceleration Over Absolutes

Absolute mention counts are nearly meaningless—a mega-cap naturally collects thousands of posts a day. What matters is the rate of change: a stock mentioned 500 times today after averaging 20 a day deserves far more attention than one steadily drawing 5,000. To make this rigorous, the Blueprint tracks a mentions-acceleration Z-score:

$$Z = (x - \mu) / \sigma$$

Here x is current hourly mention volume, μ is the 20-day baseline for that hour, and σ its standard deviation; a reading of $Z \geq 3.0$ marks an explosive awakening of crowd attention. Around it, monitor buzz volume, sentiment polarity (the bullish-to-bearish ratio), velocity (the hourly rate of change), and engagement. Polarity carries a counterintuitive lesson: the most lethal setups do not occur when chatter is 100% bullish—unanimous optimism usually means retail exhaustion. A rising bullish ratio (climbing through the 65–80% range) is constructive; a pinned, euphoric ratio near a price peak is a warning. The asymmetric sweet spot is high acceleration with mixed polarity—disagreement, not consensus, is what leaves fuel in the tank.

## The Squeeze Setup: Low Float Meets High Short Interest

Sentiment becomes an active trigger—rather than mere confirmation—in one structure: the short squeeze. Social hype is toxic unless it lands on a cap table built to amplify it, defined by two constraints—short interest of at least 20% of the float, and a free float under roughly 20 million shares. When accelerating crowd focus collides with heavy short interest and tiny share supply, it creates a short-gamma perfect storm: market makers and short-sellers are forced to buy back stock at any price to hedge, producing a vertical, non-linear eruption. This is the one case where the Blueprint leads with sentiment—and precisely because the move is violent in both directions, it comes with the strictest exit rules in the book.

## The Sentiment-Squeeze Playbook

Readers never buy a stock simply because it is trending—the signal only becomes a trade once it clears the structural filters and an entry trigger:

> THE SENTIMENT-SQUEEZE EXTRACTION SENTIMENT ACCELERATION → Mentions Z-score ≥ 3.0 on X / Reddit ↓ STRUCTURAL AMPLIFIER FILTER • Step 1 — Free float ultra-low (< 20 million shares) • Step 2 — Short interest ≥ 20% of float ↓ KINETIC EXECUTION 5-minute ORB → ride the 24–48h velocity wave → exit into the buzz peak

**The screen:** require a buzz spike of 2–5× the normal 24-hour average, a bullish ratio above roughly 65–80% and rising, and cross-confirmation from RVOL of 3–5×, price in the $2–$100 range, average volume above 500k, and a float under 50M—with a sector filter (hype in a leading theme carries further) and, above all, a genuine catalyst. **The 24-to-48-hour window:** social momentum decays fast, so the Blueprint treats these strictly as tactical sprints with a 24-to-48-hour maximum hold. Enter on a standard 5-minute Opening Range Breakout on day one of the surge; you are renting the crowd's momentum, not marrying the story. Liquidate into the peak of the buzz—selling into the late-stage demand that always chases the top—rather than holding through the reversal. Build the read on StockTwits, X advanced search, Reddit, Swaggystocks, StockGeist.ai, or thinkorswim's social-sentiment feed.

## The Quality of the Conversation, and Verification

Sophisticated traders weigh not just the quantity of discussion but its quality, because quality determines how long momentum lasts. Higher-quality sentiment centers on revenue growth, earnings revisions, new products, competitive advantages, and institutional ownership—chatter reinforcing a legitimate thesis. Lower-quality sentiment revolves around "to the moon" predictions, guaranteed-return claims, celebrity endorsements, conspiracy narratives, and coordinated buying campaigns, which fade quickly and tend to collapse hard. Social media should initiate research, not replace it: before a trending name earns a watchlist place, confirm a genuine catalyst, expanding RVOL, institutional participation, a chart breakout, and enough liquidity to enter and exit cleanly.

## The Attention Cycle

Most momentum names move through a predictable attention arc—**discovery** (experts and early institutions identify the opportunity), **recognition** (analysts, media, and professionals begin discussing it), **expansion** (retail discovers it through social media), **mania** (discussion peaks and optimism turns excessive), and **saturation** (nearly everyone who wanted in has bought and momentum stalls). The best risk-adjusted entries cluster in the first three stages; peak mention volume is one of the most reliable signs of a top. The same buzz score also means different things by regime—reinforcing trends in bull markets, rotating quickly in sideways markets, and producing only fleeting rallies in bear markets.

## The Social Sentiment Checklist and Integration

Before promoting a stock, confirm discussion is increasing rapidly (not merely high), the catalyst is genuine, relative volume is above normal, institutional buying is evident, the stock is breaking out technically, the broader sector is leading, and sentiment is supported by improving fundamentals. The more confirmations, the higher the quality of the opportunity—and the lower the odds of buying someone else's exit. The layer expresses itself across the toolkit: low-float runners on retail rotation (stocks), sector-wide hype amplified through SOXL or TQQQ (2x/3x ETFs), expanding implied volatility followed into calls (options), and longer-dated leverage on durable buzz (warrants).

## The Social Sentiment Governance Matrix

| Operational Dimension | The Retail Spectator | The Blueprint Capital Allocator |
|---|---|---|
| Information Sourcing | Follows social accounts passively, buying after an asset | Runs scrapers and Z-score filters to catch the initial |

| Operational Dimension | The Retail Spectator | The Blueprint Capital Allocator |
|---|---|---|
| | has already run 300%. | acceleration spark. |
| Psychological Stance | Operates on FOMO, feeling validated by online groupthink. | Stays clinical and detached, treating the crowd as a liquidity engine. |
| Structural Vetting | Ignores the cap table and tries to squeeze stocks with bloated floats. | Pairs buzz only with a low float (< 20M) and high short interest (≥ 20%). |
| Exit Strategy | Holds through the post-hype collapse, believing the narrative. | Exits within 24–48 hours, selling into peak volume rather than through it. |

### Risk, Discipline, and Common Mistakes

Of every layer, social sentiment is the most easily manipulated and quickest to reverse, earning its place only inside hard rules. **Manipulation and pumps:** coordinated hype can dump without warning—keep stops tight, risking no more than 5–8% per trade. **The FOMO trap:** sentiment lags price at peaks—confirm with price action, never buzz alone. **Leverage amplification:** options and 3x ETFs can erase a position on a reversal—size around 1% of capital at risk. **Noise over signal:** social works best short-term—pair it with fundamentals for anything you intend to hold. Pre-commit to entering only on multi-layer confluence, and avoid chasing every trending ticker, confusing popularity with quality, or buying after attention has already peaked.

**Blueprint Principle:** Institutional capital begins trends. Social sentiment accelerates them. Price confirms them. Treat the crowd as a measurement, never as a thesis.

## F. Institutional Buying

### Why Institutional Buying Is the Foundation

Retail investors often believe they move stock prices. They do not. The structural, multi-day trends this book relies on are funded almost exclusively by institutions—mutual funds, pension funds, hedge funds, sovereign-wealth desks, insurance companies, family offices, ETFs, and quantitative firms managing trillions. Retail volume is noise; institutional volume is the engine. The objective is not to compete with institutional money but to identify what the giants are buying and position alongside them—the conviction filter of your watchlist, confirming that an explosive setup is backed by real capital rather than fading hype. A retail trader might buy 500 to 10,000 shares in a click; an institution may need two million, ten million, or fifty million, an order that cannot be filled instantly without driving the price against itself—so institutions accumulate gradually over hours, days, or weeks, and that persistent buying pressure is what produces durable trends.

## The Footprints of Institutional Money

Institutions rarely announce their intentions; they leave a mathematically trackable trail—unusually high and sustained volume (a stock printing 2×, 3×, or 5× average across multiple sessions is rarely retail alone), repeated accumulation days and strong closes near session highs, rising relative strength against the broad market, orderly advances with shallow light-volume pullbacks, repeated support at key moving averages with higher highs and lows, and multiple breakout attempts with expanding options activity. These distinguish genuine accumulation from short-lived speculation.

## Market Microstructure: Dark Pools, Block Trades, and Icebergs

To read institutional footprints with authority, understand how giant orders actually reach the market—institutions rarely post ordinary limit orders, which would broadcast their size. **Dark pools and block trades:** private trading systems cross large orders without displaying them until after execution, but regulation requires the transaction to be reported to the consolidated tape (the Form T print) within seconds—and when a large dark-pool block prints at or above the Ask, it signals an institution paying up for size, an accumulation sweep. **Algorithmic accumulation and the floor:** when an institution is accumulation-bound, its algorithms absorb every available share down to a defined technical level—a stock touching a precise moving average and instantly sparking an aggressive, high-volume bounce with no downside follow-through marks the institutional floor. **Iceberg orders:** a large block split into small visible slices—the Level 2 book may show only 500 shares bid, but each time a retail seller dumps 500, another 500 reappear; when price refuses to drop despite obvious selling, an institution has anchored an iceberg, and the Blueprint response is to enter alongside the hidden buyer with a tight stop just beneath the floor.

## Accumulation vs. Distribution

Reading institutional intent means reading both directions. **Accumulation days:** price closes higher, volume exceeds the prior session, and the stock outperforms the broad market—several over a few weeks, amid orderly advances and strong closes, point to demand building underneath. **Distribution days:** the opposite—price declines on unusually high volume, closes are weak, and the stock repeatedly fails at resistance; watch too for failure to recover after strong earnings, a pattern of lower highs, and capital rotating out of the sector. Institutions leave just as visible a trail on the way out as on the way in, and they deploy serious capital into themes rather than isolated names—a leader inside a sector institutions are accumulating carries far more force than the same company in a neglected group.

## The Five Stages of Institutional Price Action

Stocks under accumulation move through a recognizable progression—**quiet outperformance** (the stock beats the market as volume quietly increases), **recognition** (analysts upgrade and media notices), **breakout** (price clears major resistance, RVOL expands, momentum traders enter), **reinforcement** (additional institutions initiate positions), and **public participation** (retail piles in, often where risk-adjusted reward is weakest). The best opportunities cluster in the first three stages, before widespread public enthusiasm.

## The Institutional Footprint Screen

Readers run an automated intraday screen to capture the precise moment an institutional algorithm scales up its presence:

> THE INSTITUTIONAL FOOTPRINT SCREEN THE INSTITUTIONAL SWEEP → Block trade prints ≥ 20% of 20-day ADV ↓ VERIFY ORDER ARCHITECTURE • Price action — the block prints at or above the Ask • Microstructure — persistent iceberg orders absorb retail selling ↓ THE RIDE PROTOCOL Enter alongside the algo → hard stop beneath the block-print floor

**The block-trade volume shock filter:** a single print—or a clustered series within a 5-minute window—representing at least 20% of the asset's average daily volume, with the block printing at the Ask or sweeping multiple exchanges (paying up for immediacy signals an urgent need to build a position). **The iceberg detection protocol:** watch key breakout levels for a bid that refuses to break no matter how much stock is sold into it, then enter alongside the hidden buyer with a tight stop just a few cents below the floor. Quarterly **13F filings** (via WhaleWisdom, Fintel, or SEC EDGAR) reveal ownership changes but arrive on a 45-day delay—use them only for a longer-term swing bias, and rely on real-time proxies for timing: unusual options flow (large aggressive call sweeps with real premium and bullish delta), dark-pool and block trades (off-exchange prints of 10,000-plus shares or $1M-plus notional), order flow and tape (icebergs, volume-by-price clusters, absorption on dips), and accumulation indicators. Useful platforms include Unusual Whales, FlowAlgo, Bookmap, and thinkorswim—none a crystal ball, all confirmation rather than standalone signals.

## Recognizing Healthy Pullbacks

Institutions do not buy in straight lines, and even the strongest stocks consolidate. A healthy pullback features declining volume, an orderly retracement, support at a key moving average, and a quick recovery—these pauses are not threats but frequently the lowest-risk entries the trend will offer, letting you position near the institutional floor rather than chasing extension.

## The Institutional Buying Checklist and Watchlist

Confirm relative volume is consistently above average, the stock has logged multiple accumulation days, earnings are accelerating with raised guidance, the stock is outperforming its sector, the industry is attracting institutional capital, price closes consistently near the daily highs, and pullbacks occur on lighter volume than advances. The more affirmative answers, the greater the likelihood that genuine accumulation is underway. Your highest-priority watchlist should hold names satisfying most of the following—where institutional conviction, fundamental improvement, and technical strength reinforce one another:

| Criterion | Target |
|---|---|
| Relative volume | Consistently above 3× |
| Quarterly revenue growth | Above 20% |
| Quarterly EPS growth | Above 30% |
| Accumulation days | Multiple over recent weeks |
| Technical pattern | Breakout or constructive consolidation |
| Sector leadership | Top-performing industry |
| Catalyst | Material and measurable |
| Liquidity | High enough for efficient execution |
| Pullback behavior | Light-volume consolidations |

Operationally, run this as a tiered, real-time process: pre-market, scan options flow and dark-pool prints for gappers; intraday, set alerts on large prints and promote a name to Tier 1 only on multi-layer confluence—strong institutional flow plus RVOL and a catalyst—which is where you size most aggressively. The prime setup stacks the layers: a sector leader, an earnings beat, social attention, confirming institutional options flow, and RVOL of 8×—large dark-pool buys plus unusual call sweeps in a biotech after an FDA catalyst point toward a long in the stock or calls, or a sector 3x ETF, on the breakout.

## The Institutional Rotation Model

Institutional capital tends to follow a consistent sequence—a powerful catalyst emerges and earnings expectations improve, early institutional buying begins and RVOL increases, the stock breaks out technically and additional funds establish positions, analysts raise estimates and media expands coverage, and retail participation accelerates as institutions eventually begin taking profits.

## The Institutional Accumulation Governance Matrix

| Monitoring Parameter | The Retail Spectator | The Blueprint Capital Allocator |
|---|---|---|
| Volume Analysis | Watches retail chatrooms and social hype, blind to the consolidated tape. | Monitors the consolidated tape and dark-pool prints for large block anomalies. |
| Price-Action IQ | Assumes three sideways days mean weakness and sells out of boredom. | Reads quiet consolidation on block prints as deliberate accumulation. |
| Execution Mechanics | Fights the tape, shorting stocks as they hit new | Trails the algorithmic footprint, buying where the |

| Monitoring Parameter | The Retail Spectator | The Blueprint Capital Allocator |
|---|---|---|
| | multi-month highs. | institutional floor is anchored. |
| Risk Insulation | Places wide, arbitrary stops on gut feel and gets routinely shaken out. | Sets structural stops just below the verified block print or iceberg level. |

## Risk, Discipline, and Common Mistakes

Following smart money is an edge, not a guarantee—institutions can be wrong, can be front-run, and can dump after retail piles in. **Lag and noise:** 13Fs are backward-looking, and options flow can be hedging rather than a directional bet. **Front-running risk:** institutions can distribute into retail strength—cap risk at 5–8% per trade. **Leverage pitfalls:** 3x ETFs and options amplify both directions—size them tiny, on the order of 1% of capital at risk. **Avoid the classic errors:** don't treat every high-volume day as institutional buying, don't ignore whether the stock closes strong or weak, don't chase names institutions have already accumulated, and don't confuse a short squeeze with genuine accumulation. The survivors preserve capital through drawdowns with strict sizing, diversification across three to five setups, journaling, and a standing rule to require price-action confirmation before committing.

**Blueprint Principle:** Institutions create trends. Volume reveals their footprints. Price confirms their conviction. Your objective is not to predict institutional buying—it is to recognize it early and participate while the accumulation cycle is still underway.

# Chapter 15
# The Catalyst Framework

## A. Earnings

### Why Earnings Are the Most Powerful Catalyst

If momentum is the engine that drives exceptional stock performance, earnings are the fuel—every sustained bull market produces companies whose share prices multiplied because their earnings multiplied first. No catalyst generates institutional demand as consistently as an exceptional report—and for a campaign to turn $100,000 into $1,000,000, earnings season is the richest hunting ground for tomorrow's market leaders. These are scheduled, explosive, binary events capable of 10–100% moves in hours or days, amplified through low-float stocks, sector ETFs, options, and warrants. That power cuts both ways, which is why one rule governs the chapter: **do not gamble through the report.** Holding a position into a release exposes the ledger to an unhedged binary outcome and the brutal implied-volatility crush that follows. The Blueprint treats earnings as a predictable structural disruption—you do not guess the numbers, you systematically exploit the institutional re-pricing engine after they are public, with only selective, defined-risk positioning beforehand. (The watchlist chapter taught you to find companies whose earnings are accelerating; this chapter is about trading the event itself—capturing the multi-day drift once a report fires.)

### Why Markets React Violently: Expectations, Not History

Stock prices reflect expectations, not history. Two companies can each earn $2.00 per share, yet one stock falls while the other jumps 25%—the difference is the bar each had to clear. If Wall Street expected $2.30 and the company delivered $2.00, the market is disappointed; if the expectation was $1.60 and the company earned $2.00 while raising guidance, investors reassess the entire future and reprice sharply higher. Markets reward surprises, not merely good results, and that gap between expectation and reality is the raw material of every earnings trade.

### The Four Components and the Triple-Beat

A great report rarely rests on a single number. Four elements combine: **earnings per share** (substantial year-over-year growth, a positive surprise versus consensus, ideally multiple consecutive beats), **revenue growth** (confirmation that demand is genuinely expanding—harder to manipulate than EPS), **forward guidance** (a raise signals confidence and pulls in capital), and **management commentary** (the narrative—accelerating demand, record backlogs, margin gains, new-product adoption). The Blueprint compresses this into the **Triple-Beat**: revenue beats consensus by a meaningful margin (roughly 5% or more), EPS beats decisively while showing margin expansion, and management explicitly raises forward guidance. A plain beat is noise; the Triple-Beat forces institutions to recalculate fair value.

## Acceleration, Revenue Quality, and Margins

Markets reward improving growth more than high growth. Watch the slope of EPS across recent quarters:

| Quarter | Year-over-Year EPS Growth |
|---|---|
| Q1 | 22% |
| Q2 | 39% |
| Q3 | 68% |
| Q4 | 112% |

The business here is not merely growing—its rate of growth is increasing, and acceleration commands richer multiples because investors extrapolate stronger future performance. Two quality checks refine the signal: revenue quality (the best growth comes from rising demand, higher unit sales, new-product adoption, and recurring subscriptions—not one-time transactions or unsustainable pricing) and margin expansion (improving gross, operating, net, EBITDA, and free-cash-flow margins demonstrate operational efficiency and pricing power).

## Post-Earnings Drift: The Mechanics of the Rift

When an institution encounters a Triple-Beat, its valuation models recalculate fair value at once—but a fund managing billions cannot buy millions of shares in a single session without spiking the price, so its algorithms sweep over days or weeks. That structural lag is the Post-Earnings Announcement Drift, which provides an institutional floor beneath the stock and is precisely what the Blueprint rents. The drift usually announces itself with an earnings gap—and high-quality gaps share a signature: large relative volume, a strong open, continued buying through the session, a close near the highs, and follow-through over subsequent days.

## The Pre / Through / Post Playbook

Readers run a cold, mechanical process across three phases, never holding a full position into the print:

> **THE POST-EARNINGS EXECUTION PROTOCOL TRIPLE-BEAT REPORTED** → Post- or pre-market numbers shatter estimates ↓ **THE MORNING FILTRATION** • Step 1 — Pre-market gap ≥ 4% but < 15% (avoid over-extension) • Step 2 — Opening 15-minute RVOL ≥ 3.0 ↓ **THE EXECUTION ENGAGEMENT** 15-minute Opening Range Breakout → stop-loss at the low of the day

**Phase 1 — pre-earnings preparation:** scan calendars for high-potential names—a strong historical surprise rate (beating roughly 70% of the time), upward estimate revisions, sector leadership, and "rally into earnings" relative strength. Any pre-report exposure stays light and defined-risk (a debit spread or small starter); naked longs through the event are avoided. **Phase 2 — through the release:** the morning filter is strict—the stock should gap up at least 4% but less than 15% (a larger gap invites retail exhaustion), clearing the 50- and 200-day moving averages or breaking a multi-week base. Wait the first fifteen minutes (9:30–9:45 AM EST); if RVOL is printing 3.0 or more, the algorithms are active. Place a buy-stop a penny above the high of that opening 15-minute candle, with a hard stop at the low of the day printed in those first fifteen minutes—if price breaks that low, the catalyst has failed and the position is liquidated. **Phase 3 — post-earnings momentum (the real-money layer):** trade the drift and continuation—a gap-and-go or flag breakout on high volume, confirmed by institutional options flow and social buzz—scaling and pyramiding on strength as long as the fundamentals and volume hold.

## The High-Velocity Earnings Screen and Tools

Reduce the playbook to a concrete filter: an upcoming or just-reported name with an EPS beat above roughly 8% and a guidance raise; post-reaction, a gap of +10% or more with RVOL above 4x and price holding above VWAP; a float under 50M, or a sector 3x ETF in leadership; and integration with every prior watchlist layer—RVOL, sector, institutional flow, and sentiment. Layer the tools across calendars and surprise history (Yahoo Finance, Investing.com, Zacks with its ESP predictor, Benzinga Pro, MarketChameleon, Wall Street Horizon), scanners (Trade Ideas, thinkorswim, Scanz), flow and sentiment (Unusual Whales, StockTwits, X), and charting (TradingView with earnings overlays and VWAP).

## Position Structure and Instruments

Express the trade with the leverage chosen deliberately: **stocks** as the core vehicle for a low-float runner (scale in on dips, pyramid on strength—50–200% days are possible); **2x/3x ETFs** for sector earnings waves (TQQQ on broad tech beats, SOXL on semis, held short-term to limit decay); **options** as post-print directional calls or spreads on momentum (avoid pre-earnings straddles, which the IV crush punishes); **warrants** for multi-month leverage on a sustained winner; and **blended** structures (a stock core plus long calls, or a 3x ETF plus protective puts). Example: a low-float biotech beats earnings and raises guidance, gapping 40% on 15x volume with institutional call sweeps—enter long stock or calls, or a sector 3x ETF, on the breakout, targeting a 50–100% move with trailing stops.

## The Earnings Watchlist: Three Tiers

During earnings season, sort reporters into three tiers: **Tier One — exceptional reports** (a significant EPS and revenue beat, raised guidance, expanding margins, high relative volume—immediate attention); **Tier Two — good reports** (a modest beat, stable guidance, a constructive pattern—candidates if momentum improves); and **Tier Three — disappointments** (a miss, lowered guidance, or deteriorating margins—off the momentum watchlist unless a separate catalyst emerges).

## The Earnings Catalyst Checklist

Before entering, confirm the company beat EPS expectations, revenue exceeded estimates, guidance was raised, margins are expanding and free cash flow is improving, management commentary is optimistic, relative volume is above 3, institutional buying is evident, the stock is breaking into new highs, and the sector is also leading. The more independent confirmations align, the likelier the report marks the start of a trend rather than a one-day spike.

### From Catalyst to Compounding

An exceptional report tends to set off a chain reaction, and the edge is recognizing it early—the company exceeds expectations and raises guidance, analysts increase estimates and institutions begin accumulating, relative volume expands as the stock breaks above resistance, financial media highlights the story and retail joins, and additional institutional capital reinforces the advance into a sustained market leader.

### Risk, Discipline, and Common Mistakes

Earnings create some of the market's largest one-day gains and its largest one-day declines—the discipline separates the two. **IV crush:** premiums collapse after the report, so favor post-print momentum over pre-event option longs. **Gaps and slippage:** use limit orders and size tiny on binary events; cap risk at 1–2% of capital per earnings play. **Drawdown survival:** hold no more than two or three concurrent earnings exposures, and require multi-layer confluence (RVOL, flow, price action) before committing. Avoid the classic errors—don't buy before earnings without sizing for the event risk, don't fixate on EPS while ignoring revenue or guidance, don't chase extended gaps, and don't assume every beat guarantees more upside. Most aggressive earnings traders experience 30–50%+ drawdowns; journal every play and let survival rules govern your size.

**Blueprint Principle:** Exceptional earnings create exceptional expectations. Exceptional expectations attract institutional capital. Institutional capital creates sustained momentum. Sustained momentum creates extraordinary compounding.

## B. FDA Approvals

### Why FDA Approvals Are the Ultimate Asymmetric Catalyst

Among all market catalysts, few generate larger one-day moves than a favorable FDA decision. A single approval can transform a biotech or medical-device company from a speculative research enterprise into a commercial business with measurable revenue—while a rejection, a request for more studies, or disappointing data can erase years of gains in one session. These binary events routinely produce gaps of 50–300% in small-cap, low-float biotechs, with sympathy moves in related names. Most arrive on a **PDUFA date**—the FDA's target deadline, under the Prescription Drug User Fee Act, for ruling on a New Drug Application or Biologics License Application—and because dozens land each quarter, the opportunity is repeatable across stocks, options, warrants, and biotech ETFs such as XBI or its leveraged LABU equivalent. One discipline is non-negotiable: **do not gamble on the binary outcome.** A rejection can gap a clinical-stage micro-cap down 80%

overnight—the Blueprint instead lets the binary risk clear, then trades the confirmed post-decision reaction and the multi-day institutional re-pricing. You are not predicting clinical science; you are exploiting the structural vacuum that opens after verified regulatory success.

### Why FDA Decisions Move Stocks

Biotech and medtech companies often spend years developing a single product while generating little or no revenue, so valuation hinges almost entirely on one question: will regulators approve it? Approval opens the door to commercial sales, insurance reimbursement, physician adoption, licensing, partnerships, and acquisition interest at once, and the market reprices future cash flows almost instantly. As uncertainty falls, large funds become willing to commit capital they were previously barred from deploying.

### The Anatomy of a Biotech Pricing Vacuum

The violence of the move is a function of microstructure. Small- and mid-cap biotechs typically carry a tight free float paired with high short interest, as bears wager on the high historical failure rate of trials. When an approval crosses the wire, those dynamics invert at once: trapped short sellers are forced to buy back shares at the ask (the short squeeze); healthcare funds whose mandates restrict speculative, unapproved holdings are abruptly cleared to accumulate (the institutional influx); and that wall of buying collides with a tiny, restricted supply (the float constraint), triggering a vertical, non-linear expansion. A pre-revenue science project becomes a commercial-stage enterprise overnight, and because analysts must rebuild revenue models from scratch, the asset enters a multi-day or multi-week re-pricing phase—that drift, not the binary itself, is what the Blueprint trades.

### The FDA Approval Timeline and the Catalysts That Matter Most

Understanding the regulatory path lets you anticipate where volatility concentrates: **discovery** (little attention), **early clinical trials** (modest movement), **mid-stage success** (positive efficacy data draws specialist funds and momentum begins), **late-stage Phase III trials** (often the first major catalyst, sharply raising commercialization odds), **FDA review** (anticipation and volatility build), **FDA decision** (the major re-pricing event), and **commercial launch** (attention shifts to execution and revenue becomes the next catalyst). The strongest signatures are positive Phase III results, a new drug approval, an expanded label approval (enlarging the addressable market), and the Breakthrough Therapy, Fast Track, and Priority Review designations that accelerate development and signal regulatory confidence.

### Approval Is Not Enough: Commercial Opportunity and Revenue

An approval by itself does not guarantee a successful trade—professionals weigh the commercial reality: how large the target market is, how many patients could benefit, what competing therapies exist, whether insurers will reimburse, whether the company can manufacture at scale, and whether there is a real commercialization strategy. Approval without commercial viability often produces only a temporary rally, which is why institutions ask how fast prescriptions will grow rather than selling the moment a drug clears—the most durable advances tend to come after successful commercialization, not merely after the headline.

## The Three Ways to Trade an FDA Event

There are three disciplined ways to engage a regulatory decision, and the Blueprint strongly favors the latter two. **Strategy One — trade the run-up:** buy as optimism builds, then reduce or exit before the binary event (requires the discipline to actually be out before the print). **Strategy Two — trade the confirmation:** wait for the decision and enter only if an approval is accompanied by strong relative volume, institutional buying, a technical breakout, and sustained momentum—forgoing some initial upside to remove the binary risk entirely. This is the core Blueprint method. **Strategy Three — trade commercial execution:** ignore the announcement and focus on companies already showing accelerating prescriptions, rising revenue, and strong earnings—the lowest-variance path.

## The Post-Approval Playbook

Readers never hold the stock into the announcement. They wait for the official press release or FDA database update, let the gap occur, and run a three-phase protocol:

> **THE POST-APPROVAL MOMENTUM PROTOCOL FDA APPROVAL RELEASED** → Official announcement hits post- or pre-market ↓ **THE STRUCTURAL SUPPLY SCREEN** • Step 1 — Free float < 40 million shares • Step 2 — Pre-market gap ≥ 10%, with an orderly entry corridor ↓ **DAY-1 INTRADAY ENGAGEMENT** Wait for the 10-min high breakout on RVOL ≥ 4.0 → stop at the VWAP floor

**Phase 1 — pre-FDA preparation:** scan calendars one to three months out for high-conviction setups—strong Phase III data, a Breakthrough or Fast Track designation, a positive advisory-committee vote, insider buying—favoring low-float names (under 20–50 million shares) with sector leadership. Two structural gates apply: the float should sit under 40 million shares (a bloated structure absorbs the buying and deadens velocity), and the company should hold enough cash to fund at least twelve months of commercial launch, removing the immediate threat of a dilutive secondary. Any pre-decision exposure stays small and defined-risk. **Phase 2 — around the decision:** on an approval with a strong label, let the open run for ten minutes while retail whipsaws the price, then mark the high of that opening 10-minute candle. If the stock clears it on accelerating RVOL of 4.0 or more, enter on a buy-stop or the first pullback to VWAP, with a hard stop at VWAP or the 10-minute low. A Complete Response Letter or delay means stand aside. **Phase 3 — post-approval momentum:** trade the drift—commercial-launch hype, partnerships, follow-on data—scaling and pyramiding only with continued RVOL and institutional confirmation.

## The High-Velocity FDA Screen and Tools

Reduce the playbook to a concrete filter: an upcoming or recent PDUFA with strong prior data or high historical approval odds (roughly 70%+); post-decision, a gap of +20–50% or more with RVOL of 5–10x and a float under 50M; confirmation overlays of sector leadership, institutional flow, and supportive sentiment; and price roughly $2–$100 for a workable balance of liquidity and velocity. Run a weekly routine off the PDUFA calendar (BioPharmCatalyst, FDA Tracker, Benzinga Pro, MarketBeat, RTTNews), with scanners (Benzinga Pro, Scanz, Trade Ideas), flow and sentiment (Unusual Whales, StockTwits, X, dark-pool scanners), and research (ClinicalTrials.gov, company pipelines, probability-of-approval models).

## Position Structure, Instruments, and Confirmation

Express the trade with leverage chosen deliberately: **stocks** as the primary vehicle for a low-float runner; **2x/3x ETFs** for sector amplification on a broad approval wave (XBI, LABU, held short-term); **options** as directional calls or spreads after the approval (never naked long premium into the decision); **warrants** for extended leverage on names with a real commercial runway; and **blended** structures (a core stock plus OTM calls plus a small 3x ETF). Example: a low-float biotech with strong Phase III data reaches its PDUFA and the approval gaps the stock 80% on 15x volume with call sweeps—enter long stock or calls, or a biotech 3x ETF, on the breakout, target a 100–200% move, and trail tight stops below the key intraday lows. A high-quality catalyst confirms itself through participation—relative volume above 5, strong gaps, sustained buying, closes near the highs, and follow-through—and the highest-quality opportunities align regulatory success with a large addressable market, strong IP, accelerating institutional ownership, and sufficient cash to commercialize. An approval is usually the beginning of the investment story, not the end.

## The FDA Catalyst Checklist

Before adding an FDA opportunity, confirm positive clinical data, a clearly defined regulatory milestone, a large commercial opportunity, limited direct competition, a strong balance sheet and sufficient liquidity, relative volume above 3, institutional accumulation, a constructive technical pattern, and favorable sector conditions. The more confirmations present, the stronger the catalyst—and the less you are relying on the decision alone.

## From Approval to Compounding

The strongest FDA winners follow a recognizable progression—positive clinical data with early institutional buying, the approval landing followed by analyst upgrades, new institutional ownership building as the commercial launch begins, revenue accelerating and earnings beginning to surprise, and broader investor recognition arriving as sustained appreciation develops.

## The FDA Catalyst Governance Matrix

| Operational Parameter | The Retail Spectator | The Blueprint Capital Allocator |
|---|---|---|
| Chronological Entry | Buys days before the decision on hope, exposing the ledger to an 80% overnight wipeout. | Enters only after the approval is verified, trading the multi-day re-pricing drift. |
| Supply Vetting | Chases bloated biotechs with massive floats and ongoing dilution. | Prioritizes low-float structures (< 40M shares) to maximize upward velocity. |
| Intraday Discipline | Buys the opening tick on FOMO and gets stopped out in the morning volatility. | Uses a 10-minute opening-range filter to validate true algorithmic direction. |
| Risk Management | Cancels the stop when the trade goes against them, marrying a failing asset. | Anchors risk to VWAP or the 10-minute low, protecting the core capital. |

## Risk, Discipline, and Common Traps

FDA catalysts are categorically different from earnings: many decisions are genuinely binary. A Complete Response Letter, a review delay, a safety concern, a manufacturing deficiency, an adverse advisory-committee vote, or a trial failure can wipe 50–90% in minutes. **Cap the binary risk:** risk no more than 1% of capital per trade, and never hold an oversized position through a decision. **Volatility and IV:** pre-event implied volatility is enormous and the post-approval crush punishes long premium—favor momentum continuation. **Leverage dangers:** 3x ETFs and options amplify losses—size tiny and exit quickly. **Limit overtrading:** hold no more than two or three concurrent FDA exposures, requiring full-layer confluence. Avoid the classic traps—don't buy merely because a decision is approaching, don't assume approval guarantees success, don't ignore valuation after a large gap, don't overlook dilution risk in cash-poor names, and don't confuse early-stage clinical excitement with commercial viability. Most aggressive biotech traders face severe drawdowns, and reaching 1,000% in six months depends on asymmetric winners large enough to offset the blowups; let survival rules govern your size.

**Blueprint Principle:** FDA approvals reduce uncertainty. Institutions provide the liquidity. Commercialization creates earnings. Earnings sustain momentum. The greatest opportunities arise when regulatory success evolves into long-term business success.

## C. AI Announcements

### Why AI Announcements Are a Dominant High-Velocity Catalyst

Every major bull market is defined by one or two transformative themes—railroads, the web, mobile computing—and today it is artificial intelligence. AI announcements have become some of the market's most influential catalysts, signaling new revenue, expanding margins, surging capital spending, and durable competitive advantage. In 2026, new model releases, major partnerships, chip breakthroughs, hyperscaler capex updates, agentic-AI advances, and infrastructure deals routinely spark 10–100% surges within days. But experienced traders hold one distinction above all: **not every company that mentions AI is creating shareholder value.** The retail herd chases firms that merely bolt ".ai" onto a landing page and buys the top of short-lived hype cycles; the objective is the opposite—identify announcements that materially improve future earnings. One rule governs the chapter: trade the reaction and continuation, not pre-announcement speculation, confirming with volume and price action to avoid buying the rumor and selling the news. Institutions do not buy fashionable terminology—they buy the ability to monetize technology, asking whether AI will increase revenue, reduce costs, and improve margins sustainably.

### AI Is an Ecosystem, Not a Single Industry

Many investors assume only software companies benefit; in reality the opportunity runs through an entire value chain, and the secondary beneficiaries are often where the cleanest low-float setups live: **compute and semiconductors** (AI-processor and accelerator designers, advanced-chip equipment makers, high-performance memory), **connectivity and data centers** (optical-networking suppliers, cloud and colocation operators), **power and cooling** (transformers, switchgear, electrical distribution, cooling systems, backup power—AI data centers consume enormous electricity), and **software and automation** (enterprise AI software, robotics, automation firms). This is why one of the most important secondary catalysts is rising capital expenditure by the major cloud providers—when hyperscalers lift spending on AI servers, GPUs, networking, power, and cooling, entire supply chains benefit.

### The Two High-Conviction Catalysts

Above the noise sit two structurally transformative announcement types. **The hard infrastructure win (the compute anchor)—the highest-conviction catalyst:** a small- or mid-cap data-center operator, liquid-cooling provider, or semiconductor-component manufacturer secures a certified allocation of next-generation compute (Blackwell- or Vera Rubin-class GPUs, advanced custom ASICs) or a direct sovereign cloud-infrastructure contract—near-term, guaranteed capacity expansion Wall Street must immediately model into forward capex and revenue. **The enterprise**

**implementation shock:** a legacy software or industrial company announces a proprietary, fully scaled AI integration that cuts internal operating costs by a large, quantifiable margin (on the order of 30% or more), or launches a major new subscription stream that instantly expands its total addressable market.

## High-Quality vs. Low-Quality: Hype vs. Execution

The single most useful skill is separating AI execution from AI hype. High-quality catalysts carry measurable business impact—major product launches, significant contracts, enterprise adoption, cloud-capacity expansion, partnerships with real revenue commitments, increased capex, new AI subscriptions, and revenue guidance explicitly tied to AI products. Low-quality announcements lean on marketing language—vague "AI strategy" references, speculative possibilities, undefined partnerships, pilot programs without commercial commitments. The test is simple: **how will this announcement generate revenue?** AI hype produces sharp but short-lived rallies; AI execution—accelerating revenue, expanding margins, recurring revenue, institutional accumulation—produces the durable multi-month trends. The greatest winners are not the companies that talk most about AI; they are the ones that profit most from it. So the Blueprint runs a three-tier check, demanding concrete, ideally legally binding numbers—the dollar value of a contract, the exact unit count of compute secured, or a specific margin-expansion percentage:

> THE ALGORITHMIC HYPE FILTER AI ANNOUNCEMENT HITS THE TAPE → Press release or SEC filing drops pre-market ↓ THE STRUCTURAL TRUTH FILTER • Tier 1 — Quantifiable metrics ("$50M contract," "10,000 H200 chips") • Tier 2 — Free float < 30 million shares • Tier 3 — Pre-market gap ≥ 5% on accelerating volume ↓ KINETIC EXECUTION 5-minute Opening Range Breakout → trail along the 9-period EMA

## The Pre / During / Post Playbook

AI catalysts move with unusual speed—natural-language algorithms scrape headlines within milliseconds—so the protocol is fast and mechanical. **Phase 1 — pre-announcement build-up:** monitor pipelines for earnings guidance, GTC-style conferences, expected partnerships, and model releases, watching for relative strength, insider activity, and rising buzz across the ecosystem (NVDA, AMD, suppliers, hyperscalers); any pre-event exposure stays small and defined-risk. **Phase 2 — announcement reaction:** read the details in real time and require the quantifiable metric—if the asset gaps up 5% or more on opening RVOL of 4.0+ (5x+ on the strongest setups) while holding key levels, the institutional sweep is live; mark the high of the first 5-minute candle, place a buy-stop a penny above it, and fence risk to the 5-minute opening-range low or VWAP. **Phase 3 — post-announcement momentum:** because narrative velocity decays quickly, treat these as high-speed sprints (intraday or a tight 24-to-48-hour window), trailing the stop ruthlessly along the rising 5-minute or hourly 9-period EMA—the moment a candle closes below it, the engine has stalled and the position is liquidated.

## The High-Velocity AI Screen and Tools

Reduce the playbook to a concrete filter: a major announcement (partnership, new model, capex raise) with a gap above 10% and RVOL of 5–10x; a float and liquidity filter, sector leadership, and visible institutional call buying; and full watchlist integration—social hype, an earnings tie-in, and confirming options flow. Layer the tools: news and alerts (Benzinga Pro, NowNews Pulse, Bloomberg, Yahoo Finance), event tracking (company IR calendars, NVIDIA GTC updates, AI-conference trackers), scanners (Trade Ideas, TrendSpider, Scanz), flow and sentiment (Unusual Whales across the NVDA ecosystem, StockTwits, X), and sector proxies (TQQQ for broad tech and AI, SOXL for semis).

## Position Structure and Instruments

Position structure: **stocks** as core plays in the leaders (NVDA) or ecosystem runners scaled in on dips to VWAP; **2x/3x ETFs** as the primary velocity vehicles (TQQQ for broad AI and tech, SOXL for semis and chips—higher beta, bigger swings on chip news—held short-term); **options** as post-announcement directional calls or spreads with gamma on retail flow; **warrants** for longer-dated leverage; and **blended** structures. Example: NVIDIA announces a major partnership alongside a new Vera Rubin deployment, and the ecosystem gaps on 8–15x volume with call sweeps—go long SOXL or TQQQ calls, or NVDA stock, on the breakout, targeting a 30–100%+ move with tight stops, scaling out into strength.

## The AI Adoption Cycle

AI is a structural transformation unfolding over years, and most winners climb the same ladder—**announcement** (curiosity builds), **early adoption** (first customers, modest revenue), **acceleration** (commercial adoption accelerates, analysts revise up, institutions add), **validation** (revenue and earnings exceed expectations as breakouts occur), and **leadership** (the company is recognized as an industry leader). The largest, most durable advances usually begin in the early-to-middle stages, before the broader market appreciates the long-term earnings power.

## The AI Catalyst Checklist

Before promoting an AI company, verify the announcement materially improves revenue potential, management quantifies the commercial opportunity, customer adoption is measurable, earnings estimates are likely to rise with analysts raising forecasts, relative volume exceeds normal levels, institutional buying is evident, the stock is technically breaking out, and the broader AI sector remains strong. Multiple confirmations sharply improve the odds the catalyst produces sustained momentum rather than a one-day pop.

## The AI Catalyst Governance Matrix

| Operational Axis | The Retail Spectator | The Blueprint Capital Allocator |
|---|---|---|

| Operational Axis | The Retail Spectator | The Blueprint Capital Allocator |
|---|---|---|
| Catalyst Vetting | Chases vague buzzwords and CEO hype clips on social media. | Demands quantifiable, contractually binding metrics in filings or official wires. |
| Supply Alignment | Buys heavily diluted, billion-share names that cannot sustain velocity. | Pairs verified catalysts only with low-float structures (< 30M shares). |
| Execution Horizon | Buys the top of a multi-day parabolic run and holds on blind faith. | Treats it as a 24-to-48-hour velocity rental, trailing tight along the 9-EMA. |
| Risk Architecture | Enters unhedged at the open with no structural stop and gets trapped. | Fences risk behind the 5-minute opening-range low or the VWAP floor. |

### Risk, Discipline, and Common Mistakes

AI catalysts have produced legendary runs and brutal corrections in equal measure—the speed that creates the upside is exactly what punishes the undisciplined. **Hype versus reality:** many announcements deliver a short pop followed by a "sell-the-news" fade—require multi-layer confirmation. **Leverage risks:** 3x ETFs like SOXL decay sharply in chop and reverse violently—size tiny, around 1% of capital at risk. **Rotation and fatigue:** AI leadership can fracture quickly—watch for broader shifts rather than assuming the theme leads forever. Avoid the classic errors—don't buy every company that mentions AI, don't assume a partnership automatically generates revenue, don't ignore valuation after a large run, and don't confuse speculative enthusiasm with institutional conviction. Use hard stops (5–10%), journal rigorously, and let survival rules govern your size.

**Blueprint Principle:** AI announcements attract attention. Commercial adoption creates revenue. Earnings validate the opportunity. Institutional buying sustains the trend. The greatest winners are not the companies that talk most about AI—they are the ones that profit most from it.

## D. Acquisitions

### Why Acquisitions Are a High-Conviction Catalyst

Few corporate events change a company's future as quickly as a well-executed acquisition—a deal can instantly expand revenue, increase market share, eliminate a competitor, accelerate technology, and create earnings synergies. A target frequently gaps 20–100% on the premium offer, with ripple effects across suppliers, competitors, and the sector, and unlike a one-day spike, a value-creating deal often initiates multi-month institutional accumulation. But the retail public treats acquisition rumors like a lottery ticket—rumors are frequently engineered by early insiders looking for exit liquidity, and when a rumored deal never materializes, the stock collapses. So one rule governs the chapter: **do not gamble on rumors.** Trade confirmed announcements—a definitive agreement filed on SEC Form 8-K—and the continuation that follows. The other discipline is qualitative: distinguish acquisitions that genuinely create shareholder value from those that merely make a company larger. Institutions weigh one question above all—will this acquisition generate more earnings than it costs?—buying earnings accretion, strategic advantage, and expanding cash flow, not headlines.

## The Types of Acquisitions and What Creates Value

Different deals create different opportunities: **strategic acquisitions** (a complementary business, building long-term advantage), **technology acquisitions** (capability rather than revenue—AI algorithms, cloud infrastructure, semiconductor IP), **market-expansion acquisitions** (new countries, industries, or segments), **vertical integration** (suppliers or distributors for lower costs and supply-chain reliability), and **horizontal integration** (competitors for market share and pricing power—but the most likely to draw regulatory scrutiny). The central concept is **earnings accretion**: a deal is accretive when it is expected to increase EPS after integration, and the best deals deliver both revenue synergies (cross-selling, expanded relationships, bundled services) and cost synergies (eliminating duplicate departments, consolidating manufacturing), lifting growth and margins together.

## The Two High-Velocity Trade Structures

Beyond the re-rating, two structures offer an edge. **The low-float bidding war (the multi-bid squeeze):** when a company in a hot sector—AI infrastructure, biotech, defense—is targeted, the initial bid sets a price floor, but if the target carries a micro-float (under roughly 15 million shares) and coveted IP, a competing suitor often steps in with a higher counter-offer, and the stock can trade well above the initial offer as market makers build hedges. This is the asymmetric upside of the chapter—though never guaranteed. **The arbitrage floor (and its real risk):** in a cash buyout at, say, $20.00 per share, the stock typically trades at a slight discount—perhaps $19.20—on the announcement morning, reflecting the time value of money and closing risk; that gap is the arbitrage spread, and the $20.00 offer functions as a floor. One honest caveat is essential, because the source material oversells it: the floor holds **only if the deal closes.** Merger arbitrage is a negatively skewed trade—the spread is narrow precisely because the market assigns a high completion probability, so you collect small, frequent gains against a rare but severe loss. If the deal breaks (a regulatory block, a financing failure, a material-adverse-change clause, a shareholder rejection), the stock does not fall by pennies—it typically gaps down hard, often well below the pre-announcement price. Treat the floor as conditional, size every position for a broken deal, and let the multi-bid squeeze, not the spread, be the reason you are there.

## The Acquisition Timeline

Acquisition momentum follows a recognizable sequence, and the cleanest entries come after confirmation—rumors circulate and volume rises (the highest-risk stage), the transaction is announced and analysts assess the strategic benefit, institutions analyze valuation and synergies and regulatory risk, analysts revise estimates and institutions accumulate if the deal enhances value, the transaction closes and integration begins, results start reflecting synergies, and institutions keep building as management demonstrates execution.

## The Pre / During / Post Playbook

Readers wait for the binding paperwork to cross the wire, then run a three-phase protocol against the confirmed deal:

> **THE DEFINITIVE-AGREEMENT EXTRACTION SEC FORM 8-K FILED** → Definitive acquisition agreement announced ↓ **THE STRUCTURAL RISK FILTER** • Step 1 — Verify a 100% cash offer (avoid volatile stock swaps) • Step 2 — Price trades within ~5% of the bid floor • Step 3 — Day-1 RVOL ≥ 5.0 (arbitrage desks are active) ↓ **POSITION ENGAGEMENT** Build against the floor — sized for deal-break risk → collect the multi-bid premium

**Phase 1 — pre-announcement:** scan for buildup (unusual volume, activist involvement, sector-consolidation signals) but treat this as reconnaissance, with any exposure small and defined-risk, because most rumors die. **Phase 2 — announcement reaction:** the moment the 8-K and press release hit, read the deal terms against three filters—the deal should be a 100% cash offer (a stock swap saddles the target with the acquirer's volatility), there should be no immediate antitrust or FTC flag on the wire, and Day-1 RVOL should print 5.0 or more, proving arbitrage desks are moving capital. Enter the target on strength—a gap toward the premium on RVOL of 5–10x while holding key levels. **Phase 3 — post-announcement momentum:** trade the drift—rising deal-closure probability, emerging synergies, follow-on bids—pyramiding winners while monitoring breakup fees and regulatory risk. A competing bid can gap the stock 20–40% higher; the regulatory block is the one that can gap it the other way.

## The High-Velocity M&A Screen and Tools

Reduce the playbook to a concrete filter: an announced deal with a premium of 20%+, a target gap above 15%, and RVOL above 5x; a low-float or high-beta target for extra velocity, ideally inside a leading sector with visible institutional buying; and liquidity floors of average volume above 500k and price roughly $5–$150. Layer the tools across filings and news (SEC EDGAR, Benzinga Pro, Reuters Deals, Bloomberg), deal trackers (PitchBook, Mergermarket, Wall Street Horizon, DealRoom), scanners (Trade Ideas, Scanz, thinkorswim), flow (Unusual Whales, StockTwits, X), and sector proxies (2x/3x ETFs in consolidating industries).

## Position Structure and Instruments

Express the trade with leverage chosen deliberately—and remember the acquirer is sometimes the better momentum vehicle when the market believes the deal creates lasting value, even though buyers often dip initially: **stocks** as the core vehicle for the target (scale in on pullbacks to the offer price or VWAP), with sympathy longs in ecosystem names; **2x/3x ETFs** for sector-wide consolidation plays held short-term; **options** as directional calls or spreads on the target after the announcement (on the acquirer only when strategic upside is clear); **warrants** for longer-dated leverage on extended timelines; and **blended** structures. Example: a mid-cap AI/tech company receives a $10B+ acquisition offer at a 40% premium and gaps 35% on 12x volume with call sweeps—go long the target stock or calls, or a related 3x ETF, on the breakout, target a realized 50–80% move while monitoring the regulatory path, and keep tight stops below gap support. Small-caps become targets because of unique technology, valuable patents, specialized talent, or niche leadership—but never buy one solely because it is rumored to be in play.

## The Acquisition Checklist

Before adding a candidate, confirm the acquisition strengthens the business, is expected to increase earnings (accretive), offers realistic cost or revenue synergies, can be integrated successfully, carries a reasonable purchase price and manageable financing, shows increasing institutional buying and elevated relative volume, is breaking out technically, and sits in a strong sector. Not every acquisition benefits shareholders—warning signs include excessive stock issuance, heavy debt, overpayment, weak strategic rationale, declining margins, and unrealistic synergy assumptions. After a strong, accretive deal, analysts frequently revise forecasts upward, pulling in additional institutional buying that extends momentum.

## From Catalyst to Compounding

A value-creating acquisition tends to set off a chain reaction—the deal is announced and analysts identify synergies, earnings estimates rise and institutions begin accumulating, relative volume expands as technical breakouts occur, integration succeeds as revenue accelerates and margins improve, and the company emerges as a stronger industry leader while institutional ownership keeps building.

## Risk, Discipline, and Common Mistakes

M&A produces some of the market's largest asymmetric winners and a steady supply of losers—the discipline keeps the losers small. **Deal-break risk:** regulatory blocks, financing failures, or a walk can gap the stock well below the pre-deal price—this is the defining risk of the trade; cap risk at 1–2% of capital and never treat the floor as guaranteed. **Acquirer drag:** buyers often underperform initially—avoid them, or fade short-term, unless the value creation is clear. **Leverage warnings:** 3x ETFs and options amplify both directions—size tiny and exit fast. **Rumors versus reality:** require official confirmation and volume, and never confuse a rumor with a signed agreement. Avoid the classic errors—don't assume every acquisition is beneficial, don't ignore integration or regulatory-approval risk, don't buy solely because a deal was announced, and don't overlook the impact of debt or share dilution.

**Blueprint Principle:** A great acquisition does not merely make a company larger—it makes it more valuable. Institutions buy earnings accretion, strategic advantage, and expanding cash flow, not corporate empire-building.

## E. Regulatory Approvals

### Why Regulatory Approvals Are a High-Velocity Catalyst

Markets reward certainty, and few events reduce uncertainty more sharply than a major regulatory decision. When a mining company wins an environmental permit, a bank secures a license, an energy firm clears a pipeline, or a drug maker gains marketing authorization, the company's future earnings potential can change overnight. This chapter covers the full regulatory spectrum alongside FDA and clinical decisions—FTC and DOJ antitrust clearances, EPA permits, FCC telecom approvals, FAA certifications, SEC and Defense actions, international regulators, and sector-specific rulings—often binary or near-binary, capable of sparking moves of 20–150% or more, and recurring constantly. Two disciplines define the approach: **not every approval creates shareholder value** (the best opportunities arise only when the decision materially improves future cash flows and is confirmed by institutional accumulation, elevated relative volume, and strong technical action), and you trade confirmed outcomes and continuation, not speculation. The edge lives in exploiting the re-pricing after legal certainty arrives.

### Why It Works: Certainty, Re-Pricing, and Forced Re-Allocation

Before a ruling, the market can only estimate probabilities—investors discount the valuation, analysts haircut their models, institutions cap exposure. The moment a definitive, un-appealable decision hits the public record, that uncertainty collapses, and reduced uncertainty alone often supports a higher multiple. Underneath that re-rating is a structural force: a formal ruling permanently redraws the competitive landscape, creating an immediate tracking problem for passive index funds and institutional mandates that must realign capital toward the newly advantaged sector. When a wave of effectively forced institutional buying meets a restricted share supply, the price expansion is violent and non-linear—you are not predicting the policy, you are exploiting the re-allocation it compels.

### The Spectrum of Regulatory Catalysts

The categories rank roughly from highest-conviction macro plays to the broad universe of approvals. **Antitrust clearances:** when a major merger held hostage for months by the FTC or DOJ wins a sudden, definitive clearance, the target snaps higher to close the arbitrage spread. **Appropriations and**

**subsidy mandates—the highest-conviction macro catalyst:** when a legislative body passes and funds a targeted spending bill (semiconductor fabricator subsidies, defense-production mandates, green-infrastructure grants), named recipients of non-dilutive federal cash see their growth models fundamentally altered overnight. **Compliance mandates:** updated standards manufacture a forced, inelastic demand curve that small pure-play operators with the required technology can capture. **Approvals, permits, and licenses:** product and marketing approvals, environmental permits, financial licenses, telecom approvals, and utility and infrastructure approvals, each removing a specific barrier to revenue. **Regulatory relief:** the removal of restrictions, settlement of disputes, favorable court decisions, and renewed licenses can lift profitability just as powerfully. Above all, the decisive question is whether the decision will actually generate revenue—a permit creates opportunity, it does not guarantee profitable delivery.

## The Regulatory Approval Timeline

Most regulatory winners move through a recognizable sequence, and the largest opportunities open in the middle—application (expectations and volatility build), review (uncertainty and option premium peak), approval (the decision lands, price gaps, RVOL expands), revision (analysts raise revenue, earnings, and price-target estimates), accumulation (institutions build on the reduced uncertainty), commercialization (operations expand and revenue accelerates), and compounding (earnings beat, additional funds enter, and the stock matures into a sector leader).

## The Pre / During / Post Playbook

Readers do not trade cable-news speculation or a politician's social posts. They wait for the official text to hit the public tape and run a three-phase protocol:

> **THE FEDERAL REGISTER PROTOCOL REGULATORY APPROVAL / MANDATE PASSED** → Official agency rule or bill signed ↓ **THE INSTITUTIONAL TRACKING FILTER** • Step 1 — Verify explicit, ring-fenced financial allocations • Step 2 — Confirm target free-float < 50 million shares ↓ **POSITION DEPLOYMENT** Day-1 RVOL ≥ 3.0 → enter → ride the multi-day institutional inflows

**Phase 1 — pre-approval build-up:** track agency pipelines for upcoming decisions (antitrust reviews, label expansions, device clearances, policy rulings), watching for relative strength, insider activity, and rising options flow, positioning only on strong momentum with small, defined-risk structures. **Phase 2 — decision reaction:** monitor real-time 8-Ks and agency announcements; before committing, enforce two structural gates—the action must contain explicit, ring-fenced dollar amounts or a binding legal mandate (vague "intentions to explore" are blacklisted), and the target should carry a free float under roughly 50 million shares. A positive outcome with a gap and RVOL above 5x is the trigger—enter on the first pullback to VWAP or support rather than chasing the print. **Phase 3 — post-approval momentum:** regulatory re-pricing is rarely a single day—it sets off multi-week accumulation as funds rebuild compliance baskets; trade the commercialization, synergies, and follow-on rulings, pyramiding winners with trailing stops and multi-layer confirmation.

### The High-Velocity Regulatory Screen and Calendar

Translate the playbook into a concrete filter: an upcoming or recent decision backed by strong prior data or clear strategic fit; post-outcome, a gap of roughly +15–50% with RVOL of 5–10x on a low float or inside a leading sector; confirmation overlays of an AI or earnings tie-in, institutional call sweeps, and supportive sentiment; and liquidity floors of average volume above 500k and price roughly $5–$150. Keep a dedicated regulatory calendar tracking pending decisions across industries—drug and device rulings, environmental and mining permits, energy-infrastructure approvals, banking licenses, telecom spectrum, defense authorizations, transportation certifications—and layer real-time coverage with FDA-centric tools (BioPharmCatalyst, Benzinga Pro, MarketBeat), broader regulatory sources (SEC EDGAR, FTC/DOJ trackers, EPA/FCC/FAA wires, Wall Street Horizon, PitchBook), scanners (Trade Ideas, Scanz, thinkorswim), and flow (Unusual Whales, X, StockTwits).

### Position Structure, Instruments, and Sympathy Plays

Because regulatory trends are structural and resilient to short-term noise, express them with leverage chosen deliberately: **stocks** as the core vehicle for the targeted name (a merger-clearance runner or approval winner, scaled in on dips); **2x/3x ETFs** for sector amplification held short-term; **options** as directional calls or spreads after a positive decision; **warrants** for longer-dated leverage on a multi-year commercial runway; a **synthetic long** (ATM call plus short ATM put) that replicates leveraged long exposure with minimal capital outlay but carries the full downside of the stock, demanding the same hard stop as the underlying; and **blended** structures. Example: a mid-cap biotech or medtech awaiting a label expansion or FTC clearance gets a positive ruling and gaps 40% on 10x-plus volume with call sweeps—enter long stock or calls, or a related 3x ETF, on the breakout, target a 50–120% move while monitoring implementation, and keep a tight stop below key support. A regulatory approval hits hardest when the whole sector is already drawing institutional capital, with analyst revisions and sympathy plays (competitors, suppliers, related leveraged ETFs) extending the move—trade the named winner first, but keep the ecosystem on the screen.

### The Regulatory Catalyst Checklist

Before promoting a stock, confirm the approval materially expands revenue opportunities, commercial execution can begin promptly, customer demand already exists, analysts are likely to revise estimates upward, relative volume exceeds normal levels, institutions are accumulating, the stock is breaking above resistance, and the broader sector remains strong. The more confirmations present, the lower the odds of buying a procedural headline mistaken for a transformational one.

### Risk, Discipline, and Common Mistakes

Regulatory catalysts produce genuine outlier winners and frequent, brutal losses. **Binary downside:** a denial, delay, or stricter-than-expected terms can erase 30–80% in a session—cap risk at roughly 1% of capital per trade and respect a hard stop. **Timing surprises:** agencies extend deadlines and surprise the consensus—use alerts and avoid overexposure into an unconfirmed event. **Leverage pitfalls:** 3x ETFs decay in choppy tape and options suffer IV crush—size small, and remember a synthetic long carries full stock downside. **Policy and political risk:** a change in administration or enforcement posture can re-open a question you thought was settled. Avoid the classic errors—don't buy every approval headline, don't confuse an administrative clearance with a transformational one, don't ignore valuation after a large gap, and never assume approval eliminates execution or business risk.

**Blueprint Principle:** Regulatory approvals remove uncertainty. Commercial execution creates revenue. Revenue produces earnings. Earnings attract institutions. Institutions sustain momentum. Approvals unlock value—they do not, by themselves, create it.

## F. Macroeconomic Catalysts

### Why Macroeconomic Catalysts Sit Above Everything

The greatest momentum traders share one understanding: individual stocks do not trade in isolation. They trade inside the broader context of the economy, monetary policy, capital flows, and sentiment—a company can post exceptional earnings and still fall if the macro tape is hostile, and an average company can appreciate sharply because its industry is riding a powerful tailwind. Treat macroeconomic catalysts as force multipliers: they rarely create a winning stock alone, but they decide which sectors become institutional favorites. When a major data point diverges from consensus, multi-trillion-dollar risk-parity funds, CTA algorithms, and global-macro desks are compelled to rebalance at once, forcing a violent, non-linear re-pricing across currencies, commodities, index ETFs, and high-beta equities—a single print can move an index 2–10% in a session, amplified dramatically in 2x and 3x leveraged ETFs. The goal is never to outsmart the Fed; it is to recognize when a macro change is creating opportunity and reposition before institutional capital fully responds. The governing discipline is the same: **do not gamble through the release.** Macroeconomic catalysts are broad economic events—interest-rate changes, inflation trends, employment reports, growth data, commodity moves, fiscal and monetary policy, currency shifts, and government-spending initiatives—that can influence hundreds of stocks simultaneously, and the trader's job is to follow the rotations, not resist them.

### The Holy Trinity: The Engines That Move Everything

Three recurring data engines drive the lion's share of macro-led re-pricing. **The monetary pivot — FOMC:** the Fed's rate decision and policy statement set the global price of leverage—a surprise cut or dovish dot-plot shift instantly lowers the discount rate applied to future cash flows, expanding the forward multiples of hyper-growth equities, 3x ETFs such as TQQQ, and long-dated derivatives, making rate changes the most reliable trigger of sector rotation. **The inflation regime — CPI and PCE:** a cool print (roughly 0.2% or more below consensus) signals the central bank can ease and acts as a green light for risk-on algorithms; a hot print does the reverse, and the reaction is mechanical and immediate. **The growth trajectory — payrolls and GDP:** the sweet spot is the Goldilocks signature—data strong enough to keep recession fears at bay yet cool enough to keep the Fed from tightening further—which tends to produce the cleanest risk-on trends.

## The Wider Macro Field and Sector Rotation

Beyond the trinity, several forces shape which sectors lead, and the most durable themes often come from here: **government spending** (infrastructure, defense budgets, semiconductor incentives, clean-energy and healthcare initiatives), **commodity prices** (rising oil lifts producers while pressuring transports; rising copper benefits miners and signals industrial expansion—commodity cycles often run for months), **currency moves** (a weaker domestic currency aids exporters and inflates translated foreign earnings), **geopolitical events** (conflicts, sanctions, export controls drive rapid rotation into defense, cybersecurity, domestic manufacturing, and critical minerals), and **demographic and structural trends** (aging populations, automation, electrification, and AI-infrastructure buildout support multi-year investment). Macro catalysts rarely affect every sector equally—knowing the typical map lets you anticipate where institutional capital flows:

| Macroeconomic Event | Potential Beneficiaries |
|---|---|
| Falling interest rates | Technology, small caps, consumer discretionary, homebuilders |
| Rising interest rates | Banks, insurers, selected value stocks |
| Infrastructure spending | Industrials, engineering, construction materials |
| Defense spending | Aerospace, defense, cybersecurity |
| AI investment | Semiconductors, networking, cloud infrastructure, power equipment |
| Rising commodity prices | Energy, mining, materials |
| Economic recovery | Industrials, transportation, financials |

## The Three Levels: Short-Term, Intermediate, Structural

Sort macro catalysts by how long their influence lasts. **Level One — short-term:** employment reports, inflation releases, central-bank meetings, and confidence data move markets for days or weeks. **Level Two —**

**intermediate:** rate cycles, fiscal stimulus, commodity supercycles, and manufacturing recoveries shape leadership for several months and often define a market cycle. **Level Three — structural:** artificial intelligence, electrification, automation, the energy transition, cybersecurity, and digital payments influence markets for years, and many of the greatest winners emerge here, because the trend supports sustained earnings growth over multiple years.

## From Macro Shift to Momentum

Macro-led moves tend to propagate in a recognizable sequence—a catalyst emerges and changes expectations, institutions identify the likely beneficiaries and rotate capital, sector ETFs strengthen and industry leaders break out, analysts raise industry forecasts as companies report improving earnings, and financial media amplifies the trend as retail joins and sustained momentum develops.

## The Pre / During / Post Playbook

Entering an unhedged position ahead of a major print is an account-killing mistake. The Blueprint trades the mechanical institutional re-pricing wave instead, in three phases:

> **THE FED-DAY VOLATILITY TRAP DOOR MACRO DATA RELEASE (e.g., FOMC)** → Statement drops at 2:00 PM EST ↓ **THE INSTITUTIONAL WHIPSAW ZONE** • Action — absolute execution freeze, 2:00–2:15 PM EST • Objective — let HFT market makers flush retail stops ↓ **DIRECTIONAL VELOCITY CLARITY** 2:15 PM — price clears the 15-min high/low → deploy 3x ETFs with the trend

**Phase 1 — pre-event preparation:** review consensus expectations, prior prints, and the Fed's dot plot, gauging positioning through futures, the VIX, and options skew; any bias stays light and defined-risk, and overall exposure is reduced ahead of the unknown. **Phase 2 — release reaction:** when the statement drops, high-frequency algorithms fire multi-directional sweeps to flush retail stops, so the Blueprint enforces a rigid blackout—no trading for the first fifteen minutes. You do not touch the keyboard until 2:15 PM, letting the emotional crowd get eliminated and the macro funds establish a real direction; then read the deviation and enter only once the index clears its 15-minute post-data high or low on a gap, an RVOL surge, and a hold above VWAP. **Phase 3 — post-event momentum:** trade the drift and rotation as sector leaders emerge—tech and AI on a dovish outcome, financials and energy on a hawkish one—pyramiding winners with trailing stops. Because a macro move is a systemic re-pricing, the cleanest expression is the most liquid built-in-leverage instrument available—a 3x leveraged index ETF (TQQQ for Nasdaq-100, UPRO or SPXL for the S&P 500, SOXL for semiconductors, SQQQ for inverse), held short-term, with the structural stop anchored precisely at the 15-minute post-data low. Index options on SPY or QQQ offer defined risk, warrants are usable on select macro plays, and a blended core 3x plus protective puts adds asymmetry. Example: position light in TQQQ into an FOMC meeting where dovish odds are rising—a dovish surprise produces a 4%

Nasdaq gap on 6x volume, so go long TQQQ or QQQ calls on the VWAP hold, pyramid into strength, and target a 15–40% move with trailing stops; the mirror image (a hot CPI) points to inverse exposure such as SQQQ.

## The High-Velocity Macro Screen, Tools, and Convergence

Reduce the playbook to a concrete filter: a major event (FOMC, NFP, CPI) with a surprise versus consensus of roughly 0.2–0.5 standard deviations or more; an index or ETF reaction of +2–5% or more with RVOL above 3–5x on TQQQ, SOXL, or SPY; confirmation overlays of sector leadership, institutional flow, and social buzz; and liquid instruments only. Keep a macro calendar covering central-bank meetings, inflation reports, employment data, GDP, retail sales, and manufacturing surveys, layered with calendars (TradingView, Investing.com, Forex Factory, TradingEconomics, Benzinga Pro), scanners and flow (Trade Ideas, thinkorswim, Scanz), analysis (Bookmap for futures order flow, the CME FedWatch tool), and sentiment (X, StockTwits). The strongest opportunities appear when a favorable macro backdrop aligns with a company-specific catalyst—several independent catalysts reinforcing one another is what produces the market's most durable trends.

## The Macroeconomic Catalyst Checklist

Before entering, confirm the broader economy is supporting this industry, monetary policy is favorable, institutions are rotating into the sector, commodity trends are supportive, government policy creates a tailwind, analysts are improving industry forecasts, relative volume is expanding, the stock is technically breaking out, and earnings are confirming the macro thesis. The more confirmations present, the lower the odds of fighting the tide.

## The Macro Catalyst Governance Matrix

| Operational Parameter | The Retail Spectator | The Blueprint Capital Allocator |
|---|---|---|
| Chronological Timing | Gambles before the release with short-dated options, exposing capital to binary destruction. | Holds an execution freeze until the data drops and the algorithmic whipsaws clear. |
| Instrument Selection | Trades illiquid penny stocks or warrants that decouple from macro flows. | Deploys into highly liquid 3x leveraged ETFs to capture systemic, index-wide velocity. |
| Risk Architecture | Gets shaken out by wide, arbitrary stops set inside the high-frequency churn zone. | Anchors stops outside the validated 15-minute post-release volatility boundary. |
| Market Orientation | Fights the Fed's stated path out of personal or political bias. | Stays agnostic, trailing the trend set by institutional capital displacement. |

## Risk, Discipline, and Common Mistakes

Macro-driven velocity creates the book's largest winners and its most brutal drawdowns. **Extreme volatility:** releases can swing 1–3% in minutes—use tight stops (3–8% risk) and limit size to 1–2% of capital at risk per trade. **Leverage decay and slippage:** 3x ETFs erode in choppy tape and options suffer IV crush right after the event—avoid holding leverage through uncertain event clusters. **False signals:** markets frequently fade the news—require multi-layer confirmation before trusting the first move. **Overexposure:** reduce portfolio beta before dense event weeks, and never trade against a major, established sector rotation. Don't assume every company benefits equally from a favorable trend, don't mistake a temporary headline for a lasting structural change, and respect valuation after a strong macro-driven rally. Most aggressive macro traders blow up without strict rules—backtest extensively and let survival govern your sizing.

**Blueprint Principle:** Macroeconomic catalysts create the tide. Sector leadership rides the tide. Company earnings determine which stocks become the fastest ships.

# Chapter 16
# Timing Entries

## Timing Entries — Breakouts

Finding the right stock is only half the battle—**buying it at the right time is what turns a good idea into an exceptional trade.** Plenty of traders correctly identify tomorrow's biggest winners and still lose money, because they enter too early, too late, or without confirmation. The breakout is your primary timing mechanism: it occurs when price decisively clears a well-defined resistance level—a prior high, a round number, a trendline, or the rim of a consolidation—on expanding volume, aligning your capital with the precise moment demand begins overwhelming supply. To move a $100,000 base toward a $1,000,000 target in roughly 180 days, a properly timed breakout can deliver a 20–100%+ move in days, multiplied further through 2x/3x ETFs, options, or warrants. The amateur sees a line break and buys on FOMO, then gets trapped by an engineered fakeout designed to sweep retail stops; you treat a breakout as a mechanical phase transition from low-volatility accumulation to high-velocity expansion, and trigger into it only on confirmation.

### The Economics of a Breakout

A breakout is the visible moment supply and demand flip. Before it, sellers dominate at resistance, buyers hesitate, and price drifts sideways; after it, available sellers diminish, new buyers enter, short sellers cover, institutions expand positions, and momentum traders pile in. Institutions generally prefer confirmation over prediction—they wait until earnings improve, relative strength develops, resistance breaks, and liquidity expands, then pay higher prices once conviction rises—so when you enter a confirmed breakout, you are arriving alongside size.

### It Starts With Consolidation: The Volatility Contraction Pattern

Strong breakouts rarely erupt out of chaos; they develop after consolidation, during which weak holders exit, institutions quietly accumulate, and volatility contracts. The most useful way to read that is Mark Minervini's **Volatility Contraction Pattern (VCP)**: each pullback grows shallower than the last (for example a 25% drop, then 12%, then 5%—the range tightening like a coiling spring), while volume dries up to near-zero, the tell that overhead supply has been absorbed. The tighter the contraction and the drier the volume, the more explosive the eventual expansion. Several structures express this same theme of supply tightening beneath resistance: the **flat base** (narrow range, declining volatility), the **ascending triangle** (rising lows under horizontal resistance), the **cup with handle** (O'Neil's continuation pattern, the handle shaking out weak holders), the **bull flag/pennant** (a strong impulse, an orderly low-volume pullback, a continuation break), the **high-tight flag** (a rapid advance of 80–100% or more, then tight consolidation—one of the rarest and most explosive), the **gap-and-go** (a catalyst gap that never fills), and the **volatility contraction break** (explosive expansion out of the VCP squeeze).

### Volume Is Non-Negotiable

The most common beginner mistake is buying a breakout without confirming volume—a breakout on average volume frequently fails; a breakout on heavy volume is the market voting with conviction. Layer these filters on top of the price break, because isolated technical breakouts fail often and confluence is what turns the odds: **relative volume above 3–5×** (ideally with more than 20–30% of the float traded), a strong candle closing above resistance (a holding retest is ideal), price above VWAP and the rising 9/20 EMA, a real catalyst tied to your framework, sector leadership, and an institutional/social footprint (call sweeps, rising buzz). **"Breakout + catalyst + RVOL" is your high-velocity entry signature**, and the more confirmations stack, the higher the probability of follow-through.

### The Breakout Checklist

Before entering any breakout trade, confirm a strong catalyst, relative volume above 3, sector leadership, institutional accumulation, a new 52-week high or major resistance break, strong earnings momentum, positive analyst revisions, a healthy broader market, and sufficient liquidity. The greater the alignment, the larger the size you can justify.

### The Mechanical Entry Playbook

Execute a strict, mechanical sequence so the market—not your emotions—decides whether you are filled. **1. The pivot trigger line:** define entry by the pivot high (the absolute highest point of the final, tightest contraction) and place an automated buy-stop one penny above it—if the market opens and fades, the order never fills and your cash stays pristine. **2. The 30-minute volume validation:** to eliminate morning bull traps, project the session—

**Projected daily volume = (volume by 10:00 a.m. ET) × 13**

If, by then, the asset has not traded at least 100% of its average daily volume, or its time-adjusted RVOL is under 3.0, classify the breakout as a retail illusion and cancel the buy-stop. **3. The structural stop-loss:** the moment the buy-stop is elected, anchor the stop to a technical floor—the low of the final tightest contraction (the "cheat" level), the most recent swing low, VWAP, or the rising 8-period hourly EMA—keeping risk in the 5–10% range per trade and downside boxed to one R unit (1–2% of account value). That tight box unlocks an asymmetric path to +5R, +10R, and beyond.

### Targets, Trade Management, and Scaling

**Targets and management:** take an initial 2–3R, then trail the rest with a 20-period moving average or the next resistance shelf, scaling out 30–50% into strength; the best breakouts fire in the first 30–90 minutes or immediately after a catalyst, while late-day breakouts that lack sustained volume tend to fade. **Scale in and pyramid:** take a partial entry (25–50% of intended size) on the confirmed breakout candle, add on a strong close or a successful retest, and pyramid again on a continuation breakout or new higher high (typically as price extends 10–20% with momentum intact), keeping your largest commitment behind the most confirmation. Prioritize daily and weekly breakouts for aggressive compounding—they reflect more meaningful institutional conviction than fleeting intraday moves, even when expressed through faster instruments.

## Instrument-Specific Tactics

The same breakout signal can be expressed through different vehicles. **Stocks (low-float, high-beta)** are the purest—enter on a flag or base breakout immediately after a catalyst (a low-float biotech clearing resistance on 10× RVOL the morning after an FDA approval). **2x/3x leveraged ETFs** (TQQQ, SOXL, TNA) suit sector and macro breakouts with enormous velocity, but respect daily decay and never hold a broken leveraged trade hoping for recovery. **Options:** buy calls or debit spreads on a confirmed breakout, favoring slightly OTM strikes for gamma, with post-breakout IV expansion working in your favor. **Warrants:** longer-dated leverage on sustained breakouts. **Blended:** pair a core stock or ETF with long calls, sizing the options leg so a failed breakout costs only a fraction of an R.

**Worked example.** *A sector-leading AI stock consolidates after **an earnings** beat, then breaks a 52-week high on 7× RVOL with institutional call sweeps and rising social interest. You enter the stock plus TQQQ calls on the close above resistance, set your stop below the flag low, pyramid on higher highs, and target a 40–80% move over 3–10 days.*

## New Highs, Relative Strength, False Breakouts, and Retests

Many inexperienced traders avoid stocks at new highs because they look "too expensive"; professionals think differently, because a new high means no overhead resistance, rising institutional demand, and clear leadership—a stock can stay expensive and keep getting more valuable. The best candidates also outperform their sector and the market before the acceleration becomes obvious, so use relative strength as an early filter. False breakouts are inevitable—their warning signs are low volume, an immediate reversal, a weak close, deteriorating conditions, or the absence of a catalyst—and the defense is the confluence you already require plus a tight stop. A retest is the constructive flip side: price breaks resistance, briefly returns to test it, and the old resistance becomes new support on declining volume, often a lower-risk entry than chasing an extended initial break. Stand aside when a stock is already significantly extended, volume is weak, the catalyst lacks substance, the market is deteriorating, the name has already failed multiple attempts, or liquidity is insufficient—and avoid the account-draining errors of buying before resistance breaks, ignoring volume, chasing extension, averaging down after a failed breakout, and failing to define an exit before entering.

## The Breakout Sequence

Most exceptional momentum stocks follow the same life cycle—a catalyst changes expectations, institutions begin accumulating, relative volume increases, a constructive base forms, selling pressure diminishes, resistance breaks, technical traders enter, analysts raise expectations, media takes notice, and additional institutional capital extends the trend. The breakout is not the beginning of institutional buying; it is the point where that buying becomes visible to everyone else, which is exactly why your job is to be positioned a tick above the pivot before the crowd arrives.

## The Breakout Timing Governance Matrix

| Operational Parameter | The Retail Spectator | The Blueprint Capital Allocator |
|---|---|---|
| **Entry methodology** | Buys blindly with a market order the instant a ticker flashes green. | Deploys a buy-stop order one penny above the quantified pivot high. |
| **Volume verification** | Ignores the tape and buys low-volume breakouts that instantly reverse. | Requires a 30-minute volume check confirming an active institutional sweep. |
| **Pattern context** | Chases wide, loose, erratic structures that are prone to failure. | Demands a pristine VCP with dried-up liquidity before triggering. |
| **Downside boundary** | Uses a wide stop or none at all, letting one fakeout erase weeks of gains. | Fences risk tightly behind the structural pivot low or the 8-period hourly EMA. |

## The Confluence Matrix

| Factor | High-Probability Signal |
|---|---|
| **Catalyst** | Material news or earnings |
| **Relative volume** | Above 3 |
| **Price action** | Break above major resistance |
| **Sector** | Market-leading industry |
| **Earnings** | Accelerating growth |
| **Institutional buying** | Multiple accumulation days |
| **Market regime** | Bullish or improving |
| **Liquidity** | High average daily volume |
| **Closing price** | Near the day's high |

## Risk, Psychology, and a Reality Check

Aggressive breakout trading produces explosive winners and frequent small losses, and treating risk as the first discipline is what separates traders who compound from those who blow up. False breakouts are common—require full confluence and let tight stops handle the rest; trade only names with average volume above ~1M shares or liquid ETFs so you can exit when you need to; cap risk at 1–2% of the portfolio per setup, since 3x ETFs and options amplify failures as fast as successes; and hold no more than 3–5 high-quality breakouts at once, because patience compounds faster than FOMO.

**Reality check.** *Turning $100,000 into $1,000,000 in six months requires either a 60–70%+ win rate on large R-multiples or a handful of 5–10× runners — outcomes that are rare and far from guaranteed. The aggressive approach in this book carries a real risk of substantial or total loss, and most traders who attempt this pace without discipline do not survive it. Strict rules, journaling, and hard drawdown limits (for example, de-risking at a 20–30% portfolio drawdown) are not optional refinements; they are survival requirements. Trade only capital you can afford to lose.*

### Blueprint Principle

**Breakouts are not random price movements — they are visible evidence that demand has overcome supply. The best breakouts occur when institutions, catalysts, earnings, sector leadership, and technical confirmation converge at the same moment.**

## Timing Entries — Pullbacks

One of the great misconceptions in momentum trading is that the best entries always come from buying new highs. In reality, many of the most profitable entries occur **after a strong stock temporarily retreats.** If a breakout signals that a new trend has begun, a pullback tests whether that trend is real: if buyers return and defend key support, the pullback becomes the launch point for the next advance. This is among the highest-edge timing mechanisms in the blueprint—entering closer to support means a smaller stop distance, which means a larger position for the same fixed risk, a structurally tighter, asymmetric entry that can deliver 30–150%+ when the underlying momentum stays intact. The amateur commits the cardinal sin of catching a "falling knife," buying an asset actively collapsing with no confirmation; you wait for a high-velocity leader to undergo an orderly, low-volume profit-taking phase, and strike precisely at its moving-average reconnection zone.

### Why Pullbacks Exist and Sharpen Your Edge

Markets move in waves: after a strong advance, early buyers take profits and new buyers wait for better prices while institutions keep accumulating. Large institutions rarely chase rapidly rising stocks—they wait for temporary weakness and improved liquidity, because buying into a dip reduces their market impact, and that accumulation frequently provides the support you see hold near important levels. Buying a controlled pullback gives a lower entry, tighter stop placement, a better reward-to-risk ratio, and a higher probability of continuation: entering near support shrinks the stop distance so the same percentage risk funds a larger position, a successful hold-and-bounce proves buyers are still in control, and dips offer cheaper option premiums and clean add points for 2x/3x ETFs.

## The Anatomy of a Healthy Pullback: The Liquidity Drift

Not all pullbacks are tradeable. A retreat is only worth buying when it shows clear institutional holding—a structural signature worth naming the **Liquidity Drift**, with two parts. The **low-volume cooldown:** as price drifts toward a key moving average, relative volume must contract hard, ideally below 1.0, proving institutions are not distributing. The **structural support floor:** the slide should decelerate and find an orderly cushion at an institutional defense line—the rising 8-period EMA or the 21-day EMA on the daily—where accumulation algorithms re-engage. More broadly, healthy pullbacks share a profile of declining volume, orderly price action, higher lows, limited volatility, respect for moving averages, and persistent relative strength; the absence of panic selling matters more than the size of the decline, because strong trends fall on light volume and rise on heavy volume.

## Types of Pullbacks and Confirmation

Several recognizable structures recur, all sharing the logic of orderly weakness into support within a live uptrend: the **breakout retest** (price returns to test former resistance now flipped to support—often the single strongest entry), the **moving-average pullback** (a shallow 5–15% retrace into the 9/20-EMA, 21-EMA, or 50-day), the **flag/pennant pullback** (a tight, low-volume consolidation after a sharp advance), the **channel pullback** (toward the lower boundary of an upward channel), the **Fibonacci retracement** (to the 38.2% or 50% level of the prior impulse), the **volume dry-up pullback** (the cleanest Liquidity Drift), and the **earnings pullback** (an exceptional report, then profit-taking, then renewed buying). One of the highest-quality entries of all is the first pullback after a confirmed breakout, which confirms former resistance has flipped to new support. Above all, don't buy until buyers return—wait for a bullish reversal candle at support, higher intraday lows and a moving-average reclaim, increased buying volume on the bounce, a live catalyst, intact sector leadership with institutional flow, and supportive (not euphoric) sentiment. Confirmation is what separates buying a pullback from catching a falling knife.

## The Pullback Checklist

Before entering during a pullback, confirm the primary trend remains upward, relative strength remains strong, selling volume is declining, institutions continue accumulating (no distribution), the sector remains a market leader, the catalyst remains intact, price respects major support, and the broader market remains constructive.

## The Mechanical Entry Playbook

You never buy simply because price touched a moving-average line—you run a strict sequence confirming the accumulation engine has re-engaged. **1. The moving-average anchor:** pick the reconnection zone by velocity—the high-velocity 8-EMA anchor for hyper-growth catalysts, AI names, and high-gamma options plays, or the macro-trend 21-EMA anchor for 3x leveraged ETFs and major sector leaders in an orderly multi-day correction. **2. The trigger—the first green bar:** drop to the hourly chart and wait for the first green hourly candle that closes above the high of the prior down-hour candle, the signal that intraday order-flow control has shifted back to buyers.

**Entry trigger = high of the intraday reversal candle + $0.01**

**3. Fencing the risk:** the instant the entry is elected, place the stop one penny below the recent swing low or the trigger candle's low—because you bought at a discounted support floor rather than the top of a breakout, the distance is tiny, letting you deploy a concentrated position while keeping actual 1R risk capped at 1% of the account (typically 4–8% on the position itself). Conservatively, wait for a clear bounce-candle close; aggressively, scale in 25–50% on the touch of support and add on confirmation. Targets and scaling mirror the breakout playbook—take 2–4R initially, trail with the 20-EMA, and scale out 30–50% into strength, pyramiding only with profits, never into a loser. Express the trade through low-float stocks, 2x/3x ETFs on the dip, OTM calls, or a blended core-plus-calls structure, sized so a failed bounce costs only a fraction of an R.

## Pullbacks Across Market Regimes and Common Mistakes

The same setup behaves differently by environment: in **bull markets** pullbacks are shallow, institutions buy quickly, and trends resume fast; in **sideways markets** expect more failed bounces and choppy, grinding pullbacks, so reduce size and define a maximum hold time; in **bear markets** pullbacks often become reversals and support frequently fails, so be far more selective and demand an exceptional catalyst. Avoid the recurring errors—buying before the pullback stabilizes, ignoring declining relative strength, averaging down into a confirmed downtrend, confusing a broken trend with a healthy pullback, buying simply because a stock looks "cheap," and trading dips outside your Tier 1 watchlist. Emotional averaging-down is where most aggressive traders fail.

## The Institutional Cycle, and Breakouts vs. Pullbacks

Most institutional accumulation follows the same arc, and the pullback is where you join it on favorable terms—a catalyst emerges, institutions initiate positions, the stock breaks out, retail chases, short-term profit-taking occurs, institutions add on the pullback, the trend resumes, additional institutions join, and new highs develop. Both entry styles earn their place; the best traders master both and choose based on regime and the stock's stage within its trend:

| Breakout Entry | Pullback Entry |
|---|---|
| Captures new momentum early | Offers improved reward-to-risk |
| Higher odds of immediate continuation | Lower entry price |
| Greater risk of false breakouts | Requires patience for confirmation |
| Best for explosive catalysts | Best for established trends |
| Often on heavy volume | Often on lighter selling volume |

### The Pullback Timing Governance Matrix

| Operational Parameter | The Retail Spectator | The Blueprint Capital Allocator |
|---|---|---|
| **Pullback context** | Catches falling knives in damaged names, buying below the 200-day SMA. | Buys only orderly, low-volume pullbacks above the rising 8- and 21-EMAs. |
| **Volume analysis** | Ignores the tape and buys names being distributed on heavy volume. | Requires a deflating volume signature (RVOL under 1.0) through the dip. |
| **Entry timing** | Anticipates support blindly, buying while red candles are still printing. | Waits for the First Green Bar on the hourly chart to confirm re-entry. |
| **Risk-reward density** | Suffers deep drawdowns as unconfirmed entries fracture support. | Secures asymmetric leverage by fencing risk behind the immediate swing low. |

### The Pullback Confluence Matrix

| Factor | High-Probability Signal |
|---|---|
| **Trend** | Established uptrend |
| **Volume** | Declining during the pullback |
| **Support** | Holds breakout level or major moving average |
| **Catalyst** | Still active and relevant |
| **Relative strength** | Continues outperforming the market |
| **Institutional buying** | No evidence of distribution |
| **Sector** | Market-leading industry |
| **Market environment** | Bullish or improving |
| **Entry trigger** | Bullish reversal with renewed buying |

### Risk, Psychology, and a Reality Check

Pullback trading sharpens your edge dramatically, but it still produces strings of losses with specific failure modes: many pullbacks become breakdowns (require full confluence; never buy just because a stock is down), 3x ETFs can gap through stops and options expire worthless on extended weakness (cap risk at 1–2% per setup), sideways grinding pullbacks kill momentum (define a maximum hold time), and pullback entries belong only in Tier 1 watchlist names.

**Worked example.** *An AI/semiconductor leader gaps up 25% on a major partnership, runs, then pulls back 12% to VWAP and the 38.2% Fib on lighter volume. RVOL is still 4× average, institutions are buying calls on the dip, and sector leadership is strong. You enter SOXL or the stock plus OTM calls on a bullish engulfing candle at support, set the stop below the pullback low (6% risk), pyramid on new highs, and target a 40–80% move over 3–8 days.*

**Reality check.** *To compound $100,000 into $1,000,000 in six months, you would still need several 5×–10×+ winners to offset inevitable drawdowns that can run 30–50% or more — a rare outcome, not a dependable plan, and this aggressive approach carries a real risk of substantial or total loss. The traders who fail here almost always do it the same way: averaging down emotionally into weakness. Strict journaling, backtesting every pullback setup, and hard drawdown rules (for example, cutting risk by half after a 20% portfolio loss) are survival requirements, not refinements. Trade only capital you can afford to lose.*

### Blueprint Principle

**Breakouts reveal strength. Pullbacks test conviction. The best pullbacks occur when weak hands are selling, strong hands are buying, and the primary trend remains intact.**

## Timing Entries — Trend Continuation

The biggest mistake inexperienced traders make is believing a stock that has already doubled has "missed its move." Professionals understand the opposite: **the strongest stocks often keep getting stronger, because institutional accumulation unfolds over weeks or months—not hours or days.** Trend continuation is, in plain terms, **adding capital to an active institutional freight train.** Once a strong trend is established after a catalyst breakout, these entries let you ride the impulse phase with the wind at your back, capturing 30–200%+ moves over days to weeks. The amateur refuses to buy at new highs because they feel "too expensive" and reaches instead for cheap, decaying names; you look for established structural strength and use micro-consolidation triggers to step into the trend with tightly fenced risk. Strength breeds strength—and following a confirmed trend is a higher-probability act than predicting a reversal.

### Defining a Strong Trend: The Stacked Momentum Ribbon

A trend continues for exactly as long as demand outpaces supply, and strong trends rarely end because a stock became "too expensive"—they end when earnings disappoint, institutions distribute, macro conditions shift, or the catalyst loses momentum. Define a trend with measurable metrics, not subjective drawings: a high-velocity continuation target should show the **Stacked Momentum Ribbon—**

**Price > 8-period EMA > 21-period EMA > 50-day SMA**

When the moving averages stack in that exact order, each sloping upward at a high angle, institutional buying is active across every horizon—treat the ribbon as an escalator, where a minor intraday dip into it is an entry-efficiency window, not weakness. Confirm further with a clear series of higher highs and higher lows, price above the rising 20/50-EMA and 200-day, **ADX above 25 and rising**, an anchored VWAP from the catalyst day acting as support, and sustained RVOL above 2–3×. If those are absent—ADX falling, lower highs creeping in, volume drying up—there is no trend to continue. The strongest momentum stocks climb like a staircase: advance, pause, advance again—so buy the steps, not chase the risers. Several structures offer clean continuation entries: the bull flag/pennant, the moving-average bounce (off the 9/20-EMA, 21-EMA, or 50-day), the higher-low/breakout retest, the ascending channel, tight consolidation, and the volume-confirmed extension. Volume, relative strength, and earnings together confirm a trend deserves capital—healthy trends advance on above-average volume and pull back on below-average volume, leadership persists, and the longest runs coincide with accelerating revenue, expanding margins, and analyst upgrades.

## The Continuation Checklist

Before entering a continuation trade, confirm the trend remains intact, higher highs continue developing, higher lows remain intact, relative volume expands on advances, pullbacks occur on lighter volume, institutions continue accumulating, sector leadership remains strong, the catalyst remains active, and earnings expectations keep improving.

## The Mechanical Entry Playbook

Two mechanical setups let you slice into an active trend without chasing the vertical peak. **The high-tight flag protocol** targets the most aggressive assets—low-float stocks and 3x ETFs reacting to a major catalyst: a near-parabolic flagpole of 30%+ inside a tight 3-to-5-day window, then a consolidation retracing less than 30% of the flagpole with volume well below average, triggered by a buy-stop one penny above the flag's descending intraday resistance line or the prior day's high, with the stop two pennies below the lowest consolidation shelf (1R). **The 3-bar reset trigger:** when a trend is rising steadily along the 8-EMA, identify three consecutive lower highs (three red candles), then on the fourth bar place a buy-stop one penny above the high of the third red candle—clearing it invalidates the minor pullback—with the stop one penny below that candle's low.

## Entry Style, Stops, Targets, Timeframe, and Instruments

Scale in 30–50% on the first confirmed continuation signal, then pyramid on new highs or the next pullback hold, adding only with profits; set the stop below the recent swing low, VWAP, or the 20-EMA (typically 5–10% risk); take 2–4R initially, then trail with the 20-EMA or parabolic SAR, scaling out 30–50% into strength; and hold 1–10 trading days primary. The best continuation trades line up multiple time frames—the weekly sets direction, the daily identifies the swing, the intraday refines the entry. Express through low-float stocks (add on every higher low), 2x/3x ETFs in strong directional legs (SOXL in an AI-chip uptrend, watching for decay on choppy days), at- or in-the-money calls for delta, warrants for multi-week trends, or a blended core-plus-calls structure.

**Worked example.** *A semiconductor leader breaks out on a major AI partnership and establishes a clear uptrend with higher highs and lows and ADX above 35. It pulls back to the 20-EMA on lighter volume, holds with a bullish hammer and an RVOL expansion, sector leadership strong and institutions buying the dip. You enter or add to SOXL or the stock plus call spreads, set the stop below the 20-EMA (6% risk), pyramid on new highs, and target a 50–120% move over 5–15 days while trailing stops and scaling out into strength.*

## The Three Stages of a Trend, and Continuation vs. Chasing

Trends evolve, and the stage dictates size: **Stage One (early continuation)**—a recent breakout, limited attention, quiet accumulation, the highest potential reward; **Stage Two (mature continuation)**—strong coverage, expanding ownership, steady earnings growth, the most consistent opportunities; **Stage Three (late continuation)**—widespread attention, heavy retail participation, stretched valuations, so size down. Recognizing a weakening trend matters as much as spotting a strong one—watch for heavy selling volume, lower highs, broken moving averages, declining relative strength, institutional distribution, and especially divergence (price making new highs while ADX or RVOL declines) plus climactic exhaustion volume, and exit mechanically rather than rationalizing. Avoid assuming every strong stock is overvalued, buying after a parabolic advance without consolidation, ignoring a falling ADX, fighting an established trend, and over-leveraging or staying in too long. The line between disciplined participation and emotional chasing is the difference between an edge and a gift to the market:

| Trend Continuation | Chasing |
|---|---|
| Planned and rule-based | Emotional and impulsive |
| Entered on confirmation | Entered when already extended |
| Backed by institutional flow | Unsupported by real demand |
| Risk fenced at a structural level | Random or absent stops |
| Buys strength deliberately | Buys excitement |

## The Trend Continuation Governance Matrix

| Operational Dimension | The Retail Casualty | The Blueprint Capital Allocator |
|---|---|---|
| **Trend philosophy** | Believes a stock up 50% must mean-revert, and wastes capital shorting or waiting. | Knows strength breeds strength; buys the strongest names at consolidation resets. |
| **Volume dynamics** | Chases on dying volume and gets trapped as distribution begins. | Requires a sharp volume drop through the consolidation to confirm supply is dry. |

| Operational Dimension | The Retail Casualty | The Blueprint Capital Allocator |
|---|---|---|
| **Execution entry** | Buys the peak of a green vertical bar on FOMO, then eats the pullback. | Places buy-stops at micro-pivot thresholds to force trend validation first. |
| **Risk insulation** | Uses wide, random stops after a late entry, exposing the account to deep drawdowns. | Fences risk behind the consolidation shelf or the 3-bar low, holding risk to 1R. |

## The Continuation Confluence Matrix

| Factor | High-Probability Signal |
|---|---|
| **Trend** | Higher highs and higher lows |
| **Volume** | Heavy on advances, light on pullbacks |
| **Relative strength** | Outperforming the market |
| **Catalyst** | Still active |
| **Earnings** | Accelerating |
| **Sector** | Leading industry |
| **Institutional buying** | Continuing accumulation |
| **Technical pattern** | Bull flag, tight base, or MA bounce |
| **Market regime** | Bullish or improving |

## Risk, Psychology, and a Reality Check

Trend continuation produces your biggest winners but demands patience between setups and ruthless mechanical exits: trends end—watch for divergence and climactic volume and exit mechanically; a strong ADX filter is critical, so avoid weak or sideways "trends" entirely; 3x ETFs erode during consolidation even inside an uptrend, so favor strong directional legs only; and cap risk at 1–2% per trade, pyramiding only with profits, never into losers.

**Reality check.** *To compound $100,000 into $1,000,000 in six months, you would need multiple 5–10×+ compounded runners while surviving drawdowns that can reach 30–60% — a rare outcome, not a dependable plan, and this aggressive approach carries a real risk of substantial or total loss. Most aggressive trend traders* ***fail*** *the same two ways: over-leveraging, or staying in too long. Strict rules, detailed journaling (trend-strength score, catalyst quality, R-multiple achieved), and hard drawdown protocols are non-negotiable. Trade only capital you can afford to lose.*

**Blueprint Principle**

**The greatest fortunes are rarely built by predicting reversals. They are built by recognizing exceptional trends early, respecting them while they remain healthy, and exiting only when objective evidence shows institutional demand is fading.**

## Timing Entries — VWAP Strategies

Most retail investors anchor to lagging moving averages; professionals watch something better. The **Volume-Weighted Average Price (VWAP)** is the average price a stock has traded at across the day, weighted by volume—in effect, where most shares have actually changed hands. A large fund cannot buy millions of shares at once, so it deploys VWAP algorithms to accumulate without distorting price and grades its own execution against VWAP; by tracking price relative to the VWAP line and its volatility bands, you align your entries with those institutional orders. It is not a standalone system but a timing and confirmation tool that tells you **where, exactly, to buy.** Unlike a simple moving average that treats every bar equally, VWAP weights each transaction by volume, so it answers one question—at what average price has most of today's institutional trading occurred?

**VWAP = Σ (Price × Volume) ÷ Σ Volume**

### Why Institutions Use VWAP, and How to Read It

Large firms measure execution against VWAP—buying below it is favorable, consistently buying above it looks inefficient—so their algorithms treat it as both benchmark and reference, producing two behavioral thresholds: when an asset trades cleanly above VWAP, institutional buyers control the intraday tape; when a stock pulls back to a rising VWAP and a sudden volume burst defends it, buy algorithms have triggered to protect their average entry. The simplest principle is also the most effective—above VWAP, buyers control the session and bullish momentum strengthens; below VWAP, sellers dominate and momentum weakens—so trade in the direction of the dominant trend relative to VWAP and never fight it without a strong counter-catalyst. Strong stocks pull back toward VWAP and resume higher (dynamic support), while weak stocks rally to VWAP and stall (dynamic resistance); the cleanest tape of all is the trend day, where price opens above VWAP, rebounds from it repeatedly, builds volume, and closes near its highs. Beyond session VWAP, **anchored VWAP** measures the volume-weighted average from a specific event—earnings, a breakout day, an FDA approval—and tells you whether institutions remain profitable from a transformational catalyst.

### Key VWAP Entry Strategies and Reading Extension

A handful of mechanical setups convert VWAP into an entry, all requiring catalyst and volume confirmation. The **VWAP pullback bounce** is the premier setup: after a catalyst gap, price stretches above VWAP, the first profit-taking wave (often 9:45–10:15 a.m. ET) drifts it back to the rising line on deflating volume (RVOL under 1.0), and buyers defend it with a bullish reversal candle as volume re-expands—you buy exactly where institutions are defending their cost. The **VWAP break and retest** adds on a hold of new support; the **VWAP reclaim** triggers when a weak open crosses back above on rising volume; **opening-range + VWAP alignment** gives a clean directional bias when the first 15–30-minute range holds above VWAP; and the **VWAP crossover with acceleration** signals an immediate entry when a catalyst pushes price decisively through on expanding volume. When an asset goes parabolic it stretches away from VWAP—plot standard-deviation bands (±1, ±2, ±3 sigma) to read that extension objectively:

| Volatility Zone | Market Microstructure | Blueprint Action |
|---|---|---|
| **Baseline VWAP** | Price equilibrium; execution algorithms are passive. | No action; wait for a confirmed directional move. |
| **+1 to +2 sigma** | Orderly momentum; accumulation algorithms sweeping blocks. | Hold 3x ETFs or stock; trail behind the +1 sigma line. |
| **+3 sigma or more** | Mathematical exhaustion; retail FOMO near a climax. | No-buy zone. Mean-reversion risk; scale out of longs into the spike. |

If an asset blows past the +3 sigma band on an exhaustion-volume spike, do not buy—that is where late chasers get trapped; wait for price to snap back inside the +2 band, then for it to reconnect with the VWAP baseline before deploying fresh capital. Demand confirmation before acting: RVOL above 3–5× with increasing buying volume off the line, an active catalyst, sector leadership and institutional flow, and a bullish reversal candle at VWAP. Avoid choppy or low-volume days, narrow-range names, poor liquidity, and late-day crosses—VWAP performs best in active, institution-driven sessions.

## The VWAP Checklist

Before entering a VWAP-based trade, confirm a strong catalyst, relative volume above 3, price above VWAP, sector leadership, institutional accumulation, strong broader-market conditions, bullish price structure, sufficient liquidity, and strong closing action.

## The Mechanical Entry Playbook: The VWAP Pullback Protocol

Take the highest-edge setup—the morning VWAP pullback—and execute it by rule. On a name that has cleared your pre-market catalyst and RVOL filters, the stock surges and stretches cleanly above VWAP at the open; wait for the first profit-taking wave (typically 9:45–10:15 a.m. ET) to drift price back to the rising VWAP line on deflating volume (RVOL under 1.0); place a buy-stop one penny above the high of the first 5-minute candle that bounces off VWAP; and set the stop two pennies below the VWAP line or the bounce candle's low—if the VWAP floor fractures, the institutional defense is dead, so exit immediately. Take a partial position (30–50%) on the first touch and add on confirmation; keep total risk inside 1R (4–8% on the position, with the stop 0.5–1% below VWAP); and scale out at prior highs and 2–4R, trailing the runner with VWAP itself or the anchored VWAP from the catalyst day. Express through stocks, 2x/3x ETFs, OTM calls, or a blended structure, calibrating to regime—strong bull markets keep price above VWAP all session, sideways markets whipsaw around it, and bear markets see VWAP act as resistance.

**Worked example.** *A low-float AI infrastructure name gaps 35% on a major contract win, runs, then pulls back to VWAP on lighter volume mid-morning. RVOL is still 6×, sector leadership is strong, dark-pool buying appears on the dip, and a bullish engulfing* ***prints*** *at VWAP. You enter the stock plus SOXL or TQQQ calls with the stop 5% below VWAP, pyramid on the move back above the morning highs, and target a 40–90% gain over 2–7 days, scaling out into strength.*

### The VWAP Timing Governance Matrix

| Operational Dimension | The Retail Casualty | The Blueprint Capital Allocator |
|---|---|---|
| **Indicators used** | Leans on lagging tools like RSI or MACD, buying late-stage extensions. | Anchors all intraday execution to VWAP. |
| **Pullback execution** | Buys falling stocks blindly as algorithms short them lower. | Enters only when an asset defends a rising VWAP on deflating volume. |
| **Parabolic discipline** | Chases the top of a parabolic run on raw FOMO. | Uses standard-deviation bands to flag exhaustion at +3 sigma and beyond. |
| **Risk architecture** | Uses wide, arbitrary percentage stops and takes large losses on breaks. | Fences risk just below the VWAP floor, holding it inside 1R. |

### The VWAP Confluence Matrix

| Factor | High-Probability Signal |
|---|---|
| **Catalyst** | Material and active |
| **Relative volume** | Above 3, rising off the line |
| **Price vs. VWAP** | Holding or reclaiming above VWAP |
| **Entry trigger** | Bullish reversal candle at VWAP |
| **Extension** | Inside +2 sigma, not exhausted |
| **Sector** | Leading industry |
| **Institutional flow** | Call sweeps or dark-pool buying |
| **Market regime** | Bullish or improving |

| Factor | High-Probability Signal |
|---|---|
| **Liquidity** | Deep, with tight spreads |

### Risk, Psychology, and a Reality Check

VWAP fails in specific ways: in a weak tape it acts as resistance, not support (always require catalyst and RVOL confirmation); intraday noise around the line is common (use tight mechanical stops and small initial size); 3x ETFs erode in chop even when price stays above VWAP (favor strong-trending days only); and limit yourself to 3–5 VWAP setups per day in Tier 1 names, since patience between high-quality touches compounds faster.

**Reality check.** *To compound $100,000 into $1,000,000 in six months, you would still need several outsized 5–10× winners to offset inevitable losses – a rare outcome, not a dependable plan, and this aggressive approach carries a real risk of substantial or total loss. Cap risk at 1–2% of the portfolio per trade, journal every VWAP setup (win rate, R-multiple, catalyst strength), and de-risk after a 20–25% drawdown. Most aggressive traders fail by forcing entries without full confluence. Trade only capital you can afford to lose.*

### Blueprint Principle

**VWAP reveals where institutions are conducting business. Price above VWAP suggests institutional conviction. Pullbacks to VWAP test that conviction. Successful defenses often become the launching pad for the next leg higher.**

## Timing Entries — Opening Range Breakouts

The first thirty minutes of the trading day are one of the most important battlegrounds between buyers and sellers—overnight news, earnings, economic data, institutional orders, and retail enthusiasm all collide at the opening bell, the highest concentration of institutional volume and algorithmic routing you will see all day. The **Opening Range Breakout (ORB)** captures a stock immediately after institutional conviction has been confirmed: rather than predicting the day's direction, you let the market reveal its intentions, then commit. The opening range is the price band established during the first few minutes (commonly the first 5, 10, 15, or 30—the exact window matters less than applying it consistently), and a breakout occurs when price moves decisively above its high on expanding volume. The amateur throws market orders into the morning chaos on FOMO and gets chopped by high-frequency market makers; you treat the open as a pure mechanical discovery phase, letting the market draw its boundaries before striking. Done well, ORB setups deliver fast 10–80%+ intraday-to-multi-day moves when layered with your catalyst framework, RVOL spikes, and sector leadership.

## Why the Open Matters, and the Best Candidates

Large funds usually cannot complete their orders in thin pre-market trade, so significant buying begins after the bell when liquidity is deepest, producing high volume, expanding ranges, and sustained momentum. By mapping an explicit opening-range box before acting, you wait for a definitive directional bias instead of guessing—when a stock builds that range and clears its high on an accelerating volume curve, institutional buyers are sweeping out overhead passive liquidity and driving the asset into expansion. ORBs succeed because they stack fresh information, maximum liquidity, institutional participation, rising volatility, expanding relative volume, and technical confirmation into a single moment. Restrict yourself to Tier 1 high-velocity names with a genuine pre-market catalyst—a major earnings beat or raised guidance, an FDA approval, an acquisition, an AI catalyst, an analyst upgrade, a strong macro tailwind, or clear sector leadership—and layer confirmation: RVOL above 3–5× with heavy participation, a break that holds above VWAP and keeps making higher highs, sector leadership with peers advancing, and persistent call sweeps. Avoid low-RVOL names, no-catalyst tickers, and choppy opens entirely.

## ORB Variations and the Ideal Sequence

Choose one window and apply it consistently. The **five-minute ORB (aggressive)** offers the earliest participation and fastest capture at a higher false-breakout rate—reserve it for low-float stocks (under ~20M shares), high-gamma squeezes, and rapid AI or biotech announcements. The **fifteen-minute ORB (the institutional wave)** is the default blueprint window, letting high-frequency algorithms exhaust their morning whipsaw for better confirmation—best for liquid 3x ETFs like TQQQ and SOXL, sector leaders, and major earnings gaps. The **thirty- to sixty-minute ORB** gives the strongest confirmation and lowest false-breakout rate at the cost of a later entry. The strongest ORB trades follow the same progression—a significant overnight catalyst, strong pre-market trade, a gap higher, a controlled opening range, elevated RVOL, a break above the range, continued institutional buying, and a session-long trend.

## The Mechanical Entry Playbook

Pick your window, let the range print, and trigger mechanically—never touch the keyboard before the opening range is fully established. **The 5-minute ORB protocol:** let the first 5-minute candle print and close at 9:35, place a buy-stop one penny above its absolute high with the stop one penny below its low; the tight range makes the dollar risk minuscule, allowing efficient leveraged sizing off a small 1R. **The 15-minute ORB protocol:** let the stock trade 9:30–9:45, place a buy-stop one penny above the 15-minute high, and confirm the break with a tape surge—if the high is breached while RVOL is under 3.0, treat it as a retail illusion and cancel—anchoring the stop below the opening-range low. Take 40–60% of intended size on the first breakout candle and add on a retest of the OR high as new support; stop below the OR low (typically 3–7% risk); scale out 30–50% at 1:2–1:3 R and trail the rest with the

9/20-EMA, prior highs, or VWAP; and treat 9:35–11:00 a.m. ET as the best window, fading or exiting by 2:00–3:00 p.m. unless a strong trend continues. A gap alone is not enough—demand strong opening volume, an orderly opening-range consolidation, a successful breakout, and continued institutional buying—and the better entry often comes after the initial break, a brief pullback, a successful test, and renewed buying.

## Instrument-Specific Tactics, Regimes, and Mistakes

Express the first-hour break through low-float stocks (50–150%+ same-week moves off the breakout after an FDA approval or earnings beat), 2x/3x ETFs (SOXL, TQQQ, TNA, or UPRO on AI or semiconductor news with deep liquidity, respecting daily reset), options (calls or bull call spreads as gamma ramps, with 5–10× potential), warrants (extended ORB trends with less time decay), or a blended core-plus-OTM-calls structure sized so a failed break costs only a fraction of an R. Calibrate to regime—strong follow-through in bull markets, more false breakouts in sideways markets, and frequent failures in bear markets—and limit yourself to 2–4 high-quality ORBs per day. Full multi-layer confluence lifts the win rate into the 55–65% range; a tight stop handles the rest. Avoid the account-draining errors of buying before the range is established, trading without a catalyst, ignoring RVOL, chasing extension, trading illiquid names, and holding a losing ORB hoping for recovery.

**Worked example.** *A low-float biotech receives FDA approval pre-market and gaps +35%. A clean 30-minute opening range forms; at 9:45 a.m. it breaks the OR high on 12× RVOL with institutional call sweeps and a social-buzz spike, sector leadership strong. You enter the stock plus a 2× sector ETF and calls, stop below the OR low (5% risk), pyramid on higher highs or a VWAP retest, scale out partials at +25%, and trail the rest – targeting a 60–120% move over 1–5 days.*

## The Opening-Bell Governance Matrix

| Operational Dimension | The Retail Spectator | The Blueprint Capital Allocator |
|---|---|---|
| **Opening-bell action** | Throws market orders at 9:31 a.m. on FOMO, buying the top of the morning spike. | Practices an execution freeze, letting the opening-range box form mechanically. |
| **Order architecture** | Uses market orders and absorbs toxic slippage and poor fills. | Deploys buy-stops so the trend is already moving before entry. |
| **Volume qualification** | Chases morning gaps blind to the tape, buying low-volume traps that fade. | Requires an RVOL of 3.0+ to validate authentic algorithmic participation. |
| **Risk insulation** | Holds a failed gap with no structural stop through a 10% reversal. | Fences risk just below the opening-candle low and takes an instant 1R exit if it breaks. |

### The ORB Confluence Matrix

| Factor | High-Probability Signal |
|---|---|
| **Catalyst** | Material overnight or pre-market news |
| **Relative volume** | Above 3, with active pre-market |
| **Opening range** | Tight, controlled consolidation |
| **Price vs. VWAP** | Holding above VWAP |
| **Sector** | Leading, with peers advancing |
| **Institutional flow** | Persistent call sweeps |
| **Market breadth** | Strong or improving |
| **Liquidity** | Deep, with tight spreads |
| **Risk** | Stop fenced at the opening-range low |

### Risk, Psychology, and a Reality Check

**Reality check.** *Compounding $100,000 into $1,000,000 in six months would take several 5–10×+ runners to offset drawdowns that can easily swing 30–50% of the **portfolio — a rare outcome, not a dependable plan, and this aggressive approach carries a real risk of substantial or total loss. Most aggressive ORB traders blow up by over-sizing or trading every range break. Mechanical rules, detailed journaling (ORB duration, catalyst type, R-multiple), and strict daily loss limits are mandatory for survival. Trade only capital you can afford to lose.*

## Timing Entries — Multi-Day Setups

A multi-day setup rests on one fact: **institutions cannot build a meaningful position in a single session.** Funds moving billions often need days or weeks to complete their buying, which prints recurring, exploitable entry points and keeps a trend alive long after the first move. Swing trades lasting roughly 2 to 15 trading days let you stay invested in the market's strongest trends—this is the core compounding engine of the blueprint, capturing the 40–200%+ moves that genuinely accelerate $100,000 toward $1,000,000 through repeated high-R winners. The amateur buys a chart because it "looks low" or holds an unconfirmed position over the weekend on hope; you scan for structural, multi-day consolidation that shows an explicit institutional footprint, then enter at the confluence of multi-day support and a live catalyst, aiming for +5R to +10R over a 2-to-5-day arc.

### Why They Work, and the Multi-Day Liquidity Pocket

Most successful momentum stocks follow a recognizable progression after a catalyst hits. **Day One:** a major catalyst appears and the stock trades heavy volume with strong appreciation. **Day Two:** short-term traders take profits while institutions keep accumulating; price consolidates and selling volume declines. **Day Three:** the stock holds support, relative strength stays firm, and buying resumes. **Day Four:** a fresh breakout develops as additional institutions initiate. **Day Five and beyond:** momentum continues as analysts revise estimates and media expands coverage—the richest opportunities often appear after Day One, once the market recognizes accumulation is still active. That accumulation leaves a distinctive footprint worth naming the **Multi-Day Liquidity Pocket:** a compression matrix (a tight, largely horizontal range spanning 3 to 10 days as daily ranges contract sharply) and a volume-exhaustion print (volume falling well below the 20-day baseline, empirical proof that retail sellers have run out of inventory and distribution has stopped). Read correctly, consolidation is constructive—the market loading for the next move.

## High-Probability Setup Types and Confirmation

The same liquidity-pocket logic shows up in several structures sharing one trait—supply tightening while a live catalyst keeps demand alive: **catalyst + breakout extension** (a gap, then a flag or higher-low consolidation, then a continuation leg), **the first pullback** (one of the highest-probability multi-day entries), **earnings/FDA/AI drift** (post-event momentum holding above key supports for days), **sector rotation swing** (a leadership sector pulling back to its 20-EMA or anchored VWAP, then resuming), **power-play/continuation bases** (the high-tight flag, bull flag, ascending triangle, flat base, and three-weeks-tight, all resolving over 3–10 days), **multi-day gap continuation** (Day One gaps, Day Two consolidates, Day Three breaks the Day-Two high), and **macro catalyst follow-through** (post-FOMC or post-CPI rotation sustaining for several days). A multi-day hold is only justified when backed by stacked evidence—require at least four layers before committing and re-check every morning: a live catalyst, sustained RVOL above 2.5× across several sessions (not a single one-day spike), higher highs and lows with ADX above 25, price respecting anchored VWAP or the 10/20-EMA or 50-day, persistent institutional flow with supportive sentiment, and intact sector leadership. Many strong stocks reveal their quality within about three sessions—if volume stays elevated, pullbacks stay shallow, buyers defend support, and the stock outperforms its sector, accumulation is likely still underway.

## The Multi-Day Checklist

Before entering, confirm the catalyst remains active, relative volume remains elevated, institutional accumulation continues, pullbacks occur on lighter volume, higher highs remain intact, sector leadership persists, earnings expectations keep improving, technical support holds, and market conditions remain favorable.

## The Mechanical Entry Playbook

Inside the developing structure, you still trigger mechanically: multi-day compression (3 to 10 days of tight range and dying volume), then a trigger (a buy-stop above the inside-day high or the multi-day range ceiling), then validation (intraday RVOL ≥ 2.5 in the first hour), then a housed stop (at the low of the setup matrix). **The inside-day breakout (IDB):** an inside day occurs when an asset's entire range sits within the prior day's range (the "mother bar"), the ultimate 24-hour volatility coil—place a buy-stop one penny above the inside-day high with the stop one penny below its low, the tight range allowing efficient leveraged sizing off a small 1R. **The multi-day horizontal range breakout:** when a stock builds a horizontal ceiling across five or more days, place a buy-stop one penny above the highest wick of the entire consolidation, require an intraday RVOL of at least 2.5 in the first hour, and anchor the stop below the breakout day's opening 30-minute range or nearest minor swing low.

## Position Building, Stops, Targets, and Instruments

Trigger on a confirmed pullback bounce, flag breakout, or VWAP retest within the structure; start with 30–40% of intended size on Day 1 and pyramid across Days 2–5 on strength or higher-low holds; set the initial stop below the catalyst low or 20-EMA (6–10% risk max), trailed to breakeven quickly, then with the 20-EMA or swing lows; scale out roughly 30% at 2–3R and 30% at 4–6R, trailing the remainder and exiting fully on a trend break (a lower low plus an RVOL collapse) or catalyst exhaustion; and hold 3–15 days, re-evaluated every morning against a fresh confluence check. Express through low-float stocks (80–300% swings over 5–12 days), leveraged ETFs in clear impulse phases only (they reset daily and decay sideways), longer-dated calls (2–6 weeks) or spreads rolled up and out, warrants for multi-week leverage, or a blended structure sized so a failed setup costs only a fraction of an R.

**Worked example.** *A low-float AI software company beats earnings and raises guidance hard. Day 1: a 40% gap and opening-range breakout. Days 2–4: a healthy 12–18% pullback to the 20-EMA on contracting volume that holds with bullish candles and continued institutional flow; sector leadership strong, RVOL averaging 4×. You enter and add to the core stock plus SOXL calls and warrants on the EMA bounce, set the stop below the recent swing low (7% risk), pyramid on new highs across Days 5–8, scale out at +45% and +90%, and trail the rest — a 110% realized move over nine trading days.*

## Across Market Regimes, and When Setups Fail

Calibrate to regime—trends last longer with multiple continuation entries in bull markets, shorter with more false breakouts in sideways markets, and require exceptional catalysts in bear markets. Healthy trends usually weaken gradually before reversing (watch for repeated heavy-volume selling, broken moving averages, declining relative strength, failed breakouts, and deteriorating earnings expectations), but most damage is self-inflicted—avoid believing the opportunity ended after the first breakout, chasing extended stocks instead of waiting for consolidation, confusing distribution with healthy consolidation, turning a swing into a long-term "investment" when it breaks down, and over-leveraging during a winning streak.

### The Multi-Day Setup Governance Matrix

| Operational Dimension | The Retail Casualty | The Blueprint Capital Allocator |
|---|---|---|
| **Holding horizon** | Holds decaying assets for weeks out of ego, letting time-decay destroy capital velocity. | Rotates capital into 3-to-10-day accumulation coils that are ready to explode now. |
| **Volume analysis** | Chases moves on high, distributive volume — buying the top of institutional exit blocks. | Requires a clear volume-exhaustion print confirming overhead supply has dried up. |
| **Order execution** | Throws market orders into the middle of a messy range and gets chopped by noise. | Places buy-stops just outside the consolidation boundaries to force validation. |
| **Risk architecture** | Uses wide, unquantified stops — or none — risking catastrophic overnight gaps. | Fences risk behind the inside-day low or the 30-minute breakout low (1R). |

### The Multi-Day Opportunity Matrix

| Factor | High-Probability Signal |
|---|---|
| **Catalyst** | Still active |
| **Volume** | Elevated over several sessions |
| **Trend** | Higher highs and higher lows |
| **Pullbacks** | Light-volume consolidations |
| **Relative strength** | Market leader |
| **Earnings** | Accelerating |
| **Sector** | Leading industry |
| **Institutional buying** | Multiple accumulation days |
| **Market environment** | Bullish or improving |

### Risk, Psychology, and a Reality Check

Multi-day setups produce your largest winners and your deepest temporary drawdowns, and because you now hold overnight, risk discipline matters even more: multi-day exposure means gaps can move against you (size smaller than intraday—1–1.5% portfolio risk per setup); many setups look perfect for two or three days then reverse (mechanical trailing stops and a daily confluence re-check are mandatory); 3x ETFs decay in sideways multi-day consolidations (hold them only during clear impulse phases); and greed kills compounding (define exit rules in advance—for example, any day with a lower low and RVOL under 2× = exit).

**Reality check.** *To compound $100,000 into $1,000,000 in six months, you would need roughly four to eight high-quality 5×–15× swings while surviving portfolio drawdowns that can exceed 40%. Those are rare outcomes, not a plan you can count on, and this aggressive approach carries a real risk of substantial or total loss. The traders who fail almost always do it the same way — turning swings into investments, or over-leveraging during a winning streak. Rigorous journaling (setup score, hold time, catalyst strength, outcome), strict position sizing, hard drawdown limits, and weekly performance reviews are survival requirements, not refinements. Trade only capital you can afford to lose.*

### Blueprint Principle

**One-day news creates attention. Multi-day institutional buying creates trends. The greatest opportunities belong to traders who recognize that the first breakout is often the beginning — not the end — of the move.**

## When You're Wrong on Entry Timing

This is one of the highest-leverage sections in the entire blueprint, because in aggressive 10× trading bad timing is not a possibility—it is a certainty. Even the best setups trigger late, gap against you, or stall the instant you commit. The difference between traders who survive the 180-day campaign and accounts that blow up is not avoiding mistimed entries, which is impossible; it is how ruthlessly and mechanically they respond when an entry goes wrong. When you are pursuing a 1,000% return in a hyper-compressed window with maximum capital density and tactical leverage, a timed entry that does not immediately unlock price velocity is not a minor inconvenience—it is a structural failure of the trade thesis, and dead capital in a 180-day sprint is a compounding disaster.

### The Entry Is Only a Hypothesis

Every trade begins as a hypothesis: "I believe this stock is likely to move higher because the evidence favors that outcome." You state the hypothesis, and then the market votes—your job is not to defend it but to recognize, as fast as possible, when the market has rejected it. Even the greatest momentum traders win only 50%, 55%, 60%, perhaps 65% of the time, so being wrong is normal; what separates them is that they never allow a small mistake to become a catastrophic one. Crucially, being wrong on entry timing does not mean the thesis was wrong—institutional algorithms routinely run stop hunts and false shakeouts to clear weak hands before the real continuation. When an entry fails, identify which of three situations you are in: **right thesis, early entry** (the breakout eventually occurs), **valid thesis, more time needed** (the stock consolidates first), or **wrong thesis** (institutional buyers never appear, momentum disappears, and the stock breaks support). Each demands a different response, and the only way to choose correctly is to read the tape honestly instead of forcing your ego onto the chart. The market has never seen your brokerage statement—detach your ego from your entry price; it is a scout sent to test the terrain, not a marriage.

### The Iron Vice Response: Act Instantly

When your entry timing is wrong, the position has exactly one job—prove itself quickly or be fired—and the response should be mechanical, pre-defined, and executed in seconds, not deliberated for hours:

> **Immediate Action Protocol Hit the hard stop or invalidation.** If price reaches your pre-defined stop – structural, ATR-based, or below a key moving average or support – exit fully. No "wait and see," and never move the stop lower. Typical stop distance in high-velocity setups: 4–8% on stocks and high-beta names, 6–12% on 3× ETFs, and defined premium risk on options. **Cut size early on warning signs, before the stop.** If the thesis breaks down ahead of the stop – no volume confirmation on the breakout, an immediate reversal or failure at resistance, a catalyst fade or sector rotation against you, or price stalling for more than two or three bars on your timeframe – scale out 50–100% immediately and move the remainder's stop to break-even. A small loss or a scratch always beats a full 1R loser. **No averaging down. Ever.** This is the number-one account killer in aggressive trading. Adding to a losing, badly timed position violates every principle in this book. The blueprint scales winners only.

### The Time Stop (The Inertia Rule)

The retail casualty assumes a trade is only invalid if it hits a physical price stop, holding through three sideways sessions while time decay quietly drains capital. The professional recognizes that time itself is a finite capital unit: when an entry is executed at a high-velocity pivot, the asset is mathematically required to move now.

> **The Structural Time Stop Protocol Equities and leveraged ETFs:** if the asset is not in a positive, protected position within 4 hours of execution – or it closes the day flat and sluggish inside its consolidation base – the trade is scratched. **Short-dated options:** if a contract does not show directional delta expansion within 90 minutes of an intraday breakout trigger, the position is market-flattened.

### The Instantaneous Scratch

Amateurs treat every exit as an emotional choice between a win and a loss; the fiduciary introduces a third, highly frequent outcome—the scratch, an exit at or within pennies of entry for roughly $0R or a fractional −0.1R paper cut. If you buy a breakout at $50.00, price spikes to $50.40, then reverses hard to $49.95, the timing was wrong—instead of waiting for the hard stop at $48.50 to take a full −1R loss, you trigger an automatic scratch the moment price falls back inside the breakout shelf, pulling capital back to cash unhurt for a cleaner attempt.

> [ EXPLOSIVE PIVOT ENTRY ] -> price fails to follow through | v [ RE-ENTRY BACK INSIDE BOX ] <——-+ | +-> ACTION: instantaneous scratch at break-even. Capital mass pulled back to cash, unhurt.

## Avoid the Hope Trade

Hope is not a trading strategy. When price immediately moves against you, do not panic and do not pray—interrogate the tape: Was volume weak? Did the breakout fail? Did the sector reverse? Has institutional buying disappeared? If the evidence that justified the trade has vanished, your hope should vanish with it.

## The Reset Protocol: Re-Entry Without Revenge

A failed entry is useful market data, not a verdict on your character. The fatal retail error is to take a loss on bad timing, get emotionally triggered, and delete the ticker out of spite—missing the true, multi-hundred-percent move that arrives twenty-four hours later. The blueprint trader logs the exit objectively and immediately begins hunting for a structured re-entry. Same-day, mark the chart (why was the timing wrong?), journal whether any entry rules were broken (if so, a mandatory size reduction applies to the next three to five trades), and assess whether the regime is still favorable (if not, remove the name for five to ten days). A trader is allowed a maximum of two entry attempts per setup cluster within a rolling 48-hour window: if the first is stopped on a shakeout, you may not chase it but must wait for a clean structural reset—a secondary 15-minute compression box or a successful test of the intraday VWAP line—and fire the second tranche only when the secondary pivot high fractures on expanding volume, each re-entry demanding stronger confirmation than the original. Resume normal size only after two to three clean wins or a full regime reset, and if bad-timing entries cluster, drop risk to 0.5% and retreat to cash or paper trading. Exiting and re-entering are independent decisions, not a contradiction: if you buy at $100, the stock falls to $94 and stops you, then several days later forms a proper base and you buy again at $101, the first trade protected capital and the second may become a major winner. Missing the first 3% of a move is far cheaper than participating in a failed breakout.

## Instrument-Specific Timing-Failure Responses

Professional traders view small losses as operating expenses; retail traders view them as personal failures. Stores pay rent, manufacturers buy inventory—traders pay small losses, and without them there is no business. Many large losses begin with a single dangerous thought: "I refuse to admit I was wrong." Wrong entries tend to arrive in clusters—a regime shift, weakening momentum, rising volatility—and the professional response is to become more conservative, not more aggressive. Three protections enforce this: **tilt prevention** (after a bad-timing loss, enforce a 30–60 minute cool-off or end the session), **portfolio heat** (immediately recalculate total open risk—an entry you cut early actually improves heat management), and **drawdown governance** (if cumulative bad-timing losses push you into an 8–10% weekly drawdown, halve position sizes for the rest of the week). When nothing lines up, do not force a trade—cash is a position that buys patience, objectivity, and purchasing power.

| Instrument | Why a Timing Error Bites | Response |
|---|---|---|

| Instrument | Why a Timing Error Bites | Response |
|---|---|---|
| **3× ETFs (e.g., TQQQ, SOXL)** | Extremely timing-sensitive; a wrong entry in chop decays capital rapidly through the daily reset. | Cut faster — a 3–5% stop, or an immediate scale-out on the first red bar. |
| **Options** | Theta is merciless; if timing is off, extrinsic value melts. | Exit, or roll to a later expiration only if delta and gamma still strongly favor you and you are within 1R. Otherwise take the loss. |
| **High-beta stocks** | Gap risk is highest, so a bad entry can leap past your stop. | Use limit orders and smaller initial size on potential gap plays. |
| **Warrants** | Lower liquidity means wider spreads and slower exits. | Be even quicker to exit on any sign of timing failure. |

## Turn Bad Timing Into Edge

Every mistimed entry contains information. Ask the hard questions—Was I chasing? Did I ignore volume? Was the stock extended? Did I buy before confirmation? Did I violate my own rules?—because a trading journal converts expensive mistakes into paid education. The very best aggressive traders are not those with perfect timing; they are those who minimize the cost of bad timing, keeping their timing-error cost under 15–20% of gross wins through ruthless cutting. Make the autopsy a standing template, completed for every failed entry:

| The Bad Entry Autopsy — Field | What to Capture |
|---|---|
| **Setup type** | The pattern or trigger you traded (breakout, episodic pivot, pullback, etc.). |
| **Entry reason vs. actual price action** | What you expected against what the tape actually did. |
| **Cost of the mistake** | The damage in both dollars and R. |
| **Rule broken (if any)** | The specific rule violated, or "none — clean loss." |
| **Lesson / rule adjustment** | The single change that prevents a repeat. |

## What You Do When Entry Timing Fails

| Situation | The Distorted Retail Casualty | The 10X Blueprint Fiduciary |
|---|---|---|

| Situation | The Distorted Retail Casualty | The 10X Blueprint Fiduciary |
|---|---|---|
| **Sideways drift** | Holds for days, hoping, while capital stays frozen. | Executes a time stop; liquidates within hours if velocity fails to ignite. |
| **False breakout** | Widens stops or ignores the reversal, turning a minor mistake into a major drawdown. | Deploys the instantaneous scratch to preserve capital at break-even. |
| **Post-loss psychology** | Rages – revenge-trades or abandons the name entirely. | Logs the exit objectively and watches for a structured re-entry trigger. |
| **The losing add** | Averages down to "improve" the price. | Scales winners only; never adds to a badly timed loser. |
| **The shakeout** | Deletes the ticker out of spite and misses the real move. | Runs the Dual-Attempt Re-Entry Matrix on a clean structural reset. |

## Practical Rules for Wrong Entries

Objective rules replace emotional decision-making with repeatable execution: exit immediately if the breakout fails on heavy volume; apply a time stop (scratch any entry that fails to ignite velocity within its window—4 hours for stocks and ETFs, 90 minutes for short-dated options); use the instantaneous scratch to exit at break-even the moment price falls back inside the base; never average down on a momentum trade, scaling winners only; never widen a stop simply because the trade is losing; separate the quality of the idea from the quality of the timing; limit yourself to two re-entry attempts per setup within 48 hours, each demanding stronger confirmation; reduce size after three consecutive losses and drop to 0.5% risk after a cluster of bad-timing entries; and complete a Bad Entry Autopsy for every failed entry.

## Closing Thoughts

Every aggressive trader will experience mistimed entries—that is not incompetence but a consequence of participating in uncertain markets. The defining characteristic of exceptional traders is not flawless prediction but disciplined adaptation: they recognize quickly when the market has invalidated their timing, exit without hesitation, preserve capital, and stay emotionally prepared to participate again. The trader who exits one poor entry with a small loss keeps both financial capital and psychological confidence; the one who refuses to admit the mistake usually sacrifices both.

**The Final Principle:** *the best traders are not right more often – they are less wrong when they are wrong. In the 10× pursuit, bad timing is not a failure of skill; it is expected variance. Your job is to make every bad-timing event a small, survivable scar, never a wound that threatens the account.*

# Chapter 17
# Timing Exits

## Timing Exits — Scaling Out

A defining trait of professional traders is that they devote as much attention to how they exit as to how they enter—many hunt the perfect entry yet hold no structured exit plan, so they watch large gains vanish to greed or dump exceptional trades early out of fear. **Scaling out solves both problems:** instead of selling the whole position at one perfect price, you reduce exposure in stages as the stock advances, locking in profit while keeping participation if the trend continues. In a hyper-aggressive compounding model the largest structural threat is not taking a loss—it is the **vaporization of unrealized gains.** Scaling lets you lock realized gains, permanently de-risk the remaining capital, and still leave a runner intact to capture the outsized 5x–20x+ moves that 1,000% compounding requires—a hybrid of multiple disciplined 2R–4R scalps and the occasional 10R+ runner. No trader consistently sells at the exact top, so rather than predicting the precise turning point, you profit throughout the advance. Institutions work the same way, reducing gradually to manage liquidity and minimize market impact—you should think like them.

### The Three Objectives of Scaling Out

Every scaling plan should accomplish three things at once: **protect capital** (early profit-taking converts unrealized gains into realized ones), **let winners continue** (a portion stays open to participate if momentum extends), and **reduce emotional trading** (a predetermined plan removes most of the emotion that accompanies large open gains).

### The Mathematics of the Free Trade

Scaling out literally rewrites the breakeven math of the remaining shares. The baseline is a simple 1R de-risk:

**First target (TP1) = entry price + ( 1 × initial risk distance )**

Enter at $10.00 with a stop at $9.50—your 1R risk is $0.50. The instant price reaches $10.50 (+1R), Tier 1 triggers and you sell 50% of the position: capturing +1R on half the shares banks +0.5R in realized profit, so even if the remaining 50% reverses to the $9.50 stop (a −0.5R drag), the whole trade nets exactly zero—a mathematical scratch. You have eliminated the trade's downside while keeping full exposure to a parabolic extension; from that point on, you are playing with the market's money.

### The Tactical Playbook: The Tiered Harvest

Use a rigid scale-out grid: entry with risk defined to a 1R unit, then at +1R sell 50% and move the stop on the remainder to breakeven, at +3R sell 25% and begin an 8-EMA (daily) trailing stop, and hold the final 25% for a climax spike or trend fracture. The standard plan, which you adjust for the setup's velocity:

| Tier | % of Position | Target | Trigger | Action |
|---|---|---|---|---|

| Tier | % of Position | Target | Trigger | Action |
|---|---|---|---|---|
| 1 | 30–50% | 1:2–1:3R | First major extension or VWAP break | Take profit; move stop to breakeven |
| 2 | 25–30% | 1:4–1:6R | New highs with a momentum stall | Bank gains; tighten the trail |
| 3 | Remainder | 1:8R+ | Trailing stop hit or catalyst exhaustion | Let it run, then full exit |

**Tier 1 (the capital insulator):** the instant price reaches entry plus 1R, sweep roughly half the position to cash and move the stop to breakeven—the trade is now bulletproof. **Tier 2 (the core harvest):** at +3R (or 1:4–1:6R) liquidate another quarter of the original size and tighten the trail. **Tier 3 (the runner):** insulate the final quarter from intraday noise and trail it on a daily anchor—the rising 8-EMA or the prior day's low—which keeps you positioned if the trade becomes a legendary multi-bagger. Fast scalpers (intraday ORB trades, 3x ETFs) scale heavier early, often 50% at 1:2R; multi-day low-float runners scale lighter early and trail harder. Beyond the R-multiple grid, several conditions justify reducing—technical levels (prior resistance, round numbers, a stall at anchored VWAP), an RVOL contraction after a spike, the end of a multi-day catalyst window (5–8 days after an FDA decision or earnings), catalyst fade, or total open risk exceeding 5–7% of the account—and you scale faster on objective weakness even before a price target is reached.

## The Runner, Methods, and the Profit Pyramid

The most powerful concept in scaling is the **runner**—the final portion left open after partial profit-taking, whose purpose is singular: capture the extraordinary trend, since some leaders appreciate several hundred percent beyond what first looked like a reasonable target. The partials pay for the trade; the runner is where the life-changing math lives. Scaling should travel with progressively tighter risk management—as profit increases, raise stops and let realized gains protect the remaining capital—but never move your stop to breakeven and then hold full size hoping for a moonshot, which is gambling, not scaling. Three approaches cover most situations: **equal scaling** (equal portions throughout the advance), **progressive scaling** (increasingly larger portions as price extends), and **technical scaling** (portions as resistance develops, moving averages break, or momentum weakens). The harvest maps onto three stages—recover risk, harvest momentum, and preserve the runner.

## Scaling in Different Instruments

Leverage magnifies volatility, which makes disciplined scaling even more valuable—the more leverage, the more aggressively you bank. **Stocks (low-float runners):** scale partials at key technical levels and let the core ride follow-on catalysts. **2x/3x ETFs (TQQQ, SOXL):** scale aggressively because of daily decay—never hold full size beyond 3–5 strong days, banking heavily on the first 15–25% move. **Options:** sell portions as delta increases and roll the remaining calls up and out, realizing gamma before theta erodes it. **Warrants:** longer-dated leverage permits lighter early scaling and a larger trailing portion. **Blended:** scale the stock or ETF core first, then the options last for maximum gamma capture.

**Worked example.** *A low-float AI name gaps 30% on a major partnership; you enter on the ORB and a VWAP pullback with 1.5% risk. Day 1 (+38%): scale 35% at 1:3R and move the stop to breakeven. Day 3 (+72%): scale another 30% at resistance and trail the remainder with the 20-EMA. Day 7 (+145%): the trend weakens – RVOL drops and a* ***lower high forms*** *– so you exit the rest on the trailing stop. A ~4.8R average across the position: a major compounding step taken with controlled risk.*

## Scaling Across Time Frames

| Time Frame | Typical Scaling Trigger |
|---|---|
| **Intraday** | Loss of VWAP, weakening volume, or a failed opening-range breakout |
| **Swing trade** | Resistance levels, moving-average extension, or trend exhaustion |
| **Position trade** | Major technical deterioration, earnings disappointment, or distribution |

## Market Regimes and Common Mistakes

Conditions should shape the aggressiveness of the scale-out: in **strong bull markets** trends persist longer, so smaller reductions and larger runners are justified; in **sideways markets** continuation odds fall, so quicker profit-taking is wiser; in **bear markets** violent reversals and higher volatility make aggressive scaling prudent. Scaling out is not the same as selling too soon—selling too soon is fear-driven and eliminates upside entirely, while scaling is systematic, de-risking your way through the trend. Avoid the errors that undo a good scale-out—selling the entire position after the first profitable day, refusing to take any profit out of greed, scaling without a predetermined plan, ignoring technical deterioration, holding leveraged instruments too long after a parabolic advance, and repeatedly moving profit targets just because price keeps rising.

## The Institutional Exit Cycle

Institutional selling usually develops gradually—buying pressure slows, volume declines, distribution days increase, leadership weakens, moving averages fail, analysts reduce expectations, institutions keep reducing positions, and retail finally recognizes the reversal—so scaling out early in this sequence lets you preserve gains before the broader market reacts.

### The Scale-Out Governance Matrix

| Operational Dimension | The Retail Spectator | The Blueprint Capital Allocator |
|---|---|---|
| **Profit-capture psychology** | Greed-driven; refuses to take profit at +2R, expecting the moon. | Operates on mathematical targets; treats profit-taking as a mandate. |
| **Risk transitioning** | Leaves the initial stop at the original floor and gets wiped on reversals. | Moves the remaining stop to breakeven the moment Tier 1 is realized. |
| **Ledger efficiency** | Suffers capital stagnation as winners round-trip back to losses. | Generates steady cash flow, rapidly recycling capital to liquid cash. |
| **Runner optimization** | Dumps the whole position on the first wiggle, missing multi-baggers. | Holds a protected 25% runner to capture non-linear macro trends. |

### Risk, Psychology, and a Reality Check

Scaling is mostly an exercise in beating your own psychology: the **greed trap** is the biggest killer, so define the tiers before entry; **opportunity cost** means scaling too early leaves money on the table, so balance it with your trailing rules; frequent partials raise commissions and taxes, so favor longer holds in tax-advantaged accounts where possible; and because 3x ETFs and options reverse fast, a mechanical scale-out protects capital better than a mental stop.

**Reality check.** *Even with perfect scaling, most aggressive traders still face 30–60% drawdowns between big winners, and the $100,000-to-$1,000,000 goal still requires a handful of 8–20x+ runners alongside consistent 2–4R scalps. That is a rare outcome, not a dependable plan, and this aggressive **approach carries a real risk of substantial or total loss. Without mechanical scaling rules, psychology will push you to exit too early and miss the velocity, or too late and give the gains back. Journal every exit tier with its reasoning, the R-multiple achieved, and your emotional state. Trade only capital you can afford to lose.*

### Blueprint Principle

**Great traders do not try to sell at the exact top. They harvest profits as trends mature, protect accumulated gains, and leave a portion of every exceptional winner free to become extraordinary.**

## Timing Exits — Trailing Stops

The difference between amateur and professional traders is rarely found in how they buy—it is found in **how they protect profits.** A **trailing stop** is a dynamic, one-way risk boundary that automatically tightens behind an advancing price, letting profits grow while steadily reducing downside, so you let price action, not emotion, determine the exit. It gives a high-velocity asset the room it needs to breathe and shake out retail noise, but the instant the institutional accumulation engine fractures, it triggers a market-sweep liquidation to lock in your milestone. This is the final profit-protection layer: after scaling out partials, the trailing stop lets the remaining position ride the trend-continuation phase—where many of your biggest 8R–20R+ winners come from, the exact outsized moves that turn $100,000 into $1,000,000. Unlike a fixed stop that protects against your initial loss, a trailing stop only ever moves toward protecting profit—enter at $50 with a stop at $45, watch price reach $70, and the $45 stop no longer serves any purpose. The governing philosophy: your goal is not to sell at the exact top, it is to participate in most of the trend—institutions think the same way, exiting not because a stock rose 20% but when earnings weaken, demand fades, or leadership deteriorates.

## Types of Trailing Stops and the Dual-Engine Framework

Several methods exist, each suited to different speeds and volatility. The **moving-average trail (20/50-EMA)** is most recommended—trail beneath the rising 20-EMA in a strong trend (the 8-EMA for the fastest, highest-angle moves); as long as price respects the average the trend is intact. The **swing-low trail** moves the stop beneath each successive higher low, following market structure rather than a percentage. The **ATR-based/Chandelier trail** sizes the stop to the asset's real volatility, anchored to the highest high since entry:

**Trailing floor = highest high since entry – ( 2.5 × 14-period ATR )**

The floor widens in high-volatility environments and tightens during smooth, linear expansion, insulating the position from stop-hunting sweeps. **Anchored VWAP** from the catalyst day is excellent dynamic support, **parabolic SAR** is aggressive for fast movers, a percentage trail (8–15% from the peak) is best as a floor rather than the primary tool, and a trendline stop works well in orderly advances. Time-frame matching is everything—tighten too quickly on a multi-day swing and you get shaken out by routine noise; trail too loosely on a volatile 3x ETF and a sharp mean reversion erases your gain. Two engines cover the spectrum: the **short-term velocity trail (8-EMA)** for hyper-growth equities, option sprints, and fresh-narrative breakouts (on the 15-minute or daily chart), and the **structural trend trail (ATR/Chandelier)** for liquid core positions like 3x ETFs and multi-week leaders, where multiplying true volatility by ~2.5 lets the floor breathe in volatile phases.

## The Mechanical Trailing Playbook

Trailing stops are fed into the broker as active GTC stop-market orders, not watched by hand—the point is to bypass emotional hesitation entirely: high-velocity expansion, select the engine (8-EMA for velocity sprints, Chandelier ATR for macro/3x ETFs), and on a price print below the dynamic floor, automated market liquidation fires. **The moving-average close-out rule:** on a daily 8- or 20-EMA trail, allow price to dip below the average intraday—often just market makers sweeping liquidity—but exit if and only if a daily candle closes completely below the rising average. **The prior-day-low walker:** for a vertical, parabolic climax (running ~30%+ above the 20-day average), the 8-EMA is too slow, so each morning move the stop to two pennies below the previous session's absolute low. Precise operating rules: start trailing immediately after the first partial or at +1.5R; adjust once per day or on a new swing high, never intraday; loosen the trail while the narrative is strong and tighten when news flow slows; exit fully if price closes below the trail and any of an RVOL under 2×, a lower daily low, sector-leadership rotation, or an institutional-flow reversal is present; and never widen a stop, ever. Trailing escalates in lockstep with your scale-out tiers—breakeven plus a buffer after Tier 1, a 20-EMA or swing-low trail after Tier 2, and the tightest 1.5 ATR or parabolic SAR trail on the final portion—reinforced by a time-based hybrid (breakeven by Day 2, the 20-EMA from Day 4).

## Trailing Through the Trade and Instrument Tactics

How you manage the trail changes with the trend—give room after a breakout, tighten through pullbacks, and watch volume and post-earnings behavior. Match the instrument to the trail: **stocks** add on every higher low and trail the core; **2x/3x ETFs** demand tight trails and time-based rules; **options** require rolling up and out as gamma accelerates, selling portions as theta builds; **warrants** ride multi-week trends with less decay; and **blended** positions trail the core while protecting the derivative layer first. Calibrate to regime—wider trails in strong bull trends, tighter in sideways or deteriorating tape—and avoid the errors that defeat the purpose of a trail: setting it too tight in a volatile name, moving it the wrong way, watching it by hand, and ignoring the confluence that says the trend has actually broken.

**Worked example.** *A low-float biotech wins FDA approval and gaps 45%; you enter on the ORB/VWAP bounce with 1.5% risk. Day 1 (+52%): scale 35% at 1:3R and move the stop to breakeven. Day 3 (+95%): scale 30% at resistance and switch the remainder to a 20-EMA trail. Day 6 (+180%): price pulls to the 20-EMA, holds, and resumes — the trail stays beneath the EMA. Day 9 (+240%): it closes below the 20-EMA with an RVOL collapse, so you exit the rest on the trail — a* ***massive realized*** *R-multiple on the runner with most of the gain protected the whole way up.*

## The Trailing-Stop Governance Matrix

| Operational Dimension | The Retail Casualty | The Blueprint Capital Allocator |
|---|---|---|
| **Stop customization** | Uses a static 5% stop on every stock regardless of its volatility. | Tailors the trail with ATR or moving-average metrics to fit the asset. |
| **Execution mechanics** | Manages exits by hand, panicking early or freezing as profit evaporates. | Automates via GTC stop-market orders to bypass emotional hesitation. |
| **Trend longevity** | Cuts winners at a tiny +1R out of fear, missing multi- | Gives structural breathing room so institutional capital |

| Operational Dimension | The Retail Casualty | The Blueprint Capital Allocator |
|---|---|---|
| | bagger moves. | lifts the trend. |
| **Reversal discipline** | Lowers the stop as price approaches it, breaking the rules in denial. | Treats a floor fracture as an absolute mandate to return to cash. |

## The Adaptive Trailing-Stop Model

| Market Condition | Suggested Philosophy |
|---|---|
| **Early-stage breakout** | Allow wider stops to accommodate normal volatility |
| **Strong institutional trend** | Trail beneath key moving averages or swing lows |
| **Mature momentum advance** | Gradually tighten as the trend becomes extended |
| **Parabolic rally** | Protect aggressively as reversal risk rises |
| **Weak or deteriorating market** | Reduce downside tolerance and tighten sooner |

## Risk, Psychology, and a Reality Check

Trailing turns solid trades into legendary ones, but no system avoids every loss: normal volatility can stop you out early (use ATR or EMA buffers in strong trends); giving back gains is the number-one regret (tighten aggressively past 1:6R or when multiple confluence layers fade); 3x ETFs and options erode even in mild pullbacks (favor tighter trails and time-based rules); and both "let it run" greed and fear-driven over-tightening hurt (pre-define the rules before every entry).

**Reality check.** *Trailing stops turn solid trades into legendary ones, but for the 1,000% goal you still need several 10R+ runners preserved by your trails to offset the frequent 1–2R stops, and you should expect 35–60% drawdowns between big winners. That is a rare outcome, not a dependable plan, and this aggressive approach carries a real risk of substantial or total loss. Journal every trailed trade — the trail type used, the maximum unrealized gain, the final R-multiple, and the reason for the exit. Mechanical discipline here is what separates survivors from blowups. Trade only capital you can afford to lose.*

## Blueprint Principle

**Entries create opportunity. Position sizing manages risk. Trailing stops protect wealth. The greatest momentum traders stay with exceptional trends until the market — not emotion — tells them the trend has ended.**

## Timing Exits — Momentum Exhaustion

One of the greatest mistakes momentum traders make is believing a powerful trend will continue indefinitely—no matter how compelling the catalyst, **every momentum trend eventually exhausts itself.** This is the defensive guardrail of your exit system: after you have scaled out partials and trailed stops, momentum exhaustion triggers a full or near-full exit when the explosive buying that fueled your 20–200%+ move begins to dissipate, before a sharp reversal takes the rest. It is distinct from a blow-off top—a blow-off is the violent terminal spike; exhaustion is the broader fading of buying pressure, which can arrive as a climax, a slow grind, or a catalyst that has run its course. In the most aggressive vehicles the difference is the whole account: when momentum dies, standard trailing stops give back 20–40% of peak gains before they trigger, so you learn to act on the exhaustion itself—ideally selling into the final wave of retail euphoria. Exhaustion is not a prediction; it is the recognition that the balance between supply and demand is beginning to change, well before the major decline arrives.

### The Momentum Life Cycle

Most momentum stocks move through five stages—**discovery** (few notice; institutions accumulate), **acceleration** (catalysts gain attention, volume expands), **institutional expansion** (multiple funds establish positions), **public participation** (media swells, retail buying accelerates), and **exhaustion** (institutional buying slows, profit-taking rises, distribution begins). Recognizing Stage Five is what protects accumulated gains, because every rally eventually reaches a point where institutions already hold enough, valuations stretch, and new buyers grow scarce.

### The Warning Signs of Exhaustion

Exhaustion rarely appears as a single event—treat any one sign as noise, but **three or more appearing at once is a high-confidence signal**, grouped into five categories. **Price action and structure:** failure to make new highs, a lower high or double top, bearish reversal candles (a shooting star, engulfing bar, or doji at resistance), and loss of higher lows. **Volume and extension:** the key divergence is price rising while volume contracts; a climax volume shock (an unprecedented multi-month spike, then contraction); mathematical extension (roughly 30%+ above the rising 20-day average in under five sessions, or up to 100% above the 50-day); and three to five consecutive gap-up days. **Momentum indicators:** RSI divergence (price makes a higher high while RSI makes a lower high), a shrinking MACD histogram, and an ADX that peaks and rolls over. **Catalyst and sentiment:** news flow slowing, the narrative played out, social buzz peaking, and institutional flow reversing (call sweeps turning to put buying or dark-pool selling). **Broader context:** narrowing leadership, where late in a trend only one or two names rise and deteriorating breadth signals capital rotating away.

## Three Types of Exhaustion

Exhaustion does not always look the same: **climactic exhaustion** (a huge advance, record volume, media frenzy, and emotional buying, frequently followed by a sharp reversal—the blow-off-style ending), **gradual exhaustion** (slowing momentum, declining volume, repeated consolidations developing over weeks—quieter but just as terminal), and **catalyst exhaustion** (the catalyst stops attracting incremental buyers, so even a fresh strong earnings report may fail to move price—a sign the good news is already in).

## The Exhaustion Checklist

Before continuing to hold a large position, ask: Is relative volume declining? Have distribution days increased? Are breakouts failing? Is sector leadership weakening? Has the catalyst largely played out? Are analysts becoming less optimistic? Is institutional buying slowing? Has price become parabolic? Has the broader market weakened? Multiple warning signs deserve immediate attention.

## The Exit Playbook and the Climax Liquidation Sequence

Exhaustion exits escalate with the evidence, treated as non-negotiable triggers on the final trailed portion, especially once you are +4R or beyond: scale the remaining 20–30% when the first two signals appear while the uptrend is still intact; full exit when 3+ signals are present and price closes below the 20-EMA, the trailing stop, or a key swing low; a time-based override exiting 8–12 days after a major catalyst if momentum stalls; the aggressive version for 3x ETFs and options exiting on the first clear signal plus an RVOL drop; and post-exit, move straight to cash or a new setup with no revenge re-entry. When exhaustion arrives as a violent climax rather than a slow fade, you act intraday: at parabolic extension (price ~100% above the 50-day) with a terminal emotional gap-up (8%+) stretching +3 sigma past VWAP, the instant a 15-minute candle prints below the prior candle's low the momentum engine is dead—sweep the entire remaining position into the bid rather than scaling, since waiting for the daily close can cost 20–40% of the peak.

## The Exit Decision Tree and Instrument Tactics

The whole process simplifies into three states: **continue holding** while higher highs and lows persist, volume confirms advances, and the catalyst keeps strengthening; **begin reducing exposure** when rallies become extended, distribution days appear, relative strength weakens, or the stock turns parabolic; and **exit completely** when the primary uptrend breaks, distribution becomes persistent, key support fails, and the thesis is no longer supported. Leverage compresses the time you have to react—low-float stocks can reverse 40–70% in 1–3 days once exhausted, 3x ETFs demand exit on any ADX rollover plus an RVOL collapse, and options should be sold on the first divergence or volume climax as theta and vega crush accelerate.

**Worked example.** *A low-float AI infrastructure name gaps 40% on a major hyperscaler partnership. You enter on the ORB and a VWAP pullback; through Days 1–4 the trend is **strong** and you scale partials at 1:3R and 1:6R, trailing with **the 20-EMA. On Day** 7 price makes** a marginal new high on declining RVOL, an RSI divergence appears, social sentiment hits extreme bullish levels, and ADX peaks. You exit the final 35% on a close below the 20-EMA — a ~9.4R average across the whole position, with capital freed for the next catalyst rather than tied up in a fading name.*

## From Momentum to Exhaustion

Nearly every major winner follows the same progression—a transformational catalyst, institutional accumulation, a technical breakout, accelerating earnings, sector leadership, public enthusiasm, valuation expansion, institutional distribution, momentum exhaustion, and trend reversal—so the trader who understands this cycle stops asking "how high can it go?" and starts asking the only question that matters: is institutional demand still stronger than institutional supply? Avoid believing every pullback signals exhaustion, ignoring multiple distribution days, refusing to sell out of attachment, holding a parabolic advance indefinitely, and waiting for perfect confirmation after the trend has already broken.

### The Momentum Exhaustion Governance Matrix

| Operational Dimension | The Retail Spectator | The Blueprint Capital Allocator |
|---|---|---|
| **Psychological state** | Peak euphoria; believes the stock rises forever and posts about it. | Clinical detachment; reads the extension as a mathematical trap. |
| **Volume analysis** | Thinks huge volume at the top means institutional buying is starting. | Reads huge volume at a vertical peak as terminal distribution. |
| **Exit execution** | Holds through the entire collapse, turning a win into a loss. | Sweeps 100% to cash the moment the 15-minute lower low prints. |
| **Capital allocation** | Buys more shares or short-dated calls at the peak on FOMO. | Flattens the position, converting paper profit into liquid capital. |

### The Institutional Exit Matrix

| Warning Sign | Interpretation |
|---|---|
| **Declining relative volume** | Institutional buying slowing |
| **Multiple distribution days** | Institutions reducing exposure |
| **Failed breakouts** | Demand weakening |
| **Lower highs** | Trend losing strength |

| Warning Sign | Interpretation |
|---|---|
| **Broken moving averages** | Technical deterioration |
| **Weak sector performance** | Capital rotating elsewhere |
| **Extreme media attention** | Public participation peaking |
| **Parabolic advance** | Elevated reversal risk |

### Risk, Psychology, and a Reality Check

Exhaustion exits keep your biggest winners from becoming losers, but the discipline has its own traps: strong trends pause, so require multiple signals plus price confirmation to avoid exiting a healthy consolidation; waiting too long after the signals can cost 20–40% of the gain, so act decisively; 3x ETFs and options can gap down hard, so size them smaller and trail tighter; and the "one more day" bias is deadly, so pre-define your exhaustion rules and follow them mechanically.

**Reality check.** *Exhaustion exits will save your largest winners, though you will still leave money on the table sometimes — that is the cost of protection. For the $100,000-to-$1,000,000 goal in six months, this discipline, combined with earlier scaling and trailing, is what lets a handful of 8R–20R runners carry the math, and you should still expect significant drawdowns between winners. That is a rare outcome, not a dependable plan, and this aggressive approach carries a real risk of substantial or total loss. Journal every exhaustion exit** with the signals that triggered it, the maximum unrealized gain, and the final R-multiple. Survival depends on protecting gains ruthlessly. Trade only capital you can afford to lose.*

### Blueprint Principle

Momentum creates wealth; momentum exhaustion protects it. The greatest traders are not the ones who sell at the exact top — they are the ones who recognize when institutional demand is fading and preserve the profits earned during the strongest phase of the trend.

## Timing Exits — Blow-Off Tops

One of the most profitable—and most dangerous—phases of any momentum trend is the **blow-off top**, the point where optimism becomes euphoria, buying turns emotional rather than rational, and price accelerates almost vertically in a remarkably short span. To the inexperienced it looks like the start of an even bigger rally; to the seasoned trader it usually signals that the final stage of the trend has begun. Draw a sharp line between an orderly climax run and a true blow-off: a climax is an accelerating but controlled advance; a blow-off is a violent, chaotic liquidity vortex—the last stage of an asset's life cycle before a structural collapse—where institutions quietly distribute into overwhelming public demand. This is the emergency brake of your exit system: a blow-off top lets you sell near the absolute peak of a runner and preserve the outsized gains compounding requires, while avoiding the 40–80% givebacks that destroy accounts (in aggressive compounding, protecting a 300% gain matters as much as finding the next 300% opportunity). The hallmark signs cluster together—nearly vertical price movement, unusually large daily gains, explosive volume, widespread media attention, and extreme optimism—and the mechanism underneath is brutal: the final buyers enter at the very moment the largest holders begin selling.

## Why Blow-Off Tops Occur

Every major trend eventually reaches a point where institutions already own large positions, analysts have turned overwhelmingly bullish, the media promotes the story daily, retail participation peaks, and valuations detach from fundamentals. With few new institutional buyers left, price becomes dependent on emotional buying, and once that demand weakens the reversal can be swift. The emotional arc is predictable—from "I don't believe this rally" to "this company is impressive" to "I wish I had bought earlier" to "I'll buy at any price" to "what just happened?"—and markets tend to peak when optimism is highest, which is exactly why the loudest moment is the most dangerous one to be holding.

## The Anatomy of a Blow-Off Top

No single signal confirms a blow-off; require a cluster of three or more after an extended advance, grouped into five categories. **Price action:** a parabolic trajectory break (the curve shifts from linear to near-vertical, stretching so far above the 8- and 21-day EMAs that they look flat, often 20–50%+ in 1–3 days), widening ranges with large upper wicks or shooting-star candles, an exhaustion gap (often 15%+ that opens with extreme order flow then reverses intraday into a weak close), and failed breakouts. **Volume:** climactic, record volume (often the highest of the entire move and 5–20× average) followed by an immediate contraction, plus a volume/price divergence where the highest-volume bar fails to close near its high—record volume on a failed advance is the tell. **Momentum indicators:** extreme RSI (80–95+) with bearish divergence, and a MACD histogram that spikes then collapses. **Sentiment and catalyst:** peak social euphoria ("to the moon" dominance and media saturation), an exhausted narrative, and options flow shifting from calls to puts. **Broader context:** sector leadership rotating or the broad market weakening. Healthy momentum shows orderly advances and constructive pullbacks; a blow-off shows vertical advances, emotional buying, failed rallies, and institutional distribution—one you ride, the other you harvest.

## The Blow-Off Top Checklist

Before continuing to hold a rapidly advancing stock, ask: Has price become nearly vertical? Has volume reached unusual extremes? Is the media overwhelmingly optimistic? Are retail investors aggressively chasing it? Have multiple failed breakouts appeared? Is volatility increasing? Is the stock far above its major moving averages? Has institutional accumulation slowed? Has valuation expanded dramatically? The more warning signs present, the higher the probability the trend is entering its final stage.

## The Emergency Liquidation Playbook and the 5-Minute 9-EMA Tripwire

Once a blow-off is verified on a Tier 1 position, the core rule is blunt—exit aggressively, at minimum 70–100% of what remains, and do not wait for ordinary trailing stops or further confirmation: at vertical parabolic acceleration with price gapping up 15%+ on historic volume and punching +3 sigma past VWAP, the first 5-minute candle closing below the 9-EMA triggers a 100% sweep to cash. Because the asset moves too fast for hourly or daily stops, drop to the **5-minute chart with a 9-period EMA**—allow wicks below it during minor noise, but the instant a single 5-minute candle closes below the 9-EMA the structural trend is dead, since waiting for the daily close can mean absorbing a 20–40% gap-down. Precise rules: sell 50–70% instantly on the first strong blow-off candle with a volume climax; full exit on any close below the blow-off day's low or VWAP, or on the 5-minute 9-EMA fracture; ignore "maybe it's just a pause," since blow-offs rarely resume immediately; and exit 3x ETFs and options first—they decay and reverse fastest—then the core stock. If you prefer not to flatten in one click, reduce progressively, tighten trailing stops as volatility expands, and keep only a small runner.

## Instrument Tactics and Market Regimes

Leverage magnifies a blow-off in both directions—the faster the decay, the sooner you exit. **Low-float stocks** are classic blow-off territory and can gap down 30–60% overnight, so sell hard into the volume spike. **2x/3x ETFs** are extremely sensitive—a blow-off in SOXL on AI hype often precedes a 20–40% reversal within 1–3 days as decay and redemption flows compound, so exit same-day. **Long calls** are especially vulnerable (the underlying reverses, IV contracts, theta works against you), so sell all remaining contracts into the spike where IV peaks. **Warrants** swing violently on thinner liquidity, and **blended** positions liquidate the derivative layers first. Blow-off tops cluster in late bull markets, speculative phases, and periods of widespread optimism—the more speculative the backdrop, the more violent the eventual reversal—and the historical lesson is that the company usually survives while the stock price needs time to digest excessive optimism.

**Worked example.** *A low-float biotech wins FDA approval and runs for days; you built the position through ORB, pullback, and VWAP entries, and by Day 8 it is +180% from entry. On Day 9 it spikes 35% in the first 90 minutes on 18× RVOL, with extreme social euphoria, an RSI of 92 with divergence, and heavy selling sweeps appearing. You scale the final 40% straight into the spike and fully exit by the close as it reverses below VWAP—locking in roughly 11R average across the whole position instead of watching it crash back to +60% or worse.*

## The Blow-Off Top Governance Matrix

| Operational Parameter | The Retail Casualty | The Blueprint Capital Allocator |
|---|---|---|
| **Market psychology** | Convinced a paradigm shift is underway; holds for | Recognizes a temporary, unsustainable liquidity |

| Operational Parameter | The Retail Casualty | The Blueprint Capital Allocator |
|---|---|---|
| | infinite targets. | distortion. |
| **Volume analysis** | Assumes historic volume means smart money is buying in. | Reads historic volume as terminal distribution and buyer exhaustion. |
| **Execution horizon** | Adds capital or exercises calls at the peak of the wick on FOMO. | Prepares defensively and waits for the exact structural exit trigger. |
| **Liquidation action** | Freezes in disbelief and becomes a long-term bag-holder. | Sweeps the full position to cash on the first 5-minute 9-EMA fracture. |

## The Blow-Off Top Decision Matrix

| Signal | Interpretation |
|---|---|
| **Vertical price acceleration** | Trend becoming unsustainable |
| **Record trading volume** | Potential institutional distribution |
| **Expanding daily ranges** | Rising uncertainty |
| **Media saturation** | Public participation near extremes |
| **Failed breakout attempts** | Demand weakening |
| **Heavy intraday reversals** | Selling pressure increasing |
| **Parabolic extension above MAs** | Elevated correction risk |
| **Distribution days increasing** | Institutions reducing exposure |

## Risk, Psychology, and a Reality Check

Acting on blow-off tops is what keeps your largest winners from becoming losers, and the obstacles are mostly internal: euphoria bias is the strongest enemy (pre-commit to your exit rules the moment you enter); you will occasionally exit before the absolute top (accept it as the cost of protection); false blow-offs are rare in high-conviction runners but possible in powerful secular trends (require both volume and sentiment confirmation); and 3x ETFs and options can evaporate in a single reversal session (size them knowing blow-offs are common).

**Reality check.** *Blow-off exits will save your biggest winners and free capital for the next setup, but for the $100,000-to-$1,000,000 goal you still need several 8R–20R+ preserved runners, and even with ruthless discipline you should expect violent drawdowns along the way. That is a rare outcome, not a dependable plan, and this aggressive approach carries a real risk of* *substantial or total loss. Journal every blow-off exit — the signals present, the unrealized peak, and the final R-multiple achieved — and* ***review*** *weekly. Survival depends on ruthless profit protection. Trade only capital you can afford to lose.*

### Blueprint Principle

**The strongest rallies often end with the greatest excitement. A blow-off top is not an invitation to become more aggressive — it is a warning that the balance between supply and demand may be shifting. The disciplined trader harvests profits while enthusiasm is highest and exits on objective evidence, not emotion.**

## Timing Exits — Protecting Gains

A momentum trader's first responsibility is to preserve capital; the second is to **protect profits.** There is little value in identifying exceptional stocks if the gains they generate are surrendered in avoidable reversals—every dollar preserved becomes capital for the next high-probability opportunity. This is the capstone of the exit system, the discipline that unifies scaling out, trailing stops, momentum exhaustion, and blow-off tops into an active, rule-based process that converts unrealized profit into realized capital. Without this layer, even flawless entries fail to compound $100,000 into $1,000,000, because a few large givebacks erase months of progress. So you treat every position as guilty until proven innocent: once it is in profit, the default bias shifts to defense. Momentum trading is built on asymmetry—small losses and large winners—and if you repeatedly let 40%, 50%, or 70% gains disappear you destroy the very mathematical advantage the strategy depends on. Until a gain is realized or structurally protected, it remains fully exposed to market risk; the arithmetic is unforgiving, since a 50% gain followed by a 50% loss returns you to breakeven. A trader who earns 100% and protects 70% of it compounds dramatically faster than one who lets it round-trip to zero.

### The Three Phases and the Four Pillars of the Read

Think about exits in stages: **phase one—capital recovery** (eliminate the possibility of turning a winning trade into a loser), **phase two—trend participation** (let the strongest trends run while protecting gains), and **phase three—wealth preservation** (as institutional distribution builds, shift from maximizing upside to preserving accumulated profit). Every exit decision rests on four observable factors: **price action** (while higher highs and lows stay constructive, avoid unnecessary selling), **volume** (danger arrives when heavy selling volume grows or rallies come on declining volume—volume often deteriorates before price), **institutional behavior** (protect when sponsorship fades), and **market environment** (protect more aggressively when breadth weakens or volatility spikes). The governing principle: as profit increases, risk should decrease—keep the original plan on small profit, raise stops on moderate profit, scale out on large profit, and become increasingly defensive on exceptional profit.

## The Equity Lock Mechanism

Translate that principle into mechanical rules. With high-leverage instruments—3x ETFs, short-dated options—intraday swings are violent, so you establish an unbreachable profit floor based on your peak unrealized R-multiple, the **Rule of Half-Gain Protection:**

**Emergency stop = entry price + ( peak unrealized gain ÷ 2 )**

Enter at $100.00 with a hard stop at $95.00—your 1R risk is $5.00. If the asset surges to $140.00, the trade sits on a +8R unrealized gain ($40.00); you instantly activate the lock, anchoring an automated trailing stop at $120.00 (half of the $40.00 peak profit is $20.00, added to entry), so even a catastrophic reversal stops you out at a guaranteed +4R and the trade is never allowed to decay past the halfway mark of its peak. On top of that floor, three pillars run in parallel: **Pillar 1—breakeven migration** (move the stop to entry at +1R, so risk to parent capital is zero); **Pillar 2—the two-day low lock** (for multi-day swings and leveraged-ETF positions past +3R, a hard stop two pennies below the lower of the last two completed daily lows, stepping up as the asset climbs); and **Pillar 3—the intraday VWAP shield** (for option sprints on extreme volume, once the asset has surged 15%+ and rolls over, exit on a close below the daily VWAP, which proves institutional algorithms have flipped to distribution).

## The Comprehensive Gain-Protection Framework

The equity lock is the floor; the full framework layers every exit tool into one routine, written before you enter: **tiered scaling** (30–40% at 1:2–1:3R and 25–30% at 1:4–1:6R), **mechanical trailing stops** (breakeven quickly, then the 20-EMA, swing lows, or ATR, tightening past 1:6R), **momentum-exhaustion rules** (exit the trailed portion on three or more signals), **the blow-off protocol** (sell 70–100% into a parabolic spike on climactic volume), **time and catalyst decay** (tighten or exit 8–12 days after a major catalyst if momentum stalls), and **portfolio-level protection** (if total open profit exceeds 20–30% of the account, scale everything 10–20%, and never let total portfolio risk exceed 5–8%). The hardest balance is avoiding premature exits—the resolution is objective evidence rather than emotional prediction, monitoring distribution days, failed breakouts, declining relative strength, and parabolic extension, so the more warning signs stack up, the more decisively you protect.

## The Gain-Protection Checklist

Before continuing to hold a profitable position, ideally every morning, ask: Is the primary trend still intact with higher highs continuing? Is price holding above key dynamic support (the 20-EMA or anchored VWAP)? Has institutional accumulation remained visible? Is sector leadership unchanged and the catalyst still active? Are earnings expectations still improving? Has volatility become excessive, or have multiple distribution signals appeared? Is overall portfolio exposure still within your rules? If several answers turn negative, protecting gains takes priority over chasing incremental upside.

### Instrument-Specific Protection

Tailor the method to the vehicle—the more leverage, the tighter and faster the protection. **Low-float stocks** allow wider trails early but tighten aggressively on exhaustion, since they crash hardest. **Leveraged ETFs** demand the strictest rules—tight trails (9/20-EMA or 1.5 ATR) and time-based exits, often a maximum of 3–7 strong days. **Options** are evaluated against time to expiration and IV, not just price—roll up and out or sell portions as gains accrue. **Warrants** allow more flexibility but apply the full exhaustion and blow-off rules. **Blended** positions protect the derivative layers first. Calibrate to regime—give trends room in strong bull markets, protect sooner in sideways markets, defend aggressively in bear markets—and avoid treating unrealized gains as permanent wealth, refusing to sell out of greed, ignoring distribution days, and tightening so early that you cap every runner.

**Worked example.** *A post-AI-announcement runner reaches +140% from entry; you have already scaled 65% across the 1:3R and 1:6R levels. On Day 8 it makes a marginal new high on declining RVOL, an RSI divergence appears, and social euphoria peaks. You sell the final 35% into the session for full protection — a ~8.7R average across the position, with the capital now protected and ready for the next catalyst instead of riding a 50% retrace.*

### The Institutional Wealth Cycle

Professional managers run a disciplined loop, and protecting gains is the hinge that keeps it turning—identify exceptional opportunities, build positions gradually, allow trends to mature, protect accumulated gains, reduce exposure as risk increases, and recycle capital into new opportunities. Elite traders move capital from mature trends into emerging ones rather than staying loyal to yesterday's winner, so protecting gains is not simply about selling—it is about reallocating capital efficiently. Aggressive compounding is achieved not by maximizing every individual trade but by maximizing the growth of total equity over hundreds of trades, which takes three disciplines: cut losses quickly, let winners grow, and protect gains before they disappear.

### The Gain-Protection Governance Matrix

| Operational Parameter | The Retail Spectator | The Blueprint Capital Allocator |
|---|---|---|
| **Open-equity philosophy** | Treats open profit as play money and lets big winners fade into losses. | Treats unrealized gains as real capital that must be defended. |
| **Stop adjustments** | Keeps the initial stop or removes it, hoping for a bounce in a reversal. | Uses breakeven migration and the half-gain protection floor. |
| **Technical boundary** | Relies on arbitrary mental stops and freezes when the market turns. | Automates defense with the two-day low lock and the VWAP shield. |
| **Account** | Suffers severe drawdowns, | Keeps a smooth, climbing |

| Operational Parameter | The Retail Spectator | The Blueprint Capital Allocator |
|---|---|---|
| **longevity** | destroying weeks of progress in an afternoon. | equity curve by converting gains to cash. |

## The Wealth-Preservation Matrix

| Situation | Primary Objective | Recommended Response |
|---|---|---|
| **Early trend** | Maximize participation | Allow normal volatility; avoid premature exits |
| **Healthy uptrend** | Balance growth and protection | Raise trailing stops gradually; monitor institutions |
| **Extended advance** | Preserve accumulated gains | Scale out incrementally while keeping a runner |
| **Parabolic rally** | Defend profits | Tighten trailing stops and reduce exposure |
| **Institutional distribution** | Capital preservation | Exit remaining positions; prepare to redeploy |

## Risk, Psychology, and a Reality Check

Protecting gains is mostly a battle with yourself, and the same two emotions destroy it from both sides: "let it run more" and "take everything now" both wreck compounding (define the rules before the trade and review them daily); tightening too early caps the upside that powers the whole plan (balance protection against your trend-continuation filters); and a single unprotected 3x-ETF reversal can erase weeks of gains (size these smaller from the start).

**Reality check.** *Even with perfect protection, you will still endure 35–60%+ drawdowns during losing streaks, and for the $100,000-to-$1,000,000 goal the full system — catalysts, entries, and exits — must deliver a handful of 10x+ protected runners alongside consistent 2–5R scalps. That is a rare outcome, not a dependable plan, and this aggressive approach carries a real risk of substantial or total loss. Journal every trade's protection outcome — the percentage of gains locked, the signals that triggered the exit, and the lesson. Most aggressive traders fail right here, turning winners into losers through hope. Trade only capital you can afford to lose.*

## Blueprint Principle

**Making money creates opportunity; keeping money creates wealth. The market rewards traders who protect their gains with the same discipline they use to generate them. Every dollar preserved today becomes the seed capital for tomorrow's biggest winner.**

## Timing Exits — Avoiding Round Trips

One of the most expensive mistakes in momentum trading is the **round trip**—watching a profitable trade rise substantially, refusing to protect the gain, and eventually selling at breakeven or even at a loss. You enter a high-velocity setup, watch it run +30–100% or more, then give the entire move back and exit flat—buy at $25, watch it rise to $50, then ride it back to $25, and the market's 100% gain becomes nothing. A round trip is more than a financial mistake; it is a psychological one, built from indecision, attachment, greed, and an unwillingness to accept that markets constantly change. In a compressed six-month sprint, holding a position that reverses all the way back to entry inflicts massive **opportunity cost**, freezing your capital inside a dead asset that should have been rotated into the next catalyst. This is the final line of defense for everything that came before—the objective is simple: **never allow a major winner to become a major disappointment.** Round trips rarely come from a lack of intelligence; they happen because emotion gradually replaces discipline. The amateur falls into **target myopia** (the stubborn belief that a stock must hit some arbitrary price before they're allowed to exit) and then **hope paralysis** ("I'll sell the moment it bounces back"), and institutional algorithms exploit exactly that hesitation. The emotional arc runs from "I hope this works" through "this could double again" and "it's only temporary" to "I can't believe this happened."

### The Causes — and Their Antidotes

The cure is to stop hoping and start executing mechanical boundaries that freeze profit in place. Every round trip traces back to one of a few specific failures, and each has a mechanical fix:

| Cause | Prevention Rule |
|---|---|
| **No predefined exit plan** | Write a full gain-protection plan before every entry — scaling tiers plus trails. |
| **Moving stops wider / hoping** | Never widen a stop. Only tighten or trail, mechanically. |
| **Ignoring exhaustion signals** | Full exit on 3+ exhaustion signals (RVOL drop, divergence, and so on). |
| **Holding through blow-offs** | Sell aggressively into parabolic spikes and euphoria. |
| **Catalyst decay** | Time-based exit after 8–12 days if momentum stalls. |
| **Emotional attachment** | Run the checklist every morning — no exceptions. |

### The Two Losses, and the Mathematics

A round trip creates two losses: the **financial loss** (the unrealized profit that disappears) and the **opportunity loss** (capital left trapped in a weakening position instead of redeployed)—and the second is usually the larger, because aggressive compounding depends on capital velocity, with money continually migrating toward stronger earnings, catalysts, and trends. The arithmetic is harsh: one round trip on a 5x winner can wipe out the equivalent of three clean 2R scalps, so execution, not selection, determines the result. Round trips rarely happen without notice—repeated distribution days, declining relative volume, failed breakouts, broken moving averages, and a loss of institutional sponsorship accumulate first—and the most dangerous sentence in trading is "I'll wait until it comes back." Stay loyal to the evidence, not to the position.

## The Mechanical Gain-Protection Playbook

Two simple mechanisms do most of the work: **trailing stops** (as price advances, the stop rises and downside shrinks until the market determines the exit) and **scaling out** (realize partial gains and keep a runner, so even a hard reversal leaves meaningful profit banked). Once a position moves meaningfully green, the trade flips from offense to defense-first—lock, escalate, and time-out. **1. The breakeven lock:** the instant a position reaches +1.5R to +2R, cancel the original stop and place a fresh stop at entry plus transaction costs (a ~+0.5% buffer), so the trade carries zero statistical risk to parent capital. **2. Tiered protection escalation:** at +2R to +4R scale partials and tighten to a 20-EMA trail; at +4R to +8R trail aggressively with 1.5 ATR or swing lows; beyond +8R treat the remainder as a lottery ticket. **3. The 25% maximum-retracement rule:** independently of the tiers, never let an open position give back more than 25% of its peak unrealized gain:

**Round-trip floor = peak price – [ 0.25 × (peak price – entry price) ]**

Enter at $10.00 and watch it surge to a $14.00 peak—a $4.00 open profit; the maximum allowed give-back is 25% of that, or $1.00, so the automated trailing stop sits at $13.00. **4. The time-out and catalyst clock:** if a position has reached +2R and then prints two consecutive bars that fail to make a higher high, the momentum engine has stalled—liquidate and return capital to cash—and as a hard outer bound, exit a post-catalyst trade after 8–12 trading days unless fresh positive news extends it. Every morning, run the position through an objective filter: Is the original catalyst still driving price? Is price holding above the 20-EMA or anchored VWAP? Are RVOL and ADX still supportive? Is there any bearish divergence or distribution? Is the primary trend intact and are institutions still accumulating? Is portfolio-level risk still under 5–8%? If two or more answers are "no," exit or scale heavily.

## Instrument-Specific Discipline and the Reentry Mindset

Avoiding round trips matters more as leverage rises—the same reversal that merely dents a stock can gut a derivative. **Low-float stocks** are the most prone to violent round trips: trail tightly once +4R and exit fully on any daily close below the 20-EMA. **Leveraged ETFs (TQQQ, SOXL, TNA)** carry the highest round-trip risk because daily decay erodes them even in an uptrend, so never let a 3x ETF ride more than 5–7 strong days. **Options** carry extreme theta and vega risk—even if the underlying eventually recovers, the option may not—so roll or sell on any momentum stall. **Warrants** demand the full checklist despite longer maturities, and **blended** positions exit the leveraged layers first. Much of the refusal to sell comes from fear of missing more upside; professionals dissolve it with a reframe—selling is not saying goodbye forever, since if the stock forms another breakout or catalyst you simply buy it again. The goal is to own strong trends, not permanent positions.

**Worked example.** *You enter a low-float AI name on a strong partnership catalyst and an opening-range breakout. It runs to +85% by Day 5; you scale 60% out at 1:3R and 1:6R and trail the rest. On Day 7 price stalls, RVOL collapses, an RSI divergence appears, and social hype peaks. You exit the remainder fully instead of hoping for a resumption — a +6.8R average realized, no round trip, and capital freed for the next catalyst rather than watching a 45% retrace back to breakeven.*

## The Institutional Rotation Cycle and Common Mistakes

Professional capital is rarely parked permanently in one name—it rotates through a catalyst emerging, institutions accumulating, a trend developing, momentum maturing, distribution beginning, capital rotating out, and new leaders emerging—so your job is to rotate with it. Every successful trade exists to create capital for the next one; the purpose of the win is the recycling, not the trophy. Avoid falling in love with a stock, refusing to sell because of taxes owed, ignoring repeated distribution signals, hoping a broken trend will recover, confusing a great company with a great trade, and letting ego replace discipline.

### The Round-Trip Prevention Governance Matrix

| Operational Metric | The Retail Casualty | The Blueprint Capital Allocator |
|---|---|---|
| **Open-equity vision** | Refuses to take profit, fixated on an arbitrary target or hype. | Treats open profit as liquid capital to be rotationally optimized. |
| **Reaction to reversals** | Freezes as a +4R gain falls to +2R, hoping for a return to the top. | Executes the 25% maximum-retracement stop to lock in the gain. |
| **Time-risk awareness** | Holds a flat-lining asset for weeks, tying up capital in a dead zone. | Uses the time-out rule to keep capital moving at maximum velocity. |
| **Account trajectory** | Rides a jagged equity curve that repeatedly cycles back to zero. | Builds a smoother, up-trending curve on locked-in milestones. |

### The Round-Trip Decision Matrix

| Situation | Appropriate Response |
|---|---|
| **Trend healthy, institutions accumulating** | Hold while raising trailing stops |

| Situation | Appropriate Response |
|---|---|
| **Trend healthy but becoming extended** | Scale out partially and protect gains |
| **Distribution increasing** | Tighten stops and reduce exposure |
| **Major support breaks** | Exit the remaining position |
| **New catalyst develops after exit** | Consider re-entering on a fresh setup |

## Risk, Psychology, and a Reality Check

Avoiding round trips is what separates survivors from the majority who blow up, and the enemy is almost always internal: hope bias is the deadliest (pre-commit to your rules and review them in writing before every session); missing the next leg is far better than turning a winner into a loser; and you will sometimes exit early—accept it as the insurance premium for the big runners you keep.

**Reality check.** *To compound $100,000 into $1,000,000 in six months, you would need clean, protected winners — several in the 8R–20R range — with minimal givebacks, and even with perfect rules you should expect 35–60% drawdowns between compounding phases. That is a rare outcome, not a dependable plan, and this aggressive approach carries a real risk of substantial or total loss. Journal every trade that reached +2R: did you protect the gain, did a round trip occur, and which rule was broken if one was? Review weekly. Most aggressive traders fail not on their entries but on their exits. Trade only capital you can afford to lose.*

## Blueprint Principle

**The market gives profits only temporarily; the disciplined trader claims them permanently. Never let greed, hope, or attachment turn a life-changing winner into an unforgettable regret. The greatest compounding machines are built not merely by finding exceptional trades, but by refusing to surrender exceptional gains.**

# Chapter 18
# Concentration vs Diversification

## A. Why Large Returns Require Concentration

One of the great paradoxes in investing is that the strategies designed to preserve wealth are usually different from the strategies required to create it. Diversification is a defensive, institutional protocol built to protect an already substantial fortune and to match a benchmark, and at that job it excels—but the objective of this book is the opposite: a roughly tenfold increase in capital over six months, mathematically impossible to reach by spreading $100,000 across twenty or thirty positions. Reaching it demands radical, risk-defined concentration—capital density in your highest-conviction, high-velocity catalyst setups. This chapter makes the case for the four that follow, with one non-negotiable qualifier: concentration **does not mean concentrating recklessly.** The unifying principle of this part is a single line: diversify your process, concentrate your capital—spread your analysis across catalysts, sectors, and timing methods, then commit real size to the few setups that survive the filter.

### The Mathematics of Extraordinary Returns

Large returns require meaningful exposure, and the math is unforgiving. Split $100,000 evenly across twenty positions and each holds $5,000; if one captures a legendary +100% move, the impact on the account is a mere +5%—and to double the account this way you would need all twenty independent bets to deliver home runs at once. The Blueprint instead enforces a law of capital density:

*Account Growth Velocity = Position Size % × Asset Return*

Restrict the active book to a few highly vetted, asymmetric positions and the arithmetic flips: a 30% allocation capturing a +50% structural move surges the entire ledger by +15% in a single cycle. A classic twenty-to-thirty-position book, even traded skillfully, tends to produce market-like returns that might carry $100,000 to $110,000–$130,000 over six months—nowhere near the target. Reaching 1,000% requires capturing several enormous winners, and only concentration gives a single winner enough weight to transform the account; it is no accident that many legendary aggressive traders ran highly concentrated books, often just three to eight positions, during their best runs. Diversification delivers real benefits—lower volatility, smoother returns, reduced company-specific risk—but the same spreading that smooths the ride caps the impact of exceptional winners and, beyond a point, introduces hidden drags: reduced conviction, diluted returns, slower decisions, and less research per name. Diversification does not eliminate risk—it merely spreads it—and the decisive variable is not the number of holdings but the quality of the risk management around them. The individual holds a genuine structural edge here: large funds carry hundreds of positions because regulation, liquidity, and sheer asset size force them to, while a smaller trader can concentrate into a handful of best ideas without moving the market.

## Concentration Is Not Recklessness

Many people confuse concentration with gambling, but the difference is preparation: reckless concentration means acting without research, ignoring risk, relying on hope, and refusing to exit a loser; disciplined concentration means waiting for exceptional setups, demanding multiple independent confirmations, defining risk before entry, and exiting quickly when proven wrong. The counterintuitive heart of the method is that concentrating capital does not widen your risk—it tightens it, demanding an upgrade in risk infrastructure, not a relaxation of it.

> **CONCENTRATE THE SIZE — FENCE THE RISK THE CAPITAL BASE** — e.g. $100,000 ↓ **2–3 CORE POSITIONS** — a large allocation per asset (about a third each) ↓ **THE 1R RISK FENCE** Stop distance keeps total portfolio risk ≤ 1–2% of equity Example — $33,333 allocation, stop set so the max planned loss is ~$1,000

## The Focus Filter and the Tiered Portfolio

By holding only two or three names you gain extreme situational awareness—you watch every print on the tape, every block order on the Level 2 matrix, and every shift in the VWAP bands of your targeted vehicle. When you commit, say, $33,333 to a 3x-ETF trend continuation, the stop is fenced close to the entry so absolute account risk stays at 1–2% (one to two risk units), and the tighter the structural floor (a 3% pullback line, a 5-minute opening-range low), the larger the nominal position you can carry for the same fixed risk. One honest caveat: that 1R is the *planned* loss if the stop fills near its level—an overnight gap or halt can exceed it, which is exactly why nominal exposure caps exist alongside the formula. Concentration lives inside a fixed structure: hold three to five Tier 1 core positions carrying 60–80% of capital, each with full multi-layer confluence, plus two to four smaller Tier 2 developing positions (10–20%) and a deliberate 10–30% cash buffer. Four hard limits keep the aggression survivable—never risk more than 1–2% of capital on a single trade, hold no more than 5–8% of the portfolio at risk at once, never exceed 25–40% in a single sector or theme, and never run more than two or three correlated names—and you pyramid only with profits, never into losers.

## Concentration Is Earned: The Quality Filter and the Cycle

Capital should not be allocated equally—position size should reflect conviction, and conviction must be earned through the alignment of several independent factors: a powerful catalyst, accelerating earnings, institutional accumulation, sector leadership, elevated relative volume, technical confirmation, and a supportive market. Never concentrate simply because a stock is popular, social media is excited, someone recommended it, or it doubled last week. The safest way to build a concentrated position is to scale into it—initiate a small starter, add after confirmation, and increase exposure only as the thesis strengthens—which is why concentration occurs after confirmation, not before it: screen many candidates, identify a few exceptional ones, research deeply, wait for technical confirmation, initiate, increase only if the market validates the thesis, protect gains aggressively, and rotate into the next leader.

## Instruments and a Worked Example

Conviction can be expressed across the toolkit, with discipline scaled to the leverage: **low-float stocks** are the cleanest expression of momentum and the highest concentration reward (a single 10x runner can move the whole book); **2x/3x ETFs** suit a concentrated sector bet (20–30% in SOXL during AI leadership) but are trailed tightly because of decay; **options** allow asymmetric concentration through defined-risk spreads; **warrants** are a longer-dated vehicle for multi-week catalysts; and a **blended** position pairs a core stock or ETF with an options overlay for extra leverage without raising base risk. Market conditions should always govern how aggressively you concentrate—higher concentration in strong bull markets, reduced concentration in sideways markets where false breakouts multiply, and capital preservation as the priority in bear markets. Large positions amplify emotion, so successful concentrated traders cultivate the patience and detachment to watch a large position swing without overriding the plan.

**Example.** You identify a low-float biotech with an imminent FDA decision and strong Phase III data – a Tier 1 setup. You take 25–35% effective exposure at roughly 1.5% portfolio risk, enter on an opening-range or VWAP pullback, then scale out partials and trail the rest. The name delivers +180% in nine days, and because only two or three other concentrated names are running alongside it, that single focused winner lifts the whole portfolio more than 40%.

## The Concentration Checklist

Before establishing a high-conviction position, confirm that a major catalyst is present, earnings are accelerating, institutional accumulation is evident, relative volume is above historical norms, the sector is leading, liquidity is strong, the market environment is healthy, the technical pattern confirms, and a clearly defined exit plan already exists—every concentrated position should satisfy multiple independent criteria, not just one. The two approaches are not right and wrong; they are matched to different objectives, and for a six-month compounding campaign the concentration column is the one that fits:

| Attribute | Diversification | Concentration |
|---|---|---|
| Primary goal | Preserve wealth | Build wealth rapidly |
| Number of positions | Many | Few, carefully selected |
| Position size | Small | Larger, conviction-weighted |
| Return potential | Moderate (diluted) | High (full capture of big runners) |
| Volatility / drawdown | Smoother, frequent small losses | Deeper, but recoverable on winners |
| Capital velocity | Slow compounding | Maximum velocity |
| Risk management | Important | Essential |

| Attribute | Diversification | Concentration |
|---|---|---|
| Best for | Long-term preservation | Aggressive, time-bound compounding |

## The Diversification Governance Matrix

| Operational Parameter | The Retail Spectator | The Blueprint Capital Allocator |
|---|---|---|
| Allocation Density | Spreads capital thin across 15–30 names out of fear, tracking random tickers. | Concentrates into 2–3 elite, high-velocity setups at a time. |
| Edge Exploitation | Dilutes the best ideas by mixing them with mediocre secondary plays. | Maximizes the financial reward of its single sharpest edge. |
| Risk Setup | Uses wide, loose mental stops because no position feels large enough to matter. | Applies a strict 1R structural fence and watches it intently. |
| Capital Velocity | Stagnates in a web of offsetting gains and losses, mimicking an index fund. | Recycles cash from win to win, compounding at high velocity. |

## Risk, Discipline, and Common Mistakes

Concentration amplifies losses as readily as gains, so the discipline around it is the price of admission: hold to 1–2% risk per trade and no more than 5–8% of the portfolio at risk at any time; after a big winner, do not increase size recklessly; the market always has dozens of movers, so your edge is waiting for the highest-conviction ones; and don't concentrate in low-quality companies or on social-media excitement, average down into losers, or ignore the broader market. Concentration is required to pursue 1,000% in six months, but it is psychologically and financially brutal—expect 40–70% drawdowns between winners—and most aggressive traders blow up precisely here, so survival depends on mechanical rules, journaling each position's conviction score, and the willingness to sit in cash when nothing qualifies.

## Blueprint Principle

Diversification protects established wealth. Concentration creates exceptional wealth – but only when supported by exceptional discipline. Concentrate only where the evidence is strongest, manage risk relentlessly, and never confuse conviction with certainty.

# B. Controlled Concentration

Reaching $1,000,000 from a $100,000 base in 180 days requires meaningful exposure to exceptional opportunities—broad diversification across forty names simply cannot compound that fast—but the retail public assumes concentrating into two or three positions means reckless, unhedged gambling, which leads straight to ruin. The Blueprint practices something different: **controlled concentration**, the disciplined art of holding extreme capital density in your highest-conviction ideas while keeping total portfolio risk standardized and tightly restricted. The world's best traders allocate large amounts of capital only when the probability of success is exceptionally high and the downside is clearly defined. One line frames the whole chapter: concentration without control is gambling, and control without concentration is slow death. Reckless concentration is emotional, impulsive, poorly researched, and lacking any exit; controlled concentration is evidence-based, catalyst-driven, institutionally confirmed, technically validated, and protected by predefined risk management. The single assumption that separates them is humility—every thesis can be wrong, so every concentrated position must carry a predefined plan for protecting capital before it is ever entered.

## The Core Mechanism: Risk Is Fixed, Size Is Variable

The mathematical law of the Blueprint is that portfolio risk is decoupled from position size. You fix your risk per trade—one risk unit, or 1R—at 1–2% of total equity, which on a $100,000 account locks 1R at roughly $1,000, and you never vary that dollar risk. Instead you vary the number of shares, calculated from the technical distance to your stop:

*Position Size (shares) = 1R Dollars ÷ (Entry Price – Stop-Loss Price)*

Because the stop distance sits in the denominator, a tighter stop produces a larger nominal position for the same fixed risk. Two setups make the point:

| Setup | Entry / Stop | Risk/Share | Shares (1R = $1,000) | Nominal | Real Risk |
|---|---|---|---|---|---|
| Low-float, tight stop | $10.00 / $9.80 | $0.20 | 5,000 | $50,000 | $1,000 |
| 3x ETF (SOXL), wide stop | $40.00 / $37.00 | $3.00 | 333 | $13,320 | $1,000 |

The tight-stop setup concentrates 50% of the portfolio into a single asset, yet the loss if the stop is hit is the same $1,000 as the far smaller ETF position—risk, not enthusiasm, determines size. One honest caveat the math hides: a stop caps the loss at 1R only if it fills near the stop price; an overnight gap, a trading halt, or a fast, illiquid market can blow straight through it, and that gap risk is the entire reason the nominal exposure caps exist. Capital follows confirmation, not prediction—exposure rises only as evidence accumulates, a probability pyramid from a small starter up to the maximum planned allocation once the trend, the institutions, and the market all confirm. Before any position reaches full size it should satisfy eight independent requirements: a powerful catalyst, institutional accumulation, earnings momentum, technical confirmation, sector leadership, a supportive market environment, real liquidity, and a defined exit strategy set before entry. You never fire the full allocation at once—take the first tranche (say a third of planned size) and add nothing further until that trade moves into profit and its trailing stop has migrated to breakeven; once the position is de-risked and its open risk has returned to zero, you are cleared to deploy the next concentrated allocation.

## The Hard Limits: A Portfolio Risk Framework

Controlled concentration lives inside a fixed structure of tiers with hard ceilings: **Tier 1 (high-conviction core)**—three to six positions holding 60–85% of capital, each with full multi-layer confluence including RVOL above 4x; **Tier 2 (developing)**—two to four smaller positions (10–25%); and **cash/dry powder** of 10–30%. Four hard limits cap the damage any single mistake can do: risk no more than 0.75–1.5% of the portfolio on one trade; cap exposure per name at roughly 15–25% (toward the higher end only for liquid 3x ETFs); cap any single sector or theme at 30–40%; and never run more than two or three names on the same catalyst. This exposure ceiling matters as much as the sizing formula, because even when the math on a razor-tight stop would permit an enormous nominal position, the nominal cap overrides it so one black-swan gap cannot inflict fatal damage. Dynamic rebalancing keeps the book honest—a morning review downgrades or exits any name that has lost its confluence, freed capital after a winner redeploys only into fresh Tier 1 setups, and a loser is cut to zero immediately. There is no revenge trading.

## The Correlation Audit: Diversify by Risk Driver, Not Ticker

Many traders believe they hold five positions when they actually hold the same trade five times—a semiconductor manufacturer, a semiconductor-equipment company, a semiconductor ETF, a leveraged semiconductor ETF, and semiconductor call options look diversified, but every one depends on a single industry trend. True controlled concentration evaluates correlation, not the count of holdings: hold a handful of independent opportunities—one AI-infrastructure leader, one semiconductor-equipment name, one biotech catalyst, one cybersecurity breakout—each driven by a different catalyst. If you already carry a max-size position in a 3x semiconductor ETF, you do not also open a concentrated individual semiconductor stock, and you track beta and news overlap daily, since two "unrelated" biotechs sitting on FDA dates the same week can still move together.

## Controlled Concentration by Instrument and Regime

The required discipline rises with the leverage of the vehicle: **low-float/high-beta stocks** carry the highest reward and risk, capped near 15–20% per name; **2x/3x leveraged ETFs** are the best controlled-leverage vehicle (20–30% to SOXL or TQQQ during strong leadership, trailed tightly); **options** are ideal—a defined-risk spread can put only ~1% of capital at risk while controlling 10–20% notional; **warrants** offer longer-dated controlled leverage; and the recommended **blended** structure pairs a core stock or 3x ETF with a smaller options overlay. The same playbook is dialed up in strong bull markets, reduced modestly in transitional markets, and made significantly more conservative in bear markets, deployed only when an exceptional countertrend opportunity genuinely earns it.

A Worked Example

Suppose the portfolio has compounded to $150,000 and you identify a Tier 1 low-float AI-infrastructure name with a major partnership, an earnings beat, and sector leadership. You cap risk at $1,500–$2,250 (1–1.5%) and build 22% effective exposure — about $33,000 notional — structured as a 12% core stock position, an 8% SOXL sector amplifier, and a 2% out-of-the-money call kicker. The stop sits a tight 6–8% below entry, so full risk is about 1.2% of the portfolio.

The name runs +140% over eight days. You scale out in tiers, trail the remainder, and exit on exhaustion — and that single controlled bet lifts the whole portfolio roughly 28%. Throughout, you hold only four other names, each under 20% and each driven by a different catalyst. That is the entire method in miniature: large enough to matter, capped tightly enough to survive being wrong.

## The Controlled Concentration Checklist

Before increasing any position, confirm the major catalyst remains active, earnings momentum continues, relative volume remains elevated, institutions continue accumulating, sector leadership remains intact, the broader market supports the trade, risk is clearly defined with an exit strategy already in place, and portfolio correlation remains acceptable.

## The Controlled Concentration Governance Matrix

| Operational Parameter | The Retail Spectator | The Blueprint Capital Allocator |
|---|---|---|
| Sizing Determination | Sizes on greed or a gut feeling about how high the stock will go. | Calculates size from a volatility-adjusted formula keyed to the stop distance. |
| Risk Per Trade | Swings wildly — 2% on one play, 20% on the next contract. | Holds a fixed risk unit of 1–2% of equity on every trade. |
| Position Building | Goes all-in on unconfirmed breakouts at the open. | Scales in, adding only after existing positions are locked at breakeven. |
| Correlation Discipline | Owns three tech names and a tech ETF — the same trade four times. | Runs a correlation audit, keeping active risk drivers independent. |
| Exit and Preservation | No predefined exit; capital preservation is an afterthought. | Defines the exit before entry; preservation ranks equal to growth. |

## Risk, Discipline, and Psychology

Even executed perfectly, this style is volatile and emotionally demanding, and the controls only work if you refuse to remove them after a winning streak:

expect 40–65% portfolio drawdowns during cold periods and set a hard de-risking trigger (for example, cut all sizing in half after a 25% drawdown); track beta and news overlap daily, since positions that look independent can converge in a sector flush; the most dangerous moment is right after a big win, so enforce a mandatory cash buffer and a conviction score (rate each setup 1–10 and trade only 8+); and don't confuse conviction with certainty, build maximum size before confirmation, or average down into losers. Controlled concentration is the only realistic path to 1,000% in six months, but most who attempt it blow up—almost always by stripping out the controls after a few big wins.

### Blueprint Principle

Concentration creates opportunity. Control preserves it. The greatest traders do not bet recklessly – they commit aggressively only after the market validates the thesis, and they protect capital with the same discipline they use to pursue returns.

## Correlation Risk

You can follow the rules of controlled concentration to the letter—limiting your book to a handful of names, sizing each by its stop, capping every position—and still be carrying one enormous, hidden bet, because of **correlation risk**, the silent multiplier that turns a "diversified" concentrated portfolio into a single leveraged position that moves in lockstep. A book of ten holdings can behave like one if every name responds to the same catalyst, industry trend, or macro event. Correlation measures the degree to which positions move together: high positive correlation means they fall together, the more dangerous direction. More positions do not automatically mean more diversification—a portfolio of a leading AI semiconductor company, a second manufacturer, an equipment maker, a semiconductor ETF, a 2x semiconductor ETF, and AI-hardware calls shows six securities but all depend on the same industry cycle. Allocating a third to an AI semiconductor stock, a third to a 3x technology ETF such as TQQQ, and a third to a high-gamma software-mega-cap call is not a three-pronged attack—it is a single 100% exposure to one factor: technology and growth beta. The objective is not to own many securities; it is to own independent sources of opportunity while concentrating capital in the highest-conviction ideas.

### Why Correlation Spikes Exactly When It Hurts

The cruelest feature of correlation is that it rises precisely when you need it lowest. During panics, institutions reduce exposure wholesale rather than evaluating individual companies, liquidity matters more than fundamentals, and a single macro catalyst—a hot CPI print, a hawkish Fed remark—sends cross-asset algorithms sweeping sell orders across the entire growth cluster at once, turning an intended three-unit risk into a portfolio fracture. This is the most important caveat in the chapter: in a genuine liquidity crisis, even assets that are normally uncorrelated can fall together—**decoupling reduces correlated drawdowns; it does not eliminate them**, and no "uncorrelated" slot should be mistaken for a guaranteed hedge. Correlation comes from overlapping sources to track daily—sector (same industry), macroeconomic (rates, inflation, central-bank policy), theme (AI, quantum, EVs), catalyst type (clustered FDA dates or earnings weeks), and ETF/instrument overlap (a stock, its sector ETF, and a leveraged version buy the same companies several times). Leverage amplifies every one, running from common stock (moderate) through sector ETFs, 2x, and 3x, out to options and warrants—so when several leveraged instruments all depend on the same theme, portfolio risk rises far faster than the number of positions suggests.

## Think in Risk Drivers, Not Tickers: The Tri-Sector Decoupling Matrix

Professional managers evaluate a book by risk factor, not security count, asking not "how many stocks do I own?" but "what economic forces drive my portfolio?"—AI spending, energy prices, healthcare regulation, interest rates. The strongest aggressive portfolios hold positions driven by genuinely unrelated catalysts, so each succeeds or fails for its own reason; four positions driven by AI infrastructure, biotech innovation, defense modernization, and precious metals can offer more balanced opportunity than ten different technology stocks. To hold maximum capital density without exposing the whole ledger to one factor, the Blueprint enforces zero overlapping beta by splitting the concentrated active slots into distinct vectors:

> ZERO OVERLAPPING BETA — THREE INDEPENDENT SLOTS CONCENTRATED CAPITAL CORE — split across independent drivers ↓ SLOT 1 — MICRO BETA (idiosyncratic alpha) Single-stock momentum on an internal catalyst, high RS vs. the S&P 500 SLOT 2 — MACRO / COMMODITY (decoupled driver) A non-equity or defensive vehicle — gold, energy, or rates exposure SLOT 3 — STRUCTURAL / VOLATILITY (contract mechanics) Warrants or defined-risk option structures around a binary event

**Slot 1 (micro beta)** is a high-velocity single-stock momentum setup driven by an internal corporate catalyst with strong relative strength against the index. **Slot 2 (macro/commodity)** looks somewhere other than equity-growth beta—gold, energy, or rates—with the aim of a different driver, not a hedge, since gold, energy, and Treasuries are not reliable negative correlations (in 2022, equities and bonds fell together), so treat it as factor diversification, not insurance. **Slot 3 (structural/volatility)** is driven by contract mechanics and localized liquidity—a warrant or defined-risk option structure around a binary release—largely independent of whether funds are buying or selling growth that afternoon. Translate the philosophy into hard numbers: cap correlated exposure at 25–35% of the portfolio in any single theme, hold no more than two or three names with greater than roughly 0.7 correlation, and run a daily review checking beta to the index and to sector leaders such as NVDA for AI or IBB for biotech. Use this as a working reference:

| Correlation Level | Allowed Portfolio % | Action Required |
|---|---|---|
| Low — different sectors and catalysts | Up to ~80% total | Full sizing acceptable |

| Correlation Level | Allowed Portfolio % | Action Required |
|---|---|---|
| Medium — same sector, different catalysts | Max ~30–35% | Tighter stops and smaller size |
| High — >0.7 beta or same event cluster | Max ~15–20% | Reduce immediately or avoid |
| Extreme — all tied to one macro event | Under ~10% | Stay cash-heavy or hedge |

Back the caps with hard circuit breakers: if three or more positions move more than 5% in the same direction intraday with no individual catalyst, cut total exposure by 30–50%; and after any correlated drawdown greater than about 15% over one to three days, drop to cash or single-digit risk until genuinely uncorrelated setups appear.

## Instrument-Specific Correlation Management and a Worked Example

Each instrument carries its own correlation trap: **stocks** hold the highest hidden correlation risk because low-float runners rotate together; **2x/3x ETFs** are extremely correlated to their underlying, so never hold TQQQ, SOXL, and FNGU at full size at once; **options** see correlation explode through gamma; **warrants** mask correlation until the theme breaks; and **blended** positions should offset a 3x ETF with a single-stock or macro-hedge leg rather than stacking another correlated one. Strong bull markets hide correlation risk because everything rises at once, while bear markets expose it—entire sectors decline together, leverage magnifies losses, and options bleed through falling prices, collapsing IV, and time decay—and correlation itself is dynamic, so reassess exposure continuously and rotate capital alongside institutional money.

A Worked Example

Suppose you hold four Tier 1 setups: a low-float AI software name on a strong partnership, a semiconductor runner on AI-chip news, a biotech with a PDUFA date, and a macro play in TQQQ on dovish expectations. The problem is hidden in plain sight — the AI software, the semiconductor runner, and TQQQ are all heavily correlated to the same NVDA-and-semiconductor theme, so what looks like four bets is closer to two.

The controlled fix is mechanical: cap total AI and semiconductor exposure at roughly 32%, cut size on the second correlated name, and add an uncorrelated energy or healthcare position in its place. Now, if semiconductors gap down 8% on news, the portfolio falls around 12% instead of 35% or more. Same conviction, same concentration — a fraction of the cluster risk.

## The Correlation Checklist

Before adding any new position, ask whether it depends on the same catalyst as an existing position, is in the same sector, responds to identical macroeconomic factors, would likely decline together with the others, adds genuine opportunity rather than merely increasing the number of holdings, and improves the portfolio's independent risk drivers—evaluating risk drivers, not ticker symbols, and analyzing the portfolio as one integrated system.

## The Correlation Risk Governance Matrix

| Operational Parameter | The Retail Spectator | The Blueprint Capital Allocator |
|---|---|---|
| Diversity Illusion | Owns three tech names and feels safe because the tickers differ. | Runs a decoupling check with no factor overlap across active slots. |
| Algorithmic Awareness | Blind to cross-asset correlation flows and macro-basket selling. | Tracks cluster betas and watches index correlation trends intraday. |
| Catalyst Protection | Exposes the whole book to a single macro event (an FOMC or CPI print). | Keeps active positions tied to independent, non-overlapping catalysts. |
| Drawdown Architecture | Suffers cascading stop slippage as correlated names collapse at once. | Sizes so a flush in one driver leaves the other drivers standing. |

## Risk, Discipline, and Psychology

Correlation risk is the silent killer of aggressive compounding, and it defeats traders psychologically as often as mathematically: "I have five different stocks" feels safe right up until all five sell off together; after winners, traders pile more into the hot theme, so hard percentage caps are the only reliable defense; in extreme periods a small inverse position (SQQQ or puts) or simply more cash can act as a temporary shock absorber, but don't turn an aggressive book into a permanent hedge fund; and don't confuse holdings with diversification or assume correlations stay constant. Many traders who post 200–300% in a hot streak give it all back in a single correlated crash, so reaching \$100,000 to \$1,000,000 means surviving several 40–60% drawdowns by logging a correlation score for every position and backtesting against past events such as the 2022 bear market and the 2023 AI rotation.

## Blueprint Principle

Diversification is measured by independent risk drivers — not by the number of positions. Ten highly correlated investments are often riskier than four chosen for different catalysts. Concentrate intentionally, monitor correlation continuously, and make every position earn its place by contributing unique opportunity rather than redundant risk.

# Rotational Concentration

To scale a \$100,000 base toward \$1,000,000 in a 180-day sprint, the portfolio cannot afford a single day of dead weight. Traditional concentration locks capital into a few positions and quietly bakes in opportunity cost—if a concentrated position drifts into an orderly three-week consolidation, that capital is frozen and the compounding curve flatlines while the clock keeps running. **Rotational concentration** solves the stagnation: you concentrate aggressively into only a handful of positions at any moment, but you ruthlessly rotate capital out of assets that have exhausted their near-term momentum and into the next validated catalyst. The concentration remains; the holdings change—you remain permanently concentrated in where institutional money is flowing today, pairing the velocity of concentration with a built-in survival mechanism against correlation crashes and sector exhaustion. It sits between two failure modes: static concentration risks a catastrophic drawdown when its single theme collapses, and broad diversification dilutes returns below the velocity a 1,000% campaign requires. The governing principle: concentrate in what is working right now, and rotate ruthlessly when momentum shifts.

## The Velocity Multiplier: Why Time Efficiency Compounds

Compounding is not merely a function of win rate or reward-to-risk—it is a function of time efficiency. Consider two traders, each working a $50,000 sleeve and each earning a precise +20% per trade. The static trader takes a position that surges +20% in four days, then holds it twelve more as it chops sideways: sixteen days elapsed, one +20% cycle, a $10,000 gain. The rotational trader harvests the +20% on day four and immediately redeploys into the next breakout, completing four full cycles in the same sixteen days:

*Final Capital = Initial Capital × (1 + Return Rate) ^ Number of Cycles*

*$50,000 × (1 + 0.20) ^ 4 = $103,680*

Four +20% cycles turn a single-cycle $10,000 gain into a $53,680 gain over the same window. One honest caveat: this clean curve assumes four consecutive winners with no losers, no slippage, and perfect timing—which will not happen in practice—so the realized curve is far bumpier, and only disciplined, high-quality rotations earn that edge. Underneath the arithmetic is a simple law: every dollar should either be compounding in a high-conviction opportunity or be available in cash for the next one. Leadership turns over quickly in a six-month sprint—AI and semiconductors one week, biotech and FDA the next, macro-driven financials or energy after that—and the rotational trader follows the flow rather than defending an old position. Most rotations follow a recognizable sequence (a new catalyst appears and institutions buy, relative strength improves, momentum accelerates, valuation stretches, distribution begins, capital rotates to the next leadership), so each week you ask the only question that matters: where is institutional money flowing now? Rotation expresses itself on several axes at once—sector (capital leaves a weakening group for a strengthening one), theme (AI to cybersecurity to robotics to quantum), earnings (toward accelerating revenue and raised guidance), and catalyst (industrials in a recovery, growth on rate declines, semiconductors on AI expansion).

## The Kinetic Rotation Protocol

You do not guess when to rotate; the Blueprint pulls capital out of a position the moment its efficiency decays, using an ironclad sequence:

> **THE KINETIC ROTATION PROTOCOL ACTIVE CONCENTRATED POSITION** → captures a high-angle catalyst move (+3R or more) ↓ **THE ROTATION SIGNAL** • Trigger A — a climax/blow-off exhaustion print, or a 9-EMA fracture • Trigger B — stalls flat for more than 48 hours (efficiency drag) ↓ **LIQUID EXTRACTION** Close to cash → redeploy into the next Day-1 breakout

**The apex efficiency exit:** when a concentrated position reaches +3R or more and prints a terminal exit signal—an intraday breach of the 15-minute low, or a 5-minute 9-EMA fracture—close it completely and harvest the cash rather than hoping for a second leg. **The 48-hour stagnation rule:** if a position fails to register a fresh higher high within 48 hours (two full sessions), it is classified as efficiency drag and liquidated at the market, even on a minor profit. **The rotation triggers:** act within a day or two when the name's RVOL and relative-strength ranking drop out of the top sectors, catalyst momentum fades, a higher-conviction setup emerges, or the current theme draws down more than 12–15% without recovery. **The catalyst hand-off:** scale out of weakening names using your established exit rules and immediately redeploy the freed capital, profits included, into a Day-1 catalyst breakout—capital is never left idle. Rotational concentration runs inside a fixed structure: hold three to five Tier 1 positions carrying 60–80% of capital, cap any single theme at no more than 35% even during a strong rotation, and force a rotation review after a maximum hold of roughly 8–20 trading days unless fresh catalysts extend it. The routine is daily and weekly—pre-market, rank sectors and themes by 5- and 10-day relative strength alongside upcoming catalysts, identify the strongest rotations, and execute exits and new entries with fresh, stop-based sizing.

## Instrument Tactics in Rotation, and a Worked Example

Each instrument plays a distinct role as capital migrates: **stocks** are best for targeted rotation into a specific catalyst, rotated out quickly when the sympathy move fades; **2x/3x ETFs** are the primary rotation vehicle (into SOXL during semiconductor leadership, then across to TNA for small caps or LABU for biotech) with the liquidity for low-slippage rotation; **options** suit short-term rotational conviction (buy calls in the new leader while rolling out of the old); **warrants** fit longer rotations of three to six weeks; and **blended** positions pair a core 3x ETF for the broad theme with single-stock options inside it. Never rotate because a commentator recommends it or social media is excited—rotate only when objective evidence improves—and accept the part traders dislike: rotation requires selling, because selling yesterday's leader is what creates the capital to seize the next opportunity. Pace the rotation to the tape: gradual in early bull markets, more patient in strong bull markets, accelerating in late bull markets, and shorter and less reliable in bear markets, where you raise cash and demand exceptional evidence.

In weeks one and two, you concentrate about 30% of the book in the AI/semiconductor complex – a SOXL position plus a low-float AI stock – after major announcements, and the leg contributes a +65% portfolio impact. Then the rotation signal arrives: the AI names show an RVOL collapse and RSI divergence, sector relative strength slips to fourth, and a biotech cluster with multiple PDUFA dates begins heating up.

You act on it. Scaling out of the AI positions with your exhaustion and blow-off rules, you rotate roughly 28% of capital into a biotech 2x ETF plus two low-float names with strong Phase III data. Over the next ten days, the biotech leg delivers another +55%. The compounding continues — without the major drawdown that comes from holding the old theme too long. That is the method in miniature: ride a wave at full force, harvest it near the apex, and redeploy into the next one before the old narrative rolls over.

## The Rotational Concentration Checklist

Before rotating capital, confirm that relative strength is improving in the new opportunity, earnings are accelerating, institutional accumulation is increasing, sector leadership has genuinely changed, the catalyst is becoming stronger rather than weaker, the previous leader has begun distributing, the broader market is supportive, and the new opportunity offers a superior risk-reward profile—rotate because probabilities improve, not merely because prices have already moved.

## The Rotation Reference Matrix

| Stage | Institutional Behavior | Trader Response |
|---|---|---|
| Emerging catalyst | Early accumulation | Build an initial position after confirmation |
| Strengthening trend | Increasing institutional buying | Scale up concentration with discipline |
| Mature leadership | Momentum still healthy | Hold while protecting gains with trailing stops |
| Distribution | Institutions reducing exposure | Scale out and tighten risk controls |
| Leadership shifts elsewhere | Capital rotates to stronger names | Redeploy into the new market leader |

## The Rotational Concentration Governance Matrix

| Operational Parameter | The Retail Spectator | The Blueprint Capital Allocator |
|---|---|---|
| Stagnation Tolerance | Marries a stock and holds for weeks as it chops, out of belief in the company. | Holds little tolerance for dead time — liquidates stalled names within 48 hours. |
| Capital Velocity | Completes a couple of portfolio turns in six months, limiting compound frequency. | Recycles capital through many high-quality rotations, raising the compounding exponent. |
| Profit | Refuses to sell a vertical spike | Converts vertical surges to |

| Operational Parameter | The Retail Spectator | The Blueprint Capital Allocator |
|---|---|---|
| Realization | and lets the asset round-trip with capital trapped. | cash near the apex of technical momentum. |
| View of Cash | Treats cash as an awkward waiting room and feels compelled to stay fully invested. | Treats cash as tactical energy, waiting for the next high-probability strike. |

### Risk, Discipline, and Psychology

Rotation is an edge only when disciplined; done carelessly it becomes expensive churn. Exiting too late or entering a new theme too early destroys the edge, so require strict multi-layer confirmation; frequent rotation raises transaction costs and taxes, so limit it to high-quality signals; attachment to your original theme, FOMO when you rotate out just before a dead-cat bounce, and over-rotation are the three psychological traps that do the most damage; and every new concentration still needs a defined entry, a predetermined exit, stop-based sizing, a trailing stop, and a scaling plan. Rotational concentration is the realistic sweet spot for pursuing 1,000% in six months—multiple compounding cycles while avoiding the blowups of static bets—but expect 40–65% overall drawdowns, with each individual rotation ideally capped at 15–25% of damage.

### Blueprint Principle

Concentrate where institutional money is flowing today — not where it flowed yesterday. Great momentum traders do not marry stocks, sectors, or themes. They marry opportunity, turning concentration from a static structure into a dynamic compounding engine.

## The Danger of Over-Diversification

Diversification is one of the most widely accepted principles in all of investing, and for preserving wealth it is genuinely prudent—but the objective of this book is to identify exceptional opportunities, allocate capital intelligently, and compound at an accelerated rate, and for that mission excessive diversification becomes one of the greatest obstacles to performance. Reclassify it for what it is in an aggressive campaign: **diworsification.** Spreading a finite $100,000 base across fifteen, twenty, or thirty positions does not eliminate risk—it converts active, managed, technical risk into structural mediocrity, spreading capital so thinly that even an extraordinary winner cannot move the needle. Over-diversification occurs when you own so many positions that no individual investment can materially influence performance: the book stops being a focused collection of your highest-conviction ideas and becomes an average of many small ones—and an average of the market, held with single-stock effort and higher fees, is just an expensive index fund.

## The Mathematics of Dilution

Performance depends on two things: the quality of your ideas and the capital allocated to them. The total return of the account is simply the sum of each position's weight times its return:

*Account Return = Σ ( **Position** Weight$_i$ × Asset **Return$_i$ )*

Split $100,000 evenly across twenty positions and each gets $5,000—5% of the book—so a spectacular +50% run is a raw gain of $2,500 that lands as a meaningless +2.5%, and if two other diluted names slip a routine −15% each, those small losses entirely erase the upside of your home-run trade. Over-diversification guarantees winners are too small to matter while losers quietly eat away at capital. Turning $100,000 into $1,000,000 realistically requires several 300–1,000% trades or a string of 5–15x runners captured in a compressed window, and a 10x winner inside a twenty-five-name portfolio sized equally contributes only a fraction of one turn. Diversification reduces company-specific risk, but only up to a point: past roughly a half-dozen well-chosen positions, each additional holding removes less and less risk while continuing to dilute returns, and complexity rises while monitoring degrades. There is also false comfort in numbers—in a real decline, technology, growth, small caps, and leveraged products tend to fall together, so a long list of correlated names offers only the illusion of safety. As the old line goes, diversification protects against ignorance, and over-diversification protects against success.

## The Three Structural Dangers of Portfolio Clutter

Three precise mechanisms explain why owning too many names destroys aggressive scaling. **Closet indexing:** buy fifteen growth stocks, a few 3x technology ETFs, and a basket of options, and because index funds and algorithms move whole sectors in block-baskets, you have unknowingly correlated your entire book to the broad index—taking single-stock risk and paying higher fees to earn what an index fund earns for free. **Cognitive slippage:** no one can track intraday order flow, Level 2 liquidity, and sudden macro headlines across twenty tickers at once, so a bloated watchlist leads to missed exit triggers, stops never migrated to breakeven, and execution paralysis. **Mediocrity dilution:** true anomalies are rare, often just one to three in the entire market on a given day, so forcing a portfolio to hold fifteen or twenty names mathematically requires lowering your standards, blending your top three convictions with seventeen secondary setups to fill the slots. These map cleanly to their effect on an aggressive campaign:

| Danger | Effect on Aggressive Trading | Impact on the 1,000% Goal |
|---|---|---|
| Return dilution | Best ideas get tiny allocations | Turns 8x runners into 0.3x portfolio moves |
| Diworsification | You accumulate mediocre, laggard names | The book behaves like a slow index fund |

| Danger | Effect on Aggressive Trading | Impact on the 1,000% Goal |
|---|---|---|
| Correlation creep | 20+ names share macro and sector risk | One selloff still causes a large drawdown |
| Decision fatigue | Too many positions to monitor | Missed high-velocity rotations and catalysts |
| False security | Feels responsible; breeds complacency | You avoid the discomfort outliers require |
| Opportunity cost | Capital tied up in weak setups | No dry powder for new Tier 1 explosions |

## The Cost of Attention and How Over-Diversification Sneaks In

Every position demands research, monitoring, risk management, and ongoing review, and past a certain count attention fragments and knowledge dilutes alongside capital—you come to understand many companies superficially rather than a handful exceptionally well. The strongest momentum traders know precisely why they own each position, what catalyst drives it, where the institutional buying sits, and when the trade must be exited, and that depth becomes impossible across forty names. Over-diversification rarely arrives by decision; it accumulates by drift—adding "just one more" name, FOMO on several catalysts firing at once, following advice such as "never put more than 5% in one stock," stacking 3x ETFs and options without caps, and failing to cut losers quickly. The rule of thumb that stops the drift: if you cannot name the top three reasons a position deserves capital right now, it does not belong in the portfolio.

## The Anti-Over-Diversification Rules and a Worked Example

Translate the philosophy into hard limits: **maximum positions**—five to eight at any time (three to five Tier 1 core names plus two to three Tier 2 developing); **minimum conviction**—allocate only to setups scoring 8 or higher out of 10 on your multi-layer checklist; **minimum size**—each Tier 1 position should be at least 10–15% effective exposure, with no 2–3% lottery tickets; **forced pruning**—each week, rank every position by conviction and momentum and cut the bottom two or three regardless of profit or loss; and **cash mandate**—hold 15–30% in cash as the dry powder that lets you pounce on the next rotation. Every holding should answer one question: does this materially improve my portfolio? The most effective traders are, above all, experts at saying no, and every rejected opportunity strengthens the quality of the few that remain.

The contrast is stark when the same winner lands in two different books. An over-diversified trader holding twenty-two positions across eight sectors catches a 120% biotech runner — but it adds only about 5% to the portfolio, and the month finishes up roughly 18%. A controlled trader holding four focused positions catches that identical 120% runner on a 25% allocation, which adds around 25–28% to the book, and the month finishes up 45–65% – with capital free to rotate into the next wave. Same analysis, same winning trade, radically different outcome. The difference was position count, not stock-picking.

## The Over-Diversification Checklist

Before adding any new position, ask whether it materially improves expected returns, introduces a genuinely different catalyst, is highly correlated with existing holdings, can be monitored properly, would be outperformed by simply adding to an existing high-conviction position, and dilutes your best ideas—if the new position weakens overall portfolio quality, it should not be added. The drag shows up differently by regime: in strong bull markets it makes you underperform the leaders, in sideways markets decision fatigue compounds, and in bear markets large portfolios fall together anyway as correlations rise.

## The Over-Diversification Governance Matrix

| Operational Parameter | The Retail Spectator | The Blueprint Capital Allocator |
|---|---|---|
| Portfolio Density | Owns 15–30 assets, tracking a chaotic web of tickers and random sectors. | Restricts the active book to a focused 5–8 positions that each matter. |
| Alpha Capture | Dilutes a +50% winning run down to a fraction of a percent on the account. | Sizes so a major technical advance moves the whole ledger by double digits. |
| Cognitive Bandwidth | Scatters attention across many charts, causing missed exits and stops. | Maintains complete focus over every tick of a concentrated book. |
| Selection Discipline | Lowers standards to keep buying names out of a need to stay active. | Enforces a strict filter, trading only the top-tier validated setups. |

## Risk, Discipline, and the Selective-Concentration Balance

The critical point is not "concentrate without limit"—it is to find the right balance and hold it under emotional pressure. Over-diversification feels safer and more professional, but that comfort is the enemy of an aggressive goal; there will always be more setups than capital, so your edge is selectivity, not participation; and don't buy simply to raise the position count, hold positions too small to matter, or diversify out of uncertainty instead of improving your research. Even with tight rules, expect 40–70% drawdowns—over-diversification does not prevent them, it only makes recovery slower. The balance that ties this part together: the ideal aggressive portfolio is neither recklessly concentrated nor excessively diversified—selective enough that exceptional ideas matter, diversified enough across independent risk drivers to survive a single catastrophic event, flexible enough to rotate into new leadership, and disciplined enough to protect gains when conditions change.

## Blueprint Principle

Diversification is a tool — not a destination. Taken to excess, it dilutes conviction, fragments attention, and shrinks the impact of exceptional opportunities. You build wealth not by owning the most stocks, but by owning the best ones, allocating capital intentionally, and ensuring every position contributes meaningfully to the compounding engine.

# PART V — PSYCHOLOGY, DISCIPLINE, AND SURVIVAL

## Chapter 19
# Emotional Control Under Pressure

Most traders do not lose because their analysis is wrong—they lose because, in the moment that matters, emotion overrides the plan, defeated not by the market but by themselves, not in the chart but in the chair. The setups in this book are worthless the instant fear freezes your hand, greed widens your stop, or revenge sizes your next position, and the high-velocity instruments here amplify every one of those feelings: leverage magnifies not just the money but the emotion attached to it. The goal is not to eliminate emotion—that is impossible—but to build a system that executes correctly regardless of how you feel, so emotion is present but no longer in control. Treat your feelings the way an engineer treats telemetry: data to monitor, not commands to obey. The pressure compounds with the account—as $100,000 grows toward $200,000, then $400,000, then $700,000, a 5% move that once meant a few hundred dollars now means $20,000, $30,000, or $50,000 in a session—which is precisely why the response must be mechanical rather than willful: willpower fails under load, but a rule made while calm does not. Six emotions do the most damage, each with a recognizable signature and a concrete antidote.

## Fear

Fear is the emotion of loss, and in markets its evolutionary wiring works against you. Before a trade it causes hesitation (you see a valid breakout and cannot pull the trigger, or size it too small to matter); during a trade it causes premature exits (you cut a healthy winner the moment it wobbles, banking +0.5R on a position running to +3R, forfeiting the runner the strategy depends on); after a loss it causes paralysis, freezing you out of the very next setup. Loss aversion is the engine underneath, making you hold losers while dumping winners early. **The antidote:** remove the in-the-moment decision entirely—when entry, stop, and size are defined in advance, fear has nothing to act on. Automate execution itself: place a resting buy-stop so that the instant it fills, a bracket (OCO) order deploys a hard stop and a first scale-out target. The deeper fix is sizing, because fear scales with stakes—a position small enough that losing it does not threaten you is one fear cannot dominate—so reframe the stop as a business expense, and if your heart rate spikes when you look at a position, it is too large.

## Greed

Greed is fear's twin and the more seductive, because it wears the mask of conviction—it whispers "hold a little longer," "double the size," "this one goes another 100%." It shows up as oversizing, refusing to scale out, and holding past every sensible target, fed by dopamine after a string of wins as the brain projects outlier returns in a straight line—and that extrapolation is what turns a realized winner into a round-trip back to breakeven. **The antidote:** the pre-set plan the exit chapters built—defined profit targets, mechanical scaling that banks gains on the way up, and half-gain protection that makes a giveback impossible. Decide what "enough" is before you are in the trade and feeling the pull; treat the position-sizing formula as an unbending law, with cold risk per trade capped at roughly 1–2% of equity no matter how certain a catalyst appears; scale out at predefined multiples (partials at 2R and 4R); and after an unusually large win, deliberately reduce size for the next several sessions.

## Revenge Trading

Revenge trading is the attempt to win a loss back immediately, and it is among the fastest ways to turn a manageable setback into a catastrophe. After a painful loss the mind wants restitution now—driven by cortisol and adrenaline, it oversizes the next trade, abandons the entry criteria, and often re-enters the very asset that just stopped it out. This is "tilt," and it spirals: each revenge loss intensifies the urge for the next, and an account can be cut in half in an afternoon. **The antidote:** structural and non-negotiable. A daily loss limit ends your trading when it is hit, and a hard rule requires the next trade to meet the same criteria as any other. One implementation is a two-strike rule—two consecutive stop-outs and the day is over, the platform locked—and you adopt the "best loser wins" mindset, measuring yourself by process and expectancy rather than recovering the exact dollars you just lost. Stepping away from the screen after a loss is the single most profitable thing a tilting trader can do.

## FOMO

The fear of missing out is the engine of late entries. A stock is running, screenshots of 300% and 1,000% gains flood the timeline, and the patience the method requires evaporates—you chase an extended move, buy near the top, and inherit someone else's exit, acting as the liquidity that lets institutions distribute into the parabolic wick. **The antidote:** a single internalized belief—there is always another setup. Missing one costs nothing; chasing one costs real money. Trade only from a checklist, treat a chart as either inside an authorized entry zone or in a dead zone, and the moment an asset runs more than roughly 1.5% past its defined pivot trigger, flag it as invalidated and remove it from the active screen. Observe your watchlist; do not chase it.

## Euphoria

Euphoria is the most dangerous emotion in this book, precisely because it feels the best. After a string of wins—especially explosive ones, or clearing a milestone like $100,000 to $300,000 ahead of schedule—the mind floods with a sense of invincibility, and that feeling is the direct cause of the next disaster: success breeds confidence, confidence curdles into overconfidence, size creeps up, rules start to feel like training wheels, and the account carries its largest risk at the exact moment the trader is least afraid. **The antidote:** treat euphoria as a warning light, not a reward. The moment trading feels easy and you feel brilliant is the moment to re-read your rules and reduce size. One concrete guard ties this to the equity curve—when you clear a major milestone, set a floor at the new peak, and if equity gives back even 5% from it, halve your position sizes for the next several sessions. Track process, not the scoreboard, and assume a hot streak owes more to a kind market than to your genius.

## Emotional Exhaustion

The others are acute; this one is chronic. Sustained high-velocity trading—the constant vigilance over news, catalysts, volume, options flow, and 3x-ETF positions, the emotional whiplash of wins and losses—exhausts the prefrontal cortex's executive capacity and produces real, cumulative fatigue. When it sets in, willpower breaks and decision quality degrades: you force trades out of boredom, miss obvious signals, commit sloppy operational errors, or close positions early just to escape the tension—and exhaustion lowers impulse control, amplifying every other emotion here. **The antidote:** treat your own capacity as part of the risk model. Schedule genuine time away, set a sustainable pace, and protect sleep (seven to nine hours), exercise, and nutrition as performance inputs. One protocol is a decompression cycle—roughly every twenty-one trading sessions, flatten every position to cash for a full forty-eight hours and place no new orders. A tired trader is a liability to his own account, and the decision to step back is itself a trade, usually a winning one.

*A note that outranks the trading: if the intensity of this pursuit begins to damage your sleep, your health, your relationships, or your sense of wellbeing, treat that as a signal more important than any setup. No financial target is worth your health, and persistent distress, compulsive patterns, or an inability to step away are worth taking seriously and, if needed, discussing with a professional or someone you trust.*

## The Six Emotions at a Glance

| Emotion | How it shows up | The antidote |
|---|---|---|
| **Fear** | Freezing on valid setups; cutting winners early; paralysis after a loss | Pre-defined rules and automated bracket (OCO) orders; size small enough to stay calm; reframe stops as business expenses |
| **Revenge trading** | Oversizing to win it back; re-entering angry; tilt | Daily loss limit / two-strike circuit breaker; same criteria as always; step away; "best loser wins" |
| **FOMO** | Chasing extended moves; buying tops late | "There's always another setup"; checklist-only entries; invalidate and delete extended charts |
| **Euphoria** | Feeling invincible; size creep; rules feel optional | Treat it as a warning; milestone drawdown guard; cut size; track process, not the scoreboard |
| **Emotional exhaustion** | Decision fatigue; forcing trades; sloppy errors; degraded judgment | Scheduled breaks; sustainable pace; a 48-hour cash-freeze reset; don't trade depleted |

## The Trader's Operating System

The antidotes are not six separate habits to remember under fire; they are one operating system you build while calm and run while you are not. **Predefined written rules**—entries, risk, size, and exits decided before the open and committed to paper, with no real-time deviations. **Automated execution and circuit breakers**—bracket orders place your stop and first target the instant you fill, a daily loss limit (a two-strike rule) ends the session before tilt can, a milestone drawdown guard halves your size after a 5% giveback from a new peak, and a decompression cycle flattens you to cash for forty-eight hours roughly every twenty-one sessions. **A real trading journal**—log every trade's rationale, the emotion felt, the outcome, and the lesson, reviewed weekly to expose recurring emotional mistakes. **Simulation and review**—paper-trade and replay charts to desensitize yourself before real money is on the line. **Professional support**—if emotions persistently derail your execution despite the structure, bring in a coach or a licensed professional, the way an elite athlete uses a trainer.

## Who Makes the Decision: The Governance Matrix

Emotional control comes down to one question repeated all day long: who is deciding this trade—the feeling, or the system?

| Operational dimension | The reactive trader | The disciplined operator |
|---|---|---|
| **Who decides the trade** | The emotion of the moment. | The rules written in advance. |
| **After a loss** | Doubles down to recover it. | Takes the next valid setup at the same size — or the circuit breaker ends the day. |
| **After a big win** | Feels invincible and sizes up. | Stays mechanical; the milestone guard watches for euphoria. |
| **Missing a move** | Chases it late at a bad price. | Invalidates the chart and waits, calmly, for the next setup. |
| **When depleted** | Trades through the exhaustion. | Steps away to protect judgment; takes the scheduled reset. |

## Risk, Honesty, and a Reality Check

Emotional control is the discipline most traders most underestimate and most need. The analysis is the easy part; doing the right thing while afraid, greedy, tilted, or euphoric is the hard part, and it is where the overwhelming majority of failures actually occur—not in the chart, but in the chair.

**Reality check.** *Emotional control can be trained, but it is never perfected, and the leverage in this book's instruments amplifies every emotion it describes — one more reason the aggressive path carries a real risk of substantial or total loss. Turning $100,000 into $1,000,000 in six months is extraordinarily rare; most retail traders lose money, especially with leverage, and past or hypothetical performance guarantees nothing. No* *amount of composure makes the headline target likely; it only gives a disciplined trader the chance to be among the few it works for. Put capital preservation first and let aggressive growth follow disciplined execution — never risk money you cannot afford to lose completely. And the exhaustion section is not a metaphor: if this pursuit is harming your wellbeing, that matters more than any return, and stepping back is the right call, not a failure. This is analysis of the book's framework, not financial or psychological advice; consult a licensed professional before acting.*

## Blueprint Principle

*You cannot remove emotion from trading — you can only build a system that executes correctly while you feel it. The edge is not a calm mind; it is a set of **rules made in advance that the emotion of the moment is not allowed to override.*

# Chapter 20
# Trading Like a Hedge Fund

Many retail traders believe hedge funds win because they have better research, faster computers, or privileged information. Those advantages are real, but the defining characteristic of professional trading is institutional risk management: a fund's objective is not simply to maximize returns but to maximize returns while surviving every market environment, because exceptional returns are impossible without preserving the capital to exploit the next opportunity. To scale $100,000 toward $1,000,000 in six months—roughly 47% a month, compounded—you must purge the retail-speculator identity. Here is the paradox: the larger the return you chase, the more rigid and institutional your risk architecture must be—attempt a 1,000% return with retail risk habits and you manufacture a near-mathematical certainty of ruin, and the instruments here only sharpen that edge—a 3x ETF can move 10–30% in a day. So treat your account not as a trading balance but as a one-person fund: a sovereign, risk-insulated balance sheet run with the operational rigor of a pod at a multi-manager firm. Six pillars hold that architecture up.

## Pillar 1 — Risk Management Frameworks

A professional desk governs every decision with a predefined framework. Where the retail trader asks "how much can I make?", the institutional trader asks how much can I lose, what is the probability of success, what happens if I am wrong, and how does this position affect the whole portfolio—and every trade must answer four questions before capital is committed: why am I entering, where am I wrong, how much can I lose, and how much do I expect to gain. Underneath sits expectancy: a trade is an isolated probability contract, and the only thing that matters across a large sample is positive expected value—expectancy equals (win rate × average win) minus (loss rate × average loss). The institutional obsession is asymmetric expectancy: mandate that the average win is at least two to three times the average loss (a minimum of +2R, ideally +2R to +3R), and even a 40% win rate produces a relentless upward equity curve. **The Blueprint rule:** keep a Pre-Trade Risk Diagnostic Ledger documenting the hard stop, the exact 1R distance, and the milestone that unlocks the +2R target—if a setup cannot justify a +2R expansion before major overhead resistance, it is barred. Around that core, stress-test the book with value-at-risk against a 2008-style shock, run scenario analysis (what if a 3x ETF bleeds 20% in a choppy week, or an option expires worthless), size with fractional half-Kelly position sizing, and commit every rule to writing with no discretionary overrides.

## Pillar 2 — Position Limits

Uncertainty cannot be eliminated, only contained. Earnings surprises, regulatory actions, fraud allegations, surprise dilution, trading halts, and market-wide selloffs all arrive without warning, and a position concentrated heavily enough means a single overnight gap or halt bypasses your intraday stop entirely. Position limits exist so no single mistake can permanently impair the portfolio—and the difference between institutional and reckless concentration is not the size of the position but the discipline governing it:

high conviction, predefined risk, continuous monitoring, and immediate adjustment when the thesis changes, versus emotional attachment and averaging down indefinitely. **The Blueprint rule:** enforce a hard, tiered allocation-cap system that tightens as leverage rises—the cap is only the ceiling on how much capital may sit in one place, while the 1R risk unit still does the actual sizing.

| Instrument category | Max single position | Notes |
|---|---|---|
| **Common stock / liquid ETF** | 25% of NAV | High-conviction single names; the most liquid, lowest-gap-risk tier |
| **2x / 3x leveraged ETF** | 15% of NAV | Counts at its leverage factor for exposure; rebalance daily for drag |
| **Options / warrants** | 10% of NAV | Net options delta kept at or below ~1.0× NAV; no naked short options |
| **Sector / correlated cluster** | 30% of NAV | Correlated names are treated as one position |

These caps are an aggressive-but-survivable middle setting; a more conservative operator holds single names nearer 10% of NAV, but the further the cap rises, the more a single overnight event can do.

## Pillar 3 — Exposure Management

Professionals evaluate exposure at the portfolio level, not trade by trade—a trader holding five different semiconductor names may feel diversified while owning one large semiconductor bet. Funds monitor several overlapping forms of exposure at once: sector, market, factor (whether holdings share a driver such as momentum, growth, or rate sensitivity), correlation, and leverage, tracking gross exposure (total notional) and net exposure (the difference between longs and shorts). With derivatives the danger is synthetic leverage expansion, where high gamma quietly balloons true market exposure when the market accelerates. **The Blueprint rule:** compute your true, leverage-adjusted market exposure every morning—nominal allocation multiplied by the leverage factor, so a 3x-ETF position counts at three times its dollar size—and hold true market exposure at or below roughly 150% of NAV without hedges, running higher only with explicit hedges in place. Set hard delta, gamma, theta, and vega limits, avoid naked short options, rebalance leveraged-ETF exposure daily to fight volatility drag, and harvest profit or trim delta if synthetic exposure breaches the ceiling.

## Pillar 4 — Portfolio Heat

Portfolio heat is the total capital at risk if every open stop triggers at once: instead of evaluating each trade in isolation, you ask what percentage of capital disappears if all positions hit their maximum loss simultaneously. Three positions each risking one 1R unit (1% of NAV) carry 3% heat—but the subtlety is correlation, because if those three move together the true heat in a stress event is larger than the naive sum. Heat is therefore a dial, not a fixed budget: it can expand modestly in a clean regime and must contract when the environment turns.

**Worked example.** *On a $100,000 account, a 4% heat ceiling is $4,000 of open cold risk. Three* ***trades*** *each risking 1%* ***use*** *$3,000 — inside the ceiling, with one unit of capacity left. Open a fourth 1% trade and the book is saturated at 4%. A fifth entry is prohibited, however explosive the catalyst, until you free capacity by banking a target or trailing an existing stop to breakeven (0R), which cools the total heat.*

**The Blueprint rule:** set a hard heat ceiling of roughly 4–6% of NAV in normal conditions, tightening toward the low end when volatility spikes, and count correlated positions as one. Once heat is saturated, no new position may be opened until existing risk is retired by a hit target or a stop moved to breakeven.

## Pillar 5 — Daily Loss Limits

Perhaps no single practice separates professionals from amateurs more than the daily loss limit. Every desk knows decision quality collapses after meaningful losses, and the limit is not punishment but capital preservation—it interrupts revenge trading, emotional escalation, and oversized recovery attempts before they compound into a fatal multi-day drawdown. **The Blueprint rule:** run a hard daily circuit breaker—when realized and unrealized losses across the whole ledger reach roughly 2–3% of starting-day NAV, declare a portfolio emergency: flatten every position to cash, cancel all working orders, and lock the platform for the session. Layer two more limits above it—a weekly limit (around 5–10%) that pauses trading, and a trailing limit from peak equity (around 10–15%) that cuts you to half size until you make new highs.

## Pillar 6 — Institutional Discipline

Discipline is the culture that makes every framework actually stick. Professionals rely on procedures, not motivation—and in a real fund the Portfolio Manager who pulls the trigger is deliberately separated from the Risk Officer who manages the downside and holds the authority to shut the terminal down when limits are breached. Trading alone, you must run both identities: during the session the Portfolio Manager scans catalysts and executes strictly inside the boundaries; before and after, the Risk Officer sizes positions, evaluates correlations, audits the ledger, and enforces the loss locks. That split produces the most important reframing: you judge yourself on process, not profit and loss—a perfectly executed losing trade exited precisely at its 1R stop is an institutional success, while a profitable trade taken outside your position limits is an operational failure, because it pays you for the behavior that eventually ruins the account. **The Blueprint rule:** perform a formal post-market risk audit every evening, scoring execution on rule-adherence; journal every trade and review it weekly for attribution; de-risk after both wins and losses; and build in accountability through a peer, a coach, or a journaling app.

## The Six Pillars at a Glance

| Pillar | Institutional principle | The Blueprint rule |
|---|---|---|
| **Risk frameworks** | Every trade is a probability contract; the edge is positive expectancy | Pre-trade ledger; min +2R reward; VaR / scenario tests; half-Kelly sizing |
| **Position limits** | No single mistake may impair the portfolio | Tiered caps that tighten with leverage; concentration with discipline |
| **Exposure management** | Risk lives at the portfolio level, not the trade level | True exposure ≤ ~150% of NAV (more only with hedges); Greeks capped |
| **Portfolio heat** | Measure risk if all stops trigger at once | Heat ceiling ~4–6% of NAV; correlated names counted as one |
| **Daily loss limits** | Decision quality collapses after losses | ~2–3% daily breaker → flatten and lock; weekly and trailing limits |
| **Institutional discipline** | Process over outcome; systems over emotion | Dual identity; nightly risk audit; journal; automate; be accountable |

## A Sample Risk Ruleset for a $100,000 Aggressive Account

One internally consistent starting point — a tear-out card. Backtest and paper-trade it before committing real capital, and tune the dial to your own tolerance.

- **Risk per trade (1R):** 1% of current NAV; up to 2% only on the highest-conviction setups.
- **Reward target:** minimum +2R, ideally +2R to +3R; the system is built to profit at a 40% win rate.
- **Position caps:** ≤25% NAV common stock/ETF; ≤15% leveraged ETF; ≤10% options/warrants; ≤30% any correlated cluster.
- **Portfolio heat ceiling:** ≤4–6% of NAV open cold risk; contract in high volatility; correlated names counted as one.
- **True market exposure:** ≤ ~150% of NAV without hedges; higher only with explicit hedges; recomputed every morning.
- **Daily loss limit:** −2% to −3% of starting-day NAV → flatten, cancel orders, lock the platform.
- **Weekly / trailing limits:** −5% to −10% weekly → pause; −10% to −15% from peak → halve size until new highs.
- **Discipline:** journal every trade; nightly risk audit on rule-adherence; weekly attribution review.

## Who Runs the Book: The Governance Matrix

Every decision comes down to one question: is the retail speculator or the hedge-fund risk desk running the book right now?

| Operational dimension | The retail speculator | The hedge-fund operator |
|---|---|---|
| **First question asked** | "How much can I make?" | "How much can I lose, and what if I'm wrong?" |
| **Concentration** | Emotional; averages down; ignores new information | High-conviction with predefined risk and constant monitoring |
| **View of risk** | Trade by trade, in isolation | Portfolio-level: heat, correlation, and true exposure |
| **After the daily limit** | Trades on to win it back | Flattens, locks the platform, reviews, returns tomorrow |
| **Scorecard** | Did I make money today? | Did I follow every rule? A clean 1R loss is a success |

## Risk, Honesty, and a Reality Check

The hedge-fund mindset reverses the retail instinct: extraordinary returns do not require extraordinary risk, they require extraordinary discipline. The institutions that survive across decades are the ones that prevent any single mistake from becoming fatal—secure survival first, and only then deploy capital aggressively when a high-probability edge appears.

**Reality check.** *These frameworks reduce blow-up risk; they do not eliminate it. Turning $100,000 into $1,000,000 in six months is extraordinarily difficult and high-risk, and most professionals and retail traders lose money using leverage — the 2x and 3x ETFs, options, and warrants in this book amplify both outcomes. Past or hypothetical results guarantee nothing. Institutional risk architecture is what gives a disciplined trader the chance to be among the few the target works for; it does not make the target probable. Put capital preservation first and let aggressive growth follow disciplined execution, backtest and paper-trade every rule before risking real* ***money, and*** *never risk capital you cannot afford to lose entirely. This is analysis of the book's framework, not financial advice; consult a licensed professional before acting.*

## Blueprint Principle

*You do not manage profits — you manage constraints, and the profits are the byproduct. The edge is not a better forecast; it is a risk architecture rigid enough that no single trade, no single day, and no single emotion can ever impair the balance sheet.*

**Chapter 21**

# The Family Office Approach

The family-office mindset begins with a different question. The aggressive trader asks, "How fast can I grow this account?" The family office—the private wealth structure of the ultra-high-net-worth—asks, "How do I grow capital aggressively without destroying the family fortune?" It exists to preserve, compound, protect, and transfer wealth across generations: it may invest aggressively, but it does not gamble with the core estate, because wealth is created by bold action and kept by restraint and survival. The lesson for a trader pursuing $100,000 to $1,000,000 in six months is, against the retail amateur's image of a reckless 1,000% sprint, controlled acceleration—risk taken from a position of structure, not emotion. The structure is a barbell: a large preserved core that secures the future, a smaller ring-fenced sleeve through which it can be as tactically aggressive as it likes, and a cash reserve for optionality, with the two walled off so aggression can never threaten the core. There are two nested levels: the entire $100,000 campaign is itself the ring-fenced sleeve of your broader net worth (the money that secures your life never enters this account), and inside the account you apply the same barbell—a preserved sub-core, a tactical growth sleeve where the leveraged instruments live, and a reserve.

## Capital Preservation First

The first principle orders everything else: preserve the capital before seeking to grow it—rule one is don't lose the money, rule two is don't forget rule one. This is not timidity but recognition of the asymmetry running through the whole book: a destroyed core cannot compound, so survival outranks return as a matter of sequence, and the mathematics of recovery is brutal and gets worse the deeper the hole.

| Drawdown suffered | Gain required just to break even |
|---|---|
| **A 10% loss** | requires an 11.1% gain to recover |
| **A 25% loss** | requires a 33.3% gain |
| **A 50% loss** | requires a 100% gain |
| **A 75% loss** | requires a 300% gain |

In a six-month sprint the damage is worse still, because a deep drawdown desynchronizes the entire compounding timeline. Preservation-first means a core of capital that is never genuinely endangered—diversified, lower-risk, and built to come through any single cycle intact—which funds the life and provides the psychological stability that makes disciplined aggression possible. **The Blueprint rule:** preservation does not mean sitting in cash; it means protecting the downside before pursuing the upside. Cap outright risk per trade at one 1R unit (1–2% of capital), and structure the barbell explicitly—a preserved sub-core of roughly 50–70% (cash, short-term Treasuries, unleveraged blue-chips, or protective puts), a growth sleeve of 20–40% where the 2x/3x ETFs, options, and warrants live, and a small 5–10% opportunistic slice. Never dip into the core to fund losses; replenish the growth sleeve only from profits.

### Tactical Aggression Second

With the core preserved, aggression has its place—second, and confined to the ring-fenced sleeve, sized so that losing the entire sleeve changes nothing about the security the core provides. It is also tactical rather than constant: the family office is aggressive opportunistically, waiting with patience for extreme, highly localized dislocations where risk is tightly defined but the upside is exponentially asymmetric, then striking with concentrated size the moment a real edge appears. Every aggressive action is governed by the campaign question—not "can this trade double?" but "if this trade fails, can I continue the campaign?" **The Blueprint rule:** default to conservative exposure most days and unlock the sleeve only through a binary catalyst filter—aggression is permitted when a high-probability technical pattern (an inside-day breakout, an opening-range fracture, a clean base breakout) aligns with an explosive fundamental catalyst (a triple-digit earnings surprise, an FDA decision, a major index rebalance). Keep tactical positions time-bound—days to weeks—to avoid leveraged-ETF decay and option theta, and exit ruthlessly at predefined targets or stops.

### Rotational Allocation

Family offices do not marry their positions—they rotate capital across asset classes, themes, and opportunities as conditions change, toward strength and away from weakness, concentrating the aggressive sleeve in whatever currently offers the best risk-adjusted opportunity. Capital that can move is capital that is not trapped in a deteriorating thesis, and into cash when nothing offers a real edge, because dry powder is a legitimate and often optimal allocation. The discipline lies in the difference between rotation and chasing: rotation is planned, evidence-based, and observes leadership early; chasing is emotional and arrives after exhaustion. **The Blueprint rule:** run the sleeve on a regime-based rotation documented weekly—in bull momentum into leading 3x sector ETFs or call options; into earnings season into options on individual names, then back to broader ETFs; when volatility spikes into inverse or hedged positions, cash, or volatility products; in chop or downtrend into defensive expressions or short-biased warrants—selling winners into strength and keeping turnover and option theta in check.

### Multi-Cycle Survival

A family office is built to survive every cycle—bull and bear, boom and bust, inflation and deflation—because it intends to exist across generations and knows it will face all of them. That favors robustness over optimization, giving up some upside in the best regime to survive the worst. Even a six-month campaign passes through several micro-cycles—an explosive rally, a sharp pullback, sideways consolidation, a volatility shock, a renewed breakout—and a style built only for a low-volatility uptrend gives everything back in the first serious correction. **The Blueprint rule:** match execution to the regime.

Measure broad-market conditions continuously (index VWAP deviations, ATR extensions, the VIX, breadth) and downshift mechanically when volatility expands—cut position sizes by half and pivot from multi-day structural sprints toward ultra-short-term opening-range breakouts and risk-defined option spreads. Stress-test against the worst case (a 30% gap-down in a 3x ETF, an option expiring worthless), keep a 20–30% cash-equivalent buffer, and treat a 15–20% drawdown from peak as a hard trigger to move fully into preservation mode.

## Long-Term Thinking

Underlying all of it is a horizon measured in decades rather than the six-month sprint, which only appears to contradict a short campaign. Long-term thinking is not about holding every trade for years; it is about making sure short-term decisions never destroy long-term wealth—a tactical loss in the sleeve is trivial against the decades-long compounding of the preserved core. For the aggressive trader, this framing shrinks the emotional weight of any single trade, week, or even the entire six-month attempt by placing them inside a much longer project, and the habits that protect $10 million are the same ones you must begin practicing at $100,000. **The Blueprint rule:** forget the final $1,000,000 target day to day and replace it with a micro-milestone horizon—make your only goal the flawless execution of the next trade at exactly 1R of risk, since a seven-figure balance sheet is the mathematical byproduct of stacking hundreds of risk-insulated blocks. After each major milestone (say, $250,000), lock a portion of profit back into the preserved core and reduce leverage.

## The Family Office Structure

| Capital layer | Role | Risk posture & weighting |
|---|---|---|
| **Preserved core** | Secures the future; never genuinely endangered | Diversified, lower-risk, survives every cycle; ~50–70% of the account |
| **Tactical aggressive sleeve** | Pursues outsized growth — this book's strategy | High-risk, ring-fenced, sized to be lost entirely; ~20–40%, 1R per trade |
| **Reserve / dry powder** | Optionality and a survival buffer | Cash; deployed rotationally only on real opportunity; ~5–30% |

These weightings are the dial: the more your true core is preserved outside this account, the more of the account you can commit to the growth sleeve; the more the $100,000 represents your real wealth, the closer you hold to the conservative end.

## A Sample Family-Office Ruleset

One internally consistent starting point — a tear-out card to adapt to your own tolerance, backtested and paper-traded first.

- **Preservation first:** hold ~60% of the account in the preserved core at all times; never fund losses from it.
- **Tactical aggression:** at most ~40% in the high-leverage sleeve, with portfolio heat kept within the ceiling set in the risk-management chapter.
- **Risk per trade:** 1R = 1% of capital (up to 2% on the highest-conviction setups), every trade defined before entry.
- **Tactical trigger:** technical pattern + fundamental catalyst confluence only; positions time-bound to days or weeks.
- **Rotational:** regime-based shifts documented weekly; rotate to confirmed strength, into cash when there is none.
- **Survival:** a 15–20% drawdown from peak triggers a move to preservation mode and ~50% risk reduction for several weeks.
- **Long-term:** lock profits into the core at each milestone; run a quarterly "legacy review" of process adherence, not P&L.

## The Estate vs. the Bet: The Governance Matrix

The family-office approach and the all-in gamble can pursue the same aggressive returns and meet opposite fates.

| Operational dimension | Risks everything | The family-office operator |
|---|---|---|
| **First priority** | Maximize return right now. | Preserve the core first. |
| **Aggression** | The entire account. | A ring-fenced sleeve only. |
| **Allocation** | Static; married to positions. | Rotational; toward confirmed strength. |
| **Time horizon** | This six-month run. | Many cycles and decades. |
| **Built to survive** | One cycle, if it cooperates. | Every cycle, by design. |
| **If the aggressive bet fails** | Wiped out. | The core endures; he continues. |

## Risk, Honesty, and a Reality Check

The family-office approach sits in deliberate tension with the headline premise of this book, and that tension is the most useful thing in the chapter. The book describes turning a whole $100,000 into $1,000,000; the family-office approach says you should never risk your whole anything. The reconciliation is the responsible one: pursue the aggressive attempt with a sleeve you can genuinely afford to lose, and keep your true core preserved and separate.

**Reality check.** *Structuring capital into a preserved core and a ring-fenced sleeve does not make the sleeve safe — it still carries this approach's real risk of substantial or total loss, and the headline target remains an outlier outcome that most traders, even professionals, fail to reach with* *leverage. What the structure does is ensure that losing the aggressive bet, which is the most likely result of any single attempt, does not* **end** *you: the core survives, and you live to compound and to try again. If pursuing this goal would require risking capital you cannot afford to lose — money you need for your life, your family, or your security — the family-office approach says clearly that you should not pursue it that way. Preserve the core first; be aggressive only with the slice; backtest and paper-trade before committing real capital. This is analysis of the book's framework, not financial advice; consult a licensed professional before acting.*

## Blueprint Principle

*Preserve the core, risk only a slice, and survive every cycle. Be as aggressive as you like with a ring-fenced sleeve you can afford to lose entirely — and never with the capital that secures your life. The estate must outlive the bet.*

# Chapter 22
# The Discipline of Patience

This is the chapter that resolves the central paradox of the book: the strategy is aggressive, but its core discipline is patience. The most common misconception in retail trading is that hyper-aggressive compounding requires hyper-active trading—that to reach a 1,000% return you must wrestle the tape all day. The opposite is true. A trader who is always in a position is not being aggressive but compulsive, and compulsion is exactly what the market feeds on. Real aggressive compounding is patient waiting punctuated by decisive, forceful action—long stretches of doing little, broken by rare moments of committing hard—because in an exponential growth model capital is a scarce, high-velocity resource that must not be chipped away by low-conviction noise. Patience is also the hardest discipline to practice, because the strategy's intensity and the six-month clock create relentless pressure to act: every day flat feels like a day wasted. Mastering patience means learning that those feelings are lies—that doing nothing is frequently the most profitable thing a trader can do.

## Waiting for Asymmetric Setups

Most of the time, the market offers nothing worth your risk. Patience is the discipline of waiting through all of it for the rare configurations where the potential reward dwarfs the risk—the asymmetric setups, the fat pitches—and refusing to swing at anything less. An asymmetric setup is one where the upside is several times the defined downside: a minimum of roughly three-to-one, and on the apex plays a +5R to +10R extension against a single 1R of risk. Anything outside that alignment is a symmetric trade—risking a dollar to make a dollar—and over a six-month sprint, symmetric trading is a slow death sentence, because commissions, slippage, and whipsaws erode the account before any real trend develops. Like a great hitter, you have an even greater advantage than in baseball: there are no called strikes, so you can let pitch after pitch pass with no penalty and swing hard only when the perfect pitch arrives. The trap is the opposite—when traders get impatient they lower their standards, buying weak breakouts, chasing extended moves, and increasing size to compensate, which is frustration disguised as opportunity. **The Blueprint rule:** require a dual key before any trade—the structural key (the asset coiled in a tight, low-volatility formation where risk can be fenced into a small stop) and the kinetic key (a high-impact catalyst printing to provide immediate escape velocity). If both keys do not turn, you remain an observer, demanding confluence: a clear catalyst, technical confirmation, a defined stop yielding at least 1:3, a favorable volatility setup, and a fit within the portfolio-heat and exposure limits.

## Why Inactivity Is Often Profitable

Flat is a position. Choosing not to trade is an active decision, and frequently the most profitable one, because every trade carries cost—commissions, slippage, risk, and the scarce resource of attention—and a trade taken without a real edge has negative expectancy before it begins. The profit in a trade you correctly declined is just as real as the profit in one you won; it simply never shows up as a line item. There is a subtler tax, too: a mediocre position binds your capital, so when a flawless catalyst breakout fires an hour later, your capital is trapped. This is why overtrading is the silent killer of accounts—it bleeds the account slowly through dozens of marginal trades whose costs compound quietly in the wrong direction—and it is especially profitable to do nothing in choppy, directionless, low-conviction regimes. **The Blueprint rule:** redefine the psychological state of cash. Cash is not idle money but a standing, liquid weapon—a position with zero volatility and near-infinite optionality—so scan pre-market for setups only, and if none qualifies, take no trade and spend the session journaling, reading macro, or running simulations. The patient trader who sits in cash arrives at the next great setup fresh, liquid, and fully funded while the overtraders arrive depleted.

## Trading Less, Compounding More

Trading less often compounds more. Each marginal trade you add is, by definition, lower quality than your best, so it drags down your average expectancy while adding cost, risk, and drawdown—past a few high-quality trades, more activity subtracts from the result. Consider two operators over a single month:

| Over 30 days | The over-active speculator | The patient speculator |
|---|---|---|
| **Trades taken** | 40 — trading constantly | 4 — flat for ~26 days |
| **Setup quality** | Low; whatever the tape offered | Elite; only confirmed asymmetric catalysts |
| **Record** | 20 wins, 20 losses | 2 wins, 2 losses |
| **Average win / loss** | +1.2R / −1R | +5R to +7R / −1R |
| **Gross yield** | +4R | +10R |
| **After friction & fatigue** | Flatlines to near zero | Compounds cleanly |

The over-active trader does more work, takes more risk, and ends with less, because the law of large numbers drags a stream of thin-edge trades toward their mediocre average; the patient trader, by culling everything marginal, lets a few genuine winners run to +5R and +7R. **The Blueprint rule:** cap the activity so quality cannot erode—hold to a few new positions a day and roughly ten trades a week at most, with two or three mandatory zero-trade days; scale out of winners at 2R and 4R while letting the remainder run on a trailing stop; and learn to say the sentence that may save more money than your best stock pick: "This is not my setup."

## Selective Aggression

All of this culminates in the principle that reconciles patience with an aggressive strategy: selective aggression. The patient trader is not timid—when the asymmetric setup finally arrives, he commits decisively and forcefully, sizing up within his risk limits. Patience and aggression are not opposites but two phases of the same discipline: you are patient between opportunities so you can be aggressive on them. Picture an elite marksman who sits in stillness as minor targets pass and fires with full commitment the moment a high-conviction target crosses the crosshairs—in trading, ammunition is capital, and the trader who fires constantly runs out. Because he has saved his portfolio heat and mental bandwidth through days of inactivity, he deploys concentrated capital up to the position caps, fences the downside with a tight stop, and lets the weight of the position drive a real move—then, after the win or if the market shifts, rotates back to patience and cash.

**The reconciliation.** *Aggressive compounding is not constant aggression — it is concentrated aggression. The intensity the strategy requires is spent on a few right moments rather than sprayed across all moments. Wait like a sniper; strike like a predator. The trader who grasps this is both the most patient person in the market and, when it counts, the most aggressive — and those are the same trader.*

## The Patience Pre-Trade Checklist

Before committing to any trade, ask whether this is an A-quality, genuinely asymmetric setup (reward several times the risk), whether the downside is clearly defined with a stop you will honor, whether there is a real catalyst confirmed by volume, whether the broader market is supportive and the sector showing leadership, whether the position fits inside your portfolio-heat and exposure limits, whether you are entering from discipline or from emotion (boredom, FOMO, or revenge), whether you would still take this trade if you had just missed the last three winners, and whether you can accept the full loss without emotional damage. If the answer to any is unclear, waiting is the better trade.

## The Two Modes

| Mode | When it applies | How you act |
|---|---|---|
| **Waiting (the default)** | No asymmetric setup is present — most of the time | Flat or minimal exposure; patient; protecting capital and attention; declining the mediocre |
| **Striking (the exception)** | A genuinely elite, asymmetric setup confirms | Decisive, forceful commitment — sized up within the risk limits, pressing the advantage |

## A Sample Patience Ruleset

One internally consistent starting point — a tear-out card to adapt to your own tolerance.

- No trade without the full asymmetric checklist passed.
- Activity cap: at most ~10 trades a week, with 2–3 mandatory zero-trade days.

- Cash minimum: 30–50% unless in a confirmed high-conviction regime — aligned with the family-office reserve.
- Scale out at 2R and 4R; let the remainder run on a trailing stop.
- After a loss: a mandatory 24–48 hour pause before the next entry.
- Monthly review: if trade count exceeds target and results lag, tighten the criteria further.

## Patience vs. Compulsion: The Governance Matrix

The same market hands the impatient trader and the patient one opposite results, decided by what they do in the long stretches between great setups.

| Operational dimension | The impatient trader | The patient operator |
|---|---|---|
| **Default state** | Always in a position. | Flat unless a real edge is present. |
| **View of inactivity** | Boredom to be escaped. | A profitable, active choice. |
| **Number of trades** | Many, mostly mediocre. | Few, all high-quality. |
| **Where aggression goes** | Sprayed across every move. | Concentrated on the rare right moment. |
| **Cost & drawdown** | Bled away by overtrading. | Minimized by restraint. |
| **Result** | The mediocre average — a loss. | The few asymmetric wins that compound. |

## Risk, Honesty, and a Reality Check

Patience is simple to understand and brutally hard to practice, because everything about an aggressive strategy—the intensity, the clock, the dopamine—pushes against it. The overwhelming majority of traders lose not from a lack of good ideas but from an inability to wait. Still, of all the disciplines in this book, patience is the one with the highest return on the least effort, because the trades you don't take cost nothing and save much.

**Reality check.** *Patience is necessary but not sufficient: waiting for asymmetric setups does not make them appear on your schedule, and the ones you wait for can still fail. This aggressive approach carries a real risk of substantial or total loss regardless of how selective you are, and leveraged instruments can produce rapid losses up to a total wipeout. The six-month framing makes the pressure to overtrade especially **dangerous — a** compressed **clock tempts you to force what patience says to wait for. The discipline only improves your odds of being among the few it works for; it guarantees nothing, most aggressive traders lose money, and the headline target remains an outlier outcome. Backtest and paper-trade before risking real capital, and risk only what you can afford to lose entirely. This is analysis of the book's framework, not financial advice; consult a licensed professional before acting.*

### Blueprint Principle

*Aggressive compounding is not constant aggression — it is patient waiting punctuated by decisive action. Be flat by default, decline the mediocre, and spend your aggression on the few asymmetric setups that earn it. Wait like a sniper; strike like a predator.*

# Chapter 23
# Surviving the Drawdown

Every trader who lasts will face drawdowns—stretches where the account falls from a prior high and the losses pile up faster than the wins—and in an aggressive strategy they are not a possibility but a certainty, with a deep one all but guaranteed at some point—and in a campaign built to grow $100,000 into $1,000,000 in six months, drawdowns are part of the battlefield. The drawdown itself is not the danger; the danger is the response to it. The most common reactions—sizing up to win it back, forcing trades out of desperation, trading through the tilt—are precisely what turn a survivable setback into the end.

> **The first loss is financial. The second loss is psychological. The third loss is usually catastrophic.** *The job of this chapter is to stop the sequence at the first loss.*

The recovery math is merciless and leverage makes it worse: a 20% drawdown requires a 25% gain just to break even, a 50% drawdown demands 100%, and in leveraged funds those holes open faster through volatility drag, theta decay, and gap risk. So this chapter treats a drawdown as something to be managed in a specific order, the way a pilot manages an emergency: first stay solvent, then reduce size to stop the bleeding, then recover psychologically, and only then rebuild confidence through small, clean trades and scale back up. Skip a step or invert the sequence and the drawdown deepens toward ruin.

## 1. Staying Solvent: The First Priority

Before psychology, before confidence, before any thought of recovery, comes the one non-negotiable: stay solvent. You cannot recover from ruin—a wiped-out account has no path back—so the overriding priority is to protect enough capital to keep playing. A trader who falls from $100,000 to $60,000 still has a real path back; one who falls to $20,000 faces a far harder climb; one who falls to zero is finished, and in leveraged trading insolvency is permanent. Survival is not weakness but professionalism—the market can stay irrational longer than you can stay solvent. In practice, staying solvent means cutting risk hard and early and honoring pre-committed limits: a hard drawdown cap (a loss of roughly 15–25% from peak equity triggers a full de-risk or pause, no discretion), a liquidity buffer (20–40% of capital in cash or Treasuries), no revenge and no martingale (never double up to catch up), a multi-cycle view (this six-month blueprint is one leg in a longer career), and worst-case planning against gaps, black swans, and prolonged chop.

## 2. Reducing Size: The Throttle

The most powerful tactical response to a drawdown is also the simplest: trade smaller. Position size is the throttle on the whole machine, and cutting it during a rough stretch reduces the dollar damage while you are off your game, slows the bleeding, and lowers the emotional intensity clouding your judgment. There is a hard, mechanical logic to it—when you are losing, your read on the market is, by the evidence, currently poor, so the rational move is to risk less on each judgment until the evidence says your read has returned. A disciplined trader de-risks in steps as the drawdown deepens, basing every level on current equity rather than the starting $100,000:

| From peak equity | Action |
|---|---|
| **Down ~5%** | Review every trade in the streak; cut the marginal setups; reduce risk per trade by about half (e.g., 1% → 0.5%). |
| **Down ~10%** | Cut position size to 25–50% of normal; trade only A-grade, asymmetric setups. |
| **Down ~15%** | Tighten further to Grade-A opportunities only; shift emphasis toward preservation. |
| **Down ~20%** | Stop trading aggressively; move largely to cash and the preservation bucket; minimal tactical trades only. |
| **Down 25%+** | Halt. Conduct a full system review before resuming any aggression. |

Size returns the same way it left—gradually, and only on the evidence of results. **Phase 1 (25–50% size):** trade until you string together 5–10 consecutive positive days, or 8–10 cleanly executed winning setups. **Phase 2 (50–75% size):** add slightly broader setups once Phase 1 holds. **Phase 3 (full size):** only after a meaningful recovery, typically back within 5–10% of the prior peak. Reduced size is not idle time—it is where the account is repaired, first through discipline, then through profits.

## 3. Recovering Psychologically

A drawdown is a psychological event as much as a financial one, and the most dangerous part is often not the money lost but the emotional damage that follows: shame, fear, a battered sense of competence, and a powerful urge for revenge—to win it back right now—which is what converts a drawdown into a death spiral. The first defense is to separate the drawdown from your identity: it is not proof that you are a failure but evidence that trading involves uncertainty, and the power-law nature of returns means most trades are small losses and scratches even for winning traders. The first responsibility after a drawdown is analysis, not action—distinguish bad luck from bad process by asking whether you followed your rules or broke them, whether the losses were normal variance or bad execution, whether market conditions actually changed, whether your size was too large or your leverage excessive, and whether you honored your stops. If you followed the system, the answer is patience; if you violated your rules, the answer is repair—but either way the first goal is to regain clarity, because a trader who is emotionally unstable should not be trading aggressively. Clearing the emotion takes distance and routine: a mandatory 1–5 day break when you hit a loss limit (no charts, no trading social media), journaling each trade around "what was in my control?", reframing drawdowns as tuition and data (even elite strategies carry 20–40% drawdowns), and using a trading buddy, coach, or accountability group for the objective read you cannot give yourself mid-tilt.

## 4. Regaining Confidence

Confidence after a drawdown cannot be reclaimed by a single big winning trade—trying to force it that way is just revenge trading wearing a more flattering name. Confidence follows competence, not the other way around, and competence is rebuilt one clean execution at a time. Instead of swinging for a home run to erase the drawdown, aim for base hits: make the early trades about quality, not size—smaller positions, cleaner setups, tighter risk control, partial profits, less leverage, fewer trades—and judge yourself on process rather than profit. Each clean trade, win or lose, rebuilds the evidence that you can trust yourself, and that accumulated evidence is confidence. Track consistency metrics (positive days, R-multiple adherence) over absolute dollars; only once execution improves do you scale size back up. Avoid the hero trade—the oversized position designed to erase the drawdown in one shot—because a drawdown is recovered through a series of disciplined trades, never one desperate bet. Confidence rushed is faked; confidence earned through clean execution is the only kind that survives the next drawdown.

## The Order of Recovery

| Stage | What you do | Why it comes here |
|---|---|---|
| **1. Stay solvent** | Cut risk hard; honor circuit breakers and caps. | You cannot recover from ruin — survival precedes all. |
| **2. Reduce size** | Trade small until you trade well again. | Stops the bleeding; keeps the drawdown recoverable. |
| **3. Recover mind** | Step back, journal, accept losses as normal. | Clears the tilt and revenge that deepen the hole. |
| **4. Regain confidence** | Rebuild with small, clean executions. | Confidence follows competence; scale up only as results confirm. |

## Spiral or Recovery: The Governance Matrix

The same drawdown becomes a death spiral or a recoverable setback depending entirely on the response.

| Dimension | The Drawdown Spiral | The Disciplined Recovery |
|---|---|---|
| **First instinct** | Size up to win it back fast. | Cut size and risk immediately. |
| **Emotional state** | Revenge and desperation. | Acceptance and patience. |
| **Trade selection** | Forces trades to stay active. | Waits for only the elite setups. |
| **Path of the drawdown** | Deepens toward ruin. | Stabilizes, then recovers. |

| Dimension | The Drawdown Spiral | The Disciplined Recovery |
|---|---|---|
| **Confidence** | Demanded back all at once. | Rebuilt through clean trades. |
| **Outcome** | A setback becomes the end. | A setback becomes a lesson. |

## The Drawdown Survival Protocol

When a drawdown develops, run a structured process rather than improvising. This is the whole chapter compressed into a checklist — it turns chaos into a controlled recovery.

- **Limits.** Hit a daily or weekly loss limit → stop and journal. No discretion.
- **Diagnose.** Review recent trades; separate market conditions from rule violations.
- **De-risk.** Cut position size and leverage per the drawdown ladder, based on current equity.
- **Reset.** Take the mandatory psychological break; return only when calm and clear.
- **Re-enter on gates.** Trade Grade-A setups only, at graduated size, advancing through the rebuild phases.
- **Protect solvency.** Never risk the preserved core; maintain the cash minimum; no revenge trades.
- **Resume aggression.** Only after performance genuinely stabilizes and equity approaches the prior peak.

## Risk, Honesty, and a Reality Check

Drawdowns are not a sign of failure—they are an inevitable feature of trading, and of aggressive, leveraged trading especially. What separates survivors from casualties is never the absence of drawdowns; it is the response—and the honest truth is that the natural human response is the wrong one: to reach for size and speed exactly when prudence demands less of both. The reader who internalizes the order of recovery has the rarest skill in trading: the ability to lose, and to lose badly, without being destroyed by it.

## Blueprint Principle

A drawdown tests not your analysis but your response, and the response that works is almost the exact opposite of the one instinct demands. When the account falls, protect what remains rather than chasing what is gone: stay solvent above all, cut your size to stop the bleeding and quiet the emotion, step back to clear the tilt and accept that losing streaks are normal, then rebuild your confidence one clean, small, well-executed trade at a time and scale up only as the results return. Refuse the revenge trade, the desperate size-up, the demand to make it all back today. Do that, and every drawdown becomes survivable — and surviving drawdowns is, in the end, the whole job.

# PART VI – ADVANCED COMPOUNDING STRATEGIES

# Chapter 24
# The Power Law of Trading

Trading returns are not distributed evenly—they follow a **power law:** a few trades produce the overwhelming majority of the profit, while the great mass of trades are small wins, scratches, and small losses that roughly cancel out. The year is not made by being a little bit right a hundred times; it is made by a few trades that go enormously right, sitting on top of a sea of trades that went nowhere—a Pareto distribution, an 80/20 or even 90/10 dynamic, not a tidy bell curve. This is the same shape that governs venture capital, where a single investment can return an entire fund and roughly 4–10% of deals produce the bulk of the gains, and it governs individual stocks just as completely. In aggressive trading the skew is sharper still, because leverage amplifies it: one perfectly timed 3x ETF breakout or options multi-bagger can dwarf dozens of small losses. The power law is also indifferent to which side you are on—harnessed, a few huge winners dwarf many small losses and the curve compounds; inverted, the natural human tendency, a few huge losses erase many small gains. If a few trades make the result, then your job is not to trade often but to make sure you are present, and properly sized, for the rare trades that matter—and to keep every other trade small enough that it cannot do real damage while you wait.

## Why a Few Trades Create Most Returns

The engine behind the power law is asymmetry between winners and losers: if you cut losers small at a fixed, modest risk and let a few winners run to many multiples of that risk, most outcomes cluster near zero and a thin tail of large winners carries the whole account. A speculator who takes 50 trades over six months will typically find that 40 net out to breakeven, small scratch wins, or controlled 1R losses; the entire move from $100,000 to $1,000,000 is carried by perhaps three to five massive home runs where a concentrated position captures a multi-day vertical expansion of +10R to +20R. The other forty are not failures but low-cost exploration probes. This produces one of the most liberating facts in trading: **you can be right less than half the time and still compound powerfully,** provided your average winner is several times your average loser—a trader who wins 40% of the time but whose winners are five times the size of his losers makes money handily, because the math is driven by the size of outcomes, not their frequency. Leveraged instruments widen the right tail (a 10% move becomes 20–30% in a 2x or 3x ETF, and can explode in OTM options as gamma kicks in), so a single well-chosen winner can offset ten to twenty small losers—but that same leverage widens the left tail if you let it, which is why the structure depends on keeping individual losses small and fixed. The power law is always operating; the only choice is which tail you allow to be the large one.

## Concentrating on Elite Setups

If a few trades make the result, the quality of the trades you take matters far more than the quantity. The power law rewards **selectivity**—trading only the highest-conviction, highest-expectancy A-plus setups and passing on everything marginal—because every mediocre trade dilutes your edge, adds cost and risk, and occupies the attention and capital that belong to the elite setups. Overtrading is the enemy, usually driven by boredom, FOMO, and the urge to always be doing something, but activity is not edge. Elite setups are moments when probability, momentum, liquidity, and psychology align, sharing a multi-factor confluence: strong overall market conditions and a macro tailwind in a leading sector showing relative strength; a genuine catalyst (an earnings shock, an index-rebalancing event, a major re-pricing) layered onto a clean technical base such as a multi-week volatility-contraction pattern; clearly defined downside and large upside, a minimum reward-to-risk of roughly 1:5 with risk fixed by a stop or the instrument's structure; and favorable instrument mechanics (expanding IV for long options, a low-decay window for warrants, high convexity from OTM calls on 3x sector ETFs). Grade every candidate on a checklist and fire only on the ones scoring 9 out of 10 or better. Concentration must be controlled—concentrated conviction says *"this is an elite setup, my risk is defined, my exit is clear, and the reward is worth pressing,"* while reckless overexposure says *"I need this trade to work"*—so a genuinely elite setup earns more size, but always within the survival limits. In practice that means fewer, bigger bets (roughly 5–15 elite trades over six months, not 100-plus), predefined and journaled entry criteria with no FOMO entries, and scaling out partially (for example at 2R and 5R) while trailing stops aggressively on leveraged products.

## Portfolio Asymmetry

Asymmetry is the structural principle that makes the power law work *for* you. A well-built trading book is **convex:** every position has a capped, known, small downside and an open, potentially large upside, engineered deliberately with the fixed 1–2% risk per trade, stops that bound every loss, defined-risk instruments like long options whose loss cannot exceed the premium, and the scaling and trailing discipline that lets the rare big winner run far beyond its initial risk. Contrast the symmetric trap: if you risk $2,000 to make $2,000 you need an impossible win rate—north of 80%—just to overcome slippage and fees. The goal is **positive skew:** many small, controlled losses and a few outsized gains, the exact opposite of the negative-skew profile (many small gains, rare ruinous losses) that destroys most aggressive traders—a barbell of many small, strictly-bounded risks paired with a willingness to let a few turn into large winners. Build the skew with defined-risk structures (long options or debit spreads, protective puts or collars), tiered buckets (a preservation core in cash and Treasuries funding an opportunistic growth bucket), selective hedging and rotation (inverses or VIX products to cap drawdowns), and by avoiding negative-skew traps such as indefinite holds in 3x ETFs, where volatility drag erodes them in choppy markets.

## A Worked Sequence

Take a ten-trade stretch on a $100,000 base, with the 1R risk unit fixed at $2,000 (2% of equity). The figures are illustrative of the pattern, not a promise of results.

| Trades in the sequence | Result |
|---|---|

| Trades in the sequence | Result |
|---|---|
| 5 controlled technical losses | −5R = −$10,000 |
| 3 breakeven / scratch trades | 0R = $0 |
| 1 solid tactical win | +3R = +$6,000 |
| 1 power-law outlier (a max-size 3x ETF or option run) | **+18R** = **+$36,000** |
| **Net result — a 20% win rate** | **+$32,000 (a +32% account gain in one cycle)** |

Despite winning only one trade in five, the ledger expands 32% in a single cycle: the lone outlier did not merely repair the damage of the small losses, it drove the entire account into a new compounding tier. The winner does not need company; it needs only to be large, and to have been sized to matter.

## The Shape of a Year

Across a full campaign, a disciplined power-law book tends to produce roughly this shape—again, the point is the pattern, not the exact figures.

| Outcome bucket | Share of trades | Role in the result |
|---|---|---|
| **A few elite winners** | ~1 in 10 | Produce most of the net profit for the period. |
| **Ordinary winners** | Moderate | Keep the curve rising between the big wins. |
| **Small losses & scratches** | The majority | The controlled cost of finding the winners. |
| **The occasional larger loss** | Few — capped | Must stay small; this is what inverts the power law. |

## Harnessing It vs. Inverting It

The same power law makes one trader and breaks another, decided entirely by how they treat winners, losers, and the marginal trade.

| Dimension | Inverts the Power Law | Harnesses the Power Law |
|---|---|---|
| **Return expectation** | Steady daily profits; frustrated by routine small losses. | A Pareto distribution; small losses are exploration probes. |
| **Number of trades** | Many marginal trades. | Few elite setups. |

| Dimension | Inverts the Power Law | Harnesses the Power Law |
|---|---|---|
| **Losers** | Held and hoped back. | Cut small, always. |
| **Winners** | Sold early for comfort. | Allowed to run huge. |
| **In the big winner** | Underweight, or already out. | Present, and scaled into it. |
| **Skew of results** | Negative — a few big losses. | Positive — a few big wins. |
| **Outcome** | Small gains erased by a disaster. | Big wins dwarf the many small losses. |

## The Power-Law Ruleset

Translated into a working discipline, the chapter reduces to a few rules: **track a Pareto Score**—each week, measure the share of your P&L from your top 20% of trades, targeting 70–80% or more, because if the tail is not carrying the book you are overtrading; **cap elite allocation** at no more than 3–5 open high-conviction positions at once, keeping the rest in cash and preservation; **attribute monthly**, cutting anything not contributing to the tail; and **hunt home runs inside the risk frame**, never violating drawdown protocols or daily limits, since one oversized loser can erase several winners in leveraged trading.

## Risk, Honesty, and a Reality Check

The power law is a description of reality, not a technique that guarantees the upside. Concentrating on elite setups and engineering asymmetry gives the distribution a chance to break in your favor—it does not promise that it will, and it raises variance and drawdown along the way, because a book that depends on a few big winners has stretches where those winners simply have not arrived yet. Held correctly, the power law is freeing: it relieves you of the need to be right often and focuses the entire job on two controllable things—keeping losses small and not missing or fumbling the few winners that make the year.

## Blueprint Principle

> **A few trades will make most of your money, and you cannot know in advance which ones.**

The power law reorganizes the entire craft around asymmetry. Stop trying to be right often and start engineering a book where losses are small and capped while winners are large and open; concentrate your attention and size on the rare elite setups, pass on the marginal ones, and let the few winners run as far as the trend allows. Keep the left tail short with relentless loss discipline and the right tail long with patient winners—invert it, and the same law that could have made you will quietly take you apart.

# Chapter 25
# Riding Supercycles

A supercycle is a multi-year secular trend—a structural force, technological or demographic or geopolitical, large enough to lift an entire theme for years rather than weeks. When one is underway, institutional money flows toward it relentlessly, and the strongest names produce sustained, large-scale moves that the rest of this book's setups merely try to catch in miniature. For aggressive compounding, supercycles matter because they are where the rare power-law winners live—the 5x, 10x, 50x asymmetric moves, often expressed through leveraged instruments, that can vault a $100,000 account toward seven figures in months. But a supercycle is not a promise; it is a hunting ground. This is also the chapter where being *right* is most dangerous, so the warning belongs at the front: **a true theme and a survivable trade are not the same thing.** The internet was the real supercycle of its era, and the great majority of internet stocks still went to zero—you can be correct about the decade and be destroyed by the drawdown along the way. A supercycle is driven by a structural change that compounds over years, which makes it different from a normal sector rotation lasting weeks to months: the supercycle is the tide, rotations are the waves on top of it. The theme can be real and durable while the stocks attached to it are wildly overvalued and one disappointment away from a 50% to 80% drawdown—the narrative compounds slowly while the price swings violently—so the discipline is to trade the price action that confirms the theme, never the story by itself, because the story will keep you holding all the way down.

## The Six Supercycles

Each of the following is a genuine structural driver with a distinct trading personality and a characteristic way of hurting the careless. Leadership within each rotates constantly—today's dominant name is rarely tomorrow's—so these describe the theme, its mechanics, and its risk, not a recommendation of any specific security.

**Artificial intelligence** is the broadest driver: demand for compute and automation reaching into nearly every industry at once. Its character is concentration and expectation—leadership clusters in a handful of mega-caps, valuations run rich, and the whole complex resets sharply whenever the pace of expectations disappoints. AI is not a single trade but a chain: capital flows in waves from the obvious model and chip leaders, to secondary suppliers (memory, networking, advanced packaging), to the physical infrastructure of data centers, power, and cooling, then to speculative small caps—so trade where capital is rotating now. Express it through broad AI and technology ETFs, leveraged tech or semiconductor ETFs for trending legs, and long calls or debit spreads on bellwethers around pullbacks, scaling out into strength.

**Semiconductors** are the physical layer beneath AI, devices, and data—and the most deeply cyclical theme here, booming and busting on inventory and capex cycles across designers, foundries, memory producers, equipment makers, and materials. Industry sales have run near record levels into 2026, but the cycle is the point: great companies still suffer brutal drawdowns when expectations get too high, so even in a real supercycle the entry price matters.

This is exactly where leveraged ETFs are most dangerous—a 3x semiconductor fund is savage in the down-cycle and in choppy markets—so trade the liquid sector ETFs for cleaner exposure, reserve the 3x products for confirmed trends under strict limits, and watch capex guidance and Taiwan-China geopolitics as the swing factors.

**Biotech and gene editing**, driven by medical innovation and aging demographics, is the most idiosyncratic theme: individual names live and die on binary trial and approval outcomes, gapping 30%, 50%, even 70% in either direction overnight. The theme trends, but single-stock risk is extreme, so traders often ride it through a diversified group or a leveraged biotech ETF, or only after a catalyst resolves. Stronger setups share late-stage clinical data, a real cash runway, credible institutional backing, and a clear catalyst, and the cleanest way to play the binaries is with defined-risk spreads that cap the loss to the premium, kept in smaller size.

**Energy and the power bottleneck** spans traditional production, the energy transition, the geopolitics of supply, and increasingly the power demand created by AI itself—data centers require enormous electricity, grid capacity, backup generation, and cooling, and forecasters now project some of the strongest multi-year U.S. electricity-demand growth in a generation. Its character is commodity- and macro-driven, rotating hard with the price of the underlying. The richest trades come when technology demand meets physical scarcity across natural gas, nuclear and uranium, renewables, grid equipment, and storage—so trade the rotation rather than marrying the position, and remember the direct overlap with the AI and semiconductor trades driving the demand.

**Quantum computing** is the frontier theme—enormous theoretical potential, little present profitability—giving it the highest hype-to-fundamentals ratio of the six. It trades on narrative and milestones, dominated by smaller, speculative, cash-burning names with extreme volatility: the up-moves can be spectacular and the reversals total. Separate real contracts from press releases and revenue from prototypes, keep it to a small, opportunistic tranche, express breakthroughs through OTM calls or warrants where the loss is capped, and watch for AI-quantum convergence as the catalyst that could give the theme genuine substance.

**Defense and geopolitical themes** are driven by conflict, rearmament, and multi-year government spending cycles, spanning contractors, drones, missile defense, cyber-defense, space and satellite systems, hypersonics, and battlefield AI—moving on headlines and policy more than quarterly fundamentals, which produces event-driven spikes that are hard to time. A crucial caution: defense stocks do not always rise on war headlines—in a broad risk-off move they can fall with everything else—so watch the price action, not the assumption. The theme carries ethical weight each trader must weigh; as a market theme, its defining feature is dependence on events and politics no chart can forecast.

## How to Ride a Supercycle

The method is the same disciplined machinery from the rest of the book, pointed at the theme rather than a single stock. **Confirm the money flow:** a real supercycle shows up as a sector trending on heavy volume with broad participation and persistent leadership, visible in the sector ETF, not just one headline stock—trade the theme only while the flow confirms it. **Trade the leaders and the ETFs:** ride the strongest names in the strongest part of the theme, or the liquid sector ETF for cleaner exposure, avoiding thin speculative names except in deliberately tiny size. **Scale with the trend, not the story:** add on confirmation using the pyramiding discipline, trail on the daily timeframe, and let the supercycle's persistence give your runners room while the trend holds. **Size for the theme's volatility:** crowded, high-beta themes gap hard, so leveraged theme exposure must be sized for the drawdown, not the dream. **Rotate as capital rotates:** within a theme, money moves from leaders to suppliers to infrastructure to small caps; across themes, it rotates with the macro—AI to energy to defense as conditions shift.

## The Risk Overlay

Because these themes are so powerful, the survival rules must be explicit: **cap thematic concentration**—keep total portfolio heat modest, on the order of 8%, and never let any single theme exceed roughly 10% of the book; **hold a preservation core** of 30–50% in cash and Treasuries that funds the opportunistic bucket and absorbs drawdowns; **match the instrument to the bet**—defined-risk options for binary events, 3x ETFs only for confirmed trends under strict daily limits, and larger size for the rare elite setups; and **demand confluence**, entering only when a technical breakout, a real catalyst, and cycle alignment all agree. Held this way, one or two 100%-plus thematic winners can drive the large equity jumps the campaign depends on—but only because the survival rules keep you in the game long enough to be holding them when they come.

## When the Cycle Turns

Thematic drawdowns are violent, and they are where supercycle traders are destroyed. The defining trap is that **the story stays intact while the stocks crater**—the long-term thesis is still true, the news still sounds bullish, and yet prices fall 50%, 70%, or more as the crowd unwinds and valuations reset, so a trader anchored to the narrative holds the whole way down. Two distinctions keep you alive. The first is between a pullback and a regime change: a healthy theme pulls back and resumes on its leaders, while a topping theme breaks leadership, loses its volume, and fails to make new highs even on good news. The second is between the thesis and the trade: you can keep believing in the decade-long story while being completely flat the stock, because the trade is governed by the trend and the stop, not the conviction—so when the trend breaks you exit, free to re-enter when the price action confirms the theme again. And because a turning supercycle savages leverage, the leveraged-ETF and options exposure must be the first thing reduced when the trend cracks.

| Theme | Structural driver | Characteristic risk |
|---|---|---|
| **Artificial intelligence** | Compute and automation demand across every industry | Crowded and richly valued; violent resets on disappointment |
| **Semiconductors** | The physical layer beneath AI, devices, and data | Deeply cyclical; leveraged ETFs brutal in the down-leg |
| **Biotech / gene editing** | Medical innovation and aging demographics | Binary trial/approval outcomes; huge overnight gaps |
| **Energy / power** | Structural demand, the transition, AI power needs | Commodity- and macro-driven; sharp rotations |
| **Quantum computing** | Frontier compute — potential, not yet profits | Highest hype-to-fundamentals; extreme volatility |
| **Defense / geopolitical** | Conflict, rearmament, and spending cycles | Headline- and policy-dependent; hard-to-time spikes |

## Story vs. Price: The Governance Matrix

The whole discipline of supercycle trading is refusing to let a true story override the price.

| Dimension | The Narrative Chaser | The Disciplined Theme-Trader |
|---|---|---|
| **What they trade** | The story itself. | The price action that confirms the story. |
| **Entry** | Buys the hype near the top. | Enters on confirmed money flow and leadership. |
| **On valuation** | "It's the future, so it can't fall." | Knows a true theme can still fall 50–80%. |
| **Leverage in the theme** | Max leverage on the narrative. | Sizes for the thematic drawdown. |
| **When it corrects** | Holds because the story is intact. | Exits on the trend break; story is not the trade. |

## Risk, Honesty, and a Reality Check

Supercycles are the richest source of the most painful experience in markets: being right and losing anyway. The driver is genuine, the multi-year direction may even play out as you expect, and you can still be wiped out by a drawdown your conviction would not let you sell—or by the leverage you added because you were so sure. The disciplined theme-trader captures the tailwind precisely because he never forgets it is a tailwind and not a guarantee, riding the supercycle while the price confirms it and stepping aside the moment it doesn't.

## Blueprint Principle

Supercycles — AI, semiconductors, biotech, energy, quantum, defense — are the deepest water in the market, the place where the sector and swing setups reach their full power because the biggest money is moving for years in one direction. Ride them by confirming the flow, trading the leaders and the liquid ETFs, scaling with the trend, and sizing for the violence these crowded themes produce. Honor the line between the story and the trade: believe in the decade if you wish, but let the price and the stop govern the position, and reduce the leverage the instant the trend cracks. Caught correctly, a supercycle is the strongest tailwind a trader can have; mistaken for a guarantee, it is the most expensive conviction he can hold.

## Chapter 26
# Swing Trading for Rapid Growth

Swing trading sits in the powerful middle ground between day trading and investing: the day trader seeks intraday movement, the investor waits months or years, and the swing trader captures multi-day to multi-week momentum, typically holding two to ten days. For a campaign to grow $100,000 into $1,000,000 in six months, that horizon is ideal—it lets capital participate in moves far larger than intraday scalping can reach, without the execution friction that grinds down a constant-trading curve and without the volatility drag that punishes long holds in leveraged products. The engine underneath is institutional accumulation: when a meaningful catalyst hits a stock, large funds must move enormous capital into it, and because they cannot sweep the order book in a single session without spiking their own costs, their algorithms build the position systematically over several days—creating a structured, exploitable directional runway, expressed through high-beta stocks, 2x and 3x ETFs, options, and warrants. The objective is not to trade every fluctuation but to capture the strongest segment of a move while avoiding dead money: **find stocks already in motion, enter with discipline, hold through controlled volatility, and exit before momentum decays.** The four setups in this chapter—multi-day momentum, high-beta selection, earnings continuation, and sector acceleration—are the highest-probability ways to do exactly that.

## A. Multi-Day Momentum

*Renting the 72-to-120 Hour Institutional Velocity Window*

Multi-day momentum is sustained directional strength that continues for several sessions after a breakout, catalyst, earnings report, or sector shift. It feeds on itself—rising prices draw in other traders, short-covering, options buyers, algorithmic momentum strategies, and rotation capital—so the question is never "did the stock go up today?" but "is there enough force behind this to continue for several more days?" The mental model that matters: you are not buying a company's long-term future, you are renting a 72-to-120 hour stream of institutional order flow, and your rent is due the moment that flow stops pushing the tape. A healthy setup shows rising volume on up days, shallow pullbacks, strong closes near the high, price holding above key moving averages, and relative strength versus the market—concretely, names up roughly 5–15% over five to ten sessions on expanding volume, momentum elevated but not yet exhausted. The greatest risk is chasing an extended move: a stock up 40% in two days may go higher, but the risk-reward has deteriorated sharply, so prefer early breakouts, first pullbacks, and continuation entries after controlled digestion—never the last buyer in a crowded trade.

### Why It Compounds So Fast — and the Honest Math

Rather than grinding out dozens of small intraday trades, the swing trader aims to capture the meat of a single large move—gains of 15%, 25%, 40%, 75%, even 150% from one well-timed opportunity—and a handful of them, compounded, can change the trajectory of an account. The table below shows one hypothetical sequence from $100,000 to seven figures. Read it as arithmetic, not a forecast:

| Starting capital | Gain | New capital |
|---|---|---|
| $100,000 | +25% | $125,000 |
| $125,000 | +30% | $162,500 |
| $162,500 | +35% | $219,375 |
| $219,375 | +40% | $307,125 |
| $307,125 | +50% | $460,688 |
| $460,688 | +60% | $737,101 |
| $737,101 | +40% | **$1,031,941** |

**Read the Math Honestly** That sequence assumes seven consecutive winning trades with no meaningful setbacks. Real trading does not work that way. Losses, missed entries, choppy tape, and regime changes are inevitable, and the same multiplication that compounds gains compounds losses just as fast – a single oversized loss can erase several good trades. Separate aspiration from probability. A 10x in six months sits at the extreme tail of outcomes and is reached by very few; the leveraged tactics that make it conceivable also make a total loss of capital a real and common result. Treat the figure as a direction that justifies discipline, not an entitlement. To even approach it you would need consistent, compounded returns with leverage in a sustained trend – mathematically possible, but wiped out by a few undisciplined losers.

## The Best Candidates: Where Momentum Ignites

Multi-day momentum develops around a genuine catalyst—a reason institutions are suddenly forced to own something they did not own last week:

| Catalyst | Why it ignites a multi-day move |
|---|---|
| Earnings surprises | Unexpected beats trigger forced institutional repositioning. |
| Guidance increases | Raised forward guidance often matters more than the current quarter. |
| FDA approvals | Biotech names can trend for days after a pivotal decision. |
| Breakthrough technology | AI, quantum, cybersecurity, semis, robotics, space, defense. |
| Government contracts | Large awards generate extended, multi-day momentum. |

| Catalyst | Why it ignites a multi-day move |
|---|---|
| Short squeezes | High short interest plus rising price produces explosive rallies. |
| Sector rotation | Capital flooding a sector lifts many names together (semis, uranium, defense, AI infrastructure). |

The strongest setups stack catalyst with technical alignment: a real reason to move, occurring in a name already structurally primed to break out. A catalyst without a chart is a gamble; a chart without a catalyst is a guess.

## Anatomy of the Day-1 Velocity Bar

A multi-day move announces itself with a Day-1 Velocity Bar—a daily candle that represents a complete break from prior price equilibrium, the visual signature of institutional desks caught off-balance and scrambling to reposition. It emerges from regime consolidation (the asset tightening within a multi-week shelf) into a decisive break on a surge of volume, and it must clear three filters:

> **The Three Ignition Filters Filter 1 — Closing location.** The daily close must sit in the top 10% of the session's range. A close on the highs signals buyers were in control into the bell, not exhausted. **Filter 2 — Volume confirmation.** Volume must register at least 200% of the 20-day average — proof that institutions, not a thin retail pop, drove the move. **Filter 3 — Structural break.** Price must clear a genuine historical overhead resistance level, releasing the asset from a multi-week shelf into open air.

When a high-beta equity or leveraged ETF prints this bar, closing at the peak of its range on historic relative volume and clearing structural resistance, it is highly probable that institutional execution algorithms keep buying into the next session to complete their allocation mandates. That probability is your edge.

## Confirming Strength and Entering

Beyond the ignition bar, use two or three confirming indicators—not ten. Relative volume (RVOL), current volume divided by the average for the time of day, is the most important momentum tell; price above the rising 20- and 50-day MAs confirms trend (a golden cross or a controlled pullback to the 20-day marks a low-risk continuation entry); RSI above 50–60 signals real strength while above 70–80 warns of overbought reversal risk; and MACD above its signal line with an expanding histogram indicates accelerating momentum. Three entry protocols cover the field. **Protocol A — the Day-1 closing-print squeeze:** when a stock clears a massive multi-month consolidation on unprecedented volume, buy the final closing print of Day 1 (roughly 3:55–4:00 PM ET), stepping in alongside the algorithms as they confirm control into the close. **Protocol B — the Day-2 opening-range breakout:** isolate the 15-minute opening-range high and buy the moment price fractures it on expanding volume, letting the market prove continuation and filtering out one-day flashes. **Protocol C — the Day-1/2/3 pullback:** a huge Day-1 breakout, controlled Day-2 consolidation on lighter volume (the shake-out), then a renewed Day-3 breakout above the Day-1 high as your entry, with a tight stop beneath the consolidation—often the best reward-to-risk because the invalidation level is close and clearly defined. Before committing, the core checklist demands the asset up roughly 5–10%+ over the prior 3–5 days on expanding volume, a real catalyst, a break above resistance or the 20-day MA on high volume, and—for a leveraged ETF—the underlying index momentum confirmed first; if a sane stop would be wider than your risk budget allows, you pass, no exceptions.

## Choosing Your Instrument

Match the vehicle to your conviction and holding window—each rung adds leverage and the obligation to size down and hold shorter.

| Instrument | Best used for | Trade-off to respect |
|---|---|---|
| **Stocks** | High-beta leaders with a live catalyst | Cleanest risk control; no structural decay |
| **Sector / 1x ETFs** | Confirming and expressing the broad move | Lower single-name risk; diversified |
| **2x / 3x ETFs** | Amplified plays (a 5% index move ≈ 15% in a 3x) | Outsized gains – with volatility decay; short holds |
| **Options (long calls)** | Asymmetric, defined-risk leverage on breakouts | Capped loss; convex upside; theta + IV-crush risk |
| **Warrants** | Long-dated leverage where available | Leverage with variable liquidity and terms |

## Fencing the Downside and Sizing the Risk

Trading high-beta vehicles—3x ETFs such as SOXL or TQQQ, or near-term options—means living with exceptional volatility, so tie your invalidation directly to the physics of the ignition candle and automate it.

> **The Automated Bracket Order** The instant your entry triggers, submit a non-negotiable bracket order to the broker. **Structural stop.** Place the hard stop at the mid-point (the 50% level) of the Day-1 Velocity Bar, or immediately beneath the Day-2 opening 15-minute low – whichever your entry protocol defines. **Alternative for slower vehicles.** For stocks and 1x ETFs, a 5–8% stop below entry, or a close below the recent swing low or the 20-day MA, serves the same purpose. **The discipline.** If institutional flow fails to hold these thresholds, the position is liquidated to cash automatically – bypassing the emotional hesitation that turns a 1R loss into a 5R disaster.

Define risk as the dollars lost if the stop is hit—your 1R unit—and cap it at 1–2% of total NAV per trade. On a $100,000 account that is $1,000–$2,000 at risk on any single idea, regardless of how large the position appears; use the smaller end, or less, for 3x ETFs and options. Your stop distance and risk budget together set your share or contract count—never the reverse.

## The Extraction Plan

You are renting these moves for a 3-to-5 day window, and your extraction logic must be defined before you enter. Scale in as conviction builds rather than committing full size at once—four equal tranches of 25% (initial confirmed entry, confirmation breakout, trend continuation, and trend firmly established), so your largest exposure coincides with your highest proof. Scale out into strength: at the +2R milestone, liquidate 50% of the position, lock the gain, and move the stop on the remainder to blended break-even, making the trade risk-free; alternatively scale out in 20%/30%/30%/20% tranches into successive targets. Then trail the remainder with a daily 9-EMA tripwire or a 2–3x ATR stop, forcing a full exit to cash when the asset closes below its 9-EMA or breaks the ATR trail, or when it reaches Day 5 without printing a new high—stalled momentum in a leveraged vehicle bleeds. Momentum rarely vanishes without warning: declining volume on advances, failed breakouts and gap-down reversals, clustering distribution days, lower highs and lost moving averages, negative news or insider selling, and broad sector weakness all signal that demand is leaving—exit and rotate toward the next ignition rather than hoping for a recovery the order flow no longer supports.

## Strategy Variations, Frictions, and Discipline

The same engine runs through several playbooks—choose the one that fits the regime, and do not run all four at full size at once: **breakout momentum** (fresh breakouts from consolidation or pullbacks-to-support in an uptrend, the bread-and-butter setup), **relative-strength rotation** (rank by 1–3 month performance and rotate into the top performers), **leveraged-ETF rotation** (swing between sector 3x ETFs on momentum scores, always confirming the underlying index first), and **options overlay** (calls on the strongest names for 5–10x leverage, accepting theta decay if the trend stalls). Feed them with a daily scan for percentage gainers on volume above ~1,000,000 shares, price above $5–10 for liquidity, and a verifiable catalyst. The frictions the brochure won't mention are real: overnight and news risk on multi-day holds (size down ahead of binary events), volatility decay in leveraged ETFs that reset daily and bleed in choppy stretches (short-hold instruments, full stop), options decay to theta and IV crush after the catalyst passes, and commissions, spreads, short-term taxes, and margin interest that erode the curve—model them, do not assume them away. The discipline that survives: ignore noise and trust tested rules over impulses, resist FOMO because there is always another ignition, accept that being wrong cheaply is the job, stay patient for high-quality setups, and let evidence rather than hope determine every exit.

## The Multi-Day Momentum Governance Matrix

Every rule reduces to one discipline: operate like a fiduciary of your own capital, not a casualty of your own emotions.

| Operational vector | The retail-casualty trap | The 10x Blueprint fiduciary |
|---|---|---|
| **Asset** | Buys slow, low-beta charts out | Targets high-beta anomalies |

| Operational vector | The retail-casualty trap | The 10x Blueprint fiduciary |
|---|---|---|
| **selection** | of a desire for comfort. | (≥2.0) under explosive institutional buying. |
| **Entry timing** | Chases after four vertical days, buying the absolute peak. | Enters on the Day-1 closing squeeze or the Day-2 15-minute ORB. |
| **Risk containment** | Moves or deletes stops when a position goes red, hoping for a bounce. | Locks an automated bracket at the mid-point of the ignition bar. |
| **Trade extraction** | Holds a fading trend out of greed, watching a win round-trip to scratch. | Scales out half at +2R and applies the 3-to-5 Day Sunset to return to cash. |

Distilled to working principles: trade where institutions are buying (follow the footprint, not the forum); focus on powerful catalysts and prioritize relative volume and liquidity; buy confirmed strength, not hope; add only as the trade proves itself, sizing largest where proof is highest; cut losses decisively; allow exceptional winners room to compound via the scale-out and trail; rotate capital into the strongest opportunities; increase aggressiveness only when the broad market supports momentum; and remember that survival precedes compounding—capital preserved today finances tomorrow's opportunities.

## B. High-Beta Setups

*Weaponizing Volatility Inside an Iron Risk Vice*

You cannot compound a $100,000 account toward $1,000,000 by parking capital in plodding, low-beta mega-caps—if an asset moves 1.5% on its best day, the compounding engine runs out of road long before the seven-figure mark. For a six-month 10x campaign, beta is an ally—a 3% move in the index can become +10% to +25% inside a concentrated high-beta book—but it cuts both ways, so high-beta trading demands the strictest risk control in the book: smaller position sizes than for low-volatility names (on the order of 2–5% of equity, kept within the 8% portfolio-heat cap), wider but clearly defined stops, and no emotional averaging down.

Beta (β) measures an asset's volatility relative to a benchmark such as the S&P 500, where the index itself is β = 1.0. A name with a beta of 1.5 tends to move about 15% when the market moves 10%; a beta of 2.0 moves roughly twice the market; and a vehicle with a beta of 2.5 to 4.0 does not merely climb in a tailwind—it goes vertical. **High beta is the capital lever:** by pairing hyper-responsive assets with tight technical structures, you swing a massive nominal hammer while keeping the actual capital you risk strictly fenced. The catch is symmetry—the same characteristic that produces outsized gains produces outsized losses, and high-beta names fall hardest in a correction—so this is best understood as a tool for amplifying opportunity inside a disciplined risk framework, not a shortcut to wealth. Volatility is not the enemy of rapid growth; uncontrolled risk is.

| Beta | Behavior | Implication for the 10x trader |
|---|---|---|
| β = 1.0 | Moves roughly in line with the market. | Index-like; no compounding edge. |
| β = 1.5 | About a 15% move when the market moves 10%. | Mild amplification. |
| β = 2.0 | Roughly twice the market's move. | The working floor for this strategy. |
| β > 2.0 | Extremely volatile; large moves in both directions. | Favored by aggressive momentum traders — with strict rules. |

High-beta names can deliver 10%+ single-day moves, 20%+ weekly advances, 50–100% rallies over a few weeks, and multi-hundred-percent moves during exceptional cycles—and layering leverage on top (a 5–10% index move becoming a 15–30%+ swing in a 3x vehicle) supplies the raw material for rapid compounding. Most important, **high beta is not the same as high quality:** high-beta leadership has volume, trend, sponsorship, catalysts, and relative strength, while high-beta garbage merely moves violently. The aggressive trader wants volatility with structure, always sized for the drawdown rather than the dream.

## The Volatility Filter and Elite Candidates

Enforce an unbending Beta Floor of β ≥ 2.0 (some traders screen from β ≥ 1.8), and concentrate capital into two domains only: **high-beta alpha equities** (fabless semiconductor designers, AI-infrastructure bottlenecks, and hyper-growth tech disruptors—volatile small- and mid-caps where less capital is required to move price) and **3x leveraged multipliers** (index-backed structural vehicles such as SOXL for semiconductors, FNGU for FANG+ innovation, or a high-beta S&P vehicle like HIBL). Require, before a name earns a place on the live watchlist: beta ≥ 2.0 (or ≥ 1.8 as a wider net), high relative volume and genuine liquidity (average daily volume above ~1,000,000 shares, tight spreads), a verifiable catalyst, and constructive technicals (price above the rising 20- and 50-day MAs, RSI roughly 55–70, MACD bullish, volume confirming on up days). The best candidates further share a small or mid capitalization, a strong catalyst, RVOL above 2 (preferably above 3, with exceptional setups exceeding 5–10), high short interest that can force a squeeze, and strong price momentum—new 52-week highs, clean breakouts, higher highs and higher lows. Certain sectors structurally run hot:

| Sector | Why it runs hot |
|---|---|
| Artificial Intelligence | AI software, infrastructure, machine learning, AI chips |
| Semiconductors | Chipmakers, optical networking, memory, equipment |

| Sector | Why it runs hot |
|---|---|
| | suppliers |
| Biotechnology | FDA approvals, clinical-trial results, drug pipelines (binary catalysts) |
| Quantum Computing | Small names with dramatic moves on breakthroughs or government initiatives |
| Cybersecurity | Government contracts, enterprise adoption, major security incidents |
| Defense | Geopolitical events producing powerful, sustained trends |
| Nuclear Energy | Rising electricity demand fueling strong momentum |
| Space Technology | Launch contracts, satellite communications, defense applications |

Representative names and vehicles (as of mid-2026—always verify beta and liquidity live before trading): high-beta single stocks such as NVDA, AMD, MU, ASML, and the news-driven TSLA; high-beta ETFs such as SPHB (S&P 500 High Beta) and its leveraged cousin HIBL (3x daily), plus sector 3x vehicles like SOXL and TQQQ. Micro-caps with extreme betas (5–10+) carry liquidity risk—treat them with extra caution and smaller size. *Tickers are illustrative of the instrument type, not recommendations, and beta values drift over time.*

## The Apex Setup: The High Tight Flag

High beta without technical structure is unmanaged chaos—an asset swinging 15% a day with no order is untradable, because you cannot place an intelligent stop. The magic happens when a hyper-volatile name compresses its energy into a tight, coiled shelf:

> **Anatomy of the High Tight Flag The pole.** A near-vertical explosion of +100% or more within a 4-to-8 week window, driven by a genuine institutional catalyst. **The flag.** Instead of crashing back, the asset holds its gains and consolidates sideways in a tight, orderly pattern that retraces no more than 10–20% of the pole. The shallow pullback signals that institutions are absorbing every sell order at current prices. **Why it matters.** The tightness of the flag is what makes the trade asymmetric: it places a clean, close invalidation level directly beneath your entry, so a high-octane vehicle can be traded with a microscopic, well-defined risk.

Among high-beta patterns, the shallow-retrace flag following an explosive pole offers one of the most favorable structures aggressive traders can find. Demand multiple confirmations before committing: a clean breakout above resistance or the flag's trendline ceiling, strong expanding volume (ideally 1.5–2x average) on the break, a close near the day's high, increasing institutional participation and sector leadership, and broad-market support. Two entry paths: the **pivot breakout** (buy the exact moment price fractures the flag's ceiling on expanding volume) or the **pullback-to-support** (in an established uptrend, buy a controlled pullback to the 20-day MA or a prior swing low, stop just beneath support; for leveraged ETFs and options, confirm the underlying index momentum first to avoid decay traps).

## Choosing Your Instrument

Express the high-beta view through the vehicle that matches your conviction and holding window—each rung adds leverage and the obligation to size down.

| Instrument | Best used for | Trade-off to respect |
|---|---|---|
| **Growth stocks** | Naturally high-beta single names with a catalyst | Cleanest risk control; no structural decay |
| **Sector ETFs (1x)** | Broad exposure to a fast-moving industry | Lower single-name risk; diversified |
| **2x ETFs** | Magnified sector exposure | Amplified moves; mild daily-reset decay |
| **3x ETFs** | Short-term tactical bursts (SOXL, HIBL) | Outsized gains — with real decay; short holds only |
| **Call options** | Asymmetric, defined-risk leverage (5–20x effective) | Capped loss; high gamma; theta + IV-crush risk |
| **Warrants** | Longer-dated leverage where available | Leverage with variable liquidity and terms |

## Risk Isolation: Caging the NAV

The public fears high-beta assets because it confuses asset volatility with portfolio risk—they are not the same thing. If your entry sits close to the structural floor of a tight pattern, the asset can be wildly volatile while the risk to your account stays microscopic.

> **The Tight Risk Vice Pivot entry.** Enter on the confirmed break of the flag's ceiling. **Structural stop.** The instant the entry fills, an automated stop locks immediately beneath the lowest point of the flag's consolidation shelf — frequently just 2–4% below the entry print (a 4–7% stop for wider, gappier names). **The asymmetry.** Even though the asset can surge +30% in a multi-day sprint, the actual risk to your parent portfolio is capped at a standard 1R unit. A microscopic, defined downside paired with a non-linear upside is the entire point of high-beta structure.

Define risk as the dollars lost if the stop is hit and cap it tightly: because high-beta moves are violent, use 0.5–1% of total NAV per trade (toward 1–2% only for lower-beta, cleaner-structured names), roughly $500–$1,000 at risk per idea on a $100,000 account. High beta demands a smaller share or contract count, not a larger one—the volatility does the work—and options can deliver the exposure with premium-only risk. Because the downside is caged at 1R, a single clean high-beta expansion can return +5R to +10R over a multi-day sprint: you do not need a high win rate when your structure makes winners several times larger than losers.

### Extraction, Danger Signs, and Psychology

A high-beta winner that round-trips to break-even is a self-inflicted wound, so define the extraction before you enter: bank 30–50% into the first 10–20% gain and move the stop to break-even; trail the runner with a 2–3x ATR stop or successive prior highs; exit on a break of the structural floor (the 4–7% level) with no negotiation; apply a time stop if there is no continuation after 5–10 days; and sell into strength once the catalyst is fully digested. Stand aside when high beta turns dangerous—weak volume (no institutional sponsor), extended charts (the easy move is gone), weak market conditions (high-beta names fall hardest in corrections), poor liquidity (wide spreads tax every entry and make stops unreliable), or no catalyst (volatility without a driver is noise). The same engine runs through four playbooks—catalyst-driven high-beta, relative-strength rotation, a leveraged overlay on a core stock, and out-of-the-money calls for asymmetry—and high beta tests emotional discipline more than any other style: the recurring account-enders are chasing vertical moves after the clean entry has passed, selling winners early and holding losers long, trading from FOMO, and increasing size after a loss to win it back.

### Risk Reality and the Honest Math

High beta is the most powerful accelerant in this book and the most efficient way to destroy an account; both are true at once. Volatility decay erodes 3x ETFs in choppy markets even when the underlying ends flat (short-swing tools only); gap risk can move a high-beta name 10–30% overnight straight through a stop; high-beta names fall hardest and together in a crash, so diversifying across five of them is not diversification; and big wins followed by big losers is where most retail traders blow up.

> **The Math Behind the 10x Target** To even approach a 10x in six months, the arithmetic demands roughly a 40–50%+ win rate paired with a 2:1 or better reward-to-risk ratio, chained across many trades in favorable markets. That is mathematically possible — and wiped out by a handful of undisciplined losers, a single over-sized position, or one bad gap. Separate aspiration from probability. A 10x in six months sits at the extreme tail of outcomes; the leverage that makes it conceivable makes total loss of capital a common result. Treat the figure as a direction that justifies discipline, not an entitlement you are owed. Position sizing, stops, and even-in-aggressive-mode diversification are non-negotiable, and transaction costs, taxes, and margin requirements all erode the curve.

## C. Earnings Continuation

*Weaponizing the Post-Earnings Announcement Drift*

Earnings season is the ultimate catalyst engine, and most retail traders handle it exactly backwards—gambling on options premiums in the hours before an announcement, guessing direction, and getting crushed by the implied-volatility collapse that follows the print. The 10x trader operates on the opposite side of the timeline: let the data drop, let the numbers replace the speculation, then react to what the institutions do next. When an elite company prints a genuine blowout—shattering revenue and EPS estimates, expanding margins, and raising forward guidance—it creates an instant valuation mismatch, and because large funds cannot fill multi-million-share positions in a single session without moving price against themselves, their algorithms accumulate over days or weeks. That footprint is the continuation runway, and the academic literature calls the resulting tendency **Post-Earnings Announcement Drift (PEAD):** price keeps moving in the direction of the surprise long after the report. The work of this chapter is to separate the setups where the initial reaction marks the beginning of institutional accumulation from those that are merely a one-day burst of enthusiasm—and to trade the former with structure, size discipline, and a caged downside. The edge lives in the continuation, not the print: never gamble through the report itself.

## Why Earnings Drive Momentum

Earnings season is the moment opinions become facts. A genuine narrative-changing print usually carries several features at once—revenue growth well above expectations, a significant EPS beat, expanding margins, raised forward guidance, accelerating customer or unit growth, strong free cash flow, and optimistic, specific management commentary—and the most important is raised guidance, because markets price the future, not the past. PEAD is one of the most studied anomalies in finance, documented across many markets and decades, yet it is a statistical tendency, not a guarantee: it can weaken or vanish under different conditions, and the documented edges are measured before trading costs. The market underreacts because analysts update models gradually over days and weeks, institutions accumulate over multiple sessions, investors systematically underreact to genuinely new information, short sellers are forced to cover into rising prices, and momentum traders join once the trend becomes visible—a self-reinforcing sequence of higher highs, rolling upgrades, and still more institutional buying.

## The Earnings Power Gap-Up Filter

Ruthlessly screen out minor beats—an institutional continuation run requires a fundamental shockwave, not a rounding-error surprise. Run a focused pre-market scan (around 9:15 AM ET) and demand three non-negotiable filters:

> **The Three Gap-Up Filters 1. The catalyst metric.** A major positive earnings surprise (a meaningful EPS and revenue beat — think a double-digit-percentage surprise, or a high standardized-unexpected-earnings reading) accompanied by an upward revision to forward guidance. **2. The price metric.** The asset gaps up at least +8% (large-caps) or +15% (mid- and small-caps), clearing a clean horizontal resistance level or multi-week consolidation shelf. **3. The volume metric.** Pre-market activity projects daily volume tracking toward +300% of the 20-day average — the fingerprint of institutions, not a thin retail spike.

A candidate that satisfies all three is rare, and that scarcity is the point. Beyond the gap, the highest-quality setups fuse exceptional fundamentals with clean technical action—on the day of the print: an exceptional beat, raised guidance, a strong 8–20%+ gap that holds, heavy relative volume (RVOL above 3x, preferably above 5x, with extraordinary setups exceeding 10x), and a close near the high; in the underlying business: explosive revenue growth (30%, 50%, 100%+), accelerating earnings (the market rewards the second derivative), industry leadership in transformative themes, and institutional sponsorship with a cluster of analyst upgrades.

## The Execution Setup: The 30-Minute Opening Range Box

Chasing an earnings gap blindly at the 9:30 AM ET bell is an execution error—the first minutes are pure hysteria, with wide spreads, violent two-way swings, and profit-taking from pre-market participants. From 9:30 to 10:00 AM ET you do not touch the asset; you only plot the absolute high and low of those first 30 minutes, forming a structural box, and the exact moment price breaks above the box high on expanding volume, your buy executes—giving you a confirmed intraday support floor and a clean, close invalidation level at once. The opening-range break is the sharpest trigger, but not the only valid entry: the **first orderly pullback** (to VWAP or the 20-day MA, with volume confirming the bounce, often entering above VWAP after a shallow day-1 dip of 1–3%) often gives a better reward-to-risk than chasing the gap, and the **second-stage breakout** (out of the first post-earnings consolidation) catches institutions resuming accumulation after the market digests the initial reaction. The best window is typically day 1 to day 3 after the report, with a planned hold of roughly 3 to 10+ days.

> **Worked example (illustrative).** A high-beta leader gaps +15% on a large beat plus a guidance raise, then pulls back to VWAP on lighter volume in the first session. You enter long on the volume-confirmed bounce off VWAP — in the stock, in 1–2 week calls for asymmetric leverage, or in a 3x sector ETF if the whole group is running. You target a 15–40% move over the following 4–10 days, scaling out into strength and trailing the remainder.

## Instrument, Risk, and the Drift Extraction

Express the continuation through the vehicle that matches your conviction and holding window:

| Instrument | Best used for | Trade-off to respect |
|---|---|---|
| **Stocks** | Direct plays on the leader that reported | Cleanest risk control; no structural decay |
| **Sector / 1x ETFs** | Riding a sector-wide beat (a whole group running) | Lower single-name risk; diversified |
| **2x / 3x ETFs** | Amplified sector continuation (SOXL, TQQQ) | Outsized gains — with decay; short holds only |
| **Call options** | Asymmetric post-beat upside (high gamma) | Capped loss; theta + IV-crush after the event |
| **Bull call spreads** | Defined-risk upside that blunts IV crush | Capped gain and loss; lower premium outlay |

| Instrument | Best used for | Trade-off to respect |
|---|---|---|
| **Warrants / LEAPS** | Longer-dated leveraged participation | Leverage with liquidity and time considerations |

Earnings continuation plays involve high-beta assets on enormous volume, so intraday ranges are wide—but you never accept arbitrary risk. Tie the stop to structure and automate it:

> **The Automated Bracket Stop Primary invalidation.** The instant the box high breaks and the trade is live, an automated bracket order places the stop immediately beneath the 30-minute opening-range low. **The high-velocity vice.** For ultra-aggressive or options entries, lock the stop at the VWAP line or the mid-point of the opening-range box instead – a tighter floor for a tighter 1R. **The discipline.** If the gap fails and reverses back into the box, the trade terminates automatically, protecting the parent capital. A failed earnings gap is one of the fastest reversals in the market – there is no room for a mental stop here.

Cap the 1R unit at 0.5–1% of total NAV per trade, roughly $500–$1,000 on a $100,000 account, using the smaller end for leveraged ETFs and options where post-earnings gaps are violent. A true PEAD setup can drift higher for 5 to 10 consecutive sessions as institutions complete their order blocks, so the exit framework must be patient yet mechanical: if Day 1 closes in the top 10% of its range on historic volume, hold overnight with maximum confidence; bank 30–50% into the first 10–20% gain and move the stop to break-even; from Day 2 onward trail with the daily 5- or 9-EMA; and the moment a daily candle closes below the 9-EMA, or the position reaches roughly +4R, flatten the entire block back to cash.

## When Continuation Is Less Likely

Never assume every earnings gap becomes a trend—a large share of beats fade, the classic "sell the news" reversal, with warning signs usually visible on the day: weak guidance (the market trades the future), heavy selling into the gap (large upper shadows signal distribution), light volume (no institutional sponsor), rapid gap filling (enthusiasm already fading), and broad-market weakness (which overrides single-name fundamentals). The same PEAD engine runs through several playbooks—the beat-plus-guidance play (the highest-quality fuel), sector rotation (chaining earnings within a hot group), options for asymmetry (OTM calls post-beat for 5–20x effective leverage while managing IV crush), and a PEAD long-short for hedged accounts. Let conviction grow alongside confirmation: an initial 30% position, toward 60% if the breakout holds, toward full size after a successful consolidation—and resist the largest mistake, selling immediately after a quick gain, because institutional trends persist far longer than feels comfortable, and the strongest winners deserve room to become the +4R drifts that carry a whole month of returns.

## Risk, Leverage, and the Honest Math

Earnings continuation is aggressive but must never be reckless: risk only a predetermined slice per trade, accept that some gaps reverse despite strong fundamentals, never average down into a failed post-earnings move, cut exposure when the broad market weakens, and review every trade. The earnings context adds specific hazards—"sell the news" reversals, gap and overnight risk that can move a high-beta name 10–30% straight through a stop, IV crush that can lose money on a long call even when direction is right (spreads and slightly-in-the-money strikes blunt this), and leveraged-ETF decay in choppy post-earnings consolidation.

> **The Honest Math** PEAD is a real, documented edge — and it is a thin, statistical one that survives only with fast execution, strict filters, and iron discipline. The academic abnormal returns are measured before commissions, spreads, slippage, taxes, and the very real losses from the beats that fade. Most retail traders attempting aggressive earnings plays lose money precisely because they skip the rules. Keep aspiration separate from probability. Stacking earnings-continuation winners toward a 10x in six months sits at the extreme tail of outcomes; the leverage that makes it conceivable makes a total loss of capital a common result. Treat the target as a direction that justifies discipline, not an entitlement. Position sizing, stops, and diversification stay non-negotiable, and you should backtest recent seasons and journal every trade before sizing up.

## D. Sector Acceleration

*Riding the Institutional Rotation Tide*

Individual stocks rarely move entirely on their own; they are lifted or dragged by their group. Sector acceleration occurs when a macroeconomic shift, a technological breakthrough, or a regulatory catalyst triggers a coordinated institutional rotation—global managers dumping stagnant groups and pouring billions into a theme like semiconductors or AI infrastructure—generating a structural tide that lifts leading companies together and creates multiple high-probability opportunities at once. Trading with that tide means even slightly imperfect single-stock timing is cushioned by the broader institutional buying pressure. Work strictly top-down: market direction, then sector strength, then industry leadership, then stock selection, then entry. The strongest, most reliable moves occur when three forces align—a strong overall market (the tide is rising), a leading sector (the current within the tide), and a leading stock within that sector (your vehicle on the current)—a triple alignment momentum traders call multiple confirmation, where each layer removes a category of risk. Institutions rotate in waves too large to hide: as billions enter a group, numerous stocks advance together, and the breadth of the advance becomes the signature of real conviction. Your job is to identify the wave while it is still building, not after every outlet has named it.

### The Anatomy of an Acceleration

Every acceleration begins with a single systemic catalyst and fans out through the group in a recognizable structure:

> **SYSTEMIC INSTITUTIONAL CATALYST** *Regulatory shift • AI adoption • rate-cut cycle • earnings surprise*

**COORDINATED SECTOR ROTATION** *High capital flows funnel into the group*

**ISOLATED ALPHA LEADER**
Enters an immediate vertical breakout Target for maximum-size concentration

**BETA COMPANION SPRINT**
Moves in sympathy on a delayed fuse Secondary vehicle for capital scale

The alpha leader is the name that ignites first—the breakthrough product, the blowout earnings print, the marquee contract—where capital concentrates and leadership persists longer than newcomers expect; the beta companions are the competitors, suppliers, and partners investors hunt once the leader confirms the theme, and they frequently produce the largest percentage gains because they move on a delayed fuse. The move unfolds through a repeatable seven-stage progression—ignition, re-rating, contagion, confirmation, amplification, crowding, exhaustion—with the greatest risk-adjusted opportunities clustered in the early stages, before the move is consensus.

## Following Institutional Themes

Many of the market's largest advances are driven not by one company but by durable, multi-quarter themes that pull entire supply chains higher. Learn their internal structure so that when the leader ignites, you already know where the companion capital will flow:

| Theme | Where the companion capital flows |
|---|---|
| Artificial Intelligence | AI hardware · AI software · networking · data centers · power & cooling |
| Semiconductors | Logic · memory · equipment · packaging · testing · foundries |
| Cybersecurity | Enterprise security · identity · cloud protection · network defense |
| Defense | Modernization · missiles · drones · space · cyber warfare |
| Nuclear & Power | Small modular reactors · fuel · engineering · utility infrastructure |
| Robotics & Automation | Industrial · warehouse · medical robotics · factory modernization |
| Healthcare Innovation | GLP-1 / metabolic · biotech catalysts · medical technology |
| Financials & Industrials | Rate-sensitive cyclicals · capex beneficiaries · reshoring |

As of mid-2026, the live examples worth studying include AI / power-demand broadening into utilities and industrials, GLP-1 and metabolic-health extensions across healthcare, and selective semiconductor strength—but treat any named theme as a starting point, not gospel. Every sector develops leaders sharing a profile (highest relative strength, highest volume, strongest earnings, largest institutional ownership, cleanest charts), and leadership usually persists longer than expected: the amateur reflex is to buy the cheap laggard before it catches up, but the blueprint pays up for proven leadership and lets the laggards be someone else's problem.

## The Coordinated Industry Cluster Breakout

The definitive signature of institutional acceleration is synchronicity. A single company breaking out may be an idiosyncratic anomaly, but when the industry leader, the secondary competitor, and the equipment supplier all clear their multi-week consolidation resistance within roughly a 48-hour window, that is a structural industry re-rating and your highest-conviction entry. Set alert triggers across the top three tickers, then act in sequence: the **lead trigger** fires the moment the definitive alpha leader fractures its horizontal ceiling on explosive volume (your confirmation, not your guess); the **secondary execution** shifts capital to a peer just clearing its own pivot, or a sector-leveraged ETF, if the leader is already too extended to buy with a sane stop. Core entry rules: the sector ETF breaks to new relative highs on expanding volume; prefer a pullback to the 20-day MA within an accelerating trend as a lower-risk add over chasing a vertical extension; always align with the broad market; and if the move requires a stop wider than your plan allows, you do not have a trade, you have a temptation.

## Choosing Your Instrument: The Synergy Stack

Match the right instrument to the stage and conviction of the move—each rung adds leverage and the obligation to size down and hold shorter.

| Instrument | Best used for | Trade-off to respect |
|---|---|---|
| **Stocks** | Highest-beta leaders inside the accelerating sector | Core position; cleanest risk control; no decay |
| **Sector ETFs (1x)** | Confirming and expressing the broad theme | Lower single-name risk; built-in diversification |
| **2x / 3x ETFs** | Direct, amplified plays on the rotation | Outsized gains – with decay; short holds only |
| **Options (long calls)** | Asymmetric, defined-risk leverage on leaders/ETFs | Capped loss; convex upside; time decay (theta) |
| **Warrants** | Extended leverage where available | Long-dated leverage; liquidity & terms vary |

Leveraged ETFs are the workhorses of a fast rotation, but they are tools, not investments—favor the highest-volume products to minimize slippage and actively manage every one:

| Theme | Representative leveraged vehicles |
|---|---|
| Broad tech / Nasdaq | TQQQ (3x), TECL (3x) |
| Semiconductors | SOXL (3x), NVDL (single-stock, 2x NVDA) |
| Small caps | TNA (3x) |
| Biotech | LABU (3x) |
| Financials | FAS (3x) |
| Energy | ERX (2x) |

**Setup.** Semiconductors accelerate on a wave of AI-capex headlines. A 3x semis ETF gaps up and holds above its opening VWAP while the cluster's top three names all clear multi-week resistance within two sessions. **Entry.** Go long the leveraged ETF, or buy slightly in-the-money calls on the alpha leader, on the confirmed cluster breakout – not in anticipation of it. **Management.** Plan to hold roughly 4–12 trading days, targeting a 15–40% move in the leveraged vehicle. Scale out 30–50% into the first 10–20% gain; trail the remainder beneath prior swing highs or an ATR-based stop. **Invalidation.** A close back below the breakout pivot, or a break of sector support, ends the trade – no negotiation.

## Position Sizing and the Sector Heat Ceiling

Define risk by the dollars you lose if your stop is hit—a practical band of 0.5–1% of total capital per sector play, roughly $500–$1,000 on a $100,000 account, using the smaller end for 3x products—and scale in as the thesis confirms in four equal 25% increments (initial probe, first add once the breakout holds, second add on continuation, final tranche once the trend is firmly established), so your largest exposure coincides with your highest proof. Sector acceleration's greatest gift, everything moving together, is also its greatest hazard—factor correlation—because four "different" setups in the same accelerating sector are one massive over-leveraged bet that gaps down together on a single macro headline:

**The Sector Heat Ceiling Matrix Net-Exposure Cap.** No single industry-sector cluster may consume more than 33% of total available capital in equity formats, or more than 10% of total NAV in options-premium risk. **The Structural Brake.** If you already hold a maximum-size position in a 3x sector ETF, your allowance for single-stock options or warrants in that same sector is locked at zero. This blocks synthetic over-exposure and keeps capital insulated from a systemic sector shock. **The Liquidity Reserve.** Always keep capital uncommitted so you can rotate into the next leadership group the moment it confirms. Being fully invested is being unable to act.

Leveraged ETFs reset daily and compound the path, not just the destination, so a 3x product can bleed even if the index finishes flat—use them only in short bursts timed to a clean, directional acceleration. Demand strict stacked confirmation before committing leveraged capital (sectors whipsaw and fail), respect that accelerations which rose together often reverse together, and favor high-volume instruments because liquidity is itself risk control.

## The Rotation Exit and Common Mistakes

Accelerations are fast, violent, and cyclical—capital rushes in and leaves just as quickly—so you must decide your exit logic before you enter. The cluster distribution sign: when trailing companion stocks stall or break down while the alpha leader makes a final low-volume parabolic spike, distribution is underway, and the narrowing of leadership is the tell. The moment the sector ETF or alpha leader prints a weekly candle closing below its 9-day EMA, the campaign for that group is closed—tighten trailing stops to the prior day's low or flatten to cash. Mechanically: scale out 30–50% into the first 10–20% gain and trail the remainder on an ATR stop or prior highs; hard-stop on a 5–8% adverse move or a clean break of sector support; and rotate into the next accelerating sector when relative strength weakens rather than defending a dying one. Broader signs the rotation is ending include declining relative strength, narrowing breadth, rising distribution days, weak earnings across constituents, contracting volume, and visible institutional selling. The recurring errors that forfeit the edge: buying laggards instead of leaders, chasing extended charts, ignoring weakening breadth, trading against institutional flow, clinging to declining sectors, and treating a leveraged ETF as a buy-and-hold while it bleeds to decay.

## The Sector Acceleration Governance Matrix

Every rule reduces to a single discipline: behave like a fiduciary of your own capital, not a casualty of your own emotions.

| Operational parameter | The retail-casualty trap | The 10x Blueprint fiduciary |
|---|---|---|
| **Trend identification** | Buys random charts from chatrooms, blind to industry context. | Runs a daily relative-strength heatmap audit to follow institutional flows. |
| **Stock selection** | Buys cheap laggards in weak sectors, hoping for a turnaround. | Focuses on coordinated industry clusters clearing multi-week ceilings. |
| **Instrument choice** | Reaches for max leverage with no regard to stage or holding period. | Matches stocks, ETFs, 2x/3x, options, or warrants to conviction and stage. |
| **Risk management** | Stacks multiple positions in the same sector, blind to correlation. | Enforces the Sector Heat Ceiling to cap systemic factor exposure. |
| **Exit execution** | Holds a parabolic run out of greed, riding it all the way back down. | Applies the Cluster Distribution Rule and the 9-day EMA to return to cash. |

Distilled: follow institutional money, not headlines; trade the strongest sectors before hunting individual stocks; select the leading companies within them; confirm leadership with relative strength, volume, and breadth, stacked, not single; build positions gradually as the trend proves itself; match the instrument to the stage and use leverage only when sector and market align; cap correlation with the Sector Heat Ceiling; exit objectively when leadership deteriorates; rotate capital into emerging leadership; and compound by repetition—aligning capital with the strongest trends, again and again, while preserving the flexibility to adapt.

## The Realistic Math of Compounding

Turning $100,000 into $1,000,000 is a 900% gain. Chained as sector swings, it might be expressed as several strong rotations per quarter, each captured at a favorable reward-to-risk ratio:

| Lever | What the 10x math actually requires |
|---|---|
| Per-trade reward: risk | Target 2:1 or better; never enter below it. |
| Win cadence | A handful of clean rotations per quarter, not dozens of forced trades. |
| Compounding effect | Sequential gains multiply — but so do sequential losses. |
| The fragility | A single bad rotation, over-sized, can erase several good ones. |

> **A Necessary Reality Check** Compounding is powerful, but the same multiplication that builds wealth quickly destroys it quickly. A 10x return in six months sits at the extreme tail of possible outcomes and is achieved by very few; the aggressive, leveraged tactics that make it conceivable also make a total loss of capital a real and common outcome. Treat the 10x figure as a directional ambition that justifies discipline — not as an expectation you are entitled to. The trader who survives long enough to compound is the one who sizes every position so that being wrong is survivable, refuses to widen a stop to save a thesis, and accepts cash as a position. Protect the downside relentlessly, and let the upside take care of itself.

# The Swing Trading Growth Matrix

The four setups, summarized as a working reference—the qualification that earns an entry, the vehicle that expresses it, and the horizon it tends to run:

| Setup | Technical qualification | Core vehicle | Hold horizon |
|---|---|---|---|

| Setup | Technical qualification | Core vehicle | Hold horizon |
|---|---|---|---|
| **Multi-day momentum** | Day-1 close at the apex of its range on ≥200% relative volume | High-beta growth stocks; warrants | 3–5 sessions |
| **High-beta setups** | Beta ≥ 2.0, or a structural 3x leverage multiplier | 3x ETFs; near-term call options | 2–4 sessions |
| **Earnings continuation** | PEAD gap ≥ 8% clearing overhead resistance | Liquid growth-tech / biotech; debit spreads | 5–10 sessions |
| **Sector acceleration** | Industry group leading the relative-strength rankings | Sector-leveraged ETFs | 3–7 sessions |

## The Swing Trading Ruleset

Across all four setups, the same execution rules apply—the discipline that keeps the technique from sliding into gambling: **cap the hold** at two to ten days maximum to minimize overnight and gap risk in leveraged products; **demand asymmetry**, trading only elite setups offering 1:3 reward-to-risk or better, ideally inside a live supercycle; **bound the risk**, risking about 1% per trade, keeping total portfolio heat at 8% or under, and honoring daily loss limits; **manage the winner**, scaling out 30–50% into strength at 2R–3R, trailing the remainder, and exiting decisively when momentum stalls; and **journal everything**. Held this way, a single clean 20–50% swing winner—common in 3x ETFs or options during a sector acceleration—meaningfully advances the monthly compounding path; the survival rules are simply what keep you in the game long enough to be holding it when it comes.

## Two Ways to Swing Trade: The Governance Matrix

The same setups produce opposite results depending on discipline. Contrast the gambler with the disciplined operator.

| Dimension | The Gambler | The Disciplined Swing Trader |
|---|---|---|
| **Entry timing** | Chases after a 40% two-day extension. | Enters early breakouts and first pullbacks. |
| **Reason for the trade** | A chart from a social-media watchlist. | Price, volume, catalyst, and sector all align. |
| **High beta** | Treats raw volatility as the whole thesis. | Demands volatility with structure and leadership. |
| **The earnings gap** | "I missed it," or buys the emotional spike. | Reads it as repricing; enters the continuation. |
| **Position size** | Same large size on every | Smaller on high-beta; within |

| Dimension | The Gambler | The Disciplined Swing Trader |
| --- | --- | --- |
| | name. | the heat cap. |
| **When momentum fades** | Holds and hopes through deceleration. | Exits on the stall; rotates into fresh strength. |

## Risk, Honesty, and a Reality Check

Swing trading is powerful precisely because it concentrates real size into short, high-conviction windows—which is also what makes it dangerous. The setups are genuine and the institutional flows behind them are real, but the leverage that produces the rapid gains produces equally rapid losses, and a single mistimed, oversized trade can undo weeks of progress.

## Blueprint Principle

> **Swing trading is renting institutional velocity, not guessing at charts.**

The four setups are one idea seen from four angles: institutions repricing an asset over days create a runway, and your job is to be aligned with it. Find the strongest sector, the leading names within it, the cleanest momentum or earnings setup among those leaders, and an entry where price and volume confirm—then press with high-beta vehicles sized for their volatility, manage the winner by scaling and trailing, and rotate out the instant the move decelerates. Swing trading rewards selectivity over activity: be invested when price, volume, catalyst, and sector strength all point the same direction, and be in cash the rest of the time.

# Chapter 27
# Position Scaling

*Pressing a Winner From Underneath, Never From the Top*

Scaling out, covered earlier, is how you harvest a winner on the way up. Scaling *in* is the mirror image: how you build a large position in a trade that is already working, without having taken large risk to do it—a way to have a small position when you are uncertain and a large one once the market has proven you right. Scaling is not simply buying more; it is earning the right to risk more. It rests on a single cardinal rule, the one most traders get exactly backwards: **add to winners, never to losers.** Averaging down into a losing position feels intuitive and is the classic way accounts are destroyed, because it adds size to a thesis the market is actively rejecting. But the technique is double-edged—adding to a winner raises your average cost and your position size at the same time, so a clumsy or greedy scale-in can convert your best trade into a loss. The difference between pyramiding that compounds and pyramiding that destroys comes down to the shape of the build, the triggers, and the discipline of the stop.

## A. Adding to Winners

*Letting the Market Earn Every Extra Dollar*

The logic of adding to winners is that conviction should follow evidence. You enter with a starting position when the setup is merely promising, and you add only as the market confirms the thesis—a new high, a pullback that holds and resumes, a breakout from a fresh consolidation. You are not adding because you hope to be right, but because price action is confirming that you already may be; if the first entry fails instead, the loss stays small. Three rules govern every add, and breaking any one of them is how the technique turns against you: **add only on confirmation** (a higher base, a held pullback, or a new breakout on expanding volume—never simply because the position is up); **each add is smaller than the last** (the base position is the largest, so the build stays bottom-heavy and your average cost stays well below the current price); and **raise the stop with every add** (the non-negotiable one—move the stop up so the larger blended position never risks more than your fixed maximum, ideally locking the whole position into profit). Treat every add as a brand-new trade that must meet its own criteria. What must never trigger an add: excitement, the wish for a larger profit, social-media hype, having missed the original entry, the urge to recover prior losses, or the fear of being underexposed—every one of those is emotion wearing the mask of conviction.

### The Psychology of Earned Conviction

The inexperienced trader increases exposure to losing positions, hoping to recover; the professional momentum trader does the opposite, increasing exposure only after the market validates the thesis—turning a solid 10–20% winner into a 30–60%+ result while keeping initial risk tightly controlled, because the largest size ends up in the strongest part of the move where the thesis has been repeatedly confirmed. Before committing another dollar, the professional asks a single question:

***"Has the market confirmed my original thesis?"***

If the answer is yes, they may increase the position; if no, they do nothing—or they exit. Adding to a winner is an act of mathematical optimization: when a stock or 3x ETF breaks out and immediately moves into profit, the market hands you an objective, real-time data point—the path of least resistance is up—and you act on that order flow without exposing your seed capital to unvetted risk. Far from increasing risk, this often reduces it, because the decision is a gate, not a reflex: at the initial purchase nothing has been proven and the full risk is live, while after several confirmed advances the probability that real accumulation is occurring is higher than it was at entry. Every add passes through the same decision gate:

**INITIAL ENTRY — THESIS UNPROVEN** *Small size, full stop — this leg carries the real risk*

**HAS THE MARKET CONFIRMED THE THESIS?** *Higher highs · expanding volume · profit buffer*

**NO** The market disagrees, or hasn't confirmed. Do nothing — or exit. Never add to weakness.

**YES** The market agrees and pays you first. Add into strength. Migrate the trailing stop up.

## Progressive Commitment and the Best Times to Add

The philosophy compresses to three lines: small risk, large conviction, largest commitment only after confirmation. On a $100,000 maximum allocation, a simple expression is $25,000 on the entry signal, $25,000 after breakout confirmation, $25,000 after a successful consolidation, and the final $25,000 after another breakout—every additional purchase occurring only after the stock proves itself, so that if the trade fails at any stage the remaining adds never happen and the loss is limited to the small, early exposure. In practice you scale in at two kinds of price location: on pullbacks to support (the 20- or 50-day MA, VWAP, or a prior swing low) within an uptrend, which gives the better entry price and tighter stop, and on breakouts to fresh new highs, which gives stronger confirmation. A handful of recurring situations justify an addition—each a fresh, independently-confirmed entry inside the same trend:

| When to add | What it looks like |
| --- | --- |
| **New breakout** | The stock clears fresh resistance on heavy volume; institutional buying resumes. |
| **Bull flag** | A strong advance pauses, volume contracts, the stock consolidates — then breaks higher again. |
| **Tight consolidation** | Several sideways days on shrinking volume and volatility, before the trend resumes. |

| When to add | What it looks like |
|---|---|
| **Earnings confirmation** | Excellent earnings and raised guidance bring large institutional buying; the thesis strengthens. |
| **Sector leadership** | The whole industry accelerates and the leading name grows even stronger. |

## Confirmation Before Every Add

Before increasing a position, run the same questions every time: Is price making higher highs? Is volume expanding? Is relative strength increasing? Is the overall market healthy? Is the sector leading? Has new positive information emerged? To take the nervous system out of the decision entirely, gate every add behind three hard, quantitative filters:

> **The Three-Filter Add Checklist 1. Profit buffer.** The position sits on an open profit of at least +1.5R (some traders use +1R) from the previous entry tier. **2. Structural shelf.** A clean secondary consolidation (a 15-minute bull flag or a VWAP-band reset) provides a valid support floor for the new trailing stop. **3. Insulated risk.** After raising the trailing stop, the total blended risk of the whole position computes to ≤ 0R — risk-free or in a locked-profit posture. **If all three are not satisfied, the add does not happen — no exceptions.**

## The Geometric Shape, Average Cost, and Leverage

How much you add matters as much as when. Never add equal amounts of capital at higher prices—buying the same size at $10, $11, and $12 spikes your average cost to $11, so a routine pullback to $10.80 turns a winner into a loss. Instead, make each successive add strictly smaller than the one before it:

***Next position increment ≤ ½ × prior position increment***

This decreasing, geometric shape commits the most capital where risk is lowest (the early, confirmed entry) and the least where price is most extended. Adding at higher prices naturally raises your average cost, and beginners fear this, but the goal is not to own the lowest-priced shares—it is to own the strongest trends: three adds at $50, $55, and $61 leave a blended cost well above the first purchase, yet if the stock now trades at $75, the higher average cost is paired with a far larger total profit. The fear of a higher average cost is really the fear of giving back open profit, and that fear is answered by the trailing stop, not by refusing to add. A clean progression is 25% of intended size at initial conviction, 50% after the first confirmation, 75% after another breakout, and 100% only on exceptional continuation—and after the first profitable add, move the entire position's stop to break-even, then trail it (a prior swing low, a 2–3x ATR distance, or a rising moving average) with every further add. Additional exposure can be expressed through shares, sector ETFs, 2x/3x leveraged ETFs (excellent for pyramiding a sector acceleration, but daily-reset decay means the hold stays short), call options (scale into more contracts or higher strikes as delta rises), LEAPS, warrants, and call debit spreads—reserving additional leverage for situations where both the individual trade and the broad market strongly support the thesis.

## A Worked Example

Suppose a company reports exceptional earnings and breaks out on record volume. A staged, confirmation-driven build takes 25% of intended size on the breakout, a first add after a constructive pullback holds support and resumes higher on expanding volume, a second add following another breakout with sector strength, and a final add only if the broad market remains supportive and the stock keeps making higher highs without distribution. Put concrete numbers on it with a leveraged sector play:

> **Setup.** $100,000 account; semis accelerating. Initial: $30,000 in SOXL (or NVDA), stop 5% below ≈ 0.5% account risk. Price runs +12% — the profit buffer is met. **Build.** Add $15,000 on the pullback to the 20-day MA (total ≈ $45,000; move the whole stop to break-even). Add $8,000 on the next dip or new high (total ≈ $53,000). **Extract.** Scale out 30–50% at a 20–30% total gain; trail the remainder for the runner. A ~25% average move becomes 35–50%+ on the full pyramid — with capital protected the whole way.

## When NOT to Add, and the Honest Math

Knowing when to stop is as valuable as knowing when to start. Do not add—and often, protect profits instead—when the stock becomes climactic or vertical far above its major moving averages, when volume weakens or distribution days cluster, when the sector loses momentum or the broad market enters a correction, or when the reward-to-risk on a new add no longer justifies the exposure. The most aggressive scaling belongs to phases when conditions align—strong market, healthy breadth, leading sector, exceptional catalyst, sustained accumulation—and should turn conservative when those fade. The standing risk controls apply without exception: cap one trade at ≤10–15% of the portfolio and ≤1–2% total risk, define exit criteria before each addition, avoid adding after vertical moves, recalculate total portfolio risk after every increase, and re-check that new information still supports the original thesis.

> **The Honest Math** Done with discipline — roughly 3–4 strong pyramided swings per quarter at 20–40% net each, in favorable conditions — adding to winners can meaningfully accelerate compounding toward an aggressive goal. But the same late adds that magnify a winner magnify a loser when stops are not trailed, and a single undisciplined, over-sized add can wipe out months of gains. Keep aspiration separate from probability. This is an advanced technique: master fixed-size trading first, then paper-trade and backtest pyramiding across bull, bear, and choppy markets before risking live capital. A 10x in six months sits at the extreme tail of outcomes; only a very small fraction of traders ever reach it, and the leverage and concentration involved make a total loss of capital a common result. The purpose of scaling is to improve the quality of risk taken — not simply to increase its quantity.

## The Position Scaling Governance Matrix

Every rule reduces to one discipline: let the market fund your scale while your risk stays insulated.

| Operational vector | The retail-casualty method | The 10x Blueprint fiduciary |
|---|---|---|
| **Scaling direction** | Averages down into bleeding charts to fix a bruised ego. | Averages up exclusively into winning, validated momentum. |
| **Tranche size** | Increases size arbitrarily as price extends, bloating cost basis. | Deploys a progressive geometric pyramid — each add half the prior. |
| **Risk-floor tracking** | Leaves the initial stop static, or deletes it while adding shares. | Migrates trailing stops upward with every single tranche. |
| **Execution trigger** | Adds on gut feeling or intraday hysteria. | Adds strictly on the Three-Filter Add Checklist. |

Distilled to working principles: let the market earn additional capital through confirmation; begin with a manageable position and expand only as the trade proves itself; add on constructive breakouts, orderly consolidations, and renewed momentum, never on hope; never confuse pyramiding into strength with averaging down into weakness; let position size reflect the quality of the opportunity, not your emotions; keep total exposure within predetermined limits; protect growing profits with disciplined trailing exits; concentrate capital in exceptional opportunities; and remember the objective is not to own more shares but to own more of the market's strongest trends while preserving the ability to trade another day.

## B. Pyramid Strategies

*Adding to Winners With Geometric Scale*

A pyramid is a structured sequence of adds, and the word is chosen deliberately: a sound pyramid is **bottom-heavy,** with the largest tranche at the base and progressively smaller tranches stacked on top as the trade proves itself, which keeps the blended cost low and the structure stable. The deadly inversion—adding more as price rises, so the position is top-heavy—builds a fragile tower where a small pullback wipes out the entire gain. This is the turbocharger for every setup in the book: a single well-pyramided 25–40% swing can deliver a 40–80%+ impact on the account when sized correctly. Here is a clean three-tranche build for a full position, sized bottom-heavy with a stop that rises at every step:

| Tranche | Size | Add trigger | Stop action |
|---|---|---|---|
| **1 (base)** | 50% | Initial entry on the setup | Stop below entry structure |
| **2** | 30% | First confirmation — new high or held pullback | Raise stop; position near breakeven |
| **3** | 20% | Second confirmation — next breakout | Raise stop; blended position locked in profit |

> **Worked example.** *Buy 500 shares at $20 (the base), with a stop at $18.50. The trade confirms, so add 300 shares at $23 and raise the stop to $21. It confirms again; add 200 shares at $26 and raise the stop to $24. Your average cost on the full 1,000 shares is $22.10 — well below the $26 price — and with the stop at* ***$24*** *the entire position is now locked in for a gain even if it reverses, while still riding for more. That is a pyramid working as designed: a large position built cheaply, fully protected, with open upside.*

Contrast the inverted version—200 shares at $20, 300 at $23, 500 at $26—which produces an average cost of $23.90, dangerously close to the current $26, so a routine pullback to $23 erases the entire gain. The shape is everything: the bottom-heavy pyramid is robust; the top-heavy one is a trap that feels identical while you are building it. Beyond the three core rules, a disciplined pyramid never adds below the original stop unless it is a planned re-entry, gives every add its own defined risk level, keeps total portfolio risk within limits, never pyramids into a parabolic exhaustion move, and reduces or stops adding when volatility expands dangerously—and the strongest builds occur when the stock breaks from a major base with reset expectations, sector leadership is strong, volume is expanding with shallow pullbacks, and the broad market supports risk.

## Average Up, Never Down

The two techniques are opposites, not variations on a theme:

| | Pyramiding (into strength) | Averaging down (into weakness) |
|---|---|---|
| **What the market is telling you** | It confirms your thesis. | It rejects your thesis. |
| **What should happen to confidence** | It should increase. | It should decrease. |
| **What you do to exposure** | Increase it — aligned with strength. | Increase it anyway — against the evidence. |
| **The result over time** | Capital concentrates in winners. | Capital concentrates in losers. |

While some valuation-based investment styles use averaging down deliberately, aggressive momentum trading relies on pyramiding into strength and never on averaging into weakness—that single rule prevents the most common path to a blown-up account.

## The Progressive Geometric Pyramid

You cannot scale by adding equal capital at higher prices; the fix is a geometric pyramid where each add-on tranche is strictly smaller than the one before it (next position increment ≤ ½ × prior increment). Here is a concentrated trade on a $100,000 account with the initial 1R risk set at 2% of NAV ($2,000):

> **TRANCHE 3 · APEX CAP** *500 **sh @** $12.50 (+2.5R)*

**TRANCHE 2 · MULTIPLIER ADD** *1,000 **sh @** $11.50 (+1.5R)*

**TRANCHE 1 · FOUNDATION BASE** *2,000 **sh @** $10.00 (initial entry, stop $9.00)*

**↑ Trailing stop floor migrated to $11.50 — locks +$2,520**

The full sequence: **Tranche 1 (Foundation)** buys 2,000 shares at $10.00 as price clears its pivot, stop at $9.00 (1R = $1.00/share, $2,000 total risk); **Tranche 2 (Multiplier)** adds 1,000 shares at $11.50 (+1.5R open profit)—exactly half of Tranche 1—and migrates the stop for all 3,000 shares up to $10.50; **Tranche 3 (Apex)** adds the final 500 shares at $12.50 (+2.5R) and instantly trails the stop on the entire 3,500-share block up to $11.50.

> **The Mathematical Genius of the Layout Total volume:** 3,500 shares · Blended average cost: $10.78 · Current price: $12.50 · Hard trailing stop: $11.50 Your position has expanded to a $43,750 footprint — yet because the trailing stop ($11.50) sits well above your blended cost ($10.78), the worst case on a sudden reversal is a guaranteed net profit of +$2,520. You have built a massive capital hammer while reducing the open risk to your ledger to less than zero.

## Choosing Your Shape and the Execution Rules

The geometric (decreasing) structure is the workhorse, but it helps to know the full menu:

| Structure | Layer sizing | When to use it |
|---|---|---|
| **Decreasing / Inverted** | Largest first (40–50%), then 25–30% / 15–20% / ≤10% | The professional default — commits most where risk is lowest, controls average cost. |
| **Equal-Increment** | Same size each layer (e.g. four 25% adds) | Simplest to manage; slightly higher average cost. Good for steady trends. |
| **Increasing-Increment** | Smallest first (10% → 40%) | Aggressive; risks oversized exposure late. Reserve for unusually strong, repeatedly confirmed trends. |
| **Volatility-Adjusted** | Size set by the asset's volatility | Smaller adds for high-vol names; keeps dollar risk consistent across trades. |
| **Momentum Ladder** | Add only on new highs / acceleration | Best for high-beta and earnings-continuation runners. |
| **Pullback Pyramid** | Add on retracements to 20-day MA/VWAP | Best for multi-day momentum and sector-rotation plays. |
| **Options** | Start OTM calls; add | Extreme asymmetry, but theta- |

| Structure | Layer sizing | When to use it |
|---|---|---|
| **Gamma** | as delta rises / roll up | sensitive — keep total duration 1–3 weeks. |

Confirmation comes in four flavors—technical (a fresh breakout, higher highs and lows, a bull-flag break), volume (rising relative volume, institutional accumulation), fundamental (strong earnings, raised guidance, upgrades, contracts), and market (strong indexes, healthy breadth, sector leadership)—and the same three-filter gate from *Adding to Winners* authorizes each add: a ≥+1.5R profit buffer from the prior tier, a clean structural shelf for the new trailing stop, and total blended risk computing to ≤0R after the stop is raised. The execution rules form the pyramid's operating system: initial risk of 0.5–2% of capital on the first leg ($500–$2,000 on a $100,000 account); per-add confirmation of a new swing high on volume with momentum strengthening (MACD histogram expanding, RSI 55–75); stop moved to break-even after the first profitable add, then trailed aggressively; 3–4 adds maximum with total position ≤12–15% of portfolio and never more than 2% total risk; the full pyramid held inside the 3–12 day swing window; and exit scaling that mirrors the pyramid in reverse, selling the largest, latest layers first into strength. File the layer tracker as a spreadsheet template, one row per tranche, filled before each add is authorized:

| Layer | Trigger condition | Size | Fill price | New stop | Blended cost |
|---|---|---|---|---|---|
| Initial | Breakout / pivot clear on volume | 40–50% | — | 1R below | — |
| Add 1 | +1.5R and shelf reset | 25–30% | — | Break-even | — |
| Add 2 | New high, MACD expanding | 15–20% | — | Prior swing low | — |
| Add 3 | Further new high / continuation | ≤10% | — | Trail 2–3x ATR | — |

## Multi-Week Trends, Instruments, and a Worked Compounding Example

Most of the market's largest winners advance through a sequence of constructive patterns rather than a straight line—the initial breakout from the base, an orderly pullback that holds support, a breakout from a bull flag, a strong post-earnings continuation, and a breakout to another new high—so let the trend reveal itself and add at each fresh, confirmed structure. Build exposure across instruments as conviction grows: classic share pyramiding (the cleanest expression), 2x/3x ETFs like TQQQ, SOXL, or LABU (high-octane, but daily decay forces shorter pyramids and tighter time stops), options (delta-based scaling—add contracts or roll to higher strikes as the trade works; extreme asymmetry but theta-sensitive), and warrants (leverage layering where liquidity allows). Two illustrations show the pyramid at different scales—first, a decreasing-increment structure deploying up to $200,000 on a high-conviction swing:

| Stage | Trigger | Capital added | Total position |
|---|---|---|---|
| Initial entry | Breakout above resistance | $80,000 | $80,000 |
| First add | Pullback holds support, resumes higher | $60,000 | $140,000 |
| Second add | New high on expanding volume | $40,000 | $180,000 |
| Final add | Strong post-earnings continuation | $20,000 | **$200,000** |

The largest commitment lands early, right after the breakout, while later adds shrink as the stock extends. Second, a leveraged sector-acceleration play on a $100,000 account:

> **Setup.** Semis are accelerating. Initial: $25,000 in SOXL (or NVDA shares/calls), stop 5% below = $1,250 risk (1.25%). **Build.** +12% move (~$3,000 open profit) → add $15,000 on the pullback. +8% more → add $8,000. Total position ≈ $48,000. **Result.** An average 22% gain on the full pyramid ≈ $10,500 profit – a 10.5% account boost from one ~7-day trade. **The math toward 10x.** Chaining roughly 4–6 high-quality pyramided swings per quarter at a 60%+ win rate is what mathematically supports the aggressive trajectory – if, and only if, the discipline holds on every layer.

## When to Stop, the Euphoria Trap, and the Honest Math

Pyramiding should increase the quality of risk, not merely its quantity, so before every addition reassess total exposure to the position, the sector, correlated positions, overall leverage, and the maximum drawdown if the trend reverses—a pyramid must never grow so large that one failed trade can materially damage the portfolio. Stop adding and simply manage what you hold when the asset is far above its major moving averages, shows climactic action, prints declining volume or repeated distribution days, or loses relative strength. The recurring errors that undermine a pyramid are adding on emotional excitement rather than confirmation, increasing size after the stock is already extended, ignoring total concentration, failing to raise stops as exposure grows, and continuing to add after signs of distribution—the most dangerous being the **euphoria trap**, where greed after a strong move convinces the trader to add too early or too big, raising the average cost exactly when risk is highest. Respect each failure mode: a late add can turn a winner into a loser without trailed stops; 3x ETFs plus pyramiding in choppy conditions compound losses; an overnight event hits the entire pyramid at once (use defined-risk options pyramids when gap exposure is a concern); never let one pyramided trade exceed 2% total risk or 15% of capital; and most blown-up accounts come from undisciplined pyramiding, so require journal proof of every layer.

> **Before You Pyramid — The Honest Math** Pyramid only after you have mastered fixed-size trading. Paper-trade the technique for at least three months and backtest it across bull, bear, and choppy markets before risking live capital. The same adds that magnify a winner magnify a loser when you scale into weakness, and a single late, over-sized add without a trailed stop can erase the gains of several disciplined trades. Keep aspiration separate from probability. The 4–6-pyramids-per-quarter math that supports a 10x trajectory sits at the extreme tail of outcomes; only a very small fraction of traders ever achieve it, and the leverage and concentration involved make a total loss of capital a common result. Disciplined pyramiding improves the quality of your best trades — it does not guarantee the target, and it cannot rescue a flawed process.

Distilled, the principles for pyramiding: begin with measured exposure and let the market justify every addition; increase size only after objective confirmation strengthens the thesis; keep each add smaller than the last; raise the stop with every tranche; concentrate capital intelligently rather than owning the most shares; and protect increasingly valuable positions with disciplined exits—the goal is capital concentrated in the highest-quality trends, not the most shares.

## C. Scaling Without Emotional Distortion

*De-Biasing the Execution Frame*

Every chapter before this taught you how to find and structure a trade; this is the discipline layer that decides whether any of it actually compounds. The hardest part of aggressive trading is not identifying opportunity—it is executing position-sizing decisions without emotional interference. Markets constantly trigger fear after losses, greed after gains, hope inside drawdowns, FOMO when others are winning, and overconfidence on a hot streak, and when you are pyramiding into winners and swinging volatile 3x ETFs or options, those emotions will try to sabotage every add, every trail, and every exit—one or two distorted trades can erase weeks of compounded progress. The remedy is to make position scaling rule-based rather than emotion-driven. Here is the diagnostic that cuts through it: charts do not reveal your emotions—your position size does. A trader who suddenly doubles a position without a corresponding increase in objective evidence is responding emotionally, not systematically.

### The Neurochemistry of the Expanded Balance Sheet

Scaling size has a biological trap built into it. As a position is pyramided, the dollar figures expand exponentially—a routine 1.5% intraday wiggle that once meant a negligible $300 swing suddenly flashes as a $4,500 retracement—and the unconditioned brain interprets that rapid, large-scale fluctuation exactly as it interprets a physical threat, flooding the nervous system with stress hormones.

> **POSITION SIZE EXPANDS** *Pyramiding multiplies the dollar swings on screen*

**PSYCHOLOGICAL CAPACITY THRESHOLD EXCEEDED** *Nominal size outruns emotional tolerance*

**AMYGDALA HIJACK** *Prefrontal cortex offline — fight-or-flight takes over*

**DISTORTED EXECUTION** *Panic-sells winners early • freezes when stops are hit*

Once nominal size exceeds a trader's Psychological Capacity Threshold, the cognitive brain cedes control to the emotional brain: the trader micro-manages every tick, fixates on the unrealized-PnL sidebar, and commits the two fatal errors—cutting a pristine winner far too early out of panic, or freezing when a legitimate trailing stop is breached. The brain evolved to survive danger, not to allocate capital, and that mismatch produces five recurring distortions in scaling:

| The distortion | How it sabotages your scaling |
|---|---|
| **Greed on the way up** | After a strong move you add too big, too late, or chase without confirmation — dangerously raising your average cost. |
| **Fear of heights** | Price runs fast (common in high-beta, earnings, and sector plays) and you freeze, refusing to add even on a clean signal. |
| **FOMO distortion** | Seeing others post bigger gains on the same name, you override your rules and over-allocate. |
| **Revenge / averaging down** | A small pullback feels like the end, so you add defensively to a loser instead of only to winners. |
| **Euphoria after big wins** | A hot streak inflates the next pyramid or tempts you to skip the stop entirely — "I can't lose." |

Each has the same antidote. The professional does not ask "How do I feel?" but "What does the evidence support?"—FOMO meets three questions (has the setup improved, has risk increased, does this still fit my plan?), greed meets the rule that recent profits never justify larger size, fear after a loss meets the reminder that the next great trade often arrives immediately after a difficult stretch, and hope has no place in sizing at all.

## Scaling on Evidence, Not Emotion

Every single addition must answer one question, and only one:

***"Has the probability of success objectively improved?"***

If yes, the market has earned your additional capital through confirmation—stronger price action, higher relative volume and breakouts on expanding volume, visible institutional accumulation, a still-valid catalyst with improving relative strength, and a supportive broad market. If no, the excitement in your chest is not evidence. Treat every add as a brand-new investment decision requiring its own independent justification, identically whether you are adding to stocks, ETFs, 2x or 3x leveraged ETFs, call options, LEAPS, or warrants.

## The Pre-Trade Scaling Plan

The easiest way to remove emotion is to make every decision before the emotion can arise—pre-define the entire pyramid in writing, before entry, so the market must meet your checklist, not your feelings:

| Plan parameter | Pre-committed rule (worked example) |
|---|---|
| **Initial size** | 40% of max planned position, sized to ~0.5% account risk |
| **Add triggers** | Specific price levels / technical conditions / % gain thresholds — written down |
| **Maximum layers** | 3 adds maximum |
| **Total exposure cap** | ≤ 12–15% of portfolio in any one position |
| **Stop & trail** | Move to break-even after Add 1; then ATR or swing-low trail |

**Initial.** $25,000 on the breakout above the 20-day MA. **Add 1.** +$12,000 only if price pulls back to the MA, holds, and prints a volume surge. **Add 2.** +$7,000 only on a new high with the MACD histogram expanding. **Forbidden.** Any "it feels strong, let's add more" deviation. If the trigger is not on the page, the add does not happen.

Before every addition, run the same mechanical checklist—every time, no exceptions:

**Pre-Add Confirmation Checklist** ☐ Price action: a new high, or a successful test of support on volume. ☐ Momentum: RSI roughly 55–75, MACD bullish, relative strength increasing. ☐ Catalyst: the original earnings or sector thesis is still valid. ☐ Portfolio heat: total open risk across all trades stays under 3–4%. **If any box is unchecked → no add, no exceptions.**

## De-Biasing Protocols and Guards

You cannot order a human being to stop feeling emotions while managing a large, pyramided position; the distortion has to be engineered out of the trading station. **PnL cloaking:** toggle off every flashing dollar value and display performance exclusively as percentage of NAV or R-multiples—a $5,000 pullback is terrifying, while the identical move shown as −0.5% from a local high is routine. **Intermittent screen lock:** once the scaling orders and bracket trailing stops are submitted, close the application and audit only at the open, mid-day, and into the close. **Pre-committed bracket orders:** the whole pyramid is programmed into the broker's advanced order system before the session, so the platform runs as an automated machine. Standing guards prevent creeping distortion: a maximum hold of 10 trading days per pyramid; auto-scale-out rules (sell 30% at +15% and another 30% at +25%, then trail); a daily add limit of one per position; and hard maximum-position and daily/weekly loss limits. When the urge to deviate strikes anyway, circuit breakers interrupt it—the 24-hour rule (any urge to deviate requires a 24-hour wait and a journal review), the position-size calculator (never eyeball a size), and the "mirror trade" test ("would I put this exact add on right now if I were starting fresh, with no position?"—if no, you are managing your feelings, not the trade).

## The Sleep-and-Stare Audit and Instrument Traps

Every trader has a unique baseline of emotional resilience—a size that lets one person sleep soundly gives another insomnia. If you are compulsively checking a mobile app under the dinner table, waking at 3:00 AM to monitor overseas futures, or feeling a knot of dread during market hours, your position mass has outpaced your emotional capacity: scale your aggregate size down by 33% across the board, immediately, and stay there until you can view the charts with complete detachment. Each instrument carries its own emotional trap:

| Instrument | The emotional trap | The structural fix |
|---|---|---|
| **3x ETFs (TQQQ, SOXL)** | Daily decay creates urgency bias — "I must add now before it fades." | Shorter pyramids (2–3 days between adds) and stricter time stops. |
| **Options** | Gamma euphoria: as delta rises, you add too aggressively. | Pre-set contract limits and roll rules (e.g., only roll up when 50%+ ITM). |
| **High-beta stocks** | News-driven spikes trigger FOMO. | Catalyst half-life rule: only add within ~3 days of the earnings or sector catalyst. |
| **Warrants** | Illiquidity amplifies regret on small moves. | Smaller overall sizing and stricter volume filters. |

Streaks are where discipline is won or lost. A winning streak quietly erodes caution, so increase size only if market conditions, setup quality, and risk-adjusted opportunity have genuinely improved—scale because the environment improved, never because your recent results did. A losing streak distorts the opposite way, shrinking sizes and skipping excellent breakouts; the correction is diagnostic rather than emotional—ask whether the losses came from poor execution, a strategy that no longer fits the regime, or genuinely changed conditions, and keep following the process while respecting your predetermined risk limits.

## Building the Habits and the Real-World Math

Discipline is not willpower; it is infrastructure, built on three habits. **Journal every scaling decision**—why you entered, added, reduced, and exited, plus the emotion felt at each step—because most traders discover their largest mistakes clustered exactly where they ignored their own rules:

| Journal field | What to record |
|---|---|
| Pre-trade plan | The exact written layers, triggers, stop, and exposure cap |
| Actual actions | What you really did at each scaling decision |
| Emotion (1–10) | Intensity of greed / fear / FOMO felt at each add or exit |
| Rule that held | Which specific rule prevented (or failed to prevent) distortion |
| Process score | 10/10 if you followed the plan — even on a losing trade |

**Score process, not outcome:** a trade that followed the plan perfectly and still lost is a 10/10, while a reckless add that happened to win is a failure that will cost you later. **Rehearse and stay accountable:** review past winning pyramids weekly to normalize the feeling of adding at higher prices, pair it with accountability, and protect your mental capital with the same care you give your financial capital. Disciplined pyramiding can convert an average 12–18% swing win into a 25–45% effective gain by adding correctly into confirmed strength—compounded across a series of high-quality trades, that uplift is what makes an aggressive trajectory mathematically conceivable.

> **The Honest Math** The arithmetic that would even approach the 10x target looks like a sequence of roughly 12–18 high-quality trades over six months, around a 60–65% win rate, with 2:1 or better reward-to-risk, amplified by disciplined pyramiding. Pyramiding cuts both ways, however: the same adds that magnify a winner magnify a loser when you scale into weakness, and a single distorted, oversized trade can erase weeks of compounding. Keep aspiration separate from probability. A 10x in six months sits at the extreme tail of outcomes; only a very small fraction of traders ever achieve it, and the leverage and concentration involved make a total loss of capital a common result. The discipline in this chapter does not guarantee the target — it is what keeps you solvent long enough to have any chance at it. Survival precedes compounding.

## The Emotional Distortion Governance Matrix

Every rule reduces to one discipline: cage the biochemical machine and let the system execute.

| Behavioral trait | The distorted retail casualty | The 10x Blueprint fiduciary |
|---|---|---|
| **PnL monitorin g** | Stares at flashing green/red dollar amounts, riding dopamine highs and cortisol crashes. | Cloaks all dollar values; monitors only via percentage and R-multiples. |
| **Execution delivery** | Clicks manual buy/sell on real-time panic or a desire to "make it back." | Uses pre-committed automated bracket orders — no intraday intervention. |
| **Screen logistics** | Micro-manages 1-minute ticks for hours, causing burnout and decision fatigue. | Implements intermittent screen locks, checking only at set milestones. |
| **Size calibration** | Forces sizes that induce physical anxiety, leading to premature liquidation. | Runs the sleep-and-stare audit so size matches the psychological threshold. |

Distilled: let objective evidence determine every change in position size; create scaling rules before entering and follow them; increase exposure only after the market confirms; never add from excitement, fear, or recent profits; treat every addition as a new investment decision; keep portfolio risk within predefined limits; journal every scaling decision; accept losses quickly and avoid revenge trading; measure success by quality of execution; and treat emotional control as a competitive advantage.

## Two Ways to Pyramid

The same instinct to press a winner produces opposite structures depending on discipline.

| Dimension | The Chaser (top-heavy) | The Disciplined Pyramider |
|---|---|---|
| **Add sizing** | Bigger adds as it rises. | Smaller adds each time — bottom-heavy. |
| **Trigger to add** | Excitement and FOMO. | Mechanical confirmation only. |
| **Where they add** | Into parabolic extension. | On a held pullback or fresh breakout. |
| **Stops** | Left behind; total risk grows. | Raised with every add; total risk capped. |
| **Average cost** | Creeps up near the | Stays well below the current |

| Dimension | The Chaser (top-heavy) | The Disciplined Pyramider |
|---|---|---|
| | current price. | price. |
| **A pullback then** | Wipes out the whole gain. | Finds the position already protected. |

## Risk, Honesty, and a Reality Check

Adding to winners is one of the few techniques that is both genuinely powerful and genuinely treacherous, because it amplifies position size and average cost at the very moment confidence is highest. Used as a disciplined, bottom-heavy build with rising stops, it is how a survivor turns a good trade into a defining one; used as an emotional, top-heavy chase, it is how a trader converts his single best winner into a loss—the most demoralizing outcome there is. The whole difference is the shape of the build and the placement of the stop, decided in advance and obeyed when it counts.

## Blueprint Principle

> **Add to winners, never to losers — and add from underneath, never from the top.**

Position scaling is how conviction is allowed to follow proof: a small bet while you are uncertain, a large one only once the market has confirmed you, and never a dollar of added risk to the account along the way. Build bottom-heavy, add only on confirmation, keep each tranche smaller than the last, and move the stop up with every add so the growing position is always protected. Done with discipline, pyramiding is the engine of the outsized winner; done with emotion, it is the fastest way to give that winner back.

# Chapter 28
# Tactical Use of Leverage

*Using Borrowed Power Without Letting It Destroy the Account*

Leverage is neither good nor evil—it is a force multiplier. Used intelligently, it accelerates compounding, increases capital efficiency, and lets a trader press a high-quality opportunity; used carelessly, it turns a normal losing trade into a permanent injury. **Leverage does not create skill—it only magnifies the skill, or the lack of it, that already exists.** For a campaign to grow $100,000 into $1,000,000 in six months it is genuinely tempting, because the target demands extraordinary acceleration that the linear point-moves of ordinary stock cannot generate alone. Stocks, margin, options, warrants, 2x ETFs, and 3x ETFs all magnify exposure in both directions. The professional uses leverage the way a surgeon uses a scalpel—a precise, tactical accelerator deployed only on elite setups—while the casualty uses it like a slot machine. The question is never whether leverage can help; it is whether the trader has the discipline, the liquidity, and the risk controls to survive it. Leverage is a tool, not a strategy.

## A. When Leverage Is Intelligent

Leverage is intelligent only when two conditions are met at the same time: **a genuine asymmetric edge is present,** and **the invalidation point—the stop—is structurally close.** Put a 3x ETF or a high-gamma call on a loose, erratic chart with no clear technical floor and you are merely multiplying random noise; intelligent leverage needs a compressed pattern—a tight volatility contraction, a clean 30-minute opening range—where the downside can be fenced into a microscopic space. That tight floor is the whole point, because it produces asymmetric scale: when the invalidation sits a fraction of a percent below your entry, you can swing a large nominal position funded by leverage while your actual risk to portfolio NAV stays capped at your standard 1–2% unit—a big hammer with a short handle. Beyond the tight stop, leverage deserves consideration only when the broader market supports risk-taking and the sector leads, the instrument has strong momentum and confirming volume, the catalyst is credible with a clearly defined downside, and liquidity is sufficient to exit quickly while total exposure stays survivable. With those, express it through the right vehicle—a 2x or 3x ETF during a confirmed sector surge, long calls or debit spreads after a breakout with enough time to expiration, modest margin on a highly liquid leader with a clear stop, warrants when the underlying is gaining sponsorship, or an add to a position that has already proven itself—held for short, directional bursts of days to a couple of weeks, scaling in rather than committing all at once. Respect timing above all: a correct idea entered late can still lose rapidly, and an option bought after implied volatility has expanded can lose money even when the stock moves modestly your way.

## B. When Leverage Becomes Destructive

Leverage turns destructive the moment it is held through the wrong conditions or used to satisfy emotion rather than strategy. The first structural hazard is **volatility drag**—the beta decay built into daily-resetting leveraged ETFs—

because the leverage compounds day by day, so a 3x fund held through a choppy, range-bound stretch bleeds value even if the underlying ends exactly flat, with a sideways tape quietly costing a 3x product 5–20% or more in a month. The second is the **overnight gap:** leveraged instruments are acutely sensitive to pre-market and after-hours data—CPI, Fed decisions, geopolitical shocks—and ordinary stop orders do not execute outside regular hours, so a large adverse gap jumps straight past your stop. The third failure mode is emotional and the most common: the most dangerous leverage almost always appears after a losing streak, a missed opportunity, social-media excitement, or a desperate urge to recover. Options carry their own version of this, being leverage with extra enemies—time decay, IV collapse, strike selection, and expiration—so a trader can be directionally correct and still lose. And because leverage accelerates the drawdown math, the hole it digs is brutal: a 50% loss requires a 100% gain to recover, and a 33% drop in a 3x ETF approaches a total loss. Leverage is intelligent when it increases exposure to confirmed strength; it becomes destructive the instant it increases dependence on hope.

### C. Margin Survival Rules

Margin is the most dangerous form of leverage because it can force selling—with a purchased option the maximum loss is the premium, but with margin, losses can expand past your comfort zone and trigger liquidation at the worst possible time. The broker cares only about collateral, not your thesis, so the entire job is to stay so far from a margin call that the broker never makes the decision for you. **Never use the broker's maximum:** keep account equity comfortably above 40–50%, hold normal margin usage to roughly 20–50% of the portfolio (zero in a drawdown), and never let a 30% adverse move bring you near liquidation. **Treat high leverage as short-term only:** short-dated options and heavy margin are velocity vehicles, not overnight holds—if such a position is not comfortably in profit and protected by a hard stop by late in the session, flatten it. **Put liquidity first:** never lever aggressively into thin, halt-prone, promotional, or dilution-risk names, and always keep 20–40% in cash or Treasuries. **Avoid margin into binary events:** earnings, FDA decisions, and macro prints can gap straight past stops—you intend to lose 5% and the stock opens down 25%. **Cap correlated exposure:** hold no more than one leveraged instrument per sector cluster and judge risk at the portfolio level, asking "if everything gaps against me tomorrow morning, am I still solvent?" **De-lever before the broker does:** down 5–10% from peak, cut margin by half; down 10–15% or more, go to zero and into preservation mode. One discipline runs underneath all six—price the cost of leverage into the trade, because margin interest, option theta, and ETF decay compound silently, so only take the leverage when the expected edge clearly covers its carrying cost.

### The Leverage Governance Matrix

The same instruments make one trader and break another.

| Parameter | The Destructive Gambler | The Tactical Operator |
|---|---|---|
| **Trigger for** | Deploys it out of greed on | Unlocks it only when an elite |

| Parameter | The Destructive Gambler | The Tactical Operator |
|---|---|---|
| **leverage** | loose, unconfirmed charts. | pattern has an ultra-tight risk floor. |
| **Time horizon** | Holds leveraged ETFs through chop, bleeding to drag. | Uses leverage for short, directional sprints; rotates to cash in days. |
| **Overnight risk** | Leaves bloated, unhedged margin open overnight. | Flattens or hedges leveraged exposure before the close. |
| **Correlation** | Stacks correlated 3x ETFs and options into one cluster. | Caps leveraged factors to one per sector. |
| **Risk control** | Lets the broker set the limits until a call wipes him out. | Fences every position at 1R and de-levers on drawdowns. |

## The Leverage Ruleset

The whole chapter compresses to a short standing policy:

> **Tactical leverage, in one screen. Intelligent leverage:** only on Grade-A setups inside a confirmed trend, with a tight invalidation; max 3x exposure or the equivalent options delta; scale in, adding to winners only. **Destructive avoidance:** no leverage in chop (elevated volatility or no clear momentum), into binary events, or after an emotional loss; monitor daily for decay. **Margin:** under ~30% usage normally, equity buffer above ~40%, auto-de-lever on drawdowns, and zero margin in preservation mode. **Overall:** portfolio heat ≤ 8%, about 1% risk per trade, asymmetric setups only — and journal every leveraged position with its rationale, expected path, decay impact, and exit plan.

## Risk, Honesty, and a Reality Check

Leverage is the accelerator that makes the headline target conceivable at all—and the single fastest way to end the attempt. It is genuinely powerful on the rare elite setup and genuinely lethal everywhere else, and the line between the two is thinner than it looks while you are standing on it.

## Blueprint Principle

> **Leverage is earned by the quality of the setup, never demanded by the size of the goal.**

Leverage is most useful precisely when you are already right, and most dangerous when you are trying to force the market to cooperate. Deploy it only where an elite pattern offers an ultra-tight invalidation, so a large nominal position still risks only your standard unit; use it for short, directional sprints rather than holding it through chop; protect it from overnight gaps and binary events; cap correlated exposure; and de-lever yourself before any broker can. Treat it as a way to make the impossible goal feel reachable, and it becomes the mechanism that ends the campaign in a single session.

# PART VII — THE PATH FROM $100,000 TO $1,000,000

# Chapter 29
# Designing the Compounding Roadmap

*Turning an Ambitious Goal Into a Disciplined Campaign*

A goal without a roadmap becomes emotion. "I want to grow $100,000 into $1,000,000 in six months" is ambition, but without milestones, risk limits, and allocation rules the trader swings between greed, fear, desperation, and overconfidence, and the account follows. The roadmap answers four questions—where the account should be each month, what must happen each week, how much drawdown is tolerable, and how capital is deployed as the account grows—and its central idea is that aggressive compounding is not a straight line but an escalating staircase: capital is guarded most fiercely when it is smallest, and the throttle opens only once the market has supplied a cushion of profit to trade on.

## A. The Arithmetic, and Why a Straight Line Fails

To grow $100,000 into $1,000,000, the account must multiply by ten, which at a constant rate is roughly **46.8% compounded every month**—or about 9.26% every week across the 26-week campaign. Held flat, the path looks like this:

| Month | Beginning | Growth | Target |
|---|---|---|---|
| Start | $100,000 | — | $100,000 |
| Month 1 | $100,000 | 46.8% | $146,800 |
| Month 2 | $146,800 | 46.8% | $215,500 |
| Month 3 | $215,500 | 46.8% | $316,400 |
| Month 4 | $316,400 | 46.8% | $464,400 |
| Month 5 | $464,400 | 46.8% | $681,800 |
| **Month 6** | $681,800 | 46.8% | **$1,001,300** |

The table also exposes the trap. A 10% move on $100,000 is $10,000, but a 10% move on $700,000 is $70,000, so the dollar size of volatility grows with the account. The deeper error is treating that constant rate as a quota—forcing a fixed percentage every week guarantees over-trading in low-opportunity regimes. A missed target should trigger review, not recklessness: the question is always "what does the market support right now?" never "how much do I need to force?"

## B. The Escalating Staircase: Three Phases

Because the real distribution of returns is lumpy—a few large winners drive most of the result—the roadmap schedules growth in three phases mapped to account maturity, not to the calendar, each compounding faster than the last because the operator is increasingly trading on profit the market has handed over rather than on the original principal:

| Phase | Window | Account journey | Weekly target | Operational mode |
|---|---|---|---|---|
| 1 · **Foundation** | Months 1–2 | $100k → ~$175k | +3.5% to +5% | Preservation. Single stocks and standard ETFs; leverage heavily restricted. Build a cushion without denting principal. |
| 2 · **Acceleration** | Months 3–4 | ~$175k → ~$450k | +7% to +10% | Controlled aggression. With a profit buffer in place, unlock 3x ETFs and begin pyramiding on confirmed momentum. |
| 3 · **Sprint** | Months 5–6 | ~$450k → $1M | +10% to +15% | Maximum asymmetry. Short-dated options and special-situation warrants, with principal insulated by market profits. |

As monthly checkpoints, the staircase steps through roughly $130k and $175k (Phase 1), $280k and $450k (Phase 2), and $680k and $1,000,000 (Phase 3)—slow and defensive while one mistake could cause structural ruin, then progressively faster as an ever-larger wall of market money absorbs the volatility. You build the engine and let the mathematics do the work.

## C. Weekly Targets and Cadence

Weekly granularity suits the multi-day swing rhythm. The benchmark compounded rate is around 9% a week, but it is a benchmark, not a command. In practice a week falls into one of a few types: **breakout weeks** (supercycle momentum or earnings continuation) at +20% to +40% via pyramided winners; **baseline weeks** of a handful of elite setups at 1:3 or better, producing steady single-digit-to-low-teens compounding; **flat or recovery weeks** of 0–5% or a small loss, with mandatory inactivity when no asymmetric setup is present; and **maximum-loss weeks**, where a drawdown of roughly 5–8% triggers an automatic step-down in size. A simple cadence enforces patience—plan setups and allocate buckets at the start of the week, scale into winners and rotate mid-week, then review, take partials, and journal on Friday with no fresh aggression into weekend gaps. Track win rate, average R-multiple, and the share of profit from your top 20% of trades: the objective is to stay close to the curve while never taking a catastrophic drawdown, not to hit an exact number weekly.

## D. Drawdown Tolerances

A roadmap without a braking system is useless. Drawdown tolerance works on two axes. The first is a ceiling that rises with account maturity: while the account is small and the original principal is still exposed (roughly $100k–$150k), the maximum tolerable drawdown is tightest, around 8%; it widens to about 12% in the middle tiers and around 15% past $450k, where the cushion at risk is market money rather than seed capital. The second axis is the response itself, which scales with the depth of the hole:

| Drawdown from peak | Required response |
|---|---|
| **Up to ~8%** | Normal. Heighten patience and selectivity; trim size by about 20%; take fewer setups. |
| **8–15%** | De-risk. Halve position size, shift to a preservation-heavy book, trade only A-grade setups, take a 1–3 day reset. |
| **15–25%** | Survival mode. Cut risk per trade to ~0.5%, hold gross exposure under 100%, pause new leverage, review the whole system. |
| **25%+** | Emergency stop. Move 80%+ to preservation; trade micro-size or paper only until back within ~10% of the peak. |

The severity follows from the recovery math: a 10% hole needs about 11% to climb back, a 20% hole 25%, a 30% hole roughly 43%, a 50% hole 100%, and a 70% hole 233%. Deep drawdowns destroy capital and confidence together, so the roadmap protects the compounding base above all—never averaging down a loser, with a daily loss limit of 2–4% and total portfolio heat under 8% beneath the tiers above.

## E. Capital Allocation Schedules

Capital allocation governs how much of the account is exposed at each stage, and the disciplined trader never keeps the whole account fluidly at risk. The starting $100,000 splits into three buckets that shift as the campaign matures: a **preservation core** (50–60% at the outset—cash, short Treasuries, and unleveraged broad ETFs, never risked in high-leverage plays and grown steadily by profit transfers), a **growth / tactical** bucket (30–40%—swing trades, 2x and 3x ETFs, and options in confirmed supercycle themes), and an **opportunistic** bucket (5–10%—high-convexity warrants, biotech binaries, and quantum plays in small, strictly defined-risk size). As equity grows, the schedule releases its constraints while each individual position stays bounded:

| Phase / equity | Min cash / preservation | Max invested | Max single position |
|---|---|---|---|
| **Phase 1 ($100k–$175k)** | 50–60% | ~50% | ~25% per slot; option delta ≤ 2.5% NAV |
| **Phase 2 ($175k–$450k)** | ~33–40% | ~66% | ~33% per slot; option delta ≤ 5% NAV |
| **Phase 3 ($450k–$1M)** | ~25% | ~75% | up to ~50% per apex slot; option delta ≤ 10% NAV |

Rebalance weekly or at milestones, and let a few triggers move capital automatically: after a big winner, scale out 40–60% and sweep the profit to the core; on a drawdown, shift to a higher preservation weight; on a volatility spike, raise hedges and cash; and once past roughly $600k, transfer 30–50% of each month's new gains into the preservation core to lock the campaign in. The constraint that keeps you alive in Phase 1 is the same one that lets you swing the full accumulated weight of the account in Phase 3.

## The Roadmap Governance Matrix

| Dimension | The Linear Speculator | The Disciplined Roadmap-Trader |
|---|---|---|
| **Target architecture** | A flat daily or weekly dollar quota; forces trades in bad environments. | A three-phase escalating staircase mapped to account maturity. |
| **Risk escalation** | Big risks on day one, when most vulnerable to ruin. | Leverage reserved for Phases 2–3, traded on locked-in market money. |
| **Drawdown defense** | Ignores cumulative drops until a margin call forces liquidation. | Scales size down the moment account floors are breached. |
| **Cash** | Insists on being fully invested at all times. | Treats cash as a standing weapon via a strict allocation schedule. |

## Risk, Honesty, and a Reality Check

The roadmap turns an impossible-looking goal into measurable stages, but it cannot bend the odds away from how steep the climb is. Markets do not care about your schedule, so the professional follows the roadmap without becoming enslaved to it: it gives direction, risk management keeps the trader alive, and discipline determines whether the account survives long enough to compound. Know the targets, benchmarks, drawdown limits, and allocation rules before the campaign begins, then hold them loosely enough to let the market, not the spreadsheet, set the pace.

## Blueprint Principle

Compounding $100,000 toward $1,000,000 is not a daily wage to be collected on a fixed schedule; it is an escalating staircase to be climbed in order. Spend the early weeks protecting the seed capital like a fortress, taking small, well-insulated bites; build a wall of market money before unlocking leverage. Map the milestones, enforce the drawdown floors, schedule the cash, and treat every target as a benchmark rather than an order—do that.

## Chapter 30
# Example Compounding Scenarios

*Five Engines for the Same Target — and the Failure Mode Each One Accepts*

Each path here is the same goal—$100,000 to $1,000,000 in six months—attacked with a different risk engine. These are illustrative frameworks, not guarantees. None of them lowers the bar: the underlying requirement of roughly 47% a month, compounded six times, is fixed. What the paths change is where the risk sits and what shape the outcome distribution takes—so picking a path is not picking a probability of success, it is choosing which failure mode you are most willing to risk. One path is most likely to undershoot but survive; others widen both tails, raising the small chance of actually hitting 10x while raising the much larger chance of a blow-up. Two things hold across all five: the arithmetic baseline is the same (about 46.8% compounded monthly, or roughly 9–10% weekly), and every scenario assumes the same survival rules from earlier chapters—1–2% risk per trade, portfolio heat under 8%, hard daily loss limits, a preservation bucket, and automatic de-risking on drawdowns. Real paths are lumpy: a few large winners carry the load, and the illustrative monthly runs below deliberately include the down months any honest version of these campaigns contains.

## A. The Conservative-Aggressive Path

**Mechanism.** Mostly liquid momentum stocks, the occasional 2x ETF, and a small options sleeve, with risk held to 1–1.5% per trade behind tight stops and early scaling. It aims for a relatively smooth equity curve built from consistent base hits plus the rare runner, starting from a preservation-heavy allocation (around 55% cash and core) that feeds profits back into the core as it grows.

**Illustrative math.** With about four trades a week, a 45–50% win rate, an average winner of 3R and losers held to 1R, expectancy is roughly 0.47 × 3 minus 0.53 × 1, or about +0.9R per trade — around 3.6R a week. At 1.25% per R that is 4–5% per week, or roughly 18–25% a month. Compounded, 20% a month is about 3.0x over six months and 25% a month about 3.8x.

*An illustrative run: +30%, +38%, +42%, +45%, +40%, +**55%** — about $130k, $179k, $255k, $369k, $517k, and roughly $800k by month six, short of the headline unless an extra outlier lands.*

**The honest read.** This is the path a disciplined trader could actually run — and it most likely undershoots the headline. At conservative risk the realistic outcome is 3–5x in a strong six months, which is extraordinary by any normal standard but is not 10x; reaching the target here would require an unrealistic win rate or luck into a couple of outsized runners. Its virtue is survival: drawdowns tend to stay in the 8–30% range, which the timeline can absorb. Framed correctly, it is "aim for 10x, plan to land at 3–5x, and stay in the game." Best for the disciplined trader who wants controlled aggression; its risk is simply falling behind schedule when markets are quiet.

The name is deliberately paradoxical, and the paradox is the point: it does not mean conservative investing, it means **aggressive opportunity selection fused with conservative risk management.** You are conservative in defense—capping risk per trade in an iron vice and guarding starting capital like a fortress—and aggressive in offense, concentrating capital into high-velocity sectors only when the evidence is overwhelming. Most people assume aggressive trading means maximum leverage on every position, buying every hot stock, trading every day, going all-in, and refusing to sell losers; professionals do the opposite, becoming aggressive only when probabilities are decisively in their favor and waiting the rest of the time. Deploy size only into setups showing several of powerful persistent momentum, exceptional earnings strength, visible institutional accumulation, clear sector leadership, elevated relative volume, and a genuine catalyst—while at the same moment capping the loss on every trade before entry, scaling into strength rather than averaging into weakness, reducing exposure when conditions deteriorate, and increasing exposure only after confirmation. The objective of conservative risk is not to win every trade but to survive long enough for compounding to work, because losses are geometrically expensive:

| Trader | Drawdown taken | Gain required to recover |
|---|---|---|
| Trader A | –50% | +100% |
| Trader B | –10% | about +11% |

Trader A must double the surviving capital just to return to even; Trader B barely needs 11%. This is the **Geometric Deficit**—deep drawdowns cost not just money but the compounding power of the money left, so the first objective is never "maximize every gain" but "minimize catastrophic loss," the one error compounding cannot forgive. Be clear-eyed about the arithmetic: turning \$100,000 into \$1,000,000 is a 1,000% total return, which over a smooth six months requires a compounded monthly rate of roughly 46.8%:

> $\mathbf{\$100{,}000 \times (1 + 0.468)^6 \approx \$1{,}000{,}000}$ *Equivalently, the monthly multiplier is 10^(1/6) ≈ 1.468.*

Sustaining ~47% a month is one of the rarest feats in trading, so the honest version does not pretend the curve is smooth. The deeper engine underneath every scenario is the compound-growth formula:

> $\mathbf{FV = PV \times (1 + r)^n}$ PV = starting capital • r = return per period • n = number of periods *Example:* $\$1{,}000 \times (1 + \mathbf{0.05})^{20} \approx \$2{,}653$

Every percentage gain is earned on a larger base than the last, which is why dollar gains look almost flat early and explosive late. Rather than demanding a flat 47% from day one, the path runs a **three-phase escalating schedule**: Phase 1 (Months 1–2, +28–35%/mo) trades 100% liquid common stocks and standard ETFs, capping position size at ~25% per slot and building a cushion without denting principal toward ~\$130k–\$170k; Phase 2 (Months 3–4, +35–45%/mo) steps into 2x/3x sector ETFs (SOXL, TQQQ, FNGU) only during verified acceleration and pyramids into winners, toward ~\$230k–\$315k; Phase 3 (Months 5–6, +38–45%/mo) keeps most of the account in high-beta and leveraged-ETF swings with a smaller sleeve (up to 30%) for short-dated ITM calls, toward \$650k–\$1,000,000. Risk is highest to your psychology early, when you have the least cushion, so the system keeps size modest until the account has earned the right to press.

> **A necessary caveat.** *As you will see in the scenarios below, even strong, disciplined execution frequently lands the account between $400,000 and $660,000 by the end of Month 6—not at a clean $1,000,000. Hitting the full 10x inside six months sits at the extreme upper edge of outcomes and typically requires near-flawless execution layered on an unusually cooperative market. A realistic conservative-aggressive trader often reaches the milestone in eight to twelve months. That is not failure; it is the same edge expressed at a survivable pace.*

## The Conservative-Aggressive Path Matrix

| Parameter | The Retail Casual Fallacy | The Conservative-Aggressive Blueprint |
|---|---|---|
| Growth structure | Assumes a flat, linear dollar gain every day, driving over-trading in poor markets. | Maps a three-phase escalating curve that accelerates only as market-money buffers grow. |
| Asset allocation | Gambles on illiquid small-caps or out-of-money options on day one. | Anchors early growth in liquid equities; introduces 3x ETFs and options only in Phases 2–3. |
| Risk control | Uses wide, loose mental stops to "give trades room," inviting deep drawdowns. | Enforces hard, layered drawdown brakes to keep the capital baseline safe. |
| Position strategy | Fakes diversification with many tiny positions, diluting compounding velocity. | Concentrates into two to four high-velocity targets inside accelerating sectors. |

## Worked Scenarios

The tables below are **illustrations, not forecasts.** First, trade-level compounding—no single trade doubles the account, only a long sequence of disciplined gains with uninterrupted compounding:

| Trade | Return | Portfolio |
|---|---|---|
| Start | — | $100,000 |
| 1 | +15% | $115,000 |
| 2 | +18% | $135,700 |
| 3 | +20% | $162,840 |
| 4 | +18% | $192,151 |
| 5 | +22% | $234,424 |
| 6 | +20% | $281,309 |
| 7 | +18% | $331,945 |

| Trade | Return | Portfolio |
|---|---|---|
| 8 | +22% | $404,973 |
| 9 | +20% | $485,968 |
| 10 | +18% | $573,442 |
| 11 | +22% | $699,600 |
| 12 | +20% | $839,520 |
| 13 | +19% | $999,029 |

Sustaining thirteen consecutive winners is itself extraordinarily rare; the point is structural—moderate percentage gains accumulate dramatically when losses stay small and compounding is never interrupted. Next, three monthly paths sharing the same assumptions (a 60–70% win rate, 2:1 or better reward-to-risk, 8–15 trades a month, risk near 0.5–1% per trade) but differing in how the market cooperates:

**Path 1 — Steady (most realistic).**

| Month | Net return | End of month |
|---|---|---|
| 1 | +28% | $128,000 |
| 2 | +32% | $168,960 |
| 3 | +35% | $228,096 |
| 4 | +38% | $314,772 |
| 5 | +42% | $446,977 |
| 6 | +45% | $648,117 |

**Path 2 — Front-loaded.**

| Month | Net return | End of month |
|---|---|---|
| 1 | +45% | $145,000 |
| 2 | +40% | $203,000 |
| 3 | +38% | $280,140 |
| 4 | +35% | $378,189 |
| 5 | +30% | $491,646 |
| 6 | +35% | $663,722 |

**Path 3 — With a drawdown (the most educational).**

| Month | Net return | End of month |
|---|---|---|
| 1 | +35% | $135,000 |
| 2 | +22% | $164,700 |
| 3 | –12% | $144,936 |
| 4 | +45% | $210,157 |
| 5 | +38% | $290,017 |
| 6 | +42% | $411,824 |

Path 3 is the one to internalize: the losing month is not the exception to the plan—it *is* the plan working, the rules ensuring a bad stretch is a setback you trade through rather than an event that ends your run.

## Guardrails, Allocation, and Toolkit

The equity curve should look like an escalating staircase, not a cliff face, defended in layers that engage automatically: a per-trade cap of 0.5–1% of current capital; a de-risk trigger that halves sizing units and shelves leverage if the account falls ~10–12% from its peak; and an honest ceiling acknowledging that even with these rules a bad leveraged month can still draw down 15–25%, because a stop is an intention, not a contract—in fast markets 3x ETFs and options open well past where you meant to exit. Aggression is earned in layers, each unlocked by confirmation:

| Stage | Trigger | Allocation to the idea |
|---|---|---|
| Initial probe | Setup confirmed, entry trigger hit | ~30% |
| First add | Trade moves in your favor, holds the level | increase to ~50% |
| Second add | Trend continuation, base on top of base | increase to ~75% |
| Full size | Exceptional confirmation, leadership intact | maximum planned allocation |

Aggression increases only after the market validates the thesis. A representative strong month is not a jackpot but a portfolio of outcomes—4–5 pyramided winners at +20–40% each, 8–10 smaller wins at +8–15%, and 4–6 small losses at −4–−7% cut quickly, netting +30–40% (a realistic winning stretch runs −5%, +20%, −3%, +28%, +18%—winners offsetting several small losses). Walked through, one pyramided sector-acceleration trade risks ~$800 (0.8%) on the initial leg (TQQQ shares or ITM NVDA calls), adds a layer at +12% and trails to break-even, adds another at +8% more, and scales out around +31% blended—about $4,500–$6,000 from one idea. Each vehicle is used only where its risk profile fits the phase:

| Instrument | Role in the path | Honest risk note |
| --- | --- | --- |
| Common stocks | Phase 1 foundation; liquid leaders clearing clean patterns. | Single-name and gap risk; still your safest base. |
| Standard ETFs | Diversified momentum and sector exposure. | Lower idiosyncratic risk, but trends still reverse. |
| 2x / 3x ETFs | Phase 2–3 accelerant during verified sector acceleration. | Daily-reset decay erodes returns in chop; severe losses in sharp reversals. Swing, don't marry. |
| Options (ITM, short-dated) | Phase 3 sleeve for explosive, defined-risk moves. | Time decay and IV crush; can expire worthless. Size as a sleeve, never the core. |
| Warrants | Occasional asymmetric, long-dated leverage. | Often illiquid, with wide spreads, dilution, and issuer/credit risk. Easy to overpay; trade sparingly. |

The hierarchy is deliberate—leverage and convexity are introduced after a profit cushion exists, in proportion to conviction, always with a predefined exit. Hold two truths at once: a tenfold gain in six months is extraordinary, not typical, achievable only in strong bull phases with near-flawless execution and often slipping to eight, ten, or twelve months; yet the principles that make it possible—capital preservation, selective aggression, disciplined scaling—build wealth in every environment. The real prize is a repeatable edge that compounds for years.

**IMPORTANT RISK DISCLOSURE The scenarios, tables, and figures in this chapter are illustrative examples, not forecasts, guarantees, or promises of results.** Aggressive trading—particularly with leveraged ETFs, options, and warrants—carries a high risk of substantial or total loss, and most traders who attempt extreme short-term targets lose money. Markets can deliver many consecutive flat or losing months. Leverage can move against you faster than stop-losses can protect you, and instruments such as options and warrants can expire worthless. **Only ever risk capital you can afford to lose entirely.** Nothing in this chapter is individualized financial, investment, tax, or legal advice; the author is not acting as your financial advisor. Consider consulting a licensed professional before trading, and ensure any strategy fits your own circumstances, objectives, and risk tolerance. Past performance and hypothetical illustrations do not indicate future results.

## B. The High-Volatility Path

**Mechanism.** Low-float, high-beta small caps and gap-and-go names, alongside high-beta AI, semiconductor, and biotech momentum and event-driven catalysts – fewer but larger bets, wider stops, and an explicit willingness to ride 40–60% drawdowns for the chance at explosive runs.

*An illustrative run, with the pain included: +60%, −25%, +80%, −15%, +120%, +70% – $160k, $120k, $216k, $184k, $404k, and roughly $687k.*

*Intra-week, any single week can swing +30% or −25%; two or three low-floats running 200–500% can carry the whole campaign, and an equally normal cluster of failed breakouts can cut the account by a third in a week.*

**The honest read.** This path does not raise your expected return so much as widen both tails. It has a higher chance of actually touching 10x than the conservative path, and a much higher chance of a drawdown deep enough to end the timeline – recall that a 50% hole needs a 100% gain to undo. It is closer to a lottery with an edge than to a plan; variance, not skill, dominates the six-month result. Best for traders who can stomach volatility and hold strictly to the drawdown protocols; its risk is emotional whiplash and the single unmanaged drawdown that ends the campaign.

This is the full-throttle end of the blueprint, leaning into the most erratic, asymmetric instruments in the book—small-cap momentum, biotech binaries, speculative warrants, short-dated option sprints, and 3x ETFs. It delivers the fastest potential curve paired with the deepest drawdowns. The mathematics are governed by the power law, and the path spans a spectrum: at one extreme the pure anomaly hunter accepts a ~30–35% win rate for fat-tailed outliers of +10R to +20R from warrants and binaries; at the other the full-throttle leveraged-momentum trader runs a ~55–65% win rate on big pyramided swings in 3x ETFs and options. Both rest on the same engine—a string of small, controlled losses is the cost of capturing the handful of explosive winners that drive the whole portfolio. On this path the linear idea of a steady monthly rate is thrown out; returns follow a skew-positive distribution where the average loss is capped at −1R while breakout wins yield +10R, +15R, even +20R, and out of every ten trades roughly seven are minor stop-outs while two or three explosive surges generate the entire return:

| Losers (×7) | −7R total |
|---|---|
| **Winner · squeeze** | **+12R** |
| **Winner · warrant run** | **+18R** |
| **Winner · catalyst gap** | **+20R** |

Seven −1R losers cost −7R; three outliers return +50R; the campaign nets +43R despite being wrong on most trades. The same engine runs at two intensities, set by your instrument mix:

| Expression | Win rate | Typical winner / loser | Instruments |
|---|---|---|---|
| **Pure anomaly hunter** | ~30–35% | +10R to +20R / −1R capped | Warrants, biotech binaries, OTM option sprints, micro-caps |
| **Full-throttle leveraged** | ~55–65% | +25% to +60% / −7% to −10% | 3x ETFs, options on momentum names, high-beta stocks |

The scenarios rest on the full-throttle leveraged expression's assumptions:

| Parameter | Assumption |
|---|---|

| Parameter | Assumption |
|---|---|
| **Starting capital** | $100,000 |
| **Risk per trade** | 0.75–1% of current capital (still strict, but allows bigger swings) |
| **Instruments** | Heavy use of 3x ETFs and options (long calls on momentum names) |
| **Pyramiding** | 3–4 layers on strong confirmations |
| **Frequency** | 10–20 swings per month, many in accelerating sectors (semis, AI, biotech) |
| **Win rate** | 55–65% (lower than the conservative path, due to volatility) |
| **Average winner / loser** | +25% to +60% (pyramided leveraged moves) / −7% to −10% |
| **Market** | Strong bull with sharp rotations and catalysts |

This path is defined by extreme concentration at the right moment—once an outlier trend is validated (not anticipated), the allocator runs large 25–30% tranches into the single best opportunity, with the loss pre-capped at a tight 1R and pyramiding (3–4 layers, each smaller than the last, stop ratcheting up) paused entirely during chop. Volatility produces emotional extremes, so two guardrails keep a technical drawdown from becoming an emotional liquidation—and the first is mechanical:

> **The Rule of 3 Consecutive Cuts** If the scanners trigger three consecutive stop-outs in a single week, you are programmatically barred from opening any new speculative position for the next 72 hours. This circuit breaker prevents revenge trading and stops a routine losing streak from spiraling into an unmanaged liquidation. The flat, frustrating pause is the feature, not a flaw.

Beyond it, the work is staying process-oriented when the curve is jagged: review every position daily, and remain detached during the long flat grinds, knowing two or three trades will rewrite the ledger.

## The Compounding Scenarios

**Scenario A — The Sawtooth Milestone Path.** The account opens below water after a string of stop-outs, gives back ground in Month 4, and still reaches target on two or three outliers:

| Month 1 | $92,000 |
|---|---|
| **Month 2** | **$115,000** |
| **Month 3** | **$310,000** |
| **Month 4** | **$290,000** |

| Month 1 | $92,000 |
|---|---|
| Month 5 | $580,000 |
| Month 6 | $1,000,000 |

The reality behind it: five consecutive biotech stop-outs drag the account to −8%, before a Day-1 breakout delivers +12R; a special-situation warrant cluster explodes +400% in four days, launching past $300,000; Month 4 gives back ~6% in chop; then a macro options run and an overnight biotech clearance complete the climb. **Scenario B — Explosive Run.** An ideal environment with one or two 80%+ runners; it overshoots:

| Month | Net return | Balance |
|---|---|---|
| 1 | +55% | $155,000 |
| 2 | +65% | $255,750 |
| 3 | +48% | $378,510 |
| 4 | +52% | $575,335 |
| 5 | +35% | $776,702 |
| 6 | +58% | **$1,227,591 (crosses $1M)** |

**Scenario C — The Volatile Rollercoaster (the version to internalize).** Big wins mixed with painful but survivable losses, including two negative months, surviving on ≤1% per-trade risk and paused pyramiding:

| Month | Net return | Balance |
|---|---|---|
| 1 | +72% | $172,000 |
| 2 | **−18%** | $141,040 |
| 3 | +65% | $232,716 |
| 4 | +45% | $337,438 |
| 5 | **−22%** | $263,202 |
| 6 | +80% | **$473,764** |

Two losing months totalling roughly −40% combined did not blow up the account, because per-trade risk stayed at or under 1% and pyramiding was paused during the chop—and the recovery came from one or two oversized winners. At about $474,000 after six months, this path needs strong follow-through to push past $1M around month seven or eight. That ragged, drawdown-scarred line is what high-volatility trading actually looks like.

Walked through end to end—a pyramided SOXL play on a $150,000 mid-journey account, risking $1,200 on the initial leg:

**Initial.** $40,000 in SOXL or calls on the breakout. **Pyramid.** On a +18% move with a volume surge, add $25,000 on the pullback to the 20-day MA. On +15% more, add $12,000 on the new high. Total position ≈ $77,000. **Extract.** Average gain on the full pyramid +42% — about +$32,000, a ~21% account boost from one ~8-day trade. **Repeat.** Three to five such trades in a hot month — while keeping every loser tiny — is what the explosive scenarios assume.

Reduce aggressiveness, or step aside, when indexes lose their trend, breadth deteriorates, breakouts fail, distribution days cluster, liquidity declines, or correlations spike. The standing controls—maximum risk/size/leverage limits set in advance, daily and weekly loss limits, predefined exits, and a hard rule against widening a stop on a volatile name—are what separate the survivor from the casualty.

**The Honest Math — The Highest-Risk Path in the Book** This path can deliver a 10x outcome in six months in an ideal bull market — and it has wiped out many aggressive traders. Expect 20–40% drawdowns as a normal feature, not a failure. By any honest estimate, only a small fraction of readers (perhaps 5–10%) should attempt it at all, and even they should start with paper trading and the emotional discipline of the prior chapter firmly in place. Every scenario above is an illustration of compounding mechanics, not a forecast or an expected result. The win rate can be as low as 30%, the equity curve is a jagged sawtooth, and the entire return depends on two or three outliers that may simply never arrive in your six-month window. The realistic rollercoaster (Scenario C), reaching about $474,000 with two losing months, is far closer to the truth than the explosive run — and even it assumes the bull market and the outliers cooperate.

### The High-Volatility Governance Matrix

| Operational parameter | The retail-casualty failure | The 10x Blueprint anomaly hunter |
|---|---|---|
| **Win-rate expectation** | Demands a 90% win rate; enters an emotional crisis on the first losing streak. | Expects and accepts a ~30% win rate, knowing the math relies on outlier payoffs. |
| **Drawdown behavior** | Widens stops on volatile small-caps out of hope, turning a 1R cut into a 40% blowup. | Enforces an iron 1R risk vice; treats routine cuts as the cost of hunting. |
| **Position management** | Takes tiny sizes on winners out of fear, missing the fat-tail expansion. | Runs extreme concentration (25–30% tranches) once an outlier is validated. |
| **Curve psychology** | Panics during the sideways sawtooth and changes strategy mid-week. | Stays detached during flat periods, knowing 2–3 trades will rewrite the ledger. |

## C. The Leveraged ETF Path

**Mechanism.** 3x funds such as TQQQ, SOXL, and UPRO held across days to weeks in confirmed sector trends, with short holds, pyramiding on winners, and quick rotation out of chop. The defining feature — and the trap — is daily rebalancing, which means the held return is not 3x the index over multi-day periods.

**The decay, in both directions.** In chop it bleeds: the index gains 10%, then falls 9.09% back to flat; the 3x goes +30%, then −27.3%, ending at 0.945 — down 5.5% while the index is unchanged. In a clean trend it compounds in your favor: the index rises 3% a day for five days (+15.9%), and the 3x compounds daily to 1.09 to the fifth, or +53.8% — more than three times the index's move.

*An illustrative run: +45%, +35%, +55%, +40% (after a −10% intra-month chop), +65%, +**50%** — $145k, $196k, $304k, $425k, $701k, and roughly $1.05M — the rare case that clears the bar, on the back of a sustained trend.*

**The honest read.** This path is a bet on the regime as much as the trade. Catch a sustained directional macro or sector trend and 3x daily compounding produces enormous numbers; sit through chop and the decay grinds you down even when your directional call is eventually right. Because the instrument is already 3x, a "full" position carries hidden leverage, so position sizing and time-based exits — rarely more than five to seven strong days — matter more here than anywhere. The ruin risk is concentrated specifically in sideways markets, where a single flat month can cost 10–20% to decay.

This path is engineered for the systemic allocator who wants to eliminate single-stock idiosyncratic risk entirely while keeping double-digit daily velocity—trading nothing but highly liquid 2x and 3x leveraged index and sector ETFs (TQQQ for the Nasdaq-100, SOXL for semiconductors, plus FNGU, LABU, TNA, FAS). But leverage is an amplifier, not a source of edge, and these are tactical instruments, not investments, because of one specific piece of math. Because the funds reset their leverage daily, returns over time diverge from a simple multiple of the index—the villain is **volatility decay.** The cleanest way to see it is a two-day chop:

| | Underlying index | Index value | 3x ETF move | 3x value |
|---|---|---|---|---|
| Start | — | $100.00 | — | $100.00 |
| Day 1 | +10% | $110.00 | +30% | $130.00 |
| Day 2 | −10% | $99.00 | −30% | $91.00 |
| **Net** | **−1.0%** | **$99.00** | **−9.0%** | **$91.00** |

The index ended down a trivial 1%; the 3x companion ended down 9%, nine times worse, not three. Repeat the alternating chop and the fund bleeds toward zero even as the index goes nowhere—peak-to-trough drawdowns of roughly 80–82% in TQQQ and 90%+ in SOXL have occurred. But in a clean trend it compounds in your favor: the index rising 3% a day for five days (+15.9%) compounds the 3x to +53.8%, more than three times the index. So the discipline is regime discipline—rent these vehicles strictly during clean, persistent trends and retreat entirely to cash the moment the market turns choppy, a binary switch between full deployment and full cash:

> **CLEAN LINEAR TREND** *Index trending above its anchor averages → deploy the 3x, let daily compounding surge*

> **CHOP / SIDEWAYS DETECTED** *Trend stalls → liquidate entirely to cash, freeze the curve, bypass decay*

Instrument choice dials the risk, and liquidity is a hard filter on both:

| Vehicle | Best suited to | Trade-off |
|---|---|---|
| **2x ETFs** | Moderately aggressive traders, longer swings, smoother trends | Less volatility and gentler decay than 3x — still magnifies the move |
| **3x ETFs** | Exceptionally strong momentum, clear leadership, expanding institutional buying | Amplifies gains and losses; sizing and exit discipline become critical |

Use 2x as the default in moderately strong trends and reserve 3x for the cleanest environments, restricting operations to the most-traded vehicles (TQQQ, SOXL, FNGU) where spreads are tight—thin leveraged ETFs add brutal slippage on top of decay. Hold the broader, lower-decay vehicle (TQQQ) as a core in a general uptrend and shift into the higher-volatility sector fund (SOXL) when a specific theme accelerates. The scenarios rest on these assumptions:

| Parameter | Assumption |
|---|---|
| **Starting capital** | $100,000 |
| **Instruments** | 70–90% in 2x/3x ETFs (TQQQ, SOXL primary; rotate into others on sector shifts) |
| **Risk per trade** | 0.75–1% of current capital |
| **Pyramiding** | 2–3 layers on strong momentum confirmations |
| **Hold time** | Strictly 3–10 days — decay accelerates beyond this |
| **Frequency** | 10–18 swings per month |
| **Win rate** | 58–68% (higher in trending bull markets) |
| **Market** | Bullish with clear rotations (e.g., AI / semiconductor themes) |
| **Key rule** | Exit or reduce immediately in choppy or sideways conditions |

Tie the protective stop to the underlying index's key moving averages—a moving target that rises with the trend—rather than to the leveraged fund's noisier price, because decay guarantees that overstaying a stalled trend is a slow, certain loss.

### The Leveraged ETF Governance Matrix

| Operational parameter | The retail-casual mistake | The 10x leveraged ETF fiduciary |
|---|---|---|
| **Holding duration** | Buys a 3x ETF and holds through a 3-month choppy correction, bled out by decay. | Rents the 3x strictly during verified linear trends; retreats to cash when the trend stalls. |
| **Risk insulation** | Assumes diversification protects them and sizes blindly. | Uses a moving-target stop tied to the underlying index's key averages. |
| **Liquidity profiling** | Trades illiquid leveraged ETFs with wide spreads and brutal slippage. | Restricts operations to the top few most-liquid 3x vehicles. |
| **Regime adaptation** | Fights a grinding market, guessing the bottom of a 3x fund. | Switches between bull/bear twins (SOXL vs. SOXS) or simply holds cash. |

## D. The Options-Heavy Path

**Mechanism.** Buying calls and debit spreads on momentum and supercycle names around catalysts, with occasional warrants. The appeal is convexity — a call can return several hundred percent on a move the stock itself could never make — and the enemies are theta (time decay) and IV crush (implied volatility collapsing after the event). Entries come on IV expansion, exits before the crush, and options are capped to a portion of the growth bucket to bound total premium decay.

**Illustrative math.** Because a total loss per position is common, you size small and expect to lose the full risk often. Risk 2% of the account per trade; assume a 35% win rate with winners averaging a 5x on the premium (+8% to the account) and losers going to zero (−2%). Expectancy is 0.35 × 8% minus 0.65 × 2%, or about +1.5% per trade — positive, but the 65% loss rate means frequent strings of expirations to zero, and IV crush can turn a correct directional call into a loss.

*An illustrative run: +25%, +65%, +35%, +80%, −10%, +120% — $125k, $206k, $278k, $500k, $450k, and roughly $990k — many small losses punctuated by a few 200–500% winners.*

**The honest read.** This path can close the 10x math the fastest — a handful of ten-baggers does it — and it carries the highest ruin probability and the most violent sequence risk. A bad run of expirations can halve the account in weeks no matter how right you were on direction. It is the highest-convexity, highest-fragility option: most likely to either hit the target quickly or zero out. Best only for highly skilled options traders; its risk is account destruction from short-dated contracts, oversized bets, and the binary gaps common in biotech and quantum.

This is the highest-octane track—harnessing the non-linear power of delta and gamma acceleration to control a large notional position with a small, defined cash outlay, so a favorable move lifts the option far faster than the stock. But options introduce risks shares do not: theta erodes premium every day the stock sits still, vega can move the contract independently of the stock, and a long option can lose its entire premium. The retail casualty treats them like lottery tickets (the defined downside is the premium, against uncapped upside that can run 100–500%+ on a single trade)—buying cheap OTM calls before earnings and getting destroyed by the IV collapse that follows—while the professional deploys carefully chosen contracts only when momentum, volume, and a real catalyst align. Options do not replace disciplined trading; they amplify the consequences of every decision. Four Greeks drive the premium:

| Greek | What it measures | What it means for you |
|---|---|---|
| **Delta** | How much the option price moves per $1 move in the stock. | Your friend — a 0.50 delta turns a $1 stock move into a $0.50 option move. |
| **Gamma** | How fast delta itself changes as the stock moves. | Your accelerator — a directional run pushes delta toward 1.00, compounding gains. |
| **Theta** | The daily erosion of time value. | Your enemy — it bleeds premium every day the stock sits still. |
| **Vega** | Sensitivity to changes in implied volatility (IV). | Two-edged — a post-earnings IV crush can sink a correct directional call. |

The whole craft is engineering a contract where delta and gamma work for you faster than theta and vega work against you. The retail casualty buys cheap deep-OTM calls that bleed to theta and expire worthless; the blueprint targets a hyper-specific configuration:

***Slightly ITM / ATM · Delta ≈ 0.50–0.60 · 30–45 days to expiration***

At a 0.50 delta, every $1 move in the underlying translates to about $0.50 in premium, and as the stock runs, gamma accelerates delta toward 1.00—the contract morphs into a high-leverage equity position while the maximum downside stays capped at the premium; the 30–45 DTE window gives a theta cushion. Trade only liquid contracts with narrow spreads, and on catalyst timing do the opposite of the crowd: IV swells before an earnings print and collapses after, so enter *after* the announcement to exploit the post-earnings drift, never before.

Because options can expire worthless, the path demands an unbending risk cage:

**The Option Risk Cage 1. Premium allocation cap.** Never allocate more than 10% of total account NAV to the premium of a single options position. At a $200,000 balance, the maximum single-position footprint is $20,000. **2. Risk per trade.** The premium that can actually be lost — to roughly 0.5–1% of current capital per trade ($500–$1,000 on $100,000). The defined-risk nature of long options is the whole point: size so a full loss is a survivable scratch. **3. The hard premium stop.** Set the invalidation at about −30% of the entry premium, or tied to the underlying breaking its intraday VWAP. Never — under any circumstances — hold an aggressive contract down to −80% hoping for a miracle.

Scale in by confirmation (40% initial, 30% on the confirmation breakout, 20% on post-earnings continuation, 10% on exceptional trend), pyramiding by adding contracts or rolling up to a higher strike as delta and gamma expand—never adding to a losing option because it has become cheaper. Take partial profits as a winner runs, exit losers at the predefined stop, and treat cash as strategic capital. The scenarios rest on these assumptions:

| Parameter | Assumption |
|---|---|
| **Starting capital** | $100,000 |
| **Allocation** | 60–80% in long calls (ATM to slightly OTM on high-conviction setups); 20–40% cash or small stock/ETF hedges |
| **Risk per trade** | 0.5–1% of current capital — premium only (true defined risk) |
| **Trade frequency** | Roughly 6–25 positions per month; 3–14 day holds (avoid long-dated to control decay) |
| **Win rate** | 52–62% — lower than stock trading because decay claims some correct ideas |
| **Average winner** | +80% to +300% on the option position |
| **Average loser** | −60% to −100% (often the full premium) |
| **Best environment** | Strong, trending bull markets with frequent catalysts |

Walked through—a pyramided earnings-continuation play on a $150,000 account, risking $1,000–$1,500 of total premium:

**Setup.** A high-beta name (an AMD-type leader) gaps up 12% on a strong earnings beat plus a guidance raise. **Initial.** Buy 15 contracts of 1–2 week, slightly-OTM calls (~$1,200 total premium). **Pyramid.** On a +18% underlying move (day 2), add 10 more contracts — or roll up to a higher strike. **Acceleration.** A further +15% in the underlying (days 4–7) drives gamma expansion, delivering ~280% on the full options position. **Extract.** Scale out 40% at +150% and trail the remainder — roughly $4,800–$6,500 profit (~3–4% account boost), total hold 8 days, exit before the expiration theta crush.

The recurring failures are buying extremely short-dated options, ignoring IV, oversizing, holding through expiration without a plan, and trading low-liquidity contracts—defended by a maximum premium at risk per trade, diversification across catalysts and expiration cycles, predefined exits, and a hard rule against averaging down into a decaying contract.

## E. The Momentum-Only Path

**Mechanism.** This is a methodology layered across the instruments above rather than an instrument itself: trade only confirmed strength – breakouts, trend continuation, opening-range, relative strength, high-volume sector leaders – cut weakness immediately, never fade a move, pyramid on continuation, and sit in cash when nothing is trending. The result is a lower win rate with larger R-multiples.

**Illustrative math.** A 40% win rate with average winners of 6R and losers of 1R gives expectancy of 0.4 × 6 minus 0.6 × 1, or +1.8R per trade – the strongest of the five on paper. But it comes with a long string of small losses between runners and a total dependence on a trending market.

*An illustrative run: +28%, +50%, +40%, +60%, +55%, +**65%** – $128k, $192k, $269k, $430k, $667k, and roughly $1.10M – clean when the market cooperates.*

**The honest read.** This is the engine underneath most successful versions of the other paths, and it has the best expectancy if two conditions hold: the market is trending – in chop, momentum-only is whipsawed into a death by a thousand small losses – and you can psychologically tolerate a sub-45% win rate without abandoning the system after a losing streak. It fails on regime and on discipline far more often than on math. Best for traders who can wait; its risk is missing early moves, chasing late, and overtrading weak momentum.

This is the purest form of aggressive growth, engineered for the technical purist: it ignores earnings metrics, news catalysts, and sector narratives, relying on one of the oldest anomalies in market history—price persistence, where what is strong tends to get stronger. The signal is the same regardless of vehicle (relative strength, new highs, expanding volume, rising moving averages); what varies is leverage. The purist runs it entirely unleveraged in high-beta common stocks and standard ETFs—the cleanest, most survivable version—while the aggressive variant layers a 3x-ETF and options overlay on the same momentum leaders, at the cost of reintroducing decay and crash risk. The momentum architect targets stocks at multi-year breakouts or all-time highs, where there is zero overhead resistance and no trapped sellers, isolating them through a rigid Tri-Metric Momentum Filter:

**ENTIRE INVESTABLE UNIVERSE** *Every liquid, tradable ticker*

▼

**RSI (14) ≥ 70** *Strong, persistent upward momentum*

▼

**PRICE > 50-DAY SMA > 200-DAY SMA** *Stacked, rising trend structure*

▼

**3-MONTH RATE OF CHANGE ≥ 50%** *Explosive recent velocity*

▼

## MOMENTUM LEADERS *Blue-sky breakouts at all-time highs*

Only tickers clearing all three thresholds earn capital. Relative strength is the organizing question, asked repeatedly—which stocks are outperforming almost everything else—and capital is never married to a position; it is rented to persistence and recalled the instant persistence ends. The signal is expressed two ways:

| Expression | Instruments | What you gain / give up |
|---|---|---|
| **Purist (unleveraged)** | High-beta common stocks, standard ETFs, occasionally warrants. No options, no 3x ETFs, no margin. | Removes leverage, decay, and gap-amplification risk — the cleanest, most survivable version. |
| **Leverage overlay** | Same momentum leaders expressed partly through 3x ETFs (SOXL, TQQQ) and options on the leaders. | Amplifies winners — and reintroduces volatility decay, IV/theta, and harsher drawdowns. |

The scenarios rest on these assumptions:

| Parameter | Assumption |
|---|---|
| **Starting capital** | $100,000 |
| **Focus** | Rank and rotate into top momentum names/ETFs (1-week to 3-month relative-strength leaders) |
| **Instruments** | Purist: high-beta stocks + standard ETFs. Overlay: add 3x ETFs and options on leaders |
| **Risk per trade** | 0.5–1% of current capital |
| **Pyramiding** | 2–3 layers on breakouts or pullback holds |
| **Hold time** | 4–12 days |
| **Frequency** | 12–20 swings per month |
| **Win rate** | 58–68% (strong in trends; collapses in chop) |
| **Average winner / loser** | +18% to +45% (boosted by pyramiding) / −5% to −8% |
| **Filters** | Strict: volume-confirmed breakouts or MA-support holds; avoid low-volume or >80 RSI |

Build the position as evidence improves (30% initial, 30% confirmation, 20% bull-flag continuation, 20% fresh breakout), becoming aggressive geometric pyramiding into parabolic extensions behind a trailing 9-EMA, dialed back in chop. You will never sell the exact top and must not try; let the market signal when velocity has ended:

> **The Moving-Average Tripwire The trailing engine.** While a trade expands vertically, trail it with the daily 9-EMA. As long as the daily candle closes above that line, the position is left entirely untouched. **The hard execution signal.** The minute a daily candle closes beneath the 9-EMA — or breaches the local 3-day low — the momentum spell is broken. Market-flatten the entire position back to cash. No debate, no looking back.

On the loss side the same logic applies faster—cut at a tight −5% to −8% stop the moment momentum, volume, or relative strength fails. As the account grows, holding windows tighten from three-week holds to 2-to-5 day sprints. Knowing when not to trade is part of the strategy: in bull markets deploy aggressively, in transitional markets cut size and demand higher quality, and in bear or corrective markets retreat to a 100% Cash Fortress until leadership re-emerges.

> **Setup.** A high-beta stock or ETF (a semi- or tech-leader type) breaks to a new 52-week high on 2x average volume, holds above its 20-day MA, with RSI in the 60–70 zone. **Initial.** $30,000 in the stock, a 3x ETF, or calls. **Pyramid.** After a +14% move on strong relative strength, add $18,000 on a minor pullback to the MA. After +12% more, add $10,000 on the new high. Total position ≈ $58,000. **Extract.** Hold ~7 days; scale out for an average +32% on the full pyramid ≈ $18,500 profit — roughly a 12% account boost from one trade. Then repeat with the next top-ranked momentum name.

The recurring failures are buying laggards, averaging down, ignoring volume, trading weak sectors, chasing extended moves, and holding declining stocks—defended by defining the maximum loss before entry, limiting single-position and sector exposure, sizing up only on confirmation, avoiding deteriorating breadth, and keeping cash for fresh leadership.

> **The Honest Math — Momentum Crashes Are Real** Pure momentum strategies can deliver outstanding returns in bull markets, but they are prone to sharp, sudden crashes when trends reverse. The historical record is clear: momentum works over long horizons yet can suffer multi-month drawdowns of 30–50%+ when leadership snaps. The −19% month in Scenario C is a mild version of this; a real momentum crash is worse. Every scenario above is an illustration of compounding mechanics, not a forecast or an expected result. A 10x return in six months — even unleveraged — is an exceptionally rare and uncommon outcome that depends on an unusually favorable, sustained trend that may simply not appear. The realistic path (Scenario C), reaching roughly $600,000 with a losing month along the way, is far closer to what disciplined execution actually feels like, and even that assumes the market cooperates.

## The Momentum-Only Governance Matrix

| Operational vector | The retail-casualty pitfall | The 10x Blueprint momentum fiduciary |
|---|---|---|
| **Asset selection** | Buys beaten-down, cheap stocks hoping for a value turnaround. | Targets high-beta equities hitting multi-year or all-time highs. |

| Operational vector | The retail-casualty pitfall | The 10x Blueprint momentum fiduciary |
|---|---|---|
| **Holding strategy** | Marries a stock and holds through a long downward cycle. | Rents persistence; exits the moment price velocity stalls. |
| **Regime protection** | Over-trades choppy, directionless markets and gets chopped up. | Retreats to a 100% Cash Fortress when relative strength goes cold. |
| **Exit execution** | Guesses the top out of fear, or holds out of greed into a loss. | Enforces the 9-EMA tripwire to lock gains programmatically. |

## Combining the Engines

In practice, the best roadmap is rarely a pure path—it is a blend that uses each engine where it is strongest: stocks and standard ETFs form the foundation, leveraged ETFs are deployed selectively during confirmed sector acceleration, options are reserved for elite catalyst-driven setups where convexity is worth the fragility, and the momentum rules filter every entry regardless of instrument. The conservative core keeps you solvent while the higher-variance engines switch on only when the regime feeds them. The goal is not merely to reach $1,000,000; it is to reach it without blowing up before the favorable regime arrives.

### The Five Paths Compared

The columns that matter most are the last two—not which path is fastest, but how it tends to fail:

| Path | Core instruments | Illustrative landing | Max drawdown | Main enemy | Ruin risk |
|---|---|---|---|---|---|
| **Conservative** | Stocks, some 2x | ~$800k (3–5x) | 8–30% | Undershooting | Lower |
| **High-volatility** | Low-float caps | ~$690k or blow-up | 25%+ | Deep drawdowns | High |
| **Leveraged ETF** | 3x ETFs | ~$1.05M in trend | 15–20% | Decay in chop | High in chop |
| **Options-heavy** | Calls, spreads | Fast 10x or ~zero | 15–25% | Theta, IV crush | Highest |
| **Momentum-only** | Any (method) | ~$1.1M in trend | 10–18% | Choppy regimes | Mod.–high |

### Choosing a Path: The Governance Matrix

The path is chosen long before the first trade, and the choice is behavioral.

| Dimension | The Retail Casualty | The Blueprint Capital Allocator |
|---|---|---|
| **Path selection** | Picks the flashiest path, chasing the fastest possible 10x. | Picks the path whose failure mode they can actually survive. |
| **Position sizing** | Uses the same aggressive size on every path regardless of fragility. | Sizes to the path's variance and ruin profile – smallest on options. |
| **Regime awareness** | Runs leveraged or momentum paths blind to the broader tape. | Matches the path to the regime; stands down when it doesn't fit. |
| **Outcome expectation** | Treats 10x as the base case and bets the account on it. | Treats 10x as an outlier and plans for falling short or stopping out. |

## Risk, Feasibility, and a Reality Check

None of the five lowers the bar—they only move the risk around. The conservative path is the only one whose honest expectation is survival, most likely landing at 3–5x rather than 10x; the high-volatility, leveraged-ETF, and options paths widen both tails, raising the small probability of hitting 10x while raising the much larger probability of a timeline-ending drawdown; momentum-only is the discipline that powers all of them.

## Blueprint Principle

> **You do not choose a compounding path by which one promises the fastest million.** *You choose it by which failure mode you can survive often enough to still be **trading when the rare, favorable regime finally arrives.*

All five engines target the same number, and the same arithmetic governs all of them. The conservative path trades upside for survival; the high-volatility, leveraged-ETF, and options paths trade survival for a fatter right tail; momentum-only is the method that decides whether any of them works. Pick the path whose worst case you can live through, size it to that worst case, match it to the regime, and let a handful of outsized winners—not a forced pace—carry the result. The goal does not become likely; it becomes survivable to attempt.

# Chapter 31
# Case Studies of Explosive Compounding

*What the Outliers Teach – Including the Ones Who Blew Up*

Case studies are seductive and dangerous in equal measure—seductive because a handful of traders really did turn modest stakes into fortunes, dangerous because of survivorship bias: the cases that get written about are selected because they succeeded, while the thousands who used the same methods and lost are never recorded. So read these the way a risk manager would, not the way a fan would. For each one, ask what actually drove the result—method, leverage, concentration, or simply a favorable regime—and ask what happened next, because many of the most explosive compounders are also the most spectacular collapses. The great winners share the same ingredients (concentration, timing, trend recognition, risk control, emotional discipline); the great failures share a different pattern (leverage, arrogance, poor liquidity, a refusal to reduce risk). The figures below are drawn from widely reported public accounts; some—especially the self-reported retail records—are disputed and flagged as such. The point is never the exact number; it is the pattern.

## A. Historical Momentum Traders

Aggressive momentum-based compounding is neither a modern invention nor a reckless gamble—it is a discipline, codified and documented across more than a century of markets by traders who weaponized three things in combination: structural momentum, concentrated capital, and unbending risk control. But they must be presented honestly: most did not produce extraordinary returns every month or year, several blew up—some more than once—before mastering the psychology, and their remarkable records were built through a blend of exceptional market periods, ferocious risk management, and concentration only when high-probability opportunities appeared.

> **THE CORE LESSON OF THIS CHAPTER** Great fortunes are rarely built by trading constantly. They are built by waiting patiently for extraordinary opportunities, acting decisively when they appear, and protecting capital relentlessly the rest of the time.

Despite trading across different centuries, continents, and instruments, the greatest converged on a strikingly similar playbook, little of which concerns prediction: they protected capital first and cut losses without ego, bought strength rather than bargains, concentrated during rare high-conviction windows, let winners run by scaling into strength rather than averaging into weakness, and removed emotion by trading a defined process. Each case below gives the context, the tactical architecture, the documented record with its caveats, and the Blueprint connection.

### 1. Jesse Livermore – The Pioneer of Pivotal Points

In the early twentieth century Livermore built and rebuilt multi-million-dollar fortunes trading the raw physics of price alone, reading the tape for momentum shifts long before scanners existed—the foundational blueprint for modern high-beta swing trading. He traded with the trend and the line of least resistance, never averaged down (to him the cardinal sin), and once a stock cleared its pivotal point committed serious capital and pyramided, adding size only as the market validated his direction—*the big money was never in the thinking, it was always in the sitting*. His most famous coup was shorting into the 1929 crash, widely estimated at around $100 million in that era's dollars; yet he went bankrupt multiple times, undone repeatedly by over-leverage and the very emotional distortion his own rules were designed to prevent.

> **PITFALL TO INTERNALIZE** Livermore wrote the rules and then broke them. His ruin did not come from a flawed method, it came from abandoning his method under emotional pressure and excessive leverage. The emotion-free, mechanically-scaled approach taught later in this book exists precisely to prevent his fate.

**Blueprint connection.** Livermore's pivotal points are the direct ancestor of the *Day-1 Velocity Bar* and *High-Tight-Flag* setups—buying a stock as it clears resistance into new-high territory is often exactly where the most explosive, non-linear compounding begins.

## 2. Nicolas Darvas — Box Theory and Pure Relative Strength

In the late 1950s the professional ballroom dancer Nicolas Darvas traded his way around the world by cable and telegram, ignoring tips and forecasts entirely. By his own account in *How I Made $2,000,000 in the Stock Market*, he grew an account of roughly $25,000–$36,000 into more than $2 million–$2.25 million over about eighteen months—a run that unfolded inside an exceptionally strong bull market and included real setbacks. He invented **Box Theory**: a stock in a powerful uptrend climbs like a staircase, gapping into a new range, consolidating inside a defined "box," then fracturing the ceiling into the next box higher.

> [ BOX 3 — EXTRACTION ] ceiling 60 / floor 52 ▲ breakout trigger [ BOX 2 — PYRAMIDING ] ceiling 50 / floor 44 ▲ breakout trigger [ BOX 1 — THE BASE ] ceiling 42 / floor 36

His execution was mechanical—automated buy-stops just above each box ceiling so a genuine breakout filled him automatically and a fakeout never tempted him, trailing stops pinned just beneath each new box floor, and pure reaction to price boundaries rather than opinions. **Blueprint connection.** This is the framework behind the *30-Minute Opening-Range Box* and the *Position-Scaling Pyramid*—an explosive multi-million-dollar campaign run on nothing but price boxes and trailing structural stops.

## 3. Richard Dennis & the Turtles — Systemic Trend Following and the N-Unit

In the early 1980s the commodities trader Richard Dennis turned a small stake into a fortune widely reported around $200 million, then in 1983–84 ran a famous experiment with partner William Eckhardt to settle whether trading could be taught: he recruited near-total beginners—the "Turtles"—handed them a rigid algorithmic toolkit, and funded them; by Investopedia's account they earned more than $175 million over five years. The system stripped out human subjectivity: enter long on a fresh 20-day or 55-day Donchian-channel high; size every position by a rolling 20-day ATR (labeled *N*) so a 1N adverse move equaled a fixed small fraction of equity; and pyramid in increments of N, ratcheting stops upward by rule.

> **THE MATHEMATICAL PROOF** The Turtles are the literal mathematical proof behind the *Progressive Geometric Pyramid Matrix* and the *1R Risk Vice* in this book. Extraordinary returns came not from guessing tops and bottoms, but from enforcing absolute, rule-based discipline over the downside while letting winners run.

**Blueprint connection.** Where Livermore and Darvas supplied intuition and structure, the Turtles supplied the *math*—a repeatable formula for sizing risk and adding to strength that you can encode and follow without a single discretionary judgment call.

## 4. William J. O'Neil — CAN SLIM and the Modern Synthesis

O'Neil modernized momentum investing, founded *Investor's Business Daily*, compounded a modest account into a substantial sum quickly, and built his method from a large empirical study of the market's biggest historical winners. That study produced the **CAN SLIM** framework, fusing fundamentals with technical momentum—each letter a screen the greatest winners shared before their largest advances:

| | CAN SLIM Factor | What it captures |
|---|---|---|
| C | Current quarterly earnings | Sharp, recent acceleration |
| A | Annual earnings growth | A durable multi-year record |
| N | New products / new highs | A catalyst plus price confirmation |
| S | Supply & demand | Tight float, volume on the breakout |
| L | Leader, not laggard | High relative strength vs. the group |
| I | Institutional sponsorship | Funds accumulating the name |
| M | Market direction | Only press exposure in confirmed uptrends |

He bought breakouts on heavy volume in leading stocks and sectors, held for multi-week swings in bull markets, and cut losses with a strict stop commonly cited around 7–8% below entry—his central insight being that great companies often become great stocks before the crowd recognizes them, with price and volume revealing institutional recognition early. **Blueprint connection.** CAN SLIM is the backbone of this book's *Sector Acceleration* and *Earnings Continuation* sections.

## 5. Mark Minervini — Modern, Verified, Repeatable (SEPA)

Minervini is one of the strongest modern fits for this book—a pure momentum and growth-stock trader with verified, real-money results documented through the U.S. Investing Championship, a competition audited against actual brokerage statements:

- Won the U.S. Investing Championship in **1997 with a 155% return**, reportedly while only partially invested much of the year.
- Won again in **2021 with a record-breaking 334.8%** in the $1,000,000+ division — the prior record had been roughly 119%.
- Reported **averaging around 220% annually** across a multi-year stretch in the 1990s, and a widely-cited cumulative figure exceeding **33,000%** over roughly five years (1995–1999), as he grew a ~$5,000 account into seven figures.

His method, **SEPA** (Specific Entry-Point Analysis), targets high-beta leaders in confirmed uptrends with accelerating earnings, entering on volume breakouts or controlled pullbacks (often the 20- and 50-day), pyramiding into strength, cutting losses tight (frequently 5–10%), and letting winners run under trailing stops; his **Volatility Contraction Pattern (VCP)** identifies the tightening consolidations that precede explosive breakouts. His audited returns are textbook power-law behavior—a handful of 100–500%+ winners driving the bulk of gains while 1–2% risk per trade kept drawdowns survivable.

> **THE PART READERS SKIP** Minervini blew up his trading account multiple times early in his career before the method clicked. By his own telling, the turning point was treating trading as a business and a process problem rather than a luck problem. His verified returns are real — and they were preceded by years of losses and the psychological work that prevented a repeat.

**Blueprint connection.** SEPA mirrors this book's high-beta, earnings-continuation, sector-acceleration, and pyramiding chapters almost one-for-one—living proof that strict risk control plus momentum filtering can produce 10x-class runs for a trader who has already mastered the psychology.

## 6. Takashi Kotegawa ("BNF") — The Bedroom Compounder

Kotegawa, known online as **BNF**, is the modern small-account legend. Starting around 2000 with roughly ¥1.6 million (about $13,600) and trading from his apartment, he reportedly grew that into the neighborhood of ¥15–20 billion (around $150–200 million) over about eight years, primarily as an intraday and short-swing momentum trader in the volatile Japanese market—quick decisive execution on volatile high-liquidity names, a strong preference for closing risk rather than carrying it overnight, and sizing up hard on the rare clear edge. His most famous trade, the 2005 Mizuho J-Com order-entry error, reportedly made on the order of $17–20 million in minutes—enabled partly by a brokerage "fat-finger" error, a genuine element of luck no method can reproduce on demand. BNF proves compounding from a tiny base into a fortune is *possible*; he does not prove it is *repeatable on schedule*, and his figures rest on reporting rather than audited disclosure.

## 7. The Conviction & Risk Masters

Three further names round out the lineage, each studied for a single principle. **Stanley Druckenmiller** built one of the great long-term records on a simple idea—concentrate when conviction is high and the evidence aligns, cut exposure when conviction falls—always paired with real-time monitoring and a willingness to reverse; his emphasis is *betting big when right and small when wrong*. **Paul Tudor Jones**, famous for risk control and macro timing (including a reported triple-digit return profiting from the 1987 crash), reduces his philosophy to protecting capital first, and his best-known maxim—*Losers average losers*—is a one-line refutation of the amateur's cardinal error. **David Ryan**, a multiple-time U.S. Investing Champion and O'Neil protégé, combined fundamental strength, technical momentum, relative strength, and institutional sponsorship to buy high-quality growth leaders rather than statistically cheap stocks—the clearest demonstration that in momentum you pay up for strength.

### The Historical Momentum Governance Matrix

Different eras, different instruments—one architecture.

| Master Trader | Core Momentum Weapon | Risk-Mitigation Tool | The Compounding Lesson |
|---|---|---|---|
| **Jesse Livermore** | Pivotal-point breakouts | No averaging down; cut fast | Fastest velocity occurs at new highs |
| **Nicolas Darvas** | Box-theory range fractures | Trailing stops beneath the box floor | Decouple from noise; obey price boundaries |
| **Richard Dennis / Turtles** | Donchian-channel breakouts | Volatility-adjusted N-units (~fixed % risk) | Automate systemic scaling into winners |
| **William O'Neil** | CAN SLIM volume breakouts | ~7–8% stop-loss discipline | Fuse fundamentals with technical momentum |
| **Mark Minervini** | SEPA / VCP breakouts | Tight 5–10% stops; trail winners | Verified discipline beats prediction |
| **Takashi Kotegawa** | Intraday volatility momentum | Gap avoidance; decisive exits | Small bases can compound – separate skill from luck |
| **Druckenmiller** | High-conviction concentration | Cut exposure when conviction falls | Bet big when right, small when wrong |
| **Paul Tudor Jones** | Trend + macro timing | Capital preservation first | Never average a loser |

These records were produced not by constant activity but by the repeated application of disciplined compounding, the engine being the future-value formula $FV = PV \times (1 + r)^n$. Lay the careers side by side and the shared advantage was not intelligence or prediction but discipline—accepting losses quickly, waiting patiently, concentrating selectively, managing emotion through process, and letting exceptional winners compound—and critically, their explosive periods coincided with exceptional conditions (strong bull markets, deep liquidity, clear leadership) rather than being manufactured in hostile markets. The timeless playbook maps onto modern instruments: trade only the strongest names and sectors; apply the Turtles' N-unit logic to 2x/3x ETFs (sizing down as leverage rises, trend-regime tools only); express Druckenmiller-style concentration through defined-risk options; treat warrants as survivable asymmetric bets; and across all of them scale into winners, never average into losers.

> **READ THIS TWICE Survivorship bias.** For every Livermore or BNF you have heard of, countless traders using similar aggression were wiped out and never written about. The visible winners are not the full distribution. **Markets have changed.** Regulation, high-frequency trading, decimalization, and shifting volatility regimes mean the exact conditions that produced some of these runs may not recur. Study the *process*, not the replica. **Luck is real.** BNF's J-Com windfall and the timing of several bull-market runs included genuine luck. Do not mistake a fortunate outcome for a repeatable edge. **The psychological toll is severe.** Aggressive compounding magnifies drawdowns and the emotional pressure that ruined even Livermore. Manage size and expectations accordingly.

None of this is a reason to abandon ambition—it is the reason to pair ambition with rules that keep you in the game long enough for the ambition to matter. The masters became extraordinary not by avoiding losses but by managing losses while letting exceptional trends create exceptional compounding, and surviving long enough to be there when the rare window opens is the entire game.

## B. Hedge Fund & Independent-Fund Titans

The same mechanics appear at institutional scale. The point is not that you can become Citadel; it is that the engine these allocators use—momentum capture, asymmetry, concentration, and ruthless risk control—is the same one this book hands you, scaled to a single account. Most hedge funds deliver modest single-digit to low-double-digit returns; only a select few compound explosively, and even they did not do it by taking maximum risk at all times. Read them for *process*, not replication, and remember the heavy survivorship bias.

> **THE CORE LESSON OF THIS CHAPTER** The world's greatest investors became extraordinary not because they were always aggressive, but because they knew **precisely when to become aggressive and when to become defensive** — and sized every bet so that being wrong could never end the game.

Across wildly different philosophies—global macro, statistical arbitrage, concentrated activism, multi-strategy—the great funds converged on the same habits: protect capital first, concentrate during exceptional opportunities and reduce exposure during uncertainty, let winners grow and cut losers without ego, adapt the moment the evidence changes, and think in terms of capital allocation rather than mere stock selection.

## The Macro & Conviction Titans

**George Soros** ran the Quantum Fund as an aggressive global-macro vehicle compounding at roughly 30%+ annually for decades, punctuated by billion-dollar sprints. His framework was **reflexivity**—prices actively change the fundamentals by shaping behavior—so when he spotted a trend feeding on itself he concentrated immense weight into the dislocation; the most famous example, his 1992 short against the British pound, reportedly netted on the order of $1 billion in days and "broke the Bank of England" (*to win big, you must have the courage to be a pig*), always paired with cutting invalidated positions without attachment. **Stanley Druckenmiller** produced one of the industry's greatest records—widely cited near 30% annualized over three decades with no down year, first as Soros's lieutenant (he architected the pound trade) and then at Duquesne—his method reducing to *wait, wait, then bet heavily*, concentration always paired with continuous reassessment. **Paul Tudor Jones** built Tudor on protecting capital first (*Losers average losers*), profiting spectacularly from the 1987 crash. **Michael Steinhardt** compounded at roughly 24% net annually for nearly three decades through aggressive concentrated positions and his *variant perception*—a researched view differing sharply from consensus, sized hard while policing risk-adjusted return. **David Tepper** became legendary for buying maximum pessimism (most famously battered bank securities near the 2009 bottom), while changing his mind quickly when the facts changed.

## The Quants and the Concentrated Activists

**Jim Simons — Renaissance / Medallion.** No fund has compounded like the **Medallion Fund**: from 1988 it generated average gross returns around 66% annually—roughly 39–40% net after famously steep fees—producing well over $100 billion in trading profits by exploiting fleeting statistical inefficiencies across thousands of instruments with rapid turnover and strict risk limits.

> **THE HONEST CAVEAT ON MEDALLION** Medallion has been **closed to outside investors since the early 1990s** — it is essentially an employee-only fund, and its proprietary models cannot be replicated by retail traders. The transferable lesson is not the math; it is that **consistency of process, rigorously applied with ironclad risk limits, can compound at extraordinary rates without blowing up.** Your emotion-free scaling and fractional-percent risk rules are the same principle in miniature.

**David Shaw** built D. E. Shaw into a quant powerhouse (net gains in the tens of billions) by fusing technology, data science, and systematic execution—illustrating, with the great pod shops Millennium and Point72, that diversifying *edges* is itself risk management. **Bill Ackman** demonstrates both the power and the danger of concentration—extraordinary wins (notably a 2020 credit hedge that turned a small premium into billions) alongside substantial public losses (Valeant; the multi-year Herbalife short)—proof that concentration multiplies opportunity and responsibility equally. **Chris Hohn — TCI** is the freshest proof that concentrated conviction still works at scale: in 2025 the fund earned $18.9 billion for clients, the largest single-year profit ever recorded by a hedge fund, and since its 2004 launch has compounded at roughly 18% annually to about $68.4 billion in cumulative net gains while running only a handful of positions.

## The Multi-Strategy Powerhouse and the Independent Sprinters

**Ken Griffin — Citadel.** Founded in 1990, Citadel is by cumulative net gains the most profitable hedge fund in history—roughly $83 billion-plus for investors through 2024 (overtaking Bridgewater at the end of 2022), with a record $16 billion earned in 2022 alone—run as a pod-based multi-strategy platform layering leverage and derivatives onto momentum plays.

> **WHAT CITADEL TEACHES THE RETAIL TRADER Diversified aggression.** Many independent "pods" mean no single trade can sink the firm, which is precisely what lets the winners run hot. Your retail equivalent is **portfolio heat limits** — capping total open risk (e.g. under ~3–4% of equity) so that you can press individual high-conviction trades hard without a cluster of correlated losers ending your account. **Discipline over growth.** Citadel routinely returns capital to investors when it judges the opportunity set thin — the institutional version of *raising cash when there's nothing worth trading.*

The two independent sprinters are the most directly relevant, achieved with personal capital on stocks. **Dan Zanger** turned $10,775 into roughly $18 million between June 1998 and December 1999—an 18-month, 29,000%+ run that set a world record for one-year personal-portfolio appreciation, independently verified by *Fortune* against his tax records—later reporting growth toward $42 million over roughly 23 months (that second leg unaudited). His method discarded indicators and traded only price, volume, and chart patterns (cup-and-handles, bull flags) in accelerating sectors, entering at the breakout on volume ~100%+ above average and cutting failed patterns fast with tight (~5%) stops.

> **THE PART THE LEGEND LEAVES OUT** Zanger's record run happened inside a once-in-a-generation bubble — and when it burst, he reportedly gave back a large share, suffering a drawdown on the order of **75%.** His sprint is genuine proof that breakouts can reshape an equity curve in weeks; it is equally proof that returns earned in a mania must be **defended** with the same discipline that earned them, or they evaporate.

**Kristjan Qullamaggie** (Kullamägi) is the modern benchmark—a Swedish trader who started in 2011 as a mall cop, blew up his account roughly four times in his first two years, then grew a base of around $5,000–9,000 (2013) to over $80 million by 2021 entirely with his own capital, at a self-reported ~268% CAGR from 2013–2019. His system isolates institutional footprints through three setups—the **Episodic Pivot** (entering Day 1 of a major earnings surprise where a stock gaps on historic volume), the **High-Tight Flag** (hyper-growth names compressing after doubling in weeks), and **moving-average exits** trailing the 10- and 20-day—with famously small risk of roughly 0.25–1% per trade, positions around 10–20%, and never more than ~30% held overnight.

| Master Allocator | Core Kinetic Weapon | Operational Focus | Primary Risk Rule |
|---|---|---|---|

| Master Allocator | Core Kinetic Weapon | Operational Focus | Primary Risk Rule |
|---|---|---|---|
| **George Soros** | Structural reflexivity | Macro trends & sector cycles | Exit instantly when the thesis breaks |
| **Druckenmiller** | Wait, then bet heavily | Highest-conviction macro setups | Reassess continuously; cut on new facts |
| **Paul Tudor Jones** | Trend + macro timing | Asymmetric risk/reward | Capital preservation first; never average a loser |
| **Steinhardt** | Variant perception | Concentrated, active rotation | Police risk-adjusted return relentlessly |
| **David Tepper** | Buy maximum pessimism | Distressed & macro dislocations | Stay flexible; reverse when facts change |
| **Jim Simons / Medallion** | Quant stat-arb & momentum | Thousands of small edges | Strict limits; diversified signals |
| **Bill Ackman** | Concentrated activism | Deep-research single names | Size so a loss stays survivable |
| **Chris Hohn / TCI** | Concentrated conviction | A handful of multi-year leaders | Few names, strict sizing, long holds |
| **Ken Griffin / Citadel** | Multi-strategy pods | High-beta equities & derivatives | Portfolio heat caps; return excess capital |
| **Dan Zanger** | High-volume breakouts | Tech & hyper-growth clusters | Tight ~5% stops; exit failed patterns fast |
| **Qullamaggie** | Episodic pivots & HTFs | High-beta liquid leaders | Strict ~0.25–1% risk per trade |

## The Reality of Fund Returns

It is worth anchoring this book's target against the best track records ever documented. The engine throughout is the same future-value formula, a modest repeatable edge applied across many periods.

> **READING THESE NUMBERS AGAINST A 6-MONTH 10× GOAL** Be precise about scale. Even the **greatest documented compounder in history**, Medallion, returned about **39% net per year** — and TCI's record-setting machine compounds near **18% per year.** This book's premise — $100,000 to $1,000,000 in six months — requires roughly **47% per month**, sustained, which is more than these funds make in a *year*. So who actually hit retail-style explosive numbers? The **independent sprinters** — Zanger and Qullamaggie — and they did it in **exceptional bull markets**, from **small bases**, with **personal capital**, over **months-to-years**, and Zanger then gave back roughly 75% when the cycle turned. None of them sustained a 47%/month pace indefinitely. The honest synthesis: a six-month 10× is a **stretch target that defines the aggression of the strategy, not a base-case expectation.** The durable, transferable edge in this chapter is the *capital-allocation discipline* that let these managers survive long enough to be present when the rare explosive window opened. **Surviving the bad stretches is the whole game.**

None of these funds traded emotionally, chased every headline, feared holding cash, or hesitated to cut exposure—their greatest shared weapon was the discipline to act only when the odds justified it, and decisively when they did. The defining shift is from the amateur's question *"what stock should I buy?"* to the professional's: how much to risk, what expected reward versus that risk, what the exit plan is on both sides, how much genuine conviction exists, and how it fits the overall portfolio. You will never match a fund's research staff, but you hold an advantage they cannot buy—nimbleness: you can enter and exit in seconds, concentrate without moving the market, and sit entirely in cash with no investors to answer to.

> **READ THIS TWICE Most hedge funds underperform.** The explosive names here are the rare exceptions, selected with full hindsight. The median fund does not 10×, and many close. **Survivorship bias is severe.** For every Zanger or Qullamaggie you hear about, countless traders using identical aggression were wiped out and never profiled. **High returns often hide high costs.** Leverage, fees, and concentration that produce explosive upside also produce brutal drawdowns when reversals come — as Zanger, Ackman, and Steinhardt all experienced. **You face frictions funds don't.** Slippage, smaller information edges, and your own psychology under aggressive size are real handicaps. Your strict, pre-defined risk rules are the equalizer. Backtest and paper-trade before risking serious capital.

You do not possess a fund's resources, but you possess its most important tools—speed, flexibility, the freedom to hold cash, and the ability to focus everything on your highest-conviction ideas. Adopt the disciplines that made these managers great, and that, far more than any single explosive trade, is what creates the conditions under which a 10x outcome becomes possible and survivable.

## C. Retail Trader Transformations

The same engine appears in self-directed retail accounts. Beyond the independent sprinters already covered, several documented paths show five-figure accounts growing into the millions—one frequently cited example grew roughly $80,000 into more than $4 million in under eighteen months, primarily through options on Tesla and semiconductor names during sustained earnings continuation, with many such traders leaning on 3x ETFs (TECL, SOXL, TQQQ) in strong trends. The clearest modern episode is GameStop in January 2021, when fundamental thesis, options leverage, extreme short interest, and crowd psychology collided: Keith Gill ("Roaring Kitty") testified that his position rested on publicly available information, and one well-known retail position reportedly grew from around $53,000 into tens of millions on paper at the peak—though a large share of those gains round-tripped, and many who bought late lost heavily.

> *"Wall Street has more money. The retail trader has something equally valuable—the freedom to move quickly, concentrate intelligently, and adapt without bureaucracy."*

Read every story through the lens of survivorship bias—the famous transformations are the rare successes, and almost every trader profiled started with a *tiny* account ($583, $1,500, $3,000, roughly $13,600) and compounded it over years, not a single six-month sprint. The retail trader does hold structural advantages institutions cannot use: the speed to move 100% to cash or into one setup in a second, access to small and mid-caps too small for funds, no career risk on holding cash, and radical concentration on one or two ideas. The catch is that an edge is only valuable in the hands of someone disciplined enough to use it sparingly.

## The Case Studies

Figures are drawn from public reporting and, where noted, independent audits; journalistic estimates are flagged. **Larry Williams** turned a $10,000 stake into roughly $1.1 million in twelve months in the 1987 World Cup Championship of Futures Trading—about 11,000%, still the contest's all-time record (his daughter, actress Michelle Williams, later won the same competition)—trading short-term momentum and scaling contract size aggressively in the spirit of the Kelly criterion, but only when his trend signals aligned and a profit cushion protected his seed; this was *futures*, not stocks, and the peak balance was never independently confirmed. **Tim Grittani** began in 2011 with about $1,500 and publicly documented growth to more than $13 million in trading profits (a net figure cited as high as $30 million) over roughly a decade in low-priced small-cap and penny stocks, using precise breakout extensions and exhaustion fades with a willingness to scratch a trade for a tiny loss the instant it failed—the asymmetric-R template, where a modest win rate is irrelevant if losses are capped at 1R while winners run; it took about nine months of daily effort just to turn consistently profitable. **Ross Cameron** funded an account with exactly $583.15 in January 2017, grew it to over $100,000 in about 44 trading days, crossed $1 million in 2019 (~553 trading days), and has had cumulative profits audited at roughly $18.8 million through the end of 2025—momentum gap-and-go trading at around 1% or less per trade—though $583 to $1 million took two and a half years of full-time work, not six months. **Kris Verma**, a former pharmacist, turned about $3,000 into roughly $1.6–2.1 million in under two years through systematic, backtested day trading, after losing around $100,000 early "randomly pressing buttons." The audited **U.S. Investing Championship** adds verified one-year contest records: **Oliver Kell's +941% in 2020** (accounts-under-$1M division, the highest ever in that division, after about six years of trading without making money), Minervini's +155% (1997, $250,000) and +334.8% (2021), and three-time champion David Ryan. And **Timothy Sykes** grew roughly $12,000 of bar-mitzvah money into seven figures via penny stocks before mentoring students such as Grittani. Beyond the named records, four composite archetypes recur—the Patient Trader who waits weeks then commits size only on full alignment, the Disciplined Risk Manager who reduces rather than chases after five straight losses, the Small-Account Builder who climbs $10k→$20k→$50k→$100k→$250k→$500k→$1M through drawdown-punctuated compounding, and the Career-Changer whose prior discipline transfers to markets.

| Trader | Starting seed | Span | Primary weapon | Core rule |
|---|---|---|---|---|
| Larry Williams | $10,000 | 12 months | Short-term futures momentum + position sizing | Size up only when trends align and profits protect the seed. |
| Takashi Kotegawa | ~$13,600 | ~8 years | Intraday/swing momentum on volatile names | Strike hard on clear setups; sit out the rest. |
| Tim Grittani | $1,500 | ~10 years | Small-cap / penny-stock inefficiencies | Scratch instantly; let asymmetric winners run. |
| Ross Cameron | $583.15 | $1M in ~2.5 yrs | Small-cap momentum (gap-and-go) | Risk ~1% or less; scale on confirmation; exit fast. |
| Kris Verma | $3,000 | <2 years | Systematic, backtested day trading | Trust the system's edge; never trade scared money. |

## The Mechanics, the Gamma Squeeze, and the Honest Limits

None of these transformations came from luck alone or constant activity—they came from preparation, relentless risk management, specialization in a single proven edge, patience, and continuous learning. A modern subculture of self-taught option traders has occasionally produced verified sub-$100k-to-seven-figure runs through the **gamma squeeze**: when heavy buying concentrates in short-dated calls on a low-float or heavily shorted stock, market makers who sold those calls must buy the underlying to stay hedged, feeding a self-reinforcing spike.

> **A serious caution.** *Understanding this dynamic is education; deliberately coordinating buying to force a price move is market manipulation and is illegal. Just as important, these episodes are brutally two-sided: for every early participant who captured the vertical move, many latecomers bought the top and lost most of their stake when the squeeze unwound.* ***Treat*** *the gamma squeeze as a phenomenon to recognize and respect—not a scheme to engineer.*

Across nearly every story the path runs through five stages—education, survival (keeping losses small while gaining experience), consistency (a repeatable process with documented positive expectancy), controlled scaling, and intelligent compounding—governed by the same $FV = PV \times (1 + r)^n$ formula, with consistency turning small repeatable gains into life-changing totals provided the losses in between never reset the base.

> **$FV = PV \times (1 + r)^n$** PV = starting capital • r = return per period • n = number of periods *Example: $1,000 × (1 + 0.05)^20 ≈ $2,653*

The traders who fail do the reverse on every count: trade too frequently, risk too much per position, average down, change strategies constantly, and chase excitement. Your account size does not determine your future; your discipline does.

> **IMPORTANT RISK & ACCURACY DISCLOSURE These case studies are exceptional, atypical outcomes presented for education and illustration.** They are subject to survivorship bias: famous successes are visible while the far larger number of traders who lost money using similar aggressive strategies are not. Most retail traders lose money, and most who attempt extreme short-term targets lose money. Trading stocks, options, leveraged ETFs, futures, and warrants carries a high risk of substantial or total loss. **Figures are drawn from public reporting and, where noted, independent audits; some are journalistic estimates that vary by source and have been flagged as reported rather than verified.** Nothing here is individualized financial, investment, tax, or legal advice, and the author is not your financial advisor. Replicate the process—written rules, small risk per trade, journaling, and patience—not the headline results, and consider paper trading before risking real capital. Only ever risk money you can afford to lose. Past performance does not indicate future results.

## D. Lessons from Spectacular Failures

The failures are where the real curriculum lives, because they are caused by the very behaviors aggressive compounding tempts you toward—and this may be the most important section in the book. Anyone can look like a genius in a roaring bull market; the difference between an elite 10x allocator and a liquidated tourist is almost never the quality of their offensive setups but their understanding of how easily the compounding engine throws into reverse. The people in these cases were not fools—most possessed exceptional intelligence and years of success before a single breakdown in discipline destroyed everything.

> **THE CORE TRUTH OF THIS CHAPTER** The difference between building a fortune and destroying one is usually not the ability to make money — it is the ability to **protect** it. For a book about a 10× return, this is the necessary counterweight to every chapter on aggression: **survival is the ultimate competitive advantage.**

Professionals study failure because it leaves clues, and the same handful of errors repeats across every decade. No trader wakes up intending to lose everything; the sequence is almost always identical and almost always invisible while it happens:

> SUCCESS —▶ CONFIDENCE —▶ OVERCONFIDENCE | ▼
> EXCESSIVE RISK —▶ RULE VIOLATIONS —▶ CATASTROPHE

Each step feels reasonable in the moment—which is precisely what makes it dangerous. Despite different markets and personalities, major failures share the same fingerprints: excessive leverage, ignoring or removing risk controls, averaging down into invalidated losers, emotional attachment to an entry or thesis, concentration without discipline, and the refusal to admit mistakes behind the belief that *"this time is different."* Laid out together, the outcomes rhyme:

| Case | Approach | Reported outcome | Core lesson |
|---|---|---|---|
| **Livermore** | Discretionary momentum, short selling | Fortunes in 1907 & 1929; died broke | Wins mean nothing without durable risk control |
| **Darvas** | Breakout "box" momentum | ~$2.25M (self-reported) | Method plus a bull regime |
| **Dennis / Turtles** | Mechanical trend following | $175M+ over five years (reported) | A teachable, rule-based system survives |
| **Minervini** | SEPA high-beta momentum | 200%+ in some periods (audited) | A few outliers; small fixed risk per trade |
| **Soros / Druckenmiller** | Concentrated macro conviction | ~$1B in 1992 | Bet big only on extreme edge |
| **Medallion** | Quant systematic | ~66%/yr gross over decades | The best ever is per year, not per month |
| **Meme era (2021)** | Concentrated retail conviction | ~$53k to tens of millions (paper) | Outlier regime; much of it round-tripped |
| **LTCM (1998)** | Leveraged convergence | ~44% lost in one month; ~$4.6B | Leverage plus a tail event equals ruin |
| **Archegos (2021)** | Hidden swap leverage | ~$20B wiped in days | Concentration plus leverage equals total loss |

The same story teaches opposite lessons depending on who reads it:

| Operational dimension | The retail casualty | The Blueprint capital allocator |
|---|---|---|
| **What they notice** | The size of the winners and how fast they happened. | The base rate, the leverage used, and what happened next. |
| **Survivorship** | Assumes the winners are typical and the method is replicable. | Remembers the unrecorded thousands who used it and lost. |
| **Reading** | Sees leverage as the | Sees leverage as the common |

| Operational dimension | The retail casualty | The Blueprint capital allocator |
|---|---|---|
| **leverage** | accelerant to copy. | cause of the blow-ups. |
| **The takeaway** | "If they did it, I can do it too." | "What risk control let some survive — and what killed the rest?" |

## Part I — The Institutional Catastrophes

**Long-Term Capital Management (1998).** Founded by John Meriwether and advised by Nobel laureates Myron Scholes and Robert Merton, LTCM harvested tiny pricing inefficiencies and believed its models had engineered away risk—so, because the edges were minuscule, it applied extreme leverage of roughly $25–30 of borrowed money per $1 of capital, with derivative exposure far larger.

> [ BLIND MODEL RELIANCE ] assumes historical correlations hold │ ▼ [ BLACK SWAN: 1998 Russian default + flight to quality ] │ ├─▶ volatility breaks past the model's "maximum" ├─▶ correlations converge toward 1 — diversification fails ├─▶ margin calls flood illiquid positions └─▶ forced liquidation in weeks

When the 1998 Russian default triggered a global flight to quality, the historical correlations the models depended on collapsed, margin calls flooded in, and roughly $4.6 billion evaporated in months (the fund lost about 44% in August 1998 alone), requiring a $3.6 billion Federal Reserve-organized bank rescue—*if survival depends on markets behaving normally, the strategy is already fragile.*

> **THE BLUEPRINT LESSON — LTCM The fallacy of absolute certainty.** Never let a run of wins convince you that you have beaten the market. In a six-month sprint, assume a catastrophic event is always lurking around the next corner. **The countermeasure.** Leverage must *always* be paired with a hard, pre-set stop. If you trade 3× ETFs or short-dated options, total portfolio exposure must be governed by an absolute risk limit (the *1R Risk Vice*), so that even if your entire thesis fails, the account lives to fight another day.

**Bill Hwang & Archegos (2021).** Hwang ran a private family office, using total-return swaps to synthetically hide a position empire that reportedly reached around $36 billion in exposure across a tiny cluster of high-beta media and tech names, with essentially no diversification or hedging. When ViacomCBS announced a surprise stock offering, its price fractured, triggering a cascade of margin calls; the prime brokers force-liquidated his blocks, and Hwang's roughly $20 billion personal fortune was wiped out in days while the banks lost more than $10 billion (Credit Suisse alone took a ~$5.5 billion hit).

> **AN ADDED DIMENSION — THIS ONE BECAME A CRIME** Archegos is not only a risk-management failure. In July 2024 Hwang was **convicted of securities fraud, market manipulation, wire fraud, and racketeering conspiracy** — in part for lying to his banks about the portfolio to borrow more — and in November 2024 he was **sentenced to 18 years in prison.** The lesson compounds: hiding true exposure does not reduce risk; it removes the warnings that might have saved you, and it can cross legal lines.

**THE BLUEPRINT LESSON — ARCHEGOS Concentration vaporizes wealth on the way down** exactly as fast as it multiplies it on the way up, unless a dynamic exit floor stands guard. **The countermeasure.** This is the justification for your *Sector Heat Ceiling*: an unbending cap on single-theme exposure (e.g. ~12–15% maximum), visible/listed instruments only (stocks, listed ETFs, options — never opaque synthetic leverage), and automated trailing stops on every position. No setup is ever certain enough to let one theme consume the portfolio. |

**Nick Leeson & Barings (1995).** Leeson generated early success for Barings—Britain's oldest merchant bank, founded in 1762—then hid souring bets in a secret error account while doubling down on Nikkei futures; the 1995 Kobe earthquake sent the Nikkei tumbling, the concealed losses exploded to roughly £827 million (about $1.3 billion), and a 233-year-old institution collapsed, later sold for a token £1.

> **THE BLUEPRINT LESSON — BARINGS Small losses accepted honestly stay small. Hidden losses become catastrophic.** The most expensive habit in trading is the refusal to look at — and book — a loss while it is still survivable. Your P&L must never be something you hide from yourself.

**Brian Hunter & Amaranth (2006).** Hunter's natural-gas spread positions grew so large they dominated the market; when conditions shifted, liquidity evaporated, and the fund lost roughly $6.6 billion in weeks—one of the largest hedge-fund collapses in history.

> **THE BLUEPRINT LESSON — AMARANTH Liquidity is a feature of calm markets, not a guarantee.** A position you cannot exit is not a position — it is a hostage situation. Size every trade so you can get out in a panic, not just on a quiet afternoon. This matters acutely for thin options, single-stock leveraged products, and low-float names.

**Victor Niederhoffer** built a brilliant reputation—a former Soros trader and author of a celebrated book on speculation—but sold options to collect small steady premiums while carrying hidden exposure to rare violent moves; the October 1997 mini-crash wiped out his funds, he rebuilt, and a second fund blew up in 2007 for a structurally similar reason.

> **THE BLUEPRINT LESSON — NIEDERHOFFER A strategy that wins for years can still be fatally fragile.** Never assume yesterday's market conditions persist; a long winning streak from selling cheap insurance is not proof of edge — it is the calm before the claim. Always prepare for outcomes outside the normal range, because those are the ones that settle the account.

**Jesse Livermore** appears here a final time as the cautionary case—the same talent that made ~$100 million shorting the 1929 crash also went bankrupt multiple times through revenge trading, over-leverage, and abandoning his own rules after a big win (*the market didn't beat me, I beat myself*). Past success never guarantees future discipline; every trade begins at zero.

## Part II — The Retail Failure Machine

The failures that will actually threaten *your* account are quieter, more common, and built into the very instruments this book uses. **Leveraged-ETF decay:** triple-leveraged ETFs deliver 3× the *daily* move, and the daily reset creates volatility decay that grinds value away in chop even when the index ends flat—TQQQ fell about 82% peak-to-trough in 2021–2022, SOXL collapsed roughly 91% in 2022 and suffered another ~88% drawdown into 2025, TQQQ dropped ~70% in March 2020, and a 3× short nickel ETF went all the way to zero in the 2022 squeeze—yet during the April 2025 tariff shock retail traders poured into leveraged-equity products to the tune of roughly $11 billion of inflows that month even as prices fell, the exact move that converts a drawdown into a wipeout.

> **THE BLUEPRINT LESSON — LEVERAGED ETFs 3× ETFs are short-swing tools only** — measured in days, not weeks or months. Never hold them through chop or a bear rotation. Use strict time stops, pyramid only in a confirmed trend, and respect that volatility decay is a silent, constant tax. Your emotion-free scaling rules exist specifically to override the "just hold longer, it'll come back" instinct that destroys these positions.

**Options:** the fastest way to turn a small account large and a large one to nothing—the recurring arc is a huge asymmetric win on OTM calls, euphoria, a far larger next bet, then destruction by theta decay and IV crush even when direction was right.

> **THE BLUEPRINT LESSON — OPTIONS Premium at risk is full position risk.** Govern it with the same fractional-percent rule you apply to shares (e.g. 0.5–1% of equity), because an option can go to zero in a way a stock rarely does. Scale out of winners, never let one trade dominate the book, and avoid low-probability far-OTM lottery tickets that lack a strict, identifiable catalyst.

**The behavioral spiral:** most retail ruin needs no exotic product. A trader turns $100,000 into $250,000, then gives it all back in the first correction—not from bad setups but from loss aversion: the stop gets deleted (*"it's not a loss until I sell"*), the position averages down, and one opinion holds the whole portfolio hostage. That is the mirror image of pyramiding into confirmed strength, and *successful traders become more disciplined after success while failing traders become more aggressive*. The geometric math is what makes the spiral lethal:

| Drawdown | Gain to Break Even | What It Means |
|---|---|---|
| **10%** | **11.1%** | Routine scratch — easily recovered. |
| **20%** | **25.0%** | Manageable, but already non-linear. |
| **30%** | **42.9%** | Real damage; needs a strong trend to repair. |

| Drawdown | Gain to Break Even | What It Means |
|---|---|---|
| **40%** | **66.7%** | Serious; months of progress erased. |
| **50%** | **100%** | The Death Zone begins — you must double to get back to zero. |
| **60%** | **150%** | Severe; the math is now working hard against you. |
| **70%** | **233%** | Near-terminal for an aggressive account. |
| **80%** | **400%** | Statistical ruin — the compounding engine is broken. |
| **90%** | **900%** | Effectively unrecoverable. |

> **THE BLUEPRINT LESSON — THE BEHAVIORAL SPIRAL Learn to love small losses.** A clean −1R stop-out is not a defeat; it is an active defensive victory that keeps you out of the Death Zone. Trade by percentage rules detached from raw dollar values, so a falling number cannot hijack your judgment. The deepest skill in this entire book is the willingness to take the small loss *every single time*, before it can become a large one.

Every catastrophe maps to a specific execution error, psychological root, and Blueprint defense:

| Casualty | Fatal Execution Error | Psychological Root | The Blueprint Defense |
|---|---|---|---|
| **LTCM** | Extreme leverage, no fallback stops | Hubris; blind trust in models | **1R Risk Vice** — automated invalidation on every position |
| **Bill Hwang / Archegos** | Synthetic over-concentration, no hedge | Greed; blindness to factor correlation | **Sector Heat Ceiling** — hard cap on correlated exposure |
| **Nick Leeson / Barings** | Hiding losses in a secret account | Shame; refusal to admit error | **Honest P&L** — losses booked immediately, never concealed |
| **Brian Hunter / Amaranth** | Positions too large to exit | Overconfidence in liquidity | **Liquidity sizing** — exit must be possible in a panic |
| **Victor Niederhoffer** | Selling tail risk for steady premium | Mistaking a streak for an edge | **Tail-aware sizing** — survive the rare violent move |
| **Jesse Livermore** | Revenge trading; rules abandoned | Ego anchored to being right | **Process over impulse** — rules fixed |

| Casualty | Fatal Execution Error | Psychological Root | The Blueprint Defense |
|---|---|---|---|
| | after wins | | before the bell |
| **The Retail Tourist** | Deleting stops; averaging down | Loss aversion; anchoring to entry | **Percentage rules** detached from dollar values |

## Anti-Failure Systems and the Survival Mindset

The same future-value formula that builds fortunes depends entirely on protecting PV, the capital base—every large drawdown shrinks the base you compound from, and the recovery math is brutally asymmetric. Every collapse begins with psychological deterioration, not a bad chart: the monologue shifts from analysis to hope, and catastrophe arrives not as one giant mistake but as a series of tiny compromises that compound into ruin. Here is the paradox at the heart of aggressive trading—the traders who become extraordinary usually *look* conservative, and that restraint is exactly what permits greater long-term aggression, because they are still in the game when the rare enormous opportunity arrives. Discipline is not willpower but architecture: write the rules before emotion is in the room, defining and automating a maximum position size, a hard leverage ceiling, maximum daily/weekly loss circuit breakers, a portfolio-level maximum drawdown that forces you flat, predetermined exit criteria on every position, and mandatory review after any significant loss.

> **READER EXERCISE — A HONEST SELF-AUDIT** Pull up your last ten trades and ask, for each one: *How close did I come to the mistakes in this chapter?* Did I move or delete a stop? Add to a loser? Oversize after a win? Hold an illiquid position too long? Count the near-misses honestly. The goal is not guilt — it is to find the specific rule that, written down and automated today, would have caught the error before it grew.

## Risk, Survivorship, and a Reality Check

The honest synthesis is uncomfortable. The winners share a method, but they also share something they could not control—a favorable regime and a run of good outcomes—and several of the most famous winners are also the most famous losers, the same person at a different point on the curve. The failures share a cause you *can* control: leverage, concentration, and the absence of enforced drawdown limits. Take one case from this chapter—or a recent winner you have followed—and run it through the framework: which risk rules did they follow and which did they break, how did they scale into winners and when did they take risk off, and was the result driven by method, leverage, concentration, or regime? Separate the skill from the luck.

## Chapter 32
# The Dark Side of Aggressive Compounding
*How the Traits That Win Curdle Into the Ones That Destroy*

Every chapter to this point has taught you how to press an advantage; this one is about what that pressing does to a person and an account over time—and it is the chapter most likely to keep a reader solvent. The dark side of aggressive compounding is not bad luck visited on the unfortunate; it is the **predictable shadow of the strategy itself.** The traits that make it possible—boldness, conviction, a high tolerance for risk, the willingness to size up—are the same traits that, after a run of success, curdle into the behaviors that end accounts. The strategy tends to fail not in spite of its strengths but because of them, once success removes the fear that kept those strengths in check: the same tools that can turn $100,000 into $1,000,000 can just as easily turn it into $10,000 or zero. Treat this as the operating manual for your own psychology—each of the five forces below comes with the trigger that fires it and the concrete antidote that contains it, and none of the antidotes is willpower; they are all systems built in advance. For the large majority of people who attempt this, the dark side is not the exception—it is the experience.

### 1. Blowups
A blowup is not a large loss; it is a terminal one—the loss that ends the account or the timeline outright. It is almost never caused by a single bad trade at proper size, but by the combination this book's instruments make easy: oversized positions, excessive leverage, no stop, averaging down, holding through a binary event, ignoring liquidity, and the refusal to accept being wrong, stacking until the combination becomes fatal. In leveraged products the mechanics are brutal—a 3x ETF can shed 50–90% in a sharp reversal, oversized options expire worthless, and margin forces cascading liquidations—and the retail base rates are sobering: most day traders lose money, and many aggressive accounts reach zero within months. The defining feature is that a blowup rarely begins with stupidity; it begins with success, on an almost scripted sequence—money made quickly, confidence rising, size increasing, rules loosening, a trade moving against him, refusal to exit, adding more, forced selling, permanent impairment. The math is unforgiving: a 50% loss needs a 100% gain to recover and a 75% loss needs 300%, so beyond a certain depth recovery becomes impossible—and sequence matters as much as size, a deep drawdown early (before a cushion exists) being far more lethal than the same drawdown later. **The antidote** is structural, not emotional: hard position-size limits, a cap on total portfolio heat (under roughly 8%), the pre-committed drawdown circuit breakers from the roadmap chapter, and a single organizing principle—**survival outranks speed.** You cannot compound from zero, so the first job of every position is to make a blowup mathematically impossible; making money is only its second job.

### 2. Overconfidence
After a winning streak the mind performs a dangerous trick: it reclassifies luck as skill. A favorable regime lifted every position, and the trader concludes that

*he* lifted them—attribution bias and the hot-hand fallacy working together, most powerful precisely when the account is at a new high. Overconfidence is dangerous exactly because it disguises itself as competence: losses make traders cautious, wins make them careless. The behavioral consequence is size creep—conviction rises, stops widen "because the last five worked," sizes drift up, margin gets overused, and the rules that produced the streak start to feel like training wheels, so the account carries more risk than ever at the exact moment the trader is least afraid. **The antidote** is to track process rather than P&L and default to the assumption that the regime did most of the work—after a big gain, ask honestly whether it was skill or environment, whether the plan was followed, and whether sizing up rests on evidence or ego—while keeping position sizing mechanical and fixed regardless of the streak. If anything, the right response to a hot streak is to hold size constant or trim, because reversion is most likely after extremes. Humility here is not modesty; it is risk management.

## 3. Addiction to Risk

Aggressive trading delivers rewards on a variable-ratio schedule—unpredictable wins interspersed with losses—the exact reinforcement pattern that makes slot machines compulsive. Executing max-size tranches into high-gamma options or volatile leveraged ETFs floods the reward system with dopamine, and the response is not to the money but to the uncertainty and the hit, until the activity stops being a means to a financial end and becomes the end itself, demanding ever more stimulation. The signs mirror other behavioral addictions: restlessness when flat, needing larger positions to feel anything, trading out of boredom rather than edge, checking prices compulsively, chasing to recover, hiding losses—and the tell is a change in the question being asked, from "is this a high-quality setup?" to "where is the action?" In quiet, low-volatility stretches, dopamine withdrawal pushes the addicted trader to manufacture trades where no edge exists. **The antidote** begins with mechanical rules that remove moment-to-moment discretion, scheduled time away from the markets, trade caps, an accountability partner, and an honest audit that treats "flat" as a valid and frequent position—and when volatility drops, transitioning deliberately to active observation (logging paper-traded or back-tested case studies) rather than churning. It also includes naming the problem when it is real. Compulsive risk-taking is a recognized, treatable behavioral pattern, not a weakness; in the United States, the **National Problem Gambling Helpline (1-800-GAMBLER)** offers free, confidential help, and speaking with a qualified professional is a sign of strength. Recognizing the pattern early is the most valuable skill in this chapter.

## 4. Lifestyle Inflation

Success changes spending before it changes anything else. Gains—often still unrealized—get mentally pre-spent: the trader sees the account touch $600,000 on an open swing and signs a lease on a sports car, reasoning that "one more good trade will cover it," and fixed costs rise to match the new account size until he is quietly dependent on continued trading income to sustain a lifestyle that did not exist a few months earlier. The trap has teeth: once fixed costs are committed, a normal drawdown is no longer just painful but unaffordable, forcing more risk at exactly the moment prudence demands less—and the moment a trader needs a trade to hit a number to fund real-world expenses, objective analysis is broken. Realized gains also carry a tax bill the spending ignores, and the "house money" illusion makes the cycle feel painless until it isn't. **The antidote** is a hard wall between life capital and trading capital: during the sprint, lock living expenses at their pre-sprint baseline and extract nothing from the compounding ledger for luxury, treating the capital as the fund's property until the campaign is closed and audited; withdraw profits on a fixed schedule into accounts you do not trade, set aside the tax reserve the instant a gain is realized, and refuse to let fixed costs rise on the strength of trading income. Money taken permanently off the table is the only money the strategy actually earned.

### 5. Losing Discipline After Success

This is the force that ties the others together, and the most counterintuitive: **success is the most dangerous thing that can happen to a disciplined trader.** The discipline that produces a winning run is sustained by a healthy fear of loss; success dissolves that fear, and with it the discipline—the journal gets skipped, the checklist shortcut, pre-market prep abandoned, the rules treated as suggestions, and the trader who arrived through process starts trading on feel. The result is the classic cycle: discipline produces gains, gains produce confidence, confidence erodes discipline, and eroded discipline gives the gains back, often faster than they were made—and the trader is genuinely puzzled, because nothing changed in the method except the rigor of execution, a change invisible from the inside. Discipline must actually scale up with the account, not down: a $10,000 mistake in a $100,000 account is painful, but a $100,000 mistake in a $1,000,000 account can be devastating. **The antidote** is to codify the rules in writing while you are still afraid, journal every trade with the same rigor in the good months as the bad, and adopt a deliberately paradoxical stance—treat a winning streak as a yellow flag, not a green light. Re-humble after every major gain: review the risk rules, withdraw some profit, trim size temporarily, skip the celebration trade. The moment trading feels easy and the rules feel optional is the precise moment to tighten, not relax.

### Four Structural Safeguards

Because none of these forces yields to willpower, harden the antidotes into named protocols installed in advance. **The anonymized ledger:** after a milestone, hide the raw dollar balance and flashing P&L and track performance in R-multiples and percentages only, starving the ego of the dollar figure that feeds overconfidence. **The observation slog:** when volatility falls below your threshold, switch mechanically to active observation—a few back-tested case studies a day—rather than manufacturing live trades. **The milestone reset:** the moment a target is cleared, wire a slice (say 10%) of the profit to an untouched account, treat the rest as a brand-new base, and re-apply Phase-1 defensive sizing. **The baseline-spending rule:**

keep personal spending locked at its pre-sprint level for the entire campaign, so no real-world liability can ever reach into the trading decision.

## The Shadow of the Strategy

Laid out together, the pattern is plain: each force has a specific trigger and a specific structural antidote—and not one of the antidotes is willpower.

| Force | What triggers it | The antidote |
|---|---|---|
| **Blowups** | Leverage + concentration + a tail event | Hard size limits, heat cap, circuit breakers; survival before speed |
| **Overconfidence** | A winning streak in a kind regime | Track process, assume the regime helped, keep sizing fixed |
| **Risk addiction** | Variable-reward dopamine loops | Mechanical rules, scheduled breaks, honest audit – and help if it's real |
| **Lifestyle inflation** | Pre-spending gains; rising fixed costs | Wall off life capital, fixed withdrawals, reserve taxes |
| **Discipline drift** | Success dissolving the fear of loss | Codify rules, journal always, treat winning as a yellow flag |

## Surviving Success: The Governance Matrix

The dark side is fought mostly in how a trader behaves after things go right.

| Dimension | The Retail Casualty | The Disciplined Allocator |
|---|---|---|
| **After a big win** | Sizes up and feels invincible. | Holds size or trims, and assumes luck helped. |
| **Relationship to risk** | Chases the high; cannot sit flat. | Treats flat as a valid, frequent position. |
| **Money off the table** | Reinvests everything and spends paper gains. | Withdraws on a schedule; walls off life capital. |
| **View of discipline** | Loosens the rules as the account grows. | Tightens the rules exactly when winning. |

## Reader Exercise: The Blowup Prevention Pact

Turn this chapter into something enforceable. Write your **Blowup Prevention Pact**—a signed, one-page commitment to the specific rules you will never break, even after 300% gains, reviewed monthly—and keep a **Dark Side Journal**, a running log of your personal warning signs (the restlessness, the urge to size up, the skipped routine) reviewed alongside your trades so the patterns are caught early.

# PART VIII – BUILDING POST-MILLION LASTING WEALTH

## Chapter 33
# Protecting the Fortune
*Why Keeping the Million Is the Harder Half*

Growing $100,000 into $1,000,000 is only half the battle; the greater test is keeping it. Aggressive compounding creates wealth quickly, but fast wealth is fragile — lost to taxes, lawsuits, poor structure, overtrading, lifestyle inflation, or the trader's refusal to stop behaving like a trader after success. **Hitting the target is not the finish line; it is the signal to dismantle the aggressive machine.**

The very mechanisms that grew the account — leverage, extreme concentration, high-gamma derivatives — will vaporize it just as fast if maintained past the goal: risking $1,000,000 the way you once risked $100,000 means exposing six figures to a single morning gap. So the moment the ledger crosses the target, the campaign freezes, and the operator transitions from an aggressive speculator into a defensive steward of permanent capital. The purpose of aggressive trading was never merely to make the fortune; it was to convert temporary gains into durable financial strength.

### 1. Tax Strategy
Plan taxes before the fortune is made, not after. A six-month sprint generates almost entirely short-term capital gains — positions held a year or less — taxed as ordinary income; at the top brackets the federal rate reaches the high-30s percent, and with state taxes and the net investment income tax the combined bite can exceed 40% of net profits. Frequent traders must also respect the wash-sale rule, which disallows a loss when a substantially identical security or option is repurchased within 30 days before or after the sale — deferring it into the replacement's basis, a common trap for options and leveraged-ETF traders.

The discipline is simple and immediate: **the moment you cross the target, freeze the account and calculate the liability before a single dollar is spent.** Set aside roughly 30–40% of profits in ultra-safe short-term Treasuries — a tax silo insulated from any further market exposure, correction, or error — and keep a quarterly reserve so filing season is never a surprise. The casualty waits until April, finds the reserve was traded away, and is forced to sell badly or re-enter risky trades to pay the bill.

Around that reserve, several concepts are worth reviewing with a professional: whether trader tax status and a Section 475 mark-to-market election fit (for qualified full-time traders it treats gains and losses as ordinary and sidesteps wash sales); systematic tax-loss harvesting, especially in drawdowns; tax-advantaged accounts where feasible; entity structuring for legitimate deductions; and deliberate year-end realization. None of this is do-it-yourself — work with a CPA who specializes in active traders.

### 2. Asset Protection
Once you hold a seven-figure balance sheet, your risk shifts from purely market-based to systemic legal risk. A large, unprotected personal account is a prime target for lawsuits, creditor claims, and disputes; leaving a million

dollars in a single-name retail brokerage account is a security failure. The governing principle is blunt: **trading risk should not become life risk.** Do not let one lawsuit, creditor problem, divorce, or business dispute endanger the fortune.

Protection is built in layers, from cheapest and simplest to most robust:

- **Insurance first.** An umbrella liability policy is the cheapest first line of defense and should be sized to the new net worth.
- **Legal entities.** Hold trading and investment assets in LLCs or family limited partnerships, separate from personal assets; in many states, charging-order protection limits a creditor's reach into the entity.
- **Asset-protection trusts.** Domestic (in states such as Nevada, Delaware, or South Dakota) or offshore irrevocable trusts, with spendthrift provisions, provide a stronger shield and move the core out of your personal name.
- **Titling and hygiene.** Use homestead exemptions where available, keep personal assets out of trading-margin accounts, maintain clean records, and never commingle funds.

Done well, this walls off your personal life from your accumulated wealth — the trading terminal managed under an entity rather than tied to your name. This is not a do-it-yourself area: consult a qualified asset-protection attorney and CPA, and implement the structures within weeks of a major milestone, not after a problem arises.

## 3. Diversification After Success

Concentration makes wealth; diversification preserves it. Scaling from $100,000 to $1,000,000 required concentrated, high-beta positions, but maintaining that intensity on a seven-figure base means risking six-figure swings on a single gap, and the habit of chasing high-beta anomalies has to be deliberately broken. The core capital is **permanently banned** from high-gamma options, warrants, and 3x leveraged ETFs, and is instead scattered across non-correlated, institutional-grade asset classes:

| Preservation asset class | Target | Primary mandate |
|---|---|---|
| **Broad-market index funds** | 40% | Capture foundational macro equity beta |
| **Fixed income / short-duration debt** | 30% | Liquidity and consistent yield |
| **Hard assets (real estate, gold)** | 20% | Inflation shield and purchasing-power insulation |
| **Cash reserves** | 10% | Dry powder for market dislocations |

Those weights are a center of gravity, not a straitjacket — equities might run 30–50%, fixed income and alternatives 20–40%, cash and hedges 10–20%, with the remainder in real estate, private investments, or a business. On hitting the milestone, de-risk 40–60% into this preservation bucket immediately, using tax-efficient methods — gradual sales paired with loss-harvesting, or exchange funds. Rebalance quarterly or by threshold, rotate out of the remaining leveraged positions, and treat what is left as an investment, not a trade. Even the strongest supercycle can correct sharply, so the post-success book is structured for survival across cycles, not for one more home run.

## 4. Transitioning From Trader to Investor

The final milestone is purely psychological, and it is the hardest. The operator must shift identity from a **tactical trader** — short-term, high-anxiety, speed-driven — to an **enduring investor** who is long-term and duration-driven. The trader views the market as a canvas for extracting cash velocity; the investor views it as a vault for storing purchasing power. Those who cannot shift suffer the "trader's regression" — returning to the screen out of ego and boredom, over-leveraging the seven-figure base, and handing the fortune back.

The most durable framing is the endowment model: treat the protected core as untouchable permanent capital and live only off its yield — a conservative 5% on a $600,000 core is about $30,000 a year of passive cash flow. The infinite game is won not by continuing to compound at 1,000%, but by ensuring the core survives across decades. Make the transition in phases:

- **Phase 1 (immediately).** Cut screen time, trade size, and frequency; cap any remaining aggressive allocation at 20–30% of the portfolio.
- **Phase 2 (over three to six months).** Shift the primary focus to passive, index, dividend-growth, or rules-based investing, using swing trading only opportunistically.
- **Phase 3 (ongoing).** Become a portfolio manager of a diversified mix, with professional help, under written investor rules — no day trades, a maximum single position of around 5%.

Replace the trading adrenaline with passive income — dividends, real estate — and avoid inflating your lifestyle until the fortune is fully protected and the transition complete. The strategy that built the fortune is rarely the strategy that preserves it; the final stage of aggressive compounding is not more aggression, but stewardship.

## The Fortune Protection Governance Matrix

Set against each other, the difference between keeping the fortune and giving it back is a matter of four decisions made the moment the target is hit.

| Pillar | The Retail Casualty | The Disciplined Protector |
|---|---|---|
| **Tax management** | Ignores the liability until April; trades the reserve away. | Sets the liability aside in Treasuries the moment the target is hit. |
| **Legal architecture** | Keeps the wealth in a personal account, exposed to claims. | Builds an asset-protection shield via entities and trusts. |
| **Capital allocation** | Keeps risking the whole million on concentrated leverage. | Migrates the core into diversified, non-correlated assets. |

| Pillar | The Retail Casualty | The Disciplined Protector |
| --- | --- | --- |
| **Identity** | Stays glued to the screen until the fortune is gone. | Adopts the endowment mindset and invests for the long term. |

## Your Fortune Protection Checklist

If you reach the goal, the first thirty days decide whether you keep it. A concrete starting checklist:

- Engage a CPA and an asset-protection attorney within 30 days of a major milestone.
- Calculate and reserve the taxes on all realized gains, in a separate, safe account.
- Draft a diversification target allocation and rebalancing rules.
- Put umbrella insurance and the right entity structures in place, and review them annually.
- Write a one-page "Post-Success Trading Policy" that caps aggressive activity.

## Risk, Honesty, and a Reality Check

Reaching the point of having a fortune to protect is itself the rare, outlier outcome — and even among those who get there, many give a significant portion back within a few years to taxes, lawsuits, poor diversification, or a relapse into old habits. Protecting wealth is its own discipline, and it begins the day the target is hit.

## Blueprint Principle

> **The fortune is not made when the account reaches $1,000,000 — it is made when you protect it, structure it, and keep it.**

Reaching the number is the loud part; keeping it is the quiet discipline that actually defines wealth. The instant the target is crossed, the aggressive machine is switched off: a tax reserve is fenced into Treasuries before anything is spent, the core is moved out of your personal name and behind a legal shield, the concentrated high-beta positions are unwound into a diversified, non-correlated book, and the operator stops trading for cash velocity and starts investing to preserve purchasing power. Do that, and the million becomes permanent; skip it, and the same velocity that built the fortune quietly reclaims it.

## Chapter 34
# From Aggressive Trader to Family Office Thinking

*Earning the Right to Stop — and Building Something That Outlasts You*

This is the last chapter, and the one the whole book has quietly been pointing toward. The aggressive strategy was a tool for a single purpose: to generate, quickly, a pool of capital large enough that you would never need to trade that way again. **Family office thinking is what you do once the tool has done its job** — almost point for point the opposite of everything before it. The aggressive trader's mission was multiplication; the family office's is preservation, income, continuity, and legacy — and making that transition is what changes a person's identity from speculator to steward.

A family office is the structure the genuinely wealthy use to manage capital across generations, and its governing instinct is not return but endurance: where the aggressive trader asks how much he can make this month, the family office asks how to make sure the capital is still here, intact and growing, for grandchildren who do not yet exist. You do not need hundreds of millions to adopt the mindset; you need only decide that preserving and perpetuating wealth now matters more than maximizing it — and begin the shift early, at the milestones along the way ($250k, $500k, $1M) rather than at the end.

An irony is worth naming. The family-office principles here — preserve first, diversify broadly, compound slowly, never blow up — are how durable wealth is actually built. The aggressive strategy is the exception that, if it works, buys the entrance ticket. The mature endpoint of this book is to stop being its protagonist.

## 1. Reducing Risk

The first mandate of a family office is blunt: **do not permanently lose the capital.** Everything else is secondary. This inverts the trader's posture — the trader seeks volatility because that is where fast returns live; the family office budgets it down because, once you have won, the asymmetry reverses. You now have far more to lose than to gain, and a catastrophic loss is no longer a setback but a permanent destruction of the thing the whole campaign was for. The mistake that ends most rapid wealth creators is continuing to risk $1,000,000 the way they once risked $100,000.

Concretely, measure risk at the portfolio level, target single-digit drawdowns rather than the 35–60% the aggressive strategy tolerated, and think in terms of a risk budget — how much volatility for how much expected return — rather than chasing the maximum. In practice the de-risking looks like this:

- **Evolve the buckets.** Move 50–70% of the gains into a core preservation bucket — investment-grade bonds, Treasuries, broad index ETFs, high-quality real estate — and keep only 10–20% in a tactical growth sleeve.
- **Cut the leverage.** Phase out 3x ETFs, high-gamma options, and margin; replace them with unleveraged or, at most, 1.25–1.5x exposure, targeting annual portfolio volatility under roughly 8–12%.

- **Make the drawdown cap permanent.** Institute a standing rule — for example, a 10% peak-to-trough drop triggers a full de-risk — and keep 15–25% in cash equivalents for buffers and opportunities.
- **Separate the capital.** Ring-fence long-term capital from any remaining trading capital, and move a meaningful share into protected accounts so a single decision can never reach the whole fortune.

The deepest shift is psychological. The aggressive trader's edge was a tolerance for risk; the family office's is a respect for it. A useful test for every remaining position: "Would I want my children inheriting this exact risk?" Reducing risk is not timidity — it is the recognition that the game has changed, and the capital is now the prize rather than the chip. The strategy that builds the fortune is rarely the strategy that preserves it.

## 2. Building Passive Income

A trading fortune is active — it exists only as long as you keep generating it. Family office thinking converts the lump sum into **durable cash flow that arrives whether or not you ever look at a screen again.** Income is freedom — the difference between wealth you must constantly defend and wealth that quietly supports you — and it removes the desperation that forces bad trades to pay the bills.

The building blocks are deliberately unexciting, and that is the point. A diversified portfolio throws off income from several uncorrelated sources:

| Asset class | Role | What it provides |
|---|---|---|
| **Broad equity index funds** | Growth engine | Long-term appreciation, dividends, liquidity |
| **High-quality bonds & Treasuries** | Ballast | Stable income and a buffer in downturns |
| **Real estate (direct or REITs)** | Income + inflation hedge | Recurring cash flow and a real-asset anchor |
| **Cash & short-term instruments** | Reserve | Optionality and a drawdown buffer |
| **Small aggressive sleeve** | Asymmetric upside | Capped-risk growth that keeps you engaged |

In practice that might mean dividend-growth equities yielding 2–4%, real estate or REITs at 4–8% cash-on-cash, and laddered Treasuries, private credit, or infrastructure for fixed income. Withdrawals are governed by the safe withdrawal rate — the rule of thumb that drawing roughly 3–4% of a diversified portfolio per year lets the capital sustain itself, and likely keep growing, indefinitely. Aim to live on 3–5% of the fortune (on $1M, roughly $30,000–$50,000 a year at first) while reinvesting the rest. Live within the income and the fortune is permanent; spend the principal and it is temporary. The goal is the point where your portfolio earns more than you spend — the moment trading becomes a choice, not a necessity.

### 3. Long-Term Compounding

Here the book's own headline returns in a gentler, more reliable form. The aggressive strategy chased roughly 47% a month and, as every prior chapter conceded, most often burned out. Durable compounding asks for 7–12% a year — run for decades rather than months. The contrast is the whole lesson.

The arithmetic of patience is staggering and underappreciated. With dividends and gains automatically reinvested, $1,000,000 compounding at 8% grows to about $2.16M in ten years and $4.66M in twenty, with no additional contributions at all. By the Rule of 72, a 10% return doubles capital roughly every seven years. Money left alone to compound at a modest rate over a working lifetime grows into multiples frantic trading rarely keeps, precisely because slow compounding is not interrupted by the blowups that reset the fast kind to zero.

> **The same 10x, the durable way.** *A $1,000,000 portfolio compounding at a steady 8% a year grows to roughly $10,000,000 over thirty years — the same tenfold result this book chased in six* **months, but** *achieved with near-certainty rather than as an outlier, without leverage, and without the risk of ruin that haunts every fast path. Time, not aggression, is the most powerful and most reliable form of leverage ever discovered. The trader's job was to create the seed; compounding's job* ***is*** *to grow the tree.*

Running this engine well is structural rather than clever: divide capital across time horizons — short-term trading, medium-term opportunity, long-term investment, emergency reserves, family and retirement capital — so no single decision can damage the whole; diversify globally across equities, fixed income, real assets, and select alternatives, rebalancing on a schedule or by threshold; and protect the after-tax, inflation-adjusted result through tax-loss harvesting, municipal bonds, and similar tools. A simple one-page Investment Policy Statement, setting out goals, risk tolerance, and rebalancing rules and reviewed annually, keeps the discipline honest. The family office treats time as its primary asset, and patience — letting uninterrupted compounding work across decades — is an edge available to almost no one, because almost no one can sit still. Having the capital and the temperament to do nothing is the rarest position in finance.

### 4. Legacy Capital

The final expansion is to think beyond your own lifetime. **Legacy capital** is wealth managed for people and purposes that extend past you — children, grandchildren, causes — introducing a question the aggressive trader never had to ask: what is this money actually for?

A proverb holds that wealth goes from shirtsleeves to shirtsleeves in three generations — the first makes it, the second preserves it, and the third, never having known scarcity, squanders it. Family office thinking is largely the project of defeating that proverb, and the tools are as much human as financial:

- **Estate structures.** Wills, revocable and irrevocable trusts, and dynasty trusts where permitted, to transfer wealth efficiently, minimize estate taxes, and control distributions on your terms.

- **Family governance.** A simple family constitution covering values, decision-making, and — most decisively — educating heirs, so the people who inherit the money also inherit the discipline that created it.
- **Philanthropy.** Donor-advised funds or a private foundation, to give the capital meaning beyond accumulation and provide tax benefits.
- **Succession and liquidity.** Plans for any business interests and knowledge transfer, with life insurance used for liquidity and tax-efficient transfers.

These structures are the domain of an estate attorney and a tax professional, and should be built deliberately rather than improvised. But the mindset costs nothing to adopt: the moment you begin asking who this capital serves after you, and how to hand down the judgment along with the dollars, you have stopped being a trader and become a steward of something larger than a single lifetime. Capital without transmitted wisdom rarely survives the people who earned it.

## The Transition Model

The shift is gradual, not a single switch thrown at $1M. Each milestone changes the primary goal and the main danger:

| Stage | Primary goal | Main risk |
|---|---|---|
| **$100,000** | Growth | Under-capitalization |
| **$250,000** | Acceleration | Overconfidence |
| **$500,000** | Protection begins | Giving back gains |
| **$1,000,000** | Wealth preservation | Continuing reckless risk |
| **$1,000,000+** | Family office thinking | Poor structure and lack of planning |

The higher the account rises, the less acceptable catastrophic risk becomes. The complete journey is not merely $100,000 to $1,000,000; it is trading capital, to investment capital, to passive income, to protected wealth, to legacy capital.

## The Two Mindsets

Set side by side, the journey of this book is a journey between two opposite ways of relating to money. The whole arc is the migration from the left column to the right.

| Dimension | The Aggressive Trader | The Family Office Mind |
|---|---|---|
| **Primary mandate** | Maximize return as fast as possible. | Never permanently lose the capital. |
| **Time horizon** | Six months. | Generations. |
| **Target return** | ~47% per month. | ~7–10% per year, durable. |
| **Drawdown** | 35–60%. | Single digits. |

| Dimension | The Aggressive Trader | The Family Office Mind |
|---|---|---|
| **tolerance** | | |
| **Relationship to risk** | Seeks it — it is where returns live. | Budgets it — it is what must be controlled. |
| **Measure of success** | The size of the win. | The durability of the wealth. |

## Your Family Office Transition Plan

If you reach the goal, put this chapter to work within the first sixty days. A concrete starting checklist:

- Define your post-$1M allocation — the buckets and their percentages across preservation, income, growth, and legacy.
- Calculate the passive income your ideal lifestyle actually requires, and the portfolio size that throws it off at a 3–4% withdrawal rate.
- Draft a one-page Investment Policy Statement and a short Legacy Statement defining what the capital is for.
- Schedule meetings with a CPA, an estate attorney, and a fee-only fiduciary advisor to build the structures properly.

## Risk, Honesty, and a Reality Check

As with the preceding chapter, this is a destination most attempts never reach — not because the mindset is hard to understand, but because arriving at it requires first having won and kept a fortune, which the book is honest is an outlier outcome. And even those who arrive often struggle to embrace it, because the temperament that generated the wealth resists the patience that preserves it. The reader who absorbs this chapter early gains a definition of the finish line. Knowing that the goal is to reach family-office thinking — not to trade aggressively forever — is itself one of the strongest protections against the forces that destroy those who never decided what winning was for.

## Blueprint Principle

> **The aggressive strategy was never the destination — it was the on-ramp.**

Family office thinking closes the circle the book opened. The same tenfold result chased in six frantic months is available, with near-certainty, to patient capital compounding over decades — which reframes everything that came before it. Reduce the risk once you have won, convert the fortune into income that frees you from the screen, let uninterrupted compounding do the work that no aggressive strategy can do reliably, and manage what remains for the people and purposes that will outlast you. The trader's craft was to create the capital; the steward's craft is to make it permanent. The final and highest skill in this book is knowing when to stop using the rest of it.

## Chapter 35
# The Real Goal

*What the Number Was Always Standing **In** For*

Every page of this book has been organized around a number: a hundred thousand dollars becoming a million in six months. It is time to say the quiet part directly. **The number was never the goal.** It was a proxy — a measurable stand-in for a set of things harder to put on a chart but that are the only reasons anyone pursues money in the first place. Money is a tool, a servant rather than a master; when wealth becomes the master, the trader turns restless, greedy, fearful, and never satisfied — but treated as a tool it can serve freedom, time, family, stewardship, independence, and purpose.

This final chapter is about those six things — the real goal, for which the dollar figure was only ever a tool. Naming them matters, because a goal you cannot name is a goal you cannot honor — and the trader who chases the number while forgetting what it was for risks the gravest failure of all: succeeding at the proxy while failing at the point.

There is a hard truth here, the most important in the book: the aggressive pursuit of the number can consume the very things it was meant to buy. The screen takes the time, the obsession strains the family, the risk threatens the security. Defining the real goal first is not a soft epilogue — it is the strongest protection there is against everything that destroys people who win the money and lose the plot.

### Freedom

Ask most people why they want a million dollars and underneath the answer you find freedom — not a vague slogan but the concrete kind: not being controlled by a boss, a paycheck you cannot afford to lose, a schedule someone else sets, or the need to keep showing up. Real freedom is autonomy over how you spend your days, and the wealth a trader builds is meant to create it: freedom from debt pressure, employment dependency, survival anxiety, and forced compromise.

The trap is that the aggressive strategy can quietly deliver the opposite. A trader who escapes a boss only to become enslaved to the screen — who cannot take a vacation because positions need watching, who checks quotes at dinner — has not bought freedom; he has changed masters. A trader who makes money quickly but spends recklessly, cannot stop trading emotionally, or is ruled by the fear of losing his gains is not free either. Freedom is not a large account; it is reaching the point where money no longer dictates your choices. If the pursuit of it leaves you less free than when you started, the pursuit has failed on its own terms.

### Time

Of everything discussed in this book, time is the only asset that cannot be earned back. A blown-up account can be rebuilt; a lost decade cannot. This asymmetry should reorganize how a person thinks about the whole enterprise, because the deepest irony of obsessive wealth-building is that it spends the one irreplaceable thing — time — to accumulate the most replaceable thing there is, money.

The point of financial independence is to reclaim time — to convert money, once you have enough, back into the hours and years it was supposed to free, spent on health, relationships, learning, travel, creativity, and rest. A million dollars matters not for the number but because it buys margin — to think, rest, choose, say no, and say yes to better things. So design the campaign to give time back rather than consume it — a system of rules and alerts that runs on minimal daily input, well under ten focused hours a week once the sprint is done, and real enforced non-trading periods. The right relationship reverses how most traders run it: spend money to buy back time, never irreplaceable time to buy more money than you need.

## Family

Relationships are the return that actually compounds — or quietly erodes — over a life, and they are the most common casualty of single-minded wealth pursuit. The aggressive phase tests them through stress, screen time, and emotional volatility, and the cost is often paid by the people closest to the trader: the partner who competes with the screen, the children whose attention arrives second to a chart. Wealth that costs you the people it was meant to serve is not wealth; it is a loss disguised as a win.

For most people, the family is who the money is for — which means a strategy that sacrifices them to reach the number has inverted its own purpose. So use the journey to strengthen the household rather than strain it: involve a partner in the planning (never in live trading decisions), set shared goals, and let the fortune fund genuine security — housing, healthcare, education, and generational opportunity. The healthiest version of this whole endeavor keeps people at the center, treats time with them as part of the return rather than a cost of it, and asks honestly whether the pursuit is making you a better steward of your family or merely a more distracted risk-taker.

## Stewardship

Stewardship is the shift from owning money to caretaking it — holding it responsibly, using it well, and recognizing it as a tool for good rather than a scoreboard for the ego. It is the quiet maturity the preceding chapters built toward: capital carries responsibility, both to the people who depend on it and to the uses it could serve. It calls for prudence after success, honesty in tax matters, disciplined risk, generosity, and long-term planning — and the humility to admit that supercycles, timing, and luck all helped, that no one beats the market entirely alone.

The scoreboard mentality has no finish line — there is always a higher number, a richer peer, a bigger win — while stewardship has a center of gravity: what this money is for and whether it is being used well. A steward measures success not by accumulation but by responsible use — providing, protecting, giving, building — and that measure, unlike the scoreboard, can actually be satisfied. The useful question is not “How much can I make?” but “What good should this money accomplish, and how would a responsible multi-generational steward handle this decision?”

## Financial Independence

Financial independence is the concrete milestone the whole book was reaching for, with a precise definition: the point at which your passive income reliably exceeds your expenses, so that working — or trading — becomes a choice rather than a necessity. At a seven-figure base drawn at a conservative 3–4% a year and supported by diversified passive income, that independence is within reach. It changes the trader's posture from survival to strategy: he can wait, pass on poor setups, cut risk, stop after losses, and trade from strength rather than need — no revenge trades, over-leverage, or fear-driven lifestyle inflation. It is the real target the million-dollar figure was standing in for, and for most people the number that actually buys it is far smaller than the fantasy figure.

That is a liberating realization, because the amount required to be free is set not by ambition but by your cost of living — lower your fixed costs and the finish line moves closer; inflate your lifestyle and it recedes no matter how much you make. The danger is the moving goalpost: a person who never defines "enough" can pass financial independence without noticing and keep risking the security he already achieved, chasing a number that, by definition, he will never reach because it was never fixed.

> **Define enough, in writing, in advance.** *The single most clarifying act in personal finance is to name the specific figure — the level of assets and passive income — at which you are independent, decided while you are calm rather than in the grip of a winning streak. A goal with a defined finish line can be reached and honored. A goal of* **"more"** *cannot be reached at all, and the chase does not end until something forces it to.*

## Purpose Beyond Money

The deepest layer is the one money cannot supply. Money is a means, never an end, and the people who reach a large number with no purpose beyond it are frequently the most lost of all — arriving at the destination they organized their lives around only to find it was never the point. The win feels strangely empty because winning was never what they actually needed.

Past genuine sufficiency, more money stops delivering more meaning — the satisfaction of accumulation fades as fast as it arrives, and the chase resumes for a feeling the next increment cannot provide. What endures is purpose: work that matters to you, contribution to something beyond yourself, the use of your freedom and resources in service of something you care about — a cause funded, a business built around your values, others mentored, a problem worth solving. Money can fund a purpose; it cannot manufacture one. Financial independence buys you the capacity to pursue purpose — the time, the freedom, the security — but it does not hand you the purpose itself. That you have to bring. The most successful version of this whole journey ends not with a person admiring an account balance, but with a person finally free to do the thing they were always meant to do.

## The Number Was a Proxy

Laid out together, the pattern is unmistakable: each real goal is something the money was meant to serve, and each can be betrayed by chasing the money as though it were the goal itself.

| The real goal | What it truly is | How chasing the number can betray it |
|---|---|---|
| **Freedom** | Autonomy over your days | Trading a boss for enslavement to the screen |
| **Time** | The one asset you cannot earn back | Spending irreplaceable years for replaceable money |
| **Family** | The people the money is for | Sacrificing the very people it was meant to serve |
| **Stewardship** | Caretaking capital and people well | Treating money as a scoreboard with no finish line |
| **Financial independence** | Income that exceeds your needs | Moving the goalposts so "enough" never arrives |
| **Purpose** | Meaning money cannot supply | Reaching the number and finding it empty |

## Two Ways to Hold the Goal

The same million dollars means entirely different things depending on what a person believes it is for. Contrast the two.

| Dimension | The Number-Chaser | The Person With a Real Goal |
|---|---|---|
| **What they optimize** | The size of the account. | The quality of the life. |
| **Definition of enough** | Always "more" — never arrives. | A specific figure, reached and honored. |
| **What they spend** | Time, to get more money. | Money, to buy back time. |
| **After hitting the number** | Sets a bigger number. | Lives the life it was for. |
| **Relationship to money** | It owns them. | They own it. |

## Reader Exercise: Your Real Goal Declaration

Before you place the first trade, write a one-page declaration of what the money is actually for — and keep it visible through the whole campaign, so that when emotions run hot, you have something to return to. Answer four questions:

- What does freedom look like for me — in one year, and in ten?
- How will I use the time the money buys back?
- What legacy and security do I want for my family?
- What purpose will the money serve beyond lifestyle — and what is my specific number for "enough"?

Review and update the declaration at every milestone, and read it whenever euphoria, fear, or greed take hold. It is the North Star that keeps the number in its proper place: a means, never the end.

## Honesty, and a Final Reality Check

This book has been candid throughout that its headline goal is an outlier outcome carrying a real risk of substantial or total loss. This chapter adds the deeper honesty: even success at the number is not success at the real goal, and the pursuit itself can cost a person the freedom, time, family, and peace it was supposed to provide. That is the most valuable position a reader can hold, and it is available to everyone regardless of whether the trading ever works: to know, before risking anything, that the account was never the point — the life was.

## Blueprint Principle

> **The million dollars was never the goal.**

So this is where the blueprint actually leads. Not to a balance, but to a life: autonomy over your days, time reclaimed and spent on what matters, relationships kept at the center, capital held in trust rather than worshipped, a finish line named and honored, and a purpose worth all the freedom the money can buy. The strategies in this book were instruments, and instruments are judged by the music they make. Keep the real goal in front of the number the whole way, and whatever the market does, you will have aimed at the only target that was ever worth hitting.

# Conclusion: The Survivor Compounds

*Why Staying Alive Is the Real Trading Edge*

There is a counter-intuitive truth underneath this book: **the aggressive trader who actually reaches a million dollars is not a reckless daredevil – he is a master of survival.** The amateur fixates on offense—the vertical charts, the overnight doubles, the massive wins—but in a six-month compounding sprint, offense is the commodity and defense is what keeps you alive. The traders who turn $100,000 into $1,000,000 are not the smartest, the luckiest, or the most aggressive; they are the ones who refuse to be taken out. The market is an elimination arena: you can own the best scanner or sharpest options framework in the world, but if you cannot protect your capital base through the unfavorable regimes, your edge is meaningless—you will not be there to use it. Compounding is a marathon of cycles, not a single sprint, and its power is available only to those who stay in the game long enough for the geometric math to do its work. The survivor compounds; the reckless trader disappears.

## 1. Why Survival Is the Real Edge

Most traders fail not because they never find winning trades but because they cannot survive their losing ones—they overleverage, refuse stops, average down, revenge-trade, hold through disaster, and confuse confidence with certainty. The market does not need to beat them every day; it only needs one uncontrolled event. The reason is mathematical: in a high-leverage environment the real threat is not a string of small losses but the **terminal zero.** A trader risking 20% of the account per trade needs only a short run of bad fills or one unhedged overnight gap to reach zero, and once you hit zero the game is permanently over. Picture the whole campaign as your compounded returns multiplied by a survival factor that is either one or zero—catch a dozen +500% winners but let that factor flip to zero even once, and the entire result collapses to nothing. A 50% loss already requires a 100% gain just to break even, and in leveraged products a 70–80% drawdown is often permanent. Survival preserves your mathematical optionality—it is not passive waiting but active risk management that turns a high-variance strategy into one with positive expectancy over time. The edge is not a secret setup; it is endurance: the refusal to let one bad sequence end your campaign.

## 2. The Long Game Inside Aggressive Trading

Even a six-month campaign has a long game inside it. The trader must survive bad entries, failed breakouts, sudden reversals, corrections, sector rotations, volatility spikes, missed opportunities, and the overconfidence that follows wins. Aggressive trading is not one heroic bet but a long sequence of decisions, and the survivor treats every trade, week, and month as data for the next—viewing the sprint as a single high-intensity cycle inside a multi-decade career rather than a 180-day gamble. Practically, that means reading the market as dozens of micro-regimes rather than one continuous trend: markets cycle quickly through high liquidity, tight consolidation, vertical trends, and directionless noise, and you cannot force a 1,000% curve through hostile conditions. So track the regime—the rolling 20-day average true range, whether the major indexes sit above or below their anchor VWAP—and when volatility turns erratic and price is below that anchor, recognize that the highest-probability action is often no action at all. Rotate across themes rather than marrying one, take only the asymmetric setups so you miss many moves but catch the fat-tail winners, and after big wins scale risk down and lock profits into preservation to fund the next cycle. A trader who protects capital during weak periods is not falling behind; he is preserving the ability to attack when conditions improve—treating survival through a bad regime as a genuine win, because it keeps the full capital base intact for when the environment shifts back to high-velocity growth.

### 3. The Discipline Behind Extraordinary Returns

Amateurs believe extraordinary returns require taking extraordinary risk on every trade. This is a fatal misconception. Elite returns come from keeping risk rigidly *fixed* while allowing the payoffs to scale into massive, non-linear multiples—disciplined asymmetry, not constant recklessness. The discipline behind 1,000% compounding is the ability to lock the downside inside an iron vice while leaving the upside open. In practice that is the **absolute 1R risk vice**: every position—a 3x ETF sprint, a short-dated call, an equity breakout—carries a hard, pre-set bracket that caps the loss at roughly 1–2% of total NAV, with no manual overrides; if price touches the invalidation line, the position is gone. That absolute consistency gives the equity curve a flat, controlled floor through the testing periods, which is exactly what sets up the vertical power-law moves to lift the account later. Around that vice sits the rest of the discipline, and it looks almost conservative: accept small losses as the natural tax of trading, wait for elite setups, press winners, reduce size after both wins (to fight euphoria) and losses (to protect capital), enforce inactivity when nothing qualifies, respect cash as a position, and journal every trade with its rationale, emotion, and lesson. In leveraged trading, where a single revenge trade or oversized option can erase months of gains, this discipline is the moat: without it, aggression is gambling; with it, aggression becomes strategy.

### 4. Remaining in the Game Long Enough for Compounding to Work

Compounding requires continuity—the account must stay alive long enough for gains to build on prior gains. A destroyed account cannot compound, a demoralized trader cannot execute, and a trader trapped in a deep drawdown cannot act freely. Because compounding is exponential, its power is heavily back-loaded: in a 26-week campaign the first twelve weeks look painfully slow next to the last six, where a single ordinary move can add six figures in a morning, so the trader who burns out or blows his risk rules in week four never lives to see the acceleration of week twenty. So build for endurance. A useful frame is the **longevity rule**: size your risk so the capital base could absorb on the order of a hundred consecutive controlled 1R losses without threatening structural insolvency. Underneath it sit the same survival mechanics from earlier chapters—daily loss limits of 2–4%, portfolio heat under 8%, drawdown protocols that de-risk at 10–15%, and preservation buckets—plus the emotional control, position limits, cash reserves, and humility after success that keep you executing. The goal is never to win every trade; it is to remain capable of taking the next great one. This is the formula the whole book has been building toward: survival enables positive expectancy, which enables capital growth, which—given time in the market—produces exponential wealth and the freedom that comes with it. A survivor who reaches the million and then shifts into preservation mode can realistically compound it for many years more; the trader who flames out at $50,000 or $200,000 never gets the chance.

## The Survivor Governance Matrix

The difference between the trader who compounds and the one who is eliminated comes down to where the attention goes.

| Dimension | The Fragile Casualty | The Disciplined Survivor |
|---|---|---|
| **Risk focus** | Fixates on potential profit; ignores the threat of zero. | Fixates on downside; preserves the capital base above all. |
| **Regime adaptation** | Over-trades choppy, low-probability tape out of impatience. | Calibrates to the regime; waits in cash during corrections. |
| **Loss management** | Lets losses widen in denial, digging a geometric deficit. | Enforces the 1R vice; every loss caged in a small box. |
| **Timeline** | Demands vertical returns in week one; blows up early. | Plays for longevity; survives to catch the late-cycle wave. |

## Reader Exercise: Your Survivor Commitment

Make survival a written, signed promise before the campaign begins—something to return to when a streak or a fear tempts you to break a rule. Write and date this:

> ***"I commit to being a survivor first. No trade, no streak, and no fear of missing out will ever cause me to violate my risk rules, my daily loss limits, or my preservation buckets. My edge is staying alive for the next setup, the next cycle, and the next decade. The real goal is not just the million – it is the freedom, time, family, and legacy that only a survivor lives to enjoy."***

Review it weekly and at every equity milestone. It is the simplest, most important rule in the book made personal: protect the right to continue.

## Risk, Honesty, and a Reality Check

Survival improves your odds; it does not guarantee anything. The honest framing is that this is a high-variance attempt whose base rates are punishing, and that the single best thing a trader can do to shift those odds is to make staying solvent non-negotiable.

# APPENDICES

Reference material, distilled principles, working tools, and sources to support the campaign.

# Appendix A

## The 10× Blueprint Principles

Each chapter distilled to ten working principles. Read them as a fast refresher, a pre-campaign briefing, or a daily checklist. They summarize the book; they do not replace the reasoning and caveats in the chapters themselves.

### Chapter 1 — Understanding Exponential Wealth

**1.** Pursue 10× through sequential compounding, not one heroic trade.
**2.** Compound the risk unit (1R), not the stock; raise 1R as capital grows.
**3.** Eleven disciplined ~25% gains beat one improbable jackpot.
**4.** Respect the back-loaded curve; the biggest dollar gains come late.
**5.** Remember losses compound too; every drawdown shrinks future gains.
**6.** Use convex instruments to amplify a proven edge, never to manufacture one.
**7.** Protect the compounding engine first; preservation precedes growth.
**8.** Reject jackpot-sized bets that can end the campaign before it compounds.
**9.** Let discipline execute the mathematics without emotional deviation.
**10.** Internalize that exponential wealth is a daily process, not a single event.

### Chapter 2 — The Compounding Mindset

**1.** Think in percentages and R-multiples, not dollar swings.
**2.** Adopt a process identity: a disciplined operator running a campaign.
**3.** Value consistency over brilliance; repeatable base hits compound.
**4.** Measure success by adherence to the plan, not by any single trade's outcome.
**5.** Treat patience as an active position; wait for the right setup, that's an edge.
**6.** Detach self-worth from the equity curve.
**7.** Pre-commit rules before the open so decisions are made systematically.
**8.** Embrace small losses as the cost of business and the proof your defense works.
**9.** Keep the six-month horizon in view; daily noise is not the campaign.
**10.** Cultivate the discipline to be aggressive only when the edge is real.

### Chapter 3 — The Truth About Aggressive Trading

**1.** Accept the base rate: most aggressive accounts fail, so design first for survival.
**2.** Internalize the 90/90/90 reality and the 180-day sieve.
**3.** Understand the crowd fails by design, not accident; refuse to be them.
**4.** Make survival the edge — staying solvent through bad regimes is the goal.
**5.** Emulate the few who survive through discipline, selectivity, and adaptability.
**6.** Stay disciplined throughout the 180-day campaign.
**7.** Treat every rule violation as dangerous, even if profitable.
**8.** Respect the mathematics of destruction; a few large losses end the campaign.
**9.** Run the survival cycle: protect capital, wait, strike selectively, repeat.
**10.** Clear-eyed acceptance of the odds is a competitive advantage.

### Chapter 4 — Risk of Ruin Mathematics

**1.** A 50% loss requires a 100% gain; respect drawdown asymmetry.
**2.** Cap exposure so losing streaks cannot cascade into ruin.

**3.** Protect each milestone; each month's target is the next month's starting line.
**4.** Cut losses ruthlessly before they trigger reckless recovery.
**5.** Recovery is harder; aggressive instruments magnify recovery difficulty.
**6.** Recover by reducing size, lowering leverage, and rebuilding gradually.
**7.** The steady compounder beats the brilliant gambler over time.
**8.** Lock a hard maximum drawdown that forces a full stop and a post-mortem.
**9.** Never trade to get back to even; trade the next valid setup on its own merits.
**10.** Treat the math of ruin as the binding constraint on every sizing decision.

## Chapter 5 — Understanding Market Regimes

**1.** Trade the regime, not just the stock; be aggressive only in trending regime.
**2.** Confirm bull markets with — breadth, leadership, index trend — not hope.
**3.** Deploy maximum velocity only in confirmed uptrends for 10x compounding.
**4.** Match instruments to market conditions; leverage and convexity for HPS.
**5.** Read the market stages; increase aggression early; reduce it into euphoria.
**6.** Beware overconfidence during bull markets.
**7.** Step fully to cash the moment a regime shifts to distribution or risk-off.
**8.** Controlled-aggression pledge: ferocious with an edge, disciplined without one.
**9.** Every regime is temporary; the goal is to survive the transition between them.
**10.** Predefine exposure; identify what you trade in each market environment.

## Chapter 6 — Momentum: The Engine of Fast Compounding

**1.** Trade institutional momentum, not random price movement.
**2.** Volume reveals conviction; large buyers can't hide their accumulation entirely.
**3.** Follow the strongest stocks in the strongest sectors.
**4.** Confirm institutional sponsorship before committing; follow them.
**5.** Separate true accumulation from noise using multiple signals, not a single bar.
**6.** Enter at the breakout from accumulation, not after the move matures.
**7.** Momentum concentrates institutional buying power into compounding moves.
**8.** Exit when accumulation turns into distribution: fading volume on advances, rising volume on declines.
**9.** Never confuse a low price with value; momentum rewards strength.
**10.** Watch leadership rotation for emerging opportunities, next momentum.

## Chapter 7 — Volatility as Opportunity

**1.** Treat volatility as the raw material of fast compounding, not a danger to avoid.
**2.** Volatility creates exceptional returns; a flat tape cannot produce 10× math.
**3.** Reduce position size as volatility rises; smaller positions for the same 1R.
**4.** Favor healthy trend volatility over chaos; avoid chaotic volatility.

**5.** Use volatility contraction as the setup and volatility expansion as the trigger.
**6.** Volatility creating the opportunity can also liquidate an oversized position.
**7.** Use implied volatility to improve option timing; buy cheap, harvest the spikes.
**8.** Never hold leverage through undefined volatility; you will survive without.
**9.** Let volatility regimes dictate aggression; they dictate the level of aggression.
**10.** Structure trades so expansion helps more than it hurts.

## Chapter 8 — Liquidity and Market Structure

**1.** Trade only what you can exit; liquidity is a feature of calm markets.
**2.** Size positions so you can get out in a panic, not just on a quiet afternoon.
**3.** Understand market structure ; who is on the other side of your trade and why.
**4.** Favor liquid leaders for large or leveraged positions; thin names for small bets.
**5.** Watch for liquidity evaporation as an early warning that a move is ending.
**6.** Forced liquidation is what destroys leveraged accounts.
**7.** Use liquidity-driven rallies as high-probability windows for aggression.
**8.** Account for spread and slippage; they tax every round trip.
**9.** Build exit assumptions on stressed liquidity, not normal liquidity.
**10.** Treat liquidity as a risk dimension equal to price and time.

## Chapter 9 — Trading Common Stocks Aggressively

**1.** Build the campaign on liquid, high-beta leaders capable of nonlinear moves.
**2.** Concentrate in one to five high-conviction names, never a diluted basket.
**3.** Demand clean technical structure; base, breakout, volume, before committing.
**4.** Use stocks as the controllable core and reserve derivatives for amplification.
**5.** Trail stops to protect gains as a leader extends.
**6.** Avoid low-float lottery tickets unless sized strictly as defined-risk speculation.
**7.** Add to winners; never average down into invalidated thesis.
**8.** Anchor each trade to an invalidation level set before entry.
**9.** Rotate capital toward emerging leadership as themes mature.
**10.** Hold even the best stock to the 1R risk vice.

## Chapter 10 — ETFs and Leveraged ETFs

**1.** Use sector ETFs to ride leadership groups without single-stock blowup risk.
**2.** Trade 2×/3× ETFs only for short swings in confirmed trends.
**3.** Respect volatility decay: daily resets erode value in choppy/falling markets.
**4.** Never hold a 3× ETF through chop or a bear rotation; use strict time stops.
**5.** Sector rotation guide capital toward the groups institutions are accumulating.
**6.** Limit leveraged-ETF exposure under the sector-heat ceiling.
**7.** Pyramid leverage only after the trend confirms, never in anticipation.
**8.** Understand — sponsor, liquidity, and reset mechanics — before trading it.
**9.** Leverage should amplify on proven trends, not replace them.
**10.** Exit immediately when sector leadership breaks.

## Chapter 11 — Options for Accelerated Returns

**1.** Treat premium at risk as full position risk; the rules is he same as with shares.
**2.** Use long calls to replace stock exposure, not as lottery tickets.
**3.** Prefer LEAPS and in-the-money options to reduce time decay.
**4.** Respect theta and IV crush; being right on direction may not be enough.
**5.** Use spreads to reduce decay and improve capital efficiency.
**6.** Buy convexity when implied volatility is cheap; avoid overpaying for catalysts.
**7.** Scale out of winners; never let one option position dominate the book.
**8.** Avoid far-out-of-the-money premium without a strict, identifiable catalyst.
**9.** Match expiration to the thesis horizon so time is an ally, not an enemy.
**10.** Define maximum loss before entry; options go to zero fast, unlike stocks.

## Chapter 12 — Warrants and Structured Speculation

**1.** Understand the SPAC structure before trading its warrants.
**2.** Use long-dated warrants to reduce time-decay risk.
**3.** Base the thesis on the merger target, not the warrant itself.
**4.** Exploit the asymmetry; capped downside, convex upside, but size for total loss.
**5.** Trade the definitive-agreement announcement as the catalyst window.
**6.** Respect the redemption trap and other structural risks unique to SPACs.
**7.** Compare warrants to common shares and call options before choosing.
**8.** Never confuse warrant leverage with free leverage; the asymmetry has a price.
**9.** Demand sufficient liquidity before committing size to any warrant.
**10.** Treat warrants as capped, defined-risk speculation.

## Chapter 13 — Synthetic Leverage

**1.** Treat margin as synthetic leverage that amplifies losses as violently as gains.
**2.** Keep count of total leverage including margin, options, and 2/3× ETFs.
**3.** Respect the compounding cost of margin interest.
**4.** Fear the margin call and forced liquidation more than being wrong on a thesis.
**5.** Guard against the psychology of borrowed money — it distorts judgment.
**6.** Avoid the escalation trap of meeting a margin call by adding risk.
**7.** Prefer defined-risk options over borrowed cash when appropriate.
**8.** Use margin surgically and briefly, never as a permanent state.
**9.** Keep a cash buffer so volatility never forces a liquidation at the worst price.
**10.** Treat leverage as a scalpel — precise, temporary, and respected.

## Chapter 14 — Building a High-Velocity Watchlist

**1.** Curate a small, dynamic watchlist of the market's strongest, most liquid leaders.
**2.** Admit only stocks meeting strength, volume, and structure criteria.
**3.** Refresh the list as leadership rotates; stale watchlists trade yesterday's market.
**4.** Rank candidates by reward-to-risk and catalyst proximity, not by familiarity.
**5.** Pre-define entry triggers and invalidation levels for every name on the list.

**6.** Keep the list short enough to monitor with full attention.
**7.** Track relative strength versus the index and the sector to surface true leaders.
**8.** Separate core candidates from satellite speculations.
**9.** Let the watchlist, not impulse, source every trade.
**10.** Review and prune weekly so only high-velocity names survive.

## Chapter 15 — The Catalyst Framework

**1.** Trade catalyst: earnings, approvals, deals, macro shifts can ignite a move.
**2.** Map the catalyst calendar and position before, not after, the crowd reacts.
**3.** Match the instrument to the catalyst's volatility and timing.
**4.** Separate expected catalysts (priced in) from genuine surprises (mispriced).
**5.** Define the thesis around the catalyst and exit when it resolves.
**6.** Size leverage deliberately and sized to the catalyst's risk.
**7.** Beware IV crush around scheduled catalysts when using options.
**8.** Confirm relative strength and volume expansion as the catalyst approaches.
**9.** Avoid binary bets you cannot survive being wrong on.
**10.** Commit size only when catalyst, structure, and liquidity align.

## Chapter 16 — Timing Entries

**1.** Buy high-quality breakouts from tight consolidation, confirmed by volume.
**2.** Treat volume as non-negotiable; a breakout without volume is a trap.
**3.** Use the volatility-contraction pattern to find low-risk entry points.
**4.** Prefer pullback entries into rising trends for superior reward-to-risk.
**5.** Buy where institutions buy — at structure, not after extended moves.
**6.** Define the entry trigger and the invalidation level in the same breath.
**7.** Refuse to chase; if you missed the entry, wait for the next setup.
**8.** Distinguish a healthy pullback from a trend break using volume and depth.
**9.** Anchor entries to objective patterns, not feelings of urgency.
**10.** Size the entry from the stop distance so every trade risks the same 1R.

## Chapter 17 — Timing Exits

**1.** Plan the exit before the entry; an unplanned exit is an emotional one.
**2.** Scale out in tiers to lock gains while leaving a runner for the larger move.
**3.** Free trade — sell enough to remove risk, then ride the rest with house money.
**4.** Trail stops upward as the position extends; never let a winner become a loser.
**5.** Exit into strength and momentum exhaustion, not after the reversal.
**6.** Recognize blow-off tops as harvest signals, not reasons to add.
**7.** Protect gains as aggressively as you protected capital on entry.
**8.** Avoid round-trips; banked gains compound, paper gains do not.
**9.** Let the trade structure, not hope, dictate when to take profit.
**10.** Great exits separate profitable systems from good ones.

## Chapter 18 — Concentration vs Diversification

**1.** Concentrate deliberately — over-diversification dilutes the 10x velocity.
**2.** Cap concentration with hard risk rules to avoid recklessness.
**3.** Hold only high-conviction positions under the three-basket rule.
**4.** Control factor and sector correlation under a heat ceiling.
**5.** Let position size scale with conviction and reward-to-risk, not habit.

6. Accept that concentration builds wealth when managed with stops.
7. Diversify across time and setups, not into mediocrity.
8. Never let any single position determine your financial survival.
9. Rebalance toward the strongest names as the campaign progresses.
10. Treat concentration as a calculated weapon, paired with automated defense.

## Chapter 19 — Emotional Control Under Pressure

1. Control fear, greed, revenge, FOMO, euphoria, and exhaustion.
2. Remove decisions from the moment of emotional pressure.
3. Treat revenge trading as a circuit-breaker event: stop, step away, review.
4. Ignore FOMO; missed trades cost less than chased trades.
5. Watch euphoria after wins as the most dangerous state.
6. Operate through rules, checklists, and routines.
7. Recognize emotional exhaustion and reduce size or stop before it forces errors.
8. Let the governance matrix, not impulse, decide who makes the call.
9. Separate the decision from the outcome; a good process can still lose a trade.
10. Protect psychological capital with the same rigor as financial capital.

## Chapter 20 — Trading Like a Hedge Fund

1. Run your account like a fund: written risk frameworks, not improvisation.
2. Enforce position limits so no single trade can breach your risk budget.
3. Manage gross and net exposure deliberately, especially with leverage.
4. Monitor portfolio heat — total risk across correlated positions — continuously.
5. Set daily and weekly loss limits that force a stop after a bad run.
6. Institutionalize discipline through process, not willpower.
7. Adopt a concrete ruleset sized to your actual account.
8. Define who runs the book and what authority the rules hold over you.
9. Review risk before opportunity — ask what can destroy you first.
10. Treat consistency of process as the institutional edge over the crowd.

## Chapter 21 — The Family Office Approach

1. Put capital preservation first; aggression is the second priority, not first.
2. Deploy tactical aggression only with capital you have already protected.
3. Rotate allocation toward the best opportunities while keeping a defended core.
4. Think in multiple market cycles; survival across regimes compounds.
5. Separate defended estate from at-risk bet, and never confuse the two.
6. Adopt long-term thinking even inside a six-month sprint.
7. Treat the estate as sacred and the bet as expendable.
8. Govern allocation with rules that outlast any single market view.
9. Build for durability, not only velocity.
10. Let preservation discipline license greater long-term aggression.

## Chapter 22 — The Discipline of Patience

1. Wait for asymmetric setups; most of the time the correct position is none.
2. Treat inactivity as a profitable choice, not a failure to act.
3. Trade less to compound more — overtrading bleeds capital and focus.

4. Practice selective aggression: flat by default, ferocious only on A+ setups.
5. Run a pre-trade checklist that a setup must pass before you commit.
6. Switch deliberately between patient observation and decisive execution.
7. Distinguish patience from compulsion; boredom is not a trade signal.
8. Let the market come to your price; do not chase.
9. Protect the rare large opportunity by not wasting capital on marginal ones.
10. Treat patience as an edge the impatient crowd cannot copy.

## Chapter 23 — Surviving the Drawdown

1. Stay solvent first; you cannot recover from a wipeout, only from a drawdown.
2. Reduce size immediately when in a drawdown — throttle risk before rebuilding.
3. Restore solvency, then size, then psychology, then confidence.
4. Rebuild on small, high-probability wins, not on a heroic recovery trade.
5. Treat drawdowns as information about the regime or execution, not a verdict.
6. Follow a predefined drawdown protocol.
7. Avoid the spiral — adding risk to recover faster is how drawdowns become ruin.
8. Step away to restore judgment before re-engaging.
9. Distinguish a normal drawdown from a broken edge.
10. Surviving drawdowns preserves compounding.

## Chapter 24 — The Power Law of Trading

1. Accept the power law — a few trades produce most of your returns.
2. Concentrate effort and size on elite setups; treat the rest as noise.
3. Engineer portfolio asymmetry so winners dwarf losers.
4. Let winners run; cutting them short inverts the power law against you.
5. Cut losers fast so the left tail never compounds.
6. Expect a lumpy year — long flat stretches punctuated by a few decisive moves.
7. Harness the power law instead of inverting it by overtrading and early exits.
8. Size up only when an elite setup aligns, not on every idea.
9. Measure performance over the full sequence, not trade by trade.
10. Be present and aggressive when the rare large trade finally appears.

## Chapter 25 — Riding Supercycles

1. Identify genuine multi-year supercycles or thematic waves and ride leaders.
2. Separate enduring trends from fads by breadth, duration, and sponsorship.
3. Trade price confirmation, not story; narrative can be right, the timing wrong.
4. Position in the highest-velocity leaders of the dominant theme.
5. Recognize when the cycle turns — leadership rolls over before the story dies.
6. Use supercycles as the backdrop that makes aggressive compounding possible.
7. Rotate as one supercycle matures and the next emerges.
8. Avoid marrying a theme; exit when price says the cycle has turned.
9. Let story-versus-price discipline keep you honest about narrative bias.
10. Treat supercycles as tailwinds, never as guarantees.

## Chapter 26 – Swing Trading for Rapid Growth

1. Capture multi-day momentum moves as the core swing engine.
2. Trade high-beta setups when the regime supports them, sized for their range.
3. Hold earnings continuations confirmed by price and volume.
4. Exploit sector acceleration by holding the strongest names in leading groups.
5. Define holding periods; a swing is days to weeks, not an indefinite hold.
6. Use time stops to exit setups that fail to follow through.
7. Pyramid into confirmed swings, never into stalling ones.
8. Match instrument leverage to the swing's expected velocity.
9. Bank gains on momentum exhaustion rather than round-tripping them.
10. Operate every swing within the same 1R risk discipline.

## Chapter 27 – Position Scaling

1. Add only to winners that confirm the thesis; let the market fund your scale.
2. Pyramid so added size never raises total risk beyond your 1R budget.
3. Move stops up as you add so the position cannot turn into a loss.
4. Scale without emotional distortion – follow the plan, not the adrenaline.
5. Use defined pyramid method (decreasing add sizes) rather than improvising.
6. Treat position sizing as a dynamic variable driven by confirmation, not habit.
7. Never average down into a loser; that is the opposite of scaling.
8. Bank partial profits as you pyramid to keep the trade asymmetric.
9. Let conviction plus confirmation, not hope, justify every add.
10. Keep the entire pyramid governed by the account's heat limits.

## Chapter 28 – Tactical Use of Leverage

1. Use leverage only to amplify a proven edge in a favorable regime.
2. Leverage becomes destructive – into weakness, chop, or low conviction.
3. Follow strict margin-survival rules: cash buffer, hard caps, and buffers.
4. Count all embedded leverage; options, 3× ETFs, margin, toward one ceiling.
5. Keep leverage temporary and surgical, never a permanent posture.
6. Reduce leverage first when volatility rises or the regime weakens.
7. Never use leverage to compensate for a missing edge.
8. Size leveraged positions so a normal adverse move cannot force liquidation.
9. Govern leverage decisions with a matrix, not with in-the-moment conviction.
10. Respect that leverage magnifies mistakes faster than it magnifies skill.

## Chapter 29 – Designing the Compounding Roadmap

1. Reject the straight line; design an escalating staircase of distinct phases.
2. Set realistic targets and a cadence that compounds without forcing trades.
3. Define drawdown tolerances per phase and enforce them mechanically.
4. Build capital-allocation schedules that scale size with the growing base.
5. Progress from foundation to acceleration to preservation.
6. Let the roadmap, not daily emotion, govern how aggressive you are.
7. Plan for variance; the path will be lumpy even when the system works.

**8.** Pre-decide what each milestone unlocks and what each drawdown restricts.
**9.** Review the roadmap against reality and adjust cadence, not the risk rules.
**10.** Keep the roadmap subordinate to survival: the plan adapts, defenses do not.

## Chapter 30 — Example Compounding Scenarios

**1.** Choose a strategy suited to your skills and temperament.
**2.** Understand each path's distinct risk signature before committing capital.
**3.** Options-heavy path's convexity comes with decay and total-loss risk.
**4.** Treat the leveraged-ETF path as short-swing only, never buy-and-hold.
**5.** Run the momentum-only path on liquid leaders with strict stops.
**6.** Combine engines deliberately, not haphazardly, to diversify path risk.
**7.** Match the path to the regime; no path works in every environment.
**8.** Hold every path to the same drawdown and risk-per-trade discipline.
**9.** Treat the scenarios as illustrations of mechanics, not guarantees of outcome.
**10.** Pick a path you can execute consistently under pressure.

## Chapter 31 — Case Studies of Explosive Compounding

**1.** Study great momentum traders—their successes and failures.
**2.** Note the common threads: trend timing, concentration, and ruthless exits.
**3.** Adapt their principles to modern instruments rather than copying their trades.
**4.** Respect survivorship bias; many failed using similar methods.
**5.** Learn that the same aggression built and destroyed many of these fortunes.
**6.** Extract the math behind the fortunes: asymmetric bets compounded by trends.
**7.** Apply their discipline, not just their boldness.
**8.** Heed the honest warnings before emulating any case.
**9.** Use the governance matrix to translate history into rules.
**10.** Remember that past explosive returns are lessons, not promises.

## Chapter 32 — The Dark Side of Aggressive Compounding

**1.** Treat blowups as the default risk of aggression and design to prevent them.
**2.** Watch overconfidence after wins as the leading cause of self-destruction.
**3.** Never trade for excitement instead of expectancy.
**4.** Resist lifestyle inflation that pressures the account to perform.
**5.** Become more disciplined after success, not less.
**6.** Sign a blowup-prevention pact and enforce it.
**7.** Recognize that the strategy's shadow is psychological, not technical.
**8.** Pre-commit how success will change your rules — ideally not at all.
**9.** Separate winnings from trading capital to remove pressure.
**10.** Survive your own success; it is more dangerous than failure.

## Chapter 33 — Protecting the Fortune

**1.** Protect the fortune as deliberately as you built it.
**2.** Plan tax strategy early with qualified professionals.
**3.** Use appropriate asset-protection structures.
**4.** Diversify after success; concentration built it, diversification preserves it.

5. Transition gradually from aggressive trader to long-term investor.
6. Take risk off the table in tranches as milestones are hit.
7. Separate win capital from play capital permanently.
8. Treat protection as a discipline, not an afterthought.
9. Consult qualified tax, legal, and estate professionals for personal decisions.
10. Remember that an unprotected fortune is just a large position still at risk.

## Chapter 34 — Aggressive Trader to Family Office Thinking

1. Reduce risk as capital grows; the goal shifts from velocity to durability.
2. Build passive income streams that do not depend on active trading.
3. Embrace long-term compounding once the sprint has achieved its goal.
4. Establish legacy capital designed to outlast you.
5. Follow a deliberate transition model from trader to steward.
6. Recognize when preservation should replace accumulation.
7. Protect time and freedom, not just net worth.
8. Diversify income and assets to lower single-point risk.
9. Treat the family-office transition as the natural end of the campaign.
10. Compound capital and stewardship together.

## Chapter 35 — The Real Goal

1. Remember the number was always a proxy for freedom, time, and choice.
2. Define what financial independence is actually for before chasing it.
3. Protect time and family as the true returns on the campaign.
4. Practice stewardship — capital is a responsibility, not just a score.
5. Seek purpose beyond money so success does not feel empty.
6. Hold the goal two ways: ambitiously and lightly.
7. Write your real-goal declaration and let it govern your risk-taking.
8. Measure success by life, not only by the equity curve.
9. Keep the discipline that built the wealth after you have reached the goal.
10. Let the money serve the life, never the reverse.

# Appendix B — Trading Checklists

## Pre-Trade Checklist (every position must pass)

- Regime supports aggression (confirmed trend / favorable environment).
- Name is a liquid leader with relative strength and institutional sponsorship.
- Clean structure present (base, breakout, or pullback) with volume confirmation.
- A genuine catalyst or momentum driver is identifiable.
- Entry trigger and hard invalidation (stop) are both defined.
- Position sized so the stop equals exactly 1R (≤ your fixed % of equity).
- Adding the trade keeps total portfolio heat and sector exposure within caps.
- Reward-to-risk is at least ~3:1.
- You can exit the full size even in stressed liquidity.
- You are calm, rule-driven, and not chasing, revenging, or forcing.

## Daily Operating Checklist

- Review regime and watchlist before the open.
- Confirm daily/weekly loss limits and remaining risk budget.
- Pre-set entries, stops, and targets; place orders, not opinions.
- Manage open trades by the plan; trail stops, scale per tiers.

- Log every trade in the journal as it happens.
- Stop trading if a daily loss limit or emotional red flag is hit.
- End-of-day review: what followed the plan, what did not.

# Appendix C — Position Sizing Formulas

## The risk unit (1R)

Per-share (or per-contract) risk: R = Entry Price − Stop Price (for a long). 1R in dollars is the total amount you lose if the stop is hit.

## Shares to buy from fixed fractional risk

Dollar risk allowed = Account Equity × Risk % (e.g., 1% of $100,000 = $1,000). Shares = Dollar risk allowed ÷ (Entry − Stop). Example: entry $50, stop $46, risk $1,000 → R = $4/share → 250 shares.

## R-multiple accounting

Express every outcome in R: a trade that makes three times what you risked is +3R; a stop-out is −1R. Track expectancy = (Win% × Avg Win R) − (Loss% × Avg Loss R). Roughly 36R of net gain, captured through asymmetric trades, is the arithmetic behind a 10× campaign.

## Options and defined-risk premium

For long options, treat the entire premium paid as 1R unless a stop on the option price is used. Contracts = Dollar risk allowed ÷ (Premium × 100). Never let premium-at-risk exceed your fixed fractional limit.

## Total and embedded leverage

Effective exposure = Σ(position value × instrument leverage), counting 2×/3× ETFs at their multiple and options at their delta-equivalent notional. Cap effective exposure under one portfolio ceiling.

## Fractional Kelly (sizing the edge)

The Kelly fraction f* = edge ÷ odds approximates the growth-optimal bet size, but full Kelly is too volatile for aggressive instruments. Use a fraction (commonly one-quarter to one-half Kelly) and never let it override your fixed risk caps.

# Appendix E — Momentum & Leadership Screens

## Leadership screen (find the strongest names)

- Price within ~15–25% of a 52-week high.
- Relative strength outperforming the index over 1, 3, and 6 months.
- Rising volume on advances, contracting volume on pullbacks (accumulation).
- Member of a leading sector or theme showing rotation in.
- Tightening price structure (volatility contraction) ahead of a breakout.
- Liquidity sufficient to enter and exit your intended size.

## Setup screen (timing the entry)

- Base or consolidation of adequate length and tightness.
- Clear pivot/trigger level with a nearby logical stop (small R).
- Volume expansion on the breakout or volume dry-up on the pullback.
- Catalyst or momentum driver present.
- Reward-to-risk ≥ 3:1 to the next logical target.

# Appendix F — Leveraged ETF Reference Guide

## How they work

Leveraged ETFs (2× and 3×) seek a multiple of the underlying index's return for a single day, then reset. Over multiple days, returns compound off the daily reset, so the multi-day result diverges from the simple multiple of the index.

## Volatility decay (beta slippage)

In choppy or falling markets, the daily reset erodes value even when the underlying ends roughly flat. The effect worsens with volatility and holding period — which is why these are short-swing tools, not long-term holds. Historically, broad 3× products have suffered drawdowns of roughly 80–90%+ in adverse years; treat that as the rule, not the exception.

## Operating rules

- Hold only in confirmed trends, measured in days (≈3–10), not weeks.
- Use strict time stops in addition to price stops.
- Never average down or hold through a bear rotation or chop.
- Count the multiple toward total portfolio leverage and the sector-heat ceiling.
- Verify ticker, sponsor, leverage factor, and liquidity before trading; these vary and change.
- Pyramid only after the trend confirms, never in anticipation.

# Appendix G — Options Greeks Cheat Sheet

| Greek | Measures | Trading Implication |
|---|---|---|
| **Delta** | Sensitivity to a $1 move in the underlying | Approximate share-equivalent exposure; higher delta = more directional. |
| **Gamma** | Rate of change of delta | Position direction accelerates near the strike; largest for near-dated, at-the-money options. |
| **Theta** | Time decay per day | Long options bleed value daily; worst for near-dated, at-the-money options. |
| **Vega** | Sensitivity to implied volatility | Long options gain when IV rises and lose to IV crush after catalysts. |
| **Rho** | Sensitivity to interest rates | Minor for short-dated trades; matters for LEAPS. |

## Practical takeaways

- Buy delta (direction) with LEAPS/ITM options to limit theta.
- Respect theta and vega: a correct direction can still lose to decay and IV crush.
- Use spreads to offset theta and vega while keeping defined risk.
- Treat premium-at-risk as full position risk and size accordingly.

# Appendix H — Trading Journal & Review Templates

## Daily Trade Journal (per trade)

- Date / time, ticker, instrument (stock, ETF, option, warrant).

- Setup type and regime; catalyst.
- Entry, stop, target(s); planned R and reward-to-risk.
- Position size and % of equity at risk.
- Outcome in R; exit reason.
- Rule adherence: did I follow the plan? (yes/no + note).
- Emotion / state at entry and exit.
- One lesson.

## Weekly Review

- Net R for the week; win rate and average win/loss in R.
- Best and worst trades — process, not just outcome.
- Rule violations and their cost.
- Regime assessment and watchlist refresh.
- One process adjustment for next week (cadence, not risk caps).

## Monthly Performance Audit

- Equity curve vs. the milestone plan.
- Maximum drawdown vs. tolerance; any limit breaches.
- Expectancy and distribution of R-multiples (power-law check).
- Leverage and exposure discipline review.
- Psychological audit: overconfidence, addiction, lifestyle pressure.
- Decision: maintain, throttle, or pause.

# Appendix I

## Bibliography & Recommended Reading

A curated reading list titles are grouped by theme; this list is for further study and is not a claim of endorsement by the authors cited.


### Speculation Classics

Edwin Lefèvre, *Reminiscences of a Stock Operator* (1923).
Jesse L. Livermore, *How to Trade in Stocks* (1940).
Nicolas Darvas, *How I Made $2,000,000 in the Stock Market* (1960).
Gerald M. Loeb, *The Battle for Investment Survival* (1935).

### Momentum, Growth & Technical Method

William J. O'Neil, *How to Make Money in Stocks.*
Mark Minervini, *Trade Like a Stock Market Wizard* (2013).
Mark Minervini, *Think & Trade Like a Champion* (2017).
Stan Weinstein, *Secrets for Profiting in Bull and Bear Markets* (1988).
John J. Murphy, *Technical Analysis of the Financial Markets.*
Thomas N. Bulkowski, *Encyclopedia of Chart Patterns.*
Alexander Elder, *Trading for a Living.*

### Risk, Position Sizing & Systems

Van K. Tharp, *Trade Your Way to Financial Freedom.*
Ralph Vince, *The Mathematics of Money Management.*
Perry J. Kaufman, *Trading Systems and Methods.*
Edward O. Thorp, *A Man for All Markets* (2017).
Michael W. Covel, *Trend Following.*
Curtis M. Faith, *Way of the Turtle* (2007).
J. L. Kelly Jr., *A New Interpretation of Information Rate* (Bell System Technical Journal, 1956).

### Options & Volatility

Lawrence G. McMillan, *Options as a Strategic Investment.*
Sheldon Natenberg, *Option Volatility and Pricing.*
Euan Sinclair, *Volatility Trading.*

### Trading Psychology

Mark Douglas, *Trading in the Zone* (2000).
Brett N. Steenbarger, *The Daily Trading Coach* (2009).
Daniel Kahneman, *Thinking, Fast and Slow* (2011).
Jack D. Schwager, *Market Wizards* (1989).

### Markets, Risk & Cautionary Histories

Nassim Nicholas Taleb, *The Black Swan* (2007).
Nassim Nicholas Taleb, *Fooled by Randomness* (2001).
Roger Lowenstein, *When Genius Failed* (2000).
Sebastian Mallaby, *More Money Than God* (2010).
Gregory Zuckerman, *The Man Who Solved the Market* (2019).
Scott Patterson, *The Quants* (2010).
Nick Leeson, *Rogue Trader* (1996).
Charles P. Kindleberger & Robert Z. Aliber, *Manias, Panics, and Crashes.*
Burton G. Malkiel, *A Random Walk Down Wall Street.*

# Appendix J

## Sources & References by Topic

The references below support this book's concepts, statistics, case studies, and figures. For current prices, regulations, ETF terms, and fund data, always verify primary, up-to-date sources before trading.

## Compounding math, R-multiples & position sizing

• Van K. Tharp, Trade Your Way to Financial Freedom (R-multiples, expectancy, position sizing).

• Ralph Vince, The Mathematics of Money Management.

• J. L. Kelly Jr., "A New Interpretation of Information Rate" (1956) — the Kelly criterion.

## Market regimes, stage analysis & leadership

• Stan Weinstein, Secrets for Profiting in Bull and Bear Markets.

• William J. O'Neil, How to Make Money in Stocks (CAN SLIM, market direction).

## Momentum & institutional accumulation

• Narasimhan Jegadeesh & Sheridan Titman, "Returns to Buying Winners and Selling Losers" (Journal of Finance, 1993).

• Mark Minervini, Trade Like a Stock Market Wizard.

## Leveraged & inverse ETFs (mechanics and decay)

• U.S. SEC and FINRA investor alerts on leveraged and inverse ETFs.

• Issuer prospectuses and fact sheets (e.g., ProShares, Direxion) — verify current terms before trading.

## Options, Greeks & implied volatility

• Sheldon Natenberg, Option Volatility and Pricing.

• Lawrence G. McMillan, Options as a Strategic Investment.

• Euan Sinclair, Volatility Trading.

## Retail trader outcomes & survival statistics

• Brad M. Barber & Terrance Odean, "Trading Is Hazardous to Your Wealth" (Journal of Finance, 2000).

• Barber, Lee, Liu & Odean, studies on individual investor and day-trader performance.

## Tail risk, ruin & the limits of models

• Nassim Nicholas Taleb, Fooled by Randomness; The Black Swan.

• Roger Lowenstein, When Genius Failed (Long-Term Capital Management).

## Cautionary cases referenced in the text

• LTCM (1998): Roger Lowenstein, When Genius Failed.

• Barings/Nick Leeson (1995): Nick Leeson, Rogue Trader.

• Amaranth/Brian Hunter (2006): U.S. CFTC actions and U.S. Senate Permanent Subcommittee on Investigations report.

• Archegos/Bill Hwang (2021–2024): U.S. v. Hwang (S.D.N.Y.) court records and contemporaneous reporting.

• Renaissance/Medallion: Gregory Zuckerman, The Man Who Solved the Market.

• 2021 short-squeeze episode: U.S. SEC staff report on equity and options market structure conditions in early 2021.

Note: Trading involves substantial risk of loss. Nothing in these appendices is financial, legal, or tax advice. Verify all current figures and regulations against primary sources, and consult a licensed professional before acting.

## About the Author

Frank Ikechukwu Igwealor is an economist, a California licensed attorney, a Certified Public Accountant, Certified Management Accountant, and Certified Financial Manager. Igwealor is also a California licensed Real Estate Broker since 2005. Igwealor's education includes degrees in Accounting, Economics, Business Administration, Finance, Risk Management, and Law. Igwealor lives in Los Angeles and has worked as officer and director of numerous public and private companies in the United States, Europe, Asia, the Middle East, and Africa.

www.ingramcontent.com/pod-product-compliance
Lightning Source LLC
LaVergne TN
LVHW082021200926
848481LV00010B/2896
* 9 7 9 8 9 5 1 2 1 3 0 3 7 *